U.S. Merchant Marine

Turner Publishing Company
Paducah, Kentucky

The United States Merchant Marine

Contents

From the Artist	3
General History	5
Bibliography	66
Footnotes	68
Merchant Marine Photolog	69
Merchant Marine Veterans	78
Acknowledgments	136

Turner Publishing Company
P.O. Box 3101, 412 Broadway
Paducah, KY 42001

Copyright©1993 Turner Publishing Company
All rights reserved

Created and Designed by:
David A. Hurst, Publishing Consultant

This book or any part thereof may not be reproduced without the written consent of the Publisher.

This book was compiled and produced using available and submitted information; the publisher regrets it cannot assume liability for errors or omissions.

Library of Congress Catalog Card no. 93-061016
ISBN: 1-56311-084-9
Printed in the USA

Additional books may be purchased directly from publisher.

From The Artist

The S.S. Lane Victory

It was the end of a war. Let a veteran of the war make a statement. "The job is done and I am going home." That is what is being portrayed in this picture of a Victory Ship. She is riding light with the propeller going 'flop, flop, flop' churning the water. The battle scars on her side are exuding streams of rust. The overloaded dirty waterline indicates that she has carried massive amounts of desperately needed cargo in her holds and then topped that off with a towering deck load of all sorts of war machines, She, the tired victory ship is going away, back home to be retired. There will always be memories of submarine scares, bombs exploding in the water around her, and also the echoes of gunfire. In a way, this ship seems to follow the thoughts of many of the merchant mariners who sailed her. She seems to say here, "I have lived through much. I have completed my mission. My job is done. I am going home."

In painting a cover picture for this book, I did lots of thinking. Should a wartime scene be painted with bombs dropping from airplanes, torpedoes slicing through the water, ships being blown up—fire and terror everywhere? No. The war was over a long time ago. The action is over. We relive the war only with our memories. Why not depict the end of the terrible conflagration?

With the average age of the WWII Merchant Marine Veteran hovering around the 75 year mark, we pause to think that for most of the populace around today, there are no memories of the great war. They were born after we got home! WE LIVED IT.

Jerry McClish

The SS Lane Victory, San Francisco, 1944.

Class 286, USMS, Original enrollment, Wilmington, CA. Boot training at Santa Catalina, CA, 11 July -29 August, 1944

THE UNITED STATES MERCHANT MARINE

By Michele Molnar

Throughout the centuries, they have answered a certain call - be it duty or adventure - then romanced the exotic unknown, setting out on the endless azure horizon that is the sea.

They saw parts of the world they had never heard of, and had experiences that they could never have imagined possible.

Long after leaving their last ship, the impression of the sea remains indelible for the men and women who spent days, months or years tasting the salt in the seabreeze or bracing against the pitch and roll of a ship in a storm. What washes over them is a never-ending wave of memories - the excitement, danger, loneliness, fear, tedium, first-hand education and fun.

Such is the story of the Merchant Marine.

A sailor's spirit of courage and curiosity led to the creation of a Merchant Marine in the Western Hemisphere long before the Declaration of Independence was signed - in the year 1607, to be exact.

Merchant seamen made tremendous contributions to the birth and founding of the United States. The private vessels were the backbone of the American revolutionary forces waging battle without much of a formal Navy against the British, one of the world's mightiest seapowers.

The mariners were granted exalted status by the Colonials, who issued Letters of Marque allowing them to become armed privateers in the defense of the new nation.

In 1776, there were 136 privateer merchantmen, who mounted 1,360 guns, dwarfing the official men-of-war vessels, which totaled only 31 with 586 guns. At one time or another, an estimated 70,000 American seamen served aboard the privateer vessels.

By their efforts, they contributed to victories against at least 600 British ships that were either destroyed or seized as prizes. In fact, merchantmen captured and destroyed three times as many of the British warships as did the young country's Navy frigates and sloops of war. The vessels were operated by private owners and manned by colonists who were woodsmen and fishermen as well as sailors. Some of these privateers claimed as many as 28 enemy prizes in a single voyage.

But from the beginning, it was not all glory for merchantmen. The job called for bravery, too. The British Navy retaliated fiercely against captured privateer ships, incarcerating prisoners aboard prison hulks, some of them moored in New York's East River. The conditions of captivity were an outrage against human dignity. Hundreds died of disease and malnutrition. When they died, they were simply buried without service, and their graves left unmarked in the mudflats of Wallabout Bay, where the Brooklyn Navy Yard now stands.

As the country grew into a melting pot of diversity, it was the merchant mariners who brought generations of emigrants to the United States' shores during the booming immigration years in the mid-19th century.

Merchant seamen aboard clipper ships sailed from East Coast ports around the dangerous Cape Horn of South America to the Golden Gate of San Francisco. Their contribution to the economic development of the United States could not be denied.

Again, the hardships for those who manned the ships were innumerable. Sailing ships often arrived at their destination with half their crew members lost, maimed and injured - or buried at sea. These mariners helped build America, but for so many, there was no marker dignifying their final resting place.

Life at sea was indeed horrific at times. Many crews worked eight, 10 and even 15 years without pay. Their sleeping quarters were hovels - wet, poorly ventilated and cold. The food was atrocious. Cases of brutality against seamen continued unabated for years. It wasn't until 1850 that Congress forbade flogging or other forms of corporal punishment for seamen.

Seamen fought hard for decent wages and hours, which were among the longest of an American workers, and their accident rates were the highest in the nation except for coal miners.

Shipping was a lifeblood for the mariners. But during the Civil War, there was the virtual overnight destruction of a large portion of the tonnage of material being shipped, material that could not be replaced. As a result, the merchant marine was losing its hold and the coastal villages, once thriving communities, were fast becoming dormant with ghostly docks and warehouses rotting away.

At the start of the 20th century, Great Britain was dominant in shipping, followed by Germany, Holland, Norway, France and Japan increasing their tonnage at this country's expense.

When World War I began, Great Britain was still the leader, followed by Germany, Norway, France and the United States. Then the U.S. began to build ships to handle the surging demand for vessels sailing under a neutral flag.

With the United States' entry into the war in 1917, however, this country found its efforts to supply the needs of the Allies and the American Expeditionary Forces were inadequate. The U.S. had the industrial facilities to produce and satisfy the demand, but no ships to import the raw materials needed by her industries or to export the manufactured articles sought by other nations.

Lack of ships meant the country's warehouses and docks were piled high with goods. The country's vast railroad transportation system broke down, and bottlenecks developed in light and heavy industry that resulted in unemployment to thousands.

A gigantic three-year ship-building program was launched to correct these problems. The U.S. spent more than three billion dollars, and gross tonnage of shipping material reached an all-time American high of 11 million tons.

After the boom came the bust. When the Armistice was signed, decline again set in, fueled by public indifference about world trade. The international commerce that most of America didn't care about, other countries - most notably Britain, Germany, Norway, and Japan - competed for. These countries built up their merchant marines, training them for action if necessary.

Soon, the U.S. became a second-rate maritime power. Our seamen, trained during a period of national emergency to man the cargo ships used to transport supplies, now watched foreign ships leave American harbors, their crews bidding adieu at the idle American seamen on shore.

The vessels engaged in American trade were older types. Most handled coastwise trade or operated on the Great Lakes hauling iron ore, coal and grain between the lake ports.

When the Great Depression hit, seamen suffered. Minimum standards were disregarded and the men on the ships were forced back into a life as bad as what they had endured before. Wages fell to as low as $25 a month.

Now seamen died in strikes, at the hands of police and goons. In 1934, two union strikers were killed in San Francisco and 25,000 marchers came out for their funeral processions. In 1936, 25 strikers died in New York City.

But by 1937, the tide of sentiment was shifting to support labor. Negotiations began with shipowners, and eventually 41 lines signed agreements granting wage increases averaging $10 a month, plus straight overtime of 70 cents an hour and preferential hiring through union halls, according to the "NMU Pilot" 50th anniversary issue in May 1987.

The advent of World War II changed the lives of sailors, who were now in great demand - particularly as their ships were being sunk like duck decoys in a shooting gallery.

An estimated 250,000 men served in the Merchant Marine during World War II. Estimates differ on the U.S. Merchant Marine death toll, but a conservative figure is that 6,624 were killed. When Americans who lost their lives while sailing on foreign flag ships are added, it is estimated that more than 7,000 died or were lost at sea during the war. Another 609 seamen became prisoners of war and thousands more were wounded. As of V-J day, 733 American Merchant Marine vessels of more than 1,000 gross tons were sunk.

During the first year of the war alone,

3.8 percent of merchant seamen were killed by enemy action. The death rate for members of the regular armed services during this same period was 1 percent.

From mid-January to mid-March 1942 alone, German U-boats sank 145 merchant ships in American coastal waters, killing 600 merchant seamen.

For the entire war period, 2.8 percent of merchant seamen who registered with the U.S. Maritime Service were killed - a percentage higher than the casualty rate for the U.S. Army or Navy, and second only to the U.S. Marine Corps, whose death rate was 2.9 percent.

The prevalence of danger brought fear to merchant sailors, a personal knowledge that each moment could be one's last. It brought a pervading sense that, from the calm expanse of a peaceful ocean could come a deadly torpedo. That a convoy held some safety, but danger too, when a storm and the blackness of night could send a ship off-course and into your path.

For some whose ships were hit, but who survived that tragedy, the war added the haunting horror of having to leave survivors to fend for themselves at sea - and most likely die - because subs lurked everywhere.

And the survivors, once picked up, faced more danger. They might escape the sinking of their ship, and survive in a lifeboat, only to be killed as the ship on which they were being transported took a torpedo.

Randall Bishop was sailing on a tanker when he saw three ships sunk at the mouth of the Mississippi River during one day in May 1942. "I doubt there were any survivors," he says. He also doubts that it was common knowledge at the time, because so much of what was happening was hush-hush. Indeed, 41 merchant ships were sunk by U boats in the Gulf of Mexico that month.

The "U" in U boat seemed to stand for "ubiquitous." They were everywhere. And for the most part, at the beginning of the war, they shot at defenseless merchant ships, blowing them out of the water with ease and efficiency.

Log entries from one merchant mariner, identified only as Elmer, summarize life's challenges at the time: "War is Hell." "Home for 1 hour." "Waved to family near Hell Gate." "Navy messed up orders; Navy messed up signals; Navy messed up - No pilots; Navy messed up convoy; Navy messed up berths."

Rivalries were common, but in a pinch it was "one for all and all for one."

Robert V. Giles of Woodland Hills, Calif. recalls how the "old salts" referred to academy graduates like himself as "90-day wonder boys."

"We had the little black uniforms of the U.S. Maritime Service. These were called 'U.S. Monkey Suits' by the veterans. Crawling up a Jacob's ladder with a duffle bag swinging over your shoulder, you did look awkward. Especially if it was your first time."

Old salts and wonder boys toiled together, day in and day out, 365 days a wartime year. Treachery on the high seas never took a holiday. Ships went down on Christmas, New Year's Eve, the Fourth of July.

No fewer than 120 merchant seamen who were lost in action were honored by having their names used on Liberty ships. Of these, one was eventually found alive in a Japanese P.O.W. camp, according to Capt. Arthur R. Moore, who wrote A Careless Word ... A Needless Sinking, the exhaustive documentation of merchant ships and Merchant Marines' involvement in WWII.

Moore found that 62 merchant seamen died while prisoners of war of the Japanese and two more were executed by the Japanese on Wake Island. Thirty-one U.S. flag merchant ships disappeared with all hands, with no one to tell their tale, from the *Albert F. Paul* to the *Witchita*.

Medals were bestowed upon Merchant Mariners for their service. The Merchant Marine Distinguished Service Medal was granted to heroes - those who displayed courage and selflessness in their attempts to save the lives of others. These brave mariners were recognized for putting their lives on the line for one shipmate, or dozens. They risked their lives for people who served in the Navy, the Army and Marines. Some made the ultimate sacrifice, and their seaman's medals were granted posthumously.

This is a book of stories, mostly from the Merchant Marines who served in World War II. These are the tales told by those who were there. They hint at the stories that no one can tell, which were cut short by the depths of the ocean and the fact that there were no survivors to memorialize the event or the last days of the people who experienced it.

The Merchant Marines' story from this century is a proud legacy, part of a centuries-old tradition that brought victory to our shores again and again.

1935 -1939

It was the United States "calm" before the storms that would become the Second World War, a time for planning a trained Merchant Marine. Starting to emerge from the Depression, the country was sensing a serenity and predictability that its citizens embraced and wanted to retain. The lives most people lived were about to change forever, but they didn't realize it yet and the troubles of the world seemed far from our country's shores. Most people wanted to keep it that way.

Witness Richard A. Bradford's recollection of a scheduled West Coast run by a passenger ship:

'Like Clockwork, Even in Dense Fog' Reminiscences of a 1935 Ordinary Seaman on a Coastwise Passenger Ship
By Richard A. Bradford, Des Moines, Washington

In 1935, I made my first ship, as an ordinary seaman on the *S.S. H.F. Alexander* of the Pacific Coast Steamship Company, also known as the Admiral Line.

The "H.F.", as everybody called her, was the fastest and biggest of the four Admiral Line passenger ships. She was a triple-screwed steam turbine vessel, originally built for cross-Atlantic runs.

The *H.F.* made a round trip from Seattle to Los Angeles Harbor like clock-work, via Victoria, B.C., San Francisco, L.A., San Francisco and back. Calling every week, she sailed on a tight schedule that meant just about all ships running the Pacific Coast could predict when they would sight the *H.F.*

I often thought in later years what a responsibility old Captain Hansen had: some sailings running through fog along the coast, always running full ahead with just the magnetic compasses, radio direction finder and depth sounder. I remember on several occasions helping the A.B. on watch send a heavy lead, waxed on the bottom, down to the sea bed. Then we shared the tough job of cranking it back up to get a sample of the bottom to identify, among other things, the color of the sand. The sample was taken to the bridge while the *H.F.* was holding steady at 22 knots running through fog.

The *H.F.* carried some cargo, had four sets of cargo-handling gear and a big deck gang: bosun, bosun's mate, carpenter, three quartermasters, A.B. watchman, three A.B. daymen, nine A.B. watchstanders and six ordinaries, which meant one quartermaster, three A.B.'s and two ordinaries on each watch, the rest being day workers except the night A.B. watchman.

The bosun's name was Frank Webb, a former prize-fighter and patrolman for the Sailor's Union of the Pacific during the big 1934 waterfront strike. He treated us ordinaries O.K. When we were in Los Angeles on a hot day, he'd knock us off at about 10 a.m. so we could go swimming on the ocean beaches. He eventually became a longshoreman in Seattle.

The pay was $45 per month with the ordinaries getting no overtime. Any overtime was given to the A.B.'s, and that wasn't much because with the dayman and watch on deck, there was about enough to tie up and let go during the daytime.

We ordinaries each stood two hours' look-out on the weather wing of the bridge at night and spent the rest of the watch on standby. I had the 8-to-12 watch most of the time. The A.B. watchman would come and get a standby when some passenger didn't make it to the rail. This was frequent, as the passenger list was constantly changing.

The day watch mopped up and wiped down the entire boat deck as the *H.F.* "blew tubes" at night and splotches of soot were waiting every morning. After we finished that, we'd put the mops on a heaving line at the stern and wash them in the sea while having a smoke. Then it was polishing brass fittings on the deck railings, or washing the promenade deck windows. When at sea, garbage accumulated from being in port. This was piled on a lower shelter deck aft to be shoveled overboard into "The Big Locker".

We broke watches every Monday morning in Seattle and by 2 or 3 p.m., we had the entire ship washed down, wooden decks barberized, and everything ship shape. Then we were knocked off until 8 a.m. Tuesday, when we once again started the weekly run.

In the passageway, outside the midships crew mess room, the number of passengers aboard was always posted. It was in excess of 500 at times.

We sailors were quartered forward, two decks down, beneath the steerage passengers (all men in one big room with single bunks.) We sailors, some 18 of us in one big fo'c'sle, remember many times the green seas covering the portholes as we slammed into prevailing northwest swells, heading north. The *H.F.* would plunge up and down, heading north, and she would constantly roll, heading south, as the northwest swells hit her quarter.

The *H.F.* was a good job in those days, a good "feeder" with fresh milk and cream always, and baked goods on the table as I remember. I was 18 at the time.

Her last year in coastwise service was 1936. The following year there was another strike. A recession hit in 1938, so she laid in Alameda estuary in San Francisco Bay until being pulled out for troop service in World War II.

U.S. Launches First Efforts to Train Its Merchant Mariners

In 1936, Congress passed the Merchant Marine Act, which defined our country's basic Merchant Marine policy and established the Maritime Commission as the government agency responsible for the long-range ship-building program and Merchant Marine planning.

One year later, the commission started building cargo ships to replace the slow (10- to 11-knot) ships that had been turned out during the last part of World War I until 1920.

The Merchant Marine Act also called for "trained and efficient personnel." These four words gave birth to the United States Maritime Service, according to Commodore Telfair Knight, who was commandant of the service.

The first commission chairman ordered that a study be launched to determine the training requirements of merchant seamen. Luckily, the U.S. government got its Merchant Mariner education program underway well before Pearl Harbor and the imminence of war.

In November 1937, the commission submitted an economic survey on the American Merchant Marine, pointing out that: "The United States is the only major power which does not have extensive facilities for training young men for a career in the Merchant Marine."

Knight recalled that all phases of the problem had to be studied: the types of men to be trained, in what numbers and the nature and scope of courses.

"It was two years before a workable plan had been evolved and training was initiated at Hoffman Island," Commodore Knight wrote in the January 1946 issue of "MAST Magazine."

Swinburne and Hoffman Islands were obtained from the Procurement Division, and training began on September 6, 1938. A second training station - this one on Government Island in Alameda, Calif. - was opened two weeks after Hoffman Island. On May 6, 1939, the *American Seaman* was commissioned and attached to Hoffman Island. At about the same time, the reconditioning of the sailing vessel *Joseph Conrad* and three other small ships was completed. These were assigned as auxiliary trainers.

About 2,500 applications had been received by the time Hoffman Island was just over one month old. Of these, more than half were deemed eligible for training. By the end of the year, 389 licensed and unlicensed men were enrolled.

At first, all enrollees were experienced seamen being trained so they could do their jobs more efficiently. Most were temporarily unemployed because of a recession that hit the maritime industry.

Students were taught without textbooks and without a regular class format.

"A completely standardized course would not have been practical, even if there had been one, because individual trainees varied greatly in age, intelligence, education, sea-going experience, training and, particularly, in temperament and ambition," Knight wrote.

Licensed and unlicensed personnel were trained together until February 1939, when a school for officer trainees was completed at Fort Trumbull. "When Hoffman Island became exclusively a training station for unlicensed personnel, it was possible to organize the courses to better advantage," Knight recalled.

As the training program progressed, it became apparent that basic training for service in the Merchant Marine was essential. Steps were taken to enlarge the training program to include apprentice seamen. This change of course met with considerable opposition, at first, because it conflicted with prevailing economic conditions: the supply of merchant seamen outpaced the demand for them on ships.

By August 1939, though, the authorization was granted to train inexperienced men.

The Civilian Conservation Corps seemed the most likely recruiting grounds for unlicensed positions in the Merchant Marine. The C.C.C.'s Advisory Council approved the idea since it seemed a worthy means of preparing its men for private employment. For its part, the Maritime Commission found in the C.C.C. a "source of young men who had already demonstrated their ability to live and work together in closely organized groups," according to Knight.

Candidates were chosen from C.C.C. enrollees between 18 and 23 years old who had completed satisfactorily one year of enlistment. They were given medical exams with health standards only slightly less rigorous than those of the U.S. Navy.

"High requirements as to character were established, and enrollees were called upon to take an oath and sign a commitment to serve one year at sea in the American Merchant Marine after completion of the year's training course," Knight wrote.

The first class enrolled at Fort Dix, N.J. on October 26, 1939. They entered the Maritime Service as apprentice seamen at $21 a month, plus subsistence and clothing, and began training on the *American Seaman* early in November.

Jerry McClish, now president of the International Society of Marine Painters, recalls being in the C.C.C., and what it was like to be among the first to graduate from Gallups Island Radio School.

C.C.C. to Merchant Marines: He Was Volunteered for the Transformation
by Jerry McClish, Bradenton, Fla.

When a C.C.C. officer's orderly asked

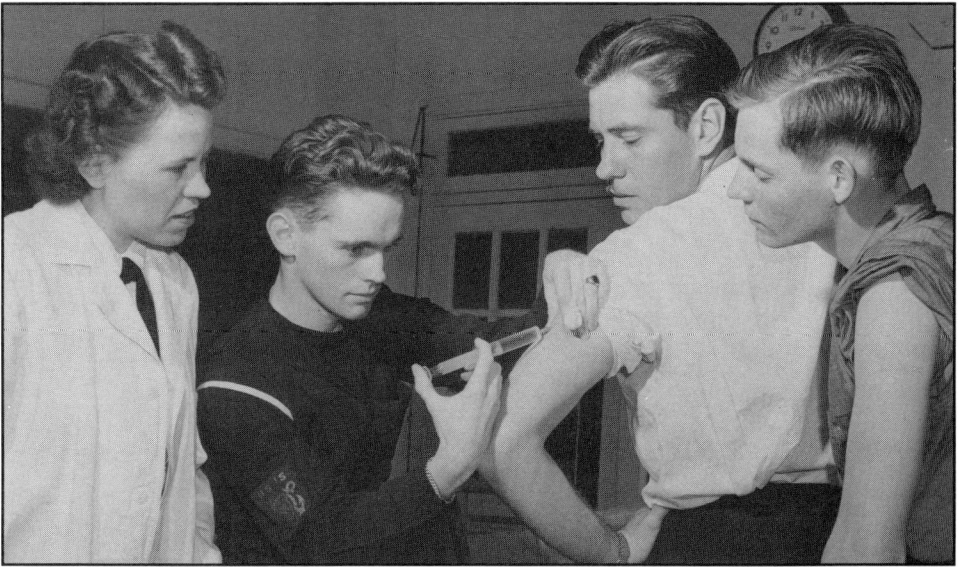

Part of the initiation—shots. Here a student under a nurse's supervision inoculates another, Sheepshead Bay, NY, 1945. (USMS)

7

me in June 1940 what I thought about the Maritime Service, I told him I didn't really know anything about it except that it apparently had something to do with ships and the sea.

I remarked, "Anything would be better than remaining in the C.C.C.," whose camps were run by Army personnel with about the same regimental routine. When I made that off-hand comment in Indiana, I meant to convince the orderly that he should accept an appointment in the Maritime Service, which he did. But the quota was full for the first round, and when the second round came up a month later he decided to stay because he was in love. That didn't stop him from making a decision about my future: he and the company clerk elected to submit my name, without informing me.

It was a total surprise on a Wednesday when the Lieutenant in charge asked if I wanted a day off to go home before departing on Friday. I asked, "Where to?" and he replied, "Fort Dix, N.J." That's when I found out that this country boy was in the Maritime Service.

The troop train I took was loaded to the hilt with recruits from all over the midwest. Arrival at Fort Dix was somewhat disheartening. We were assigned tents for accommodations, and everywhere outside the tents there was rain and knee-deep mud. Inspections were held with recruits lined up in muddy ruts while a very neat officer rode by on a very clean white horse.

A few days later, we were placed aboard buses and sent off to an undisclosed location. In the New York Navy Yard, we were quickly sent to board the *S.S. American Seaman*. It was July 1940, and we were out to sea - many of us for the first time.

On the first day, we were issued the regular Navy uniform - the 13-button britches, a pull-over blouse with the square collar hanging down the back. It was just great until "mal de mer", or something like that, lined up many of the apprentice sailors along the side of the ship to feed the fish.

Several days later, after I had thoroughly polished and repolished many objects on the bridge and cohorts had chipped paint over and over, we were called to muster on deck. About 1,000 responded to muster. After inspection, there was a general call for 500 volunteers for radio school.

"Anything would be better than what we were doing now," I thought. Operating a radio had to beat brass polishing any day. I stepped forward - and then looked forward - to pounding brass rather than polishing it.

The *S.S. American Seaman* dropped us off in Boston and we were ferried out to Gallups Island. It was easy to see why such a rugged group had been picked for Day One. Any self-respecting fellow who was accustomed to the modern amenities of life would probably have swum back to Boston - or wherever he started from. I was used to kerosene lamps, a wood-heating stove and an outhouse, so honestly this was a shade better.

The buildings - an abandoned quarantine station - were vintage 1900, or earlier. The head was a single pipe running along the wall with bell-shaped openings sticking up for those in need. Temporary shower stalls were ready in wood enclosures outside. In one of the old houses on the island, the explorers among us found a complete bathtub with running water. It was a deep secret for a discreet few. What a luxury!

Our group was assigned many jobs, and really helped organize the school. Workers were brought in from the Boston area, and soon classrooms and barracks were taking shape.

The fundamentals in our first classes were mainly in seamanship, pyrotechnics and lifesaving. Then electronics and its associated theories were introduced. It soon became evident that there was a distinction between "soon-to-be-seamen" and the possible "Future Maritime Radio Operators".

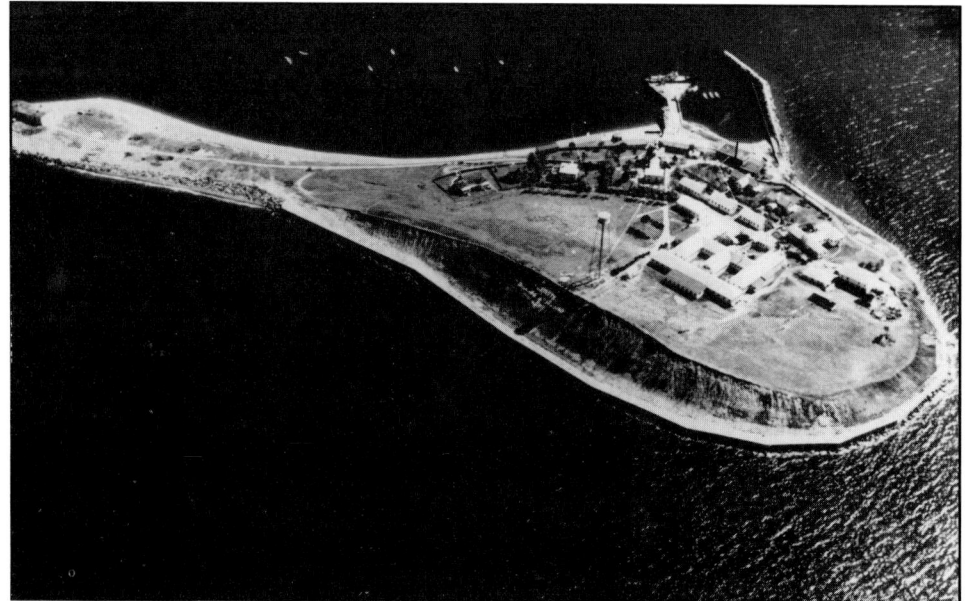

Gallups Island Radio School, Boston, MA.

Outside of the textbook learning, there was a special challenge: typing on a mill. Many of us knew touch-typing, but for those who had little acquaintance with such a contraption, learning code and type simultaneously was tough.

At this time, Hitler was rampaging through Europe with his notoriously quick, but efficient, Blitzkriegs. Accordingly, there were weekly Friday afternoon "weeding-out" tests called "Blitzkriegs." Fail one and you were restricted for the weekend liberty to Bean Town. Fail two - or maybe it was three - and you were relegated to become a seaman and be shipped out. That quickly and efficiently whittled our initial 500 fellows down to about 250.

I was on Gallups Island nearly 18 months. The initial classes got a longer, more leisurely and lengthy education than later groups. Our 10-man whaleboat crews trimmed the Navy and Coast Guard units on Boston's Charles River.

Finally, Graduation Day arrived. We had to pass a 50-question test administered by F.C.C. personnel, which we prepared for by reviewing a book appropriately called, "Questions and Answers." Most of us passed. Then came the CODE. Some breezed right through it; others froze with an iron fist. Finally, with hearty encouragement, most of us dit-dahed our way through to a Second Class Telegraph License. It was a proud day.

I was offered a teaching job on the island, but the call of the sea was too great. After all, we had watched many ships ply their way down the channel, which ran right by us, on their way to distant and mysterious ports, while we sat on that island real estate.

Shortly, I was en route to New York and the United Fruit Company's Great White Fleet in August 1941. My first ship was the *S.S. Carrillo*, out of Boston, on its way to the glamorous tropical port of Cortez, Honduras.

Before the war, it was kind of nice. I had a white uniform, white shoes, the epaulets. It was the first time I ever saw a full set of silverware.

Training policies and procedures were continually changed and refined as the Maritime Service confronted a need for seamen that burgeoned with our growing war effort.

A decision was made to separate apprentice seamen from experienced personnel, at least during the first months of training. After careful study, a 10-acre St. Petersburg, Fla. waterfront site was chosen as most suitable for the fourth shore station, to be devoted exclusively to training apprentice seamen. The property was donated by the City of St. Petersburg.

Neutrality Act of 1939 Sidelines Thousands of Seamen

Intent on keeping the United States out of war, Congress passed the Neutrality Act of 1939. Withdrawing many American ships from established European routes had the ripple effect of jeopardizing the livelihood of an estimated 10,000 seamen. New York was the port most affected.

An antidote? Training. As many as 4,000 of these seamen could be absorbed into the rapidly expanding Maritime Service. Gallups Island was enlarged to handle 800 more men. Collectively, facilities were made available that could turn out 8,000 seamen annually.

But despite the government's efforts to sidestep involvement in troubles abroad, European unrest escalated, convincing our leaders to "batten the hatches" and prepare for war. Part of the heightening activity for readiness was a renewed emphasis on the merchant fleet, and a mammoth shipbuilding effort was launched.

A West Coast training station for apprentice seamen was established at Port Hueneme in San Fernando County, Calif. Later, when the United States entered the war, this training station was turned over to the Navy for war purposes and the Maritime Service's training activities were moved to Avalon on Catalina Island, where buildings were already available.

To meet the ever-increasing need for trained seamen, the course for apprentice seamen was reduced from one year to nine months, then, in March 1941, to six months. As an emergency measure, regular courses for experienced unlicensed personnel and officers were suspended, so that all facilities could be devoted to training apprentice seamen for unlicensed positions, and qualified unlicensed personnel could be trained to obtain licenses as third mates and third assistant engineers. As demand continued to increase, four new training vessels were purchased and additional buildings were added to the shore stations.

In April 1941, when it became clear that the C.C.C. could not provide the number of men needed for apprentice training, the Maritime Service launched a system of general recruiting and the following month a nation-wide publicity campaign was underway. Enrollment of apprentices doubled in the quarter ending June 30, 1941, and almost doubled again during the next quarter.

Evidence of the pre-war program's effectiveness came when it was compared to the World War I experience, Knight said. Throughout the war, American merchant ships were operated by the War Shipping Administration as a civilian service. During World War I, the merchant fleet was, by successive stages, largely absorbed into the Navy. Had that war lasted much longer, the entire merchant service would have undoubtedly been militarized, Knight indicated.

More ships were needed, too. The Maritime Commission increased its production schedule for building cargo ships to 100 per year. Within a year, the timetable would be sped up again to a rate of 200 ships annually. The U.S. had to make up for its past sins of omission in the ship-building arena. It had to get on track for the challenges ahead.

1940

The first Merchant Marine ship to become a casualty of the Second World War was sunk a full year before Pearl Harbor, in the Bass Straits off Australia.

The *S.S. City of Rayville*, a freighter carrying 2,500 tons of lead ingots, struck a German-laid mine on November 9. Third Engineer Mack B. Bryan, one of her crew, lost his life in the incident, making him the first Merchant Marine casualty of World War II. The rest of the 36-man crew was rescued by local fishermen in two motorboats.

Five other merchant ships were sunk before our formal entry into the war.

Before the start of the war, merchant ships were privately owned and controlled by shipping companies for the transport of commercial cargo. Seamen signed shipping articles - normally for a period of not more than a year - that designated the nature of the voyage and its destination.

With the advent of World War II, the peacetime requirements and procedures changed. More than a year before the attack on Pearl Harbor, the Coast Guard began training merchant seamen in gunnery and other military subjects. The Naval Reserve also trained merchant seamen in military-related fields.

The world was on the verge of war.

1941

The shortage of ships had become apparent to President Franklin D. Roosevelt, as he received reports of heavy shipping losses in the European war. In January 1941, FDR authorized building 200 standard, prefabricated freighters of about 7,800 tons each. The price tag would be $350 million, with the first vessel expected to be complete in a year. Producing the ships quickly and producing many of them took top priority.

Hugo Schramm, transportation writer for the China-Burma-India Veterans Association's publication, "Sound-off," described this time of accelerated shipbuilding in his Fall 1990 "Ships Column:"

"FDR refused to say whether the ships would be turned over to Britain. Many would. Two months later, the Maritime Commission let contracts for the first 137 vessels. It was the beginning of the Liberty Ship program."

The Liberty was a modification of an earlier (1897) British design. Simple and economical to build, it proved that all-welded construction would work, and ushered in the era of prefabricated mass production.

The ships were built to last five years, and cost from $1.5 million to $2.3 million each to build. There were 19 yards building Liberty ships. Almost one-third of the workers producing them were women.

Some agreed with FDR, who referred to the new Liberty ships as "ugly ducklings." Others found names that were less favorable. But they accomplished what they were designed to do: deliver the goods.

Kaiser shipyards built the most, breaking production records over and over. Speed was of the essence in the race to get America's goods to the fighting forces abroad.

Schramm writes: "The Kaiser people tell the story of a lady who had been asked to baptize a ship. She arrived on the launching platform, was given the usual magnum bottle of champagne but there was no ship. Asking if a mistake had been made, a desk admiral told her to start swinging the bottle at once, for not only the stem but indeed the whole ship would arrive at any moment.

"The man who was responsible for the Liberty ship program was then 60-year-old Oregonian Henry J. Kaiser." A high school drop-out, he was the industrial leader of World War II. Kaiser began his illustrious career as a 'go-fer' with a highway construction company. Besides his war-time shipyards in Richmond, Calif. and other U.S. seaports, Kaiser supervised the construction of the Boulder-Coulee and Bonneville Dams, which Army engineers had predicted could not be erected the Kaiser way. He also collaborated on the Oakland Bay Bridge.

In August 1942, Kaiser told a Senate

SS John W. Brown, one of two remaining operational Liberty ships. Based in Baltimore, the Brown and her sister Liberty, the SS Jeremiah O'Brien in San Francisco, serve as museums and bases for Merchant Marine veterans' groups.

subcommittee that he had never seen a shipyard until 1940, but now he could deliver 70-ton flying boats in 10 months and larger ones in 14. At that point, Kaiser shipyards had completed 100 10,000-ton ships and reduced the building time of each to 46 days.

Kaiser hit his all-time record in September 1942, when his shipyard turned out the *Joseph Neal* in 10 days.

"All told, (Kaiser) was able to launch about 1,500 Liberty ships, almost one-third of all U.S. maritime production," wrote Schramm.

The Liberty's design called for a welded hull, rather than a riveted one, which had been the prevailing marine practice of the day. A welded hull made the ship strong, but difficult to maneuver in storms since it didn't "give" to the motions of the sea as a riveted hull would.

Even before the United States' new Liberty ships rolled out of production and into the high seas, negotiations were afoot to acquire a whole fleet of idle Danish ships to add to the nation's seagoing force.

In February 1941, the U.S. Maritime Commission announced that the American flag would be raised over 58 vessels all berthed in North and South American ports. Many Danish seamen from these ships served in the American Merchant Marine throughout the duration of the war.

The transfer represented a compromise in a stalemate between representatives of the British Shipping Ministry and the Danish operators over which country should operate the ships.

American-owned companies were allowed to charter the ships for Western Hemisphere and Pacific Ocean service, thus releasing British ships for pressing duty in the North Atlantic.

This deal left the Pacific to the American Merchant Marine. The British agreed to withdraw their ships in the Pacific. The United States agreed to take over there.

By May 1941, pressure was mounting. On May 21, a German U-boat sank the *S.S. Robin Moor*, an American freighter of the Robin Line in a South Atlantic neutral zone. En route to North Africa, the *Robin Moor* was stopped at sea by the submarine's commander. Her crew was given 20 minutes to abandon ship. Then she was summarily shelled and sunk by torpedo.

Bob Burton, a member of the Seafarers International Union who was aboard the *Robin Moor*, recalled the puzzling incident for the editors of a pamphlet entitled, "SIU at War" a few years later.[1]

The sub came up to the four lifeboats and gave their inhabitants some bread before drawing off and shelling the vessel. The German sub commander "knew we were American, for there were big American flags painted on our hull," explained Burton.

Happily for Burton - who survived two subsequent torpedo attacks on ships he served on - his lifeboat was adrift for only 15 days before being picked up by an English ship and taken to Cape Town.

FDR echoed Burton's bewilderment about the incident when he delivered a special message to Congress on June 20.

"The submarine did not display its flag, and the commander did not announce his nationality," FDR said. "The *Robin Moor* was sunk without provision for the safety of the passengers and crew. It was sunk despite that fact that its American nationality was admittedly known to the commander of the submarine, and that its nationality was likewise clearly indicated by the flag and other markings.

"The total disregard shown for the most elementary principles of international law and of humanity brands the sinking of the *Robin Moor* as an act of international outlaw.

"Its general purpose would appear to be to drive American commerce from the ocean wherever such commerce was considered a disadvantage to German designs; and its specific purpose would appear to be the interruption of our trade with all friendly countries.

"We must take it that notice has now been served upon us that no American ship or cargo on any of the seven seas can consider itself immune from acts of piracy. Notice is served on us, in effect, that the German Reich proposes so to intimidate the United States that we would be dissuaded from carrying out our chosen policy of helping Britain to survive.

"In brief, we must take the sinking of the *Robin Moor* as a warning to the United States not to resist the Nazi movement of world conquest. It is a warning that the United States may use the high seas of the world only with Nazi consent.

"Were we to yield on this we would inevitably submit to world domination at the hands of the present leaders of the German Reich.

"We are not yielding and do not propose to yield."[2]

Unfortunately, neither did the enemy.

By September 1941, gunnery training of merchant crews had been authorized on 83 Panamanian flag vessels. In October, President Roosevelt asked Congress to lift the ban on arming merchant ships, saying it was not fair to deny merchant seaman the means of defending their lives and their ships while "sailing the seas on missions connected with the defense of the United States."

One month later, Congress complied with the president's request and authorized merchant ships to be armed. Merchant seamen began to get additional military training in gunnery, handling barrage balloons, wartime communications, gas warfare, swimming through burning oil and enemy ship spotting at night.

Normal peacetime requirements about specific information in shipping articles also changed. The Secretary of the Navy ordered that particulars about a ship's destination, the duration and nature of the voyage could be excluded from the articles.

Seamen were expected to sign onto ships with "unknown" as the defining characteristic of the trips.

Robert Giles, who sailed in the latter part of the war, devised a simple but clever system to let his wife know about where he was during the war.

Before he left, Giles gave her a map with men's names written on different islands in the Pacific, where he expected to be sent. The second sentence in his letters to her would be the tip-off. "Tell John to pay the $10 he owes me" would signal his wife to check the map for the island labeled "John."

Although he had often left a port by the time she heard from him, it gave her some idea of where her husband had been.

The first Liberty ship, the *S.S. Patrick Henry*, was launched September 27, 1941. The day was observed as "Liberty Fleet Day," and it was still some 10 weeks before Pearl Harbor. Her maiden voyage was to Suez, via Cape Town with stores for the British in Egypt.

December 7, 1941 - A Fateful Day Aboard Ship for Far-Flung Sailors

The Japanese attack on Pearl Harbor on December 7 has been the subject of intense attention and scrutiny by historians because of the element of surprise and the staggering losses it engendered on U.S. soil. It was a defining moment in the war.

But few have pondered the individual incidents of Japanese aggression elsewhere on that day, which were tell-tale predictors of their intentions.

The first American target sunk by a Japanese submarine in World War II was not anywhere near Pearl Harbor. It was the *S.S. Cynthia Olson*, a steam schooner manned by civilian seamen of the U.S. Army Transport Service. The ship was attacked 1,000 miles northeast of Hawaii at least 17 minutes before the initial detection of enemy planes headed for Pearl Harbor.

Maritime historian Charles Dana Gibson, who served during World War II as a seaman in the Army Transportation Corps and the Merchant Marine, has been credited with uncovering a U.S. Army message in government archives revealing details of the Japanese submarine attack on the *Cynthia Olson*.

The *S.S. Lurline*, 300 miles away, received a radio distress call from the transport - but neither the ship nor its 33-member crew and two U.S. Army passengers were seen or heard from thereafter.

In his book "A Careless Word...", Moore reprints a letter dated December 26, 1941 to Mrs. Carlson Berthel of San Pedro, Calif, apparently a relative of one of the crew members, from a C. H. Kells, Lt. Colonel, Q.M.C., Assistant about the incident.

It reads, in part:

"It is regretted that no definite information can be given you of the fate of the crew of the CYNTHIA OLSON. The Army, however, has not given up the whole crew of this vessel as lost without a trace.

"It is true that early on the morning of

December 7 the CYNTHIA OLSON sent an SOS stating she was being attacked by an enemy submarine. Nothing further was ever heard from this vessel or the crew. The Japanese press announced the vessel had been torpedoed and sunk. Our Army and Navy used all means possible to locate some trace of this vessel or its crew ..."[3]

The letter is full of conjecture, offering hope that some of the crew could have escaped in life boats and made it ashore, or that the ship might have been "torpedoed by a Japanese submarine, that this submarine took aboard it the members of the crew and, as is customary in cases of this kind, will keep such information a secret until the submarine returns to its home base or to a port where the crew can be put ashore."

Such hopes, of course, were fruitless for Mrs. Carlson, for the USAT, and for countless others as the war progressed and more and more Merchant Marines were missing in the line of duty.

S.S. President Harrison's Master Runs Ship Aground to Render it Useless to Japanese on Pearl Harbor Day

Another amazing footnote to the Pearl Harbor attack originated on the *S.S. President Harrison*, a passenger ship that was intentionally run aground in the Yangtse River just after Pearl Harbor so the Japanese couldn't use it as a troopship to further their imperial goals.

Alas, despite the captain's valiant stand, the ship was only moderately damaged and it eventually was repaired for service by the Japanese.

Moore described what happened that fateful morning:[4]

When the *President Harrison's* master received word about Pearl Harbor, he tried to slip out of the Yangtse River below Shanghai. It soon became apparent that he would not succeed in getting away from a Japanese cruiser and liner blocking his way, so the captain ordered the ship run aground at full speed in the hope of rendering it useless to the Japanese.

The captain also ordered that his 166-man crew prepare to abandon ship before it struck the shoreline of Shewieshan Island. Three crewmen drowned abandoning ship; the rest made it safely to shore.

"The master was sentenced to a six-month jail sentence at the Japanese Naval Station in Sasebo, Japan for beaching and wrecking the *President Harrison*. The remaining deck and engineer officers were kept as prisoners of war by the Japanese. The rest of the crew was interned in Shanghai as civilian enemy nationals. Ten months later, all these crew members were interned in various civilian camps in the Shanghai area. Later in the war, some officers and crew members were sent to work in the coal mines at Hokkaido, Japan.

"The ship was later salvaged by a Japanese salvage firm, repaired and named the *Kakko Maru*, then later renamed *Kachidoki Maru*. She was torpedoed and sunk by the *U.S.S. Pampanito* in the South China Sea on September 12, 1944 while en route from Singapore to Japan. On board were about 900 Allied prisoners of war. Those prisoners who were saved were picked up by Japanese submarines and returned to prison camps."[5]

Twelve of the President Harrison's crew members died as captives of the Japanese.

Although these stories are among the most dramatic of merchant mariners on December 7, 1941, seamen on land across the country and scattered on waterways throughout the world knew their lives would forever change when they heard about the Pearl Harbor debacle.

Devastating and definitive, the Japanese actions catapulted the country into war. The U.S. could no longer rely on a position of "neutrality."

Here's how Jerry McClish remembers that fateful day, and how it changed his life at sea: "I was on the *S.S. Hiburas* about 80 miles south of Mobile inbound when the message came across, 'To all merchant ships - The Japanese have bombed Pearl Harbor. Repeat, the Japanese have bombed Pearl Harbor. This is no joke.' We were at war.

"A trip or two later, while moored at the New Orleans city docks, a crew of painters came aboard and presto, the ship was all gray - including the windows. Then came radio silence and the start of BAMS (short for Broadcast to Allied Merchant Ships.)"

BAMS were broadcast by the War Department in Washington at least twice a day. "The broadcast was a list of call letters for all the ships that had radio traffic coming up. If your ship was on the list, you had to sit and wait for the message to come up." When BAMS messages for the vessel arrived, McClish dutifully copied them.

Many times McClish took the messages to his Norwegian skipper, a Capt. Fuglestad, who chose to ignore them, saying sheepishly to McClish, "Sparky, we never received that message, did we?"

Rather than stay on course with the convoy, the captain would give instructions that maneuvered the ship away from the pack. Mariners who went to sleep as part of a convoy awoke without any ships in sight.

Many veteran skippers like Capt. Fuglestad had dedicated their lives to the sea, and they did not take kindly to being ordered around by the U.S. War Department. Especially when they thought the orders could jeopardize their lives and the lives of everyone aboard ship.

To these captains, the convoy system did not represent strength in numbers, but more aptly senseless regimentation. Convoys, in their view, were no better than sitting ducks bobbing together in a pond. Mavericks - or renegades - like Capt. Fuglestad broke out of convoys, on the theory that subs were less likely to follow a single ship than they were a group of ships.

"During the early days of the war, along torpedo alley, which was the South Atlantic coast, there was never a night that we did not see a burning ship on the horizon, after the very steady 'dit dit dit dah dah dah dit dit dit' followed by the position. Sometimes there was a goodbye rather hurriedly. Then you would wonder if they ever made it to the lifeboats," McClish recalled.

"I was lucky. We were chased only once, about 100 miles south of New Orleans. Since our ship was riding high, it was possible that the sub did not want to waste a torpedo on an empty vessel."

War Shipping Administration Created

Shortly after Pearl Harbor, President Roosevelt, by executive order, created the War Shipping Administration (WSA) as a temporary war agency responsible for acquiring control over and operating all American merchant vessels other than those assigned to the Army and Navy.

Then, the WSA took control of all off-shore merchant vessels under various types of charters, while the Maritime Commission concentrated its energies on the ship construction program. As the use of these vessels was transferred from the private operators and assigned to the government, the WSA appointed the private steamship

Pearl Harbor Day

companies as government agents to carry out the many intricate details involved in the technical phases of steamship operation.

Through the the WSA, most merchant seamen became employees of the United States, and 75 percent of merchant shipping was allocated to Army and Navy cargoes. In addition to equipment and ammunition, merchant ships transported military and civilian personnel to war zones, including the great majority of more than seven million Army personnel transported overseas.

Decisions about the escalating war were coming from Washington at a feverish pace. Unfortunately for the seamen lost in unescorted ships along the East Coast of the United States, some important decisions were being side-stepped.

Ian Miller, founder of the Sons and Daughters of the U.S. Merchant Marine Veterans of W.W. II, describes the tenor of the times in his article for the Seamen's Recognition Day program, in observance of the 40th anniversary of 'V-E' Day:

"After December 7, 1941 and the attack on Pearl Harbor, the U.S. sent almost any ship that would float off to the West Coast in preparation for a Japanese invasion that never did materialize. In the meantime, there was a very real war taking place off the East Coast. Prior to Pearl Harbor, the Navy had been escorting foreign merchant ships from American ports to Iceland. Yet they refused to do likewise for our own ships when it was needed most. This attitude of indifference in our high command was to cost the lives of hundreds of merchant seamen.

"Oddly, the chief saving grace for the men of the Merchant Marine came from Germany. Hitler stubbornly refused to allow Admiral Donitz the number of U-boats that he wanted to send to American waters. Operation Paukenschlag signaled the mass slaughter of merchant shipping off our coast. Instead of the hundreds that the press of the day spoke of, there were relatively few U-boats.

"But these sliced through our merchant shipping like a hot knife through butter. Battle hardened U-boat commanders came to our shores expecting a continuation of the convoy battles they had faced in the North Atlantic. They could not believe what they found. City lights were shining bright, aids to navigation were on, and best of all, there was no U.S. Navy to counter-attack.

"At first the merchant ships were unarmed and many a German sailor looked aghast as merchant seamen were cremated alive when their tankers were torpedoed. In spite of repeated pleas from our British allies who had the experience, our Navy top brass steadfastly refused to use a convoy system. The merchant ships and the men of the Merchant Marine became mere cannon fodder. At night, with the lights of cities like Miami ablaze, U-boat commanders had only to sit and wait while the ships paraded in front of them. In the morning, the local resort owners would complain to authorities about the oil, cargo and at times mangled and dead merchant seamen that were washed up on their beautiful white beaches.

"The concern was not for the poor devils of the Merchant Marine; rather it was for the negative effect on the tourist trade. This callousness was to be a preview of the regard that we as a nation would have for those who sailed in our merchant ships during the war."

Caught in War: Joseph Vernick Becomes P.O.W.

An oiler on the *S.S. Ruth Alexander* in October of 1941, Joseph Vernick thought he would make one more trip before considering his sister's invitation to live and work in Honolulu.

"When we left Honolulu, instead of going directly west we headed south. And we started blacking out portholes," he recalls. At stops along their route, Vernick and the crew watched Australian and New Zealand troops getting ready. War appeared to be imminent.

"We arrived in Manila on the day of Pearl Harbor. What great timing," he observes wryly. Within 10 days, Manila itself was under fire. Sixty-eight ships were sunk in the air raids.

One day, Vernick emerged from an air raid shelter across the street from where the *Ruth Alexander* was docked to discover that the ship had hastily departed - apparently on orders, as word of the Japanese invasion came - leaving some of her crew behind. (She was subsequently attacked in the China Sea by Japanese bombers on December 31, 1941, sinking a few days later.)

American President Lines put Vernick and the other stranded crew members up in a hotel and asked them to help out. Vernick and four others volunteered to help the Army run supplies to Corregidor and Bataan in light boats during the last weeks of December 1941.

When word came that the Japanese were invading Manila, Vernick helped smash cases of liquor from warehouses so the Japanese wouldn't get it, and handed out food to the Philippine people.

Finally, on January 3, 1942, the Japanese got to the hotel where Vernick was staying and rounded up everyone. It was the beginning of his nearly three and a half years in captivity.[6]

First he was interned at the University of Santo Thomas for one year, then he was sent with other younger prisoners to a camp 60 miles away called Los Banos. This camp eventually filled up with men, women and children as the Japanese conquered more territory.

Hunger was the prevailing condition that afflicted Vernick and his fellow P.O.W.s. Prisoners could also be subjected to brutal beatings, or if they tried to escape, execution.

"The first year wasn't bad because as long as they thought they were winning the war, the Japanese were magnanimous. But as the Americans got closer, capturing island after island, the Filipinos realized the Americans were coming back. They were digging up their arms and bolos and starting guerilla action. This created a serious disruption of our food supply in camp," Vernick told Jaffee.[7]

Leaves became a staple - even morning glory leaves, despite their sand-paper quality. A dog or cat was a delicacy, a feast. At one point, Vernick and two friends decided to break into the compound that stored supplies for the Japanese. After casing the place for several nights, they chose a cloudy, drizzly night to break in with the help of a screwdriver. Almost discovered by a Japanese sentry - which would have meant certain death - they managed to remain undetected in the shadows and come out with corn, brown sugar and cigarettes.

Their near-miss with the authorities came only a few weeks before their liberation.

"On February 23, (1945) we were virtually starving. The Japanese called us for roll call, and they were going to execute us all. They lined us all up. Two thousand of the people they were going to execute. Somehow I think our military heard about it....

"We heard planes. I went out there and you could see 11 or 12 planes. We didn't know what they were. All of a sudden, little black things dropped out...Sure enough, I could see the white star. All of a sudden those little black dots turned into parachutes. The next thing I knew, parachute troops came down right in the middle of the camp. Guerrillas were in the back of the hills."[8]

Soon, amphibious tanks came into the camp and, in the midst of Japanese resistance, started picking up the prisoners. Vernick survived the liberation.

Once out in the rehabilitation camp, it was discovered that he had beri-beri. Vernick became ill from eating the routine food - such as eggs and ham - that was being given to the starved prisoners. When officials realized what was happening to the ex-P.O.W.s, some of whom died from eating rich food, they cut back to rice rations until the starving people could digest more complex foods.

Vernick was brought back to the U.S. on the *Admiral Capps*.

"Of the 123 merchant mariners in our camp, many died - some even after returning home from beri-beri," says Vernick.

As president of the U.S. Merchant Marine Veterans of World War II, Vernick spearheaded the acquisition of the S.S. Lane Victory to be a "living monument to those mariners who perished for the security and freedom which we all now enjoy." He is loathe to talk about himself and his war experiences, but relishes any opportunity to talk about the ship, which is docked in San Pedro, Calif. More about the Lane Victory later in this book.

1942 - Merchant Mariners Face Unprecedented Danger

In his book <u>Operation Drumbeat</u>, Michael Gannon called it "The Atlantic Pearl Harbor." That phrase aptly describes the devastation that was visited on the Merchant Marine along the Eastern seaboard, in the Gulf of Mexico and in the Caribbean in late 1941 and early 1942.

But he maintains that few people realize

the impact of this carnage of lives and vessels was more crippling than the Pacific catastrophe because of its debilitating effect on the British and United States' war efforts.

"The losses by submarines off our Atlantic seaboard and in the Caribbean now threaten our entire war effort," lamented Army Chief of Staff General George C. Marshall in June of 1942.

One month before, FDR underscored the importance of the Merchant Marine, proclaiming: "The war is now five months old and we have had our answer. Two million men have been called to the colors. In far places and near, our soldiers, our sailors, our air pilots, the beleaguered men of the Merchant Marine have shown the stuff of heroes. Everything we have asked of them they have delivered. Everything - and more."

"Beleaguered" was an understatement. "Defenseless" would have made the description more complete.

Many Merchant Mariners felt that what they needed - primarily guns for self-defense, and gunners to use them, were not being installed at all - or as quickly as they should be - on the older, vulnerable ships on which they risked their lives.

Laying in wait along the coast shipping lanes, German submarine pilots could choose their targets like marksmen at a shooting range.

The coal-burning *City of Atlanta* went down on the morning of January 19, 1942, as she passed Diamond Shoals, North Carolina headed for New York City.

Within five minutes of being torpedoed, the ship sank and she took 43 men to their deaths. There were three survivors. The following account is based on the "Seafarers Log" of January 26, 1942:

"The *City of Atlanta* was steaming northbound, just rounding Hatteras at about 2 a.m., when it received the first torpedo. No prior warning was given and the first the crew knew of the presence of enemy subs was the violent explosion that all but tore the Atlanta out of the water. The survivors are certain that the torpedo must have hit the boilers, blowing them up, and accounting for the rapidity of the sinking.

"Immediately after launching the torpedo, the submarine came to the surface and began to shell the ship. One shell went directly through (the room of Robert Fennell Jr., oiler.)"

Earl Dowdy, AB, was also off watch and in his room when the attack came. "By some miracle he was able to get into his life belt and onto the deck. Most of the life boats had been smashed and he dove overboard. Dowdy swam violently to get away from the ship before she went under.

"Over his shoulder he could see the deck gang trying to launch the only remaining life boat. They succeeded in getting it into the water and started to pull away. Before they could pull two strokes, the Atlanta gave a mighty shudder, and then rolled over on top of the life boat, crushing it and taking it to the bottom of the ocean.

"The water was churned to a froth as the ship disappeared from view. Gear, broken life boats, and great planks from the bridge were tossed in the air wildly.

"Then, as the icy waters calmed, a blinding searchlight flashed on them from the conning tower of the lurking submarine. The white light snapped off, and the black hull of the submarine quietly sank beneath the surface of the water. Dowdy swam to a piece of the wreckage. It was a long plank and he grasped one end of it. Soon other survivors swam over to the planking. Ten men grasped the improvised life raft. Then began the long cold vigil, waiting for some ship to pass that would rescue them."

The water was cold. Few men had been able to get the life belts. Many were wounded. One by one, their grasp on the plank relaxed - they slipped beneath the water. Dowdy watched them go - helpless. After the first hour there were only five left. Two more went during the next hour. The three remaining men talked, and then sang a little to keep their spirits up. And then Dowdy was alone.

For six hours Dowdy clung to his raft. At 8 a.m. the *Seatrain Texas* appeared on the horizon. Dowdy yelled and waved his arms. Against many odds, the ship saw him, launched a boat and picked him up.

As Dowdy was pulled into the boat, the *Seatrain* quartermaster spotted Fennell and (George) Tavelle, 2nd mate. They had been drifting separately on wreckage.

Fennell's leg was badly torn by the shell that had gone through his room, and he was barely conscious when he was picked up. In the explosion that had awakened him from a sound sleep, the entire side of Fennell's room had been blown away.

"I started up the passageway and felt my right foot buckling. I pulled up my trousers and saw just one bloody mass. I kept on going up the passageway and suddenly remembered my wife's picture hanging on the wall. I went back down to get it. It wasn't on the wall, so I looked around and found it had been thrown on the bunk by the force of the explosion. I took it out of its frame, folded it twice, and put it in my pocket."

When he was rescued, Tavelle was suffering from exposure and only lived because of the prompt first aid treatment he received aboard the *Seatrain Texas*.

The waters off Cape Hatteras were indeed treacherous, populated as they were by enemy subs. A dozen ships had been sunk in this area within a two-week period.

And so it was that, within less than a week of the *City of Atlanta*'s sinking, the *S.S. Venore* met the same fate about 20 miles southeast of the cape. But her story is an even more riveting one, because she fell victim to a ruse by the German U-boat commander.

Here's how "The SIU at War" pamphlet from the Seafarers International Union of North America recounted the tale:[9]

A Nazi Trick Sunk the S.S. Venore

This freighter went down off the Carolina shore with her skipper, the radio operator and 18 members of the crew.

After spending 38 hours in an open boat, 21 survivors were picked up and taken to Norfolk, where they described the trickery used by the Nazis in sinking their ship.

Masquerading in the dark as a light ship, the sub blinked a code message for the *S.S. Venore* to come closer. While the unsuspecting freighter changed her course and veered off to see what the light ship wanted, the sub's gun crew was aiming its deck gun. When the *Venore* came within range, they opened fire, sending several shells into her. Soon thereafter, two torpedoes smashed into the ship almost simultaneously.

"Two crashes so far. Will keep informed. Think swimming soon," read the first message from the *Venore's* radio operator.

Two minutes later a second message snapped out: "Torpedoed twice. Ship still afloat, but listing badly. Captain requests assistance immediately."

The *Venore* was going down fast but

HIGHEST W. W. II CASUALTIES

Members of the U. S. Merchant Marine serving aboard U. S. cargo ships and tankers during W. W. II suffered a greater percentage of war related deaths than did the nations regular armed forces combined.

Branch of Service	Total Number Who Served	War Deaths	Percent of Members	Odds of Being Killed
ARMY	11,268,000	234,874	2.88%	1 in 48
NAVY	4,183,466	36,958	.88%	1 in 114
MARINES	669,108	14,733	2.94%	1 in 34
COAST GUARD	241,093	574	.24%	1 in 417
TOTAL:	16,361,667	287,139	1.76%	1 in 57
MERCHANT MARINES	215,000	6,795	3.16%	1 in 32

Sparks stuck in his shack, tapping out messages that helped direct rescue ships to the spot.

At 1:22 a.m., the last message came: "Cannot stay afloat much longer."

The freighter must have plummeted to the bottom after that, because another message was started but never finished. Sparks went down with the ship.

After spending 38 hours in an open boat, 21 survivors were picked up and taken to Norfolk, where they described their ordeal.

Crew members who weren't killed in the torpedo blasts succeeded in launching several boats, but two of them swamped in the heavy seas and some of the men were drowned.

Survivors in the boats that pulled away from the ship feared that they would be shot by machine guns, so they lay in the boats' bottoms, not daring to take their place at the oars. For several hours, they drifted until they were sure the sub was gone.

During the next day, several ships passed without seeing them.

Allen Horton, who was on watch in the crow's nest when the *Venore* first saw the fake signals, had this to say about the Nazi strategy: "They fooled us completely. The light blinked in code that the vessel was a lightship. She told us to come over near her. We started toward her, still thinking she was a lightship, when a shell hit us in the bow. It didn't do so much damage, but we were called to our stations.

"Then the submarine moved around to our port side and a torpedo hit us. A general alarm was sounded. That sub, when it circled us that time, signaled with her lights as if she were a buoy. But she didn't fool us that time and when the second torpedo struck us, we were as ready as we could be. But without guns it didn't mean much."

Going to Sea, and Being Lucky

"I was on the East Coast and sailed coastwise through the carnage. I saw ships sinking and oil slicks where ships went down. But I safely sailed the East Coast to the Gulf on a tanker several times," recalls John O. Smith, now first vice president of the U.S. Merchant Marine Veterans of World War II.

Smith estimates that merchant mariners were in direct danger about 15 to 20 percent of the time they were at sea during World War II. But since no one knew when trouble lurked beneath the water or over the horizon, it could make for some tense traveling.

Raised on the Chesapeake Bay in Virginia, Smith answered the lure of the ships he watched coming and going on the waterfront. The excitement their destinations promised intrigued him. "I knew no matter what I did I'd never make enough money to see the world," he says.

So at the age of 16, he made his first working voyage on a ship and he hasn't stopped since.

When the war started, Smith tried to join the Navy, but he was told that he was more valuable in the Merchant Marines. So he sailed as chief engineer on various ships in various war zones. Ships on which he sailed were attacked by submarines and aircraft. "I've seen torpedoes go by on each side of the ship. But I was most fortunate to escape injury."

Once, he escaped a Murmansk trip because the ship he served on broke down. He figures that need for repair might have saved his life. Since his ship couldn't join the convoy, she was sent alone to the Persian Gulf.

In 1943, a ship on which Smith served received a radio message than an E-boat was in the South Atlantic in their neighborhood. "We immediately changed our course and escaped," he explains.

Smith experienced every shade of weather, too, from hurricanes and tropical heat to ice and hail storms. But again, there was never any major damage to his ships from poor weather.

Convoys could be as troublesome as they were comforting, especially when ships broke down at night and stopped, dead ahead. "The little blue light on the stern in front of you would be all you could see. It was well-hidden."

Did all this excitement conspire to scare him?

"I was too young and stupid to think about it. I always had the feeling that 'it wouldn't happen to me'."

Aboard the many ships he worked on, Smith observed "an endless variety of human nature." Even in the most hair-raising moments, his shipmates did not show their fear. "The bulk of them may have been scared in their hearts, but they'd never show it."

After the war, Smith kept to the sea. He was the City of Long Beach's chief engineer who worked on the *Queen Mary* when she was brought to her new berth in the U.S. from Southampton in 1967.

"They sent me to England to learn the complex utility systems on the *Queen Mary*. I was with her for her 40-day historical trip from Southampton, when we went around Cape Horn to Long Beach."

He stayed with the *Queen Mary* for seven years. Now, he is a dedicated volunteer with the *S.S. Lane Victory* in San Pedro.

Stopping to Pick Up Stranded Man on Raft, Against Orders

Michael Morow started going to sea at the age of 14 as a deckboy/cabin boy on the *Seagull*, a German sea tug running in the English channel between Antwerp and London in the early 1920s. He came to the U.S. in time for the Depression. Jobs were

scarce, and he rode mostly tankers through the early '30s.

Soon after the war broke out, Morow shipped as quartermaster on the *S.S. Argentina*, taking troops to Australia just a few months after Pearl Harbor. Here's how he described some of his wartime experiences in the "NMU Pilot" of August 1986:

"We sailed all by ourselves without any convoy because there was a big push on in New Guinea against the invading Japanese. From there we went into the Caribbean. There, while I was on the 4-to-8 watch, we spotted a man on a raft. It was strictly against the rules to stop in this kind of situation because there were so many subs in the area and they were known to set this kind of a trap.

"But Captain Simmons said, 'Stop the ship. Open the sideports and get this man aboard as soon as you can.' The operation took just a few minutes and we all held our breath until the ship got underway again. The captain was a good man and a fine seaman. Later I sailed with his son, a second mate, on the Panama Line.

"Next I shipped aboard a Hog Islander to Casablanca where we lay in the harbor almost a month waiting to discharge our cargo of ammunition. We were originally bound for Murmansk. They had issued us Arctic zoot suits and fur vests. Lucky for us we had engine trouble and could not sail, because that whole convoy we were supposed to go with was wiped out."

March brought no relief for the merchant mariners. Vessels of all kinds went down at an average of more than one a day in March.

In <u>Operation Drumbeat</u>, Gannon recounts the March 4 meeting in the nation's capital between members of the Tanker Committee of the Petroleum Industry War Council and representatives of the Navy and War departments.

By then, 65 ships had been sunk along the East Coast and in the Caribbean, of which 27 (41.5 percent) were tankers. At that rate, an industry spokesmen told those gathered, there would only be 125 tankers left of the 320 available for the region. Another 3,000 merchant marines would die. And the oil supply would drop to intolerable levels, both for U.S. domestic needs and to further the war effort, for the U.S. or its Allies.[10]

These projections were well-founded. "During March, vessels of all kinds went down at an average of more than one a day."[11]

Gannon continues: "Daunted by the appalling losses of the past seven weeks, merchant seamen who in the first weeks of the war had proved eager to sign on for new sailings after being torpedoed, were now increasingly demoralized by the sinkings, especially engine room men on tankers, who were leaving in troubling numbers. In the past chief mates complained about men who got drunk in port or were hard to handle; now they complained about not finding enough men to make a crew. One master reported that on reaching home port, 13 of a crew of 30 disappeared. Aggravating the problems of deteriorating morale and crew shortages was the belief of some Navy and shipping officials that certain crewmen were Axis sympathizers who had been induced by enemy agents in various New York and Brooklyn bars ... to divulge sailing times. But most Navy officials dismissed this possiblity as irrelevant since, as one said, 'The submarines could lie off focal points up and down the coast and await the arrival of ships without having any previous knowledge of sailing times'."[12]

Submarine commanders did not have to resort to espionage reports and the persuasiveness of spies. They could just lie in wait and watch, secure in the knowledge that a target would sail along the heavily traveled shipping route. If daytime duty seemed too hazardous for their taste, the U-boat commanders could wait until nighttime, when the shoreline would be lit like a centenarian's birthday cake.

In fact, in March Admiral King requested only a "dimout", not a "blackout" along the Eastern Seaboard.

Gannon details the dire consequences of the decision: "On the very day that King was rejecting blackouts, the 7,610-GRT American freighter *S.S. Lemuel Burrows* was torpedoed and sunk by *U-404* off Atlantic City, New Jersey. Twenty crewmen died. The second engineer, who arguably had a better picture of the situation from his lifeboat than King had from his desk, reported that the lights of a New Jersey beach resort doomed his vessel...The engineer added, 'We might as well run with our lights on. The lights were like Coney Island. It was lit up like daylight all along the beach'."[13]

No general blackout was declared along the East Coast. Shielding and dimout was as drastic as Admiral King cared to be, with a concurring nod from the Army. Civilians weren't eager to assist under their own initiative, and the U-boats continued to prevail.[14]

Another casualty in this holocaust was the *S.S. Barbara*, a combination passenger-freighter of the Bull Line.

The *Barbara* was one of the first to be lost in the Windward Passage between Haiti and Cuba, on a warm night in March that made the war seem far-removed. But a German sub's torpedo that hit the bunkers midships shattered the 2:30 a.m. Caribbean quiet.

Again, the "The SIU at War" booklet details what happened next.[15]

John Taurin, the quartermaster, felt the

jolt, dressed hurriedly and ran on deck to find that flames prevented him from reaching the boats.

Although three rafts had been put over the side, Taurin and Bosun Charles Rooney were too late and found themselves stranded on the after part of the ship.

Preparing to "swim for it," they noticed the gangway secured to number 5 hatch.

"It was better than nothing," Taurin said, so they cut the lashings, dumped the gangway over the side and dived into the water.

A passenger joined them. The three survivors paddled away on their precarious float as the sub started shelling the *Barbara*. They devised a see-saw system with Taurin, the heaviest of the three, paddling at one end to balance the gangway. The other two survivors kept to the other end.

Smoke from the burning ship settled like a fog that kept them from seeing other rafts and the sub. Waves were washing over them almost continuously. In the morning, they watched a shark circle them a number of times, then swim away. In a few hours, more appeared and by afternoon six or seven kept vigil around the shipwrecked men.

The motion of their feet as they paddled to keep afloat kept the sharks at a distance, but never chased them away.

Escaping the sinking *Barbara,* the men were covered with bunker oil. As the sun rose, the oil caked on them like tar. Combined with the salt water they unavoidably gulped and the increasing intensity of the sun, they eventually became unquenchably thirsty.

As the seas swelled higher the second night, they had to fight harder to keep their heads out of the water. Knowing that sharks were waiting for them to tire and drop off added to the strain.

In the morning and afternoon of the first day, planes passed high overhead without spotting them. When the planes passed at the same time on the second day, Taurin knew they hadn't drifted very far. He could see the mountains of Cuba and Haiti on either side, a reassuring presence that meant warships would probably be out searching the area.

"I determined to hang on at any cost," he said. Neither he nor Rooney spoke, because they could barely move their tongues. Hanging on, they ducked the spray that broke over the gangway and continued kicking their legs to keep the sharks away.

Sadly, the third man - a Puerto Rican passenger - could withstand the struggle no longer and released his hold on the gangway on the afternoon of the second day. For awhile, the sharks were absent.

After the passenger died, Taurin's weight depressed his end of the raft, almost drowning him before he could adjust the balance of the gangway.

Rescue came finally on the fourth day that the two men had gone without food or water. As Taurin was trying to decide whether to hang on a little longer or let go, a seaplane flew over, circled several times, then left. Several hours later a destroyer picked them up. By then, their tongues were so swollen they could barely breathe.

In A Careless Word, Moore indicates that two rafts containing 27 crew members and 10 passengers reached shore safely. Another life raft, with the master and 16 others, was rescued by a Navy sea plane several miles off Porta l'Ecu, Haiti two days later. A fourth raft with 21 survivors landed on Tortue Island after three days at sea. An Able Seaman walked across the island to get help from the Haitians, who sent one of their Coast Guard boats to retrieve the survivors.[16]

It wasn't only the Eastern seaboard that suffered losses in early 1942. War was being waged in the vastness of the Pacific Ocean and beyond, in the Indian Ocean and the South China Sea.

Another dramatic story - revolving around the *S.S. Bienville* , an unarmed freighter - originates in this region. The fact that there is anyone left to tell the tale is largely to the credit of Capt. Robert Spearing, who acted on his intuition while in Calcutta, and ordered the construction of four big life rafts. These were placed on the fore and after well decks, a fortuitous choice as events unfolded.

The *Biennville* , which had left the states on December 16, 1941, discharged its cargo in Suez and proceeded to Calcutta. There, some 5,000 tons of ore and general cargo were loaded and she left for home on April 4, one among a fleet of unescorted merchant ships.

Three days later, the *Biennville* 's crew heard the ominous sounds of heavy firing.

The collection of true war experiences from "The SIU at War" fills in the details:[17]

"I had 'Sparks' tune in and he got S.O.S. reports from all around us. The fleet of merchantmen had split up by this time and we were sailing alone. Things looked mighty bad," Capt. Spearing recalled.

Japanese planes had appeared overhead and dropped two bombs when the ship was about 25 miles off the coast. The *Biennville* crew stood and watched as one bomb made a direct hit on No. 2 hatch, while the other smashed squarely into the port side forward.

Fire broke out in No. 2. All hands rushed to fire stations while the skipper swung her around toward the coast. Less than 10

minutes later, the fire was almost under control when the planes returned. The two bombs they unleashed this time were near-misses.

But at 7:30 a.m. - 17 minutes after the initial attack - it became clear the *Biennville* would be attacked again when a large ship was spotted on the horizon and it was identified as a cruiser.

"At first we thought it was a British warship in response to our S.O.S.," Capt. Spearing said, "but our hopes were quickly dashed, for she was a Jap heavy cruiser."

Behind the cruiser was a carrier and two destroyers, a task force that had raided Colombo (Sri Lanka) the day before.

"As soon as I identified the cruiser as a Jap, I rang STOP on the engine room telegraph and the black gang shut down the entire plant before coming on deck. Those boys had nerve. They didn't get a bit excited. Then I gave the order to abandon ship."

When they came on deck, the black gang watch below went to number 3 boat. As they started to lower away, the destroyer opened fire at them, killing or wounding all hands. The boat was shattered and the men fell helplessly into the sea.

As number 2 boat started down, the cruiser's second turret opened fire. "We saw the flash, and almost at once the shells smashed into our hull, rocking the ship and splattering pieces of deck plate and showering tiny steel fragments all over the place," said Capt. Spearing.

Number two boat was split open by the concussion, and several more men fell into the sea. Number four boat was also torn open by the blast. An unstoppable fire now raged aboard the ship.

A third salvo from the cruiser smashed into the *Biennville*, tearing open the deck plates, smashing the booms, cutting down all the standing rigging and blowing rivets across the decks. Several men, including the skipper, were badly wounded by flying steel.

It was then that Capt. Spearing's life rafts proved pivotal. Though only half the crew was left, some of whom were badly wounded, those unable to walk were placed on a raft and told to "hang on."

"We just sat there because the rafts were too heavy for us to put over the side," the skipper remembered. "We could see Japs lining the rails of the cruiser, watching the show as they threw the fourth salvo at us."

This time, the cruiser's shells blew a hole in the *Biennville*'s side and she started to settle. Luckily for those left, the ship settled on an even keel. Part of the vessel's cargo was freed, including 500 monkeys bought for Rockefeller Foundation experiments. In confusion, monkeys ran all over the decks, chattering and clinging to the men on the life rafts.

As the ship went down, the *Biennville*'s survivors were sucked under the water with her, including the wounded men who clung to life rafts.

"It seemed like an eternity before the buoyancy of the raft overcame the downward pull of the ship's suction and shot us to the surface like a rocket," recalled the Captain.

Survivors who had been clinging to bits of wreckage were picked up by the life raft. Moments later, they all thought they would be killed by a Japanese pilot who dove his plane straight at them. But he leveled off at 500 feet and flew off to the carrier, probably taking publicity photographs of the scene for Japanese media.

As the Japanese task force moved away, several men swam to the number one boat, which was still afloat and had drifted far astern. The boat appeared to be in good shape.

Before getting into the lifeboat, the second cook died of severe stomach wounds. An AB who had both arms shot off at the shoulder still found his sense of humor, saying: "Look at the shape I'm in. Ain't this a hell of a fix?" Alas, he died soon thereafter and both men were buried at sea from the lifeboat, with the skipper - who was lying with severe leg wounds in the bottom of the boat - reciting the traditional burial service of the sea.

The second mate was seriously wounded when a piece of deck plating tore through him. Although he begged to be thrown overboard, his mates refused. So he clenched his teeth and didn't say one word after that.

"I didn't think there was courage like those men had," said Capt. Spearing.

After recovering from their shock, the men started rowing toward the coast. They landed at the village of Kaliput on the morning of the 18th. Villagers swam out and guided them through the surf.

As soon as possible, the British sent stretchers and people to carry them. The 24 survivors were borne through the jungle to a distant hospital. Too badly wounded and weak from the trip, five of the men died during the next two days.

Of the *Biennville*'s crew of 43, 19 finally reached the U.S. Of these, nine were torpedoed on a Liberty ship while en route home from Suez.

And so it went, again and again. Statistics can never capture the terror, the sadness, the human tragedy of the multitude of Merchant Marine lives lost at sea during World War II in oceans around the world.

In April, the U.S. Navy's Eastern Sea Frontier war diary identified the East Coast as "the most dangerous area for merchant shipping in the entire world." Insurance companies refused to write policies on merchant vessels, according to Michael Gannon's account of this period.[18]

The Atlantic convoy system was organized in May. But because of a lack of armaments and a scarcity of escort vessels, it wasn't until October 1942 that all American merchant ships were armed.

Robert W. Morris, a Merchant Marine veteran from Pineville, La. remembers that newspapers printed the tally in terms of tons of shipping lost by month.

"There were very few planes to patrol, and even fewer patrol boats from the Navy or Coast Guard. We simply did not have them. This was when the newly organized Civil Air Patrol was put to work flying their own or Club planes to patrol the Atlantic Seaboard. Men and women alike amassed thousands of hours in 1942. Sometimes, when they spotted subs on the surface, their calls to the military were answered. But usually there were no planes or patrol craft close enough to catch them."

The war toll mounted. By the end of 1942, 3,200 merchant seamen were dead or missing.

While reports of disaster after disaster came in, many ships did make it through under the most difficult conditions. And life went on in its quirky, stranger-than-fiction fashion.

Jerry McClish recalled serving on the *Santa Marta*, which ran aground outside of Barrios Harbor (Guatemala.) Having slid up on a gently sloping mud flat, it was so high and dry that "we were nearly in dry dock," he remembered.

Subs lurked in the water all around, but they didn't fire on the ship. At one point, three ships with unusually long hawsers tried to pull the ship off. The *Santa Marta* never budged.

At last, a salvage vessel from Merrit and Chapman in New York arrived. When the *Santa Marta* finally moved, she took on a severe list. "I took pictures of the crew trying to launch a lifeboat from the high side. Also pictures of the purser clasping the money box ready to go. The ship could not have sunk, even rolling over. Her 55-foot beam would have stuck up considerably from the surface of the water, which was only 17 feet deep.

Surviving S.S. *Beatrice's* Sinking and Other Adventures

The *S.S. Beatrice* was carrying raw sugar near Jamaica on May 24, 1942 when a German submarine started shelling it.

When it was on fire from stem to stern, the crew abandoned it, according to the second mate's reminiscences.

Assigned to the second boat, he and three sailors lowered it with some of the crew aboard. The boat fell and became unhooked in a heavy ground swell, leaving the four of them on ship.

"We got to the after-main deck and crawled behind the hatches to the life rafts, which were made of barrels, and let them go overboard. I took two of the sailors by the hand, as they could not swim, and we were able to get onto the raft. We could have been killed, but the German submarine crew did not fire at us."

The *Beatrice* sank at sundown in the Caribbean Sea. "The next morning we spotted a plane and the smoke of a ship, but they went out of sight. That evening we saw smoke again. It seemed to be getting nearer. We were spotted and picked up by a Norwegian corvette, and taken to Kingston, Jamaica. The crew in the lifeboat arrived the next day."

Moore reports that one man in the 31-

man crew perished when his raft drifted into the line of shell fire from the sub.[19]

For every "hit" taken by the Merchant Marine, there must have been countless near-misses.

Malcolm Hinchcliffe of Glendale, California spent five harrowing months in the North Atlantic on the *Norluna*, a small three-hatch vessel built for a one-day run on the Great Lakes. Once, a torpedo missed the ship by only 10 feet.

Hinchcliffe signed on as an AB in Boston on July 14, 1942. The ship set sail for Halifax, Nova Scotia, where it joined a large convoy headed for England. At Torpedo Junction, four ships - including the *Norluna* - left the convoy and headed toward Iceland.

While Hinchcliffe was at the wheel at 2 a.m. the next morning, the ship on the *Norluna*'s portside was torpedoed. "The Navy gun crew, standing watch with a 3-inch gun on our stern, told us the torpedo had missed the *Norluna* by only 10 feet. It just rolled us," Hinchcliffe recollected.

"Our captain gave orders to turn around to pick up survivors. We were able to pick up some men. The torpedoed ship had been carrying large pilings to build a dock in Iceland. In the heavy sea we could not get to men clinging to the pilings, who were begging to be picked up.

"We had to leave them as a submarine had been spotted, and our lifeboats were filled to over double their capacity.

"Two of the men I helped pull out of the water said they had been torpedoed twice before. They both were floating in the water in rubber suits, which kept them afloat and warm. Another man we rescued died and was buried at sea."

The other two ships with their corvette escorts went on to Iceland. But for four days and four nights, the *Norluna* zig-zagged, taking shots at a submarine several times a day.

The *Norluna* finally completed its run to Iceland, then continued on to Hudson Bay. In November, the *Norluna* dragged anchor in a river in Labrador and had to be abandoned. The crew was transported to Boston, where it was discharged on December 14, 1942 - five months to the day after Hinchcliffe signed on.

Bob Morris, Friend from Louisiana Sign on as Seamen Same Day...

When Bob Morris, now of Pineville, La. signed up to be a merchant seaman, he went to the shipping commissioner's office in the Federal Court House, where Captain W.W. Woods helped him fill out the necessary forms and papers.

Just as they were finishing, in walked Billy Fontain, a friend he who shared his passion for taking flying lessons. They met at an airport, where an hour of flying in a new Taylorcraft, with instructor and fuel, cost $5. After each lesson, they spent a week comparing notes about what they had learned and saving money so they could take another lesson. In June 1941, at the age of 16, Morris and Fontain shared the thrill of completing their first solo flights.

Here, their lives diverged. Morris went to Mobile, Ala. to work in a drug store, then returned to school where he occasionally ran into Fontain. Their paths also crossed at the airports, but they were not close friends at that time.

Then came their coincidental meeting at the sign-up.

Bob recalls waiting while Billy completed the paperwork to attain his "instant merchant seaman" status. Their ID numbers were one digit apart. They marveled at their success as they wandered down to the Seafarers International Union Hall.

Jobs were going at a brisk pace. "No one professed to know where the ships were bound, but some seemed to have this top secret information," Bob Morris wrote years later. The two friends signed on for the *S.S. Alcoa Rambler*, Fontain as an ordinary seaman and Morris as a wiper. But when the time came to sign the articles, it was discovered the Union man had sent too many men. Morris was disappointed that they could not make their first trip together. He returned to the Union Hall for another try.

It was February 1942, and the friends would not meet again for several months. When they were reunited, Fontain filled Morris in on his trip with war cargo from Mobile to Philadelphia, where more supplies were taken aboard, then on to Scotland where 20-millimeter Orlican anti-aircraft guns were mounted. From Scotland, the ship sailed in a convoy of 50. Final destination: Murmansk, Russia.

At this point, the U.S. Navy Armed Guard was still on the drawing boards, and not in the turrets. So Fontain was one of the merchant seamen trained as a gunner. He brought back tales of endless, sleepless days and nights thanks to the unwelcome combination of German air attacks and the extended Arctic light. He told Bob what it was like to "hit the deck" as a Stucka dived toward them, and to see a bomb falling from the plane out of the corner of his eye. The weather was so cold, Billy reported, that the guns would only get out one shot, then freeze up.

On the way to Murmansk, German airplanes and submarines sank many of the ships in the convoy, and more on the return trip to Scotland. Only four of the original ships in the convoy made it back to the United Kingdom.

It was a rude awakening for Fontain, who said he slept 24 hours at a time when the air raids were over. In Russia, he watched as women helped unload ships. He felt the constant eyes of the Russian secret police, as they followed the ship's crewmen wherever they went when they were ashore.

All this was sobering news. "Billy's account was very harrowing. He was indeed a very shaken and changed 17-year-old," Morris wrote.

First Trip Includes Close Call on Eve of 17th Birthday

By contrast, Morris' first job was as a mess boy on the *S.S. Alcoa Shipper*. It wasn't exactly his first choice - but at least it promised a much-needed paycheck at the end of the trip.

Carrying general cargo to the Caribbean - including hundreds of barrels of gasoline in the No. 4 hold near the engine room - it called in Laguaira, Venezuala, then a chain of islands called the British West Indies (Windward Islands.) Dropping off cargo at Trinidad and Barbados, Morris felt like a tourist on a sightseeing trip, until the ship pulled into a beautiful round harbor with a narrow entrance named Castries, St. Lucia.

The *Alcoa Shipper* dropped anchor because two British troop ships - the *Lady Nelson* and the *Umtata* - were tied up at the only two docks.

It was the eve of his 17th birthday, and Morris cleaned up the mess hall after dinner then settled down with a book at about 8:30 p.m. for an hour of reading before he fell asleep.

"At about 10:30, everyone on the *Alcoa Shipper* was jolted to full awareness by the sound of a terrific explosion," wrote Morris, who jumped out of his bunk to see what had happened. Looking toward the dock, he saw a second explosion as a torpedo struck amidship on one of the docked troop ships. "All the people on the *Alcoa Shipper* expected our ship to be hit any second. It did not happen. Those barrels of gasoline would have surely put some sport into the game," Morris wrote.

"Tragically, both (troop) ships were loaded with British soldiers and both sank in only a few minutes in shallow water, while still tied to the dock. The death toll was terrific. Many were East Indian troops."

A near-melee ensued as all the townspeople were running down to the dock to see the devastation, while the ships' survivors were running to the dock to get away from the ships. After an hour, a C-47 flew over the scene with a huge search light - to no avail.

The *Alcoa Shipper* unloaded its cargo on barges the next day and continued on its way to Martinique and Guadeloupe. The ship's crew never heard another word about the incident.

In the mid-1950s, Morris saw an article in Reader's Digest *about the tragedy, which shed more light on what had occurred. British West Indies Navy lookouts were posted on either shore of the narrow entrance to the harbor. Their telephones connected them only to the Chief of Police's office.*

When they saw the submarine come into the harbor on the surface, the lookouts dutifully notified the police station, only to be told they should call the military since it wasn't the police's job.

The lookouts followed on foot along the shore - in a screaming rage - as the sub circled, then torpedoed the ships as it swung around. They steamed out of the harbor with impunity. Their intelligence was up-to-the-minute. Mission accomplished to perfection, they left without firing a shot at the Alcoa Shipper.

Morris and his wife returned to Castries years later as visitors and found a white-haired black policeman who was there when the ships were sunk. They exchanged stories of this amazing experience.

Sailing in Uncertain Times, Mysterious Things Happen

Returning from the trip aboard the *Alcoa Shipper*, Bob Morris collected $300 - more money than he had seen in his life. "How could anyone have such adventure and excitement and see all those beautiful islands and be paid all this money?" he wondered as he took a bus home to tell his parents about his experiences.

Morris reports that his mother wanted him to join the Navy "where there wasn't so much danger." But he was undeterred by her arguments and signed on as an ordinary seaman to an "old rust bucket," the *S.S. Panama City*, carrying general cargo to Jamaica. On the way back, the ship was routed to New York.

"By this time, the submarine menace was so great that ships traveling on the East Coast did so only in daylight, and would anchor in the safest harbor they could find along the coast each evening about sundown," Morris wrote.

"The *Panama City* made the first landfall near Titusville, Fla., dropped anchor, and continued up the coast to the general vicinity of Brunswick, Ga. the following day to swing at anchor there that night. About 4 a.m. the next morning, preparations began to get underway for the next day's run. A Coast Guard patrol vessel pulled up and headed straight for the shore. When it got light enough to see, it was time to go.

"Unbelievably, the Coast Guard men were climbing all over what appeared to be a submarine. The ship weighed anchor and the crew members never heard anything about what at least 20 people saw. Many years after the war, a number of stories were published about a German submarine, which ran aground in the vicinity of Brunswick. Anything is possible.

"The *S.S. Panama City* continued north with all available hands as lookouts, and anchored in the Charleston and Wilmington areas as they progressed up the coast," wrote Morris, who was assigned to the midnight-to-4 a.m. watch and slept until about 10:30 every morning.

As the ship approached Cape Hatteras, Morris was awakened by a tremendous explosion that seemed to come from the aft part of the ship. He grabbed a life jacket and ran out on deck to find that most of the crew was already there and looking aft, out to sea. No one was preparing life boats, but Morris felt sure the *Panama City* had taken a torpedo.

An engineer told Morris that the Navy gun crew - who were under the command of a 19-year-old bo's'n mate second class - had spotted a submarine just breaking surface, and had fired the 5-inch gun at it. The bo's'n mate gave the order to fire again when they had the sub in their sights. They complied, but no one could tell if they had hit it. They reloaded, but did not fire again.

"The ship's radio man contacted the station he had been assigned to, and within minutes, two Civil Air Patrol planes were over the area where the sub was supposed to have been. One was a Stinson Reliant and the other looked like a Curtis Robin. They circled the spot a long time while the ship remained on course. After a few minutes, one of the planes caught up with the ship and flew around it, very close to the water. The two people in the plane gave a thumb's down sign, and flew toward the shore.

"In about 30 minutes, an Army North American AT-6 came from astern and the air crew did the same thing. It could be surmised that they had seen an oil slick and maybe some debris. As usual, the ship's crew never heard a word about it. Anyway, the young bo's'n mate and the gun crew were the heroes of that day. After the war, it was learned that German subs released fuel oil and ejected debris from torpedo tubes as a ploy in a tight situation. But just maybe, someday, a submarine hull will be found in the Cape Hatteras area, with a shell hole in it."

It was an otherwise uneventful trip to New York harbor.

Once back in Meridian, Miss. with his family, Morris did not tell his mother any more sea stories after this. But he continued to go to sea, have more adventures, and eventually survive the sinking of a ship that was sunk by a sub. (See 1943 and Morris' account of serving on the maiden voyage of the *S.S. John Drayton*.)

Torpedoed on Three Ships in Three Years, Bob Burton Lives to Tell About It

First, Bob Burton escaped the *S.S. Robin Moor* before it was blown apart in one of the early incidents of German submarine activity (see 1941.) He survived 15 days in a lifeboat, which was picked up by a British ship and taken to Cape Town.

Burton's second close call occurred 14 months later when the *S.S. Robert E. Lee*, a passenger ship, was sunk in the Mississippi Delta in the afternoon of July 29, 1942.

"It's very strange, now that I look back on it, but I can't tell much about what took place because I don't know," Burton explained in "The SIU at War" booklet.[20]

"Everything happened so fast. I was talking to the engineer when there was a terrific crash. I was knocked down and hit my head on something. After that I don't remember a thing until I awoke in the water. The engineer and the cadet on my watch were both killed. I have no idea how I ever got out of the engine room."

"The water woke me up in a hurry, and realizing what had happened, I began swimming. Luckily, I was quite a ways from the Lee when she went down, stern first."

Burton swam for his life, eventually making it to a raft and climbing aboard. About an hour later, a sea plane spotted them and picked them up.

His third close encounter with death-by-torpedo came almost a year later, on the *Samuel J. Kirkwood*, a Bull Line liberty ship.

The account in "The SIU at War" picks up the story:

"As fireman-watertender on the *Kirkwood*, Burton was once again below at the fateful hour. The torpedo hit at 11:30 p.m., crashing into the ship with a reeling impact between four and five holds.

"Burton was thrown onto the floor plates and barely missed hitting his head on one of the burners. 'Luckily, I didn't,' he says, 'because I didn't have much time to get out as it was.'

"The third engineer stopped the engine and Burton cut out the fires. While the third ran up the engine room ladder, Burton chose the emergency ladder up through the fire room ventilator. He looked up the ladder snaking its way to the bridge deck...

"He says, 'It was very quiet down below then - and dark. I went up the ladder like a monkey, bumping myself against the ventilator. But I didn't care about that. Then right near the top, when I almost had my head out the 'spout,' something caught my shoe. I was stuck. My foot wouldn't budge. I couldn't go up and I couldn't go down. It was terrifying - like a nightmare. I remembered reading about the men who were trapped like that on the *Repulse* when she went down, and I pictured myself going under with the *Kirkwood*, caught like a rat in that ventilator.

"'It was only a couple of minutes, but it seemed like an hour before one of the Navy gunners came up, grabbed me around the

shoulders and pulled until I came free.'

"Here Burton has a good word for his shipmates and for the Navy gunners of the *Kirkwood* .

"'My boat was still at the davits when I got to the boat deck. They saw that I was missing and they had delayed lowering away until I had time to show up. They saved my life.'

"Although the *Kirkwood* sank in a few minutes, the boats were handled so efficiently no one was hurt or lost.

"After 11 days adrift, they were spotted by a patrol plane, which directed a warship to their rescue."

Getting trapped in the frantic rush to abandon ship was a predicament worth contemplating. Imagine squeezing through a porthole to safety.

In the *Robert E. Lee* disaster, such was the fate of one John Marshal, who mercifully found his way out.

Here's his story, as told to "The SIU at War" editor:[21]

"I was laying on my bunk, dozing, when the torpedo hit. I grabbed my life jacket and ran forward, but I came to a big hole in the deck.

"Lots of steam was rising out of it, so I turned and ran all the way aft to the fan tail. Then I found the door to the after deck jammed tight. I figured the ship was going down quick because she was beginning to list. But there wasn't any exit - just a little porthole.

It was mighty small, but it looked big to me right then, and I said, 'Porthole, here I come.'

"I still don't remember how I got through, but I must have dived. The next thing I knew, I had a mouthful of water and the Lee was going down too close for comfort."

A recent clipping from the "NMU Pilot," published by the National Maritime Union, features another survivor's tale from the *Robert E. Lee*.

John Radix, a retired NMU member from Brooklyn, was on the ill-fated ship. He was asleep in his bunk when the *Lee* was torpedoed. Unable to stand because of fractures in both legs, he pulled himself to the jagged hole in the side of the ship that was left by the torpedo. He dropped into the water, somehow keeping himself afloat until rescuers picked him up. After several operations, he was serving aboard ships again - within two months.

(He received his NMU book in New Orleans in 1943. Three years later, he was promoted to chief steward, and remained in that rating until he retired in 1971.)

The *Robert E. Lee*'s sinking sent a message to Americans living in the South. The waters only 25 miles from their shore could not be considered safe.

A patrol boat was accompanying the Alcoa passenger ship, which was on its way to New Orleans from Trinidad, when it was hit about 25 miles from the mouth of the Mississippi. Moore reports in <u>A Careless Word</u> that the *Robert E. Lee* carried 270 passengers - most survivors of previously torpedoed American ships - 131 crew members and six Naval Armed Guard. Ten crew members and 15 passengers were lost.[22]

S.S. *Honomu* Sunk on Murmansk Run;
Captain Strand Taken P.O.W.

The Arctic route to Murmansk proved to be one of the most treacherous expanses of sea during the war. Some considered it suicidal. Besides the generally harsh weather in the area, it was a favored spot for German attacks. Little wonder it earned the named "Bomb Alley."

It was here that Capt. F.A. Strand's crew of the *S.S. Honomu* struggled valiantly, then eventually lost, in July 1942.

The Matson ship fought a running battle for days with German bomber and torpedo planes sweeping "Bomb Alley," only to fall victim to a Nazi submarine.

An article from a Matson Company publication described the captain and crew's ordeal, in Strand's own words.

Sailing from the East Coast, the freighter left Iceland on June 27, 1942 as part of one of the largest convoys ever to attempt to fight its way to Murmansk, carrying weapons and war materials for the embattled Russians.

Units of the British fleet guarded the convoy because the Merchant Marine vessels in it were barely armed. The *Honomu*, for instance, carried only .30-caliber machine guns.

As they approached the dangerous waters, Nature provided protection that man could not in the form of low clouds and fog. The first German planes attacked at 4 a.m. They launched a running battle over several days, with bombs and torpedoes raining on the convoy.

The *Honomu* survived as the crew fought its way along. In the Barents Sea, the escort vessels left the merchant ships, which were expected to make their way alone to their destination. In the case of the *Honomu*, that destination was Archangel, Russia.

It was July 5, at about 2:30 p.m., when a German submarine's torpedo struck. Minutes later, another hit near two holds where explosives were stored, but miraculously they did not detonate.

All but one lifeboat was destroyed by the torpedoes' explosion and subsequent fire.

Strand ordered his men to abandon ship. Nineteen made their way in the remaining lifeboat; the remainder found places on four rafts with the captain boarding the last one to leave the ship.

Within minutes of getting to the water, the submarine loomed out of the overcast. An order came from the conning tower that the captain identify himself.

"That's where I made my mistake," Capt. Strand told the reporter. "I did."

Ordered to board the submarine, he learned that the German high command planned to destroy the effectiveness of the Allied Merchant Marine by capturing its trained captains and chief engineers. So while the U.S. was in the midst of its frenetic ship-building program, the Germans thought they might disable that fleet by collecting all the trained and qualified captains they could.

Once aboard the U-boat, Strand found himself witnessing a successful attack on a British merchant ship, which sank.

Then, a German "friendly fire" incident imperiled his life. A German plane attacked the U-boat, apparently because the sub failed to relay proper identification signals while running on the surface.

The vessel was jarred, but not damaged, although its companion sub was rendered incapable of submerging by the shelling.

Finally, the two submarines returned to their mother ship on the Norwegian coast, near Kirkness.

Strand's captors decided to fly him to Germany, where he was to be interrogated about vital information to the Nazi war effort. An Allied bombing raid forced the trip to be postponed a day.

The flight to Oslo skirted Strand's native country, where he had lived until he was seven. In Oslo, where coincidentally his sister lived, Strand was confined in an old fort.

When Strand mentioned his sister - whom he hadn't seen since she was six and he was seven - a German officer arranged for the two to meet. Their reunion was made

SS Jeremiah O'Brien passes underneath the Golden Gate Bridge.

even more bittersweet because Strand could no longer speak Norwegian and she did not understand English.

"The German officer said it was the darnedest thing he ever saw," Capt. Strand said. "We visited for all of 10 minutes. She made arrangements for my father to come see me the next day, but the Germans shipped me out before he could arrive."

The trip from Oslo to Germany was made by freighter in a guarded convoy. Strand was taken to Wilhelmshaven, a giant German naval base. After several weeks of questioning by the Germans, Strand was assigned to a prison camp near Bremen.

Strand survived with a tedious, sparse routine. He ate one mid-day meal, which consisted of five potatoes, a bowl of soup or mush, one-seventh of a loaf of black bread, a little sugar or margarine, and hot water. The captive's weight plummeted from 190 pounds to 157 during his months of confinement.

On January 15, 1943 in Switzerland, Strand was exchanged for a German prisoner under the terms of the Geneva Convention, which required that he agree not to take up arms against Germany or its allies again.

And what of the rest of the *Honomu* 's crew of 37 seamen and four British gunners? Moore reports that two were killed in the engine room's explosion, 10 died of exposure in the lifeboat, as did one of the British gunners.

The chief mate was in charge of the lifeboat, on which they raised a sail to tow the four liferafts. On July 16, the chief mate decided to cut the rafts loose and continue alone. The 21 survivors on the raft were sighted on July 18 and picked up by two British escort vessels.

The lifeboat was sighted on July 28 by a German submarine. The only men alive were five crew members and three British gunners, who had been without food and water for six days. They were all taken aboard the sub and eventually held as prisoners of war in Germany until hostilities ended.[23]

CONVOY
By Flare Fredricksen
Plymouth, WI

Freighter-Tanker-Transport
Escorts laying ash can patterns
The Irish Sea,
A clear night,
"Sleep tonight with your clothes on."
Nerves - Nerves - Nerves.

LIFE Magazine Draws Attention to NMU's Role in War Effort

U.S. civilians continued to learn about the Merchant Marines' activities by reading about them in newspapers and magazines back home.

On August 24, 1942, "LIFE" carried a story entitled "NMU: It is a Union Fighting a War." The article praised the gargantuan and highly hazardous job undertaken by seamen, and related staggering statistics.

"From its 4,000,000 men, the U.S. Army has lost to date 1,381 soldiers killed. From its 600,000 men, the Navy has lost 3,420 sailors killed. But from its small number of 50,000 men, the National Maritime Union has lost 1,800 killed.

"These figures, startling in their frankness, show to what an extent the National Maritime Union is fighting the war. Most of these union men, manning tankers and freighters, met death by torpedo. They died bravely in the flaming darkness of a foreign ocean - as bravely as any soldier or sailor ever died. They believed in freedom so they gave their lives for their country. They are heroes.

"The survivors are equally heroic. Returning to the union hiring hall, where they have received a medal for being torpedoed to add to their union badge, they have shipped out to sea again. From seeing the shape of the war in Suez, Murmansk and Cape Town, they know that war is dirty and tough and cruel. They have got the taste of blood in their mouths.

"The National Maritime Union knows how to fight. In five stormy years it has fought with rival unions, with Congress, with shipping companies and with the public. Today, with all its hard-won gains toward decent living conditions, threatened by war, it is fighting again. It has promised that no union ship will leave port without a full and adequate crew. In spite of sinkings and terror at sea, it has kept its promise."

Accompanying the article are two photographs: one shows seamen gathered in front of NMU headquarters, an $85,000 building in New York. Hanging from its third to fifth floors are banner-like signs: "National Maritime Union-C.I.O." and "Keep 'Em Sailing" the top two banners read. "Thousands of N.M.U. Members Continue in the Service - We Deliver the Goods" and "Hundreds of N.M.U. Members Have Already Lost Their Lives in Defense of Their Country" trumpeted the middle two signs.

And at the bottom, in large bold letters: "Buy U.S. War Bonds" and "Open A Western Front Now."

A caption with that photograph explained: "The Union and its members have already bought close to $300,000 in war bonds."

The other photograph shows a U.S. Merchant Marine American eagle badge, with the "We Keep 'Em Sailing" motto emblazoned along the bottom, and a torpedo pin attached underneath, connoting a survivor of a torpedo attack.

M.S. *American Leader* Sunk by Germans;
Survivors Turned Over to Japanese, Who Keep Them as P.O.W.s
By George William Duffy

George William Duffy graduated from the Massachusetts Nautical School on September 23, 1941. Little did he realize then that war would break out in 10 weeks, or that he was embarking on an epic journey that would find him spending 34 months as a Japanese P.O.W. Here is his version of the events that followed graduation:

When hostilities commenced, I was Junior Third Officer in the brand new motor vessel *American Leader*, which was alongside Pier 1 in the port of Manila in the Philippine Islands.

After witnessing the initial bombing raid on vessels at anchor off the piers, and on the U.S. Naval Base at Cavite, we put to sea on the night of December 11, bound for Sydney, Australia. We arrived there on Christmas Day. (For accomplishing this "escape," Haakon A. Pedersen, the *American Leader* 's master, was awarded the United States Lines' Distinguished Service Medal.)

On St. Patrick's Day, 1942, we returned to Boston and several days after that, New York. The cargo we had loaded in Australia and New Caledonia was safely delivered, and we restocked our holds full of trucks, steel, barbed wire, combat boots and sundry other military items. Lashed to the deck were nine twin-engined bombers.

The *American Leader* was strengthened, too, in a sense. It was fitted with a single, antiquated four-inch cannon, two .30-caliber Lewis guns and two .50-caliber anti-aircraft machine guns. A U.S. Naval Reserve Ensign and eight Naval enlisted men were brought aboard to service and man these armaments.

By the end of April, they joined us and we were all back at sea.

This time our destination was the Persian Gulf, which we reached in late June. By mid-August, the discharging/loading cycle again accomplished, we were homeward bound with 10,000 tons of sheet rubber, liquid latex, opium, rugs, Latakia tobacco and dozens of other Middle Eastern products crammed under, and loaded onto, the deck of our 400-foot long, 13 1/2-knot freighter.

The last port of call had been Colombo, Ceylon (now known as Sri Lanka.) It was there that I recall reading an article in a daily newspaper concerning the activities of the German Navy in the South Atlantic Ocean. It appeared that the British and American Naval authorities feared that one or more German commerce raiders were loose.

These heavily armed vessels were actually freighters or small passenger ships converted to military use. Their guns were carefully hidden. Equipment such as scouting aircraft and fast torpedo boats were out of sight in spaces that once carried bananas, cocoa or timber, or whatever a normal peacetime merchantman would carry.

Thus, these raiders were something to fear, not only for their fire power, but because they could be practically on top of their unsuspecting victims before the danger could be perceived.

On September 7, 1942, we left Cape Town - alone. The Royal Navy people assured us that the Germans we had read about had "gone home."

Our being alone was not unusual, of course. The day of the large, escorted convoy had not yet arrived. In fact, with the exception of a few hours in the Caribbean earlier in the year, we had traversed the oceans of the globe without a vestige of any protection from the Allied naval forces.

This solitary voyage was to be a long one. We were headed for New York, but via the Pacific Ocean! The Germans were creating so much havoc with their U-boats in the mid- and North Atlantic, that our British Admiralty dictated routing that would take us westward, and then southwest to the Straits of Magellan, then north along the west coast of South America to the Panama Canal. From there, we presumably would find some protection for the last leg up the East Coast of the United States.

We never saw the Straits of Magellan. On September 10, in a position about 850 miles west of Cape Town at about 2000 in the evening, the *American Leader* was attacked and sunk by the German raider *Michel*. Of the 49-man merchant crew, 10 were lost. One of the gun crew was killed. Several hours later, the *Michel* returned to the scene, and from three rafts, picked up the survivors and made them prisoners of war.

There were already two Americans aboard the German ship - wounded crewmen from an American tanker that was sunk seven weeks before. Two nights later, the British freighter *Empire Dawn* fell to the *Michel* and 22 of her 44-man crew joined us in the crowded prison quarters.

Our captors were strict with us, and understandably so, as they could not risk any chance that we would cause problems for them. Essentially, our treatment was fair: we were given the same food as they received and in the same quantities. We joined them for movies and listened to the same music and announcements spewed out by the ship's PA system.

During our time in the *Michel* she met up with several other German ships. In early October we were transferred to one of them, the supply tanker *Uckermark*. There, things were both better and worse. The living accommodations for the officer prisoners were above the main deck in the fo'c'sl; the unlicensed crew member prisoners were lodged well below deck in a storage space that afforded no escape if the tanker fell into difficulty.

Her skipper had been a prisoner of the British in New Zealand in World War I. Therefore, he understood our plight and tended to be quite lenient with us. We were free to come and go on deck from sunrise to sunset, and he made no objection to our attempts at determining his ship's position each noon. He was most solicitous towards us, as was evidenced by the number of checker boards, chess sets and playing cards that were delivered to our quarters. In addition, we received many dog-earred copies of German books and magazines, most of which we couldn't read, but at least they had pictures.

(One of these pictures, which Duffy clipped and was able to keep in his possession throughout his captivity, ultimately became the inspiration for a statue in New York harbor memorializing merchant seamen who lost their lives at sea. For more on the amazing story of the castaways, and Duffy's preservation of their photo for decades - only to discover that they had all died, see the section entitled "American Merchant Mariners' Memorial.")

Capt. Pedersen joined him (her skipper) every day for a drink and a copy of the day's radio news from Berlin.

But the bleak side of our predicament was that we were bound for the Far East - probably Japan.

And so it was, two days after our arrival in the roadstead of the harbor at Tandjong Priok, outside the great city of Batavia, Java, that a group of Japanese officers came on board, and we were unceremoniously handed over.

That was November 6, 1942.

I managed to eke out an existence over the following 34 months, but it was a most difficult time. For awhile, I remained on Java, living in three prisoner-of-war camps and working at a variety of jobs: loading ships, building roads, growing vegetables, and so on.

In June of 1944, I went by ship to Singapore and from there to Sumatra, where about 5,000 Allied prisoners and an untold number of native and Indian laborers constructed a railway through swamps, almost impenetrable jungle, and a rolling, hilly countryside. Hundreds of British, Dutch, Australians and Americans succumbed to the hard labor, the malaria, the dysentery, and injuries which came with the territory.

On the day the Japanese surrendered, we completed the job!

It was not until mid-October of 1945 that I returned to my hometown of Newburyport, Massachusetts, after an absence of three and a half years.

My parents had received a few messages from me during those years, <u>but not until after I had been declared missing in action, my life insurance paid, and my estate finalized by the Probate Court</u>. (It is an interesting commentary that the first word from the Japanese indicating that I was alive and a prisoner came on the morning of Easter Sunday, 1943 - Resurrection Day!)

The Germans, to my knowledge, never reported to anyone that they had sunk the *American Leader* and captured the 47 survivors.

To say that we had a difficult time with

Seaman Gordon J. Frazier (left row front) and fellow instructors from US Maritime Service Training Base, Sheepshead Bay, NY on weekend pass at Coney Island, 1944.

the Japanese is an understatement. Two of our crew - Sidney Albert and Steve Pekich - died as a result of the tropical diseases and malnourishment which plagued us on Sumatra. Seventeen others drowned in the sinking of Japanese prison ships - the *Tomahaku Maru* by the *U.S.S. Tang* on June 26, 1944, and the *Junyo Maru* by H.M.S. *Tradewind* on September 18, 1944. Of the 58 men who manned the *American Leader* when she departed New York that fateful Sunday afternoon in April 1942, only 28 came home in 1945!

And so it is today and every day, after I arise, that I look out the window of our home here at Seabrook Beach, New Hampshire towards the Eastern horizon where the Good Lord is giving me another day.

A fitting tribute to Capt. George Duffy was paid on Maritime Day 1992 (May 19), when he was the first veteran to receive a Pacific War Zone medal for his service in the Merchant Marines during World War II.

The award was presented by Secretary of Transportation Andrew Card aboard the rehabilitated Liberty ship, the John. W. Brown, *which was docked in Washington, D.C. at the time.*

These awards from the United States Maritime Commission were unveiled for the first time that day: the Atlantic War Zone; the Pacific War Zone; the Mediterranean-Middle East War Zone and the Merchant Marine Defense medals. The last honors service in the Merchant Marine between Sept. 8, 1939 and the attack on Pearl Harbor.

Liberty Ship *S.S. Stephen Hopkins* and German Raider Battle Fiercely in South Atlantic; Both Ships Lost

Only four months after she was christened, the *S.S. Stephen Hopkins*, a Liberty ship, was carrying coal from Cape Town to Bahia, Brazil in the South Atlantic, when she was double-teamed by the *Steir*, a German sea raider, and its escort, the *Tannenfels*.

Outnumbered and outgunned, the *Stephen Hopkins'* crew put up a formidable resistance in the morning of September 27, 1942.

Hugo Schramm, transportation writer for the "CBIVA Sound-Off," recounts the tale in his Fall 1990 Ship's Column.

Visibility was reduced to two miles when the raider opened fire at long range on the *Stephen Hopkins*. Within four minutes, the U.S. ship replied so strenuously that a writer in the German War Diary estimated that the crew was firing away with six 4.7-inch guns and lighter weapons.

"In fact," Schramm writes, "the *Stephen Hopkins* had replied with her only armament: a single 4-inch gun giving a 31-pound broadside to an adversary armed with six 5.9-inch guns, six smaller ones, two torpedo tubes and two Arado seaplanes on a launching pad."

Speed was another area where the *Stephen Hopkins* was outperformed. The *Steir's* speed was 14 knots, compared to a mere 9 knots for the *Stephen Hopkins*.

Still, the raider had been hit 15 times in less than 10 minutes, causing burning oil to begin spreading on the ship. As the *Steir's* crew abandoned ship and was brought aboard the *Tannenfels*, her supply ship, the *Steir* exploded and disappeared.

In the meantime, the survivors of the *Stephen Hopkins'* crew were also abandoning ship. Fifteen of them reached the Brazilian coast after 31 days on a raft. The remaining 42 men, including the ship's master, had to be given up as lost at sea.

By October of 1942, the country's armaments factories were able to catch up with the demand and nearly all American merchant ships were armed.

But by then, thousands of ships and lives had been lost. A whole generation of ships was sacrificed at sea in the rush to move materials and supplies. The SIU pamphlet describes some of them: bluff-nosed tankers built in World War I; Lakes and Hogs; stubby colliers; ore carriers; West Coast and Kearny ships.

Among the casualties from another era was the *S.V. Star of Scotland*, a stately 1887 six-mast schooner.

Her history is as fascinating as her last voyage. Built in Scotland, she sailed as the *Kennilworth* until steam-powered ships sidelined the wind ships.

She was reincarnated as a gambling ship, the *Rex*, and anchored with the *Tango*, another gambling ship, beyond the three-mile limit off Long Beach, Calif. There, speed boats brought high rollers to her tables.

Rerigged and outfitted for the Second World War, she set out for Cape Town, manned by an SIU-SUP crew out of San Pedro.

"The big sailing ship was such an unusual sight, tearing along in the trades with all sail set, that an American sub commander surfaced one day just to board and look around. He was amazed at the size of her," reported "The SIU at War."[24]

The *Star of Scotland* made Cape Town safely, where Robert F. Kennedy of New York (no relation to the late senator) boarded her as an AB as she was headed for Brazil.

Following is Kennedy's account of the events that unfolded, and the fate of the crew, as told to "The SIU at War."

"We were 10 days out and making about seven or eight knots in a heavy sea when the mate came in the fo'castle and said we could discontinue the lookout because the danger zone was passed. But we didn't agree with him and decided to keep a lookout anyway. One of the 8-12 ABs went on watch.

"That was just before 8 on Friday morning, November 13. At 8:13 we heard a shot. It came from out of the sun and we couldn't tell whether it was a sub or a raider. Then there were several more shots. They fell ahead of us and we saw the splashes. The fifth shot hit the fo'castle on the fore deck and it started to blaze."

The skipper ordered the crew to abandon ship, but they were carrying a big square sail on the foremast and couldn't get it in. Even when they dropped all the other sails, the big ship was still doing four or five knots. One lifeboat was smashed by shell fire, but they luckily got the other over the side and pushed away without swamping.

The mate, the only man lost out of the crew of 17, fell into the water trying to slide down the falls into the boat. Although his fellow crew members threw him a life ring, he was soon swept far astern.

A crew of young Germans lined the deck of the big U-boat, which had two mounted deck guns, watching the *Star of Scotland* burn and joking with the men in the boat.

By then, Kennedy said, the schooner had lost most of her way and two German sailors came up close and boarded her, taking all the provisions, slop chest and other gear. Captain Constantin Flink was taken aboard the U-boat and questioned. When he explained that he was the only one able to navigate the lifeboat to land, he was permitted to rejoin the other survivors - after promising he would not command another ship sailing against Germany.

After awhile, the sub commander threw them a line, gave them bread and cigarettes, and towed the boat around for about two hours looking for the mate. But he was nowhere to be seen. The U-boat's crew told them they were lucky not to be Englishmen. "If you were English, we would have machine-gunned you," he said.

With only a compass for navigation, the captain set a course for South Africa and bet the crew he could make it in 20 days.

They didn't have much food. The boat was crowded and the days were tedious and exhausting, but Kennedy apparently seemed nearly casual about the often dangerous 1,040-mile trip to land.

"Of course, there were some exciting moments. One day, two dolphin and a swordfish got into a battle right beside the boat. They split the rudder and almost capsized us. For a few minutes it was like one of those movie thrillers where the hero totters around on the edge of a cliff."

Star of Scotland crew members had to be resourceful to keep themselves alive on their arduous journey. They dried flying fish that flopped into the boat, and ate them. One day when the tins of powdered milk were all gone, they caught a dolphin and boiled it in a bucket. A broken oar was used for the fire.

They also rigged a sail on several oars lashed together. On the 20th day, as Captain Flink had predicted, they made land in Angola, having averaged 50 miles a day and traveled more than 1,000 miles.

Controversy Arises Over Militarization of Merchant Marine

How separate was the Merchant Marine from the armed forces? How voluntary was the service of seamen? These questions remained the subject of fiery debate for years after the U.S. declared victory over the Germans and Japanese.

The "NMU Pilot" examined this issue in

detail in a November 1979 issue.

Although there was no blanket deferment of seamen, there was a de facto deferment. The Selective Service regulations - Local Board Memorandum 115-H (B) - read in part:

"Service in the Merchant Marine, considering its importance to the war effort and the hazards involved, is so closely allied to the service in the Armed Forces that men found by the Local Board to be actively engaged at sea may well be considered as engaged in active defense of the country. Such service may properly be considered as tantamount to military service. Therefore, when a Local Board finds a man actively engaged in the Merchant Marine or in training therefore, it should give serious consideration to his occupational deferment."

Beyond this directive, many men who could have enlisted in the armed forces were diverted into the Merchant Marine. These potential enlistees were informed by military personnel that they could better serve their country by joining the Merchant Marine.

Second Mate Dennis A. Roland is one person who fit into that category. His inability to get officials to reactivate his Naval Reserve status set off a chain of events that each compounded the injustice of the one before.

Roland became a P.O.W. of the Germans, then the Japanese. He was among those forced to help build the infamous Bridge over the River Kwai.

An article summarized this part of Roland's story:

"It still goes through his mind that, by rights, he shouldn't have been on a freighter (American Export Lines' *M.V. Sawokla*) that was sunk near Madagascar by a German surface raider," the article reported.

The raider succeeded in sinking two more Allied ships before starting for Japan. Since it was blocked from escaping into the Atlantic by Allied naval forces, the raider's crew handed Roland - along with 88 other prisoners - to the Japanese. Finally, Roland was interned in Thailand at Kwai, where 1,200 of the 1,600 prisoners died.

He was liberated when the war turned against the Japanese.

Roland would not have had to suffer untold hardships had his frequent efforts to activate his Naval Reserve status been successful.

"The Navy kept telling me I was more important to the war effort in the merchant marine," Roland told the reporter.

The Merchant Marines' independence from the traditional branches of the U.S. armed services set it apart. But Merchant Mariners played no lesser role than did their counterparts in other branches of service..

In 1942, some controversy arose surrounding the issue of whether the Navy Department should be empowered to take over the Merchant Marines.

Admiral Simons proposed that the Navy assume the responsibility for operating the merchant fleet for efficiency reasons, and that the officers and seamen serving aboard the vessels be inducted into the Navy.

For his part, Navy Secretary Frank Knox announced that a study was being undertaken to investigate the transfer of the Merchant Marine into the jurisdiction of the Naval Reserves.

However, the maritime unions and private ship-owners both argued that such a transfer would be self-defeating. They argued successfully that the existing arrangement of private ownership under WSA supervision should be improved. It made more sense than scrapping a workable organization in the middle of the war and trying to replace it with a brand new military administration.

Great Britain's experience was cited in their argument, as was the lack of Navy unanimity on the proposed transfer.

The plan received a blow when FDR announced his disapproval of the idea and questioned the effectiveness of the proposed Navy transfer. As Commander-in-Chief, Roosevelt said, his approval would be a precondition to such a move, and he would not approve this course of action.

On May 2, 1942, FDR sent Senator George L. Radcliffe a letter that said, in part:

"I have your letter of April 10th in which you refer to the current rumors that the officers and seamen of the Merchant Marine are shortly to be turned over to the Navy Department. I agree with you that at the present time such a move is not necessary, and would be unwise ..."

The following year, the Deputy WSA Administrator spoke before the NMU convention, summarizing the government's opinion of the matter:

" ... I believe that we have successfully refuted those who would have us believe that the Merchant Marine could be better run under the armed services."

Training Efforts Expand to Keep Up with Demand for Mariners

As soon as the U.S. was in the war, the training program for Merchant Marines grew at an incredible rate, reported Commodore Knight.

"Courses were intensified, periods of training reduced. In the latter part of 1942, the largest training station for merchant seamen in the world was opened at Sheepshead Bay, where 10,000 men could be quartered and trained. Schools for radio operators were opened at Gallups Island and at Huntington, New York. The latter station was subsequently moved to Hoffman Island.

"In 1942, the Maritime Service foresaw that there would be a need for trained emergency medical men aboard ships, because of the increased possibilities of injury and sickness. It was decided to combine the duties of hospital corpsman with those of the uunior assistant purser, and on December 7,

Sheepshead Bay, NY, 1944

the Hospital Corps School was opened at Sheepshead Bay. The Purser School was already in operation."

Other schools were opened during the war to upgrade both licensed and unlicensed personnel at the principal ports. Several schools were provided for the training of specialists, such as diesel engineers, turbo-electric engineers, high pressure geared turbine engineers, junior engineers, pumpmen, carpenters and electricians.

The U.S. Maritime Service Institute in New York conducted correspondence and extension courses to be taken by men while they are at sea.

'Give Cadets Most Dangerous Assignments,' Captain Says
By Lester E. Ellison, Basking Ridge, N.J.

My sea career started October 12, 1942, when I reported to the U.S. Merchant Marine Academy. My first trip to sea was on the freighter *M.S. West Grama,* built in 1919 in Los Angeles. She was deliberately sunk on June 8, 1944 as part of the Goosenberry 1, breakwater in Mulberry "A", an artificial harbor at Omaha Beach off the Normandy coast. It was sad to see the first ship I sailed on being sunk.

The captain on the *M.S. West Grama* had very little use for cadets. His orders were: "Give cadets all the dangerous assignments. If they get killed there would be very little lost." This trip ended April 17, 1943. Under this captain, I learned what work was and how to do it.

During 1942 and 1943, there were not enough deck or engine officers to man the Liberty ships being built. The *S.S. William H. Prescott* was ready to sail, and did not have a third mate. Much to my surprise, I was asked by the U.S. Merchant Marine Academy to go aboard as third mate, based on the very favorable recommendation from the captain of the *West Gramma*. By that time, I was beginning to get premature gray hairs, most of them from sailing the *West Gramma*.

By now I had a healthy fear of captains. The fact that I was now a deck cadet - sailing as third mate on only my second trip to sea - would have made old sea captains turn over in their graves.

I will be forever thankful to Captain Richard Dean and the American President Lines for the education they gave me aboard the *William H. Prescott.* At age 21, I was the youngest officer aboard ship and Wilbert Black, at age 72 the 1st assistant engineer, was the oldest. It was sailing on ships like the *William H. Prescott* that make you want to go to sea. This voyage ended August 31, 1943 in New York City.

Ellison was pivotal in convincing the New Jersey Legislature to extend veteran's status to New Jersey seamen who sailed for the United States during the war. The bill granting this status was signed by the governor on January 16, 1992.

S.S. President Coolidge's Sinking, Heroism Beyond the Call of Duty

The *S.S. President Coolidge* was carrying more than 5,000 Army troops on October 26, 1942, when she hit two mines in quick succession nearing Espiritu Santo Island in New Hebrides.

Patrick C. Olson, a Merchant Marine officer, received the Distinguished Service Medal for his actions to save an Army officer. The incident was described in the citation that accompanies the medal.

"Listing heavily and sinking rapidly, (the *Coolidge*) was run aground on a reef to gain time to debark the troops. Olson was making a final search for stragglers or injured when the ship rolled over port side.

"Hauling himself up the slanting deck, he reached the starboard side which was now nearly horizontal and only a few feet out of the water, when he heard cries for help coming from deep within the hull. By this time the ship, pounded by the surf, was slowly sliding, stern first, off into deep water.

"But Olson, completely disregarding his own safety, crawled to an open side port from whence the cries came. An army officer was trapped by the rising water in the ship's hull, and the critical angle of the smooth deck made unaided escape impossible. Olson made several attempts to lower a rope ladder, only to have it blown away from the outstretched hands of the drowning man by the blast of escaping air forced out of the ship by the rapidly rising water.

"Quantities of broken glass and other debris, blown through the vent with great velocity, cut into Olson's face and arms, but he persisted in his heroic rescue attempt until the ship suddenly slipped to the bottom, sucking Olson down with her. When the ship struck bottom and the vacuum of her plunge was broken, a violent discharge of imprisoned air shot Olson to the surface where he was soon picked up by a rescue boat.

"Though unsuccessful in his heroic attempt, his magnificent courage, which sustained him literally into the depths of death, was in keeping with the finest traditions of the United States Merchant Marine."

The award was signed on May 22, 1945 by E. Scott Land, Chairman.

S.S. Alcoa Pathfinder Torpedoed; Surviving Sub, Lions, Crocodiles

News of merchant ships being sunk sometimes made the hometown newspaper only when a sailor returned home to tell how he survived the ordeal.

Harold Locktov returned to Oakland, Calif., where he told a reporter about his escape from the *S.S. Alcoa Pathfinder,* and from danger in the wilds of Africa.

Locktov, who was 20 at the time, sailed on the freighter delivering a cargo of war material to Cairo, Egypt. The ship was attacked on its return, at about 2 a.m. on November 22, 1942, south of Mozambique.

"We had no intimation of the attack until the torpedo struck us," Loctov told the reporter. "At that, it felt more like one of our own guns being fired. The torpedo struck in the engine room, killing all three men on watch there, as well as the third cook, who was asleep on deck just above where it struck. Our other casualty was the radio operator.

"The ship went down awfully fast, and, except for the men on watch, none of us were able to get away with shoes or clothing other than what we were sleeping in.

"Soon after we hauled away in the lifeboat, the submarine surfaced and came charging down on us. I thought sure we were going to be run down. But it stopped short and the commander came out of the conning tower. In excellent English, he asked us our identity. Then the U-boat hauled away. It was a big sub - I imagine it must have been about 300 feet long.

"We were about 15 miles off the coast, and with a life raft in tow we rowed in and set up a camp."

The newspaper account continues: "As the shipwrecked sailors landed on the beach, from the banks above appeared a big force of wild-looking natives, each armed with a long spear."

Locktov is quoted as chuckling: "Boy, I sure thought we were scheduled to go into the cooking pot. But the natives proved friendly and one of them agreed to act as a guide to the nearest British outpost."

Locktov, another sailor and the native guide - who spoke no English - started out across the country. It was a two-day trip, and during the night the trio became entangled in heavy marsh country.

After getting out of that, they came into plains with high grass. Eventually, they reached the outpost and the British sent back a truck to pick up the other survivors. The British also notified the two that the country threy had traversed was notorious for its crocodiles and lions. When the crew was assembled again, a Royal Air Force plane

Return from LeHavre.

came and took them to Durban, after which they returned to New York.

Merchant Marine Suffers Greatest Loss of Life on Single Ship When 133 Go Down with S.S. Coamo

It was December 9, 1942 when the passenger ship *S.S. Coamo* was torpedoed by a German U-boat off Bermuda. Not much can be told about this vessel's sinking, because all hands died at sea and no Allied ships were nearby to witness it.

But one fact sets this sad statistic apart: the *Coamo*'s demise cost more lives than any other single U.S. flag merchant ship's sinking during World War II.

Records obtained by Capt. Arthur Moore do indicate that the *Coamo* was on its way to New York, via Lands End, England, when she was sunk. She had left Gibraltar on November 26, 1942 in a convoy.

When the British Admiralty detached the *Coamo* from its convoy, she proceeded independently toward New York. Alone in the vast expanse of the sea, the *Coamo* was downed by U-604, taking 133 merchant seamen with her.[25]

Christmas Cheer from World Leader's Message To Brave Merchant Marines

As stories about the loss of lives became more and more common, it must have been more and more difficult for merchant sailors to find the emotional reserves to celebrate any holiday. How did "glad tidings" and "merry" and "happy" fit with a Thanksgiving-Christmas season plagued by ships being torpedoed to the depths of the ocean?

Randall Bishop of Laguna Beach recalls the meaningful Christmas Eve greetings his ship received from British Prime Minister Winston Churchill in 1942.

"It was a Christmas gift that gave a lift. From the Gulf of Mexico, we pulled into the hazy Sabine River. Then we slowed down to take on the pilot.

"One the way up to the refinery, a new tanker shot by us with 'Merry Christmas' on her code flags. We didn't have time to answer.

"We had been at war for a year - a year of wholesale, pitiless slaughter of our merchant fleet, mostly tankers delivering crude oil to the giant oil refineries on the Atlantic seaboard.

"When we tied up in Port Arthur, Texas, they informed us that the new tanker that passed us had been sunk. The workmen swarmed onto the ship, began loading and said we would be in the Gulf before daybreak. It was raining and black as ink. When we slipped out into the Gulf, the only thing we had to navigate with was the captain's 60 years in these waters. We didn't hug the coast - we shaved it.

"When I left the wheel to get a pot of coffee, I passed the radio shack, and Sparky handed me a telegram. I showed it to the crew and they all smiled.

"In the wheelhouse, the captain said, 'Randy, keep that telegram for posterity.' And I did.

"The telegram read: 'To the American Merchant Marine - behalf of the British Empire and myself, we wish you a Merry Christmas - Winston Churchill'."

Two Heroes Die Saving Crew Members in Stormy Sinking of S.S. Maiden Creek on New Year's Eve 1942

Danger came in many forms to those who manned ships during World War II - not the least of which was savage weather.

One such storm, on New Year's Eve in the North Atlantic, claimed the *S.S. Maiden Creek* as it was bound for New York with a load of ore. The ship hit a severe storm off Block Island on December 30, 1942.

Aaron McAlpin, then a 54-year-old member of the *Maiden Creek*'s steward department, recalled that dreadful year's end for "The SIU at War." He was one of 31 survivors.[26]

For 24 hours, the ship was pounded by the seas. On the afternoon of December 31, after losing one of her boats and all of her rafts, she sent out an urgent S.O.S. Seas were breaking over her decks, and the ship was filling fast.

Another vessel came up late in the afternoon, signaling them to abandon ship. But the captain delayed, hoping to bring the *Maiden Creek* in. It was a fateful decision.

After circling several times, the rescue ship went away. Later it was learned that the ship's captain mistakenly assumed that the *Maiden Creek* had been torpedoed and didn't want to endanger his ship by staying around.

"Just about dark, she started to go down by the head, and the skipper gave the order to abandon ship. The waves were terrific - at least 30 feet high - thudding against the deck houses and giving her a terrific pounding. Worst of all, it was cold and all of us were soaked by the spray.

"We used the starboard boats. Number one got away first. It hit a big sea, but the crew knocked the blocks out in a hurry and pulled away without smashing. It was mighty good seamanship. We wondered if we could do as good.

"Our number three was next, but it was evident that someone would have to stay on board and handle the lines if we were to get away.

"Joseph Squires and Harold Whitney, the deck engineer, volunteered. They lowered us away very carefully, timing it so we'd hit the water at the right moment. No one seemed a bit nervous or excited. A wave broke over us but we didn't swamp.

"We had to fend the boat off to keep from being smashed against the hull and a few seconds later, the sea carried us away from the side of the ship. When Squires and Whitney slid down the falls we were too far away and they had to drop into the water. Whitney disappeared. Squires started swimming with all his might, but he couldn't reach us. The Captain threw him a line and tried to maneuver the boat over to him, but the waves were too strong. After a few minutes, we lost sight of him."

Besides paying tribute to the two men whose skill and sacrifice launched the boat, McAlpin also commended the expert seamanship that kept them afloat in such terrific seas. "We had some mighty good men on that ship," he says. "They knew what to do and worked like a team under Captain Cook."

Late that night, they saw a distant flare, followed soon by several more. It was probably from number one boat, but there was nothing they could do to help her or communicate, and the boat was never seen again.

On New Year's morning, the cold, exhausted men were pelted by a sleet storm. A breaking sea filled McAlpin's rubber suit with water and soon after his feet began to freeze.

McAlpin believes the other ship reported their position, because several planes flew over. It was to no avail, though, due to a heavy overcast.

"We were going up and down like a roller coaster," McAlpin said. "One wave hit us so hard it cracked a seam in the boat. From

U.S Army transport Lakehurst, Hampton Roads, Norfolk, VA, 1943.

then on we had to bail constantly to stay afloat. The men at the oars worked like demons to keep us from capsizing. Captain Cook had the tiller."

The seas moderated somewhat on January 3. The survivors made a sea anchor with blankets and got some rest from battling with the oars.

During the day, a plane spotted them and dropped rations, water and whiskey. Later the *S.S. Staghound* picked them up.

By that time, McAlpin was experiencing the deep sleep that comes to those who are freezing to death.

"It was the damnedest thing," he says. "I thought I was making coffee - I went through the whole routine, just like I did in the galley. It even tasted good - all in my mind, of course."

Another seaman almost jumped out of the boat, hallucinating that it was tied to a dock.

After their rescue, the *Staghound's* surgeon estimated that a few more hours' exposure would have proven fatal for all.
Postscript:
 • *After several months in an English hospital, McAlpin returned to the U.S., incapacitated for further war-time sailing.*
 • *A Liberty ship was christened the* S.S. Joseph Squires, *to commemorate the heroism of its namesake. The Liberty ship* S.S. Thomas Crawford *honors AB Thomas Crawford, who also was lost in the Maiden Creek's sinking.*
 • *Another ship bore the Maiden Creek name the* S.S. Maiden Creek II. *She took two torpedoes, and was declared a total loss on March 18, 1944 near Algeria. Six crew members and five Navy men were lost.*[27]

1942 ended and another year began. Already the toll of merchant mariners dead or missing was 3,200.
1943
"Delivering the goods" wasn't getting much easier in early 1943. But the vital supplies still got where they needed to go.

In May, President Roosevelt paid merchant seamen the following tribute:

"The men of our American Merchant Marine have pushed through despite the perils of the submarine, the dive bomber and the surface raider. They have returned voluntarily to their jobs at sea again and again, because they realize that the life-lines to our battle fronts would be broken if they did not carry out their vital part in this global war."

Indeed, seamen were valued because they were critical to the war effort. A seaman who attempted to resign during a voyage, or otherwise violated military policy, faced military court martial. Because of their importance, merchant seamen were exempted by Congress from being inducted into the armed forces for as long as they continued to serve in the Merchant Marine. Draft boards were instructed to ask whether any registrant with sailing experience was willing to accept employment in "active oceangoing service" and, if so, to refer him to the Merchant Marine.

Then-Director of the Selective Service General Lewis B. Hershey wrote to the local draft boards:

"Service in the Merchant Marine, considering its importance to the war effort and the hazards involved, is so closely allied to the service in the armed forces that men found by the local board to be actively engaged at sea may well be considered as engaged in active defense of the country. Such service may properly be considered as tantamount to military service."

Answering the nation's call to duty, many mariners signed on for additional voyages at the expiration of their terms.

"During the war, the turn-over in the Merchant Marine was one-fourth the pre-war rate," according to the historical background in a lawsuit filed in 1987 by the Washington offices of the law firm Proskauer Rose Goetz & Mendelsohn.

It was during this year that FDR said: "The men of our American Merchant Marine have pushed through despite the perils of the submarine, the dive bomber and the surface raider. They have returned voluntarily to their jobs at sea again and again, because they realized that the life-lines to our battle fronts would be broken if they did not carry out their vital part in this global war."

**Confusion Ends in Escape from U-boat Destruction;
One-Fourth of 88-Ship Convoy Not So Lucky
By Frederick R. Michelsen
(As told in the "NMU Pilot," March 1987)**

It was early January 1943. I was Third Mate on the *William C.C. Claibourne*, a new Liberty ship named after the Governor of Louisiana. I had been sailing three years with the NMU on deck.

In May of 1942, I sat for my Third Mate's license at 42 Broadway. I passed and was sent to San Pedro by the War Shipping Administration. There I shipped on another Liberty and spent six months taking war materials to the Aleutians (Dutch harbor) and South East Alaska.

Now I was back in New York and sailing again after a short leave. This time, as I recall the articles, we were heading east to a point in the Atlantic, and then (wherever) the master would direct or be directed and back to a final port of discharge in the United States for a period of at least 12 months.

We had loaded explosives at Cavins Point, New Jersey and deck cargo at the Brooklyn Army base. About 8 p.m. on January 6, 1943, we up-anchored off St. George, Staten Island and along with many other ships slipped down the lower bay out to sea.

It was a frigid night, around zero temperature. I was glad to be relieved at midnight to go below as I had stupidly worn cotton socks instead of wool. In those war years, we stood our watches on the flying bridge in what we called "the dog house." It offered little protection, being made of canvas and pipe.

After rounding Sandy Hook, we headed south until we were joined by more ships out of Hampton Roads. Once gathered, we were 88 ships, headed east along the 35th parallel. Our position was in the rear, about the third column from the last, if memory serves me.

We were down to the marks with many tons of bombs and munitions. Ships like ours were put in the rear of the convoy, in the "coffin corner" as they called it. Fair weather held for the first 10 days or so. Fire, boat and gunnery drills were held.

Our armament consisted of two water-cooled 50-caliber machine guns with which to fight off the Luftwaffe and U-boats ... The enemy knew where we were and had been following us for days. Every so often, one of our few Navy escorts would drop back and let loose a few depth charges to hold the U-boats at bay.

The evening of January 19, 1943 found us near the Azores. I went on watch at 8 p.m. A Nor'easter sprang up and started to blow spit. About this time the convoy commodore sent a signal from his Christmas tree, a vertical iron mast with several arms like branches, carrying multi-colored lights. The signal was GREEN-GREEN-RED, (meaning a 45-degree emergency turn to starboard) to be executed upon extinguishing the signal. When a signal was sent by the commodore, it was to be repeated by all ships, since the convoy was spread out over a large area of ocean. That way everyone would get the message and know what to do.

What happened next I don't understand to this day.

Someone put up RED-RED-GREEN, which meant 45-degree emergency turn to port! I called the captain. Now (it seemed) half the convoy had put up RED-RED-GREEN, and the other half GREEN-GREEN-RED!

While all this was going on, the storm was building and we were feeling it. Suddenly, the commodore's signal light went out. Now came the grand finale: half the convoy went to port and half to starboard.

I said to the captain, "Let's not go to starboard," as we had deck cargo and it would bring the storm on our port beam. He agreed and ordered the helm to steer north 360 degrees from our former course of 90 degrees. After this, while we made a course northwards, the rest of the convoy sailed out of sight.

All that night, Sparks, the radio operator, said the air waves were jammed with the signal for "I have been torpedoed," which was S.S.S. not S.O.S. We heard later that the ships which went down-wind, obeying the GREEN-GREEN-RED signal, were easy prey for the U-boats which followed them - some on the surface - and picked them off like ducks in a shooting gallery.

The *S.S. City of Flint* was lost in this action. She had been interned in Norway earlier in the war, but was released by the Nazis. So through that night some of the world's best American merchant seamen ... drowned in fuel oil, were blown to bits, burned alive and gave the sharks a fine meal. Later reports said 22 ships - one-quarter of the convoy - went down.

The next day we sailed all alone, nothing in sight around the horizon. But we knew we were not safe yet, since there were plenty of U-boats between us and Gibraltar. For the next eight or nine days, we steamed various courses. When we drew near to Gibraltar, we dodged the Spanish merchantmen. The U-boats had a habit of hiding beneath them, and then coming up on you. Surprise!

We finally reached Gibraltar and rejoined what was left of our convoy. You didn't get much sleep in Gibraltar, as all night small patrol boats dropped small depth charges to ward off frog-men who might swim out from the Spanish mainland and attach mines to the bottom of the ships at anchor.

From Gibraltar, we went to Oran and Arzeu in North Africa and discharged our cargo. We took sand ballast at Port Said and returned to New York about 60 days after leaving it. Naval Intelligence questioned us about what had happened to the convoy, but we heard no more about it.

Meanwhile, my draft board was looking for me. When I told the lady in charge that I'd been at sea, she snapped, "That's no excuse. Don't you know there's a war on?"

Two Ships Collide in Convoy During Fierce
North Atlantic Winter Storm
By D.F. Cameron

I was a young cadet-midshipman aboard a grossly overloaded freighter, plowing through a wintry sea in convoy off the coast of Labrador.

It was January 1943. The purpose of the convoy is to elude an attack by enemy submarines. But the convoy itself is an extremely dangerous operation because of the close proximity of one ship to another. There is a terrible fear of collision. This fear is constantly with you. It tends to pucker-up your innards, especially during the long, bitter, cold dark nights when not a glimmer of light is allowed.

To know that just behind you there is a giant tanker loaded with aviation gasoline following close in your wake. On both sides and just forward of your bows there are three other vessels carrying thousands of tons of high explosives. It is not a story of heroism, but rather a story of quiet desperation and fear.

Back at the Academy, we were told that the individual ship was expendable. Only the convoy was important. If each ship only made a one-way trip, it was acceptable. But we had not made it to the war zone yet, and we were nowhere near ready to deliver our cargo, when the captain gave the abandon ship order.

It was a bitter cold, dreadful night amidst a raging North Atlantic snowstorm off the coast of Labrador. The Atlantic Ocean in these latitudes is the color of phlegm regurgitated from the bowels of Hell. The din of the general alarm bells and the wailful mourn of the ship's steam whistle mingled with the gale-force wind and blowing snow in a night as black as coal.

It was in itself enough to frighten a real old salt. But a boy of only 18 summers, not having to shave yet and less than a week out of Halifax, and here we were - going down.

As I stood on the vibrating, slanting, snow covered boat deck with my arms wrapped around a stanchion, I thought that the torpedo must have hit up forward of the No. 3 hold. Yet I did not hear the explosion, nor feel the shock of the impact.

I could hear our engine order telegraph ringing violently and a powerful searchlight was turned on at the port wing of the bridge. It stabbed the night with its beam.

It was then that I saw a big "Hog-Island" freighter. Her beam was to our bow and she was wallowing heavily into the deep troughs as we were. She was rising up on the great crests as we were. We had hit a ship.

Our bows were plunged deep into her midships just beneath her bridge, where her engine room would be. Then I saw little red lights rising high into the sky of blackness, and realized that each light was a seaman caught in the crest of a giant sea. The little red lights were attached to our life jackets and activated upon contact with the sea water. As fast as they appeared, these lights would disappear into the stormy night.

"Soon, my light will be one of them," I thought. "Davey Cameron will meet Davey Jones on his terms in his sea."

Jim, my father, will be pissed off at me for losing a brand new ship and 10,000 tons of badly needed supplies. "Holy," my mother will cry, and light a million candles for my soul.

Here, Mr. Cameron's reminiscences end. But the reader can take heart in the knowledge that the mere fact he wrote them in 1988, signifies that he survived this treacherous collision.

Veteran Merchant Officers Admitted to Maritime Service

On January 7, 1943, Supplement 1 was added to General Order No. 23 of the War Shipping Administration, admitting qualified and experienced officers already in the merchant fleet to the Maritime Service.

The reasoning behind this change was that the officers could then wear the Maritime Service uniform and insignia, and be enabled to serve better under war conditions, according to Commodore Knight, commandant of the U.S. Maritime Service.

Under this program, 24,976 men were appointed as officers in ranks commensurate with their positions aboard ship. All of these officers agreed to undertake additional training in the Maritime Service.

S.S. Dorchester's Sinking Claims 675 Lives,
Including 102 Crew Members

Twenty-five minutes after it was struck by a torpedo on February 3, 1943, the passenger ship *S.S. Dorchester* sank, taking with her 675 individuals - U.S. Army personnel, Danish citizens, Naval Armed Guard, civilian workers, U.S. Coast Guard personnel and merchant mariners.

According to Capt. Arthur Moore's research, it was the second largest loss of Merchant Marine life in the war.

Moore's account[28] is that the *Dorchester* was traveling in convoy from St. John's Newfoundland to Narsarssuak, Greenland with the passengers, general cargo, lumber, and 60 bags of mail and parcel post.

Confusion reigned because the torpedo, which struck near the engine room on the starboard side of the ship, did not make much noise. With a huge hole blown into the *Dorchester's* hull, flooding occurred quickly.

Three minutes after the torpedo hit, the master ordered that the ship be abandoned. Many of the passengers, making no effort to leave, evidently did not realize how dire the situation was. Only two of the ship's 14 lifeboats were successfully launched.

Four U.S. Army chaplains gave up their lifebelts to soldiers who had none. Survivors spoke of the calm attitude of these four men, who went down with the ship.

Among the survivors were 28 crew members, 44 civilian workers, three Danish citizens, 12 Navy gun crew, seven Coast Guard personnel and 135 Army personnel.

Merchant Mariner Recalls Dangerous Times, Lucky Escapes

George Read was aboard the *S.S. Fairfax*, the *Dorchester's* sister ship, when the *Dorchester* was hit. He recalls that many who reached the lifeboats froze to death in the horrendous cold.

Here are excerpts of his tale, as told in a program for Seamen's Recognition Day, 1985:

War Stories to Remember
By George Read

In 1943, I joined NMU. I shipped on the *S.S. Fairfax*, Clyde Mallory Lines, as quartermaster. I was on her one year. We made the "Greenland Run" without convoys, only zig-zag. Under the ice was our U-boat enemy. We ran cargo and troops to all the bases in Greenland. I was there three times.

The weather in Greenland was cold - 40 degrees and 50 degrees below zero. The *Fairfax* was a small passenger ship. She carried 400 troops or so...

Next I went to New York and the old NMU Hall, with open jobs by the hundreds every day! I looked at the board. A new Liberty ship out of Portland, Maine, the *S.S. Joseph Squire*, was crewing up. We joined a convoy out of Halifax and crossed the Atlantic with general cargo. En route one ammunition ship was sunk and one Liberty ship was hit by a U-boat. We discharged in Liverpool. Every night the Germans dropped bombs, and ships around us were sunk in the harbor. We shifted to Southampton where we took gunnery school and training on mustard gas decontamination.

Next we lay in Caens for seven weeks. No shore leave - only captains went ashore for meetings. Finally the day came. V.J. Day, Omaha Beach. I never saw so many airplanes - 2,000 or more - fires ashore and tracer bullets flying all over.

There were about 5,000 dead, some with their full packs on. It was something that I hope will never be repeated again.

Back to England and a trip to Glasgow, and then aboard the *S.S. Nemalo*, another Liberty ship fully loaded. We thought she was coming to the U.S., but when I saw the deck cargo - locomotives - I didn't know what to think.

Then we got the word: "Come get aboard. Destination unknown." We headed north and picked up a convoy to Murmansk and Archangel. When we came back, we had lost 60 ships. The majority were stranded by the weather and the Germans took advantage of it. On our ship we carried back four different crews that we picked up, some in bad shape. We discharged them in Scotland and started back to the States. Our stores ran out. We ate corned beef hash three times a day.

Back at the NMU Hall, my buddy Philip Proctor decided to go West. Over 100 of us, all NMU, took a troop train heading for San Pedro. As soon as we arrived, the ships were waiting for us. We rode the tanker Brookfield, running to Panama for 10 months, supplying the Navy with fuel. Back in San Francisco went bosun on the troop ship *S.S. Marine Serpent* for a year.

One day we saved some flyers off a Catalina airplane that sank. I received a letter from President Truman. I still have it, and some medals ....

Here, Read points out that medals don't pay doctor bills. "Breathing chemicals in tanks and breathing gas, living in old ships with asbestos during the war, didn't help anybody's health," he wrote.

His thoughts were penned before U.S. Merchant Marine World War II veterans achieved the status they deserve, but he added these words: "I have an idea. Since our government cannot afford recognizing us old-timers, we should ask the Russians, the British and the French to acknowledge our service during the war. After all, if it wasn't for us, Europe would be a Big Russia."

Tale of a Lucky Ship, and a Not-So-Lucky One

Henry Dooley went to sea as an AB during World War II, and summarized his many experiences for "The NMU Pilot" in March 1985, as part of a commemoration of V-E Day.

Reading his detailed account, it would be difficult for anyone to refute that merchant mariners "saw action" during their wartime service.

The *S.S. John Hayward Payne*, on which Dooley sailed from Norfolk, Va. to Oran, Algeria in March 1943, seemed to be protected by an invisible shield.

While Dooley went ashore in a bum boat, 100 yards away a Navy small boat took a direct hit and all Navy boys were killed.

Then in the invasion at Gila, Sicily, a German radio bomb hit a Liberty ship stocked with ammunition and all hands were lost. That tragedy occurred less than 1,000 yards from the lucky *John Hayward Payne*, he recalled.

The situation grew even more macabre, if such comparisons are possible in wartime, when Dooley witnessed the waters off Scoglitte, Sicily filled with the bodies of young American paratroopers - shot down by American gunners in what he said was a tragic mix-up.

"While unloading a huge tank, our jumbo boom broke and the tank and soldiers went to the bottom," Dooley wrote.

He watched helplessly as more merchant ships went down while awaiting the invasion in Berzerti North Africa.

"On arrival at Salerno, Italy, the German planes were raising havoc. Several bomb-loaded ships were sunk. The British battleship *Warspite* and U.S. Cruiser *Georgetown* took direct hits. The *Georgetown* lost several hundred men."

But the lucky *John Hayward Payne* remained untouched, serenely sitting in the middle of the harbor.

Anchored in Gibraltar on the way home, disaster struck again - to someone else. Two ships next to the *John Hayward Payne* were blown up by underwater divers from Spain.

Dooley figured that the *S.S. Casimer Pulaski*, on which he shipped out from Castle Island, South Boston on Feb. 4, 1944, was as unlucky as the *John Hayward Payne* was lucky.

Carrying a full load of ammunition for Russia, it avoided trouble for three days. Then submarines hit two tankers in the convoy in which the *Casimer Pulaski* was traveling.

"Our torpedo nets broke, fouled up the propeller, and we lost the convoy," said Dooley. "All deck cargo was lost in a storm."

The ship proved to be in such poor shape that it discharged its cargo in Bristol, England and returned to the States.

Leaving Boston again, disaster revisited the *Casimer Pulaski*. A sub attack broke up the convoy, and in the night storm the *Pulaski* smashed into a Norwegian ship, on which all seamen but four (rescued by the *Pulaski* crew) went down.

Damage to the *Pulaski* landed it in the East Boston shipyard for one month. The day came to set sail, and a boom dropped, killing a shipmate.

Proceeding in convoy, the *Casimer Pulaski* once again saw action in Northern Scotland where a submarine attacked. Several ships in the convoy were sunk, by both torpedoes and collisions.

"We carried Canadian troops to the invasion of France, and while returning to London in the English channel, were attacked by E. Boats.

"A torpedo went through our ship at No. 2 hold. While we were being towed up the Thames River to the shipyard, the first buzz bombs hit London. We were in Canningtown Prince Albert Shipyard for three months. That area was the target for continuous bomb attacks during our stay.

"1946: My first ship after the war hit a reef off Belfast, Ireland. And sank."

Bob Morris, Friend Reunited in What Would Prove to Be Ill-Fated Trip Aboard *S.S. John Drayton*

Billy Fontain and Bob Morris teamed up again as they took "the world's longest bus ride" to Baltimore, which Fontain had heard was the world's best place to ship out of. After checking in at the union hall, they were shortly on their way to Wilmington, N.C. to board a new liberty ship in the local shipyard.

There, they joined the *S.S. John Drayton* "shakedown" cruise, then sailed with the ship to New York to pick up its war supplies and the Navy Gun crew that would defend it.

"After the ship's crew battened the hatches, the stevedores loaded 26 Sherman tanks and 10 Douglas A-20 bombers on deck.

As the days went by, it became obvious that the cargo was going to Russia. Billy Fontain had his hat set: he was not going back to Russia. That was his prerogative, since the crew had not signed the articles," Morris wrote.

Fontain was so concerned that the friends approached the captain to see whether or not he could confirm that the *John Drayton* was Russia-bound. The captain told them only that the ship was not headed for Murmansk.

That assurance wasn't enough for the 17-year-olds, who conducted a little scouting mission of their own. In the warehouse where the ship was being loaded, Morris and Fontain then discovered cases labeled "Bandar Shahpur" and "Abadan" (Iran). That satisfied Fontain and he agreed to proceed with the trip.

"This ship and cargo would have been a prize for any sub crew. The *John Drayton* made the same slow, hazardous trip down the Atlantic coast, sailing only in daylight, and anchoring each night. That was the order of the times. Unknown to the crew, the ship was to sail to Panama via Guantanamo, Cuba, through the Panama Canal and down the West Coast of South America to avoid submarines. They would continue on around Cape Horn to Capetown, South Africa for refueling and resupply. From there, their orders took them up the East Coast of Africa, via the Mozambique Channel west of Madagascar, to make their way to the Persian Gulf. The crew, ship and cargo would travel nearly three-quarters of the distance around the earth to deliver the goods.

"The *John Drayton* anchored in Guantanamo Bay for a number of days for reasons unknown to the crew. A Navy launch came to the ship one day to take a mixed group of Navy gunners and ship's crew for training on the naval base. This was for 20-millimeter anti-aircraft guns. After some hours of classroom training, they were taken to a firing range and all the trainees had a turn at shooting at an airborne sock target towed by a Grumman JF-2 Duck. So far as anyone could tell, the target landed intact.

"The Navy man in charge of training the group then said it was about time for garbage detail, and that all the trainees should be there to see it. Everyone thought they were going to be put to work. Instead, they gathered on a 20-foot cliff overlooking the Caribbean, as sailors threw a large quantity of garbage into the ocean. The water was quite clear and they saw hundreds of fish of every species imaginable gather for the feast. Some were huge, some were colored, some were spotted. They did not seem to be predators, even though most were in a frenzy to get all they could in the least amount of time. It was a unique show for the people off the ship."

Swan Dive Turns Shark Scare for Merchant Marine Cadet

Morris recalled that the *John Drayton* was the first ship he had been on with cadets from the Merchant Marine Academy on King's Point, N.Y. "These were fine, clean-cut young men who were serious about learning all they could about steamships, engines and navigation. They were neat and very proper when they went ashore."

One memorable cadet was proud of his physique and his diving ability. He demonstrated the latter by diving from higher and higher decks into Guantanamo Bay, receiving enthusiastic encouragement from those who happened to be watching at the time.

"The flying bridge on fully loaded liberty ships was probably 40 feet from the water," Morris wrote. One day, with a fairly large audience gathered below, he climbed to the flying bridge. Once there, though, he deliberated for a long time about whether he should attempt this particular dive. The crew offered exceptional amounts of support, encouraging him to "take the plunge."

Finally, he climbed over the handrail and pushed off for a swan dive. About the time he reached a horizontal position in the dive, he looked down and saw what everyone else suddenly spied: a shark about 3-feet long hovering in his approximate splashdown area.

"The swan became a back-pedaling, clawing, screaming boy, who somehow managed to hit the water feet-first with a terrific splash. He went for the ship's ladder and the shark took off in the opposite direction. End of diving."

Voyage of *S.S. John Drayton* Continues

After few days after the excitement of the diving incident, the ship encountered a tragedy when a third assistant engineer in his 70s died in a boiler malfunction. A steam valve he was opening had failed, nearly decapitating him. The old man was a retired engineer who wanted to contribute in the country's time of need, and he died in her duty.

The ship stayed in Cuba for another month while engine room repairs were made. While there, the crew saw many ships gather in Guantanamo Bay. "At the time, no one knew it, but this was part of the North African invasion force," Morris wrote.

When the repairs were finished, a small convoy formed and the ships were escorted to Colon, Panama to prepare for the canal trip.

Both born sightseers, Morris and Fontain strolled through the city.

Leaving the canal zone, the *John Drayton* sailed south along the west coast of South America, passing Colombia, Ecuador and Peru, then changing course to go directly towards Cape Horn.

"Off the coast of Chile, the seas began to build. The weather was clear, but the waves were monstrous. For four days the ship was picked up like a toy on the crest of a mountain, only to be lowered to the depths of a valley caused by these running seas. To look up at the waves from the stern of the ship left fear in the hearts of all hands. If the ship had gotten abeam of the waves, surely it would have capsized," Morris wrote.

Forty-four days after leaving Panama, the ship arrived at Capetown and dropped anchor at Table Bay, where the crew was treated to a show of natural splendor.

Table Mountain is a 4,000-foot flat plateau which rises out of the South Atlantic Ocean. Capetown is built on the slope at the base of the mountain. Clouds flowed off the top of Table Mountain like a waterfall, then disappeared into "thin air." Local residents called this phenomenon the "Tablecloth."

From here, the ship headed east around the Cape of Good Hope. For many days, they steamed close to the African shore past Port Elizabeth, Durban, Lourenco Marques (which Morris would become better acquainted with later,) and up the Mozambique Channel until they cleared the Comoro Islands. Then they sailed straight-away for the Persian Gulf.

The *John Drayton* arrived in Abadan, Iran early in January 1943, then went up the Tigris and Euphrates Rivers, anchoring near Khorramshahr where it waited to take a turn at the docks to be unloaded. They unloaded the tanks and planes finally, but spent at total of three months in the area before leaving.

This gave Fontain and Morris and their crewmates plenty of time to explore date plantations, ride bum boats, hitchhike rides on Army trucks to Basra, Iraq and explore the region. Bob Morris celebrated his 18th birthday on March 8, 1943, in Khorramshahr, a long way from Meridian, Miss.

"Finally, all the cargo was unloaded and the ship sailed back down the Persian Gulf and anchored overnight near the Gulf of Oman. The boys put lights over the side to read the draft. Huge 10-foot snakes were attracted to the lights, for the entertainment of the crew," Morris wrote.

Here, too, phosphorus in the water treated the crew to "amazing displays of lights on waves, ship's wakes and bow waves."

Leaving April 1, the ship sailed for three uneventful weeks from the Persian Gulf toward Capetown.

Then came the evening of April 21.

Morris Survives Sinking of *S.S. John Drayton*; His Friend from Back Home Didn't

Bob Morris remembers that the seas were running high, with spray splashing over the bow of the *John Drayton* that night. They were in the Indian Ocean, at about the same latitude as Durban, South Africa.

He was on the 4-to-8 watch, and had just been relieved from his one hour and 20 minute turn at the wheel steering the ship. Morris stopped at his locker for his black leather jacket and rain coat because it was a cloudy, cool evening. Then he assumed his look-out post on the bow, joining a Navy gunner who was also stationed there.

It was dusk, about 7:15 p.m., when the gunner grabbed Morris' arm, saying "Look! Look!" Two trails of bubbles were visible as torpedoes passed from starboard to port, about 10 feet in front of the bow. In a split second, the ship passed over them. Being closest to the phone, the gunner picked up the receiver and reported to the bridge what they had seen.

"The captain immediately began a zig-zag course pattern and set off the general alarm. Every man on ship became a lookout, with the exception of the black gang on watch in the engine room.

By 7:40 p.m., it was pitch black. When Morris and the gunner were relieved just after 8 p.m., they were told that the captain had called off extra look-outs since no one could see in such total darkness.

The captain told Morris and the gunner he thought he had seen two submarines with his field glasses, and they in turn told the captain what they had seen.

Then Morris went to throw his raincoat on his bunk, joining Fontain in the mess hall.

"Did you really see a torpedo?" Fontain asked with some doubt in his voice. Before Morris could answer, a torpedo hit the starboard side of the ship in the engine room. It was not as loud to Morris as he had expected. But it was still as lethal.

"Immediately the lights went out and they heard the sound of steam blowing below. Everyone grabbed a life jacket and headed for the lifeboat deck for instructions at their assigned lifeboats. The officers were assessing the damage, but nothing happened for several minutes," Morris remembered.

Morris recalls that Fontain came over and told him he should come over and look at Fontain's lifeboat. "There was nothing to see. It had been blown off by the explosion. They waited together for several minutes, with no one thinking about the sub. But the people on the sub had not forgotten. They began to shell the ship," Morris wrote. "The order soon came to abandon ship."

Morris' assignment was to install the drain plug in the bottom of his lifeboat while it was being lowered away. The second mate was in charge of this lifeboat, and he began to pass several navigational instruments to Morris - one of which was the ship's chronometer. Fontain was on the boat deck, helping people get into the boats. He looked over the side and called to Morris jokingly, "If you make it home and I don't, tell them I went down fightin'." Morris said, "O.K."

About the time the lifeboat hit the water, Morris recalls that he became very busy because the sea was rough. Some men were coming down life lines. Others were tossing their clothing into the boat. In the chaos, a messboy in Morris' lifeboat prematurely released the toggle from the painter (the 1-inch rope that tows the lifeboat alongside the ship if the ship is still making way so that people can continue to get in.) Only 11 people had gotten into a lifeboat built for 22. A dozen or more people were left swinging on life lines with nothing but ocean beneath them.

Morris had been yelling to his friend to come down the life line, when he realized what had happened. That was the last time Morris ever saw Fontain.

The lifeboat began drifting behind the ship as the sub crew pounded more shells into the *John Drayton*. As they broke out the oars to row out of the line of fire, someone said that the sub had fired 25 rounds when he quit counting.

"The sea was so rough that one by one the fellows became incapacitated by seasickness," Morris indicated - all except a fireman who was in the engine room when the torpedo hit and Morris himself.

The fireman was laying on his stomach in the boat because he had cut his back climbing through a ventilator pipe getting out of the boiler room. He had no shirt. Morris found a shirt and coat for him, then uncovered the boat's rudder and put it in place. He found the sea anchor and tossed it over the side so the boat would be heading into the waves. They drifted for awhile. His fellow survivors were too weak with seasickness to help.

The shelling had ceased. It was pitch black when they heard the sound of a diesel engine coming out of the darkness. In a few minutes it drew closer. Then the submarine pulled up along the lifeboat.

Meeting the Enemy: Stepping Aboard a German Sub

"Everyone able to think was frozen in fear, because of the stories of merchant seamen being gunned down from submarines. Someone on the sub had a megaphone and began yelling, 'Are you English?' a couple of times. No one said a word. The sub crew threw a heaving line into the lifeboat," Morris wrote.

Seeing a man on the submarine with a machine gun pointed at them, Morris decided to grab the line and make it fast.

"One man come aboard," commanded the voice behind the megaphone, as they pulled the boat close to the side of the sub.

The waves lifted the lifeboat and slammed it onto the rounded hull of the sub, then it slid off as the waves subsided. No one in the boat made an effort to move. Most were unable.

The injured fireman said, "Morris, please go. They will tear the lifeboat up soon." So he went to the side of the lifeboat, and when the big wave lifted it so it was even with the sub deck, he leaped into the hands of four Italian sailors.

Morris felt the heat from the deck gun as he was led to the conning tower. A dim shaft of light from the open watertight door at the top of the conning tower cast illumination on the frightening scene. A man who appeared to be in full uniform spoke to him in English. He asked if they were English. Where had the torpedo hit? How many were killed? What was the name of the ship? What was the cargo? Where was it bound? Where had the ship been? All the answers seemed well-received until Morris informed them that the ship was empty.

"He is lying," a short, stocky fellow with a burp gun kept telling the captain.

"They did not seem to recognize the names of the ports, spoken in 'scared Southern'," Morris wrote. "Much of the information was relayed down the conning tower. The officer was quiet for several moments, then said, 'Goodbye'."

Morris could not believe he was to be released so easily. He asked the course and distance to the coast. The office responded with another curt "Goodbye." The man with the burp gun offered his opinion again: "He is lying."

But Morris was allowed to walk a short distance. He waited for the right wave, and jumped back onto the lifeboat, without any assistance. Morris released the heaving line and the sub moved away, into the darkness.

"The same people were seasick, so there was no help to put the heavy mast up in the rough weather," wrote Morris, who stayed awake all night, "electrified with the experience." Questions raced through his mind. How did the sub crew find their boat in the darkness? Was it compassion that caused them to ask how many were killed? Was theirs the only lifeboat approached?

Later Morris would learn that the Italian submarine Leonardo da Vinci *was responsible for the demise of the* John Drayton- *and that of 30 men aboard her.*

Awaiting Rescue with Shipwrecked Crewmates

"At daybreak, George Bowman, a young AB from Brooklyn, began to stir and together they put up the mast and sail. George was the senior 'officer,' but he was overcome with seasickness again," Morris recollected, so he took the compass and steered a good course to the west. When the sun came up, he felt relaxed and warm enough to fall asleep at the tiller. An hour or so later, he awoke to find that some of his compatriots were recovering. With a good breeze, they made headway.

The only one who complained was the messboy who had severed the lifeboat's ties to the *John Drayton* too soon. Even before the torpedo hit the ship, the messboy had been unpopular. He was ostracized for his obnoxious, gossip-mongering attitudes. But when he claimed it had been "his job" to set them free of the ship, he became persona non grata. So when he dared complain about their plight, and remarked that they were all going to die, "a cook half his size named Randolph Scott shut him up," Morris reported.

The survivors sailed west all day and everybody took turns at whatever chores came up under the directions of "Captain" George Bowman.

On the morning of the second day, they heard and saw a single engine airplane that was reminiscent of Lindbergh's *Spirit of St. Louis*. It appeared to be heading east at about 4,000 or 5,000 feet. Since they had no way to signal the pilot, they simply watched helplessly as he flew out of sight.

No one drank any of the water, nor ate any of the rations stored in the lifeboat. The same thought seemed to be on everyone's mind: "save it until we can't do without it any longer."

"By the end of the day, everyone was

'head's up,' so George set watches and divided up the chores," Morris recounted. "By noon the third day, someone on lookout - standing at the mast - reported he saw a buoy. All hands stood up. It wasn't a buoy. It was a Swedish ship named the *Gottenberg*, which in due course picked them up, lifeboat and all.

The survivors learned that they were heading south, and probably would have made Antarctica in a few weeks. The ship was bound for Lourenco Marques, Portugese East Africa (now Maputo, Mozambique.)

They were given lodging in an old wooden hotel in the middle of the city by the American Counsel, then moved to a beach hotel.
Since Portugal was neutral, few Allied ships called there. It was a full month before a ship was routed in - another liberty - and they had to sign on as crew members (no pay) because of some quirk in the law.

Wherever he went - in Lourenco Marques and en route to the U.S. - Morris repeatedly asked about other survivors of the *John Drayton*. At Durban, South Africa, they learned that eight people had been picked up from another lifeboat, which originally held 30 survivors. They had been adrift for 30 days. At a hospital in Durban, four died from the eight who had been rescued. No names were available to them.

These survivors had been spotted by a plane on about the fourth day. They assumed they would soon be picked up, so they divided and used all their rations and water. Rain squalls came. The inclement weather made it impossible for search and rescue ships to locate them. The captain of the Drayton was among the rescued survivors who lived, and he confirmed this story to Morris about five months later.

Finally, Morris found a reliable source with news about Fontain. Billy Fontain had lasted about two weeks before dying of exposure and drinking the salt water.

Recuperating in Capetown Amid Rowdy Merchant Mariners

After their ordeal, what was apparently a bad case of the flu forced Morris and Bowman into a detour from their repatriation. They wound up in Capetown to recuperate, where merchant seamen were looked on with some distrust.

The two men were placed in different rooms in a nursing home, where they stayed for two weeks. For several days they didn't know where they were. When they were about to be dismissed, a woman told them apologetically that merchant seamen were denied access to hospitals in Capetown because of "a long history of bad behavior."

From first-hand experience, Morris knew what she meant.

As he was beginning to recover, Morris found himself next to an English merchant seaman with a broken leg - suffered in a fall from his ship onto a wooden fender that kept the ship clear of the dock. The British fellow had been drunk at the time.

His mishap hadn't sidelined his rowdy spirit, though. One day when a nurse was bending over Morris to take his temperature and pulse, the Englishman seized the opportunity to pinch her in the thigh. Startled, she hit Morris in the middle of his chest, knocking the breath out of him. Then she turned on the offending Brit and "beat the devil out of him," finally picking up a book and landing a decisive blow to the groin.

The Englishman recuperated nonetheless, and on the day of his release was met with buddies from his ship. Already inebriated, they brought a bottle for him. Eventually, they all staggered out and within an hour he was back in the same bed - having tripped going down the front steps of the nursing homes and broken the same leg again.

Bowman and Morris began taking walks around the nursing home to regain their strength. Within a couple of weeks they were well enough to sign onto another ship to be repatriated in the U.S. This ship went to Buenos Aires.

With no money, the men made do wearing Portugese Army shirts and pants, a pair of dungarees and checkered shirts. They managed to get in some sightseeing, and in the meantime learned that still other *Drayton* survivors were on a ship that was sunk on the way home.

The ship that Bowman and Morris took arrived in New York the same day the Italians surrendered. Morris still had few clothes and no money. They were housed in a Seaman's Bethel in the Battery - on credit. Finally the steamship company gave them a draw of about $200, with no promise of when they would get their pay straightened out. They had been gone two weeks short of one year.

While in New York, Morris learned that there were 15 other survivors, bringing the total to 26 of the orginal crew of 41 and 15 Naval Armed Guard. He heard that many survivors had been interviewed on a radio show. And he discovered that the young radio operator, who was disabled, had been killed during the shelling while sending SOS positions on the emergency frequencies.

Captain Earl Norman also survived the *John Drayton's* sinking, and Morris credits the captain with being instrumental in helping him get all the paperwork completed upon their return. The captain also filled him in on the tragic loss of life among the crew.

After a week in New York, he once again returned to Meridian.
His adventures continued when he joined the *S.S. John Calhoun* (See below.)

S.S. *Michigan* Takes Torpedo on Way to Oran, Algeria
Reminiscences of Henry G. Quirk

The *S.S. Michigan*, a freighter built in 1919, wasn't the most welcome sight he had

SS HF Alexander at her regular port.

seen in his short 16 years, as Henry G. Quirk of McAlester, Okla. remembers it.

Looking at her in the Brooklyn, N.Y. shipyard, Quirk beheld a dead ship with no heat. It seemed ancient to him, and very quiet - "similar to a graveyard on a foggy night."

Picking up general cargo in Boston, the ship returned to New York where Sherman tanks were loaded for the trip to Oran, Algeria.

"Maybe they were what absorbed the impact of the torpedo," Quirk surmised many years later. A deck load of Army gliders finished off the complement of war supplies.

"Was all this to defeat General Rommel of the German Afrika Korps? Years later I realized that was its destiny," writes Quirk

Customs searched for diaries. No cameras were permitted. Especially no radios were allowed on board. Quirk recalled a fellow who brought only one record with him - "Friendship," by Judy Garland - and then over-played it until it disappeared mysteriously one night. No one would have to ever hear it again.

"We departed New York for we did not know where. The old rust bucket plowed through and rolled with the best of them. I heard Chief Engineer Driscoll complaining about water in the oil. Weather permitting, I enjoyed being on deck. I did not concern myself with what ocean we were in. But I heard a mate say he was glad to be out of the Atlantic due to wolf pack subs," Quirk writes.

They made the crossing and saw the famous Rock of Gibraltar. That morning, a French troop ship joined the convoy. Later Quirk learned that it held 1,700 people, including hundreds of French Sengalese Moroccan troops bound for desert combat against Rommel, the "Desert Fox." The *S.S. Del Norte* was on the *Michiga's* port beam, and the troop ship behind the *Del Norte*. It turned out that the *Del Norte* carried special troops. Just as the merchant seamen on the *Michigan* had no way of knowing that at the time, they had no way of knowing that they would take the place of those troops on the *Del Norte* 's return voyage.

It was April 30, 1943, and the next day was to be arrival day in Oran, North Africa (Algeria.) "I took out my black shoes, and checked my 'going-ashore' rags, not knowing I would never see them again. Believe me, I never again shined a pair of shoes the night before arrival. Any port, any ship."

"7:50 a.m. I was looking at the clock mounted on the starboard bulkhead above a mess table. The messhall was thwartships. The torpedo struck No.2 hatch area and she sank immediately up to the bridge. If the bulkhead to the engine room gave, or if it had hit the engine room, we all would have been lost. I ran aft on the wood catwalk for a life preserver, then returned to the portside lifeboat," he recalls.

As it was, all aboard - 38 crew members and 24 Naval Armed guard - survived.

Quirk recalled that a black gang fellow was slacking the fall too fast, and the A.B. was too slow slacking on the cruciform bit.

"We're lucky we did not lose the lifeboat ... Many of us shoved off as quick as possible," he said.

"There was an explosion and it looked like the sun setting. We guessed it was a high octane tanker. It hit the troop ship. We never did learn the name of it. I don't know how many ships were hit. We just drifted, it seemed like hours. The bodies from the French troop ship were drifting all around. The French Sengalese were short, and their uniforms were made of heavy wool, dark brown and they were brown-skinned. They looked like 10-year-old boys. Many of the whites were in white orderly clothes.

"Finally we got to a British corvette, one of two in the area. They had been dropping depth charges. I imagine those in lifejackets in the water felt it worse than we did in a lifeboat. In the meantime, we watched the old *Michigan* stern up and disappear. All I could think about was my comfortable black shoes, all shined. We were sprayed with oil, and not comfortable. But it was good to be alive."

Although Quirk reports that they discussed cutting the life jackets and letting the bodies floating around them sink to a respectable grave, no one made a move to do so.

"We finally maneuvered up to a corvette that had been sitting still, trying to pick up any sub noise. There were many troops up against the stern, dead. Finally a sailor on the corvette threw down a heaving line. We attached it to a cleat on the boat. One of the engineers went up a Jacob's ladder they threw down. Even though he had an artificial leg, he went up so fast.

"The horns started to blow on the corvette, and the screw started, and we were being towed. The line was jammed on our cleat. Luckily I had on a sheath knife, and was able to cut the line. We drifted around all the debris. Finally, a corvette let us go aboard."

Conditions aboard were nothing to write home about. It moved like a roller coaster. Survivors rescued on canvas cots hung by chains and ate off of dirty plates because demand for food exceeded the ability to clean the plates.

"We finally arrived alongside the pier in Oran. So many on that small corvette went to dockside, it looked like we would capsize until the sailors yelled. We were loaded in an Army truck and taken to the uptown area by the Red Cross mess hall to eat. Just to be in a safe haven felt great."

Staying in the Metropole Hotel for the merchant navy, the occupants took their chairs out in the hall the first night to talk and reassure one another after their ordeal.

Quirk remembers the bed bugs. They drove him to sleep on the floor that first night. The next day, though, he befriended soldiers who invited him to share their quarters. So for the next two weeks he had his accommodations upgraded and slept in a bunk with a mattress cover filled with straw.

"The Red Cross gave us a total of two meals and then said, 'Find a restaurant.' But we had no money. Finally the captain gave me $11 - a draw against wages," wrote Quirk.

But since they had only been out to sea a few weeks, and then the ship was sunk, Quirk's and his crew mates' pay would stop accumulating the day the *Michigan* went down.

When the *Del Norte* was ready to set sail for New York, Quirk got aboard for the 22-day trip.

"It took all day, waiting to go through F.B.I., customs, etc. The F.B.I. told me I should register for the draft as my age showed 18. I was scared to admit to being only 16, for fear they would make a federal problem ... Then a lady who drove a United Seaman's Service station wagon told us how lucky we were. A fellow who lost three ships in a row had been killed by a New York taxicab..."

When Quirk returned home for his 30-day survivors' leave, he registered for the draft but did not divulge his true age.

"I am happy to see that some of the history of the World War II Merchant Marine is being recorded for future generations. I write this in memory of all seamen lost, but not forgotten. I believe in Guardian Angels, as I must have one," Quirk concluded in his letter.

Crew Saves Gasoline-Packed *S.S. Daniel Huger*

The *S.S. Daniel Huger* traveled in the same convoy as the *Michigan*, but mercifully avoided being torpedoed. Ten days later, however - on May 9, 1943 - the Liberty ship was attacked by German bombers as she was being unloaded at a dock in Bone, Algeria.

The crew had only 60 seconds warning to man their guns before 17 German planes started a high-level bombing attack.

Two bombs fell close aboard the *Daniel Huger*, showering shrapnel on the decks and fatally wounding a gunner and the third mate on the port side of the bridge. Bomb fragments fell into the No. 5 hold, starting a fire among the barrels of gasoline.

The captain ordered her abandoned, after flooding the magazine and throwing live ammunition over the side, because the ship could explode at any moment.

Here is the account of what happened next, as told to "The SIU at War".[29]

"When the fire brigade arrived, however, it was decided to try and save the ship with foamite - a dangerous job which necessitated volunteers going aboard, entering the hold next to the fire and playing a hose on the heated bulkhead to keep the flames from spreading.

"One of the volunteers was the ship's purser, Alexander Waigandt of Astoria, Long Island. Going into No. 4 hold and directing the work of volunteer SIU crewmen who took turns going down with him, he kept water playing on the heated bulkhead.

"For his initiative in leading themen in this dangerous job, Waigandt was awarded the Merchant Marine Distinguished Service Medal."

Their valiant efforts saved the ship.

Convoy Meets Hurricane in Caribbean, But Is First to Avoid Loss of Ships in Torpedo Alley

Reminiscences of Paul Buhman

When this Vancouver, Washington resident thinks back to May 21 - June 6, 1943, it stirs memories of a Panama Canal-to-New York convoy that saw once-in-a-lifetime weather. He was a fireman aboard the Liberty ship *S.S. Amos Kendall*. It was the ship's maiden voyage, and his first outing as a fireman.

Buhman's is a detailed account of the danger of everyday life in a convoy, compounded by the uncertainties of the weather. His ship joined the convoy outside Limon Bay. Here's his story:

I was in the engine room on watch when we started out to open sea. We soon found that being in a protective convoy was not to be compared with traveling alone. The top speed of the convoy was set by the fastest speed of the slowest ship. To complicate things further, we continually zig-zagged on our course. There were over 75 ships in the convoy - tankers, freighters, and Navy escort vessels. When all ships were directed by the command ship to turn 20 degrees port in concert, we trusted they would all execute the instructions correctly. We were only a few hundred yards apart, and a collision could happen very quickly..

To hold our exact place in the convoy, we continually received instructions from the bridge. "Up two revolutions." We would respond by opening the engine throttle a third of a turn. "Down three revolutions," we would be told a few minutes later, and we moved the throttle valve a half-turn close. Each turn of the ship's propeller would push the ship about 16 feet forward, depending on the load, current, wind, and so on. This convoy's speed was six knots, more or less.

Whenever we changed engine speed, it affected the steam demand. If the engine was slowed very much, I had to cut off one burner on each boiler to compensate. Otherwise, the excess steam pressure would "pop" the safety valve - something a good fireman never wanted to happen. The opposite was true when more speed was required. All three of us on watch in the engine room and fire room were fully occupied at all times in a convoy. This activity was to continue for the next 13 days from Panama to New York, a distance of about 2,000 nautical miles.

Three hundred miles north of Panama, in the Caribbean Sea, we encountered a violent tropical storm. I had never been in a tropical storm at sea before, and I hoped later that I would never be in another such as this one.

For the next two days we received the full force of the storm. The ship pitched and rolled at angles I never knew possible. We had tied everything down in the engine room. Barrels of oil, boiler compound and spare parts were securely fastened to posts and rails. Water in the bilges would go rushing across the bottom of the engine room and crash into the side of the ship. When the ship rolled the opposite way, the water went crashing back. It was difficult, if not impossible, to keep the bilge pumped dry since the water moved constantly.

The second assistant engineer had the same problem with water in the boilers, where he was trying to keep it at the proper level. Too much water in the boiler could carry over into the engine with devastating results. Too little water, and the boiler tubes would melt down. When the ship rolled to starboard, the water in the port boiler sight glass would be full and the starboard sight glass would show empty. With the next roll, everything was reversed. This is where I got acquainted with, and learned the meaning of the phrase, "educated guess."

The engine room was not the only department that was having problems. The steward's department was almost closed down. The cooks could barely cook, since the pots and pans slid around on the range. With much persistence, they were able to prepare a limited number of dishes. The coffee urn was fastened down, so coffee wasn't a problem. They could also fry eggs - which came out scrambled - and make hot cakes. But we were lucky. The Navy destroyer escorts were only one-fourth the length of our ship, and cooking on them was impossible so their crews were on cold rations for three days.

Our messmen were resourceful. They wet down a bedspread and used it as a tablecloth. This method kept dinner plates and coffee cups from sliding.

Several old-timers remarked that they had never before been in such a storm. Hurricane was the proper designation. The wind and rain were relentless.

Ropes had to be strung from the midship house to the various stations - bow watch, forward and aft gun tubs, etc. - so the deck hands and gun crews could man their stations. At times, several feet of water would wash over the deck. No lights were allowed. Total blackout was in effect since we were in dangerous waters. For once, I was pleased that I worked in the engine room.

Somber speculation was also forming among the crew members that the ship might break in half, as some Liberties were prone to do. With our holds weighted with a cargo of copper, we were like a huge roly-poly in the water. Our draft was 27 feet forward and 30 feet aft. Midship at the Plimsoil mark, the reading was 1'3" above the center line. We were loaded to the allowable maximum.

When I got off watch at 0800 on the third morning of the storm, I went topside and as I looked out on deck, was greeted by bright sunshine. The sky was mostly clear, and the wind had subsided. The ship however was still rolling heavily, as the sea had not yet begun to calm in the wake of the storm. The swells were still in excess of 25 or 30 feet.

In heavy seas, there are two good places to observe and feel the action of the ship - the

Crew of SS Stephan T. Mather, 1943, Basra.

bow and the stern. I made a brisk dash to the aft gun tub, a distance of 125 feet. Standing in the tub was not unlike riding a fast elevator. When the heavy seas plunged the bow down, the stern would rise to a high viewpoint. We were on the starboard side of the convoy and in a middle position from front to rear. Off to the port side, you could see four or five miles and many rows of other ships. When the ship pitched the next time, the bow would be up and the stern down. All you could see then was water all around you. It was like being in the bottom of an emerald bowl, with water at the edges.

Starting down the ladder to the deck, I stopped in utter bewilderment. There, just below me, stood a German Shepherd, wagging his tail, tongue part-way out of his mouth.

The dog belonged to the first mate, who had purchased it in Chile and kept him out of sight until the crew was on the last leg of the voyage home. If crew members had seen the dog before, they too might have wanted one and the ship could have come to resemble a floating zoo.

I reached out and patted the dog's head, saying something like "Nice doggie." The first mate informed me the dog did not understand English, and he was working on it. How intriguing. A dog that knew more Spanish than I!

The first mate and the dog walked around the aft corner of No. 5 hatch cover on the port side, waiting for the proper moment to make the dash to the midship house. The dog stood obediently at his side. When the port deck cleared of water, after the roll, the mate said, "Come on boy," and headed across the open deck at a fast run. The dog started along with him, then stopped half-way.

When the first mate saw what had happened, he crouched down to urge the dog on. "Here boy, here boy," he called frantically, then tried something in Spanish, but the dog wouldn't budge. More frantic coaxing by the mate, but the dog stood with his head tipped, ears alert, apparently confused.

The ship was beginning its roll towards port. In a few seconds, the deck was covered with three feet of water. The dog was swimming above deck. As the ship righted herself, the dog still swimming, went over the side with a rush of water. Though the ship was moving slowly, there was no way to reach the dog. He was swimming alongside, about 10 feet out. A large gentle wave caught him, he rode the crest and then disappeared from sight at the bottom of the wave's trough. The next time I saw the dog, he was 50-feet astern and swimming as hard as he possibly could to catch us.

I ran to the midship house and went to the upper deck, hoping to help in some way. The mate ran to the bridge and tried to get the captain to stop the ship. The captain refused. He then tried the radio man to request that the destroyer escort directly behind us would pick up the dog. The radioman had orders: "COMPLETE RADIO SILENCE IN CONVOY." The mate found help. A Navy signalman from the gun crew would send a message with our "blinker light" to the destroyer escort: "WATCH FOR AND RESCUE DOG OVERBOARD DIRECTLY IN YOUR PATH." He sent this message several times with no response. Finally, after a long wait, the destroyer escort responded: "NEGATIVE TO REQUEST."

We were told, sometime later, that in these waters infested with German submarines and raiders, a rescue attempt even for a man overboard was prohibited.

I returned to the main deck and went to my fo'c'sl. I had missed breakfast, but was in no mood to eat after what I had witnessed. It was an incident I shall never forget.

At the pay-off in New York, we were told that our convoy was the first to pass between Cuba and Haiti (Torpedo Alley) without a loss of any ships.

Taking Training on Catalina Island, 1943
By John L. Dahl

It was May 1943, and I was getting ready to graduate from high school in Park City, Utah. World War II had been in progress for 18 months, and the boys in my class were trying to decide which branch of the service they would be in. I had not yet made up my mind, but was not enthused about the Army, Navy or Marines.

There was a lot of publicity about the Merchant Marine at the time due to many ships being sunk, and there were posters in the post office advertising for recruits. I thought that this was another branch of the service, so just to be different, I told all my friends that I was going to join the Merchant Marine. My commitment was made.

In September, when I turned 18 and became subject to the draft, I went to the U.S. Maritime Service recruiting office in Salt Lake City and signed up for training at Catalina Island. At that time, the U.S. Marines were fighting in the Solomon Islands, the Allied forces had just invaded Italy, and Germany was being pounded from the air in preparation for "D-Day" in June 1944.

A few days later I joined several other recruits from Utah, Idaho, Montana and Colorado, and we boarded a train for Los Angeles. We were picked up by a bus and spent our first night sleeping on a cot at a warehouse on the dock in Wilmington, where the *S.S. Avalon* was berthed. The next morning we boarded the ship and sailed to Catalina Island for three months of training. Catalina was largely taken over by the Maritime Service during the war to train merchant seamen for the War Shipping Administration.

After receiving inoculations, a crewcut and a supply of clothing consisting of dungarees, one blue and one white sailor uniform, a pea jacket, shoes, underwear and a sea bag to carry them in, we were assigned to a cabin in a villa just off Catalina Avenue. These cabins were small plywood shacks with no bath and no heat. There were four bunks. Meals were served in Boose Brothers Cafeteria, one block down the street.

We were assigned to a section with 40 trainees under the direction of one section leader. Bill Flannegan, who had graduated from Maritime School and already made a few trips to sea, was our leader. He was highly respected by our section. We spent six weeks in basic training, where we learned how to march, how to swim in the frigid water at Crescent Beach, how to fire the 20-mm and 5-inch guns from the patio outside the casino. At the Yacht Club, we also learned how to launch lifeboats, abandon ship and swim through burning gasoline. In another class, we learned about ship construction and nomenclature.

After basic training, we were assigned to specialty training in deck, engine room or steward department schools. I selected engine room, and was transferred to the beautiful St. Catherine Hotel on the beach just north of the casino. This was once a resort hotel, but we found the amenities lacking with no maid service and four bunks to a room.

In the classroom, we learned about engines, boilers, pumps, generators, evaporators and condensers. We tested our knowledge as crewmen on the *S.S. Avalon*, and the *S.S. American Sailor*, which cruised around the island. While at the hotel, the island was hit by a severe winter storm which beached and destroyed several private yachts. Some of our trainees volunteered to help tie down boats and save them.

We finished our training around Christmas in 1943. I managed to get home for the holidays, but on January 4 I had to report to the Maritime Station on N.E. Sandy Boulevard in Portland, Oregon. There, I awaited an assignment for my first ship.

My Merchant Marine career lasted for the next 10 years, during which I sailed on 16 ships, through World War II, the Korean War and then through the Lend Lease program. I eanred the War Shipping Administration awards for service in the Pacific War Zone, the Atlantic War Zone, the Mediterranean Middle East War Zone and the Merchant Marine Combat Bar. I made four trips around the world, working in capacities from wiper to first engineer. Little did I know what I was getting into when I signed up for the Maritime Service, but it turned out to be a great opportunity to see the world and serve my country.

Two Ships Collide in Port-to-Port Passing;
Survivors Describe Ordeal

Transporting ammunition meant carrying danger, even in the most routine maneuverings of a ship.

On June 1, 1943, seamen were reminded of that simple truth when the *S.S. John Morgan*, a Liberty ship on her maiden voyage, and the tanker *S.S. Montana* collided just before dawn off the Chesapeake Capes. Eighty-four lives were lost between the two ships.

The two ships were passing one another when the *John Morgan* suddenly changed course and headed directly for the *Montana*.[30]

The St. Louis Post-Dispatch carried an account from two survivors, with the headline: "Explosion of Ammunition Ship 'Terrifying,' St. Louisan Says; Two Survivors of Collision Assert Public Does Not Realize Danger of Merchant Service."

The explosions were so powerful that the freighter sank within a few minutes and debris was showered on a Coast Guard ship a quarter of a mile away.

Robert Yoffie of St. Louis, had only been in the Merchant Marine six days when he had to swim for his life through burning oil. The Post-Dispatch spoke to him and his friend, Billy Irby of Houston, Texas, a fellow seaman, before they once again set sail.

Irby, then 21, had been in the service for three years when the collision occurred. He escaped the burning ship by crawling out a porthole on the poop deck and jumping 35 feet into the water.

"The main deck was a mass of flames and smoke, so we couldn't make it to the lifeboats. The captain, the first, second and third mates were burned, but someone gave the order to abandon ship. Our problem was how to get into the water."

Yoffie found his way out through an iron door and was picked up by the Coast Guard at about 6 a.m., after clinging to a raft for an hour. "The gasoline burned in a big blaze, with thick smoke. I thought it would blow up, but it didn't, and I swam like hell to get away from that ship," he told the reporter.

The Post-Dispatch concluded this way: "Proud of their insignia of the United States Merchant Marine, they observed that it does not receive the distinction or recognition the work merits. Inland, especially, they said, storekeepers have thought they were trying to impersonate the Navy when buying sailor uniforms.

"Pointing to glamor advertisements of men and women in the armed forces, they asked, 'Where do you see anything about what the Merchant Marine is doing? It's not understood what it is doing, except in the coast shipping towns'."

Little did these young men, who had been through such a harrowing experience, know how far the ramifications of their astute observations would reach.

**Seaman Serves Happily on S.S. El Estero,
In 1943 It Catches Fire and Must Be Sunk Near Statue of Liberty**

Kevin H. King of Somerville, Mass. served in World War II, Korea and Vietnam. When he looked back at his years of service for the "NMU Pilot" in March 1985, it was his adventures on the S.S. El Estero that he focused on most.

King joined the El Estero in December 1941 as a wiper in England. She was an American ship under the Panamanian flag, armed with four 30-caliber machine guns on the bridge and a 4.7 anti-submarine gun aft. There was no gun crew at the time they headed out to sea to pick up a convoy.

"At this time, I was only 19 years old. My last ship was a coal burner. This one was burning oil. It made about 8 knots. Well, we picked the convoy up and headed out to sea. We were about seven days out when the engine broke down at night. The chief engineer put everybody in the engine room to work to try to fix it.

"The convoy wished us good luck and left. We had to wait a few hours to let the engine cool down. Well, we fixed the cylinder, buttoned her up and got underway. The captain said we were heading for St. Johns, Newfoundland. We could only make four knots. We were all alone. Sitting ducks," King said.

Still, they made it to St. Johns where they heard about Pearl Harbor from the surveyors who came aboard. Shipyard workers and longshoremen labored around the clock to prepare the El Estero for the trip to New York.

"Going ashore one night, I happened to see some of our cargo on the dock. It was marked 'USSR'. We departed from New York on 13 January 1942 for Halifax, Nova Scotia. I'll remember that day as long as I live. The Normandy was burning at the dock uptown. She tipped over. That was the French Lines. They flooded her to put the fire out, and she capsized," King said.

When the captain handed out the Arctic gear, it came with a little advice: don't lose any of it. Three days later, they hit freezing weather and they had to keep the Arctic gear continuously.

"It was no joke trying to get through the ice pack. You could see the German reconnaissance planes over on the horizon. The destroyers would fire on them to scare them off," he explained.

The temperatures worsened, to 35 degrees below zero, then 45 degrees below zero, Fahrenheit. The wind and snow picked up to blizzard conditions, and the captain was forced to slow the ship. When the storm broke, all the forward cargo was hanging over the side. For the safety of the ship, the deck gang chopped with axes to free it.

Finally some Russian destroyers with icebreaker bows came along and got a bow line on. "The captain told us later that they told him they were looking for us," King said.

"We would put on the radio and get Lord Haw-Haw. He would say, 'I'm broadcasting to you seamen. Don't sail American or British ships. Go home. Think of your family and your wife. Some of you got in here, but not many will leave." He meant the ships.

"Well, we got some of the ships in. It would be good if we got half the convoy in. Some British ships made it too. We went without our escorts, the H.M.S. Eclipse and the H.M.S. Trinidad - two destroyers - because they got shelled off Norway."

Lord Haw-Haw said they wouldn't make it to Murmansk, but they did, despite the storm, the docks being bombed at night and the sinking of a nearby British ship.

"Our crew went to the air-raid shelter. They told us not to use the guns. They said the shore batteries would take care of them. A bomb hit the stack on another ship. She was across the other side of the dock from us. We talked to some of the crew the night before we left Murmansk.

"We got attacked two days out. The captain told us to drop the smoke screens into the water. We did and finally made it back to Iceland. The Navy told us we were very lucky. I saw in a paper two years ago where some divers went down and took $70 million or $80 million worth of gold off our escort, the H.M.S. Edenberg. She was a good destroyer.

"I stayed on the El Estero running to the military bases in the Caribbean, bringing back bauxite from Georgetown. I got off in August 1942 and took a ship called the S.S. Capira.

"We got torpedoed seven days out of New York. It was 4 a.m. in the morning when the torpedo hit. The second mate said 'Get the raft.' I let it go and went overboard. A wolfpack of subs attacked us. We lost the engine room oiler fireman and the chief engineer, who was on deck when it hit. A Canadian corvette picked us up 200 miles south of Iceland.

"Well I went back to the company, U.S. Lines. I went back on the El Estero, running to England, back and forth until she went afire alongside the ammo dock at Cavens Point, N.J. in 1943. The Coast Guard had to sink her right alongside the Statue of Liberty. She was loaded with 5-ton bombs for the Air Force in Britain when she caught fire. They thought she might blow up, along with half of New Jersey.

"Next I was on the S.S. Alexander Wilson in 1944. We made the invasion June 6, 1944. They sent us to Cherbourg, where we lay in the English Channel off the Isle of Whyte for about three weeks."

1944

The era of the "ugly duckling" was drawing to a close. Liberty ships had served their purpose. They had been built fast. They had delivered supplies throughout the world, powered by a steam reciprocating engine. And more than 2,700 of them had been constructed since the Liberty Ship program was launched.

Now a call went up for a new emergency ship, one designed to last longer than five years.

There was demand for a faster, more efficient ship, one that sailed at 15 knots or more compared to the Liberty's plodding 11 knots. A steam turbine engine proved to the be answer.

Shippers thought such a vessel could be more commercially viable to ply the world's trade routes once the war was won. The millitary wanted a better ship for its own stand-by purposes, too. The Liberties had been plagued by hull fractures, so design improvements were necessary to prevent that problem as well.[31]

The so-called "Victory" ship program was started in 1943. On February 28, 1944, the United Victory - the first of the new line of ships - was launched by the Oregon

Shipbuilding Corp.

Another 530 Victory ships followed her to make their way into the world's waterways, of which 414 were cargo ships and 117 were transports.[32]

And who would sail these ships?

A recruiting poster from this time portrayed a determined-looking mariner, jaw set, duffle bag slung over his shoulder. Bold letters beneath the drawing declared:

> **"You Bet I'm Going Back to Sea!"**
> Register at your nearest U.S. Employment Service Office
> **U.S. MERCHANT MARINE**
> War Shipping Administration
> Man the Victory Fleet

Merchant seamen participated in all the major invasions of World War II, from North Africa to the Aleutians, from the South Pacific to Italy and France.

Often, they participated as part of the first-wave assault forces where they saw front-line fighting.

"Of all the invasion bridgeheads, none have been 'hotter' than Anzio, where many SIU seamen delivered food, equipment and explosives that enabled Clark's men to hold on and eventually join the drive on Rome," as reported in "The SIU at War."

Allied landings began at Anzio on January 22, 1944. Allied attacks commenced eight days later. In mid-February, the Germans began their own major attack on the Anzio beachhead, at one point almost breaking through a U.S. division on one front. Despite several offensives by the Germans, they were held at bay and in early March they were forced to resort to a defensive stance.

First-Hand Account—Anzio Invasion

Thomas D. Walker Jr., then listed as a Baltimore resident, gave his first-hand experiences at Anzio to "The SIU at War." Here's how he captured it:[33]

Loaded down with gasoline, ammunition, food and other supplies, Walker's ship arrived at Anzio from Naples at 8:30 a.m. on a Sunday. Two hours later, they found themselves in the midst of a heavy air raid. By noon on their first day, the German artillery on the heights beyond the town had them spotted and opened up with their 16-inch heavy artillery.

"The Army stevedores called the big shells 'whistling whillies' and paid no attention to them, saying you never hear the one that hits you and if you did, it wouldn't be any use worrying anyway. They could hear the big shells coming, and then see them hit the bay in a geyser of spray and a cloud of black smoke. Water would still come down after the smoke had blown away. One hit amidst gasoline or ammunition would have sent the ship sky-high in a grand display of pyrotechnics. But they were all near-misses - at least while Walker was there."

It appeared that the Germans had scored some hits, though. A sunken Liberty, a wrecked British cruiser and an assortment of smashed landing craft on shore were testimony to those losses.

"The Nazis tried to eliminate the supply ships during the first night with a high-level attack preceded by flares. A barrage of red fire kept the planes too high for good aim, and they missed the ship with a rain of bombs. But they made up for it by smacking an ammunition dump on shore and blowing it up like a 4th of July celebration.

"On Monday a Liberty came in flying a barrage balloon, which was all the distant artillery needed for range. In a few minutes shells started coming over like baseballs, with occasional heavies thrown in for good measure. One big 'whistling whillie' smashed the water astern of Walker's ship, and rocked it like a beam sea in a North Atlantic howler.

"During the daytime Germans and beach-head forces kept up a constant artillery duel. The sky seemed polka-dotted with shell puffs. Occasionally during the day the Luftwaffe would try a sneak dive-bombing attack, or send over Junker 88s high above the patrolling umbrella of Allied P-40s. Their observers also made frequent visits, so high up only the condensation from their exhausts could be seen across the sky. Radio-controlled glide bombs were used, too; a weapon which soldiers said had been successful against shipping and supply dumps."

By their fourth day, the alarm rang and Walker ran on deck to see several planes directly overhead. One plane dived through a barrage of anti-aircraft fire and bombed a Liberty that was discharging ammunition (the *S.S. Elihu Yale*, which went down February 15, 1944.) The bomb dropped in her No. 4 hold, leveling the vessel's entire after section. (Most of the *Yale's* 45-member crew and 40-man Armed Guard survived; however, two ordinary seaman, a messman and two Navy men were killed.[34])

"Another bomb just missed an LST loaded with gasoline. And a third blew off the stern of a destroyer.

"Most memorable of his experiences at Anzio, according to Walker, was the sight of American bombers going over for a raid on German artillery positions. Many of them were shot down and the men could see the big ships burst into flames, spiral crazily and then crash into the hills, or disintegrate in the air amidst smoke and fire.

"During five hectic days at Anzio, Walker's ship had 65 alerts, 48 raids and 35 direct attacks on the harbor shipping in which bombs fell close by."

***S.S. Lawton B. Evans* Downs Five German Aircraft at Anzio**

It's one thing to at least be on the right side of the fighting in a war. The *Lawton B. Evans* found itself behind enemy lines at Anzio.

The ship's third cook recalled the scenario, after its convoy traveled from Hampton Roas, Va., carrying food and medical supplies to Naples, Italy.

"As the front lines were just north of Naples, we could see and hear the gunfire at night. Also the air raids," wrote one cook.

In Naples, they reloaded with a number of types of ammunition. The upper sections of holds No. 2 and 3 were set up for troops. Returning to the harbor, the *Lawton B. Evans* joined a small convoy of landing craft and supply ships heading north along the coast of Italy.

"Around midnight, we observed search lights along the coast, under complete blackout. We were informed: 'You are now behind German lines and will participate in the invasion of Anzio around daybreak.' We discharged our troops to smaller craft under cover of heavy gunfire from the U.S. Navy, and began to discharge cargo into small craft (called Ducks.) As the Germans regrouped, the next eight days were absolute hell.

"To keep from being a stationary target, we pulled anchor and moved at slow speed while unloading to avoid the fire of a railway gun in the hills, which would only fire during daytime to avoid detection. The air strikes were heavy and often. We changed the meal schedule so we would be ready for the attack.

"During attacks, I worked loading AA magazines in a munition storage area. The *Lawton B. Evans* was credited with downing five German aircraft at Anzio.

"I don't know how much death I saw. I saw strong men break and cry like small children. One Liberty ship was completely blown from the water. Some of the cargo (ammo) landed on our deck. We returned to Naples for minor repair and loaded German prisoners in holds No. 2 and 3, and returned to Hampton Roads, Va."

* * * *

The need for extreme caution continued. A poster signed by the Naval Control Service Officer of Halifax, N.S., and dated February 1944 warns: "LIGHTS MAY MEAN DEATH WHILST IN CONVOY. Your ship MUST be kept thoroughly Blacked Out at all times, otherwise you are endangering all ships in the convoy and the Lives of Everyone in it! Signal Lamps and Navigation Lights, if used at all, must be DIMMED to show the absolute minimum of light necessary!
Offenders will be dealt with drastically! You disregard this warning not only at your own Peril but unfortunately at the Peril of Everyone in the Convoy!"

Directions on the poster advise that it is to be posted in prominent places throughout the ship.

Perils of Supply: Treacherous Trip to Alaska
By Orval Miller, Third Engineer

Much has been said about the hazards of the North Atlantic in the wintertime and the fury of a China Sea typhoon, but an excursion to the Bering Sea in January 1944 ranks with the best (or worst) of them for miserable sailing conditions.

The *S.S. Richard J. Cleveland*, a Liberty tanker, had been shuttling between San Pedro, Calif. and Pearl Harbor, Hawaii, hauling "bunker C" and passengers. (Thirty-two west-bound "volunteers" from the federal prison on Terminal Island housed in two bunkhouses on the boat deck. Apparently, a war-time program allowing inmates to volunteer for active military duty out of the slammer.)

Imagine the surprise and consternation of the crew, after topping off the tanks, securing the gear, waiting the arrival of our usual contingent of "passengers", to have the military trucks pull up with arctic gear for the Navy gun crew instead of the chain gang from the prison. The sailors were pleading with the skipper and anyone else available to provide similar gear for them, or at least let them go ashore to purchase warm, weather-proof clothing, as none had been supplied to the slop chest. Armed military guards prevented anyone from leaving the ship and we began our voyage with summer clothing and swim suits. Our destination was no longer Pearl Harbor, but Dutch Harbor, Alaska.

It was a dark and stormy night. The Pacific wasn't living up to its name and the farther north and west we went the colder and more violent the wind and seas.

Most discussions (arguments) in the ward room centered around the question, "Where the hell are we?" because, due to the severe weather, a navigational sight of any kind - sun, moon, stars, horizon - was not available. The propeller was out of the water as often as it was in, causing constant "throttle watches" to keep the engine somewhat under control. Estimating the effectiveness of the propeller, the strength and direction of the current, wind and seas etc. became a constant struggle to determine where we were. Some 24-hour runs would result in a net loss of 10 to 20 miles, according to some estimates.

The engine crew wasn't coping much better. Having a constant throttle watch left little or no time for maintenance or service work. An unbelievable amount of condensate was returning to the hot well. It was difficult to get the fuel oil warm enough to transfer it to the settlers.

Oiling the engine, cleaning burners and strainers, blowing tubes, testing boiler water, and so on, was all difficult because maintaining your footing required holding onto something secured. The generators couldn't be changed because the oil in the circuit breakers was frozen and prevented moving the switches. The steam line to the anchor windlass froze and split a joint of pipe. Because seas were coming over the bow and the spray was freezing into shards of ice like razor blades and needles, no one had gone forward to make sure the equipment was still turning over. After the storm eased, fog and calmer seas allowed us to jury rig a repair of the steam line and progress was made toward Dutch Harbor.

At breakfast one morning the third mate mentioned that if the calculations were at all valid we should make Unimak Pass sometime on this morning watch. Fog and rain alternated, and the seas were not really calm. About 0945 the engine room telegraph went from full ahead to full astern in one sweep of the needle. Fortunately, we were in position to act immediately and were able to back down before hitting the rocks adjacent to Unimak Pass. We learned later the light had been moved so that it would be easier to service and maintain. Apparently our charts did not reflect these little changes. Nonetheless it did verify again the old adage that it is difficult to compete with experience.

The irony of the situation was that the second mate was a towboat skipper with many years experience, but the Coast Guard would not grant him an unlimited license because he had towed coastwise using piloting and dead-reckoning techniques and they required navigational experience. He was told if he made a trip offshore as a second mate they would lift the restriciton. This man had put us right where we headed for in spite of miserable weather conditions and limited or no opportunity to navigate.

After negotiating Unimak Pass and consulting with a passing fishboat, we arrived at Dutch Harbor in the afternoon only to find the submarine nets drawn closed to protect the harbor. Another storm was expected and we were told to head out into the Bering Sea to ride out the storm. Again, a dark and stormy night, the difference being the wind seemed to come from all directions at the same time with rain, sleet, hail and snow swirling around.

Early on the 2000-2400 watch there was an extremely loud KA BAAM! A few seconds later the engine (with full steam) stopped. DEAD STILL. We immediately closed and then apprehensively opened the butterfly throttle valve. The engine seemed to respond in a normal fashion. We didn't know what had happened. Did we hit a mine? Were we torpedoed? What made the engine stop? Did we hit the bottom? A quick survey of the engine room, shaft alley, and fireroom found nothing broken or under water. This information was given to the bridge when they phoned asking "What happened?"

Due to the limited or rather non-existent information and the perilous sailing conditions, the skipper decided to have all hands stand by - just in case - and told the watch to have all personnel standby and be prepared to abandon ship if necessary. Apparently the only thing heard or understood was the "abandon ship" part because someone grabbed the whistle cord and gave the customary signal to abandon the ship.

The engine room crew interpreted this to mean that the individuals topside were about to leave or were no longer there, so they began to shut the engine and boilers down. It also occurred to us that if the ship couldn't live in this storm, the likelihood of a tin lifeboat surviving, even if it could be launched, was nil. A phone call to the bridge: "What the devil is going on up there?" The response: they were only making preparations to abandon ship and to keep everything running.

About this time, either due to loss of footing, concentration, or consciousness, the bridge lost control of the steering and the ship broached. The ship rolled to port to the extent that the engineer laid prone on the engine column and the fireman was hanging from the work bench. We feared the ship was going to turn turtle. Slowly, very slowly, it recovered, and in due time resumed its accustomed pitching and rolling.

The oiler was late returning from the usual calling of the midnight-to-four watch. He reported the passageways jammed with all hands - sailors, stewards, gunners etc. - wearing everything they owned plus a lifejacket. It was difficult to use the passageways and almost impossible to locate anyone. Individuals he did locate said they were obeying the skipper's orders and were preparing to abandon ship. He never did locate the second engineer, but the chief and others were in the boat deck passage singing hymns accompanied by a Hawaiian AB and his ukulele.

The following morning it was discovered that the starboard side and main deck just forward of the midship house were broken. The hull would open and close with the seas, the port side acting like a hinge. We made Dutch Harbor later that day and when the ship was tied up the eight-to-12 engine watch was finally relieved.

Pumping began immediately of the starboard cargo tanks since Dutch Harbor was almost out of oil and we wanted to see the extent of the rupture and assess the damage. The fracture was in a void area so no fuel, cargo or machinery space was flooded. Best of all, it was possible to weld it without gas-freeing tanks. Navy CB's made the repair after the ship was trimmed drastically to the port side.

When repairs were nearly complete, military personnel eligible for rotation back to the lower 48 states were invited to come aboard. An announcement to Naval and Marine contingents resulted in a "No thanks, I'll wait" response. (They were rotated every four to six months.) When the offer of 32 bunks in dog houses, requiring arctic gear, headed for Seattle, was made to the Army contingent, a priority system had to be used. All the Army passengers had over 30 months' service at this desolate post.

We made an uneventful but beautiful trip via the inside passage to Seattle where corrective structural work was performed in the shipyard.

Sitting on a Powder Keg: The First Voyage of the *S.S. Poland Victory*, the Third Victory Ship

By John L. Dahl, wiper

After becoming certified as a fireman/watertender, I was shipped off with some of my new friends (from Catalina Island) to Portland, Oregon to be assigned to a ship. It was March 1944 when I found myself a crew member waiting on the dock for the *S.S. Poland Victory* to be delivered from the Oregon Ship-building yard. This was the third Victory ship to be built.

I had three sea bags packed with everything I owned. Captain Leonard Duks walked down the dock saying "Hello" to each of the crew members. When he asked me what my job was, I replied, "Wiper, sir." Looking at all my sea bags, he commented that it wasn't necessary for me to bring my own rags.

After boarding our new ship, we found the three wipers shared quarters in the small deckhouse on the fantail, over the propeller and under the 5-inch gun. We had to hold tight to our bunk rails during heavy seas to keep from being pitched out. Once our supplies were stocked, we headed down the Columbia River to San Francisco.

The wiper's first job at sea was to clean the bilges under the engine, and the boilers. Those who weren't already seasick soon became sick in the rocking, sloshing, oily-smelling bilges. In San Francisco, we received orders to proceed up the Sacramento River to Port Chicago, where we took on a full cargo of ammunition.

I was impressed at how carefully the cargo was handled. (Three months later, Port Chicago was destroyed and hundreds of people were killed when another ship blew up at the same dock.)

By this time, the Americans had turned back the Japanese in New Guinea and were working their way up the north coast from Milne Bay to Lea, Madang and Weewak. The *Poland Victory* headed out under the Golden Gate Bridge, bound for New Caledonia. In a couple of weeks, we pulled into Neumea, where we joined a convoy headed for Milne Bay. Once there, we were circled by a destroyer. Using a megaphone, someone from the destroyer called out and asked if we were the *Poland Victory*. When this was confirmed, they told us to follow them at our top speed. The rest of the convoy went to anchor. We later learned that we were headed for Hollandia in Dutch New Guinea, which was about 200 miles behind Japanese lines.

The American Army had just established a beachhead at Hollandia, and it was short of ammunition. Our ship arrived while fighting was still going on, and we anchored out in the bay. G.I.'s started unloading our ship immediately with use of L.C.I. barges. They were anxious to return to their foxholes at night, however. That was when Japanese aircraft usually came over. The Navy ships in the bay went out to see when enemy aircraft were in the area, but the *Poland Victory* remained at anchor until our cargo was unloaded. This took about three weeks. Every night, we thought it might be our last.

Our ship's crew became well-acquainted with some G.I.s. They appreciated our fresh food in place of their K-rations. In return for our food, they helped us arrange a little "shore leave" to go visit the front lines near the airport, where fighting was still going on. They gave us a lift ashore and equipped us with rifles. Then we took a jeep to the dangerous area where shots continued to ring out, and we picked up a few souvenirs along the way.

This sounds crazy now, but 18-year-old boys do not worry about such things. That's why they make good soldiers. Fortunately, we returned to the ship without any holes in us.

When our ship was almost unloaded, and the ammunition was neatly stacked on the beach, a lone Japanese plane came over one evening and dropped a bomb right in the middle of it. They said more G.I.s were killed from the resulting explosion than were lost in the invasion. Ironically, it turned out that our shipload of ammunition did more harm than good for the war effort. I was thankful that the Jap plane did not pick our ship as a target.

No one knew why it hadn't, except that our anti-aircraft guns were in action whenever enemy planes came near, but the soldiers ashore only had rifles. On one occasion, one of our gunners forgot to take his finger off the trigger while following an incoming plane and shot up our own flying bridge. Fortunately, no one was injured.

On our return trip we headed for New York via the Panama Canal, with a stop at Jucaro, Cuba to pick up a load of sugar. As we left Panama, we passed through an area where ships were being sunk by German U-boats. We traveled at top speed in a zig-zag path and remained at general quarters. My station during general quarters was to pass powder casings for the 5-inch gun. Once while doing this I lost my footing when the ship pitched, and I dropped the shell casing. I can remember chasing it around the deck, wondering what it would take to make it go off. Fortunately, I caught it and the only damage was a few smashed fingers.

That night we passed a lifeboat, and the occupants were signaling us with flashlights. We had orders not to stop for any reason and had to continue on. The Coast Guard was active in the area, picking up survivors, and we all hoped these people were rescued.

After leaving the U-boat area we entered the Caribbean, where we experienced a severe hurricane. We were all glad when the trip ended in New York and we were able to go home for a few weeks.

I missed New Guinea so much that I went there again on my next two ships, the *S.S. Neptunes Car* and the *M.S. Island Mail*. My second visit was within two months, but this time the Army would not let us go ashore. They were still mopping up snipers, and they said it was too dangerous. My third trip was about three months later. At that time, Hollandia had been built up with a seaman's club, an outdoor theatre, bars, and everything else a sailor needs - except girls.

All's well that ends well, but I would not want another trip like Voyage #1 on the *Poland Victory*.

Evaluating Maritime Service Training the Hard Way: Signing Onto a Ship for Dangerous Mission

**By Lt. Commander William F. Schepler, U.S.M.S.
Chatsworth, Calif.**

When I arrived in New York, it was the first day of Spring 1944, but there was a snow storm. I had been helping to train men for the

Four crew membes of the SS William Baton on shore leave in Bari, Italy. Rolf J.C. McVickar, AB; James M. Berry, OS; Carm Tintle, AB; Harold Shermond, AB.

U.S. Maritime Service at the Catalina Island training station, and I wanted to see firsthand how they were doing.

In a very short time, I signed onto a Matson Liberty troop carrier, the *Stephen A. Douglas*. A few weeks later, we were headed for the Mediterranean in a large convoy.

It was a rather uneventful crossing until the day our war zone bonus went to 100%. That night, we went through the Straits of Gibraltar. On my watch, a German submarine's torpedo missed us.

The next night, again while we were on watch, all hell broke loose when the convoy came under a large German air attack. Our chief engineer came down to see whether the three of us needed anything. He was nervous, never stepping off the bottom rung of the ladder. I didn't blame him. Only a few months before, his ship had been torpedoed and it had sunk so fast that they didn't get any boats away. Later we heard that the German who had chosen our ship to destroy was in turn destroyed by our gun crew.

At breakfast I asked the British convoy commander who had crossed with us where he thought the German planes had come from. "No doubt Spain," he said. But we also had Naval bases in the Azores of Portugal, another "neutral" country. So it looked like we would be earning our bonus.

After unloading our troops in Oran, we docked next to a sunken Liberty ship, settled with its buckled decks on the bottom. It had been bombed and sunk by an Italian frogman. So we knew why our sleep was being disturbed by men on our side, dropping small bombs to discourage a recurrence of that event.

We learned another startling fact. Just about the same day we left Charleston on this trip, the Germans had hit a Liberty troop ship with one of their new radio-controlled glider bombs. Like so many others, this troop ship also carried munitions. That was the *S.S. Paul Hamilton*, the most costly Liberty ship disaster of the war (in terms of total number of casualties.) Five hundred and four men died from that one bomb. *(Capt. Moore lists the casualties as 504 U.S. Army Air Force personnel, 47 merchant crew and 29 Naval Armed Guard, for a total loss of 580 lives.[35])*

Did that German crew receive the Iron Cross? If they did, they received it posthumously. The plane was brought down by a British gunner just as the *Paul Hamilton* blew up.

We spent the next five months crossing the Mediterranean, back and forth with trucks and equipment and countless thousands of full 5-gallon jeep cans of gasoline for the fast-moving Allies pushing up the boot of Italy. We called at ports like Palermo, Bari, Brindisi, Naples on the North, and Tunis and Oran in North Africa.

Bari had only recently been reopened for use. The sight that met us was about 16 or 17 ships on the bottom of a rather shallow harbor. We were told this was all the work of one German plane. That wasn't quite the case - but almost!

It was about five months before - sundown on December 2, 1943 - that the British were unloading a large convoy when the typical lone German observation plane made its usual flight to look things over. Very little attention was paid to him. But the Germans must have liked his report, because they sent a small group of bombers back to take advantage of the well-lit target. It was common in Italy at the time to fully illuminate when working cargo.

That night, the Germans hit the jackpot. They directly or indirectly sank 17 ships in about 20 minutes and got away with almost no losses.

When we arrived five months later, there were still merchant seamen coming aboard begging for any berth, any job, just to go home. The Italians who worked the cargo moved very slowly; their hearts weren't in it. But one afternoon, we had an air attack alert. Those slow-moving Italians took off on a dead-run out of the port area. Their memories were good.

What they didn't know at the time - nor did we - was that an American Liberty that had been blown up had 60 tons of mustard gas aboard. This created much needless pain and suffering that could have been avoided if the medical people had known what they were dealing with. Also, this could have been the reason these seamen were being kept in Bari: to keep the secret in Bari. Even today it isn't well-known that we had poison gas available to us if our leaders felt it was necessary.

When we arrived in Naples, the Germans had only left the week before, and time bombs were still going off in public places like the main post office.

Sometimes our convoys were escorted by Italian destroyers. I remember once when the convoy commander signaled for a change in course and the destroyers sent off four depth charges.

But it was on the way home in convoy that we were in our most dangerous position. Again, it was on my watch. The water in both boilers disappeared. We had no choice; we had to secure the fires and drop out of the convoy.

We can thank our young first engineer for his keen eyesight. He determined that one boiler was full and the other partly empty. So fires went back into the full boiler and water was pumped into the other to bring the water into sight.

It was three hours before we were back in our place in the convoy. We were lucky! If it had been a year earlier, there would have been more U-boats around and I wouldn't be writing this story.

Also, I had my answer: Our trainees were doing a mighty fine job.

Going "undercover" to learn about the life of Merchant Marines was a tactic undertaken by two more unlikely candidates at the time of the Normandy Invasion.

The excitement their ploy generated is described below:

Incognito Congressmen from New Jersey, Pennsylvania Join Convoy to Check Up On Merchant Mariners

By Captain Claude D. Phillips

In May 1944, just days before the Normandy Invasion, I signed on as third mate on the *S.S. Esso Utica,* a brand new T2-SE-A1 tanker.

The vessel was under the command of Captain Herbert A. "Lord" Nelson, a fine seaman and an excellent shipmaster. The maiden voyage from Sun Shipbuilding, Chester, Pa. was to Aruba to load a full cargo of aviation and motor gasoline. Upon arrival in New York Harbor, she anchored near the George Washington Bridge to load a deck cargo of P-38 planes and await convoy. Shortly prior to sailing, Captain Nelson returned via launch from the convoy Commodore's meeting with two new steward department utilitymen in tow.

There were about 40 ships in the convoy, including two troop ships, so we had good escort - an aircraft carrier and about six destroyer escorts. Nevertheless it wasn't a smooth voyage, as we still lost a number of vessels during the transit.

It soon became apparent to the officers amidships that the new utilitymen weren't regular seamen. We had no idea who or what they were, but assumed they were FBI or even Naval Intelligence, as there had been a lot of sabotage of merchant ships.

Of course, in those days there was no "entertainment" aboard ships for officers or crew. You were either standing watch, practicing abandon ship drills, or sleeping, with any spare time you might come by used for reading or writing. So it became easy to "have a little fun" at the expense of the "greenhorn" utilitymen.

Coming off watch I'd often summon one of them to my quarters and pretend to be upset because my bunk wasn't made up properly, or the toilet wasn't cleaned very well. After a "dressing down," I would require them to do the job over! They took all of this good-naturedly. The time passed and in due course we arrived in Liverpool, England.

I happened to be on watch as we passed in and Captain Nelson instructed me to send a sailor aft and request the new utilitymen to report to the bridge. As they came up the port wing ladder - dressed in top hats, tails and striped pants - Captain Nelson came out on the bridge wing and said to me, "Mr. Phillips, I would like for you to meet two of your congressmen, Gordon Canfield of New Jersey and Hugh D. Scott Jr. of Pennsylvania."

When the vessel docked, they were met by an entourage of the diplomatic corps, as well as many of the news media. Articles appeared about the voyage in a number of national and international publications. I understand they subsequently visited General Eisenhower's headquarters and were briefed on the invasion before returning to the U.S.

After his return, Congressman Canfield

spoke at the Nov. 15, 1944 Propeller Club meeting in New York. The "Ships Bulletin" for October to December 1944 quotes him in part as follows:

"I am a member of The House Committee on the Merchant Marine, and I am proud to add that I am a tankerman. With Congressman Hugh D. Scott Jr. of Pennsylvania, I shipped incognito as a utilityman on the *Esso Utica*, a tanker carrying 128,000 barrels of high-octane gasoline.

"I learned more about the Merchant Marine from this experience than I have from taking testimony over a period of 45 months on the House Committee."

Both Scott and Canfield were active supporters of American seamen and a strong American Merchant Marine. They earned the respect of seamen of all time by risking their lives on that voyage "to see first-hand how the men of the Merchant Marine were faring," when they could have been safe and secure in Washington, D.C.

Canfield passed away some years ago. I have maintained occasional contact with Scott over the years. Of course, he was elected to the Senate and elected Senate Minority leader a number of times.

In 1948-'49, he was National Chairman of the Republican Party. At that time I was sailing as master of the S.S. Pan Florida and was at sea on Election Eve, November 1948. It appeared to me and many others, including the publishers of the "Chicago Tribune," that Truman would be defeated and Tom Dewey the next president of the United States. Accordingly that night I sent a radiogram from the ship to Senator Scott congratulating him for his efforts on Dewey's behalf. The rest is history, of course.

After leaving the senate, Scott practiced law in his Washington firm for many years, and has since retired and lives quietly in the Virginia suburbs of Washington. I spoke with his secretary recently (August 1992) and Senator Scott sends his regards and best wishes to all American Merchant Mariners, and especially those veterans and shipmates from World War II.

Normandy Invasion Sustained by Merchant Mariners' Efforts

In the winter and spring of 1944, southern England was transformed into a huge armed camp and staging area for the most massive seaborne assault the world had ever seen, the Allied invasion of France.

Operation Overlord, under the supreme command of General Dwight D. Eisenhower, was planned to land the First United States Army on "Omaha" and "Utah" beaches in Normandy.

The invasion fleet of thousands of Navy vessels, merchant ships and landing craft carried out pre-invasion minesweeping and shore bombardment, and the actual landing of an assault force of 176,000 men and 20,000 vehicles.

The vast armada moved out of ports all along the English coast, and the first units appeared off the Normandy beaches early in the morning of June 6. Among them were the ubiquitous Liberty ships.

The logistics involved were mind-boggling. Merchant ships did a tremendous job supporting the troops, a vital factor in the invasion's success. Once ashore, troops needed mountains of ammunition, food, guns and equipment to keep fighting.

Hundreds of ships maintained a supply shuttle between England and the French coast after the initial landings. Later, they ran to Cherbourg, Antwerp and other captured ports as soon as they could be reopened.

In the first 20 days after D-Day, the shuttle ships delivered 189,000 vehicles and 1.7 million men, as well as food, fuel, shells and other supplies of every conceivable description - from typewriters to telephones, from bombs to beds and bandages.

Normandy Invasion: Lester Ellison Among Those Building Artificial Harbor at Omaha Beach

The Normandy invasion constituted a massive Allied effort and the beginning of a decisive turning point in the war. Counted among the Allied naval forces preparing to confront the Germans were two battleships, two monitors, 23 cruisers, 105 destroyers, 1,076 other warships like minesweepers and anti-submarine vessels, 2,500 landing craft and 2,700 merchant ships.

"After sailing on various Liberty ships, I went to work for the Army Transportation Corps as the mate on a U.S. Army tug, and I was soon on my way to Europe," explains Lester E. Ellison of Basking Ridge, N.J. "This was February 1944."

The next few months were occupied by training off the coast of England. "Little did I know that we would be at Omaha Beach at 0600 on D+1 to build and operate an artificial harbor," he said.

For their training, Ellison and the 9-member crew on U.S. Army Tug ST 761 practiced moving the "Phoenix" units and concrete block ships that would be sunk to create Mulberry A, an artificial port that the Americans undertook (with Mulberry B, by the British) to permit the landing for the invasion of Europe.

"These had never been moved before through the English Channel. We trained under various conditions, taking off from the Isle of Whyte off the coast of England into the channel. There was a tremendous tide and the current there is very swift," Ellison recalled.

Each tug was assigned to a different work area. In Ellison's group, six tugs were required to hold one block ship in position while it was being sunk.

"They (the block ships) had dynamite charges in them, which just blew their bottoms out. The tugs had to hold them in position while they sank in 15 or 20 feet of water."

Besides sinking concrete blocks designed to make the harbor, old and newer ships consigned to this purpose were sent to the bottom. Among them was the *S.S. West Grama*, the first ship on which Ellison had served.

Participating in preparations for the Normandy invasion was particularly hazardous duty. First, there was the matter of proximity to the explosives designed to scuttle the ships. Then there were the Germans firing away at anything that moved in the harbor or on the beach. The danger of being struck by a "floating mine" was ever-present. And then there were activities that, because of the size and complexity of the invasion, couldn't go by "standard operating procedure," like their tug's first orders.

"We were assigned to move a barge loaded with ammunition and explosives onto a beach that had not been cleared of mines. It was just one of those things you're told to do, and you do it," he said. Usually, the beach would have been swept for mines first. "But they really needed the ammunition. They just wanted it on the beach," he recalled.

Luckily, Ellison and his crewmates carried out their assignment without mishap. But he thinks back to how deadly the Normandy invasion proved to be.

"It didn't get dark until around 11 o'clock

Atlantic scene.

at night. Then we would tie up alongside a ship and get some sleep. The first thing we'd have to do the next day is to remove the bodies that had washed up between the tug and the block ships. We saw so many. They were dead soldiers. Not hundreds, but thousands," he said.

It took about nine days to build the artificial harbor. For the better part of four of those days, they were under severe fire. On the 10th day, gales began that ruined much of their handiwork.

"It was the worst storm they had had in 30 or 40 years. During most of that storm, we did rescue work evacuating soldiers off the phoenixes who were on their gun crews," Ellison explained.

After the gales subsided on June 22, Ellison and the rest of the crew were among the people helping to restore Mulberry A as much as possible. Merchant ships were used to plug the holes in the breakwater.

Then they settled in among the forces operating the harbor.

At this time, Ellison's tug was under the command of the U.S. Navy. "Even at this date, it's hard to explain to anyone that you were a Merchant Mariner sailing with the U.S. Army Transport under the command of the U.S. Navy. We arrived at Omaha Beach on June 7, 1944 and we were there until August 28, 1944."

Ellison keeps among his papers a commendation letter from the commander of Task Force 128. It reads, in part: "To the officers and men of your craft, I wish to convey my heart(felt) commendation for an assignment well done off the U.S. Assault Beaches in the Baie de la Seine during the Allied invasion of France in June 1944. Your craft served with the U.S. Naval Forces under my command and rendered loyal and efficient service which contributed to the successful accomplishment of the mission. It was a pleasure to have such an able and willing team in my organization."

As to the specifics of his tug's contributions, Ellison keeps a memorandum dated 10 August 1944, marked SECRET, from the Harbor Master of U.S. Naval Advance Base 11. It reads, in part:

"1....the formation of an artificial harbor was the most important (activity undertaken by the tug,) during which time subject tug assisted in the siting of over fifty (50) Phoenix units, weighing from three to six thousand tons each, and twenty-three (23) blockships. The formation of this artificial harbor made it possible for the successful landing of many important troops, vehicles and supplies. Besides assisting in the siting of the above, subject tug has also assisted in many salvage operations and general harbor tug work.

2. During the period from 6 June 1944 through 10 August 1944, subject tug has not missed one day or night of operations from any reason and has been ready for any assignment at any time.

3. In adequately performing the above duties, it has sometimes been necessary to expend the subject tug and its gear, becuase of the nature of its duties, at times in the open channel, in all conditions of wind and weather, day or night, subject tug received a most serious pounding, which accounts for the present condition of the tug and its gear.

4. To the Officers and men of U.S. Army Tug ST 761, we express our sincerest gratitude for a difficult operation very well done, under most trying conditions of wind, weather, and enemy action."

Experiences Aboard 'Station Ship' at Utah Beach for Normandy Invasion

Another participant in the Normandy invasion preparations was Don Naish of Dryden, Mich., who served as chief engineer aboard the *S.S. Thomas B. Robertson*.

The Liberty ship had been converted to a transport that could handle 700 troops besides its crew and the armed guard.

Crossing the channel, men were dropped over the side of the ship to paint signs on it: "Port Direction" in huge letters on one side and "Ferry Control" on the other.

At Utah beach on June 7, the *Thomas B. Robertson* became headquarters for the Navy personnel who ran the beachhead. They lived on and operated from the ship.

"Once we dropped the hook, business picked up in a hurry. We would have as many as 50 LCVPs, LCMs and every other kind of landing craft imaginable tied up to us. We stored all the Naval craft in the area with stores, fuel and water. Sometimes the ship looked like a mother duck with a whole flock of ducklings, especially at night," Naish remembers.

"The first couple of days at the beachhead, we had to move occasionally because the Germans had a mobile 88 battery that was giving everyone fits - until it was silenced," he explains.

A battleship laying seaward of the *Thomas B. Robertson* lobbed huge shells at gun emplacements on the beach.

"I never did know what ship it was, but I sure remember those shells whistling overhead."

After a few days of air raids, things quieted down. Naish remembers the last air raid was on August 8. The *Thomas B. Robertson* continued as "nerve central" at Utah Beach for another three months until bad weather forced it to leave.

Chief Mate's Log on *Eleazar Wheelock* Reveals Harrowing Travels

Logs kept practical records for ships, but even the most mundane entries left evidence of the travails of ship's crews during wartime.

These sparse excerpts from the log entries of the *Eleazar Wheelock's* chief mate in 1944 demonstrate just how active service during this period could be:

<u>6 June 44</u>: Sailed aong the South coast of England in a convoy with 40 Liberty ships. 1 Liberty ship and 1 Transport hit by mines. Transport burned and sank in about 2 hours.
<u>7 June 44</u>: Anchored 4 miles off French coast (Omaha Beach.) Cruisers and battleships are shelling shore continuously.
<u>9 June 44</u>: 1/2 mile from beach. Shot down 2 planes, 1 gunner hit.
<u>11 June 44</u>: Heavy air-raid about 0400 hours. Shrapnel from anti-aircraft fire fell on decks.
<u>18 June 44</u>: Log writer went ashore in afternoon, 6 miles inland. Many houses not destroyed. People still live in area with many gardens and cattle.
<u>20 June 44</u>: Many women wearing German uniforms acting as snipers taken prisoner by U.S. forces. Several Japs were brought in who assisted German sniping. Germans using pilotless planes.
<u>22 June 44</u>: Transport came in, discharged troops and, while proceeding to sea, hit a mine and sank in about 10 minutes.

With records like these, it could hardly be refuted that the U.S. Merchant Marines "saw action" during the war.

When President Franklin D. Roosevelt signed the GI Bill in June 1944, he acknowledged just how vital the mariners' contributions had been and virtually promised that seamen would be next in line for recognition. Little did he - or anyone - know that such status would be another 44 years in the making.

Here are FDR's words in June 1944: "I trust Congress will soon provide opportunities to members of the merchant marine who have risked their lives time and again during this war for the welfare of their country."

Japanese Atrocities at Sea

"These were indeed dangerous years for the Merchant Marines," Randall Bishop of Laguna Beach reports.

A veteran mariner who has his A.B. papers, Bishop saw the following account from an Englishman in a Honolulu newspaper. Bishop kept it, and used it in a letter to the editor of his hometown newspaper. The excerpt from Lord James Blears is as follows:

"From Dec. 13, 1943, to the end of the war with Japan, all Japanese submarine commanders received orders from Vice Admiral Sakonju and Vice Admiral Hisao Ichioka, Commander of SUB-RON 8, to sink all enemy ships, take (if possible) the captain and several other survivors aboard their ships for interrogation, then kill them and kill all remaining survivors of the sunken ship.

"This the majority of them did with Samurai swords, pistols, sledgehammers and machine guns.

"Between Dec. 13, 1943 and October 1944 in the Indian Ocean alone, Japanese I-boats sank and massacred the crews of eight allied ships including the *S.S. Tjisalak*, which was sunk on March 26, 1944 by the Japanese submarine the I-8 commanded by Tatsunoki Ariizumi.

"British, Dutch, Indonesians, Australians and an American (female) Red Cross nurse - 103 people total received the above treatment. All were murdered in cold blood with the exception of five. Three Dutch officers, one British Indian seaman, and myself: Second Radio Officer J.R. Blears (British). How we survived the swords and machine guns and being left for dead 1,200 miles from land is another story.

"I, (Lord James Blears), feel that these facts should be noted in memory of my shipmates and hundreds of others who were murdered and who are not around to write about it.

"Peace on earth to all."

S.S. Jean Nicolet - Legacy of Enemy Brutality

The *S.S. Jean Nicolet*, its passengers and crew, fell victim to the Japanese policy of eradication on July 2, 1944 in the Indian Ocean.

A Liberty ship, she was carrying general cargo and a crew of 41, as well as 28 Navy armed guards, 30 passengers and a U.S. Army medic.

According to Capt. Arthur Moore's account,[36] no one died in the aftermath of two torpedoes ripping into the ship, or the subsequent shelling of the *Jean Nicolet*. Everyone was able to abandon ship safely in four lifeboats and two rafts.

Apparently a few men escaped in a small raft under the cover of darkness. The remainder were taken aboard the Japanese submarine where many were murdered with bayonets or beaten to death by brutal clubbing with rifle buts.

When a plane was heard overhead at about 2:30 a.m. on July 3, the Japanese vessel submerged. The survivors who were still on deck were left there to drown, which many did, with their hands tied behind their backs.

Moore reports that, despite the thorough efforts of the enemy to kill everyone, 23 people (out of the 100 originally aboard the *Jean Nicolet*) were rescued between 10 a.m. and 2 p.m. by the *H.M.I.S. Hoxa*. The *Jean Nicolet's* master, who had been taken prisoner by the sub's crew, was never seen again. Thirty crew members, 19 Navy men, 27 passengers and the Army medic perished in the atrocity.[37]

Remember Port Chicago: Serving on Ammo Ships Required Bravery

By Louis Schiavon, Carefree, Arizona

Naturally I share a strong camaraderie with all World War II merchant seamen, as they were generally unpretentious free spirits, certain of off-shore duty. However I hold a special affinity for those who sailed the ammunition ships.

They knew the extra exhilaration of exclusion from convoys, dodging submarines and kamikazes while astride thousands of tons of explosives. They were the creme de la creme.

The faint-hearted eliminated themselves. I'm personally aware of one who purposely contracted gonorrhea in Kelso, Washington to avoid signing articles. Another brushed his gums with a stiff toothbrush until they bled. He was excused because of "trenchmouth." Still another carried something in his armpits until he acquired a fever (wet tobacco, I believe.)

I have long been deeply disappointed that the 67 merchantmen who were vaporized in the explosion of the Liberty ship, *S.S. E.A. Bryan* and the *S.S. Quinault Victory* (on July 17, 1944) at Port Chicago (California) have not been memorialized as have been the Navy C.B. stevedores involved. The mariners' monument should be no less grand. After all, the explosion occurred on the least hazardous leg of their proposed journey.

Ammunition was being loaded onto the Bryan *when the explosion took place, setting off a chain reaction with the ammunition being loaded on to the* Quinault Victory *next to it. Both ships were virtually leveled, as was the small town of Port Chicago. Fragments of the vessels were found two miles away, and the blast was felt up to 200 miles away. On the ships alone, 110 men were lost - including Naval Armed guards.*[38]

No other branch of the service exceeded the bravery or the risks of merchant seamen, yet they've never been accorded the respect and recognition they deserved. It still hurts to remember one incident. After returning from a nine-month trip to the South Pacific on the Liberty ship *S.S. E.A. Burnett*, loaded with 5,000 tons of bombs, and having encountered numerous kamikaze attacks, participating in an invasion, and various and sundry other such experiences, the elderly mother of one of my best friends called me a "draft dodger."

I remember thinking, "If you only knew what it felt like to spend nine months wondering which second of which day you would be blown to bits, you'd think it a tough way to avoid the draft." However, neither my friend nor I said anything. But we both knew that, although he was in Army communications, he had never heard a shot fired in anger. He was accorded the generous G.I. benefits, while I and all of my fellow merchant seamen patiently waited for those same benefits as promised by President Roosevelt in 1945. It's a good thing we were patient, becuase it was over 40 years before they were forthcoming.

Despite the lack of appreciation, I'm proud to have served in the Merchant Marine and I am convinced that the war would not have been won without us.

Fighting Five Storms at Sea to 'Deliver the Goods' Leaves Nerves Frayed, But Ship Intact

By Frank E. Bland

When Frank E. Bland of Wichita, Kansas recalls excitement on the high seas during World War II, one trip in particular comes to mind. He was an oiler aboard the Liberty ship *Walter L. Fleming*, which endured not one, not two - but five - major storms in a September 1944 to February 1945 trip.

We pick up his story at the start of the trip, in Baltimore, where they loaded cargo destined for India via the Mediterranean Sea, the Suez Canal, the Red Sea and the Indian Ocean to Madras then Calcutta, India.

"From Baltimore, we were sent to Norfolk, Va. to join the convoy. While waiting for all the ships to arrive, we were anchored a mile or so off-shore. During this time, a hurricane went up the east coast with winds clocked at 130 mph.

"During the height of the storm, we were running the main engine at three-quarters speed just to keep the strain off the anchor chain. While this was happening, the galley caught fire when some grease slopped out of a can the cooks were thawing for use."

The fire seemed a minor problem compared to what happened next: an English ship in the line next to the *Walter L. Fleming* broke its anchor chain and started drifting toward them.

"Its steering gear would not respond and it drifted across our bow," Bland remembered. Two Englishmen stood poised with boat hooks they planned to use to fend off from the *Walter L. Fleming*. " I doubt if the boat hooks would have been sufficient to prevent contact. We didn't connect. The Englishmen ended up on the beach, bow first. This was not an encouraging start for the voyage," Bland recollected. "The storm finally ended and we departed for the Rock of Gibraltar."

Wartime troop transport, SS W.H. Gordon, became a passenger ship after the war.

Their ship was storm-free for thousands of nautical miles, until they left Colombo, Ceylon for Madras, India. It was the monsoon season, and the *Walter L. Fleming* encountered a typhoon. Here, Bland continues:

"The rains came frequently while we were in Madras. The heat and humidity were almost suffocating. We went from Madras on up to Calcutta to unload the rest of our cargo. Again, we ran into another typhoon.

"There were no other storms until we reached Alexandria, Egypt on the way back to the states. At Alexandria, the British requisitioned all our beef and pork. They gave us mutton for it. They also took all of our cigarettes and all of our fuel oil, except what they determined we would need to make the return trip to New York City. What they didn't allow for was the foul weather.

"Almost immediately after leaving Alexandria, we got into another storm. This storm plagued us all the way through the Mediterranean and out into the Atlantic Ocean. The ride home was rough, as we were almost empty and riding high in the water. We had 300 tons of opium in the No. 2 hold, and 300-plus monkeys in cages on top of the No. 4 hold. The opium was to be used as a substitute for morphine. The monkeys were for a hospital in Brooklyn, who wanted them for experiments.

"We didn't have any more storms until we got close to Bermuda. There we got into another hurricane. The captain logged that, in one 24-hour period, we went 24 knots backward.

"All of these storms had delayed us considerably. The delay and the slower speed caused us to use most of our fuel oil. The fuel oil shortage got to the point that we had to pump sea water into the storage tanks and float the fuel oil, so the pumps could pick it up. The oil was put into the settlers, and the settlers were heated to boil off the water before it could be used to fire the boilers. It was not a fuel-efficient operation.

"Under normal conditions, we would have had two boilers making steam and keeping pressure in the range of 250 to 275 pounds. At this point, we were down to one boiler and only 150 pounds of pressure. The lower pressure slowed us even further. I don't know how the word got out, but a sea-going tug showed up to give us a tow. Since we were still making headway at a speed better than they could have towed us, they just ranged along with us in case we did finally run out of oil.

"We made it into Norfolk on our own, under our own steam. We were 1,000 miles short of New York City. After refueling and taking on some fresh food we made it up the coast to Staten Island. There, we unloaded the opium and monkeys. We had to break ice in the East River, making our way to the pier on Staten Island. It was February, and it was cold.

"Storms at sea were always a problem. Eating and sleeping at times were very difficult. The location of your bunk could be part of the difficulty. I do know that tempers and nerves are on edge after a few days of fighting the stormy weather. Anyway, we made it back and that was what it was all about."

Life Aboard *M.V. Yaquina Head*, a Deep-Sea Tug

The *M.V. Yaquina Head* was a 195-long, twin diesel-engine powered tug that holds vivid memories for Doyle Bales, oiler.

He remembers sailing on it in March 1944 and towing the *S.S. John Worthington*, a tanker that had been torpedoed, from Galveston to Corpus Christi, Texas. The tanker miraculously survived a German torpedo that tore completely through the ship - from starboard to port aft of midships - missing the engine room by about 25 feet. "With all this damage, the boat came in under her own power with only two injuries and no fatalities. Other than the very visible torpedo holes in the hull, that was all the tug's crew knew of the attack," he explains.

In May 1944, the *Yaquina Head* picked up two cement-type barges at Mobile, Alabama and headed for Hawaii. The barges, which had to be moved by sea-going tugs, were equipped with diesel generators, pump room and steering rudder, but they had no main engine room or propulsion system. They served as floating fuel storage and refueling vessels that could be moved where needed in the war operations at sea.

One night in the calm Pacific, on the 12-to-4 watch, the bridge issued "slow" then "stop engines" orders. At the same time, the tug's horn blasted.

"I was sent scurrying topside for a report. Seems the Navy crew on board the barges, or at least the head one, went to sleep from boredom, and that barge wasn't following us at all. Between our powerful search light, and the blasting horn, we managed to arouse everyone from a good nap and proceed to Hawaii."

It took them 38 days to make the voyage to Hawaii - seven longer than a sister tug who got there at the same time but had left a week later.

Returning home at the top speed of 12 knots, they stopped only so the captain could do some "sea turtle fishing" - giving the crew a gourmet treat.

"In six months on this tug, the longest voyage was Hawaii and back. In disgust, I signed off for a short leave and then grabbed the Liberty ship *S.S. Francis Asbury*. A fateful decision. The *Yaquina Head* had a boring trip to Antwerp, Belgium. The *Asbury* 's outing was anything but boring.

The *S.S. Francis Asbury*'s Sinking: Doyle Bales' Tale of Survival

Again and again, World War II stories demonstrate that the difference between life and death can rest in a split-second decision that, when it's made, seems insignificant. In retrospect, it's a fateful choice.

Doyle Bales signed onto the *S.S. Francis Asbury* as oiler on September 23, 1944. Less than three months later, the ship was lost in the Bay of Ostend, Belgium after an acoustic mine struck near the engine room.

The *Francis Asbury* had left in the fourth convoy into Antwerp after the Battle of the Bulge. It was the fourth ship in the fourth column of ships. The year, of course, was 1944.

Bales recalled some of the momentary decisions that had life-and-death implications on that December 3.

"As oiler of the second watch, I left the engine room at 4 a.m. I had considered taking the first watch this trip, but the first engineer was not yet aboard. The second engineer and I had been working together very well, so I again chose the second watch. None of the first watch engine room crew survived the direct hit. This was my first stroke of luck.

"The explosion from the deep mine blew gunners' crewmen 40 to 50 feet into the air from the gun tubs. My body lie 24 inches under a steel beam above my bunk. The explosion blew me into this beam and knocked me unconscious. My bunkmates called my name. When they didn't hear an answer, they assumed I was safely out on deck.

"When I came to, the water in the fo'c'sle was already eight- to 12-inches deep. Dazed

Liberty ship sunk outside LeHavre harbor.

and struggling for survival, I made my way to the deck and saw a lifeboat 150 to 200 yards away. My instinct then was to give it a try before the ship went down. At this moment, the young man at the helm that morning joined me and advised me there was still a life raft to be launched. His leg had been wrenched by the explosion, but his mind was more clear than mine at the time.

"As he pounded the pintle hook to release the raft, I watched for anyone in the way. The Navy signalman panicked and dove overboard so I had to call a halt to the launch for awhile. Soon, as the Navy man floated out of sight, we finished launching the raft. Once aboard the raft, I pulled three more fully-clothed and very heavy shipmates on with me. The Navy flagman was never seen again."

Wearing only trousers and T-shirt, Bales cut the lines free from the ship. Shipmates used their bodies to shield him from the cold.

An English trawler picked up survivors at about 4 a.m., when water temperatures dipped to 40 degrees.

"We lost seven crewmen and three officers, along with seven of our Navy Armed Guard. The chief enginner died beside me in the rescue boat. His quarters, I was told, got the full force of the boiler explosion from below."

Bales lists the following unusual occurrences from the shipwreck:

• Fighting to survive does strange things to people. A Navy bos'n clung to his binoculars from the time the ship was hit until he was rescued. He had been blown so high from the gun tub that he could look down into the smoke stack. When he "landed" and recovered, he assisted in lowering the lifeboat, then rowed with those binoculars still in hand. At no time was he aware of his stranglehold on the binoculars until rescuers asked him to release them.

• Everyone - except one Navy Armed Guard member - was covered in sea water and bunker oil in their escape from the ship. He avoided the messy predicament because, as he stood on the railing holding a cable, a wave lifted a life raft beside him and he was able to step aboard - clean and dry.

• The deck engineer, a Danish seaman, surmised that the *Francis Asbury* had been hit by more than one torpedo. He should have known; this was his third shipwreck in World War II.

Bales had a final note of praise for Captain Jean Patrick, who rescued the survivors from yet another channel-crossing to get to London. A trawler took survivors to Terneuzen, Holland, and from there the Army transported them to London, aboard empty cargo planes - thanks to the captain.

Opening Antwerp's Port, and Hitler's Failed Promise

Anthony Laich of El Monte, Calif. was second assistant engineer on a Liberty ship that, on Novermber 28, 1944, was part of the first convoy into Antwerp. Opening the port here improved the supply position of the Allied armies, preventing shortages.

On its way from Cherbourg to Antwerp, two ships directly in front of Laich's were hit by tattle-tale mines, designed to go off after a number of ships had passed over it. The disabled ships pulled out of the sea lanes and sank.

Laich remembers going through the locks to get into the Antwerp harbor, and being on a streetcar in the city when the buzz bombs came over. They sounded like an outboard motor, but they packed deadly explosives. The one that came closest to him landed in the Belgian soldiers' barracks, and was a dud.

Despite Hitler's announced intention during the Battle of the Bulge to bomb the locks and strand all the merchant vessels, he was unable to carry out his threat. Laich counts himself among those who were glad of it.

'Japanese Suicide Victims Floated by ...'

When James Lacy Smith of Escondido, Calif. recalls his experiences aboard the T-2 tanker *S.S. Scotts Bluff* in late 1944 and early 1945, it's a memory filled with searing images that illustrate the tenor of the times.

The Navy crew aboard used the ship's anti-submarine armaments - two fifties on the fantail and two on the bridge - to avert Japanese air raids while the *Scotts Bluff* was in port, delivering aviation gas to the B-29 base in Saipan.

"There were bloated bodies floating alongside us - mostly Japanese civilians, suicide victims - and in the distance we could see people jumping to their deaths from the high cliffs to the rocks and water below.

"The local Yank radio signed on at eight-bells every morning with 'Dancing in the Dark'. Four days of this, then we joined up with a six-knot convoy headed for the Canal and wound up delivering barrels of Marianas sea water to Boston Harbor. With a full load of high-test gas on board, and with Smith at the wheel first watch, convoyed to the English Channel where we laid dead in the water on a night of full moon until the Navy took care of a Wolf Pack. Then up the Thames to Shellhaven. Saying 'So long' to Horatio Lord Nelson in Trafalgar Square and the V1 and V2s, we headed west, outriding a giant North Atlantic storm solo, and ending the five-month odyssey at Port Arthur, Texas."

Waiting there was a telegram from California bearing news of the birth of his daughter, Susan Katherine, on March 13, 1945.

Memories of Transporting British Refugees on Still-Treacherous Murmansk Run

It was just before Christmas 1944 when 38 ships gathered off the coast of England to form a convoy to Murmansk, recalls J.M. Stanley of Santa Barbara, Calif. Well-escorted, the ships made their way to Murmansk Harbor unscathed.

But unloading the ships' cargo was another matter. "We were bombarded every night, and could only work in daylight hours - of which there were few," he wrote. Despite the shelling, apparently no ship was hit in port.

As they were preparing to leave, the British brought 25 refugees - mostly women and children, and a few old men - to be taken to Scotland. Their village had been destroyed by the Germans. They had been picked up on the beach by a destroyer, and now the convoy's ships were accepting small groups as passengers.

Most of the children had no clothing and were wrapped only in blankets. Everyone aboard donated clothing and the women tore it apart to make appropriately-sized outfits for the children.

"The next morning, icebreakers came so we could leave early and go through the straits single-file before daylight. We formed a convoy before noon, and almost immediately three landward ships were torpedoed. The convoy immediately changed course and the escorts left to try to destroy the subs and pick up survivors."

The ship on which Stanley served proceeded north and met a British carrier near North Cape, then continued down the coast of Norway. Soon after daylight the next day, a plane attempted to bomb the

Shipboard celebration.

45

carrier, but missed.

"From then on, we were under attack by JU-88s, medium bombers that came in at low altitude. Our planes were constantly fighting them off, but there were too many of them. The noise of the guns, the diving aircraft and rough weather were deafening. At least four guns fired at all times.

"Our ship shot down three planes, but how many they (the Axis) lost I never knew. Berlin Radio came on the second night bragging about the sinking of 10 ships. It was too rough for subs to attack, but the planes continued to pound us during the daylight hours for six days until we came within range of land-based aircraft from England.

"We apparently lost 18 ships - all with refugees aboard." The refugees on Stanley's ship were among those who were safely deposited back in Scotland before the ship completed a safe North Atlantic crossing.

Christmas Letter Highlights Role of Merchant Marine

It appeared that the efforts of merchant seamen were not going unnoticed. Their contributions were cited in a Christmas letter by E.S. Land, administrator of the War Shipping Administration, to "The Men of the United States Merchant Marine" dated December 25, 1944:

For three years, the mettle of the Nation and the stamina of our fighting men have been tested in a ruthless war. Long months before our troops set foot on foreign soil, the men of the American Merchant Marine had been in the fight. The dark days to Murmansk, to the United Kingdom, to the Mediterranean and to the Pacific are not to be forgotten, nor are those whose lives were given to the cause of freedom. Words cannot express the gratitude that all of us feel for the magnitude and the success of your accomplishments.

As we enter the fourth year of the war we may hope that our armed forces, sustained by the labors of the 180,000 men of our fighting Merchant Marine, will bring the inevitable victory to the United Nations.

Let us pledge among ourselves on this anniversary of the birth of the Prince of Peace our unrelenting efforts to finish the task, that in the future Christmas may be celebrated in a world of peace among those we love. May God be with you, this Christmas and always.

1945

The reputation of the Merchant Marine's contribution to the war effort had reached the highest ranks in the Army and Navy.

Witness these remarks.

From General Dwight D. Eisenhower, Commander-in-Chief of the European Theatre: "Every man in this Allied Command is quick to express his admiration for the loyalty, courage and fortitutde of the officers and men of the Merchant Marine ... When final victory is ours, there is no organization that will share its credit more deservedly than the Merchant Marine."

$$$ Pay Day $$$

Pats on the back were welcome. But was it worth it? The fear? The long hours? The boredom? The loneliness?

One ordinary seaman explained the pay scale this way:

"My pay was $85 a month base pay, plus 50 cents an hour overtime. When our ship reached half-way overseas into the war zone, we got 50 percent of our base pay as a bonus. When we were in the war zone such as in England itself, we got 100 percent of our base pay. So with my base pay, my overtime and the bonuses on an average 3 1/2 month round-trip, I was paid about $500."

Hardly a king's ransom.

Bob Morris of Pineville, La. shared these thoughts: "Since the Merchant Marine was considered a commercial operation, it was not considered a part of the military services. There were no provisions for veterans' benefits of any kind. The unlicensed crew members were paid anywhere between $87.50 to $100 per month, plus $100 per month bonus, only while in war zones. There was no clothing allowance, sick leave, vacation credits nor retirement."

Receiving $300 for his first voyage, on which he saw two British ships torpedoed, Morris in his youthful wonder couldn't believe he could see so much adventure, such beautiful scenery and still receive such a princely sum.

But after he survived the sinking of the *S.S. John Drayton*, and had been out of the U.S. for two weeks shy of one year, he returned to New York to receive a draw of about $200 but no promise of when his pay would be straightened out.

Then, after his disastrous experience with the first mate on the *John C. Calhoun*, (See 'Mutiny on the High Seas?' below,) he was forced to resort to extreme measures to collect his back pay for almost a year's service on the ship. No amount of calling or correspondence brought results, so he contacted the other crew members and found they all were having the same experience.

The Calhoun Athletic Club (buddies who served aboard the ship) gathered again in Atlanta and took off for the New York headquarters of the Bull Line Steamship Company to force the issue. They got paid.

The American populace had no idea how merchant seamen's pay could suddenly cease. If his ship was lost, or if he was captured, he received no residual pay. There are documented cases of mariners who spent multiple years as P.O.W.s, without receiving any recompense for their time in captivity.

Why They Signed On

Some were too old to serve in the more traditional branches of the military. Indeed, veteran seamen today remember working alongside men in their 70s who wanted to serve their country.

Other mariners had been rejected for medical reasons. Perhaps their specialized skills made them more valuable to the Merchant Marine than they would be in the Army, Navy or Marines. And some clearly did not know what they were getting into, figuring the Merchant Marine had to offer a better life than digging foxholes.

Melvern Schroeder described his thoughts on joining this way: "A world turned upside down, taken to the 10th power. That's what it seemed to this naive youth from the wheat fields of Kansas. Why I happened to choose the Merchant Marine, about which I knew little, remains hazy. There were mixed reasons, precipitating factors. Among them, certainly, lurked the imminence of the draft board summons that would deny not only my freedom, but also my freedom of choice," explained Schroeder, who joined the U.S. Maritime Service in March 1944.

He used his time at sea to discover the world, to learn about the diversity of people, to discover the writings of philosopher Will Durant, and to discover himself.

Abandon ship drill, SS Santa Paula with two female crew members: Edna Doyle in white kerchief, Mary Claire Jones, center.

Jinx-on-Board? Water Spout Stirs Scare

Surrounded by danger every day, nerves were often frayed. Richard S. Warren of Lancaster, Pa., who was second radio officer on the *S.S. James Bowie,* remembers how one particular incident pushed his "superstition" button.

Early in January, 1945, the ship was in the Gulf, on its way from New Orleans to the Pacific. Warren was in the Officer's Mess wtih Captain W.F. Allison when the general alarm sounded during dinner.

Seeing the look on the captain's face, they knew it wasn't a drill and everyone headed for their stations.

"When I arrived on the bridge, the mate was pointing out a huge disturbance on the water some distance off port-side. When he spotted this, his first reaction was that a U-boat was surfacing and he sounded the alarm. But the captain quickly identified the disturbance as a water spout, a tornado at sea. We were far enough away that we were in no danger. The all-clear was sounded and we returned to our now-cold supper."

Later that evening, though, Warren was talking with the second engineer who confided in him that, when the alarm sounded, he guessed that he was going to get wet again.

Apparently the second engineer had three times before been aboard Liberty ships sailing from Gulf ports. And on all three occasions, they had sunk and he had survived. He thought he had picked a "goner" again.

The second engineer didn't want word to get out about his track record. "He didn't want anyone to think he was a jinx," Warren recalled. "I wished he hadn't confided in me, though, because it took awhile to overcome that feeling of a 'jinx-on-board'. However, we made it to the Philippines, and back to Seattle, without any further encounters with real or pseudo-subs."

Supporting MacArthur's Liberation of the Philippines

For Loring W. Wordell, signing up with the Merchant Marines was his choice after being rejected for the Navy because of a poor right eye.

"I swear it was the same doctors who refused me before, but I passed the physical," he explains.

After the rigors of Gallups Island Radio School, he took his first assignment in February 1944, on the Liberty tanker *Alan Seeger.* The captain he served under there was ordered off the ship after the Federal Communication Commission discovered that he ordered the ship's Autoalarm to be shut off because it occasionally was tripped by voltage differentials.

After a trip around the world on another ship, Wordell was assigned in November 1944 to the *Jacques Cartier,* bound for the liberation of the Philippine Islands.

"We left Los Angeles on Thanksgiving Day of 1944 and arrived at Finch Haven, New Guinea on Christmas Day. From there, we proceeded along the north shore of New Guinea to a port called Hollandia, which was to be the marshalling point for the ships that would make the invasion. We were probably the third ship to arrive, so we waited there over a month for all the ships to gather and for the time to be right for the invasion," he recalls.

The *Jacques Cartier* was made the commodore ship of a 100-ship fleet, which worked its way northward to the port of Tacloban on the island of Leyete. "At that time, we were bringing American citizens out of the Philippines. An invasion had been made, and these people were liberated from the Japanese and being repatriated home."

Escorted from Leyete through the San Bernardino Straits by two destroyers, the *Jacques Cartier* and its companion ships threaded their way around and through the many islands for two days without buoys or light. All navigational aids had been destroyed.

"Then we made our way northward into Lin Gayan Gulf, which is 100 miles north of Manila. The invasion had already been made." Anchored off-shore, the *Jacques Cartier* and other ships acted as floating warehouses. Cargo was discharged by LCMs with 50-ton capacity as supplies were needed, one day at a time.

After several weeks of unloading cargo, Wordell and his crewmates headed to Brisbane, Australia to pick up aircraft parts bound for Manila. After several more weeks waiting in Manila Harbor to discharge the cargo, they got a berth on the dock to do so, took on fuel and water and were sent home.

"We were mid-Pacific on the way back to Los Angeles when the first atomic bomb was dropped, and only a few days later the war was over."

General Douglas MacArthur had the highest praise for the merchant mariners who participated in the American invasion of the Philippines. His remarks:

"On these islands I have ordered them off their ships and into foxholes when their ships became untenable targets of attack. At our side they have suffered in bloodshed and death. The high caliber of efficiency and courage they displayed ... marked their conduct throughout the entire campaign in the Southwest Pacific. They have contributed tremendously to our success. I hold no branch higher in esteem than the merchant marine service."

Bless Those Barnacles: Surviving U.S.-Laid Mines, After Going Adrift in a Tanker, and Other Adventures

Robert V. Giles of Woodland Hills, Calif. recalls hair-raising near-misses in his 1943-'45 service in the U.S. Merchant Marine, and how a sense of humor and ingenuity helped everyone survive the stresses of war.

His most dramatic moment came in mid-1945 when he was purser aboard the *Yamhill,* a tanker full of oil that went adrift in the Pacific coming out of the Panama Canal. The oiler in the *Yamhill's* engine room - a veteran seaman - accidentally leaned against the shut-off button and the ship lost power.

"We drifted into the mine fields, and dropped anchor," Giles recalled. When a nearby Navy ship's officer heard what had happened, he radioed *not* to put down anchor, after which the *Yamhill's* Russian lend-lease skipper decided to pull up anchor.

When it surfaced, a cable with three mines attached came with it. The Navy ship pulled alongside and cautiously snipped off the mines, which hadn't detonated because they were covered with barnacles. Then it beat a hasty retreat, leaving the *Yamhill* to restore power and back out of the treacherous waters alone. Since the mines had been laid by the U.S. some 30 feet down, and since the oil-laden tanker reached a depth of 30+ feet, it was a nerve-wracking five or more hours wondering whether the propellers would slice through the barnacles that had accumulated on the mines.

Burial at sea, SS Santa Paula.

Giles remembers the incident as one that "broke the boredom" of endless hours at sea. The skipper had given orders for everyone to prepare to abandon ship during the 4-mile departure from the minefield, but gallows humor prevailed. "We won't need lifeboats here," Giles said. "We'll need a parachute to get back down."

For its part, the Navy ordered every ship away from the tanker. Despite the danger it was in, the *Yamhill* made it out in one piece. The Navy discovered that barnacles could render their mines worthless. Giles and the rest of the crew were eternally grateful they hadn't been blown sky-high, in U.S. territory and even worse, a non-bonus area.

Another incident on the *Yamhill* found everyone willing to put themselves in danger to help save the life of one Navy Armed Guardsman.

As purser, Giles also was responsible the "first aid" duties aboard ship - except that he had no formal training to support the job description. "I used to tell everyone, 'Don't get sick'," he recalls.

But on the way to Manila, someone did. The Navy man complained of pain in his lower right side, and Giles determined it was appendicitis. So he sent the man to bed and started a rotation of crew members to keep ice on the 18-year-old's side around the clock. Two days later, the sick man emerged saying the pain was gone, but he didn't look well. Assuming his appendix had burst, Giles consulted his medical book, which said the patient should be operated on as soon as possible.

"I had to get all officers and delegates to agree that they would give permission to break radio silence. Within 12 hours, a small Navy ship with a doctor aboard came by and had us lower him to their ship where he was operated on at once. We continued on to Manila, then heard he was in Guam, healthy and awaiting a new ship."

In his two-year stint, Giles experienced two other near-misses while on the *Fort Donelson*. Anchored in Ulithi, Micronesia in March 1945, the tanker was attacked by Japanese suicide planes and survived. Then, on the way to Guam, the tanker was chased for 48 hours by a Japanese sub, which fired two torpedoes and missed. "They were poor shots," Giles said simply. Gunners manning the *Fort Donelson*'s five-inch cannons kept the sub at bay.

Giles recalls another shock as well - the news in April that FDR had died. His passing left a void that was about to be filled by Harry ... Who? For a country that had grown accustomed to living with the anxieties and uncertainties of war, the executive transition was yet another one as battles raged on.

Kamikaze Hits *S.S. Hobbs Victory* After Valiant Fight

The maiden voyage of the *S.S. Hobbs Victory* would prove to be her last. She had left Richmond, Calif. in early 1945 but it was just after Easter when she set out from Ulithi Atoll for "Destination X" - the invasion of Okinawa.

J. Edward Laughton of Salinas, Calif. - a second mate called "Big John" by crew members - describes the intensity of the last days of the *Hobbs Victory*.

Two days out, the convoy she was in encountered a hurricane complete with winds of 100 knots. Contending with the weather, the seven-ship convoy changed course and arrived two days late in the tiny islands of Kerama Retto five miles south of Okinawa.

They felt secure anchored between two large Navy ships, until an order was sent: "All merchant ships carrying explosives or gasoline will proceed out of their present anchorage to one around the smallest westerly island." Carrying 6,000+ tons of ammunition, the *Hobbs Victory* joined the *S.S. Pierre Victory* and the *S.S. Logan Victory* in their lonely sail to an unprotected part of the island.

Less than an hour after dropping anchor, Japanese suicide planes "came out of nowhere, it seemed," Laughton wrote. One Zeke crashed into a Navy LST (Landing Ship, Tank). Loaded with fuel oil, the ship became an instant inferno. The other was a Betty, which came straight toward the fantail of the *Hobbs Victory*.

"This twin-engine enemy plane looked like a two-story building bearing down at the stern of the ship. A top-notch gun crew opened fire with all it had - a 5-inch 38 aft, four 20-mm. along each side and a three-inch 51 forward. The five-inch projectiles puffed explosions right in front of the nose of the plane as it came in. These caused the Betty to take a 90-degree turn to the left, and head for the broadside of the *Pierre Victory*, which was still unalerted because of the enemy's quick attack."

When it was only 200 yards from the *Pierre Victory*, the kamikaze was brought down by the 20-mm. crew on the *Hobbs Victory*.

Captain Izant came running and ordered Big John Laughton: "Get hold of the chief engineer and tell him to get up a full head of steam. We're getting out of here."

Laughton had just passed along the order when he saw a kamikaze crash into the *Logan Victory*, hitting her broadside midship. The ship's cargo of ammunition didn't blow immediately, giving some crew members and Navy Armed Guard time to evacuate.

The attacks continued, with the *Hobbs Victory* skipper directing maneuvers to get the ship out of what seemed to be a "sitting duck" anchorage.

"Before clearing the last tiny island, the Hobbs' guns were still busy firing at what appeared to be another Zeke hovering in the shadows of the island and getting ready to make a run on the ship. All guns on the port side opened up on the plane, as it tried to gain altitude. Just then, the crew saw the insignia of a U.S. Navy Hellcat, and firing ceased. The plane had been hit, but the pilot managed to bail out to safety.

Heading for open sea, Captain Izant and the crew hoped they could elude kamikazes. After eight hours of torment, they enjoyed a 15-minute reprieve. Then a Zero came in four points off the port bow, swinging like a pendulum 30 to 40 feet above a calm sea to elude the gunfire that was pouring its way.

"Tension aboard this bucket of dynamite was at an all-time high. Mouths were dry and prayers were uttered as the 20-mm tracers poured into the Zeke. Smoke poured from the underside of the plane, but alas it was too late. The momentum carried the kamikaze through the radio shack," Laughton recalled.

The engine room took the direct hit, with smoke, steam and fire pouring forth. Luckily, the ship didn't immediately blow. Survivors loaded the injured on lifeboats. Some tripped life rafts and jumped in after them. Rescue boats from shore helped pick up survivors.

At midnight, the count was in. From a 99-man crew, 13 perished. And the *Hobbs Victory*, which was on fire and adrift in the ocean, finally succumbed to the pyrotechnics of its "cargo doomed to boom," as Laughton calls it.

Wreckage in the English Channel, 1946.

Dud Torpedo Leaves Crew Counting Blessings

The *S.S. Colby Victory's* survival - after being struck by a torpedo - is a dramatic tale told by Jim Heine of Livermore, Calif.

On a crystal-clear moonlit night in the Indian Ocean, the *Colby Victory* was making its way from Melbourne, Australia to Calcutta, when it met up with a solo Japanese sub.

Heine was awakened by the piercing sound of the general alarms and the realization that the chief mate and chief engineer were preparing to launch the lifeboats. When he looked to the starboard side, Heine saw the reason for the excitement: sitting in the water 200 yards parallel to the *Colby Victory* was a trolling submarine biding her time before releasing a torpedo.

At 17 knots, the Victory ship was already navigating at "full speed ahead." Outrunning the sub was an impossibility.

"The brilliant midnight moon was casting a sparkling sheen on the glassy sea. In effect, it was inviting every enemy vessel in the area to attack. I was scared to death as I searched the heavens looking for planes. The ear-deafening alarms were sounding loud and clear, and the enemy was still patrolling us on the starboard.

"At this moment there was no doubt that a prayer or two couldn't hurt. Jake, an AB and confirmed atheist ... was truly traumatized by our most unhealthy predicament. The last I saw of him, he was on his knees praying ... making all kinds of promises to the Lord, asking forgiveness for his past sins and promising to change his ways if only he could survive our inevitable demise."

Then came an anguished voice calling out: "Torpedo! Torpedo! Torpedo!" Everyone could see it, a surface cruising missile with bright dancing phosphorus flashing from its fin as it darted through the water. It was on target. Midships.

As the torpedo rammed into the side of the *Colby Victory*, Heine looked heavenward. "It was so immediate that all I could say was, 'Holy Christ, nothing happened.' The ship didn't explode. The torpedo was a dud! The good Lord heard Jake's plea for mercy and spared all of us."

Jumping out of the gun tub, Heine ran over to where the torpedo hit the thick steel plates and saw a huge crater. The sub had vanished into the swelling waters below.

Heine concluded that the sub commander was returning to his Japanese home port with one last torpedo when he came across the *Colby Victory*.

V-E Day: Merchant Mariners' Job Continues

On May 8, 1945, Americans throughout the world celebrated victory in Europe.

The message came to merchant ships via Mackay radiogram:
GERMANY HAS SURRENDERED UNCONDITIONALLY. CEASE FIRE HAS BEEN ORDERED FROM 2201Z EIGHT MAY - REPEAT 2201Z EIGHT MAY. PENDING FURTHER ORDERS ALL EXISTING INSTRUCTIONS REGARDING THE DEFENSE SECURITY AND CONTROL OF MERCHANT SHIPPING ARE TO REMAIN IN FORCE. MERCHANT SHIPS AT SEA WHETHER IN CONVOY OR SAILING INDEPENDENTLY ARE TO CONTINUE THEIR VOYAGES AS PREVIOUSLY ORDERED.

The following day, this radiogram went out from the WSA's Land:
FOR ALL UNITED STATES VESSELS X THE END OF ORGANIZED RESISTANCE IN GERMANY BRINGS NO LESSENING OF THE TASK OF THE UNITED STATES MERCHANT MARINE X CLOSING OF HOSTILITIES IN THE EUROPEAN THEATRE MEANS TO THE MARITIME COMMISSION AND WAR SHIPPING ADMINISTRATION A SITUATION UNCHANGED BASICALLY EXCEPT FOR A SHIFT IN EMPHASIS IN TIME AND PLACES X THERE WILL BE NO LESSER DEMAND FOR SHIPS OR FOR MEN TO SAIL THEM X TO THE MEN OF THE MERCHANT MARINE I EXTEND MY HEARTFELT THANKS FOR A JOB WELL DONE AND MY UTTER CONVICTION THAT YOU WILL CONTINUE YOUR ACHIEVEMENTS IN THE DAYS AHEAD IN THE SAME MANNER X

Indeed, danger did not disappear in the European theatre with the Germans' surrender.

The "SIU Log" reports an incident on June 4, when the *S.S. Colin Kelly* hit a mine as she headed up the Straits of Dover for Antwerp, Belgium. An oyster-type mine made contact with the hull at the engine room and blew a hole in the ship "big enough to drive a truck through." Miraculously, none of the men below at the time were lost or injured and she was able to be towed to Tilbury for repairs.

It turns out the "little Liberty that could" had a long history of thwarting danger. Nine Nazi swastikas adorned her stack, bearing witness to the action-packed voyages she had seen in the Mediterranean.

The *Colin Kelly* took part in the invasion of Sicily, during which her gunners shot down five planes in one day of heavy air raids. A heavy storm in the Atlantic Ocean in December 1944 claimed two of her crew when they were washed overboard.

Mutiny on the High Seas? Threat Backfires in Two Cases

Tensions often mount on ships as crew members' close proximity and personalities cause conflicts. Some skippers handled authority well; others had problems managing their people and their own sense of power, however misplaced it may have been.

Nils L. (Whitey) Pearson of Lake Elsinore, Calif. found himself in the middle of one such situation in 1945 on the tanker *S.S. Pequot Hill*.

As boatswain, Pearson was ordered to strip the lifeboats at sea, and to paint them inside and out. "Lifeboats are your only means of salvation. You don't strip the lifeboats, and take all the survival gear out, when you're at sea," he reasoned.

The captain thought differently. When Pearson refused the order, he advised the boatswain it was a direct order. Pearson again refused. Then the captain ordered Pearson to work the entire deck gang as soon as they came off watch. The deck gang held a meeting, after which they told Pearson they did not intend to work any overtime.

"I advised the captain that the deck gaing would turn out off-watch only if it was for the safety of the ship," Pearson explained. "He asked for my keys and placed me under house arrest and charging me with mutiny."

Pearson was confined to his cabin, where the captain showed up a couple of days later, asking the boatswain to reconsider. "He urged me to change my mind and work the deck gang to strip the lifeboats and to chip the paint on the deck. Since we had just been strafed by a Japanese plane after leaving Aniwetok, and this incident had all happened in the international waters, I stood my ground and again refused the order."

The situation prevailed until they

The Esso Utica damaged from collision with sub.

49

reached Panama, where the *Pequot Hill* was met and escorted into the harbor by every armed service on hand. The crew and officers were questioned in a hearing aboard ship. After the inquiry, the captain was escorted off the ship, fined and sent home.

Another captain replaced him, and Pearson completed the trip as acting chief, paying off in Philadelphia on November 8, 1945.

Aboard the *S.S. John C. Calhoun*, a Bull Line Liberty ship, allegations of mutiny were also raised on a trip in 1944, recalls Robert W. Morris of Pineville, La., an able-bodied seaman on this ship's ill-fated last voyage.

He describes the *Calhoun's* first mate as "a megalomaniac pscychopath, totally unpredictable, (someone) who tried to rule by fear and intimidation." This first mate looked at all seamen as draft dodgers. His favorite threat was: "I'll have you put in the Army."

"Even the most naive person on the ship knew this was not possible, so all crediblity was lost," explains Morris, who often fell victim to the worst punishment the first mate could dream up - cleaning grease from the cargo winches.

Anchored in Oro Bay on the New Guinea coast, the crew started their routine repair work. "The deck crew put stages over the side on both the bow and stern to scrape and paint the hull. With this arrangement, they could work in the shade most of the time," said Morris, who was carrying out his regular detail with the winches.

This was successful for several days, until the first mate decided the crew should work on the bow - in the direct heat of the sun - rather than on the stern in the shade. Viewing it as harassment, the deck crew walked past him and went to work on the stern.

Unbeknownst to them, the mate had the radio operator call ashore to report to the MPs that the crew on the *John C. Calhoun* had mutinied.

"Everyone was amazed when a boatload of MPs, armed to the teeth, climbed up the jack ladder. The first mate met them, and soon everyone on the ship gathered around out of curiosity. The first mate named the mutineers and told them he was having them put in the Army stockade," said Morris, who was not involved, but the first mate told the MPs to "get that one too" in the round-up.

Morris knew that civilians could not be put into the stockade, based on a conversation he had had several weeks before.

But everyone got into the Higgins boat, with the first mate keeping his distance from the mutineers. They landed at a makeshift dock, where they were loaded into an Army truck and taken to the barbed-wire enclosed stockade. The first mate had a long talk with the Army officer, and left. Thirty minutes later, the Army officer told the "mutineers" that they were free to go back to the ship.

In no hurry, they ate in an Army chow line and took in an open-air movie. After the movie, the seamen offered the soldiers a steak dinner for a ride back to the ship. The celebrating went on past midnight.

"After a few weeks at anchor, some Coast Guard people came aboard for a hearing. They took and held the seaman's papers for the boys involved. It's like the IRS before an audit. They attach all financial accounts, whether the victim is guilty or not," Morris said.

Then the *John C. Calhoun* itself met an unfortunate fate. While most of the crew was off watching a movie on another ship, the *Calhoun* was tied up against another ship. Suddenly, the audience heard an explosion. One of the crewmen said, "I hope that explosion was on the *Calhoun* and it sinks. That's one way to get off of it."

It was indeed the *Calhoun*, with flames shooting from the No. 4 hold where gasoline had been stored. The crew on the ship it had been tied up to had used fire axes to cut the hawsers and set the ship adrift before the movie-goers could get aboard. Tug boats came and nudged the *Calhoun* toward a beach a short distance away. It sank by the stern, up to the poop deck in water. Despite efforts to put out the fire, the ship burned for two more days.

Eventually, the body of a 20-year-old soldier was found in the No. 4 hold. One theory held that he was looking for beer or whiskey, which was rumored to be among the cargo on the ship, when the explosion occurred. The explosion could have happened when he turned on a non-sparkproof flashlight (which was recovered at the scene) that ignited the gasoline vapor-and-air mixture.

In the meantime, more allegations were leveled at the crew by the first mate, including "failure to respond to an emergency," "failure to go to fire stations" and "failure to follow orders." Another Coast Guard inquiry was inconclusive, but more crew members' papers were taken.

While the *Calhoun* was being repaired, the crew volunteered for other ships, and the War Shipping Administration complied by assigning them to another Liberty bound for San Francisco.

Once there, Morris and another crew member went to see a federal court judge assigned to the case of the seamen who had had their papers revoked. After examining their records, and spending two hours questioning them, the judge exonerated them and ordered the Coast Guard to return their papers to the seamen.

The Calhoun *was returned to Norfolk, Va. and placed in a bone yard where she was cut up into scrap metal after the war. But members of the*

Loaiing Boxite aluminum ore.

"Calhoun Athletic Club" - buddies who met on the ship and who shared many beers and adventures together - kept in touch for 48 years. Club members include: Morris, Blewett Odom, Herbert Akins and Raymond Scribner. Odom and Akins died in 1993.

Crew Uses Herculean Efforts to Save S.S. John Rawlins from Air Attack, Fire, Typhoon

Occasionally, despite a slew of dangers, a Merchant Marine crew escaped unscathed but its ship succumbed.

Such was the case with the *S.S. John Rawlins*, which was struck by a torpedo on July 27, 1945 while discharging her cargo in Okinawa's Naha Ko harbor.

Following the air attack by the Japanese plane, which left a gaping 20-by-30 foot hole in No. 3 hold, the "Fire" alarm sounded. The ship's cargo of kerosene and lubrication oil in the stricken hold had been turned into a raging inferno. The heat threatened 1,600 drums of white aviation gasoline in No. 2 hold, so it was flooded, sinking the ship lower in the water.

Although the engine room bulkheads began to buckle under the intense heat, no major damage occurred there. The *John Rawlins'* crew fought the fire in shifts for 42 hours before finally getting it under control.

The ship was taken to Buckner Bay in Okinawa for repairs. It was there on September 16 that the ship met its next foe - a typhoon. Under the direction of Captain Emil Hrubik, the crew labored intensely to save her again. Their valiant maneuverings were finally defeated by the ferocity of the storm.

When the *John Rawlins* began dragging her anchors, no effort of the crew or engines could stop her. All hands were ordered into life jackets and to the midship house for safety. Eventually the ship was driven on the reef and engineers were ordered topside for safety. When the storm passed, the ship had sunk in about 28 feet of water.

She was declared a total loss, but the crew miraculously avoided injury.

Transporting German P.O.W.s Across Atlantic, Returning with GIs

With the war in Europe officially over, there were thousands of people to bring back. But there were also people to repatriate in Germany, and Lawrence W. Ashton of Hilton Head, S.C. vividly recalls the fascinating trips he had as purser on the *S.S. Kingston Victory* transporting them.

Alfred Thompson, Albert Offredo, Thornton Gogoll, SS Occidental, Helsinki, Finland, 1946.

"The troops we carried from Boston to LeHavre were elite German prisoners of war who had been captured - largely from the Russian front - and incarcerated in a P.O.W. camp in Arkansas or Oklahoma. They were doctors, college professors, artists and other well-educated men who had been sent to the Russian front because they were unsympathetic to the Nazi philosophy," Ashton explained.

Once in Europe, these former P.O.W.s would participate in the Allied military's reconstruction of the West German goverment.

"As an example of their educational level, the man assigned to clean my office spoke five languages, so we had many political and philosophical conversations," he said.

When the winter seas of 1945 became seasonally rough, the German doctors took charge of the more serious injuries (like broken legs) that resulted while Ashton, the pharmacist mate, looked on.

"Upon reaching LeHavre, we disembarked our German P.O.W.s and boarded 3,000 returning G.I.s. There was plenty of room for everybody on the way over, but the bunks were stacked six high on the return trip. I will forever remember touring the ship's hold with the Army chaplain trying to boost morale. This was a difficult task because when the man on the top rack wanted to vomit from sea sickness, it had a contagious effect all the way down to the bottom rack."

Ashton sailed on the *Kingston Victory* for three of those crossings - taking German P.O.W.s and bringing back G.I.s. Sometimes they sailed through minefields off the coast of France.

"But I was too young to be concerned, and frankly too excited and busy to care. This must be why young people make the best soldiers and sailors," Ashton remarked.

San Francisco Victory Parade Honors Corregidor Hero and His Son, Capt. Jonathan Wainwright V

It was a time of joyous and thankful celebration across the country, as men and women began returning home. Victory parades were the order of the day.

On September 10, 1945, San Francisco hosted one such parade, and a particularly poignant reunion beween Lt. Gen. Jonathan Wainwright, who conducted the heroic defense of Bataan and Corregidor after MacArthur left the Philippines, and his son, Capt. Jonathan Wainwright V, then a 13-year veteran of the U.S. Merchant Marine.

Besides making their way down Market Street together, the two spent time aboard the *S.S. Lakeland Victory*, the ship which Capt. Wainwright had recently taken under his command.

The last time the father and son had been together was in September 1940, when the general was transported to Manila on his son's ship. At the time, the general was concerned he would miss out on the war he predicted for Europe.

Far from "missing out," Gen. Wainwright led extensive, valiant defenses in the Philippines before being forced to surrender to the Japanese with his 15,000 men. He accompanied his men on the Bataan Death March and survived to be a P.O.W. in Manchuria until the end of the war.

Meanwhile, his son was carrying on in his father's heroic tradition. In September 1943, Capt. Wainwright commanded a Liberty transport taking troops and supplies to the hard-won Salerno beachhead.

"As we went in a lot of fireworks kept picking at us," he told a newspaper reporter. "On the fourth day, a 500-pound bomb from a Stuka dive bomber hit the ship on the portside, and she caught fire. I ordered all the ship's crew off. We lost 26 men then and more died in hospitals later. The next morning, the ship blew up, scattering debris all over the harbor."

When Lt. Gen. Wainwright inspected his son's new command, he seized the opportunity to compliment the Merchant Marine, saying he thought it would be a big factor in the postwar economy. He also said he was proud that his son had dedicated himself to such a fine service.

Wainwright's sentiments were shared by the highest commanders in the U.S. Navy.

As Admiral Ernest King put it, "During the past three and a half years, the Navy has been dependent on the Merchant Marine to supply our far-flung fleet and bases. Without this support, the Navy could not have accomplished its mission. Consequently, it is fitting that the Merchant Marine share in our success as it shared in our trials."

A newspaper clipping of the day tallied the score as follows. When WWII ended, the American Merchant Marine:
• Numbered 6,000 ships;
• Almost equaled the entire world's pre-war tonnage;
• Comprised two-thirds of the world's post-war total;
  before World War II, only one-fifth of the world's shipping flew the American flag;
• Was three times the size of Britain's; before World War II, it
  had been only half of Britain's;
• Was five times bigger than pre-war;
• Had cost $22.5 billion;
• Had lost 743 ships.

1946

Post-war America became enmeshed in the most massive war-to-peacetime transition ever attempted.

Some merchant mariners couldn't get home fast enough. Others had discovered a way of life that suited them, and wondered what opportunities might be ahead.

Herman H. Jones of Las Vegas, for example, sailed T-2 tankers and Victory ships. He signed onto his first ship - the *S.S. Axtell J. Byles* - in 1943 as a wiper, then held a variety of positions - as junior engineer, oiler, galleyman, F.W.T., pumpman/machinist - on 23 more ships over the next seven years.

Jones' account of his travels demonstrates the shift in need as the type of goods to deliver changed. In late 1944 and early 1945, he traveled on the *S.S. York* in convoy carrying 100-octane gas, fighter planes and Army trucks to South Wales, U.K. and then Birkenhead, England.

In early 1946, he was junior engineer on the *S.S. Hampden Sydney Victory* as she brought back U.S. troops from Marseilles, France. The day after arriving in New York with the troops, they set out again to bring back more than 900 women military personnel and nurses from Le Havre, France. Hitting a North Atlantic storm on the way back, he observed: "What a sick bunch of women!"

Clifford B. Moore, too, remembers the poignancy of bringing back homesick G.I.s aboard the *S.S. Sea Porpoise*, a C2 convertible cargo/troop carrier.

Although his ships never engaged in wartime hostilities, Moore did have a startle. Upon entering the English channel in 1946, he heard explosions in the distance.

"Knowing the war was technically over, I inquired and learned that the French and English people spent many daylight hours in row boats with rifles hunting and detonating mines placed by the Germans during the early part of the war. A small shipping channel had been cleared and marked to safely allow for navigation into most French and English ports," he indicated.

Meanwhile, Jones spent May to July hauling horses on the *S.S. South Bend Victory*. First, 750 mares pregnant with mules were transported from Newport News, Va. to Gdynia, Poland. From there, the ship went to Montreal, Canada where 750 wild horses were loaded and taken to Poland.

"What a trip! Nothing like waking up in the morning in the middle of the Atlantic Ocean and smelling hay and fresh horse crap," Jones said.

North Atlantic storm, December 1945.

Gen. Jonathon Wainwright, fourth from left; his son, Capt. Jonathon Wainwright V, second from left, aboard SS Lakeland Victory, San Francisco, 1945. Lt. Joe Karr, second from right.

In May 1948, he was aboard the tanker *S.S. AMPAC California* when Israel became a nation.

"The shooting started and we had to stay off the outside decks, as the small-arms fire was whizzing everywhere. We had several bullet pock marks on our ship."

It was on this voyage that Jones stopped in Marseilles and married his long-time girlfriend. In 1950 he left the Merchant Marine.

"Sailing was a great experience and gave me a trade to make a good living to raise my four children," wrote Jones, who became a stationary engineer in several large Detroit, Mich. factories.

In fact, training given to merchant mariners laid the groundwork for many veterans seeking peacetime employment. To get an idea of the enormity of the training effort, Commodore Telfair Knight, commandant of the U.S. Maritime Service, enumerated the following statistics in a <u>Mast</u> Magazine article:

From 1938 to Nov. 1 1945:
- Seven training stations and seven training ships were developed;
- From these, 248,431 men were schooled and upgraded, and made ready to "deliver the goods" to the many fighting fronts of the global war.
- Of these, 148,344 held entry ratings;
- 22,570 deck and engineer officers were trained up from the ranks;
- 7,727 radio operators;
- 4,956 purser-pharmacist's mates;
- 28,976 other specialists;
- 35,858 men were upgraded to higher rank.

- In addition, 7,115 officers were trained by the U.S. Merchant Marine Cadet Corps and 2,707 officers by the five State Maritime Academies.

Further, Comm. Knight wrote: "Maritime Service-trained men performed admirably throughout the war. They stood up under bombs and torpedoes, in addition to the regular hazards of life at sea. Taught at training stations how to man a gun, they gave heroic assistance to the Navy gun crews.

"During training, they learned the use of the latest life-saving devices available and with these saved many lives. However, many lives were lost, particularly during the early days of the war. The Merchant Marine suffered the highest number of lives lost, in proportion to its size, of any branch of the service.

"The heroism of the men of the Merchant Marine did not go unrecognized. Admiral King, General Eisenhower, Admiral Nimitz, General MacArthur, to name a few, have all paid tribute to the American merchant fleet."

Admiral Chester Nimitz's words spoke of the crucial importance of the Merchant Marines to future conflicts. He said: "This war has fully confirmed the necessity for a strong...merchant marine...so that it may be employed as an auxiliary of the Amry and Navy in time of war."

Earliest Efforts to Gain Veteran Status Launched

Shortly after the war, the Merchant Seaman's War Service Bill was introduced in the U.S. House of Representatives. It was the first of many unsuccessful attempts to grant veteran status to merchant mariners.

At the time, the "New York Times" wrote: "At least there should be an effort to recognize the dignity of the service to give thousands of disabled merchant marine veterans some distinction from members of the civilian population who have taken no risk and suffered no injury connected to the war."

Adventures in Vietnam, and Beyond on 1947 Trip Aboard Liberty Ship
By Ken Gossett, Thousand Oaks, Calif.

In early 1947, the S.S. Joshua L. Chamberlain, with its 38-man crew, left San Pedro, Calif. to carry various cargo - including steel military barges - from Seattle to the French Foreign Legion fighting in Vietnam. From there, they traveled to Singapore, Norfolk Island with supplies for the descendants of the Mutiny on the Bounty, Australia, New Guinea, Indonesia and South Africa. It was quite a trip, starting with a horrendous storm churning 75-foot waves in the North Pacific.

When we arrived at the Saigon River it was tricky maneuvering up the snake-like turns, with many Japanese ships sunk along the way creating navigation hazards.

Saigon was a bustling city full of Legionnaires from all over Europe. About one-third of them were ex-German soldiers imprisoned by the French at the end of the war. They had been given the option of staying in prison or "volunteering" for the Legion. They marched in goose-step with all of the commands given in German. Very few Frenchmen were in the Legion. I immediately felt all of the hositility generated by the years of war toward these "Nazi" troops.

However, after a few cognacs in a

sidewalk cafe, I settled down and began to talk with some of them. The group I was with had no one who spoke English, but I found a Czechoslovakian who spoke Spanish, so I translated for the Americans to him, and he to German and someone from German to French.

The best currency in those days was cigarettes. I did not smoke, but would buy my two cartons from the slop chest at 50 cents per carton every week. I had accumulated 10 cartons to trade, but customs did not permit us to take them ashore.

While drinking in a dance hall with native girls, we became friendly with a Legionnaire and a French sailor off a French warship. When they found out I had cigarettes, the Legionnaire ran out into the street, stopped a jeep, and jumped into the front seat. The sailor and I got in the back.

We went to the ship and got the cigarettes, then sat on them in the back seat like hens over eggs. At the customs gate, the native customs officer wanted a bribe. The Legionnaires refused and a real confrontation took place. Finally we were ordered out of the jeep, and there was the evidence!

The customs man said we were under arrest, and he was going to take us to the most foreboding looking jail one can imagine in downtown Saigon.

Suddenly, the driver turned off the road and started out through the countryside at high speed. The customs man was still sitting on the side of the jeep with his underling, and loud arguing continued. The gist of the dispute was that the Legionnaire would be sent to a place worse than the civilian jail - their base in the country. At that time, the countryside belonged to the communists at night, and they would shoot any Europeans who ventured out there.

I was scared to death, making as small a target as possible in the back seat. Suddenly, the customs man pulled out a pistol and pointed it at me, ordering the jeep to stop. I was yelling "Stop" in every language I could think of, and the driver complied.

When the customs men stepped off, the driver threw the motor in gear and took off, leaving them to walk back a couple of miles to town. We circled around and went downtown with the cigarettes, sold them and had a party.

The next day the MPs came looking for me, but I was asleep on the Poop Deck and no one could find me. They said they would be back the next day. What a scared 19-year-old I was that night. When they returned, they interviewed me in front of the captain and made it clear they wanted the Legionnaires, not me. I told them I knew nothing about the incident and, since my French was so poor, I could not recall the French names anyway. They left and I walked them to the gangway. As they walked down, the Legionnaire was walking up the dock shouting greetings to me and waving. I tried to get him to stop, but he continued and actually passed them on the gangway.

They did not say anything to him, and the incident was over....

Taking supplies to the descendants of the Mutiny on the Bounty, we had to move twice a day to the lee of the island and could only unload during high tide into whale boats. I spent time on the island and found the people delightful. They had no jail. The only work was unloading a ship every six weeks and caring for their gardens. There was a well cared-for graveyard going back to the days when the British operated a prison there. One grave was for a 16-year-old boy off a whaling ship killed by a "miscreant" over 100 years before.

Then we went to Brisbane and Sydney, Australia, on to Rabaul, New Britain, Lae and Port Moresby, New Guinea.

The jungle had already reclaimed the big Navy base at Port Moresby, where we picked up thousands of empty 55-gallon oil drums left by our forces during the war. The aborigines would roll those drums out of the jungle and down the dock 24 hours per day. The rumble was constant and nerve-wracking.

There was no recreation except alcohol available, and our systems could not take

SS Spring Hill Deck Dept. AB.

SS American Navigator

both the heat and the drinking. Three of our crew had mental breakdowns in one week, including the radio operator who threw the radio over the side. He was locked in the hospital, and we sailed on to Surabaya, Indonesia with a radio operator, but no radio. (The ship could not sail without a radio operator.)

The Dutch were at war in Indonesia. The troops were Dutch Marines trained for six months at Camp Le Jeneue, N.C. They all spoke excellent English. In fact, the joke was that the only ones who did not speak good English were the Americans!

Here we saw small children of 7 or 8 and women working or the docks. An old man would herd the children with a long stick, striking them if they did not perform their tasks. We could hear gunfire outside the city, but we were relatively safe.

Back to New Guinea for another load of empty drums, and on to Durban and Port Elizabeth, South Africa. We went around the Cape, headed for Norfolk, Va. The seas were so strong going south toward the cape that we logged over 200 miles in one 24-hour day pushed backwards!

Nine months and four days after leaving California, we finished our memorable voyage.

1948

In a September issue of the "New York Times," Frank Zack of the Merchant Marine Veterans of America, offered his impassioned view, reflecting the sentiments of the day - and for four decades to come - among his fellow mariners:

"Our seamen were trained to man guns, assigned battle stations on guns aboard ship, participated actively in every invasion, wore the uniform of the United States Maritime Service and sailed ships that had guns mounted fore and aft for the purpose of attack, not self- defense.

"They were subject to court martial from the time they left the States until they returned. They received ribbons and medals for heroic service far beyond the line of duty. They swore allegiance to our country.

"Never once through our government's advertisements in the papers, magazines and radio were the words 'civilian employment' used.

"In fact, these men were led to believe they were joining a part of the armed forces. They volunteered their services. They sailed the Murmansk run. They established a 'bridge of ships' across the Atlantic. They lost over 7,000 men and 1,700 ships through enemy action. Is that civilian employment?"

1950s - Korean War Calls for Merchant Marines

It wasn't long before Korea took center stage in the minds of Americans whose lives once had been ruled by another war.

Mariner Ray Maurstad played a pivotal role in that conflict. In fact, he demonstrated a unique ability to be in the "right" place at a critical moment in history twice in the decade - first at the outbreak of the Korean War, and later as the first radio operator to receive the *Andrea Doria's* distress call. (More about that later.)

In 1949, Maurstad took an assignment in Pusan, South Korea to establish a Merchant Marine academy there. He was training Koreans on six 2,500-foot Baltic coasters. World events interrupted his mission.

Maurstad, then 22, was chatting with a friend from Seoul on his ham radio on a Sunday morning, June 25, 1950. Suddenly, the friend's messages became urgent. A large force of North Koreans had just crossed the border and was invading South Korea at Seoul.

Acting immediately, Maurstad relayed the news to Gen. MacArthur's headquarters in Tokyo. For the next two weeks, until they were evacuated to Japan, Maurstad and another operator manned the radio around the clock.

"The Army set the equipment up in a mess hall and I radioed while my wife stood guard in our living room with a loaded shotgun," Maurstad said. Eight months pregnant, she was evacuated to Japan where her husband later joined her.

The Korean War reactivated the need for a larger fleet of seaworthy vessels and a strong Merchant Marine. Ships - and sailors - who had been mothballed suddenly found their services in demand again.

Loring W. Wordell remembers having taken a job ashore in 1950 that proved unsatisfactory, and calling the union office in New York, then getting his licenses renewed and his papers in order.

"The union found me a ship on May 18, 1951, the *S.S. Greeley Victory*," Wordell remembers. It was to be a two-week voyage to Europe and back. Little did he know that, thanks to the demands of moving goods for the war effort, that voyage would extend to eight months.

In Rotterdam, they loaded fertilizer bound for Korea. Since the Suez Canal was in jeopardy, the captain decided to take the long route across the Atlantic and through the Panama Canal. It took 50 days to get to Korea, by which time the fertilizer had become packed "solid as a rock." It had to be removed with pick axes.

Discharging the cargo at Pusan, the *Greeley Victory's* crew scoured the holds then pointed the ship for Masan, a port 100 miles to the west. There, they loaded vehicles that had been damaged, bombed and wrecked for transport to Sasebo to be rebuilt.

"We did the shuttle between Korea and Japan many times . Our last port was Inchon before returning home December 1951."

Ships that had been mothballed in eight National Defense Reserve Fleets around the country as surplus after World War II duties, were taken out of "reserve" status and prepared to deliver supplies to yet another front.

In the line-up was the *S.S. Lane Victory*, a victory ship that was completed in 1945 just as the war was winding down. She had eight outings before being assigned to the reserve fleet. Her eventual destiny promised a finer fate than any other Victory ship - refurbished and docked in San Pedro, Calif. as a living memorial to the merchant mariners who lost their lives in World War II. She is also a National Historic Landmark. (Read more about her below.)

But in October 1950, the *Lane Victory* set sail for Yokohama, Japan fresh with military supplies from the Oakland Army Base. Unloading her cargo there, the crew went ashore and discovered how slowly Japan was recovering from the war.

In his book, <u>The Last Victory: The Life and Times of a United States Victory Ship 1945-1992</u>, Walter W. Jaffe describes the Korean experiences of the *Lane Victory*.

In late November, the ship arrived at Inchon, South Korea - empty - with the crew not knowing what its cargo would be. "The next thing we know, we had 3,000 prisoners of war being put on board the boat," Third Mate Gil MacMillan said, and he was in charge of feeding them.[39]

Rice was the meal, and MacMillan reported that maintaining discipline with the help of an armed guard was essential, or there would have been food riots. It was a two- or three-day trip to Pusan. Three P.O.W.s died on the trip. MacMillan guessed it was from malnutrition.

Their next cargo was an even tighter squeeze - civilians from the evacuation of Wonson. While they scrambled to get the refugees aboard, they were being shelled from shoreside and the city seemed to be exploding.

The count leaving Wonson was 7,009 refugees. A baby was born on the one-day trip to Pusan. Everyone except the crew disembarked there.

After the *Lane Victory* had been cleaned up from the unsanitary conditions created by overloading the ship with human cargo, she was sent to Hungnam. There, under the cover of fire from a U.S. cruiser and two destroyers, 3,834 troops, 1,145 vehicles and more than 10,000 bulk tons of cargo were loaded under combat conditions. The *Lane Victory* was one of seven merchant ships involved in the evacuation, along with 21 Navy vessels. Troops and equipment were deposited in Husan.

After one more Hungnam-to-Pusan trip, the *Lane Victory* left the war zone, where it had been for one month. A long month. After a break in Sasebo, Japan, they headed back to the war zone on Christmas Eve, 1950 for about two weeks, before returning to Japan, then San Francisco in early 1951.

It wasn't long before she was headed to Louisiana to pick up more military supplies, then back to Korea and what was considered the tedious work of shuttling from port to port between Japan and Korea transporting whatever was needed for the war effort. From late June through August, she was relieved of military duties and instead did commercial transport for American President Lines to the Philippine Islands, Guam and Burma before returning to San Francisco.

The *Lane Victory* did more service,

carrying supplies to Korea - once a load of ammunition for the war effort.

For the *Lane Victory*, and plenty of other merchant ships brought out of mothballs for the Korean War, three years of war meant another flurry of activity and usefulness. When the war was over in 1953, so was their value and they - like she - were decommissioned that year and put back into storage.

As always, war wasn't the only hazard facing merchant mariners. The weather posed its usual unpredictable peril.

February 18, 1952 delivered a deadly storm in New England that broke up two tankers - the *Fort Mercer* and the *Pendleton* - off of Chatham, Mass., a little fishing port on Cape Cod. The tankers apparently broke apart at almost exactly the same time. Seven of the crews of both vessels were known to have died; 13 - including the *Pendleton's* 38-year-old skipper - were unaccounted for and another 32 were rescued by the light of flares.

One man was lost while Coast Guard rescuers were taking 32 seamen from the stern of the *Pendleton*. Another five perished when they leapt from the tossing bow of the *Fort Mercer* and missed the bouncing life rafts. Still another, wearing a lifejacket, was lost when he jumped off the *Pendleton's* bow in an effort to reach a nearby Coast Guard motorboat.

An Associated Press report indicated that it was a daring, split-second rescue by the light of flares off Chatham Bar that saved lives.

Ray Sybert, the Pendleton's chief engineer from Norfolk, Va., described the Coast Guard rescue as "nothing short of miraculous. Here were four young men working in the dark against terrific odds."

Flares were dropped from a circling plane to light the scene. The Coast Guard's 36-foot open life boat made repeated passes at the *Pendleton's* stern to pick up one individual at a time.

Bernard C. Webber was the boatswain's mate first class who was in charge of the lifeboat. "We lost our windshield on the way out. The snow kept hitting my face so hard I could hardly keep my eyes open. I couldn't see much, and had to steer mostly by instinct. I was strapped to the wheel so I wouldn't get tossed overboard. The other men were knocked to the deck time after time.

"Some of the men from the stern of the *Pendleton* were half-handed down to us. The others had to make clear jumps. The very last was a big guy called 'Tiny'. (Later identified as George Myers, who weighed 350 pounds.)

"He got on our boat but fell off. Just then a big wave caught us and we banged against the side of the tanker. He was crushed. We had to let him go to save anybody, but that guy died a hero. He handed down probably half the survivors we did get."

The Orlando Sentinel-Star reported the first-hand account of Edward A. Gallagher, a survivor of the *Pendleton*, on which he served as second engineer.

He was on watch in the tanker's engine room when the *Pendleton* was torn apart by 50- and 60-foot waves. "It sounded like thunder, or like a torpedo had hit the ship," he said.

Once on the deck, Gallagher saw the bow of the ship drifting about half a mile away, with eight people aboard the section. They were lost and presumed drowned.

Gallagher described the stern portion, in which most of the crew had been sleeping, as unsteady. Their biggest fear was that the section would capsize, since the waves seemed on the verge of flipping them over. "I never thought I'd make it," he remarked.

A lifeboat rescued them, but it too was nearly turned upside down in the enormous waves.

"We had a whale of a scare and a good drenching as the lifeboat heeled," Gallagher said at the time. Having been in many storms after 12 years at sea, Gallagher reported this to be the worst.

Radio Operator Maurstad Receives *Andrea Doria* S.O.S.

Ray Maurstad remembers July 26, 1956 as a slow night aboard the *Robert E. Hopkins*, an oil tanker en route from Massachusetts to Texas after discharging her cargo. Most of the crew was asleep when 28-year-old radio operator Maurstad received an S.O.S. signal from the sinking *Andrea Doria*.

ANDREA DORIA TO ALL STATIONS: DISTRESS, DISTRESS. JUST COLLIDED WITH ANOTHER SHIP. WE ARE LISTING, IMPOSSIBLE TO PUT LIFEBOATS AT SEA.

Maurstad radioed back: ROBERT E. HOPKINS TO ANDREA DORIA: YOUR DISTRESS MESSAGE ACKNOWLEDGED. PLEASE STAND BY FOR OUR POSITION.

Then he sounded the alarm to rouse the crew. "All any of us could think of was

APL C-10 Class includes MV President ADAMS, MV President JACKSON, MV President KENNEDY, MV President TRUMAN. Length 275 meters, beam 39 meters, displacement tonnage 77065, Speed 24 knots.

getting there as fast as possible. We had only one picture in our minds as we headed for the crash site - hundreds of people drowning in that icy blackness, screaming for help."

An Italian luxury liner, the *Andrea Doria* had collided with the *Stockholm*, a Swedish liner off the New England coast. While the *Andrea Doria* went down, taking 51 people with her, the *Stockholm*, her crew and passengers survived the accident.

Heavy fog and the need to navigate around a fishing fleet by radar slowed the *Hopkins* as she made the 45-mile trip to the disaster scene. Three other ships had arrived first, and rescued most of the survivors.

"The *Doria* had a heavy starboard list and was about to capsize when we finally arrived and lowered our lifeboats," Maurstad reported. He and his mates rescued the last passenger aboard, a naked man clutching the stern of the doomed liner.

"He had been partying and was asleep in his cabin, unaware the ship was sinking. When he awoke, he had to crawl up the bulkhead wall, using the sink and towel racks, to reach the passageway."

The "last survivor" was one of 1,655 passengers and crew members who made it off the *Andrea Doria* alive.

1960s - Vietnam Creates Renewed Need for Merchant Marine Fleet

"When the Vietnam war came on, I could see that there was a good possibility that my services could be used," Loring W. Wordell remarks. He was right.

Wordell was one of the veteran seamen who once again found themselves in greater demand as the U.S. became involved in another conflict across the ocean. Ships, too, found renewed significance and became liberated from their "reserve fleet" status.

According to Walter Jaffe's account, 172 victory ships were taken out of mothballs for Vietnam service, carrying one-third of the war cargo sealifted to support U.S. involvement in the war. Some 6,000 American merchant mariners manned the ships.[40]

The *Lane Victory* was brought of her Suisun Bay hibernation in August 1966. For two months, work was done on the ship to prepare her to be part of the Vietnam Sealift. She made 14 voyages, including some carrying ammunition from the East Coast through the Panama Canal to Southeast Asia.[41]

That first Vietnam voyage offered up a real "first" for veterans of previous wars - leaking napalm. Luckily, the crew contacted MARAD (the Maritime Administration) and the Navy for instructions, and found out that it was not a serious problem.[42]

As the war wore on, opinions diverged. Debates raged about whether it was necessary for the U.S. to be involved in Vietnam. People opposed it in different ways.

Ironically, the only Christmas the ship spent in the U.S. in her active career was also the year she became the target of one of the more unusual forms of war protest. On December 28, 1967, the *Lane Victory*, docked in Port Chicago, Calif., received an anonymous call that a bomb had been planted on board and would go off in an hour and a half. A security search team was sent aboard, but no bomb was found after their thorough investigation.[43]

Another potential danger evaded on the *Lane Victory*.

Ships Carrying Explosives Collide in Saigon River; No Fire Results
By Loring W. Wordell

My assignment was the *S.S. Meridian Victory*, October 1967. We would load up with explosives here on the East Coast, go south through the Panama Canal and over to Vietnam. It was more or less six weeks either way, so that round-trip would be about three months.

The first voyage, we went into Nahtrang and discharged the cargo there. The next voyages were to Cam Rahn Bay, then Danang, Bangkok, Thailand and then home to the states.

Because of circumstances on the ship, I decided it was a good thing to leave, so I transferred from the *Meridian Victory* to the *S.S. Barre Victory* in September 1968.

The *Barre Victory* was doing the same thing - loading up with explosives and going to Vietnam. This time we went up the Saigon River to Cat Lai and discharged the cargo. Carrying 10,000 tons of explosives, we went up the Saigon River about 100 miles. The cargo was discharged onto barges, which were to be towed up river to Long Bein.

The captain of the tugboat allowed me to go with them on one of their trips upstream. We had five barges in tow. The wheelhouse and bridge of the tug were armor-plated and fitted with gun mounts. We were sniped at on two occasions and asked for aircraft to be sent in. They bombed and strafed the sniper position.

Back on the ship, with the holds empty and ready to head home, we were loaded with 4,700 tons of unstable explosives bound for Yokuska, Japan to be disassembled and rebuilt.

On our way down the snake-like path of the Saigon River, we encountered another vessel coming upstream carrying 10,000 tons of explosves. She was rounding the curve as we were about to enter. It soon became evident that a collision was imminent, and that I should brace myself.

Where was she going to hit us? Seconds at a time the picture changed and to my surprise, she hit within 10 feet of where I stood. The two vessels lurched. Grating, tearing and grinding sounds could be heard as she moved past us, destroying the bridge wing, lifeboats and deck house for over 200 feet along our port side. Then contact was broken.

It was remarkable that no fire erupted, since the lifeboats' crumbling spread gasoline everywhere.

We put into Yokohama at the Mitsubishi Shipyard a week or two later, and spent three weeks having three-quarters of a million dollars worth of repairs done so we could bring the ship home.

When the ship was about half-way home, mid-Pacific, we received a message stating that she was to be laid up and to prepare for that before we entered the U.S.

In December of 1968, the *Barre Victory* was put into the reserve fleet and I went home for the Christmas holidays.

After this incident, Wordell did not go to Vietnam again. The union assigned him to the Montpelier Victory, a 50,000-ton tanker owned by Ari Onassis. He made trips from Cook Inlet, Alaska carrying crude oil out to Los Angeles or San Francisco with a round trip about every two weeks.

By 1969, anti-war sentiment was even more vocal. Protestors were finding new and more outspoken ways to demonstrate their anger. One of these was to take private yachts into waterways and block ships leaving ammunition piers. How times had changed. Now, merchant ships had to be escorted by Coast Guard cutters until they were in open waters. Such was the case for the *Lane Victory*, as she navigated from Port Chicago to San Francisco Bay. The *Lane Victory*'s escorts bid her farewell at the Golden Gate Bridge.[44]

Arriving in Southeast Asia had its moments too. The Saigon River continued to pose problems. Crew members were issued flack jackets and told to stay inside as it was navigated. On November 27, 1969, she docked at Newport on the river and came close to having a bomb planted on her by a Viet Cong swimmer. When guards spotted the saboteur under the docks near the ship, he was killed immediately. The incident sent a scare through crew members, who refused to stay on deck stowing the lines as the ship headed down river to the sea.[45]

S.S. Badger State Abandoned After Bomb Cargo Shifts; 25 Crewmen Lost

Danger, as always, lurked in the holds of the ship where the cargo they were transporting could cause disaster.

That's what happened with the 459-foot *S.S. Badger State* on December 26, 1969. Carrying bombs and rockets equal to 2,000 tons of TNT, the ship ran into trouble when the weather turned turbulent and some of her cargo broke loose.

One hour after she was abandoned by her 39-man crew about 600 miles northeast of Midway Island, the *Badger State* was racked by explosions in the starboard stern section.

A Greek ship picked up 14 crewmen, apparently including the skipper Charles Wilson, while a U.S. Air Force rescue plane dropped life rafts and die markers for those still in the water.

"When the sun went down yesterday, some of the missing men were seen clinging to life rafts in mountainous waves. Three ships and a circling rescue plane stood by during the night," according to a United Press International account in the "New York Times."

"But when dawn broke under leaden skies, with rain squalls reducing visibility at times to less than a mile, there was no sign of the missing men.

"In the all-night search, a circling Air Force plane dropped flares and life rafts."

By December 28, one body had been recovered from the 50-degree water. Four other bodies were spotted, but it was impossible for ships to recover them in the surging seas. A single ship patrolled the mid-Pacific in fading hope of finding survivors.

Finally, the 25 missing crew members were given up as lost. The bombs had been picked up in Bangor, Wash. and were on their way for use by the Air Force in Danang, South Vietnam.

"Merchant seamen throughout the world focused on the incident," Jaffee reported.[46]

The *Lane Victory* made her last Pacific crossing in April of 1970. When she returned to San Francisco, she was sent to the reserve fleet, where she would remain until her "rescue" by World War II Merchant Marine veterans, bent on turning her into a museum ship/memorial to their fallen compatriots.

"After all," says Joseph Vernick, president of the U.S. Merchant Marine Veterans of World War II, "Merchant Marines do not have graves like the Army. They lie at the bottom of the Seven Seas. They died for the security and freedom which we all now enjoy."

Mariners' Fight to Gain Recognition After World War II

Merchant Mariners' battle to receive veterans' status took ten times longer to win than it did for the Allies to prevail in World War II itself.

By 1988 - when Merchant Marine veterans of World War II finally succeeded in getting their just due - government officials estimated that only 90,000 of the 250,000 who served in the war were still alive to see the victory.

Standing in the way during the more than 40-year struggle were many veterans who had served in the Army, Navy, Marines and Air Force. National leaders of the Veterans of Foreign Wars and American Legion repeatedly voiced their opposition.

The age-old obstacles of ignorance and prejudice seemed to keep the campaign against seaman alive. Perceptions that mariners earned high wages, while facing little or no wartime peril, hampered legislative progress. The impression that seamen were "draft dodgers" seemed to dog them.

Mariners watched while the Secretary of the Air Force granted veterans' status to 14 civilian groups, including: a group of dieticians and physical therapists from World War I; civilian construction workers on Wake Island in World War II; members of the Women's Army Auxiliary Corps who declined to serve in the military when that group was militarized in WWII, and women who ferried planes from the U.S. to England in WWII. But Merchant Mariners just didn't qualify.

James L. Burnett Sr. from Mobile, Ala. shared his sentiments in a March 1982 letter to the "NMU Pilot". It read, in part:

"I want to convey my strongest resentment toward the Secretary of the Department of Defense and the Secretary of the Air Force for denying us veterans benefits...

"To emphasize my deep hurt..., I would like to say that undoubtedly they were not there in World War II, Korea or Vietnam as I was. Our ships were loaded with airplanes, ammunition, food, clothing, gas and oil - and everything needed to help win a war!

"I volunteered in the U.S. Maritime Serve in May 1944 at the age of 16 and was issued a uniform of my country which I still have and want to be proud of. I was trained under the complete control of the U.S. Coast Guard at Sheepshead Bay, Brooklyn, N.Y. I was put aboard ship by my U.S. government in time of war (1944) and was assigned to battle stations in all theatres of war - the North Atlantic, Mediterranean, South Pacific, England and later Korea and Vietnam. I served my country for 21 years before leaving the merchant marines.

"Since then I have received four medals from my government for this service, plus several campaign ribbons. I also have one medal from a foreign government for helping to liberate that country in World War II.

"If our service was so meritorius, then why is the Pentagon so biased against us - so few who did so much...

"I do not know what they mean by active military service. My life was in danger in all theatres of the war. We were under complete U.S. governmental control in these areas of war. We had guns on our ships. We had battle stations and we helped man the guns. We furnished all war areas with guns, ammunition, airplanes, tanks, food and men. President Roosevelt called us his fourth line of defense!..."

Similar sentiments come from Charles de la Motte of Westlake, Ohio, who also wrote to the "NMU Pilot". Assigned to the Liberty ship *S.S. John Walker* in May 1942, he saw much action on her until January 1946. He sailed on her to Northern Russia, Molotovsk and Murmansk without convoy or escort, and was attacked by six German planes. They lost their second mate in a bombing raid. Then they sailed to Algiers, Oran, Naples, Anzio, Normandy, Belgium. They were also in the invasion of Sicily.

He reminds us of the old saying:

"In times of war and not before,
God and the sailor we adore.
When peace is declared and all is righted,
God is forgotten and the sailor slighted."

By the mid-1980s, the sustained effort to carry the message of Merchant Mariners' exemplary service started to get through to the powers-that-were - particularly after a lawsuit was filed.

In February 1985, the "NMU Pilot" reported that a government review board would hear new arguments "in the prolonged drive for official recognition of the decisive role of seamen in achieving victory in World War II, and consideration of their right to GI Bill benefits."

Three applications presenting the case were given to the review board: one from an AFL-CIO Ad Hoc Committee, including the NMU and other maritime unions; another from seamen who took part in Operation Mullberry during the invasion of France; and a third from Charles Dana Gibson, World War II ship's officer, marine consultant and maritime historian.

Gibson made a case that merchant seamen and Army Transport crews should be eligible under a law passed in 1977.

This appeal failed.

In 1986, a lawsuit was filed after merchant seamen and their organizations had exhausted all administrative procedures and appeals available to them in their efforts to win recognition of their wartime role.

The plaintiffs were the AFL-CIO and Edward Schumacher, Lester Reid and Stanley Wilner.

Schumacher, who sailed AB and second mate during the war, took part in the invasions of North Africa, Sicily and Normandy. He also sailed on the treacherous Murmansk run. After the war, he quit the sea and joined the Smithsonian Institution as an artist and scientific illustrator. He retired as the Smithsonian's director of scientific illustration.

Reid sailed in the Atlantic and Pacific Theatres of War, including the Battle of Leyte Bay in which General MacArthur recaptured the Philippines.

Wilner served on the *M.S. Sawokla*. (The *Sawokla* was sunk off Madagascar in November 1942 by a German raider. The survivors were turned over to the Japanese. They spent the next four years in P.O.W. camps and helped build the Bridge over the River Kwai.) Wilner was a shipmate of Dennis Roland, whose experiences led him to devote much of his life to obtaining justice for American P.O.W.s.

The Washington offices of the law firm Proskauer Rose Goetz & Mendelsohn handled the suit, which was filed in the the U.S. District Court for the District of Columbia. Its content was included in the testimony for H.R. 1235, the Merchant Seamen's Benefits Act.

On May 7, 1987, the Subcommittee on the Merchant Marine of the U.S. House of Representatives' Committee on Merchant Marine and Fisheries held a hearing on the Merchant Seamen's Benefits Act and two related bills.

Excerpts from the testimony that day:

"The United States is the only country engaged in the Second World War which has not honored their own merchant mariners," from the National Council, Maritime Academy Alumni Associations.

From Charles April Lloyd, 1987

chairman of the U.S.N. Armed Guard WWII Veterans: "Speaking in behalf of my other Armed Guard brother, Lonnie Whitson Lloyd, killed in action May 5, 1945 aboard the *S.S. Black Point,* sinking three miles off the coast of Port Judith, R.I., which also took 11 lives of the merchant crew, I can only repeat what he told my family as I listened after he had returned from a trip to Murmansk, Russia ... 'We are not allowed to say one word of where we have been or what we saw or did ... But I will say this much - for three days and nights we were under enemy attack without any sleep and the only food or water that we got was what the merchant seamen brought to us at our gun stations. When this war is over, and if I survive, I will tell you things that you would not believe civilized people would do. It's hard to believe I have been to a place where it was kill or be killed.'

"I saw the fear of facing death that he went through and I am sure all the men of those ships, whether Navy or merchant seaman, suffered the agony and fear, regardless of how brave they were... Most all these merchant seamen were trained in helping the gun crews by bringing ammunition, loading and unloading, hot shellman and other duties at the gun station that the Armed Guard performed.

"Many below deck, such as the engineers, could only pray that the ship would not be hit, for their chances were slim indeed. Many were scalded from the broken, hot steam pipes and if they made it to the lifeboats, they would have to spend many days before being rescued. Brother Whitson had survived the sinking of the *S.S. Expositor* on February 22, 1943 and broke down emotionally. Here was a man who volunteered to serve his country and was as brave as they come, but a brave man can stand but so much. The merchant crews were there under the same conditions, trying to end the score of December 7, 1941 and to see that the supplies were delivered to their sons and friends that had elected a different branch of the service in which to serve. Many of these men were over-age for the draft, could not pass a physical for regular service and had special maritime skills that you just don't learn over night."

From Ian A. Miller, president and founder of The Sons and Daughters of U.S. Merchant Mariners of World War II: "...The American merchant seaman of World War II was a volunteer who put his life on the line for his country. He did not tarry behind awaiting a draft notice... He sailed into the thickest of the fray, at times aboard unarmed ships and after coming into harm's way he sailed again. His casualty rate cries ou tin mute testimony to his courage and service. The American merchant seaman did not falter when his country was at war. ...

"And what has been his lot as a result of this unselfish and brave service? He has for over 40 years been the victim of national neglect. He has been denied the benefits and rewards heaped upon those who served in the same ships with him... He has been denied a place in the parade when we honor those who served our country and laid down their lives for our freedom in mortal combat with the enemy..."

Charles Dana Gibson, the marine historian and himself a veteran of the Merchant Marine, entered this testimony: "World War II is the sole example within our nation's history when our merchant fleet was placed under naval instructions and naval discipline which prohibited - come what may - a master and his crew from surrendering their vessel to the enemy. It was also the only period wherein government orders mandated that no U.S. merchant ship was to be abandoned as long as its guns could be served.

"During our Revolution, the War of 1812, the Mexican War, the Civil War, and in World War I, no such orders were ever issued. During the early years of our nation, masters of privateers, although authorized to arm, attack and seize the enemy's shipping, were allowed a complete freedom of choice. The decision to fight and perhaps die in the process was left up to them. In World War II, no choice was allowed."

Finally. January 19, 1988. Perhaps it should have been called V-Day for U.S. World War II mariners, because it's the date they were finally conferred veteran status - as long as they served aboard ocean-going merchant ships in World War II.

Edward C. Aldridge Jr., Secretary of the Air Force, decided that those who had served on such ships between December 7, 1941 and August 15, 1945 would be considered "active duty".

The record indicates that he was acting on a recommendation from the U.S. Department of Defense's Civilian/Military Service Review Board.

It was a victory in a particularly long, hard-fought battle.

In his National Maritime Day Proclamation that year, President Ronald Reagan stated, "The importance of the merchant marine to our national defense was never more clear than in World War II when, at a cost of more than 6,000 lives and with a loss of 733 ships, the American merchant marine never faltered in delivering cargo for our Armed Forces throughout the world."

"After 43 years we became veterans so we can have a plot in a military cemetery," wryly observes Joseph Vernick, president of USMMVWWII.

But Vernick was working diligently -

with John O. Smith, the organization's first vice president and Dan Rapaport, secretary - to make sure a more lasting memorial would be forthcoming. (See chapter on *Lane Victory*.)

American Merchant Mariners' Memorial

Few statues have a history as rich in human pathos as that of the American Merchant Mariners' Memorial, anchored in the waters of New York Harbor off Battery Park.

Seven castaways were photographed in a life raft by the Germans who had sunk their ship, then left to perish. Their photo, published in a national German magazine, was discovered and clipped by an American merchant seaman who was a P.O.W. of the Germans at the time, George William Duffy. [See Folder 4, #11 for photo.]

Duffy managed to get the photograph when he was a captive of Captain von Zatorsky on the *Uckermark*, a German supply tanker. The tanker's captain had himself been a P.O.W. - during World War I - so was sensitive to the plight of the Americans aboard, who were permitted to play checkers, chess and cards, and to read old copies of German books and magazines.

Here is Duffy's story about the mysterious photograph.

Mariners' Memorial: Preserving Castaways' Photo for Posterity
By George William Duffy

One day I was skimming through a copy of "Berliner Illustrierte Zeitung," issue 27 of 1942. Interestingly, I came across a photo essay of the sinking of an American oil tanker by a German submarine. This was the sort of slick little weekly that we get with our Sunday papers today.

One of the published photos showed seven survivors of this tanker, all of whom were quite visible and perhaps identifiable. So, in the naivete that age 20 affords, believing that war would not last too long, and thinking that these seven fellows would someday appreciate seeing themselves after being sent scrambling for their lives, I tore the page out, folded it and hid it with my meager belongings.

In 1945, when I was repatriated to the United States, that newspaper page had survived with me! Efforts were made at that time to identify these castaways, but without success. In the mid-1970s, the photo of the men was published in several <u>Port of Boston Handbooks</u> which I edited, and also in the Massachusetts Maritime Academy Alumni Association's "Bulletin." Ultimately, in the early 1980s, Captain Arthur R. Moore, then in the process of producing his monumental <u>A Careless Word ... A Needless Sinking</u>, contacted me. In short order, it was determined that these fellows had been in the U.S. tanker *Muskogee*, which was lost with all hands in March 1942.

ALL HANDS!

And here I had in my files for over 40 years a picture of seven of her crew, taken from the U-123 which had torpedoed her ship and left them to perish in the North Atlantic Ocean!

Captain Moore published all of the German photographs in his book, and it is now possible that two names may be placed under two of the faces. I have not, however, personally seen the evidence to substantiate these claims. Positive identification is at hand, though, of the man in the center of the group of seven. This fellow was the *Muskogee's* chief mate, Morgan John Finucane of Fall River, Mass.

Curiously, Finucane graduated from the Massachusetts Nautical School in 1928 - 13 years prior to my graduation from the same school. This connection eventually led me to snapshots and a yearbook photo of that era.

While Moore and I - and others - were trying to solve the riddle of the raft and its seven unfortunate occupants, another group of people in New York City had created a corporation for the purpose of erecting a memorial to all merchant seamen who had been lost at sea in peacetime or in war in the history of this country.

An Arts Advisory Committee, headed by Charles Dana Gibson of Camden, Maine, eventually chose as the theme and the inspiratic for the proposed memorial the picture of the seven castaways.

"It is the starkest portrayal ever caught on film depicting the toll the sea can extract from a ship's company. It is a circumstance that spans the ages," Gibson wrote.

On October 8, 1991, in the waters of New York harbor just off Battery Park, a bronze sculpture by the famed artist Marisol was unveiled before a large crowd of Merchant Marine veterans, industry leaders, labor leaders, family members, next-of-kin

SS Lane Victory. Above with tugs alongside heading to drydock. Right, out of the past, ready for the future.

of deceased seamen, clergymen of three denominations and, most fittingly, before me, George William Duffy, who had the foresight, intuitiveness and probably the gumption to save the German news page which became the marvelous and impressively thought-provoking American Merchant Mariners' Memorial.

Finding Inspiration from the Sea

The beauty and majesty of the ocean, the adventure and intrigue of the sea, all conspire to incite creativity. Merchant mariners often have the idle time at sea, the inspiration and the inclination to produce songs, poems, paintings and crafts. Letters home have conveyed significant meaning and deep feelings.

Jack Butcher (a.k.a. "Square Knot Jack") took a seaman's utilitarian knowledge and turned it into an art form.

The "NMU Pilot" of April 1983 describes Butcher's handiwork, which was on display at the Green Rooster saloon near 23rd Street and Seventh Avenue in New York.

Butcher started shipping on U.S. ships in 1942, after a stint in the British merchant navy.

Although he sailed on the deadly Murmansk run to Russia in World War II, and sailed in the Korean and Vietnam wars, he escaped all areas of conflict "with nary a scratch."

"Jack is one of a dwindling breed of seamen whose career spans the old days of tar, hemp and manila rope and the new high technology ships such as the LNG (liquified natural gas) carriers," the "Pilot" wrote.

Butcher used his considerable marlinspike skills to create decorative knot boards that display knots with names as intriguing as the knots are attractive. There are rose knots, a star knot, ship's bell, carrick bend, wheel knot, four blade screw, monkey fist, Tom Fools knot, Chinese ceremonial knot, handcuff hitch, Turk's Heads, a bowline on the bight, reef knot, eye splice, short splice, sheepshank, Japanese bowline and a sailor's breast plate (from the days sailors wore heavy woven rope mats to protect themselves against cannon grape shot.)

Ship's captains are among the customers who have bought the rope boards, some of which use gold metallic cord.

Another creative outlet for the inspiration of the sea is painting. Jerry McClish of Bradenton, Fla. has converted his natural talent and love for the sea into a thriving profession as an artist.

President of the International Society of Marine Painters, McClish works in watercolor and oil. "Doing sketches of native sailboats complimented by the translucent and sometimes totally transparent water inspired me to paint watercolor," he said.

"The portrayal of any work of art on paper or canvas is a challenge that requires inspiration, dedication and much work. While living a carefree life on my sailboat in the Bahamas several years ago, it occurred to me that I was in Homer country so why not resume the art career that had been put aside more years than I care to remember."

Now McClish has a drawing class on public television, and has conducted workshops in 20 states, as well as Europe and the Bahamas. He has also written instructional books on drawing and painting.

One of McClish's works is a painting of the *S.S. Lane Victory*, which is on sale at the ship's museum shop. His work is also on display in the Boston Marine Gallery, the Boston State House and the Kings Point Merchant Marine Gallery.

Writing is another way mariners try to capture the depth of feelings that they experience about their seagoing careers. Flare Fredricksen of Plymouth, Wisconsin is a prolific poet who evokes both the grit and glory of life at sea. This is one of his offerings:

Wanderlust

I grow tired of the reeking docks
and the filth clogged water
that smells of land.

And the smoke-filled skies,
and the buildings rise -
My heart yearns for the seas.

The clouds won't have to be
the cleanest white,
nor the sky the clearest blue.

As long as the salt is in the air
and the lubbers line
points true,

To wherever the wind
and the tide, may carry
this restless soul of mine.

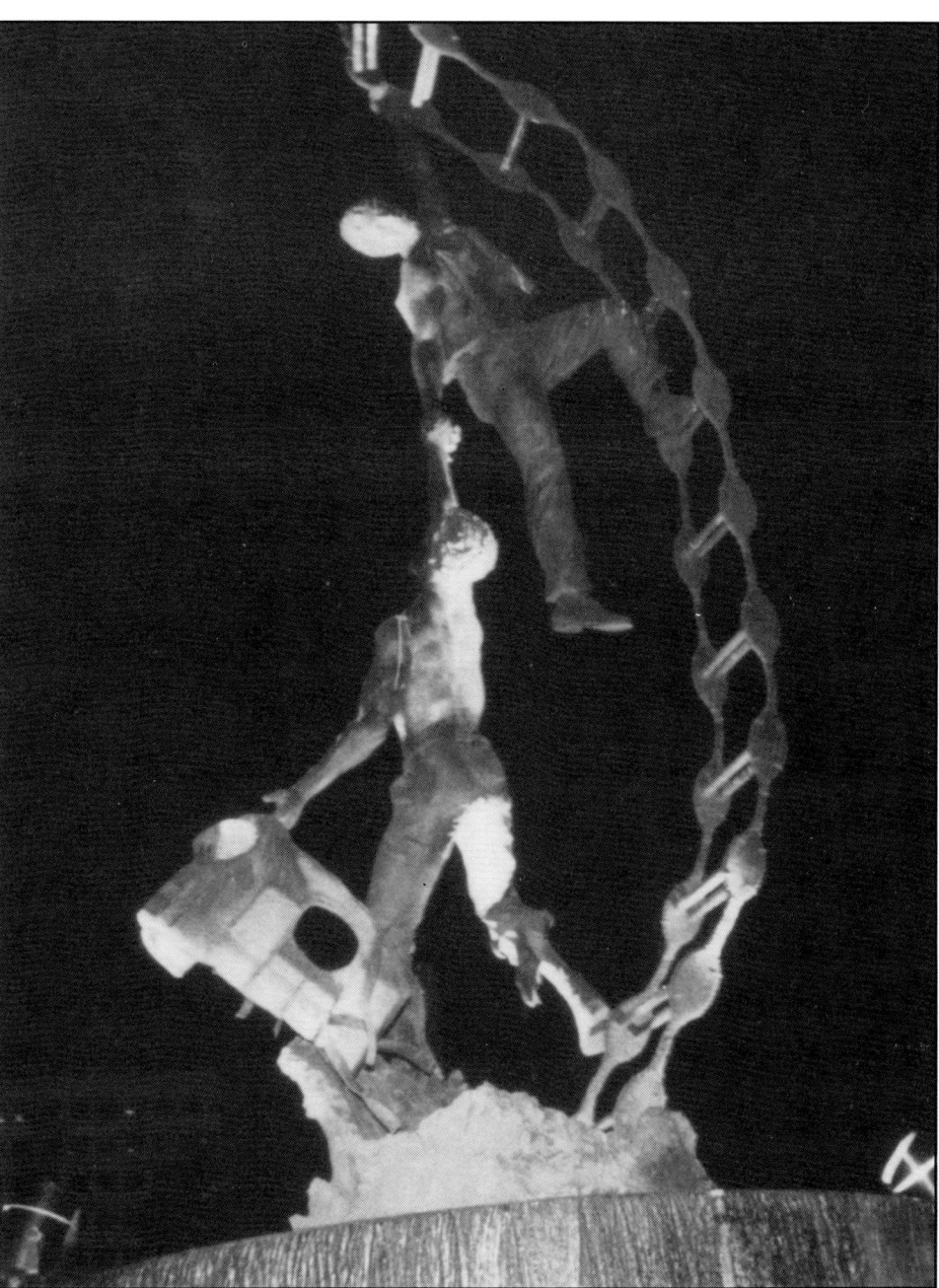

Merchant Marine Memorial WorldPort, L.A., San Pedro, CA.

Doing Good Deeds for Fellow Man

Veteran mariner Frank Liberatore of Winter Park, Fla. is one of the American veterans who has been working to help Chi Hsii "Charlie Two Shoes" Tsui in his efforts to become an American citizen.

"Charlie" was an 11-year-old when he and the 6th Marine Division got together in China in 1945, according to an article in the Fall 1991 issue of the "CBIVA Sound-Off."

The Marines adopted Charlie - feeding and clothing him and sending him to school. They were unable to bring him home with them at the end of the war. But Tsui never forgot the Americans' kindness.

In 1962 he was stripped of his citizenship, placed under house arrest and lost his job when he refused to join an anti-American campaign. By 1980, though, U.S. relations with China had improved. Tsui began writing to his American friends and three years later he came here to visit the people who had helped him 35 years before.

They banded together to help him again. In 1985 he was granted an indefinite stay of deportation, and permitted to bring his family to the U.S. Tsiu, his wife and three children live in the Chapel Hill, N.C. where they own and operate a restaurant.

Liberatore was among those who petitioned Congress to grant Tsiu's family permanent residency status. They succeeded in 1992. Now citizenship is being sought.

Liberatore's efforts, and those of countless other mariners on behalf of their fellow man, show how a seaman's life touches the lives of many others.

Joseph DiMattina, who sailed in World War II soon after recovering from tuberculosis because of the shortage of skilled seamen, reminded mariners of this fact in an article he wrote for the "NMU Pilot" in July 1977 called "Ambassadors in Shirt Sleeves."

"During wartime, merchant seamen not only 'Delivered the Goods' and 'Kept 'Em Sailing,' but they helped the civilians ashore in whatever country they happened to be."

Whether it was offering left-over food to the French in early 1945, or carrying contributed clothing to the people of Bremerhaven, Germany after the war, DiMattina participated in - and witnessed - acts of generosity and kindness from his fellow mariners. He saw it again in the Korean War, when clothing was donated to an orphanage in Inchon.

"Wherever you go in this world, remember that you are often the only example of an American that people see. If you can do some kindness, do it. But a base act never! Always be a fine 'Ambassador in Shirt Sleeves,' the kind of person your country deserves."

Women of the Merchant Marines

While men have dominated the Merchant Marines for years, women have "surfaced" now and then in the seafaring tradition.

A biography called "Captain Mary", published by the Kings Point Merchant Marine Museum, tells the story of an unusual woman who took to the seas and taught navigation during the war.

The book, which is summarized by Francis J. Walsh Jr. in the July 1992 "Anchor Light," details the life of Mary Parker Converse, who earned a master's license for steam and motor vessels from the U.S. Department of Commerce.

Born in 1872, she was a society matron who, as the wife of a wealthy shoe manufacturer, raised their five children. But then her life took an unusual course. Her marriage ended in an era when divorce was rare. When her husband died later, she was left in comfortable circumstances.

Living in Denver, Colorado, Mary felt the call of the sea, and a need to "be worthy". She satisfied both needs by signing on as an unpaid apprentice, traveling aboard various ocean-going vessels. Shortly before the U.S. entered World War II, she passed her government examination and received her master's license.

She never served as an officer at sea. But at the request of the Navy, Mary set up a school in her Denver home during the war to provide navigation training to V-7 program candidates and other maritime trainees. She received much acclaim and media attention for her unconventional activity.

In 1961, she died in California at the age of 89.

Edna Doyle Liberatore, now of Winter Park, Fla. and Mary Jones made headlines on Christmas Day, 1968 when they were profiled as "bona fide ordinary seamen, entitled to sail on the deck of any seagoing vessel."

The article, which appeared in the "Newark (N.J.) Star-Ledger", pointed out that each is an accredited wiper. And they both passed the Coast Guard test for "lifeboatman", so they are qualified to man the oars, serve as coxswains on the tiller or handle the lines, blocks and davits of any lifeboat used by a ship to carry away its crew and passengers in the event of a sinking.

The two women were sailing as waitresses aboard the Grace Lines passenger ship *Santa Paula*, a job they held since joining the Merchant Marine in 1957.

"We can rig a bo's'n's chair and stage and ladder. We can tie all knots. We can make the short splice and the long splice and we can paint and we can chip," Liberatore told the reporter at the time.

For her part, Jones chimed in: "And we studied navigation, attended safety meetings and we can work the winches and haul the lines, too."

The two women earned their sea status after the Coast Guard came aboard the *Santa Paula* in New York to make a movie while giving the crew its quarterly tests. The Coast Guardsmen thought it would be fun to have women in the lifeboat for that drill, so the ship's captain referred them to the two waitresses, and suggested they join the boat crew.

The Coast Guard "probably tongue-in-cheek" told the women they could be accredited as lifeboatmen if they passed the standard tests. Much to everyone's surprise, the women took the Coast Guard at their word, went for the tests and received accreditation.

"As long as we were there, we asked to get endorsements as ordinary seamen and wipers, which doesn't call for any special qualification," Liberatore said.

It took a little arm-twisting to get the Coast Guard officer to go along with that, but his superiors advised him he should give them the endorsements.

PRESERVING THE LEGACY: Museum Ships for the Merchant Mariners

For those who have never sailed on one, it is difficult to imagine the majesty of a ship or to understand the human history that made it come alive.

There is nothing like stepping aboard to understand and absorb not only the sights, but the sounds and the smell and the feel that make a ship a special place.

Thanks to the efforts of tireless volunteers, people who love ships and the legacy that they contain, it is possible to visit three World War II-era ships in the U.S. and get a taste of how the war was won.

The S.S. Jeremiah O'Brien: Liberty Ship Museum in San Francisco

The *S.S. Jeremiah O'Brien* is a Liberty ship that was built in 57 days in 1943 at the New England Ship-building Corporation yards in South Portland, Me. During World War II, the *O'Brien* made seven voyages, operating in both the Atlantic and the Pacific theatres, from Omaha beach to Calcutta.

The *O'Brien* was named for a Scotch-Irish lumberjack from Machias. He commanded a merchant ship that captured the first British Navy vessel in the Revolutionary War's first naval battle on June 12, 1776.

One of 2,750 identical Liberty Ships, the *O'Brien* was intended to last just for the duration of the war. She has demonstrated a much greater longevity.

Liberties were built by shipyard workers who had little experience and sailed by crews who had limited sea time. Most of the workers and sailors were taught their trade during the war.

Former crewmen report that the *O'Brien's* gunners engaged enemy aircraft during the Normandy campaign, and that she was the possible target of at least two bomb attacks and one torpedo. During the first days and weeks after D-Day, she visited the hazardous beachhead 11 times carrying vital weapons and supplies.

On her last voyage, from July 1945 to January 1946, the *O'Brien* stopped in Australia, Calcutta, Shanghai and Manila before returning to San Francisco. She brought 11 Australian war brides to join their American husbands. Since there were no passenger accommodations on board, the women used a vacant gunner's quarters in the after deck as a dormitory.

At the end of the war, she the *O'Brien*

was mothballed in Suisun Bay for 33 years prior to being saved as a memorial.

Her initial rescue came in 1962 by Admiral Tom Patterson, wjp was on special assignment surveying Liberty ships for the Maritime Administration.

He was checking 15 a day to decide which would be the first to be scrapped. When he saw the *O'Brien*., Patterson realized she has different. He explained his sentiments to writer Walter Jaffee: "She was completely unaltered... All the charts were there, from Normandy to the Pacific. The glass was intact in the license frames on the bulkhead. The wartime instructions were posted alongside the Mark XIV gyro. The station bill signed by the captain was in the right place. The captain's night order book at Normandy beach was in a desk drawer.

"There were only minor indents in the *Jeremiah O'Brien's* plating and little hull pitting. The blueprints of the ship were mounted in the passageway abaft, the wheelhouse intact. The oak joiner work throughout her quarters was beautiful to behold. The ship was a time capsule."

Not knowing what he could do with the *O'Brien*, Patterson nonetheless put her name at the bottom of the scrap list, designating her the "least desirable for sale." Keeping her from being tapped for sale or spare parts, Patterson eventually pulled together a group of people who had an interest in preserving the ship.

Volunteers went to work making the rusty, dirty old ship look and run like new. It was steamed to a shipyard in San Francisco under its own power, restored and docked at Fort Mason. As of June 1993, more than 425,000 hours of work have been donated by the unpaid crew to keep her fit and seaworthy for cruises.

The *O'Brien* now serves as a living tribute to the men and women who built and sailed such ships. Owned by the U.S. government, she is under the authority of the Maritime Administration, which had the foresight to save her from the scrapyard. She is associated with the San Francisco Maritime National Historical Park.

Saving the *S.S. Lane Victory*: A Victory for Merchant Marines' World War II Veterans

The *S.S. Lane Victory* is a Victory ship that was named after Isaac Lane, a self-educated ex-slave who became an Episcopal Bishop and founded Lane College, in Jackson, Tennessee, in 1882. His granddaughter christened the ship, which was built in 1945 at the California Shipbuilding Company in San Pedro, Calif. The ship was operated by American President Lines for many years, then by Pacific Coast Transport Co.

Besides transporting military cargo in World War II, Korea and Vietnam, she also transported Korean refugees and Korean prisoners of war. The *Lane Victory* sailed in peacetime carrying commercial cargo around the world.

The ship was repainted gray, and

LANE COLLEGE HONORED BY MERCHANT MARINE TIES

"Lane College, from its beginning, has served as a source of inspiration for the youth of the CME Church. Today it stands as a symbol of Christian education for youth of all faiths, creeds, colors and nationalities.

One of the great honors attributed to this College was that of having a Liberty ship named after its founder, Bishop Isaac Lane. Liberty ships were the pride of the United States Merchant Marine. These ships were used to transport men, materials and foodstuffs to the war front during the Second World War and Korean War . . .

Those of us who are alumni of Lane College look with pride upon the SS Lane Victory. It is "our" ship and we beam with an abundance of vainglory when she is honored. Lane College and its administration will continue to be part of the SS Lane Victory family. its history is, and will continue to be, inextricably interwoven into the fabric of our history."

Arthur L. David, PhD, Interim President, 1992

Joe Johnson, Personnel dept.; Anne R. Cooke, historian, and George Thacker, Registrat at founder's grave.

Frank and Edna Doyle Libertore at founder's grave.

mothballed in 1970 at Suisun Bay, San Francisco, California. There the ship was a member of the Reserve Fleet until being donated to United States Merchant Marine Veterans of World War II (USMMVWWII) by an Act of Congress in 1988. On October 18, President Ronald Reagan signed the bill conveying the ship to the organization.

When she was towed 400 miles from Northern California to her current home in 1989, the *Lane Victory* almost was not permitted into Los Angeles harbor because prior approval to give her a berth had not been granted.

But using the same resourcefulness that got them the ship in the first place, the veterans stuck to their guns - and continued full steam ahead. They have been back and forth with the Harbor Commission, but it seems the *Lane Victory* will be berthed in San Pedro for the forseeable future.

Ask John Smith how they got through it all and came out with a ship and a place to put her, and he has a succinct, three-word response: "Bluff, luck and guts."

Since all other Victory ships are to be scrapped by 1995, the *Lane* promises to be the last Victory. She measures 455 feet long, 62 feet wide and 28 feet draft. With five cargo holds, she weighs in at 10,750 deadweight tons. Fuel consumption per day is about 40 tons.

The *Lane Victory* is a museum ship and living memorial. In 1990 she was granted the National Historic Landmark designation.

Besides being a frequent location of filming for television shows and movies, the *Lane Victory* is a popular tourist attraction that makes day cruises to Catalina Island several times a year.

Part of the excitement is that the ship comes under mock attack by Nazi airplanes to evoke the feeling - if not the fear - of its wartime service.

The *S.S. John W. Brown*: Restoring Liberty Ship in Baltimore

Moored two miles east of Baltimore's Inner Harbor is the *S.S. John W. Brown*, the last of three Liberty ships launched in special Labor Day ceremonies at Bethlehem Fairfield Shipyard.

It was in this same Baltimore shipyard that FDR made his Liberty Fleet Day address in September 1941 at the launch of the first Liberty ship, the *S.S. Patrick Henry*. And it was this Baltimore shipyard that built 384 Liberty ships, the most of any shipyard, according to "S.S. John W. Brown: Baltimore's Living Liberty", a 1991 booklet written by Sherod Cooper and published by Project Liberty Ship, which is restoring the *Brown*.

The *Brown* slid down the ways into the Patapsco River at 1215 on 7 September 1942, 42 days after her keel had been laid and seven months ahead of schedule. Few vessels in history have had as long a record of continuous service in war and peace as the *Brown*, which was named after an early 20th century labor leader.

She saw action at the legendary Anzio beachhead, came under fire during the invasion of the South of France, and braved mines, storms and submarines as she carried cargoes to Europe and the Middle East. During one trip, she carried 151 Royal Navy sailors and officers who were survivors of a torpedoed ship on their way home for reassignment. On the way back, she brought 500 German P.O.W.s from Field Marshall Erwin Rommel's Afrika Corps.

February 21, 1944 was probably the most hair-raising in the Brown's history. The Liberty ships *S.S. Peter Skene Ogden*, some 500 yards ahead of her, and the *S.S. George Cleeve*, some 850 yards off her starboard bow, were torpedoed. Both vessels were total losses and had to be beached.

Some five months later, the ship's routine was disrupted for a celebration in recognition of a visit to the Naples harbor by King George VI of England. The merchant crew strung a line of flags from the bow to the tops of the foremast, mainmast and mizzenmast to the stern, and the gun crew mustered at their stations in dress whites.

Leaving the Bay of Naples on July 29, she passed a British destroyer on which Prime Minister Winston Churchill stood, waving a "V" sign to the men on the ships departing for the invasion of Southern France. On August 17, the *Brown* experienced six alerts, but was not attacked.

Returning to Naples in convoy, she picked up 500 P.O.W.s and 33 guards bound for Hampton Roads. The *Brown* continued her voyages - the only blip coming from problems with her port boiler, which was

SS Jeremiah O'Brien, Liberty museum ship.

repaired. She arrived in England on V-E Day.

The *Brown* completed her post-war voyages in 1946, then she was loaned to the City of New York for educational purposes. She became an annex of the Maritime Department of the Metropolitan Vocational High School - later the Food and Maritime High School, and finally Park West High School.

She was berthed in the East River until 1967, when she was moved to a spot on the Hudson River for the rest of her life as a schoolship. Students learned about deck, engine and steward's department roles, as well as radio operation, the duties of the purser and boat building. They learned how to swing out and lower lifeboats, and how to handle them under oars and sail.

When the class of 1982 graduated, the Board of Education chose to retain a more traditional classroom environment, and to return the *Brown* to the U.S. government.

Four years earlier, a group had formed to preserve the *Brown* when she was no longer needed for education. Ultimately, the *Brown* found a home not in New York, but in the Port of Baltimore. She was re-dedicated there on Labor Day 1988.

Home to the Museum of the Naval Armed Guard and numerous other displays, the *Brown* is a living, steaming tribute to the men who served, and died, in the Second World War.

Normandy 1994 - Mariners Prepare for Historic 50th Anniversary Voyage

Many things in life seem to come full circle. For Merchant Marine veterans, the opportunity to participate in the 1994 Normandy Convoy represents a huge circle spanning 50 years.

The convoy, comprised of the *S.S. Jeremiah O'Brien*, the *S.S. John W. Brown* and the *S.S. Lane Victory*, will gather on the East Coast and travel to France to commemorate the Normandy Invasion.

The two West Coast ships, having much farther to travel, will leave their respective ports in April 1994 for the trip around to the East Coast, meeting the *Brown* in New York for a celebration before beginning their trans-Atlantic voyage.

In mid-May under Naval escort, the convoy will steam to Halifax to pick up a Canadian naval escort, then continue across the Atlantic to Southampton, where more festivities will await.

The big event will be the trip across the English Channel to Normandy, arriving the morning of June 6 where massive commemoration activities are planned. The Army will stage a jump by airborne divisions that participated in the invasion and Rangers will scale the cliffs at Point du Hoc.

Lying just offshore will be the three U.S. ships, symbolizing the greatest naval armada in history. Amphibious troops will re-enact the landings at the various beaches and restored military vehicles will be displayed by the hundreds.

After the Normandy ceremonies conclude, the ships will visit 45 European ports - both on the Continent and in the United Kingdom - throughout the summer months. Each ship will carry in her tween decks a U.S. Trade Show of products.

It will cost $5 million total (about $1.7 million per ship) to make the ships ocean seaworthy, purchase fuel, stores, insurance and to cover associated costs. All three ships will have to drydock for repairs before the trip.

AMERICA WORKS*Normandy '94 will raise most of the money by getting sponsorships - goods, services and money - from major corporations. A bill introduced to Congress in January 1993 would provide each ship with $700,000 by scrapping some 50-year-old Victory ships and turning the proceeds over to each of them.

Crew members - no more than 60 per ship - all will be volunteers, taken from the ranks of membership. Since the voyage will last six months, provisions are being made to change crew members at specified points. No passengers will be carried on the trans-Atlantic leg of the voyage. However each ship will carry 800 passengers across the channel to the Normandy beachhead.

In a pamphlet outlining the convoy, one page poses the question, "Why Do It At All?" The response is an all-encompassing one, reflecting seamens' attitudes that have spanned the ages.

"We always say that these fine old ships are a celebration of the American Spirit, that Can Do attitude that accomplished miracles during World War II when, in our country's darkest hour, its citizens rose to their greatest triumphs and government and industry cooperated as never before.

"This trip will demonstrate to the world that this spirit still lives today."

SS Lane Victory, restored.

SELECTED BIBIOGRAPHY

A Careless Word - A Needless Sinking, by Capt. Arthur R. Moore. Published by American Merchant Marine Museum at the U.S. Merchant Marine Academy, Kings Point, N.Y., First published 1983, fifth edition 1990.
An exhaustive documentation of the catastrophic losses suffered by the American flag Merchant Fleet, both in ships and personnel, during World War II.

A History of Ships and Seafaring, by Canby Courtlandt. Published by Hawthorn Books, New York, 1963.

A Maritime History of the United States: the Role of America's Seas and Waterways, 1st edition, by K. Jack Bauer. Published by University of South Carolina Press, Columbia, S.C., c1988. Series: Studies in Maritime History

American Merchant Ships, 1850-1900, by Frederick C. Matthews. Published by Marine Research Society, Salem, Mass., 1930.

American Sail, a Pictorial History, 1st edition, by Alexander Kinnan Laing. Published by Dutton, New York, 1961.

Americans Who Have Contributed to the History and Traditions of the United States Merchant Marine, by US Merchant Marine Cadet Corps. Published by US Merchant Marine Cadet Corps, Kings Point, N.Y., 1943.

America Sails the Seas: the History and Romance of America on the High Seas from the 15th to the 19th Century, by Frank Charles Bowen. Published by R.M. McBride and Co., New York, 1938.

America's Maritime History, by Archibald Campbell Denison. Published by Putnam's, New York, 1944.

America's Maritime Legacy: a History of the U.S. Merchant Marine and Shipbuilding Industry Since Colonial Times, edited by Robert A Kilmarx with contributors Lawrence C. Allin...[et. al.] Published by Westview Press, Boulder, Colo., 1979. Series: A Westview Special Study.

A Million Ocean Miles, by Edgar T. Britten. Published by P. Stephens. Distributed by Sterling Pub. Co., New York, 1989.

Battle of the Oceans, by William Edward Bennett. Published by Liveright, 1944.

Captain Fraser's Voyages, 1865-1892, by Thomas Garry Fraser. Published by Norton, c1979.

Captain Mary, by Mary Allen Converse. Published by Kings Point Merchant Marine Museum, 1987.

The Colonial Clippers, by Basil Lubbock. Published by Brown, Son, and Ferguson, Glasgow, c1968.

Conquest of the Seas: the History and Adventure of Sea Ships, by Frank Charles Bowen. Published by McBride, New York, c1940.

Deep Water Days, by Oliver G. Swan. Published by Macrae, 1929.

Dynamite Cargo - Convoy to Russia, by Frederick Sawyer Herman. Published by Vanguard, 1943.

Eastward the Convoys, by William Greenough Schofield. Published by Rand McNally, Chicago, 1965.

Famous American Ships: Being an Historical Sketch of the United States As Told Through Its Maritime Life, by Frank Osborn Braynard. Published by Hastings House, New York, c1956.
German and Japanese submarine operations on the East and West coasts of the US in 1942 and our merchant marine's struggle against them.

Fire on the Beaches, by Theodore Taylor. Published by Norton, 1958.

The Flight from the Flag: the Continuing Effect of the Civil War Upon the American Carrying Trade, by George W. Dalzell. Publishedb y the University of North Carolina Press, Chapel Hill, c1940.

Great Ships Around the World, by Penrose Scull. Published by Ziff-Davis, New York, c1960.

Greyhounds of the Sea: the Story of the American Clipper Ship, by Carl C. Cutler. Published by the US Naval Institute, Annapolis, Md., c1960.

In the Days of the Tall Ships, by R.A. Fletcher. Published by Breatands, New York, 1928.

The Invisible Billionare, Daniel Ludwig, by Jerry Shields. Published by Houghton Mifflin, Boston, c1986.

The Last of the Windjammers, by Alfred Basil Lubbock. Published by Charles E. Lauriat Company, Boston, 1927.

The Last Victory: The Life and Times of a United States Victory Ship, 1945-1992, by Walter W. Jaffee. Published by United States Merchant Marine Veterans of World War II, 1991.
Documents ship, from its building, through service in World War II, Korean War and Vietnam, and its rescue and refurbishing to become a world-class museum ship and memorial.

The Last Voyage of the Quien Sabe, by Lars Skattebol. Published by Harper & Brothers, New York, 1944.
Survivor of ship torpedoed by German submarine on return trip from Africa tells the tale.

Lewis and Dryden's Marine History of the Pacific Northwest: an Illustrated Review of the Growth and Development of the Maritime Industry, from the Advent of the Earliest Navigators t o the Present Time, by E.W. Wright. Published by Superior Pub., Seattle, Wash., 1967. With sketches and portraits of a number of well known marine men.

Liberty Ships, the Ugly Ducklings of World War II, by John Bunker. Published by the Naval Institute Press, Annapolis, 1972.

Lifeline, by Robert Carse. Published by Morrow, 1943. The ships and men of our merchant marine at war.

Long Haul, the United States Merchant Service in World War II, by Robert Carse. Published by Norton, 1965.

Lucky Penny, by Harry Schorsch. Published by Eldonna Lay and Associates, El Cajon, CA, c1991.

The Mercantile Marine, by E. Keble Chatterton. Published by Little, Brown, Boston, 1923.

Merchant Sail, by William Armstrong Fairburn. Published by Fairburn Marine Educational Foundation, Center Lovell, Maine, 1945-1955.

Merchant Ships of the World: Being an Illustrated Descriptive Annual of the World's Merchant Ships, edited by Frank C. Bowen and F.J.N. Wedge. Published by Sampson Low, London, 1923.

Merchant Steam Vessels of the United States, 1790-1868, by William M. Lytle. Revised and edited by C. Bradford Mitchell with the assistance of Kenneth R. Hall. Published by the Steamship Historical Society of America. Distributed by the University of

Baltimore Press, Staten Island, N.Y., 1975.
"The Lytle-Holdcamper list," initially compiled from official merchant marine documents of the United States and other sources.

Naval and Maritime History: an Annotated Bibliography, 4th edition, by Robert Greenhalgh Albion. Published by Munson Institute of American Maritime History, Conn., 1972.

Ocean Traders: from the Portuguese Discoveries to the Present Day, by Michael W. Marshall. Published by Facts on File, New York, c1990.

The Old Merchant Marine: a Chronicle of American Ships and Sailors, by Ralph Delahaye Paine. Published by Yale University Press, New Haven, 1919. Series: Chronicles of America Series. V. 36.

Operation Drumbeat: The Dramatic True Story of Germany's First U-Boat Attacks Along the American Coast in World War II by Michael Gannon, Harper & Row Publishers, New York, 1990.

The Ordeal of Convoy NY 119, by Charles Dana Gibson. Published by Ensign Press, P.O. Box 638, Camden, ME 04843, in 1973. (Still available by writing to publishers.)
Narrative history of a convoy of seagoing tugs, harbor tugs, yard tankers and barges owned by the US Army, left New York bound for England.

The Pacific Coast Maritime Shipping Industry, 1930-1948, by Wytze Gorter. Published by University of California Press, Berkeley, 1952-54.

Pictorial History of American Ships: On the High Seas and Inland Waters, by John Durant. Published by Barnes, New York, 1953.

Purser's Progress by Tom O'Reilly. Published by Doubleday, Doran & Co. Inc., Garden City, New York, 1944.
Humorous saga of the S.S. Mulligan Stew and its new purser.

Queens of the Western Ocean, by Carl C. Cutler. Published by U.S. Naval Institue, Annapolis, 1961.

The Rise and Decline of US Merchant Shipping in the 20th Century, by Ren'e De La Pedraja Tom'an. Published by Twayne Publishers, New York, Maxwell Macmillan, Canada, Maxwell Macmillan International, New York, 1992. Series: Twayne's Evolution of American Business Series. No. 8.

The Sea and the States; a Maritime History of the American People, by Samuel Wood Bryant. Published by Crowell, New York, 1947. Series: The Growth of America Series.

Seafarers and their Ships: the Story of a Century of Progress in the Safety of Ships and the Well-Being of Seamen. Published by the Philosophical Library, New York, 1956.

Sea Lanes in Wartime, by Robert Greenhalgh Albion. Published by Norton, 1942. Edition: The American Experience.

Sea War; The Story of the U.S. Merchant Marine in World War II, by Felix Riesenberg, Jr., Rinehart & Co. Inc., New York, 1956.

Selected Articles on the American Merchant Marine, by Edith May Phelps. Published by H.W. Wilson, White Plains, N.Y., 1916.

Shanghaiing Days, by Richard H. Dillon. Published by Coward-McCann, 1961.

Ship Recognition: Merchant Ships, by Laurence Dunn. Published by De Graff, New York, 1961.

Ships of the US Merchant Fleet, by John A. Culver. Published by Denison Pr. Distributed by De Graff Distr., Weymouth, Mass., 1965.
Brief listing of representative types of vessels used in passenger, cargo, towboat, and other services, with 113 photographs and descriptive notes.

"The SIU At War," booklet edited by John Bunker, published by the Seafarers International Union of North America, August 1944.

Sole Survivor by Ruthanne Lum McCunn. Published by Design Enterprises of San Francisco, P.O. Box 14675 San Francisco, CA 14675.
Account of Poon Lim's 133 days surviving in the South Pacific on a wood-and oil barrel life raft after sub sank the SS Belmond, on which he was a crew member in 1943.

Square-Riggers on Schedule, by Robert Greenhalgh Albion. Published by University Press, Princeton, 1938. Edition: The New York Sailing Packets to England, France, and the Cotton Ports.

A Statistical Analysis of the World's Merchant Fleets; Showing Age, Size, Speed, and Draft by Frequency Grouping. Published by U.S. Dept. of Commerce, Maritime Administration, Washington, Dec. 1957-.
Includes merchant ships of 1,000 gross tons and over. Excludes ships owned by the military forces. The ships of each country are subdivided into 4 major groups: combination passenger and cargo ships, bulk carriers, tankers, and freighters.

The Story of the American Merchant Marine, by John Randolph Spears. Published by Macmillan, New York, c1915.

The Sway of the Grand Saloon; a Social History fo the North Atlantic, by John Malcolm Brinnin. Published by Delacorte Press, New York, 1971.
"A Seymour Lawrence book."

There Go the Ships, by Robert Carse. Published by Morrow, 1942.
Experiences of a former newspaper reporter who shipped aboard a merchant vessel carrying suplies from the US to Russia.

Trouble on Board: the Plight of the International Seafarers, by Paul K. Chapman. Published by ILR Press, Ithaca, N.Y., c1992.

We'll Deliver, by C. Bradford Mitchell. 1977 United States Merchant Marine Academy Alumni Association, Kings Point, New York.
A full history of the U.S. Merchant Marine Cadet Corps.

The Western Ocean Packets, New Edition, by Alfred Basil Lubbock. Published by Brown, Son, and Ferguson, 1956.

Yankee Ships, an Informal History of the American Merchant Marine, by Reese Wolfe. Published by Bobbs-Merrill, 1953.

Yankee Ships in China Seas; Adventures of Pioneer Americans in the Troubled Far East, by Daniel MacIntyre Henderson. Published by Hastings House, New York, 1946.

Youth and the Sea: Our Merchant Marine Calls American Youth, by John J. Floherty. Published by J.B. Lippincott Company, Philadelphia, New York, 1941.

FOOTNOTES

FOOTNOTES

1 Bunker, John (ed.), "The SIU at War," published by the Seafarers International Union of North America, August 1944, p. 9.
2 Ibid.
3 Moore, Capt. Arthur R., A Careless Word ... A Needless Sinking, published by the American Merchant Marine Museum at the U.S. Merchant Marine Academy, Kings Point, N.Y., fifth edition 1990, p. 334.
4 Ibid, p. 227.
5 Ibid.
6 Joseph Vernick's story is based on a personal interview with him and the account he gave to Walter W. Jaffee, as told in The Last Victory: The Life and Times of a United States Victory Ship, 1945-1992, published by the United States Merchant Marine Veterans World War II, San Pedro, Calif., 1991, pp. 221-229.
7 Jaffee, ibid, p. 224.
8 Ibid, p. 228.
9 Bunker, "A Nazi Trick Got the Venore", ibid, p. 7.
10 Gannon, Michael, Operation Drumbeat: The Dramatic True Story of Germany's First U-Boat Attacks Along the American Coast in World War II, Harper & Row Publishers, New York, 1990, pp. 342-343.
11 Ibid.
12 Ibid, p. 343.
13 Ibid, p. 344.
14 Ibid, p. 345.
15 Bunker, "Death in the Windward Passage," ibid, pp. 26-27.
16 Moore, ibid, p. 28.
17 Bunker, "The Saga of the Biennville," ibid, pp. 29-31.
18 Gannon, ibid, pp. 342-343.
19 Moore, ibid, p. 29.
20 Bunker, "Three Strikes But not 'Out'." ibid, pp. 22-23.
21 Bunker, "Tight Spot!", ibid, p. 23.
22 Moore, ibid, p. 238.
23 Moore, ibid, p. 130.
24 Bunker, ibid, pp. 13-14.
25 Moore, ibid, p. 59.
26 Bunker, "The Story of the Maiden Creek," ibid, pp. 10-11.
27 Moore, ibid, p. 178.
28 Moore, ibid, p. 77.
29 Bunker, "They Saved the Ship," ibid, p. 46.
30 Moore, ibid, pp. 405 and 409.
31 Jaffee, ibid, p. 6.
32 Ibid, p. 10.
33 Bunker, "Action at Anzio," ibic, pp. 25-26.
34 Moore, ibid, pp. 86-87.
35 Moore, ibid, p. 217.
36 Moore, ibid, p. 146-147.
37 Ibid, p. 146.
38 Ibid, pp. 397-398.
39 Jaffee, ibid, p. 97.
40 Ibid, p. 152.
41 Ibid, p. 277.
42 Ibid, p. 159.
43 Ibid, p. 178.
44 Ibid, p. 197.
45 Ibid, pp. 201-202.
46 Ibid, p. 204.

Statue at Massachusetts Maritime Academy, Buzzard's Bay, Mass.

American Merchant Mariner's Memorial

Merchant Marine Photolog

Ed and Ginny Cala, Bob and Betty Gilz at Earl Carol's, Sunset Strip, New Year's Eve, '43. On liberty from Catalina Island,

Volunteers at a merchant seaman's booth in New Orleans, March 1946.

Panama Canal, 1946, from SS Israel Singer.

SS Silas Weir Mitchell, 1946.

SS Stephan T. Mather, Basra, 1943.

Korean Refugees aboard the SS Lane Victory

December 1950, 7009 Korean civilians were transported from Hungnam to Pusan

Sheepshead Bay, 1943.

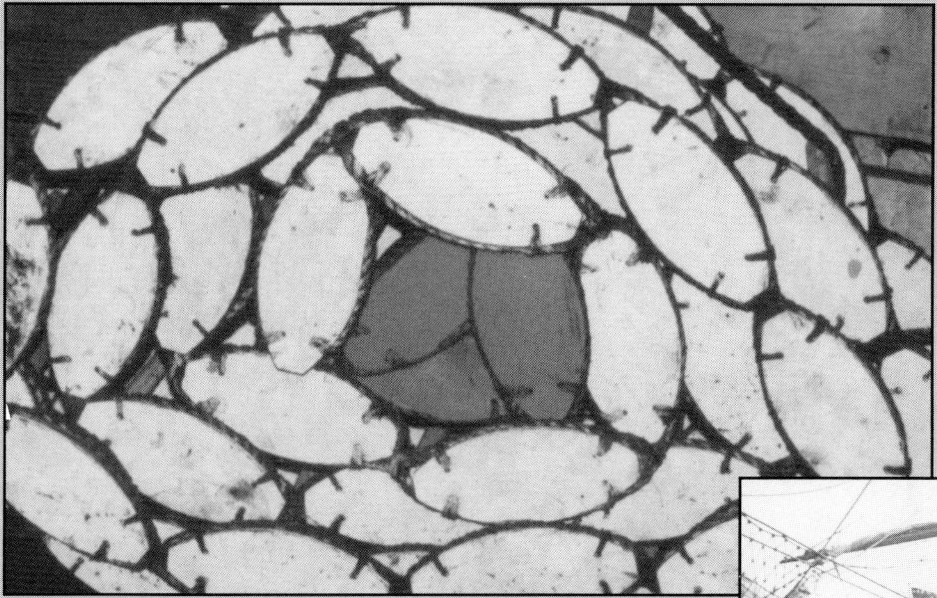

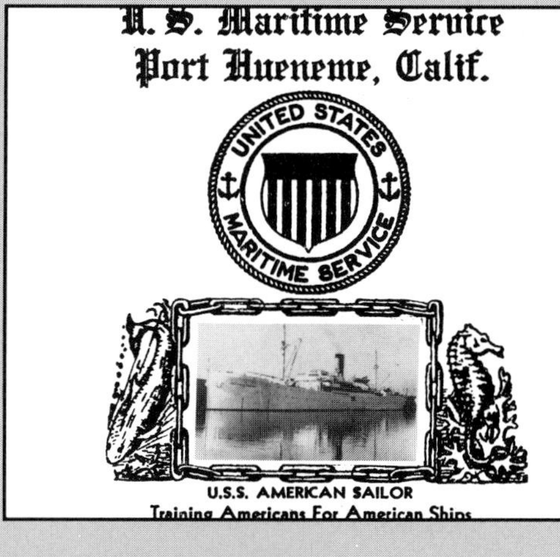

Above, Jacob's Ladder on display on SS Lane Victory. Above right, Training ship card. Right, squarerigger merchant marine training ship, St. Petersburg, FL, 1941.

Crossing the Equator

Clockwise from right SS Occidental; SS Occidental; SS Isaac Singer; Koloa Victory.

After a trip to Liverpool, England, SS Benjamin F. Coston.

Sunset on the Carribean, SS Jeremiah O'Brien

SS Occidental Victory

Sheepshead bay, 1944

U. S. Merchant Marine Veterans

Twelve crew members of MS Ariaga

Dining room personell

CHARLES ACEBO, was born Dec. 5, 1914 in Montpelier, VT. First Acebo born in USA. His parents are Spanish. Graduated San Pedro, CA High School 1934. He joined the Merchant Marines Feb. 27, 1939 in San Pedro, CA.

He served on the *Minnesotan* as wiper, Coastwise (March 1940). Served on *Olopana* O/seaman, Intercoastal (May 20-1940 to Aug. 1, 1940. Served on *Hamakua,* as wiper Intercoastal, Aug. 24, 1940 to Sept. 24, 1940.

Sailed on a Matson freighter to Honolulu. Served with 7th Div. and 63rd (C) Engr., 44th Div. U.S. Army Aug. 20, 1941 to June 23, 1947. ETO (France), longshoreman/marine clerk for 29 years.

His memorable experiences include returning from the East Coast off the Coast of Lower California. He was at the wheel. It was a beautiful day, the ocean was like a mirror. A perfect set-up for day dreaming and that is exactly, what he was doing. Suddenly, in barges, the 1st mate yelling "where in the hell are you going?"

Charles quickly recovered from his trance and realized he was quite a few degrees off course. Heading toward a reef and disaster. (that happened on the *Olopana*. She was a part of convoy PQ 17 and sunk going to Murmansk. (heard on cable TV) either A&E or Discovery Channel how ironic, many lives would have been saved if only he would have been allowed to continue his day dreaming. Then Maybe Not!

His mother, known as (La Montañesa) had one of the first boarding houses for seamen, beginning in the late 1920s through the 1940s, San Pedro, CA.

Retired as a Marine clerk, visiting the victory lane in 1969.

WINFIELD H. ADAM, sailed as chief purser - pharmacist's mate during WWII on SS *Maria Mitchell* from Sept. 9, 1943-April 6, 1944 and on SS *Albina Perez* from Feb. 22, 1945-Aug. 15, 1945.

Has Victory Medal, Honorable Service Button, Presidential Testimonial Letter, Pacific, Atlantic, Mediterranean, Middle East War Zone Bars, Combat Bar with stars, and Merchant Marine Emblem. USCG discharge dated Aug. 15, 1945. Attended Hospital Corps School, Sheepshead's Bay April 24, 1944-Aug. 12, 1944. Is retired captain USCG. Next of kin is wife, Marilyn.

He is a member of AMMV JWB Chapter.

KEISTER N. ADAMS, born Oct. 23, 1932 in Winchester, VA. After high school, he graduated from Virginia Tech (BS) and University of Maryland (MS). He attended the U.S. Merchant Marine Academy basic school in San Mateo, CA and sailed as a cadet midshipman (Engine) on the Cuba Victory to Okinawa in early 1945 and to South America. Later, he served as a junior engineer on the S.S. *Mandarin* to South Africa.

After WWII, he taught school in Virginia and Maryland and was then employed by the U.S. Department of Agriculture until he retired in 1982. He was the deputy administrator for Commodity Operations when he retired and, among other duties, was responsible for purchasing and shipping all of the food commodities provided to foreign countries under Title II of P.L. 480. Thus, he maintained a close relationship with most steamship companies in the booking of ships and transport of commodities overseas and continued his interest in the American Merchant Marine.

He was a member of the Washington, D.C. Propeller Club and is a member of the Annapolis, MD, Kings Point Club. He also belongs to John W. Brown Project Liberty Ship as well as the U.S. Merchant Marine Veterans of World War II.

He resides with his wife Ann in Annapolis, MD.

MARK ADAMS, General counsel and original PLS founding chairman. (TUD O-N 1988, p.4; N p.3).

PERRY R. ADAMS, was born Dec. 10, 1923 in Corona, CA. He joined the Merchant Marine March 1943 at Sheepshead Bay. Assigned to M/V *Forallon* on Nov. 1, 1943 *as* purser/Phm, serving in the Atlantic and Pacific. Left ship on May 10, 1946. He took part in Normany Invasion. Ship towed cement blocks from England to build artificial harbor at Normandy.

When the war ended and the wartime ocean going tugs were taken out of service, he returned to California to return to college. During the next two summers, was able to ship out as purser-Phm. After leaving college went to work with Pacific Far East Line. Sailed as purser-PhM for about 18 months and was then brought ashore as assistant port purser. Was employed by PFEL for the next 26 years. Was then employed by Bulk Food Carriers, a small west coast shipping company as treasurer and chief financial officer. The company was bought out and for the next 10 years, (ending in 1990) headed his own consulting business retiring in 1990.

Has been quite active in American Merchant Marine Veterans in San Francisco. Currently, he puts out the monthly newsletter. He is also writing a book on World War II Merchant Mariners who were awarded the Merchant Marine Distinguished Service Medal or the Merchant Marine Meritorious Service Medal. Hopes to have it published in 1993.

Married and has two children, four grandchildren. Now retired.

ELMER F. ADLER, sailed as 3rd assistant engineer during WWII. Attended Fort Trumbull, New London, CT. Holds Atlantic, Pacific, Mediterranean Middle East War Zone Bars. He is married to Mary. Member of AMMV JWB Chapter.

EUGENE H. AIREY, resides in Baltimore, MD. AMMV charter member JWB Chapter Oct. 14, 1989.

RALPH ALBERS, resides in Falls Church, VA. Graduated from USMS Gallup Island Radio School. Sailed as radio officer aboard the U.S. Army ship *Wistera*. Made the first contact with WSC (Tuckerton, NJ shore station) on 500 kcs. using the *Brown's* main transmitter on May 24, 1992 at the mouth of the Potomac on the way to Alexandria, VA.

Member of Project Liberty Ship, Radio Committee and GIRA.

BENJAMIN F. ALBIZ, resides in Potomac, MD. Sailed as cadet/midshipman-deck, ordinary seaman, able bodied seaman during WWII. Served 32 months (December 1943-August 1946). Has Atlantic and Pacific War Zone Bars and Victory Medal. Attended Sheepshead Bay and Kings Point completing 3rd and 4th class resigning in good standing. Benjamin's next of kin is brother, Paul Ibitz, 1800 Girard Ave., South Minneapolis, MN. He is member of AMMV JWB Chapter.

FRANCIS J. ALLEN, was born Aug. 31, 1923 in Baltimore, MD. He joined the Merchant Marine at Sheepshead Bay, NY in December 1942.

Served on SS *Joseph Stanton* as mess. Stationed around the world, Panama, Australia, Persian Gulf, South Africa, South America and New York, 1943. SS *Herman Winters* coal passer, abandoned at sea, in Atlantic, March 7, 1944. SS *John Murphy,* O.S. United Kingdom, Atlantic, 1944. SS *David Bushnell*, O.S., United Kingdom, SS *James Moore*, AB, North Africa, Italy, France, Atlantic and Mediterranean Sea, 1944, SS *James Pettigrew*, A.B., Mediterranean, SS *Park Holland,* DK maint., Mediterranean, end of war at sea, 1945, SS *Pedro Menandez,* A.B., S. America Cont., *Paul Hamilton Hayne*, Mediterranean, *Pacific Victory*, Bos'n, North Africa Middle East, Trieste, Italy, Portugal, Mediterranean, SS *Cygnet II,* Bos'n, U.K.

Flying Chipper, North Africa, Suez, India, Singapore, China, Japan, Guam, Israel, Italy, SS *Saxon*, North Europe, shuttle between Japan and Korea, Korean War. *Pioneer Wave*, New York, Far East, Borneo, South and East Australia, A.B. *African Dawn West,* South E. Africa. Quit September 1954.

He was a tavern owner for 35 years. Resides in East Baltimore, MD.

GRANT H. ALLEN, was born March 25, 1918 in Dallas, TX. Moved to the West Coast in early 20s and graduated from San Pedro High School 1935. Commenced going to sea on small coastal and harbor vessels 1939. Master of the kelp harvestor "C.L. Argues" 1940/1943. Graduated from U.S. Merchant Marine Officers Candidate School, Alameda, CA, 1944.

Sailed with American Mail Line on SS *Cape Ann* as 3rd mate, 2nd mate and ch. mate during 1944 and 1945. Sailed ch. mate on *Thomas A. Hendricks* and *Ida M. Tarbell* 1945/1946.

Sailed as master on various cargo and miscellaneous vessels 1947-1962.

Joined Global Marine Inc. an offshore industry company, in 1962 in management capacity and retired from same in 19483. Presently resides in San Pedro, CA.

ROBERT S. ALLGAIER, sailed as radio officer during WWII. Attended Sheepshead Bay and Gallups Island. Has three War Zone Bars. He is married to Nancy and they reside in Potomac, MD. He is a member of AMMV JWB Chapter.

PAUL B. ALMQUIST, was born Aug. 18, 1925 in Hastings, MN. He joined the Merchant Marine October 1944 in Minneapolis, MN. He took training at Sheepshead Bay and Hoffman Island, NY, Radio Officers School.

Served on MS *Cape Juby,* as radio operator, stationed in North Pacific, July through October 1945. SS *Sacajawea,* as radio operator, stationed in Pacific, November 1945 through January 1946. SS *Longview Victory,* radio operator, stationed in Pacific, February 1946 through November 1946.

His memorable experiences include being in convoy from Eniwetok to Philippines. Attacked by Jap fighters north of Truk. Seeing destruction in Manila Bay. Greeted by pretty girls in Manila.

Employed 1947-1977 with Frontier Airlines, 1952-1992, owner of Hertz Rent-a-Car franchise, 1972-1992, owner of Holiday Inn franchise. He is married and has three daughters, and will retire June 1993.

BILL ALWOOD, reported to the Merchant Marine School at San Mateo, CA in July of 1944. He was assigned to the tanker *Grande Roude* at San Pedro in December, a midshipman.

He made two trips to the Ulithi Atoll in the Caroline Islands. On the first trip they had two submarine attacks just as they were entering the harbor. The lead ship was torpedoed in number three hold which contained lumber. The captain beached her and it was their lucky day as number four and five holds contained munitions. Later, the sub shot one into the harbor hitting a LSI which was starboard of them. They had casualties. He feels that if the LSI had not been there, they would have been hit.

In July of 1945 he was sent to Kingspoint LSI. In September 1945 he left Kingspoint and signed on the *James L. Breck* in Philadelphia as an oiler, for a trip around the world. Arrived in San Francisco in May of 1946 and was discharged.

Bill resides in Columbus, OH with his wife Carol. They have four children and eight grandchildren.

He is a retired self-employed florist and landscape architect.

The thing he liked the most about serving in the Merchant Marines was those "salt water showers".

OSWALD AMOS, was born March 15, 1905 in Narva, Republic of Estonia. Arrived in New York in 1926 as seaman on Belgian freighter *Caucasia*. Married Tyyne Sundwall in Albany, NY in 1927. One son Ronald, was born in 1935.

Oswald became naturalized American citizen in 1940. Served in Merchant Marine from 1943 to 1945 as ship's carpenter on liberty ships: *Jonathan Trumball* to the British Isles; *Henry B. Brown* to the Mediterranean; and *Ben F. Dixon,* twice, to Scotland, and then to Murmansk.

Underwent U-boat attack in Irish Sea. Then during Murmansk run in convoy his ship *Ben F. Dixon* shot down German bomber during air attack. During stay in Murmansk, Oswald was arrested by Soviet police and jailed overnight because he spoke Russian learned as a child in Estonia.

Formerly a carpenter and dockbuilder, he resided in Mount Vernon, NY and Lindenhurst, NY. Now lives in retirement home in Leesburg, FL.

MILTON E. AMOSS, sailed as 1st assistant engineer during WWII. Has Atlantic and Mediterranean War Zone Bars and Combat Bar. Attended Fort Trumbull. His next of kin is his sister Elizabeth Noon, who resides in Baltimore, MD. He is a member of AMMV JWB Chapter.

CHARLES E. ANDERSON, was born January 1922 Vladivostok, Siberia (father officer serving in U.S. Navy).

Graduated engineering college and first shipped out of San Francisco on SS *Paul Shoup* (oil tanker) in 1942.

Sailed 2nd assistant engineer mainly liberty ships. Pacific, Atlantic, Mediterranean 1942-1946. Was aboard the SS *Edwin T. Meredith,* liberty ship which was cited by Adm. W.F. Halsey for its participation in rescue operation of survivors of torpedoed troop ship SS *Cape San Juan* in the Pacific in November 1943.

Retired in 1982 as vice president manufacturing after 30 years in the electronics industry. Resides in Forestville, CA where he manages family real estate interests.

E.L. ANDERSON, served as chief engineer aboard the SS *Ponce de Leon*. See ship/crew listings.

RICHARD LEE ANDERSON, sailed as deck cadet, AB, and third mate during WWII. Has Atlantic, Pacific, Mediterranean, Middle East War Zone Bars and Combat Bar. Due Russian Medal for the Murmansk Run.

Attended Kings Point Merchant Marine Academy. Graduated Fort Trumbull Officers School in 1944. Article appeared in *The Evening Sun* of Dec. 16, 1944 announcing seven ensigns graduated at Fort Trumbull. These seven Baltimorians, included Patrick L. Whalen, Albert F. Johnson, John Kukia, Carroll H. Cooper, Frank Douglas. (See Sunpaper article quote listed below under Patrick L. Whalen). Sailed on SS *Argentina,* SS *Thomas Kearns,* SS *Jeaquin Miller,* SS *Leopold Damresch,* SS *Montgomery City,* SS *Steel Engineer,* SS *Richmond,* and SS *Esso Reading.*

Richard is a member of AMMV JWB Chapter and resides in Baltimore, MD.

ROSS TERRY ANDRUS, was born Nov. 17, 1926 in Magna, UT. Entered the Merchant Marine November 1944 in Salt Lake City, UT. Served on SS *William P. McArthur* as second radio officer, stationed in San Francisco, Eniwetok, Ulithi, Okinawa, Yokohama, Inchon and San Francisco. SS *Sherman O. Houghton,* as chief radio officer, stationed in San Francisco, Vancouver, Portland, Kobe and Seattle. *General W.H. Gordon,* as third radio officer, stationed in San Francisco, Shanghai, Hong Kong, Manila, Hong Kong, Shanghai and San Francisco. SS *Lane Victory,* as chief radio officer, stationed in San Francisco, Los Angeles, Panama Canal, New York City, Baltimore, Raumo Finland, Grangemouth, Scotland and Norfolk.

His memorable experience includes spending three days and nights in a typhoon between Ulithi and Okinawa. Lost part of deck load of lumber. Life boats stove in. Gun covers torn off. Inches of water blown in and sloshing back and forth on radio room deck. Unable to sleep due to roughness.

He was Copper Millman 1947-1950; Army radio operator 1950-1952; TV repairman 1952-1954; broadcast radio and TV engineer 1954-1973; electronics mechanic 1971-1985; cost estimator 1985-1990.

Married to Helen Mellor in 1954. They have sons and daughters, Shauna, Colleen, Barbara, Allen, Dawn (deceased), Blair, Glenn, Leilani and Dale. He retired Nov. 30, 1990.

ROBERT F. ARMENTROUT, sailed as AB during WWII. Has Pacific War Zone Bar. Attended Sheepshead Bay.

Married to wife June and they reside in Warren, MI. He is member of AMMV JWB Chapter.

NORMAN MATHUS ARMIGER, (See Norman A. Matthews)

RAYMONDE ARMOUR, resides in Baltimore, MD and is member of AMMV JWB Chapter.

EARL W. ARNOLD, was born Jan. 1, 1919 in a small farm town of Huntley, NB. It was always his dream as a small boy in looking to the horizon over the flat lands of Nebraska that some day he'd go over it and see what's on the other side. He wanted to come to a sea cost and get on a ship and travel. He did not know just how all of this would fit together but he's sure it would all fall in line in due time. He wanted to go to the South Sea Islands to Australia and Calcutta India on over to Egypt to see the Pyramids and to full his dram it was a must that he make that one trip that would take him around the world.

He accomplished all of that on the first two ships he had gone to sea on which were two liberty ships, the *Mark Hopkins* and *Ferdinand Westdahl.*

He chose San Francisco as his seaport the Sailors Union in San Francisco had a school to teach seamanship and that's where he started to become a seaman. Seaman at the Union hall had the privilege of picking their own ship.

The first ship he picked for his first trip was a liberty ship, the *Mark Hopkins,* named after prominent San Franciscan who made a name for his self when at the time track and trains were laid across our country. The cargo to be carried on the trip was ammunition and it was to be taken to New Caledonia in the South Pacific from there it was to take a cargo of Nickel Ore from New Caledonia to New Castle Australia in turn bring back a load of coal to New Caledonia.

They were then dispatched to go to the Tonga Islands at Tonga Ta-Boo to take cargo off of another liberty ship that had gotten torpedoed on it's way to it's destination. While there our ships crew had been invited to attend a Saturday night dance on the island. In going to the dance they see a table full of cakes that the women folks had baked for this occasion, at intermission each cake is auctioned off unknown as to who baked each cake. If you bought one of the cakes a polynesian woman that baked this cake would come over and tell you that she baked it and asked to share it with you. Did he buy a cake? He sure did and had fun in sharing it with the young barefooted lady. After loading all of the cargo they were going to take off the torpedoed ship the captain of their ship had the King of the Island bring his dancing group over to the ship and put on a native Polynesian dance, which was fantastic.

He found the Polynesian people of the South Pacific friendly and the most care free style of life a person would want. After taking this cargo to its destination they were then ordered back to San Francisco.

CHARLES (CHUCK) ARNOLDY, was born in Tipton, KS, June 27, 1927. Dropped out of the tenth grade in Englewood, CO and trained at Catalinia Island Training Center May 28, 1944 - Oct. 28, 1944.

Sailed on the following ships between the following dates:

SS *Simon Bolivar,* Oct. 7, 1944-May 23, 1945 as messman/hotshellman; SS *Salina Victory,* July 11, 1945-Sept. 5, 1945, utility/hotshellman; SS *Cape Race,* Oct. 9, 1945-Feb. 6, 1946, ordinary seaman; SS *Loyola Victory,* Feb. 13, 1946-May 7, 1946, acting AB; SS *Solano,* May 13, 1946-June 3, 1946, Ordinary; SS *Hawaiian Banker,* May 6, 1947-July 28, 1947, Acting AB; SS *Marine Swallow,* Aug. 20, 1947-Oct. 1, 1947, Ordinary; SS *Sunset,* Oct. 16, 1947-Dec. 2, 1947, AB/QM; SS *Ampac Los*

Angeles, Dec. 17, 1947-Feb. 5, 1948, AB; SS *R. Ney McNeely,* Feb. 18, 1948-March 31, 1948, AB; SS *Cornelia,* April 15, 1948-June 1, 1948, AB.

When Charles came home he met a perfect woman - bye bye sea.

He worked as a carpenter (and apprentice) for nine years, electronic technician for seven years, and employment counselor for 23 years, raising two fine young ladies during the meantime. Remained close friends with Tom Noakes, who went to sea with him in 1944, seeing him every month. He has enjoyed retirement since 1987 and will answer all letters promptly.

B.W. (WES) ARRANCE, was born April 3, 1923 in Farmingdale, NY. He joined the Merchant Marine November 1942. Received maritime training at Sheepshead Bay, Brooklyn, NY.

Served on SS *John W. Brown,* wiper, to North Africa with troops doctors and nurses to Algiers, returned with 500 of Rommel's Afrika Corps. Attacked by enemy planes on return, all O.K.

SS *Gutzon Borglum,* oiler, to England (London) all mixed supplies. Out at night during the Blitz attack (young kid). Wounded that night, O.K. Quite a sight and experience.

SS *Gutzon Borglum,* oiler, to Persian Gulf with "Lend-Lease" supplies for Russia to Abadan and Basra. Returned by way of Durban and Cape Town, S.A. to Buenos Aries for wheat and then to New Orleans.

Also served on SS *Peter V. Daniel* as oiler, SS *Watertown,* oiler. Both trips to England, Liverpool etc with various supplies, MV *Cape Porpoise,* MV *Wild Rover,* MV, *Cape Pembroke,* 3rd engineer, to South America.

After *Peter V. Daniel* attended Officer's training at Ft. Trumbull, New London, CT. Received 3rd engineer's license. Any horsepower, all oceans. Left the sea in 1947.

His most memorable experience includes the violent North Atlantic in the winter, returning to New York. The violent Indian Ocean on way to South Africa and the Cape. The aircraft attack, the sub attack's and the Blitz in London. The very memorable trip up the Amazon to Manus, 1,000 miles. Small town at that time, brought back raw rubber and Brazil nuts.

He was awarded the Atlantic War Zone Bar, Mediterranean-Middle East War Zone Bar, Combat Bar (with stars), New York State Meritorious Service Medal.

He has donated all of his ship discharges, all of his original seaman's papers, tickets and the original third engineers license, ID and passport to the museum aboard the *John W. Brown.* He is a member of the American Merchant Marine Veterans Chapter aboard the *John W. Brown.*

He and his wife were on board the *John W. Brown* for her "Matron Voyage".

Member of Project Liberty Ship and AMMV JWB Chapter. Note: He is looking for Herb Leiblein or L Leiblien who was best man at his wedding.

LAWRENCE (LARRY) W. ASHTON, was born Sept. 16, 1923, Brockton, MA. Attended Northeastern University. Joined Maritime Service Dec. 11, 1944, Boston, MA.

Boot camp and purser/pharmacist training, Sheepshead Bay. Graduated Aug. 1, 1945. Medical residency at Brighton Marine Hospital, MA.

Ships sailed as purser/pharmacist mate include liberty tanker *Albert G. Brown,* coastwise to Galveston, TX. One trip Aug. 31-Sept. 17, 1945.

Troop ship SS *Kingston Victory,* three trips. Boston to LeHavre, France and return. September 1945 through December 1945. Transported 300 German prisoners of war to LeHavre to assist the Allied Military Government. Returned each trip with 3,000 GI's.

Completed military obligation with several trips on the M/V *Coastal Messenger* to Cuba, Jamaica and Haiti - Jan. 3, 1946 through Jan. 2, 1947.

Employed 36 years with General Electric Medical Systems. Retired December 1983, and lives with wife Mary on Hilton Head Island, SC.

GERTRUDE K. ATKINSON, sailed as junior assistant purse-nurse during Korean War and Vietnam War.

She served on ST Mandoil, SS John Paul Jones, SS *Admiral Dewey, SS National Mariner,* SS *National Liberty,* SS *National Defender,* and ST *Western Hunter.*

Gertrude is registered nurse and is married to William. They reside in Baltimore, MD. She is a member of AMMV JWB Chapter.

WILLIAM JAY ATKINSON, was born Jan. 13, 1913. Graduated New York State Merchant Marine Academy 1933. Sailed almost continuously from then until early 1975 when retired. Employed by numerous steamship companies, most, if not all, no longer in existence. During WWII torpedoed once, tanker *William C. McTarnahan,* in Gulf of Mexico. 1943-1944 first officer, Army Transport Service. June 1944 enrolled in USMS as lieutenant commander for upgrading license to master.

First ship as master *William Grayson* operated by Black Diamond Lines for W.S.A., thereafter sailed mostly as master until retirement. Life member of Project Liberty Ship, and member of American Merchant Marine Veterans, Council of American Master Mariners, U.S. Naval Institute.

DONALD R. ATWOOD, sailed as purser during WWII. Attended Sheepshead Bay. Holds Atlantic, Pacific and Mediterranean War Zone Bars.

Donald is married to Violet and they reside in Baltimore, MD. He is a member of AMMV JWB Chapter.

LOUIS BACKSTGON, was chief engineer on SS *Ernest W. Gibson* from April 23, 1946-August 1, 1946. After armistice it was first cotton ship to Japan.

Louis resides in Scarsdale, NY.

BENNY B. BACON, served as purser on the SS *Richard Randall* (TAL, May 92, p.5.). He is a member of USMMVWII.

STANLEY R. BAKER, born Sept. 6, 1924 in Oakland, CA. Enlisted U.S. Navy (Class M-1) at age 18. Maritime Training Station at Avalon, CA Dec. 26, 1942. May 4, 1943 sent to San Francisco, CA for sea duty. Endorsed as an ordinary seaman with a lifeboat certificate.

First ship was the *William H. Aspinwall* (Liberty), San Francisco to the Hawaiian Islands, then through the Panama Canal to New York. Next was the *William Sharon* (Liberty); *Bald Eagle* (C-2) as able seaman; *Cape May* (C-2); *Napier* (C-2); *Trade Wind* (C-2); *David R. LeCraw,* boatswain; *Cape Gaspe* (C-2) and the *A. Frank Lever* (Liberty) as third mate.

Married in 1946 and settled in Alameda, CA where they now reside. Retired after 40 years of law enforcement in the San Francisco Bay area, but he still misses the sea!

JAMES BALDWIN, sailed as chief engineer on SS *Sinclair Texas* (tanker) plus a hundred more. He now resides in Newark, DE.

JUDSON D. BALDWIN, enrolled in the United States Maritime Service Jan. 5, 1945 at Norfolk, VA. He graduated from the United States Maritime Service Training Station, Sheepshead Bay, NY.

Ships sailed on: *Carl Schurz, Louis Marshall, Alexander White* (Liberty), *Woodstock Victory, Berkshire, Plymouth, Bon Air Seam* (Collier) ordinary seaman, able bodied seaman.

He was awarded the Pacific, Atlantic and Mediterranean Middle East War Zone Bars by the War Shipping Administration confirming active service with the United States Merchant Marine in those war areas.

An ordained Baptist minister, he retired from the active pastorate in 1992 after 37 1/2 years. Judson lives with his wife, Isabelle, in Stuarts Draft, VA. He is a member of U.S. Merchant Marine Veterans World War II and Project Liberty Ship.

VERNON L. BALDWIN, was born Nov. 10, 1925 in Bend, OR. He joined the Merchant Marine in San Francisco in May 1944.

Served on SS *Frank Joseph Irwin* (Liberty Ship), SS *Costa Rica Victory,* SS *W-H Berg* (Tanker), SS *George D. Printice* (Liberty), SS *Lorado Victory,* and SS *Marine Arrow.*

His memorable experience includes the trip around the world. He will never forget the summer of 1945 in Okinawa and until the war was over. They were raided night after night, but never hit.

He has one daughter (Patricia Golden).

Retired in 1989. Printer, travels, camps, fishes and golfs.

DOYLE E. BALES, was born May 18, 1918 in Denison, KS. Completed school in the Midwest. Joined the Merchant Marine September 1943 in Kansas City, MO. Trained at Sheepshead Bay, NY December 1943 helped lay up a Great Lakes freighter in Detroit for the winter.

Joined the MV *Jaquina Head* and deep sea tug.

Sailed on the SS *Francis Asbury* and liberty cargo ship which he lost when it hit a deep mine at Ostead Belgium. Next was the SS *Monroe*, 1919 steam turbine, then a very old coastwise tanker out of San Pedro the SS *TeJou*. Doyle went to work for the motor truck division of International Harvester and retired in 1983 as outside parts and service salesman for a local Clark forklift dealer.

Doyle has lived in Bakersfield, CA since 1952 with his wife Naomi and three children.

Doyle is a life member of MMV WWII San Pedro and National Liberty Ship Memorial, San Francisco. Doyle and Naomi are still employed part time and enjoy their R.V. trailer in Lake Tahoe.

ALFRED R. BALFIELD, sailed as third, second, first assistant and chief engineer during WWII. Had bow blown off when ship hit mine. Attended Sheepshead Bay in 1943 and MARAD Schools.

Marine engineer for Navy - NAVSEA. Married to Camille. They reside in College Park, MD. Alfred is a member of AMMV JWB Chapter.

RAYMOND J. BARIBEAU, was born Sept. 8, 1927 in Chicago, IL. Joined the Merchant Marine on June 27, 1943 in Chicago, IL. They were sent for basic training in Sheepshead Bay in New York. After about 13 or 14 weeks of training a group of them were sent to Philadelphia, PA. He was assigned to a liberty ship, the SS *Minor C. Keith* which was docked at a place called Hog Island. They sailed the next day, for God knows where, he cannot recall what the cargo was. At that time they had the Navy Armed Guard to man the gong, plus the blimps, and Navy ships. They picked up a convoy soon after that. He even wore his life-jacket to bed. About two days before they entered the Mediterranean Sea, they were attacked by German U-boats. They were hit by a torpedo at about the No 2 hold. The Captain (Capt. Puispeau) ordered to abandon ship. He was one of the lucky ones to be in one of the life - boats. This happened about sun-set. The next morning he counted 13 life-boats and four-rafts. He was told later that out of 38 Navy Armed Guard and 48 Merchant Marines only 56 survive. This is something you only see on T.V. or in the movies. The next morning a German U-boat, "I never will forget the number U-169" surfaced and he told them to come along side. The Captain gave them biscuits and water and also took a prisoner. He was able-bodied seaman.

He never can remember his name. They used to call him "Red" because he had a red beard and hair. Many years later he had the privilege of sailing with "Red" on a United Furit Company ship (passenger and cargo) the SS *Chiriqui* out of New Orleans, LA. He signed aboard as a relife bos'n. He doesn't know what happened when he was taken prisoner on the U-boat, but it seems, he was not the same person. He was told that he wrote a book about his experience on the U-boat, it's called "U-boat Prisoner." They were picked up by a English Corvette soon after that and brought to Southhampton, England. They left England on the SS *Lyman Abbott* an Army transport ship, and docked at Norfolk, VA. He went to sea many years after this, and his last experience was in Havana Cuba. While on board the SS *Chiriqui*. Castro shot up the ship and they forced to leave. He stopped going to sea in 1962. Tried out for the police department, they say he did not pass the test. Got a job a the Boeing Aerospace Company in N/O. Got a job at the Boeing Aerospace Co. in N/O. That built the Saturn that took the men to the moon, worked there for over 20 1/2 years. Then took a job at Martin-Marietta manned space systems that builds the E/T Tank for the space shuttle. He retired on May 1, 1991.

Married has one daughter, four grandchildren, two great grandchildren. Enjoys fishing, boat model building and traveling.

GEORGE H. BARK, donated two liberty ship hurricane cabin lamps. He is a member of AMMV Gulfstream Chapter. He resides in Ft. Lauderdale, FL.

ERNEST E. BARKER, was born June 15, 1926 on Arkansas cotton farm. Ages 16-17 worked in Kaiser Swan Island shipyard in Portland, OR. Joined Merchant Marine 1944; trained at St. Petersburg, FL.

Sailed on 17 ships as fireman, oiler, 3rd and 2nd engineer, 1944 to 1953: SS *Christenson, Richardson, John W. McKay* - 1945, *William B. Leeds* - 1945, *Elgin Victory* - 1945-6, SS *Junior* - 1946, *Spartenburg Victory* - 1946, *Pine Bluff Victory* - 1947, *Tillie Lykes* - 1947, *Hawaiian Citizen* - 1947, *Scott E. Land* - 1947, *Mahlon Pitney* - 1948, *Elko Victory* - 1948-1949, *Arizona* - 1950, *Bedford Victory* - 1951, *Adelphi Victory* - 1952, *China Trader* - 1952, *Rock Springs Victory* - 1952-3.

Celebrated end of WWII on liberty ship *John W. McKay* high and dry on a coral reef; it had buried its nose in the reef at high tide the night following departure from Manila. January-June 1946, made four trips on troopship returning German POWs and bringing GIs home from Europe. Sailed around world-22 ports-on SS *Scott E. Land* (C-4) 1947. Made three trips to Korea during Korea War: *Bedford Victory* - 1951; *Adelphi Victory* (ammunition) 1952; *Rock Springs Victory* (ammunition) 1952-3.

Sailed on K-41 sailboat to New Zealand and Australia in 1982 accompanied outbound by son Bill. Single handed from Bunderburg, Queensland to New Caledonia and Tonga mid 1983. Joined in Niefu, Tonga by son, Bruce for 30 days and brother, Sid for week. Returned to California late 1983 - 202 days at sea, 17002 miles: slow freighter.

A visit to the past: January-April, 1991, sailed as second engineer on SS *Banner* to Dammam, Saudi Arabia. Semi-retired attorney at law residing in Redondo Beach, CA.

WILLIAM N. BARNARD, was born Dec. 16, 1926 in Colorado. Graduated North Denver High June, 1944. Enlisted USMS Dec. 13, 1944, Denver. Catalina January and February 1945 to Seattle graduate station.

Ships sailed SS *Bering*, 1945; SS *Thaddeus S.C. Lowe*, liberty ship, 1945; SS *Notre Dame Victory*, 1945 (later made history as Great Lakes ore carrier, *Cliff's Victory*); SS *Mericos Whittier*, tanker, 1946; SS *China Victory*, 1946 (Calship's first AP4 type - carried hull No. 1 plate); SS *Benjamin Goodhue*, Liberty ship, 1946-47 (rescued survivors from SS *American Farmer*, damaged in collision in Atlantic).

Received certificate of service April 3, 1947. Worked as plant operator for Shell Chemical Co. 1949-1982. Retired and lives with wife Evelyn in Commerce City, CO. Charter life member of USMMVWWII, proud to be listed as crew member of *Lane Victory* in dedication brochure.

GEO. LEON BARNETT, was born Sept. 2, 1926. Graduated Warrior, AL, May 1944. Drafted June 1944 and declared 4F. Joined Merchant Marine August 1944, called and shipped to St. Petersburg, November 1944 for training. Transferred to USAHS *Ernest Hinds*, Charleston, SC, February 1945. Mediterranean zone until October 1945.

October 1945 signed on T-2 tanker SS *Camp Namanu* as quartermaster. Discharged February 1946.

Married Jean Griffin April 1946 and had three sons. Became Pure/Union Oil distributor April 1955, Decatur, AL and retired September 1971. He resides in Hartselle, AL.

WILLIAM B. BARRETT, was born Jan. 8, 1923 in Water Valley, MS. He joined the USMS cadet, September 1942 in New Orleans.

He served on the SS *Gatun* (freighter), cadet, New Orleans, Cuba, Costa Rica; SS *P.E. Crowley* (Laker), cadet, New Orleans, Pacific Islands, West Coast; USAT Y-6, (Army tanker), 2nd mate, New Orleans, Australia, New Guinea; SS *William Borah* (Liberty), 3rd mate, New Orleans, Panama, Philippines, West Coast, San Francisco, Seattle; SS *Fred Joyce* (Liberty), 2nd mate, New Orleans, West Africa, Italy, France, Yugoslavia, Boston, Baltimore.

His memorable experience includes serving on Army tanker (Y-6) in New Guinea for one year. Visiting Genoa, Dubrovnik, Manila, Abidjan and many other fascinating places.

He left the Merchant Marine in October 1946.

He is a nationally recognized authority on economic development, was executive director of the North Mississippi Industrial Development Association for twenty-five years. In this capacity he directed the area development activities for over 100 communities in twenty-nine counties. More than 600 industries located in the region during his tenure. On March 1, 1986, Barrett started his own company, William Barrett Associates, Inc., offering executive search, placement and counseling services to community and development organizations. He veered into the political spectrum in the spring and summer of 1987 by serving as state campaign manager for Maurice Dantin, a democratic candidate for governor of Mississippi. For four months in 1988 Barrett acted as a consultant to the Lower Colorado River Authority, Austin, TX. LCRA implemented an economic/industrial development program to enhance job opportunities in forty-three rural central Texas counties. He assisted in developing community assessment and retention tactics, broad marketing strategies, and executive evaluation/recommendations.

He attended the University of Mississippi, is a graduate of the U.S. Maritime Service Officers School in New London, CT, and served in the U.S. Maritime Service for four years.

Upon separation from the service he joined radio station WELO in Tupelo, MS. He began a career in economic development as manager of the Marion County Chamber of Commerce in Columbia, and from there he advanced to the Mississippi Department of Economic Development in Jackson, serving as manager of the industrial division for several years.

Barrett completed the Institute of Organization Management sponsored by the Chamber of Commerce of the United States at the University of Georgia, and the Economic Development Institute sponsored by the American Economic Development Council and the University of Oklahoma.

His professional affiliations include: American Economic Development Council, Mississippi Economics Council, Mississippi Association of Chamber of Commerce Executives, Mississippi Industrial Development Council, Mississippi Manufacturers Association, Newcomen Society of the United States and Southern Industrial Development Council.

Married to Jane Hosmer and they have daughters Elizabeth Barrett, Manhattan, KS and Rebecca Ringensberg, Nashville, TN.

VERNON BASEMAN, resides in Fallston, MD. He is a member of AMMV. Charter member JWB Chapter, Oct. 14, 1989. (TUD O-N, 1991 pg. 12).

EDRIC S. BATES, was born April 12, 1916; Brooklyn, NY. Graduated from high school, Ligonier, PA. Class of 1934. January 1934 Pennsylvania National Guard until leaving the State. He outfit was the 103rd Medical Regt., 109th Ambulance Co. This was the last horse drawn ambulance company in the USA.

1935-1947 Sea time:

Ships sailed aboard. SS *Turriaga*, OS, dry cargo; SS *Veragua*, OS and A.B, pass cargo; SS *Tanamo*, A.B., dry cargo. SS *Western World*, QM, Pass; SS *Pennsylvania*, QM, pass; SS *Beecon*, A.B., tanker; SS *F.Q. Barstow*, A.B. tanker; SS *Exmouth*, A.B., cargo. SS *W.L. Steed*, A.B. tanker; SSTC *McCobb*, bos'n, tanker; SS *Wards Island*, A.B., sludge; SS *Mobile Oil Jr.*, 3rd mate, tanker; SS *Dorchester Jr.*, 3rd mate, troop; read Captain Arthur R. Moore's book, page 77, he did not make that voyage, but he sailed on the previous one, SS *Barron Hill*, 2nd mate, tanker; SS *Carlon Ellis*, chief mate, tanker, SS *J. Howland Gardner*, chief mate, tanker.

1938-1949: U.S. Naval Reserve.

1949-1966: U.S. Coast Guard, active duty, ret.

Maritime service at various times:

1935 Hoffman Island, New York; 1937 sailing ship: Joseph Conrad: 1941; Ft. Trumball, CT; first officer candidate class; 1947-1948, USMS American Seaman; 1948-1949, USMS, American Mariner; 1942 first USNR officer aboard Hoffman Island to releave USCG; 1941, third mate license was dated Dec. 7, 1941; 1947 last Merchant Marine discharge dated Dec. 7, 1947.

Also had duty aboard USS *Texas* 1939; USS *President Adams*, 1949; USS *Consolation*, 1947-1949; 1972, B.S. degree; University of Florida, Gainesville, FL; 1972, retired from all endeavors. Traveled world wide - suffered mid stroke in 1986. Been partying ever since

U.S. Coast Guard vessels: USCG cutter *Jonquil* - XO; *Persens* X.O. - C.O.; *Willow* - C.O.

He and his wife Marion are charter life members of USMMVWW II and charter members of the East Central Florida Chapter.

REAR ADMIRAL RICHARD BAUMAN, (TUD pg. 26, O-N, 1991) Captain Rick Bauman, chief officer of the restored SS *John W. Brown*. Graduated from Kings Point in 1975 and is a Maryland pilot (TUD, spring, 1992, p. 12).

ELMAR J. BAXTER, was born in Los Angeles Aug. 30, 1924. Graduated Loyola High 1941, attended Loyola University, joined U.S. Merchant Marine Cadet Corps 1943.

Shipped out as deck cadet-midshipman on liberty ship SS *Jack London* to Alaska/Aleutians and again to Guadalcanal/Bougainville in South Pacific. Completed deck officer training U.S. Merchant Marine Academy, Kings Point, NY, graduating 1945 as a third mate in USMS, and ensign, USNR. Sailed as junior third mate on converted Liberty ship troop carrier SS *Lucretia Mott* 1945 ferrying 1,500 U.S. soldiers to Europe. After war, sailed as mate for Moore-McCormick Lines between New York and Brazilian ports on C-1 ships SS *Cape Cumberland* and *San Antonio*.

Elmar came ashore in 1946 to join Hearst's International News Photo in Los Angeles, writing first television news show on West Coast. In 1952, he became travel and outdoor editor of Los Angeles Herald-Express and later the merged Herald-Examiner, writing daily columns for 16 years.

After handling publicity for Princess Cruisers in its early days, he was named public relations officer for Port of Long Beach. During a 20 year second career, he directed the Port-sponsored TOPSail '84, Tallship Olympic Parade of Sail honoring Los Angeles Summer Games, and was founding director of International Seafarers Center in Long Beach Harbor.

Elmar retired in 1990 but remains active in maritime matters. He was 1990 recipient of Outstanding Personal Achievement Award from Kings Point Alumni Association, it is a Lifetime Honorary Member of U.S. Propeller Club, Port Employee of Year, and served on American Merchant Marine Veterans Memorial Committee. He lives in Huntington Beach, CA with his wife and Academy sweetheart Jeanne.

PAUL E. BELCHER, SR., was born Oct. 16, 1923 in Rosendale, MO. Attended school at Central High School, St. Joseph, MO, Jan. 15, 1942.

After school he went to Portland, OR to work in the Kaiser Shipyards building liberty ships, LSTs, and tankers. He liked the ships so much he joined the Merchant Marine in May 1943 at Kansas City, MO and was sent to Sheepshead Bay, Brooklyn for training.

Served on SS *Relief,* (tug), OS, 1943; SS *King S. Woolsey,* (liberty), OS, Newport News to Oran, 1943; SS *John Davenport* (liberty), wiper, Norfolk to Murmansk, 1944; SS *Amer. Trader,* (tanker), OS-AB, Norfolk to Spain, 1944; SS *Samuel Johnson* (liberty), OS, Norfolk to England, 1944; SS *Laura Bridgman,* (liberty), OS-AB, New York to Philippines, 1945; SS *Wm. Paca* (liberty), OS, New York to Belgium, 1945; SS *Robert G. Ingersoll*, OS, New York to France, 1946.

CHARLES BELLINGER, served as AB on the SS *Thomas Donaldson* during June 1944 (VWOA News Letter, winter 1992).

JOSEPH BENEDICT, sailed as ordinary seaman, third mate, second mate and chief mate during WWII. Has Atlantic and Mediterranean War Zone Bars. Attended: Sheepshead Bay and Ft. Trumbull.

He is married to Evelyn and they reside in Timonium, MD. Member of AMMV JWB Chapter.

ROBERT (BOB) BENNET, sailed as junior third mate on the SS *Lane Victory,* 1949-1950 (TAL May 1992, p.5).

HELEN BENTLEY, honoray chairman, PLS and honorary member AMMV JWB Chapter. She resides in Towson, MD.

JACK O. BERG, was born April 16, 1927 in Omaha, NB. He joined the Merchant Marine March 1945 in Chicago, IL. Served on SS *Jubal A. Early,* radio officer; *Charles H. Marshall* (all liberty ships) in the Atlantic, Pacific, Mediterranean, and Gulf of Mexico.

Shot down kamikaze and other incidents at Okinawa. Almost ran aground at Naples, Italy. Sixty-three degree roll in storm off Cape Hatteras. Today, Jack is amazed to think that he could have went from high school in a quiet mid-western town to kamikaze attacks at Okinawa, in less than two months time and with no training. Graduated Springfield, IL High School 1945 (in absentia). U.S. Army, Signal Corps instructor, Korean War era. AT&T Communications Supervisor, 38 years service.

He has two children and one grandchild. Retired June 1986. Spends time catching up on amateur radio and other projects around the house.

ROY C. BERG, graduated from the New York State Merchant Marine Academy in 1941. Sailed as chief engineer and was a commander in USMS. Was first assistant engineer on the SS *Harriet Beecher Stowe*.

He now resides in Huntinton Station, NY.

WILLIAM BERGIN, resides in Linthicum, MD and is a member of AMMV JWB Chapter.

ROY BILLMARK, was born July 2, 1925 at Winnepeg, Canada. He grew up in Minneapolis. Joined the Merchant Marines July 1943 and trained at Sheepshead Bay, NY as cook and baker.

He sailed on SS *Montery*, (troop ship), two trips; SS *Texas*, (tramp cargo); SS *John Bidwell*, (liberty); SS *James Fergus* (liberty); SS *Carter Braxton* (liberty); SS *Thomas Hart Benton* (liberty), two trips; SS *Rainbow* (C2 victory) nine months aboard.

Port of Call: Panama, Hawaii, New Guinea, Noumea in Caledonia, Suva in Figis, Puerto Rico, South Hampton and Portsmouth England, Marsielle Cherbourg and Le Havre France, Rio de Janeiro, Brazil, Ghent Belgium, Montevideo Uruguay, Santiago & Valparaiso Chile,

Callao Peru, Punta Bay Ecuador, Leg Horn Italy, Piraeus and Saolinka Greece, Shanghai and Tsingtao China; Yokohama Japan.

Home ports: New York, New Orleans, San Francisco.

All experiences were memorable. Some good and some not so good.

He was officially discharged March 6, 1947 and spent 15 years with Milwaukee Railroad, 20 years in propane gas and heating, general building contractor and beef cattle farmer 20 years and then retired.

He is now living at farm in Milaca, MN with wife Joyce. They have six good children who are up and gone well.

He is very proud to have been part of the U.S. Merchant Marine in WWII. He is however, ashamed of the way they were treated after it was done. What would they have done without them? Veterans status in 1988 was nice and appreciated but unfortunately meaningless to most. As of 1992 they are ineligible for membership in the VFW and he has a real problem with that in view of their casualty rate in foreign waters, the high seas and even off our shore shipping. This is a put down they didn't need with their Veterans status and certainly do not deserve. "God Bless Us One and All Anyway."

RANDALL BISHOP was born in Swampscott, MA on Feb. 5, 1921. He served in WW II as a Merchant seaman. In 1942 he was on an old tanker (*William M. Burton*). In 1943 he took a tanker from Philadelphia to the South Pacific. They had 150,000 barrels of sub fuel. From San Francisco, he got a Liberty ship and took it to Calcutta, India, where they had a heavy air-raid. Next port of call was Durban, South Africa where they took on coal as a ballast. Then on to Brazil, where he was hospitalized in a jungle hospital with a fever.

 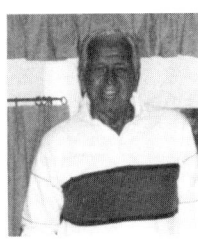

As soon as he got back he got another Liberty at Hogs Island, the big ammo dump near Philadelphia. They left with 10,000 tons of ammo — deck cargo was stacked to the flying bridge. Getting across the North Atlantic was rough. When they arrived London was on fire from the buzz bombs. They were turned around and sent to Scotland where they were anchored for about a week. When they got the word they dashed across the channel to Cherbourg. Then they left England with a load of coal for ballast and headed home on the North Atlantic. Bishop was on the sea till the war ended.

In 1945 he shipped on the old army transports (troop ships) bringing troops back from the major islands in the Pacific, Japan, Korea and China. One summer he shipped on the Great Lakes, then on sea going tugs and banana boats to Central America. During Vietnam, he was on a tanker carrying JB4 jet fuel to Wake Island.

His hobby is tracking down old ships. Bishop travels almost continually. He is a member of the S.S. Lane Victory. His awards include President Truman's Citation Letter, The Victory Meda, The Merchant Marine Combat Bar, The Pacific War Zone Bar, The Atlantic War Zone Bar.

JOHN ALLISON BLACKBURN, was born July 20, 1926 in Walter Reed Hospital, Washington, DC. He joined the Merchant Marine April 1944 at Baltimore, MD at the age of 17.

He took training at Maritime Service Training Station, Sheepshead Bay, NY (Sec 138).

Served on the *William Moultrie* (liberty ship), utility man, 1944, Atlantic and Mediterranean; *Albion Victory* (Atlantic), messman, 1945, Atlantic; *John Greer Hibben* (liberty), wiper, 1945, Pacific; *Cody Victory*, wiper, 1945; Atlantic/Mediterranean; *Walter M. Christiansen* (liberty), oiler, 1945-1946, Atlantic; *Thomas Heyward*, (liberty) wiper, 1946, Atlantic.

His memorable experience includes joining the U.S. Army in July 1946. Served in Korea and Germany. Discharged November 1952. Joined Pulaski County (VA) Sheriff's Department February 1956, retiring June 30, 1986 with 30 years service. Retired with rank of major.

Married to Violet Miles Blackburn since Feb. 12, 1953. Has one son, two granddaughters. He is a member of the American Legion, VFW and lives in Pulaski, VA.

FRANK E. BLAND, was born at Piedmont, KS July 30, 1925. Graduated high school at Piedmont May 1943. Enlisted Maritime Service. Sworn in at Kansas City, MO July 17, 1943. He was sent to Sheepshead Bay Training School, Brooklyn, NY. He received fireman-oiler training. Graduated Baltimore, MD Nov. 22, 1943. He served on the following ships and dates served.

Alcoa Guard, a Hog islander, as a fireman on trip to Cuba, Nov. 24, 1943 to Dec. 24, 1943. *Robert G. Ingersoll,* Liberty ship, as oiler on trip to the Persian Gulf Jan. 31, 1944 to June 2, 1944. *Walter L. Fleming,* Liberty ship, as fireman on trip to India, Aug. 28, 1944 to Feb. 5, 1945. *Fort Henry,* T-2 tanker, as an oiler on trip to India, Persian Gulf, Italy, Africa, Trinidad, and Guam, March 17, 1945 to Sept. 9, 1945. *William Thornton,* Liberty ship, as 3rd asst. engineer on trip to France June 15, 1946 to July 31, 1946. *Dwight W. Morrow,* Liberty ships, as 3rd asst. engineer on trip to Germany, June 13, 1947 to Aug. 8, 1947.

Recalled to active duty Nov. 13, 1945 at Houston, TX. He was sent to Alameda, CA for engineering officer training. Released from active duty March 15, 1946 at Alameda, CA. Completed training at Alameda resulted in his being issued licenses: A38787-any horsepower steam ocean going vessel. A33125-any horsepower diesel ocean going vessel.

He operated a service station. Owned a petroleum products bulk agency. There has been a large variety of endeavors. He retired from 20 plus years of selling life insurance. The time that he spent in the Merchant Marine fleet plays a large part in his memories.

BILL BLISS, (See John Hird)

CHARLES F. BLOCKSTON, sailed as first and third assistant engineer during WWII, Korean Conflict and Vietnam War. Was taken as POW during WWII and sunk twice.

Attended Hoffman Island in 1940 and Fort Trumbull in 1945. Served as oiler on SS *Carlton* out of Philadelphia on March 7, 1942 which was torpedoed and sunk on July 5, 1942. USCG Certificate of Discharge states: "Place of discharge at sea (torpedoed)." Date on discharge is Feb. 28, 1945. Captain was R. Hanson. (TUD Sept. 1992, p. 33).

He is a member of AMMV JWB Chapter and resides in Hurlock, MD.

HAUS P. BLUM, SR., sailed on Liberty ships as AB and Bosun until December 1952. Visited the *Brown* on May 3, 1992. He resides in Collensville, VA.

MARSHALL BLUM, was among the survivors of the SS *Mary* that was lost due to enemy action. He is married to Maureen Blum and they reside in Baltimore, MD.

MELVIN F. BOCKELMAN, was born Dec. 9, 1927, joined the Merchant Marine 1944, took training at Catalina Island, sailed on SS *West Celeron* to Pearl Harbor with lumber. Next sailed on SS *David Belasco* to Saipan Island with war supplies, last sailed on SS *McKittrick Hills* (T-2) with aviation gasoline to Manila Philippines.

After war finished high school, joined U.S. Army Air Forces served in England, Hawaii and U.S. Strategic Air Command. Retired as chief master sergeant in 1966. Joined Kansas City, MO Police Department and developed the Police Computer System ALERT I and II.

FREDERICK J. BOLD, sailed as radio officer during WWII and Korean Conflict. Has Atlantic, Mediterranean and Middle East War Zone Bars. Attended Sheepshead Bay and Hoffman Island Radio School

Married to Bonnie and they reside in Baltimore, MD. Frederick is a member of AMMV JWB Chapter.

JOHN C. BOND, sailed as fireman and oiler from June 5, 1945 to April 4, 1948. Attended Sheepshead Bay. Enrolled at Baltimore, MD on Nov. 25, 1944 and came out as F 2/c. Sailed as fireman for three short trips to Alaska then as an oiler.

He is married to Dorothy and reside in Baltimore, MD. John is a member of AMMV JWB Chapter.

MIKE BORING, PLS member and a sport diver who has visited the wreck of the Liberty ship SS *John Morgan* (TUD O-N 1988, p.3).

LOUIS GABRIEL BOSSO, was born March 30, 1927 in Staten Island, NY. He joined the Merchant Marine Aug. 10, 1944 at Sheepshead Bay.

He served on ships: *Robert Toombs* (liberty-South Atlantic SS Co.), oiler, New York, Baltimore, MD, Italy, Dec. 3, 1944 to Feb. 23, 1945. SS *Arthur M. Hulbert,* oiler, Philadelphia, PA, France, March 19, 1945 to May 28, 1945. SS *Claymont Victory,* oiler, New York-Germany, Nov. 27, 1945 to Dec. 26, 1945. SS *Madawaska Victory,* oiler, New York-France, July 11, 1945 to Aug. 21, 1945. SS *John A. Donald,* oiler, New York-Italy, May 6, 1946 to July 4, 1946. SS *Warrior* (waterman SS) oiler, New York-Korea, May 19, 1947-Aug. 25, 1947.

He worked for Proctor and Gamble for 40 years. Retired in 1987. He was married for 47 years. He has three children and five grandchildren. He is now retired and fishing.

HARVEY LEE BOSWELL, born Jan. 12, 1928 in Wilson, NC. Joined the U.S. Maritime Service in 1944. Attended Sheepshead Bay Maritime Service Training Station. Shipped via troop train with several train car loads of boots to Seattle, WA and was ordered to the SS Eric V. Hauser as a wiper. Ship went to Honolulu loaded with war supplies, then to several South Pacific islands, joined a convoy and then into Okinawa.

While being unloaded at Naha, Okinawa the Japanese planes came over nighly on air raids. His most memorable experience — Against all rules, Boswell, a couple of messboys and an O.S. put on life jackets and jumped overboard to swim to an Army Transport Ship that was having movies that night. While they were in the water, a

Jap air raid started. A strong undertow caught Boswell, and had it not been for a messman, he would have been swept out of the harbor. A Navy smoke boat (each M.M. ship was assigned a smoke boat to hide the ship from Jap planes) picked them up, and took them to the Army Transport. They were ordered back to their ship and threatened with a court martial.

He sailed on over 25 ships and visited 32 countries in his short eight years at sea.

Boswell was paralyzed from the waist down in a fall in 1952 while serving on an oiler on a matson ship, the SS *Hawaiian Retailer* while ashore in Kauai. Spent over a year in Marine Hospitals in S.F., Seattle, and Norfolk. After coming home in a wheelchair in 1954, he went back to his first love, carnival business and after forty years he's still with it, for it, and love it.

OTIS L. BOUCHIE, JR., was born May 25, 1923 and was raised at Fort Kent, ME on the U.S.-Canadian border. His family moved to Florida in 1938. In October 1942 at Tampa, FL he shipped U.S. on his first ship the SS *Thermo*. He had no prior maritime or Navy training. The old square head bos'n chased him from stem to stern, he was a good teacher.

In 1943 he started shipping acting A.B. on Liberty's and T-2 tankers. They carried tanks, airplanes, ammunition, bombs and hi-test gas to all war zones. In May 1944 he got his war-time A.B. ticket at Baltimore, MD. Otis was in the invasion of South France. They carried free French troops and they returned to North Africa with German POWs. They made shuttles to Sardinia and ports north of Naples in the push for Rome. He made a career of the Merchant 1942-1966.

He retired on a National Maritime Union AFL-CIO Service Pension. He worked as a licensed security officer from 1966-1982. Otis fell victim to cancer of the larynx and left the work force.

He has been married over 50 years. They have five children, 13 grandchildren and two great-grandchildren. "I was lucky to have sailed WWII, Korea and Vietnam unscratched. I thank God."

DANIEL J. BOYLAND, served as purser on board the SS *James Bowdoin* on its maiden voyage and kept a personal diary of the trip. He has obtained the official and secret logs from the National Archives as well as the Navy convoy record and gun crew log. He is looking for information concerning torpedo defense nets as to their height of the booms, the length they extended over the sides of the ship and depth they went into the ocean.

Daniel resides in Burbank, CA.

JOHN BOYLSTON, president, PLS. (TUD Nov. 1988, O-N, 1991, p.24 and Sept. 1992, p.28; TAL May 923, p.1). He resides in Solomons, MD.

JOSEPH P. BRACKEN, (TUD O0N, 1991, p.16).

POWHATAN S. BRADBIE, sailed aboard American Flag Merchant ships during WWII. He is member of AMMV JWB Chapter and now resides in Pasadena, MD.

RICHARD A. BRADFORD, was born July 31, 1917 in Sparks, NV. He joined the Merchant Marine in 1935 in San Francisco.

Served on the following ships.

1935, SS *H.F. Alexander*, O.S., passenger, coastwise, Pacific. 1936, SS *General Pershing*, O.S., passenger - Cargo, Pacific. 1943, SS *John T. McMillan*, O.S., cargo, Pacific. 1944, SS *Kohala*, A.B., cargo, Pacific. 1944, SS *John H. Marion*, A.B., tanker, coastwise, Pacific. 1944, SS *Cape Mendocino*, A.B., troop-cargo, Pacific. 1944, SS *Tejon*, A.B., tanker, coastwise, Pacific. 1945, SS *Carl Schurz*, A.B., troop-cargo, Alaska. 1945, SS *John H. Marion*, A.B., tanker-coastwise, Alaska. 1945, SS *Maunalei*, A.B., cargo, Pacific. 1946, M.V. *Lucidor*, A.B., cargo, Alaska.

After paying off *Lucidor* on Dec. 9, 1946 he worked nine months for the U.S. Maritime Administration as a material checker, inventorying stores and equipment aboard ships involved in bare boat charters or vessels going into layup.

HENRY E. BRADLEY, attended USMSTS at Sheepshead Bay, December 1943-April 1944. Sailed as 3rd engineer on SS *Biddle*, SS *Evans*, and SS *Walter Ranger*.

Henry now resides in Wilmington, DE.

ROMEO G. BRANSON, was born Jan. 25, 1923 in Washington, DC. His family moved to Newport, RI on his fourth birthday, remained there for elementary through high school. Returned to Washington, DC at 18, worked as a projectionist in the theater for two years.

Enlisted in the Merchant Marines in June 1943 in Sheepshead Bay; received 2nd Cook & Baker's endorsement. One year later upgraded to chief cook's endorsement through National Maritime School.

Sailed intermittently as chief cook, 2nd cook, messman to 1946. Spent a year attending school in Rhode Island, returned to sea, working intermittently ashore.

In 1957 he attended New York Business School for two years, emerging as a fledgling court reporter. Worked in the Philadelphia Common Pleas Court as official reporter until retirement in 1983. Currently work by appointment.

Hobbies include photography, motorcycling, traveling, taking computer courses, amateur radio. Married to Enid, teaches school and shares similar hobbies. They have no children.

"I would love to hear from any old shipmates."

OSWALD BRETT, (TUD O-N 1991, p.8)

DEREK BRIERLY, (TUD O-N, 1991, p.11)

SAMUEL V. BRITT, is member of AMMV charter member JWB Chapter Oct. 14, 1991. He resides in Charles Town, WV.

CHARLES R. BROOKS

CLYDE BERTRAM BROWN, was born on Aug. 17, 1922 on the Island of St. Vincent in the West Indies. Emigrated to the United States with his parents July 1923. Attended elementary and high schools in St. Vincent and Brooklyn, NY.

Joined the National Youth Administration was trained as an auto-mechanic 1941-1942. Then went into the U.S. Maritime Service in February 1943 at Sheepshead Bay, NY and graduated with oilers, fireman, and watertender's papers July 2, 1943.

Shipped out on his first tanker the SS *Caribbean*, some of the other ships sailed on were the SS *Kernstown*, the SS *PanPennsylvania*, the SS *Eufala Victory*, etc. For many months crossings were made from refineries in Curacao and Aruba to England with high octane aviation gasoline.

His last trip was to the Philippines on a C type ship to take troops and return troops back to the U.S. He received his last discharge after the war in October 1945.

Enrolled at NYC Technical College earned an associate degree in Electrical Technology, worked several years as a senior engineering technician. His next job was with the Department of Electrical Installations, supervising the installation of the first computerized signal light system in the City of New York, retiring after 25 years of service in 1990.

He married Anna Carty in 1943 and have three children, Rodney, Darryl and Regin, looking foward to our retirement in the State of Florida.

LESLIE G. BROWN, was born Oct. 10, 1922 in Bay Shore, NY.

He joined the Merchant Marine August 1941 and trained at Hoffman Island, NY. Sailed on training ships, the three mast schooners—*Vema*, the patrol craft—*Kimball*, the Hog Islander—*Empire State*.

Discharged Feb. 1942. Went to work March 1942 with Standard Oil Co. of New York. Sailed the Atlantic on three tankers—SS *American Arrow*, MS *Brillant*, SS *Sea Hound*. His memorable experiences include sailing the Atlantic with the tankers and going by men on life rafts.

Enlisted in the US Navy in Sept. 1942. assigned to the Third Naval Dist. of New York. He served on several ships until he left the Navy in 1946.

After leaving the Navy, he worked for the Sperry Gyroscope Co. for 18 years and then Grinnan Aerospace Co. for 18 years before retiring in April 1983. He lives with his wife, Norma in New York.

ROBERT M. BROWN, CAPT., was born Sept. 24, 1901 in Eustis, FL. Joined the Merchant Marine in 1921 in New York City.

Brown was Master of the Liberty Ship *Oakley Wood* from her launching to the end of WW II in the Philippines. He made five north Atlantic convoy crossings in WW II, to Europe, Murmansk, Russia, and one unescorted via the Panama Canal to the Philippines. He also made one trip of about three months as captain of a T-2 tanker. His memorable experiences include sleeping with a pillow over his head because of buzz bombs.

After he left the sea he worked with Captain Wainwright as a marine surveyor out of Jacksonville. He owned and operated a 50-ft. diesel deep-sea fishing charter boat out of St. Augustine. His wife died in 1969 and their daughter Roxie lives in St. Augustine. He has three granddaughters—Mary, in the Navy Reserve as a Chief Petty Officer, Lynne, who works in a small boat building plant and Ronna, the youngest, a dental assistant.

WARREN E. BROWN, was born Oct. 15, 1920 in Baltimore, MD. Started going to sea in August 1937 as a wiper on the SS *Dorothy* (bull line) chartered to Isthimian SS Co., to South and East Africa, England and Germany. Fireman on SS *Arlyn*, fireman on SS *Helen* (coastwise), fireman on SS *Flomar* (intercoastal), oiler on SS *Flomar*, fireman on SS *Santore* (Baltimore to Cruz Grande, Chile). Note: They were southbound on Sept. 1, 1939 when war was declared in Europe, painted American flags on sides of ship. Fireman on SS *West Madaket* (intercoastal), oiler on SS *Steelore*, oiler on SS *Schoharie* (May to August 1940) (to Egypt, Aden, Visagapatam, India) oiler on SS *Sundance* (September 1940 to January 1941) to Honolulu, Japan, Sumatra, Bintan, Honolulu, Mobile, AL) The Japs had signs in store windows "We don't want your Yankee dollars". Oiler on SS *Robin Locksley* (March 1941 to July 1942) (South and East Africa and Suez) In Port Elizabeth on Dec. 7, 1941. Coming home in January 1942 (not allowed to use radio receivers!) Skipper decided to hug East Coast where they would be "safer". MISTAKE! But they were lucky and got into Boston o.k. Next trip on Locksley to Suez! Running alone. Then oiler on SS *Alcoa Prospector* (September 1942 to March 1943) to Suez, Malta (convoy Portcullis), Buenos Aires, Montivideo, NY (via Straits of Magellan) Running alone except Malta convoy.

Got second assistant license April 1943. Went back on SS *Robin Locksley*. To Ascension Island, West Africa, NY. Next trip to South and East Africa (via Cape Horn outbound) and Buenos Aires (14 WRENS boarded there! they took them to New York) Running alone. (Sailed as licensed junior engineer, 4th assistant engineer, 3rd assistant engineer, 2nd assistant engineer, 1st assistant engineer on the SS *Robin Locksley* from 1943 to 1946.) In December 1943 they (SS *Robin Locksley)* started running in convoy to U.K. and later to France until end of the wear. Then back on peacetime run to South and East Africa.

Got chief engineer's license in 1946, Steam or Motor, Unlimited horsepower. In 1946-1947 made several coastwise trips on M/V Coastal Harbinger (1st assistant). In 1947-1948 made intercoastal trip on SS *Bessemer Victory (2nd assistant)*. Went back on SS *Robin Locksley* 1949-1950. Made several trips on M/V *Floridian* in 1965-1966 (1st assistant and chief engineer).

Most memorable experiences:Getting hit by a dud torpedo at 0450 hr. while on watch in the engine room. It hit in the machine shop! Early 1945.

Sailing in the Malta Convoy "Portcullis" (loaded with coal in #1, aviation gas in #2, anti-aircraft ammunition in #3, bombs in #4, food in #5 and a deckload of aerial torpedos), with an extremely heavy escort. And being cheered by the people in Malta as they entered the Grand Harbor. (December 1942)

Bringing survivors home. They brought home survivors of the SS *Robin Moor* (torpedoed May 21, 1941). SS *Sagadahoc* (torpedoed Dec. 3, 1941). And many others from various ships. They picked up one man three times out of the five (5) times he got hit! Name was Bob Burton - he was on the *Robin Moor*.

A fire in #1 hold, with ammunition in #2! The fire was in the mail. The postal inspector said it was sabotage. It was discovered at about 2300 hr. The lookout's feet got hot! He was on the foc'sle head and it was cold that night. It took till noon the next day to extinguish the fire. (March 1942).

A fire in the stack which set the boatdeck awning on fire. They were loading aviation gasoline in leaky five gallon cans in #2 and you could see the vapor rising out of the hatch! They were in Port Sudan, loading cargo for Malta (November 1942).

Other employment: Worked for a major insurance company as a boiler and machinery inspector and safety engineer. Worked as a safety director in private industry. Still holds valid chief engineer's license, unlimited horsepower, steam and motor, issue #12-10.Retired Nov. 1, 1990.

Lives with wife, Jane, in Longwood, FL. He has three daughters, one son (tugboat captain), five grandchildren and one great grandchild. He is now taking an even strain fore and aft.

Made the "Matron Voyage" on the SS *John W. Brown*, Sept. 21, 1991 and plans on making the "Matron Voyage" on the SS *Lane Victory*, Oct. 3, 1992. STEADY AS SHE GOES.

WILLARD R. BROWN, sailed as messman, utility and O.S. during WWII. Attended Sheepshead Bay from November 1944-February 1945 served on SS *Augustine*, SS *Patrick B. Whallen*, SS *Richard J. Hopkins* and SS *Malcolm*. Also worked at Bethlehem-Fairfield Shipyard from 1942-1944.

Has Merchant Marine Emblem, Honorable Service Button, Presidential Testimonial Letter, Atlantic, Pacific, Mediterranean and Middle East War Zone Bars and Victory Medal.

Married to Charlotte and they live in Severn, MD. He is a member of AMMV JWB Chapter, secretary.

WILLIAM R. BRUNER, was born Aug. 2, 1923 in Trumann, AR. Graduated from high school in Decatur, IL on June 5, 1942. Classified 4F by Selective Service.

Sponsored and trained by the Sailors Union of the Pacific in San Francisco, CA.

Signed on the SS *President Grant* May 15, 1943 as an ordinary seaman. Sailed to Noumea, New Caledonia with 2,000 Army engineers.

Signed on the liberty ship SS *Philip Kearny* as an ordinary seaman. Sailed to Port Chicago, CA for cargo of munitions. Returned to San Francisco. Advanced to able bodied seaman (acting). Sailed to Hawaii, Solomon Islands and the Coral Sea.

Signed on the liberty ship SS *William J. Palmer* as an able bodied seaman (papers) Feb. 1, 1943. Sailed to Port Hueneme, CA. Loaded penalty and deck cargo and departed for Hawaii, Marshall and the Mariana Islands. Returned to San Francisco Oct. 10, 1944 after eight months and ten days at sea. Final discharge.

Went back home to Decatur, IL. Married and never returned to the sea. Retired to Lake Mary, FL with 26 years of employment with automatic totalisators of Newark, DE Oct. 1, 1988.

RAYMOND R. BRUNK, was born March 31, 1922 in Akron, OH. He joined the Merchant Marine December 1942 in Los Angeles, CA.

Served on SS *Richard March Hoe* (liberty), (fireman-w/t) April 11, 1943 to June 28, 1943. SS *Cape Victory* (victory), fireman w/t, July 28, 1943 to Oct. 4, 1943. SS *Henry Miller* (liberty), fireman w/t, Dec. 31, 1943 to May 23, 1944. SS *Lawrence Gianella*, (liberty), fireman w/t, July 1, 1944 to May 12, 1945. SS *Lane Victory*, (victory), fireman w/t, June 27, 1945 to Aug. 29, 1945. S/T *Newberg* (3rd asst. eng.), Nov. 12, 1945-March 4, 1946, T-2 Tanker. S/T *Fort Clatsop* (3rd asst. engr.) April 25, 1946 to June 13, 1946, T-2 Tanker.

His memorable experiences includes delivering troops and supplies for invasion of Attu, in the Aleutian Islands. Ship *Richard March Hoe*, 1943. Delivered troops and supplies for the invasion of the Philippines at Leyte Gulf. Ship, SS *Lawrence Gianella*, 1944. Proceeded on a voyage around the world via the Suez Canal.

Received training on Catalina in early 1943, January through March.

Worked for McDonnell Douglas Space Division as field eng.

He is a volunteer crew member on the *Lane Victory*, helping with the restoration, engine room.

WALTER F. BRUNNER, sailed as oiler and F/T during WWII. Attended USMSST as Hoffman Island. Awarded Merchant Marine Emblem, Atlantic, Pacific, Mediterranean, and Middle East War Zone Bars. Sailed on *Simon Maberger, Isaac Coles, James W. Johnson, Robert E. Peatry, Samuel Gomper, Skidmore Victory, Kingsport Victory* and *Texarkana Victory*.

Married to Josephine and they live in Oxford, MD. He is a member of AMMV JWB Chapter.

GEORGE R. BRUSH, JR., was born Nov. 16, 1927 in Amityville, NY. He joined the Merchant Marine June 1944 in New York.

Served on SS *Fredericksburg*, SS *Ouachita Victory*, SS *Henry A. Dobson, Frederkksburg*. Served in the South Pacific for most of 1945. Sailing between Curacoa, Netherland, W. Indies and Australia. *Ouachita Victory* was one of the first American Merchant ships into Scandinavia after WWII (later 1945).

His memorable experiences include *Ouachita Victory* ran around north of Stockholm. Ship was listing badly with several large holes. Finally rescued by a number of salvage ships and towed to Gothenburg, Sweden for lengthy repairs.

Assistant vice president and director ITT World Communications. 37 years service with ITT, five additional years as director with Comsat and Contel (now GTE).

Married to Marion A. Brush. Married 44 years. They have four children, George III, Carol, James and Kathleen. They also have ten grandchildren.

JOHN BRUSZO, was born Sept. 27, 1925 in Nesquehoning, PA. He joined the Merchant Marine Oct. 5, 1943 in Philadelphia, PA.

Employed at Central Railroad of New Jersey. Single an retired Aug. 15, 1988.

ROBERT A. BRYAN, sailed as cadet, 3rd mate, 2nd mate, and master during WWII. Attended Kings Point. Awarded National Defense Bar, Atlantic and Pacific War Zone Bars.

His son, Thomas E. Bryan, is his next of kin. Robert resides in Martinex, CA and is a member of AMMV JWB Chapter.

KENNETH BRUCKELMEYER, sailed on SS *New London* and was wounded. He received the Mariners Medal 47 years later. Refer to ship/crew lists.

He is a member of AMMV MW Chapter.

PAUL H. BUHMAN, was born Sept. 21, 1922, Camas, WA. Joined Naval Service, Portland, OR, September 1942, assigned apprentice seaman, Class M-1, USNR. Sent to USMSTS Port Hueneme, CA for boot training.

Helped move training station from Port Hueneme to St. Catherine Hotel, Catalina Island.

Ships sailed: *Amos Kendall* (fireman/wt) Liberty ship 1943, Pacific and Atlantic; *Dunham Wright* (fireman/wt) Liberty ship 1943, South Pacific; *Czechoslovakia Victory* (oiler) 1944 North Pacific; *Elmira Victory* (oiler) 1944 South Pacific and North Pacific; *Cape Georgia* (oiler) 1944-1945 North Pacific and South Pacific.

In 1949 he went to work at Crown Zellerbach Paper Mill Camas, WA as electrician, retired 1984.

At present he has several Koi ponds for a hobby and volunteer as a "Watchstander" (Guide) at the Oregon Maritime Center and Museum, Portland, OR. He and his wife Peggy live in Vancouver, USA.

RICHAEL A. BURKE, graduated as ensign, USMS from USMMA in 1946. Served on Liberty ships, etc. He resides in Newark, DE.

HETZEL M. BURTON, sailed during WWII, Korean and Vietnam Wars and peacetime. Is 78 years old and retired. He is a member of AMMV JWB Chapter. He resides in Gulf Shores, AL.

JACKSON J. BUSH, was born Nov. 27, 1925. Graduated from Central High School, Madison, WI June 1943. Joined the USMS September 1943. Took training and graduated from USMSTS Sheepshead Bay, Brooklyn, NY November 1943. Transferred to USMSGS Baltimore, MD and assigned to: SS *Pomona* as OS convoyed to Halifax, NS and on to London, England. Later sailed on the following Liberty ships during the period of April 1944 to February 1946 as a member of the deck department.

SS *Robert H. Harrison,* North Africa and Mediterranean ports; SS *James M. Gillis,* Scotland and Murmansk, Russia; SS *Marion McKinley Bovard,* North Africa and Italy; SS *James E. Howard,* South America, Chile and Canada; SS *Cornelius Gilliam,* Trieste and other Italian ports.

Entered the U.S. Army February 1946 and retired from the Army in February 1967. Served both in Korea and Vietnam. Upon retirement from the U.S. Army, Joined the Brown County, WI Sheriff's Dept. and recently retired from the Sheriff's Department.

ROBERT J. BUSHER was born Oct. 2, 1923 in Petaluma, CA. He joined the service on Jan. 6, 1943 and was sent to Catalina Island. Busher signed up for radio school and got his combo blinker/beeper and learned the code. He passed the review board and was shipped to New York for about nine weeks and then on to Gallups Island.

Joined the Liberty ship *SS Sidney H. Short*. The first voyage for the *SS Sidney Short* began on Jan. 28, 1944 and ended Dec. 23, 1944. Some of the places they were in: Milne Bay, New Guinea, Australia, Hollandia, Goodenough Island Noomfoer Island.

Memorable experiences include staging in Hollandia, joining a large convoy including 6 Liberties, all loaded with landing mats, gasoline and 105 shells. He remembers the gunner from Kentucky who was asleep when an air raid began. When large pieces of shrapnel started landing along side of him, he picked off the tail feathers on a Jap bomber and it crashed into a Navy tender tied up to the *SS Augustus Thomas*, leaving her with no power and booms out.

Busher's date of discharge was March 1, 1946. He attained the rank of Ensign, USMS and received the Pacific Theater & Combat Bar.

He got married June 22, 1946, raised three sons, worked 41 years in the hay, grain and feed business and retired in 1987. His hobbies are fishing and hunting and traveling from Fairbanks to Flagstaff visiting his family. He got his ham license in 1992.

ED BUTCHER, shipped out at age 15 as AB, 1945-53, spending two years shuttling between Japan and Korea taking in fresh equipment and supplies and bringing out damaged equipment, tec. (TAL 4/92, p.7). Buther lives in Swansea, SC.

ROBERT A. BUYS, resides in Gretna, VA and is a member of AMMV JWB Chapter.

LEO B. BYRNS, sailed as OS, AB, messman during WWII. Has Merchant Marine Emblem, Atlantic, Pacific, Mediterranean and Middle East War Zone Bars. Attended Sheepshead Bay.

His skills include, construction and flooring.

Kenneth L. Byrns of Caledonia, MI is Leo's next of kin. Leo is a member of AMMV JWB Chapter.

NELSON M. CALEY, was born Nov. 19, 1926 in Canton, OH. Boot training, Section 667, Sheepshead Bay Nov. 20, 1944. Hoffman Island Radio Training January 1945, Section 37-R. Graduated Hoffman Island June 29, 1945.

Ships sailed: Liberty-*Francis E. Siltz,* 2nd operator July 30, to Sept. 20, 1945 Italy and return. Liberty-*Francis E. Siltz,* chief operator Sept. 21, 1945 to Sept. 4, 1946, Mobile, Panama, Tacloban, Manila, Sidney, Brisbane, Manila, Finschhafen, Sidney, Brisbane, Manila, Nagoya, Yokohama, Portland, OR. Liberty-*Abraham Baldwin,* chief operator Jan. 6, 1947 to April 15, 1947. Norfolk, Rotterdam, Norfolk, Antwerp. March 23, 1947 lost rudder north of Azores-drifting. March 30 tug arrives from New York. April 14, 1947 finally arrive at New York under tow, 33 days after leaving Antwerp.

Worked Ohio Bell Telephone Co. for 35 years, retiring Nov. 30, 1983. Thankful every day for the electronic training received at Hoffman Island. Licensed amateur operator W8EAR since March 1949.

TOM CAIRNS, sailed as FWT on SS *John N. Maffit*. Subsequently sailed ATS in various engine positions and eventually sailed as third assistant engineer.

Tom resides in Riverton, NJ.

DAVID F. CAMERON, was born in 1924 in Malden, MA. He joined the Merchant Marine 1941 in Boston, MA. Served on SS *George Davis,* cadet, in Wilmington, NC.

His memorable experiences include convoy to Murmansk USSR 1943. Collision near Arctic Circle with "Hog Island" freighter, no survivors 27 years on passenger ships, tankers and freighters as 2nd, 1st engineer.

He is now a hard rock miner, San Juan Mountains, western slope of Rocky Mountains, chief engineer, the "Independence: Silver Mine.

David received the Victory Medal, Mediterranean Middle East War Zone Bar, Pacific War Zone Bar, Atlantic War Zone Bar, Merchant Marine Combat Bar, The Vietnam Service Bar and the Philippine Liberation Ribbon.

HENRY CAP, in 1942 at the age of 16, he quit school to join the U.S. Navy but was turned down because of a congenital ear defect. After being rejected by everyone else including the draft and Sheepshead Bay Maritime School he went to work on a harbor tug. After 90 days he secured ordinary seaman papers and shipped out on October 25th on a tanker bound for England. Fortunately he was never torpedoed or went through an air raid. He believes that the rough storm they passed through on their return was partly responsible.

After the war he shipped on and off until 1953. At the present time he is married 44 years and has sired four children, three boys and a girl. He is retired from Local 361 Brooklyn as a rigger ironworker.

JOE CARBO, sailed as chief engineering on the SS *Remsen Heights*. Donated framed poster of ship stack insignias to PLS.

ARCHIE H. CARPENTER, sailed as mess boy and radio officer on one ship October 1945 to April 1946, SS *Samuel Griffin* (Todd-Houston). Attended Sheepshead Bay, Gallups Island and Hoffman Island.

Archie is married to Bonnie and they reside in Bradenton, FL. He is a member of AMMV JWB Chapter.

ELMER LORD CARTY, was born in Rockville Centre, Long Island, NY Feb. 6, 1902. Graduated New York State Nautical School training ship *Newport* May 15, 1920. Joined *Standard Oil* of New Jersey, third mate August 1927.

WWII served tankers carrying aviation fuel, heating oil and water for Aruba. Torpedoed April 16, 1942 50 miles east of Los Hermanos off coast of Venezuala. Chief mate of ship *Heinrich von Riedemann*. Became master *S.B. Hunt* May 30, 1942 at 40 youngest skipper Standard Oil Fleet.

Logs Nov. 23, 1942 on missing. Coast Guard assures Captain Livingston Roe; *Glenpool*; *Esso Augusta*; *W.H. Libby*. They have no records after Oct. 18, 1944. May be period running convoys to England, Iceland, Murmansk and under control of Navy. They guarantee still there.

Served as Commodore of convoys many times. Awards include Merchant Marine Defense Bar Service from Sept. 8, 1939 to Dec. 7, 1941; Atlantic War Zone Bar (twice); Merchant Marine Combat Bar with Stars.

Licensed operate steam and motor vessels any gross tons any oceans; 1st class pilot New York Bay and Harbor, Galveston. Asked to join Pilot's Association in both places.

Resigned last command *Esso Utica* after seven years April 14, 1953 because of illness. Operated Captain Carty's Cottages, Newfound Lake, New Hampshire until death May 17, 1963. He was a master Mariner.

Esso Utica was one of the first super tankers. It was a great honor that Dad was given command of one.

RALPH L. CATT, graduate of USMA, Kings Point. Sailed on five oceans including and called at Murmansk, Russia.

Ralph resides in Milford, DE.

THOMAS L. CAUTHEN, sailed as radio officer during WWII on board T-2 tanker SS *Carniflex Ferry,* Sept. 24, 1945-December 1945. Sailed from Galveston, TX to Philippines. From January 1946 to February 1947 sailed with Cities Service Oil Co. as purser aboard various tankers on coastwise and South American trips. Enrolled in USMS at Birmingham, AL on Dec. 7, 1944 and attended Sheepshead Bay as apprentice seaman. Transferred in February 1945 to USMS Radio Training School, Gallups Island, Boston, MA graduating Aug. 31, 1945. Has FCC TLT Radiotelegraph and Radiotelephone license. Has certificate of substantially continuous service in the USMM for period of service Dec. 7, 1944 to Feb. 3, 1947. Also has Presidential Testimonial Letter.

Thomas is married to Jean and they reside in Baltimore, MD. He is a member of AMMV JWB Chapter.

JOHN A. CAVALLIO, resides in Kingsville, MD and is a member of AMMV JWB Chapter.

PAUL R. CAVANAUGH, sailed as fireman 2nd class, utility and oiler during WWII. Was sunk. Attended Sheepshead Bay.

He is married to Leona and they reside in Baltimore, MD. He is a member of AMMV JWB Chapter.

FRANK CHERKAIS, was born Feb. 12, 1916 in Kiev, Russia. Taken to U.S. by uncle, a butcher in Philadelphia. At age 24, in 1940, two buddies seamen got him drunk and put him aboard a small tanker in port of Philadelphia. He was awakened by an old timer and asked where am I? The old salt said, "first trip?" Uhuh! here's a hair of the dog that bit ya and handed him three fingers of rye whiskey. "You're a wiper, go down to the engine room and take a bucket with you. On second thought, better take two buckets, one for you, and one for the engine room. "He never forgot that." Trip was only eight days from Philly to Boston and back. Seasick every minute of the trip. "Never again you bastards" (his two buddies who shanghaid him) and they laughed and said he'd be out in 10 days on his own and he did and kept sailing until 1974. Last trip broke down and hospital.

The Coast Guard lifted restrictions on alien seamen for WWII duration and allowed a small quota to sail foreign and coastwise.

He did have a U.S. Merchant Mariners document #2129508 and a resident alien card and was member of National Maritime Union.

Sailed on rivers, great lakes, coastwise, foreign in ratings. He served on SS *Coaldale Victory,* chief butcher, LeHavre troops; SS *Grand River,* albe seaman, Bristol-Curacao, *Joshua Lippincott,* able seaman, Panama, S. Africa, Durban, Port Elizabeth.

His memorable experience includes Murmansk run 1945. November attacked off Oslo by Stukas subs and battleship. Lost around 18 ships. He was on a 20mm on starboard deck aiding gunner *J. Lippincott* Nov. 2, 1945 to April 3, 1946. They made it home pockmarked.

Frank is now retired at the age of 76 but would like to make one more trip. He is building a 15' plywood boat.

"I was known as a rebel, an atheist, a commy and an agitator until 1974 when I made a phone call to the 700 Club on T.V., a Christian program. A young man led me in prayer confessing my sins unto God and asked Jesus Christ to come into my life. A 180° change since and has become a minister of the Gospel and wants to return to Kiev to preach to the Russians."

ALOIS F. (LOU) CHERNEY, sailed from 1941-1946 as oiler, deck engineer, 3rd assistant engineer, 2nd assistant engineer and chief engineer. Enrolled in U.S. Maritime Service Training Station at Fort Trumbull on May 18, 1942. Graduated on Sept. 18, 1942 with 3rd Assistant Engineers License and Commission as ensign (E) in USMS. Sailed on SS *Suwied,* SS *Greylock,* SS *Clamar,* SS *William Pepper,* SS *Marie Meloney,* SS *Gracie Abbott,* SS *Benjamin Williams,* SS *John Merrick,* and SS *Nashua Victory.*

Awarded the Atlantic, Mediterranean-Middle East, and Pacific War Zone Bars, Merchant Marine Defense Bar and Combat Bar and Presidential Citation. Donated copies of BAMS Messages announcing proclaiming end of war in Europe received on board the SS *John Merrick* while at sea.

Alois resides in Silver Spring, MD.
He is a member of AMMV JWB Chapter.

LORN C. CHURCH, was born July 1, 1917 in Boulder, CO. Joined Merchant Marine Oct. 13, 1942 training Catalina, CA.

Served on SS *Coney,* oiler June 8, 1943 to Oct. 2, 1943. *Jhon G. Brady,* oiler and deck engineer Oct. 5, 1943 to June 27, 1944. SS *Horace,* oiler, 1944. SS *Cape Henlopen,* fireman and watertender, Aug. 30, 1944 to Nov. 20, 1944. SS *Typhoon* fireman and watertender Dec. 4, 1944 to May 27, 1945. SS *Knox Victory,* junior engineer July 19, 1945 to Nov. 2, 1945.

Discharged Sept. 15, 1944 USNS San Diego, CA. Married 34 years to Pear V. Church, two step children, Robert and Dorothy.

He is a retired plumbing and heating contractor.

LOUIS N. CIRIGNANO, was born Oct. 6, 1925 in Passaic, NJ. Graduated Passaic High School 1943. Enlisted at 18 in 1943. Attended the Sheepshead Bay, Brooklyn, NY. Maritime training school.

First liberty ship was the SS *Thomas Wolfe,* served in the stewards dept. The trip was 13 months North Atlantic, English Channel D-Day invasion of Normandy beaches, carrying cargo, supplies, troops, made 30 trips to beaches, French ports of call with Southampton, England is base port of call. Received combat, North Atlantic ribbons etc. Later sailed on SS *Joseph Hews,* SS *Richard Rush,* SS *James Jackson,* SS *Raphael Semmes* etc. until 1946.

Returned to sea in 1949. Served in the U.S. Army 1950-1951 during the Korean War.

Attended Montclair State Teachers College 1952-1956 BA degrees. Returned to sea after graduation sailing on Seafarers International Union ships (Stewards and Deck Depts.)

Began full-time teaching in 1967 after earning MA degree from Paterson State Teachers College. Retired from Lodi, NJ Public School System as a Special Education Teacher in 1988.

Served on the Passaic Board of Education for 18 years active in legion, education, civic organizations etc. He's a bachelor and lives in Passaic, NJ and Hallandale, FL.

BARD N. CLAAR, was born Feb. 19, 1921, Rexford, KS. Graduated Oberlin, KS May 1941. Sworn into Coast Guard July 23, 1941 at Omaha, NE. Assigned to Hoffman, Island, Staten Island, NY through January 1942. Trained on Empire State and three masted schooner, Vema as cook. Assigned to MS Aurora in Philadelphia, PA. Did not sail on her went back to NYNY joined National Maritime Union.

Ships sailed on SS *Toteco* Feb. 5, 1942 through April 8, 1942, tanker, messboy and 2nd cook, Atlantic Ocean; SS *George Wythe,* May 9, 1942 through May 15, 1942, freighter, 2nd cook, Atlantic Ocean; SS *Western Queen,* May 29, 1942 through June 1, 1942, freighter, mess boy, Atlantic Ocean; MS *Arriaga,* (Paniminian Flag) June 13, 1942 through June 23, 1943, tanker, 2nd cook, torpedoed June 23, 1942 in Carribean of Columbia S.A. (ship lost)

(*Scottish Bard,* original name), Sept. 10, 1942 through Sept. 30, 1942, freighter, 2nd cook, Carribean, Atlantic; SS *Esso Harrisburg,* Nov. 1, 1942 through March 29, 1943, tanker, 2nd cook, Atlantic, Pacific; SS *Esso Norfolk,* May 9, 1943 through May 4, 1943, tanker, 2nd cook, Atlantic; SS *Esso Providence,* July 19, 1943, through Feb. 16, 1944, tanker, wiper, Atlantic, Mediterranean (bombed in Augusta, Sicily, Aug. 24, 1943. Not Lost); SS *Esso Bedford,* March 23, 1944 through July 7, 1944, tanker, fwt, South Atlantic, Carribean. SS *Esso Raleigh,* Aug. 11, 1944 through Sept. 13, 1944, tanker, fwt, Atlantic, Gulf; SS *Esso Washington,* Oct. 20, 1944 through July 3, 1945, tanker, 2nd cook, Atlantic Gulf, Pacific. (Ran aground at Eniwetok, in Marshall Islands. March 14-45 ship lost; SS *Esso Dover,* Aug. 4, 1945 through Aug. 15, 1945, tanker, oiler, South Atlantic.

Married on Friday July 13, 1945. Worked for Safeway Grocery, farmed, owned Old General Grocery Store all in Western Kansas. Operated Coop Gasoline tank wagon. Went to work at Boeing, Wichita as tool and die maker September 1951 and retired from Boeing as tooling supervisor Feb. 1, 1980. Now garden, bowl, fix cars and cooks for his wife. He now lives in Wichita, KS.

ROBERT E. CLAPPIER, was born May 16, 1925 in Minneapolis, MN and graduated from Lewiston High School, Lewiston, MN and graduated from Lewiston High School, Lewiston, MN. Joined the Merchant Marine in 1943. Took training at Sheepshead Bay, NY and advanced training at Baltimore, MD.

Ships sailed: *Michael Tracy,* Atlantic; *A.J. Cermak* liberty ship, 1944, in Atlantic, Mediterranean and Middle East; *Joseph Holt,* Liberty Ship 1944, in the Atlantic, and 1945 in the Pacific. Returned to Minnesota and attended Winona State, Winona, MN, North Dakota Sate at Fargo, ND and University of Minnesota. Was a science instructor, and later a high school principal in Minnesota from 1948-1985.

Retired 1985 from South Washington County Schools, Cottage Grove, MN. Bob remains active doing maintenance work for his son, Dr. Ronald Clappier, and doing substitute teaching.

Bob lives with his wife Jeanne (Speltz) in Woodbury, MN. They also have a daughter Suzanne who is married and lives in Wisconsin.

ROBERT "BOB" L. CLARK, Z648554, was born July 10, 1929, in Venice, CA. In September 1945, at the age of 16, he went to sea with the Army Transport Service on board a small cargo ship, FS398, which was a reefer ship. They delivered Thanksgiving dinner to troops on Kwajalein Isle. These were the first real fresh "frozen" turkeys they had had in years.

For ten years he sailed steadily on various ships for the U.S. government and the Sailors Union of the Pacific. He worked on cargo and troop ships, on tankers and animal transport ships. While he was on the *Plymouth Victory* ship they took 800 Peruvian cavalry horses from Germany to three ports in Greece for their cavalry.

He also had the privilege of working on the last Liberty ship to be built and delivered-the *Albert M. Boe,* a four large hatch "Boxed Aircraft Transport" ship.

On April 26, 1952, he was aboard the SS *Wm. Eaton,* a standard Liberty ship. He'd just gone off watch at 2345. They were passing Tokyo Bay on the way south from the Northern Island to Korea with a full load of coal. The weather was heavy and it was raining. There was no bow lookout (on the flying bridge) when the ship went aground on To-Shima Island at 0020 (a.m.) The two port lifeboats were launched to get the crew to a destroyer that the Navy had sent to rescue them, but they could not get close to them. He was put in command of the #4 lifeboat and they rowed some two hours or more before a whale boat reached them and towed them to the destroyer.

The *Eaton* worked on the rocks for four to five days and finally broke in two, forward of the bridge, and came to rest along side the bow. It was declared a total loss. He was thankful for lifeboat training! In his experience, he believes that was the only ship lost during the Korean conflict. That was his most memorable experience at sea.

He retired at the age of 51 from the San Francisco Bay Naval shipyards, where he'd served as a rigger and foreman rigger for nearly 20 years.

He has been married twice. Working part-time on private R.R. Pullman car "Virginia City".

FLORIAN CLARK, sailed as fwt and wiper during WWII, Korean and Vietnam Wars. Holds Atlantic, Mediterranean Middle East, Pacific War Zone Bars and Combat Bar.

Married to Mary and they reside in Baltimore, MD. He is a member of AMMV JWB Chapter.

WILLIAM G. CLARY, JR., sailed as chief mate during WWII, Korean and Vietnam Wars. Has Victory Medal, Mediterranean Middle East, Atlantic and Pacific War Zone Bars and Vietnam Service Bars. Attended Sheepshead Bay, Kings Point, Radar School 39 Broadway, NMY and MM & P School in Baltimore. Lt.jg., USNR retired.

Has daughter Patricia Stern, his next of kin, who resides in Miami, FL. William is a member of AMMV JWB Chapter.

SAMUEL A. CLAUSS, sailed as oiler at start of WWII and was chief engineer at end of WWII. Has combat with stars, Merchant Marine Emblem, Atlantic, Mediterranean, Middle East War Zone Bars.

Samuel is married to Norma and they reside in Towson, MD. He is a member of AMMV JWB Chapter.

HARRY COHAN, sailed as 3rd engineer on SS *Thornstein Veblen.* He resides in Rahns, PA.

PHILIP J. COMBA, sailed as FWT and oiler during WWII. In the Suruj Archipeligo in the Philippines the ship was strafed and one or two armed guard members were wounded. The ship was the SS *Harrington Emerson* out of San Francisco. Was on the Murmansk Run in early 1944 on the SS *Gilbert Stuart* from March 1, 1944 to May 31, 1944. Is supposed to get medal. Has the Pacific, Atlantic, Mediterranean Middle East War Zone Bars.

He is married to Mary and they reside in Delmar, MD. He is a member of AMMV JWB Chapter.

IVAN F. COMMONS, was born Aug. 28, 1915 in Colusa County, CA. Joined the Maritime Service in July 1944 and trained at Catalina Island until October 1944. Sailed on the *Alice H. Rice* (oiler), Liberty ships with general cargo to Guam. October 1944 to January 1945.

Sailed on the *Canada Victory* (oiler) February 1945 to April 1945 to Okinawa where a Japanese suicide plane sent her to the bottom with 7,000 tons of ammo aboard.

They escaped with the loss of only two lives, one Merchant seaman and one gun-crew member. The rest of them were pulled from the water by Navy crews and were placed aboard a Navy hospital ship which left for San Francisco several days later, and they landed in S.F. on May 30, 1945.

He joined the San Joaquin County, CA Sheriffs Department in January 1946 and retired on April 1, 1970. Since that he has enjoyed a very active retirement, traveling extensively and is involved in numerous volunteer community projects.

CHARLES K. CONDRAY, sailed during WWII.

He now resides in Finksburg, MD and is a member of AMMV JWB Chapter.

DELANCY L. COOK, resides in Lutherville, MD and is a member of AMMV JWB Chapter.

CARROLL H. COOPER, (See Sunpaper article quote listed under Patrick L. Whalen.)

HERB COOPER, was a deck cadet aboard the SS *Sebastian Cermeno* with 3 1/2 months of his six months sea time completed. Along with twelve months of intensive shore training he would be eligible to get his 3rd mates license. The *Cermeno* was sunk by German U-boat-511 off Madagascar. Herb was one of the 72 person who survived the torpedoing. Upon arriving back in the U.S. Herb heard that his "Lifeboat and Survival" time did not count as sea time. He shipped out on another Liberty ship for a short voyage which turned out to be 13 months long. Herb got his 3rd Mates license in December 1945. Heidnrich (Henry) Pahls was torpedo officer aboard the U-511 enroute to Japan for delivery to the Japanese navy. On Jan. 24, 1992 these two former combatants of WWII met at the Oregon Maritime Museum. (AMMV, summer 1992, p.20).

SHEROD COOPER, sailed as cadet 1945-1946. Project Liberty Ship historian and director (TUD spring, 1992, p.8). He now resides in Hyattsville, MD.

BURNELL C. COSBY, graduated from USMMA February 1945. Sailed on the SS *Flying Scud* (C-2) in the Pacific. Also sailed as 3rd assistant on the SS *Elinor Wylie,* SS *W.M. Roundtree* and the SS *Joshua Chamberlain.*

During the Korean War served as lieutenant USNR on the USS *Newport News* (CA 148) and the USS *Siboney* (CVE 112).

Burnell resides in Wilmington, DE.

THOMAS A. COSTER, resides in Baltimore, MD and is a member of AMMV JWB Chapter.

CHARLES COX, JR., resides in Baltimore, MD and is a member of AMMV JWB Chapter.

ROBERT G. COX, was born Aug. 6, 1923 in Philadelphia, PA. Entered University of Pennsylvania September 1941. Left to enter Kings Point in February 1943.

Shipped as a cadet on the *James Bowie* to Bizerte N. Africa, Casablanca and Hull, England. Back to the academy February 1944. Graduated and got 3rd mates license in November of 1944. Shipped on *Frederick W. Taylor* to Antwerp in January 1945 to New Orleans and then Liverpool.

Took time off July and August 1945 sat for and got 2nd Mates license. Shipped on the *Cyrus H.K. Curtis* September 1945 to Palermo, Cagliari and Naples back to Baltimore and out again to Dubrovnik, Yugoslavia. Returned to University of Pennsylvania in February 1946 and graduated February 1948.

He is a retired insurance broker. Married and has two sons and two grandchildren.

CHARLES A. CRABBIN, (deceased), Project Liberty Ship secretary from 1988-1992 (TUD, spring 1992, p.5).

ROBERT E. CROZIER, sailed as fireman during WWII. He is married to Dorothy, his next of kin and is a member of AMMV JWB Chapter. They reside in Burton, SC.

DENNIS J. CULLEN, resides in Baltimore, MD and is a member of AMMV JWB Chapter.

ROBERT CUNDIFF, was born Feb. 27, 1927 in Pittsylvania, County, VA. He enlisted in the Maritime service Jan. 22, 1945 in Norfolk, VA.

Took maritime service training at Sheepshead Bay.

His memorable experience includes: taking train cross country to Long Beach, CA. First ship was *Southwestern Victory,* around the world, May 1945- September 1945. Long Beach, Australia, India, Naples, and New York. Shipmate was Jim Thorpe who was sailing as carpenter. Sailed as wiper.

Other ships sailed as fwt - *Costa Rica Victory, Baylor Victory, DePauw Victory* and *Loyola Victory.* Last trip SS *Oran M. Roberts,* June 1948.

Married in Danville, VA in 1948. Now retired has four children and four grandchildren.

MELFORD D. CUNNINGHAM, joined USMS in August 1944 at Detroit. Left Sheepshead Bay October 1944. Continued sailing until 1947.

He now resides in Prescot, MI.

RICHRD J. CUNNINGHAM, attended Sheepshead Bay in 1944. Sailed as OS. He now resides in Milford, CT.

ROBERT PAUL DAERR, was born May 17, 1928, in Greensburg, PA. Entered service May 1944 at the age of 16 in Pittsburgh, PA. Attended boot camp at Sheepshead Bay, NY.

Served on: SS *Oscar S. Straus,* OS, liberty tanker, North Africa; SS *John Fairfield,* OS, liberty ammo ship, Italy; SS *ATS Uruguay,* OS, troop ship Army, England, France, Belgium; SS *Cahawba,* OS, T2 Tanker - India,

Bairain, (Persian Gulf), Australia, South and Central American, Hawaii, Japan, Dutch West, Indies; SS *Mauvilla*, Act. AB, T2 tanker, Wales, UK; M/V *Swift Arrow*, deck maintenance, Army cargo, Germany.

His memorable experiences includes being fired on and helped sink submarine, Mediterranean. 1945 caught in hurricane off Okinawa, hull split forward of midship housing, ship stayed together. Temporary repairs at Pearl Harbor, dry dock at *Colon*, Panama Canal Zone, installed belly band.

Other employment: Senior chief petty officer, U.S. Navy, 1953-1977 retired. Over the road driver, Chemical Leaman Tank Lines to 1985.

Married twice, four children, two boys, two girls. Lives with wife Chloe and daughter Valerie in North Huntingdon, PA. Today he is loafing, skating, hiding from the BOSUM.

DANIEL B. DAHL, was born Jan. 1, 1917 in Fosston, MN. Joined the Merchant Marines in Minnesota in 1942. Went to Sheepshead Bay training station in New York. Shipped out March 4, 1943 on Liberty ship SS *Judah P. Benjamin*, ran unescorted through the Panama Canal, around the horn of South Africa and Egypt. The trip took 7 1/2 months, on return trip they met an English ship off Capetown. They waved and moments later they heard a great explosion, the English ship sun in three minutes. He believes they were not torpedoed because they were empty. He worked in stewards department as saloon mess. Other Liberty ships he sailed were:

SS *James DeWolf*, November 1943 to March 1944; SS *Charles Carrol*, May 1944 to October 1944; SS *William Beaumont*, December 1944 to April 1945; SS *David Holmes*, May 1945 to August 1945; SS *Anna Dickinson*, September 1945 to November 1945.

One trip on above ships they sailed in a 100 ship convoy with Navy escort. As he recalls they lost two or three ships, the convoy split off Portugal, most of convoy went to the Mediterranean, they went to Casablanca. Another trip they went to Italy stopping in Brindisi, Bari, and Ancona where the ship was unloaded and war supplies, Jeeps, etc were driven to the front in Rimini where fighting was heavy.

He married after the war. He has three children, nine grandchildren and five great grandchildren. He is retired from engineering and lives in Glendale, CA.

JOHN L. DAHL, was born Sept. 16, 1925 in Park City, UT. Graduated from Park City High School 1943. Joined the U.S. Maritime Service in October 1943 and received training at Catalina Island. He was assigned to the SS *Poland Victory* (the third Victory ship built), as wiper. A load of ammunition was carried from Port Chicago to the invasion of Hollandia in Dutch New Guinea.

After the first trip John worked his way up to first engineer and sailed on 16 different ships between 1944 and 1953. In addition to *Poland Victory* he sailed on *Neptune's Car* (1944-1945), *Island Mail* (1945), *Ann McKim* (1945-1946), *Malden Victory* (1946), *Eagle Wing* (1947), *Mormac Wren* (1947), *Lou Gehrig* (1947), *Iraq Victory* (1947), *President Tyler* (1948), *Jeff Davis* (1948), *General Walker* (1950), *Alfred Victory* (1950-1951), *Robin Wently* (1951), *Lafayette Victory* (1952), *Hawaiian Retailer* (1952-1953). John served in WWII and the Korean War. He received the Merchant Marine Combat Bar; Pacific War Zone Bar; Atlantic War Zone Bar; and the Mediterranean Middle East War Zone Bar.

After leaving the sea John attended the University of Utah. In 1956 he was employed by Royal Insurance as a boiler inspector and safety engineer. In 1964 he joined C.N.A. Insurance as branch loss control manager in Salt Lake City. He was transferred to Pennsylvania as loss control manager for the eastern states in 1971. In 1975 he was transferred to San Francisco where he retired in 1990.

John now lives in Pleasant Hill, CA with his wife of 37 years Eileen. They have two grown children and three grandchildren.

PHILIP JOHN DAILEY, looking for the owner of "Eddies Bar & Grill" that was patronized by SIU seamen. It was located on the corner of Pratt and South Streets in Baltimore. His last contact was in 1955. Philip died March 1, 1991. He had heart surgery. He is survived by his wife.

HENRY G. DALE, served as radio officer from 1942-1946 and now resides in New Castle, DE.

JOHN D. (JACK) DANIEL, was born May 20, 1920 in Rochester, NY. He joined the Merchant Marine in 1938 at New York State Merchant Marine Academy.

Worked for United Fruit Co. for 31 years, six months and five days in all engineering positions from 3rd assistant to chief engineer.

Presently also a volunteer Maritime Industry Museum SUNY Maritime College. On June 12, 1942 was on SS *Sixaola* when she was torpedoed in Caribbean and sunk at 2130 hours by a German submarine. Lost 29 people, spent 48 hours in lifeboat. Since 1971 stationary engineer in heating plant, serving 12,325 apartments.

His wife is deceased and his has son Robert and grandson Ian. Forced retirement U.F. Co. Still actively employed.

WILLIAM H. DANLEY, JR. was born Nov. 5, 1929 in Eureka, CA. He joined the Merchant Marine in San Francisco, CA.

Served on the SS *Fort Raleigh*, T-2 tanker, OS-Q, South Pacific; SS *New World Victory*, OS, Japan-South Pacific, Philippines.

He is now busy gold mining.

JAMES W. DAVIS, attended Sheepshead Bay in November 1944. Made 24 trips.

He now resides in White Plains, MD.

RICHARD JOHN DEITER, enlisted in the Merchant Marine Nov. 23, 1943 at Kansas City, MO. Took his training at Sheepshead Bay. Graduated Feb. 19, 1944, aboard USS *George Washington* (Army vessel) at Boston, MA to London, England, back in port Philadelphia, PA. After leave, home in Kansas aboard USS *John Bartrum*, San Diego, CA, May 28, 1944 for the Philippines Island by Australia, New Guinea. Work the Manila Bay, Oras Bay and Leyte during the invasion.

Arrived in Port Seattle, WA February 1945. Left to Kansas and was married, returned to ship at New Orleans, LA. Grain freight to Oran Algeria, Africa, and back to New York port. While on leave a farm accident occurred and he was admitted in the Winter General Veterans Hospital for four months. This ended his career as seaman with Maritime Service.

Merchant Marines gave him the opportunity to see the world, the different culture of people in all these countries.

DOUGLAS E. deKEYSER, AMMV charter member JWB Chapter Oct. 14, 1989. He resides in Pasadena, MD.

ROLAND F. DEMBECK, sailed as wiper, oiler, and ordinary seaman during WWII. Has Combat Bar, Atlantic, Mediterranean and Middle East War Zone Bars and Victory Medal.

He is married to Betty and they reside in Spring Hill, FL. He is a member of AMMV JWB Chapter.

MATTHEW DIBELLA, sailed as utility, messman and Army 2nd cook during WWII. Was sunk and damaged. Has Atlantic, Pacific, and Mediterranean War Zone Bars and Philippines Liberation Ribbon.

He is a restaurant manager and chef. Married to Terry, they reside in King of Prussia, PA. Matthew is a member of AMMV JWB Chapter.

ANTHONY DIMAGGIO, was born Aug. 29, 1924 in Corona, NY. He joined the Merchant Marine Oct. 26, 1942 in Pass Christian, MS. Third mate's license issued June 1945.

Served on SS *Henry B. Brown*, deck cadet, February 1943 to July 1943; USAHS *Thistle*, wheelman, January 1944 to May 1944; USAHS *John J. Meany*, wheelman, June 1944 to January 1945; SS *Wm. E. Pendleton*, third mate, June 1945 to November 1945; USAT *Blanche F. Sigman*, third mate November 1945 to June 1946; USAT *Maritime Victory*, third mate, July 1946 to August 1946; SS *Vanderbilt Victory*, third mate, September 1946 to July 1947; SS *George F. Patten*, third mate, August 1947 to October 1947; SS *Topatopa*, third mate, October 1947-December 1947; SS *Malden Victory*, fourth mate, February 1948 to October 1948.

After completing basic cadet training at USMMA Pass Oct. 26, 1942-Feb. 10, 1943, Christian, MS he was granted 10 days leave in New York which was his home. Upon completion of his leave he reported to war shipping administration 39 Bway, NYC for ship assignment as a deck cadet. Another deck cadet, two engine cadets and Anthony were assigned to a liberty ship being built in Baltimore, MD, the USS *Molly Pitcher*. They were living in a hotel in Baltimore. When the company decided it was costing them too much money for S&Q and since the SS *Molly Pitcher* wasn't completed and was only at the outfitting dock. The company ordered U.S. back to the WSA office in New York for reassignment. It was only a few days and he was assigned to the liberty ship SS *Henry B. Brown* which was also in Baltimore, MD at the outfitting dock right next to the *Molly Pitcher*. He stayed with the *Henry B. Brown* while it was completed (three weeks) and sailed as deck cadet on its maiden voyage. He was 18 years old and they were sailing in convoy for Casablanca, North Africa.

His gun assignment was the 20mm on the flying bridge port side forward. About midway across the Atlantic they started getting attacked by U boat wolf packs every evening at 6:40 p.m. General alarm was sounded daily at 5 p.m. so they and the convoy could be prepared while at his assigned gun station on the flying bridge he couldn't help but notice the liberty ship behind his ship was always out of line either to the port or starboard of the column.

Finally around the third or fourth evening of attacks by the Wolf Pack and as he was staring astern the ship behind his was way out of line to the port when a torpedo hit it midship right under where he was assigned on the *Henry B. Brown,* needless to say a loud explosion on impact and a column of water shot into the air twice the height of the masts. The ship rolled violently and drifted back through the convoy. His ship was first in their column and the torpedoed ship was second. He arrived safely in Casablanca and upon conversing with other ships docked from his convoy. He was able to find out that the ship torpedoed was the *Molly Pitcher* and that it didn't sink but was destroyed by their destroyers and escorts to prevent a menace to other convoys. He wasn't able to find out about casualties until the great book A *Careless Word a Needless Sinking* was published. According to the casualty list the deck cadet survived. When he thinks of it he can still clearly see the torpedo hitting the SS *Molly Pitcher* where he probably would have been standing.

Employed as mate at Staten Island Ferry. Director New York Inland and Harbor contracts MEBA 22 years. He is widowed and has two children, Patricia and Stephen. Retired Feb. 1, 1987. He is enjoying retirement in Florida.

DONALD A. DITTMER, was born July 12, 1927 in Ann Arbor, MI. Enlisted July 11, 1944, Federal Building, Detroit. Arrived at Sheepshead Bay, Brooklyn, NY, Aug. 14, 1944. Attended Engineers School Vocational Training. 1st Ship - Sun Ship and Dry Dock: *San Pascual* - Maiden Run - T-2 Tanker. Gasoline to Avonsmouth/Bristol England from Port Arthurs, TX; 2nd ship, *Mobile Bay,* gas and oil to Shell Haven - Graves End England from Arkansas Pass, TX, (tanker); 3rd ship, *Esso Baytown,* gas and oil to Essex, England (tanker) from Bayonne, NJ; 4th ship, SS *Henry George* (Liberty), from Port Hueneme, C.B. base-Oxnard, CA to Eniwetok and Okinawa.

Got caught in storm (typhoon) Oct. 3, 1945 off Okinawa. Discharged at San Pedro Dec. 18, 1945. Got home in time to be drafted to serve in the Korea Occupation with the 7th Div. Inf. and 11th Abn. (Signal Corp) as a radio operator (CW Code).

Retired from the State of Ohio, Steam Engineering Div., 22 years service as a stationary engineer. He now delivers prescription drugs to hospitals and pharmacies, part-time and is a part-time musician.

EDWARD H. DOBLER, was born Oct. 31, 1927 at Brooklyn, NY. Attended Catholic School. Quit VoTech Training and enlisted USMS October 1944, New York. Completed boots, USMSTS Brooklyn, NY, Sheepshead Bay, had the honor to train aboard SS *Mariner* (C-3) and the *Vema,* three masted schooner both training ships. Graduated 2nd Cooks and Bakers School also from Sheepshead Bay.

First ship, SS *Bessmer,* Standard Oil, tanker, coastal and shipyard out of Baltimore, MD, 2nd cook and baker. Second, SS *John S. Copley,* liberty, cargo, out of Baltimore, MD, to Rio, San Paulo, S.A. and return Baltimore,

2nd cook and baker; third, SS *Hawaiian,* shipper C-3, out of Baltimore, MD. Troop ship, "three" 3 (trips) CBI Theatre, last trip via Singapore to Seattle, WA, ordinary seaman and act AB, fourth SS *Marine Falcon,* C-4, out of Seattle, WA, Act A.B., troop ship, Occupation Forces, nurses, Red Cross personnel, Yokosuka, Japan and return Seattle "Shipping Strike". Fifth, SS *Maiden Creek II,* cargo, out of Seattle Act, A.B., Vancouver, BC partial load lumber, Coos Bay, OR, top off and deck load lumber, depart San Pedro, CA, refuel, top off stores, some crew replacements etc., depart San Pedro, CA through Panama Canal to Amsterdam, Holland, return Lake Charles, LA.

It appeared the Korean War loomed over the horizon so yours truly opted for the U.S. Navy. Advanced from seaman to chief warrant officer, ships boatswain. Retired August 1970 after serving in both fleets from amphibious crafts and ships, cruisers, carries, oceanographic, survey ships, naval station investigator, Argentia NFLD. Armed Forces Police, Naples, Italy and Navy Recruiting Service, New York.

Employed various super markets as meat cutter and manager, Upstate, NY. Moved to Jordan, MT 1983. Became Garfield County Sheriff 1985. Retired as sheriff 1991. Presently (July 1992) Reemployed as special deputy.

"In my opinion he owes his success first to his Catholic training school, second to the valuable education received both academic and practical while a member of the USMSTS and USMM and later the U.S. Navy Charter Life Member #149 USMMV WWII.

HAROLD DODGE, was born Nov. 16, 1926. Graduated Imlay City Michigan. Sailed Great Lakes, age 17, on *Hazen Butler,* one of few wooden hatch ore carriers so turnover was great and went from deckhand to deckwatch in two weeks. Shipped out of New York by way of war shipping administration. Alocoa Trader, Hog Islander to Antwerp and spent 10 days over New Years 1945 in Buzz Bomb Alley. Liberty ship, *Hart Crawe* around Cape of Good Hope to various ports or Eastern Africa. Carried a mixed peace time cargo and skeleton gun crew, and was in Beria, a neutral Portugese port on V-E day.

Maiden four trips on converted troop carrier *William Victory* to Europe. Three Caribbean and South America trips as A.B. and quartermaster on T-2 tanker, *Jordan Valley,* Liberty ship, *Frederick W. Galbraith,* load of coal to Antwerp, liberty ship *Tarleton Brown* to Marseilles.

Retired NAPA jobber in Imlay City.

FRANK E. DOUGLAS, (See Sunpaper article quote listed under Patrick L. Whalen.)

MAJORIE DOVMAN, former membership secretary of Project Liberty Ship, when the project was in New York.

She resides in Forest Hills, NY.

EDNA DOYLE, was born May 22, 1922 in Indiana. First ship 1957, cruise ship *Santa Rosa,* Grace Line Co. sailing from New York to Caribbean for three months. Returned to sea in 1958 and remained on the *Santa Paula,* Grace Line for 15 years. After all American Cruise ships

were sold she sailed on freighter and container ships as cook, spent another 15 years at sea and retired in 1987 with 30 years sea service. Life member of the USMMVWW II; Representative of Florida and Chapter Organizer, East Central Florida Chapter secretary.

Merchant Marine awards to civilians; Vietnam Service Medal earned while serving on the SS *American Ranger* ammunition ship to Vietnam. To her knowledge, she is the only American female Mariner who has been awarded the Vietnam Service Medal.

She now lives in Winter Park, FL married to a Merchant Mariner, Frank Liberatore, retired with 45 years sea service. Mother of two, grandmother of six and great grandmother of six.

HORCE B. DREVER, served as cadet from July 1941-December 1942. Sailed on SS *Santa Rose* from September 1941-April 1942. Attended USMMA from June 1942-December 1942. Sailed on SS *Richard Henry Dana* as 3rd mate and 2nd mate from January 1943-September 1943. Served in U.S. Navy.

He now resides in Rydal, PA.

JOSEPH DREYHAUPT, sailed as wiper, oiler, electrician during WWII attended Sheepshead Bay.

He is married to Elizabeth. They reside in Knoxville, MD. He is a member of AMMV JWB Chapter.

ANTHONY P. DUBINSKI, sailed as 2nd mate. Sailed during WWII and Korean War. Ship was damaged. Attended U.S. Merchant Marine Academy at Kings Point in 1945.

Holds Atlantic, Mediterranean-Middle East, and Pacific War Zone Bars and Victory Medal. Skilled as industrial specialist (ship construction).

Married to Mary and they reside in Silver Spring, MD. He is a member of AMMV JWB Chapter.

GEORGE WILLIAM DUFFY, upon graduating from Massachusetts Nautical School in September 1941, was employed by United States Lines in their MS American Leader. In early 1946 returned to U.S. Lines in *Britian Victory* (3rd officer), *James Bennett Moore* (chief officer), *Marine Marlin* (2nd officer), *Ethan Allen* (chief officer/master), *American Miller* (chief officer), and *American Judge* (chief officer/master). Current license - unlimited master, issue 8-11.

Since coming ashore have worked in a variety of Marine-oriented businesses; sail making, yacht and fishing boat sales, ocean cargo solicitation, vessel management, boarding, and agency work. Between 1975 and 1985 edited five bi-annual *Port of Boston Handbooks*.

In 1990 was elected "Alumnus of the Year" by the Massachusetts Maritime Academy Alumni Association. Is presently employed part-time as boarding agent for Consail International of Boston, MA.

Married 41 years to Margaret Doyle and they have two daughters, and five granddaughters.

A.O.H. TONY DUVAL, was born on May 8, 1917 in the Netherlands where he attended and graduated from the Netherland Merchant Marine Academy in Amsterdam in

1939. He served as apprentice and 4th officer with the Holland America Line and on board the old *Nieuw Amsterdam* which at that time was converted into a troop carrier capable to carry at that time was converted into a troop carrier capable to carry 6,000 troops for the Royal British Army. Towards the end of the war he joined Waterman Steamship Company and served as second mate on the Liberty ships *Francis G. Newlands, James Smith* and *George B. MacFarland*.

In 1948 he moved to New Orleans in charge of foreign vessels operation department of a large steamship agency and later joined Shell Oil Co. as Marine manager in their Delta Division for the offshore operations near the mouth of the Mississippi River. Since 1965 he has been a Marine consultant and surveyor in the Middle East and presently since 1981 a Marine appraiser as well with the firm of Noble, Denton and Associates in Houston, TX where he made his home. In this position he has, among other assignments, been involved with approval of ocean tows of remaining Victory ships and T-2's and other ex-World War II vessels, going to their last resting places, generally a foreign scrap yard.

Presently living in Houston with his wife Peggy, he still has not been able to understand the meaning of the word "retirement".

JAMES J. DVORAK, was born Oct. 13, 1921 in Plattsmouth, NE. Moved to Nampa, IA in 1924. Worked at Oregon Shipyards 1942 on liberty and victory ships. Took training at Santa Catalina 1943.

Sailed *W.M. Irish*, OS May 8, 1943-May 20, 1943; *James M. Goodhue*, O.S. may 24, 1943-Dec. 6, 1943; *M.V. Cape Henry*, A.B., Feb. 9, 1944-May 28, 1944; *Cape San Blas*, July 17, 1944, A.B., Sept. 8, 1944; *Cape San Blas*, Sept. 9, 1944, A.B., Dec. 14, 1944; MV *Cape Igvak*, A.B., Jan. 16, 1945-Aug. 17, 1945; SS *Newberry Victory*, bosun, Sept. 24, 1945-Dec. 12, 1945; SS *North Platte Victory*, Jan. 7, 1946, carpenter, Feb. 12, 1946, Feb. 13, 1946, bosun, March 13, 1946. March 27, 1946, carpenter, Aug. 7, 1946; Aug. 8, 1946, third mate, Sept. 6, 1946.

All ships sailed in the Pacific Ocean.

GERALD EARLY, resides in Corning, NY. He is a member of AMMV JWB Chapter.

ROBERT R. EDELMAN, sailed as AB and deck maintenance during WWII. Has Pacific War Zone Bar. Has a barrage baloon license. Attended Hoffman Island.

His next of kin is his daughter, Kathleen Jovan, who resides in Severna Park, MD. Robert resides in Phoenix, MD. He is a member of AMMV JWB Chapter.

RICHARD MCEWAN EDISON, was born July 10, 1909 on a farm outside Grand Rapids, MI. They lived in town winters so he went to school there.

His business career included learning hotel management by on-the-job training at the Pantland Hotel followed by class work at Cornell University. He then learned accounting at Davenport Business School and began work at Baxter Laundry, however, the Depression ended that. Fortunately, he was hired by the Muir Drug Co. and began in the Dayton store.

In 1933 he married Marion Kimes and in 1935 opened his own drug store in Fostoria, OH where he still reside.

In March of 1943 he joined the Merchant Marines and began training at Sheepshead Bay. After further training in the Staten Island Hospital, he graduated as a purser pharmacists mate. He sailed on the SS *Popham* Nov. 10, 1943 to June 24, 1944, then SS *Pan Gulf* from Aug. 7, 1944 to Nov. 20, 1944, next on SS *Robert Ellis Lewis* Jan. 22, 1945 to March 21, 1945 and lastly on the SS *Frederick Bouchard* from May 3, 1945 to Oct. 17, 1945 when he signed off in Manila due to illness. He got back to managing his drug store, playing bridge and enjoying his family, Marion and their three daughters Sarah, Judy and Ann.

JOSEPH EDMONDS, attended Hoffman Island as PLO. Sailed on SS *American Mariner,* SS *Thomas Fitzsimmons* and SS *William Prouse.*

AMMV founding president, JWB chapter. Charter member October 1989. He resides in Crownsville, MD.

CHARLES T. EDWARDS, was born Dec. 13, 1924 in Sacramento, CA. He joined the Merchant Marine in San Francisco, CA in 1943.

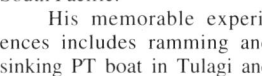

Served on *Amy Lowell,* messman, South Pacific; *Blue Ridge Victory,* utility man, South Pacific; *Alcoa Patriot,* third cook, South Pacific; *Fair Isle,* butcher, South Pacific.

His memorable experiences includes ramming and sinking PT boat in Tulagi and painting an American flag on their stack. Rest was just routine bombing and strafing by Japanese. They were in first convoy that went back into Philippines.

He has eight children, eight grandchildren, and three great grandchildren. Vice president, general manager, Spectra American Color Lab, Sun Valley, CA.

JOHAN A. EHRENSVARD, was born July 4, 1919 in Sweden. He joined the Merchant Marine in 1937 in Sweden.

Employed with Chevron Shipping Co. Master and pilot since 1960.

1970-1971, periods as mooring master; 1975-1978, observed sea trials, accepted delivery and spent first 2-3 months in command of each of five newly built tankers. 1977 and 1982 attended Marine Safety International Shiphandling simulators at La Guardia. Retired Oct. 1, 1985 under special severance program established on account of jobs becoming surplus.

January 1948-September 1949, Baker School of Navigation, San Diego as instructor; July 1946-July 1947, Swedish M/S *Sven Salen* as third officer; September 1941-September 1945, various U.S. vessels as AB up to including chief mate; June 1938-July 1941, various Scandinavian vessels as apprentice and AB; June 1937-August 1937, af *Chapman* (sail) Royal Swedish Navy as apprentice.

September 1941-August 1945: October 1941 to May 9, 1942, *West Chetac,* AB, South and East Africa; July 15, 1942 to Feb. 1, 1943, *William Johnson,* bos'n, England and North Africa, intense submarine attacks. Intense air attacks in NA Harbors; Feb. 24, 1943 to May 3, 1943, *Peter Helms,* AB, U.S. East Coast to U.S. West Coast; June 27, 1943 to Jan. 13, 1944, *James Harlan,* 3-2M, New Caledonia, Chile, U.S. East Coast, Cuba, Scotland; Feb. 26, 1944 to April 10, 1944, *Peter Helms,* AB, *Hawaii;* April 1944 to July 10, 1944, *Elcedro,* 3rd mate, Alaska; September 7, 1944 to Jan. 22, 1945, *James Lawson,* 2m, New Guinea; Jan. 30, 1945 to Aug. 24, 1945, *Laura Drake Gill,* 1M, Guam, New Guinea, Okinawa.

EARNEST W. ELLIOTT, sailed as 3rd mate sometime in 1944 on board the liberty ship *Russell A. Alger.* Donated hurricane lamp from the *Alger* to the *Brown.*

LESTER E. ELLISON, was born March 17, 1922 in Mt. Vernon, TX. After graduation he went to New York City to go to school at the United States Merchant Marine Academy.

During World War II, he sailed on various Merchant ships. Sailed as cadet, third officer, second officer, first officer and master.

In 1945, he married Jeannie Hidalgo. Jeannie is a native of Manhatten, New York City. They have two daughters, Leslie and Lisa, and five grandchildren.

Most of his professional career has been spent in the nuclear power industry. His function has been to assure the quality of the plant.

In 1957, he went to work for Ebasco Services in New York City. At present, he operates five companies overseas for Ebasco. His function is as follows: Managing Director, Ebasco B.V., Rijswkjk, The Netherlands; Vice President and Managing Director, Ebasco Italia SrL, Milan Italy; Vice President and Managing Director, Ebasco Deutschland GmbH, Dusseldorf, West Germany; Director and General Manager, Ebasco Overseas Corporation, Rijswijk, The Netherlands; Director, Ebasco Services Singapore Pte. Ltd., Singapore.

He is very fortunate that Jeannie can travel with him as he has worked all over the world including Communist China.

GEORGE A. ELLWOOD, was born May 23, 1928 in Toledo, OH. He joined the Merchant Marine Oct. 16, 1944 in Toledo, OH.

Served on SS *James Whitcomb Riley,* ordinary seaman, New York City, NY; SS *Royal Oak,* ordinary seaman, New York, NY. U.S Army Hospital Ship *Shamrock,* ordinary seaman, Wilmington, CA; U.S. Army transport, *President Buchanan,* ordinary seaman, Wilmington, CA.

Served in the U.S. Navy for nine years; 25 1/2 years U.S. Navy Reserves. Father sailed on Great Lakes, ore carriers (USNR May 23, 1986). Working as a senior piping designer/estimator.

EDWARD ARTHUR ENGEBRETSON, was born Dec. 16, 1926 in Brooklyn, NY. Joined the U.S. Maritime Service in January 1945 at Sheepshead Bay,

NY. Selected for Hoffman Island Radio School in March 1945. Graduated on Sept. 14, 1945 as warrant radio officer.

Served on the following U.S. flag ships (tankers): *Delaware Sun*, *Chester Sun*, *Trimbles Ford*, *San Pasqual*, *Fredericksburg*, *Monmouth*, *Pueblo*, *Gulf Solar*, keytanker as well as freighters/passenger ships: *Santa Isabel*, *Santa Paula*, *Santa Olivia*, *Independence* and *Exchange*. All as radio officer from November 1945 through 1964.

Joined Mackay Radio and Telegraph Company (AC&R) as a Marine sales representative in mid-1961. Later Mackay Radio became a part of ITT International Telephone and Telegraph Company) and he retired in January 1986 as director of Marine sales.

He worked as a marketing manager with COMSAT TECHNOLOGY PRODUCTS from January 1945 through March 1987 selling the first portable INMARSAT Communications Systems to the News Services, U.S. Navy, Egypt, Palace Communications in Sultanate of Oman and many other Government Services in the U.S.A. He established his own company "Global Communications Inc." in May 1987 and has been active ever since as a manufacturers representative in military and commercial communications products.

Ed lives with his wife Arlene in Raleigh, NC and they have been married 41 years. They have three daughters- Carol (Special Education teacher in Virginia Beach, VA); Nancy (veterinarian in Raleigh, NC); and Karen (public health nurse in Roanoke Rapids, NC).

JOSEPH L. ERDMAN, sailed as F/W-oiler during WWII, Korean Conflict and Vietnam. Has Atlantic and Pacific War Zone Bars. Attended Sheepshead Bay September 1942 to January 1943.

Mary Drew, Joseph's sister is his next of kin. She resides in Maumeee, OH. Joseph is a member of AMMV JWB Chapter and resides in Baltimore, MD.

ERICK L. ERICKSON, he was born Feb. 16, 1925 in Libby, MT and before the age of two his parents moved to Seattle, WA where he was raised and grew up on the Duwamish River.

They lived in a two-room shack that was built on logs which went up and down with the tide.

Needless to say they were very poor and his father who worked part-time in Bremerton Navy Yard paid $3.50 a month to a brick yard which owned the property where they were moored for rent. Another $3.00 for water which was piped along the beach which all residence who mainly were commercial fisherman and Merchant Mariners used.

One Merchant seaman who was away at sea most of the year let him live and sleep in his one-room shack while he was away Times were tough and jobs were few.

When lumber freighters would tie up at the near-by lumber docks he would go aboard he wash dishes for the cooks and messman and in exchange receive a full meal.

Often as he would row his boat alongside the freighters the longshoreman would throw over lumber dunnage which he would tie together to form a raft and when he got all he could handle safely he'd row it all back home, separate it into lengths and sell it for $8.00 per month. Often the longshoremen felt sorry for him and not only dunnage was thrown over the side to him but #1 grade lumber as well. On one occasion a long shoreman thought perhaps he could use a cant hook and he was lowering it over the side to him on a rope he was warned that someone was coming so in his haste he just let it drop from about 20 feet above water. When it hit the boat it broke a floor board which stopped it from going clear through his boat.

When he was 16 John Manni's a merchant seaman, whom he shared his cabin with asked him if he'd like to join the Merchant Marine so he took him up to the union hall and introduced him to the union officials.

School was just out for the summer as it was around June 5 or 6, 1941.

The union official told him that if he wanted a job he'd have to be at the union hall early every day and wait each day until a job showed up. Shipping out was slow and the old timers had first chance on all the jobs that showed up on the boards. He was also told that if he missed a day he'd lose his place in line so he showed up every day hoping to land a job.

On one occasion a fellow Merchant seaman had passed away and as they read his obituary one member yelled out "we don't care about his life's history," What's his shipping number?

After waiting patiently day after day ships would come and go then finally on Sept. 5, 1941 a wiper was needed for the SS *Satartia*. No one wanted the job as it was sailing for Shanghai, China and most men preferred a coast wise run so they could be home more often.

At around 2:00 p.m. the desk clerk told him to get his gear together, along with $65.00 to join the union and report back as soon as possible and he'd have a bus ticket ready for him as the *Satartia* was down in Aberdeen, WA.

He jumped on his bicycle and peddled home which was about three miles up stream. On such a short notice it was a miracle that he and his mother could come up with $65.00, but tucked away behind dishes were a few dollars here and there even underneath a rug next to the floor boards was found just enough to make up the $65.00 needed. He made his way back to the union hall and got his bus ticket to Aberdeen. Arriving late in the afternoon he asked around if anyone had seen the *Satartia* at the lumber docks. Nobody seemed to know for sure and one fellow told him the *Satartia* was here in the morning and pulled out after loading headed for China. At this time it was getting dark and he thought for sure he'd missed his ship. Feeling mighty low he prayed "Lord" somehow please help me, as he walked down the road with intentions to hitchhike back to Seattle, he stuck out his thumb and the first car stopped and picked him up. When he told him his story how he missed his ship he said he knows where the ship is its over in Hoquaim only five miles away. It happened the fella that picked him up was none other than the port commissioner. He drove him right up to the ship and dropped him off at the gangplank.

Finding his way back to the engineers quarters at the stern he met an oldtimer by the name of Patty Taylor one of the oilers and who's broken accent matched the name perfectly. Patty must have been in his middle or late 60's and he insisted they both go ashore together for one last drink before sailing. He told him he didn't drink, but he insisted they walk over to the nearest tavern which was only a block away from the dock.

He didn't drink beer but for every bottle Patty drank he ordered him a coke. Needless to say he was glad when Patty finally called it quits and he was thankful the ship was close at hand.

The next day they left *Hoquiam*, WA for Shanghai, China and he had made a friend for the duration of the time that they were together aboard the SS *Satartia*.

ROWLAND J. (ERIC) ERICKSON, was born Dec. 3, 1914 in Two Dot, MT. The Erickson's moved to Long Beach, CA in 1921. Eric graduated from Polytechnic Hi in 1933. He was employed by the Press Telegram as a district manager from 1933 to 1944. He joined the Merchant Marines in February of 1944. After graduation he served as a training officer for MSTS on Catalina Island. In November of 1944 he made a pier head jump and sailed aboard the *William B. Wilson* as an ordinary seaman. The *William B. Wilson* unescorted and carrying a military personnel and supplies successfully completed a round the world voyage in New York, March of 1945. Returning

to the Port of Los Angeles Eric crewed aboard the coastal freighter Yorba Linda and the Tugboats of Wilmington Transportation through 1946.

He received a B.A. from Harbor Junior College in 1952 for Civic Endevor in the harbor. Eric retired in 1981 as manager of a diesel engine overhaul shop in Wilmington, CA, having received a commendation from the U.S. Navy for overhauls done on a minesweeper and LSTs. He resides with his wife, Beverly, in Hesperia, CA.

HERCULES P. ESIBILL, sailed during WWII, Korean War and peacetime. He is a member of AMMV JWB Chapter. He resides in Catonsville, MD.

BURTON J. ESPY, was born May 26, 1927, Louisville, KY. Graduated Fern Creek (KY) High School, 1945.

Joined Merchant Marine 1945, trained at Sheepshead Bay, NY. Left Merchant Marine 1948.

Served on *Cassius Hudson*, fireman, New York based, *Blue Ridge Victory*, fireman, New Orleans based, *Sidney Lanier*, oiler, New Orleans based, *Cape Breton*, oiler, New Orleans based, *Coyote Hills*, watertender, New Orleans based.

Since leaving the Merchant Marines, Burt has had a exciting and rewarding life and a varied career, from working as a accountant for the L&N Railroad to raising pheasants and ducks for a hunting preserve he owned. He had a successful career as a home and commercial contractor which merged into the Espy-Heavrin Real Estate, Inc. firm. His latest business venture is a secondary mortgage purchasing company which operates in 10 states.

He is married to Harriett Wright and has four children. Linda Espy, a legal secretary; B.J., Jr., a contractor in Florida; Anna Jean Murphy, a registered nurse in Little Rock; and Kim Wright, operates her own beauty shop in Brandenburg.

An avid golfer, Burt has a 10 handicap and plays at Hillcrest Country Club in Brandenburg. At his winter home in Bradenton, FL, he plays at Palma Sola Gulf Club.

BILLIE LEVI EVANS, was born Sept. 14, 1923 in Nash, OK. Joined the Merchant Marine in Wichita, KS. Sworn in maritime Jan. 26, 1943 in Kansas City, MO. Took training at Sheepshead Bay, NY May, June, July 1943. Sent to Officers Cadet School, St. Pete, FL. August 16, 1943. Graduated October 1943. Left San Francisco for Pacific November 1943.

Served on *Clinton and Clive*, as skipper, Australia to New Zealand, 1943. Q-123 *Gen. Eichenberger*, flag ship, 2nd officer, New Guiana 1944-1945; *Barbara C*, liberty ship, deck, Philippines 1945.

His memorable experience includes invasion of N. Guiana, Hollandia and Leyte. Took exams in Providence, RI in fall of 1945. Obtained unlimited 2nd officer license. Philippine bombing of harbor.

He was employed with Texas Oil Co., Sampson Construction Co.

Married for 49 years and has one son, one daughter and three grandchildren.

Framed and ranched near Cheyenne Wells Co. 1946-

1988. Active in Masonic lodge and Christian Church. Retired farmer-rancher. Still active to help. Lives with wife June of farm near Arapahoe, CO.

CLIFFORD E. EVERT, was born Nov. 8, 1922, Republic, KS. Graduated Republic High School, attended Kansas Wesleyan University. Enlisted Merchant Marines 1942 at Wichita. Trained at Sheepshead Bay, NY. Sailed on Standard Oil tankers as ships purser/pharmacist mate. Home port New York City. Received grade of Lt. jg. 1945.

Sailed to *Esso Washington* January to June 1944, five trips across North Atlantic to England. *Fred W. Weller* July to December 1944, three trips to Pacific. *Esso Dover* February 1945 to May 1946, eight trips to Pacific and South Atlantic. *Esso Annapolis* July 1946 to April 1947, 15 trips to Caribbean and South Atlantic.

Married Jetty Linden 1947. Lived in Republic, KS 1948 to 1953. Moved to Santa Ana, CA 1953. Retired as maintenance superintendent from city of Tustin 1986.

One daughter, Leslie and three grandchildren. Lives with wife, Jetty in Santa Ana, CA.

JULIAN (JERRY) FAAS, he was with the Riverside County sheriff's office when the Japs attacked Pearl Harbor, he had just finished installing the first police two way radio system in the stations and cars of this county.

He heard over the radio that the Merchant Marines needed radio operators for the merchant ships that was in 1944 so he went to San Pedro and got his Coast Guard papers and the War Shipping Administration sent him to San Francisco where he was assigned to the liberty ship SS *James S. Lawson.*

He joined the SS *James S. Lawson* during August 1944 which was located at Navy supply depot in Oakland, CA. The ship took off for San Pablo, CA where they tied up there for several days while they loaded dynamite, torpedoes, war heads and bodies.

They returned to the Oakland Supply Depot where they loaded on four PT-boats that had came down the coast from the Alaska detail. Two PT boats were loaded forward and two boats were loaded aft.

They took off for the South Pacific, however, when leaving the dock they had a very severe port side list and when entering the ground swells outside of the Golden Gate that port side list was really something, being new on a ship every time the ship would list to the port side and stop and then finally straighten, he thought for sure the old liberty ship was going to roll over on the port side but it always came up.

He hit the sack and when he awoke the next morning the ship was sailing so beautiful they used up fuel to straighten up the ship.

They sailed south and crossed the equator on Sept. 29, 1944 and they had a great party for most of the crew and officers of the PT-boats and they unloaded the dynamite, torpedoes, war heads and bodies at a pontoon dock that the Navy had built for such purposes.

While they were unloading the dynamite and demolitions etc. they had an attack and the *Mt. Hood* which was anchored several miles from their ship got hit and blew up. It must have been loaded with ammunitions because it just disappeared sent pieces of metal in all directions. It made that mushroom cloud just like the first atomic bombs that he saw at a later date.

The huge tidal wave almost put them up on the beach and they were lucky that some of that dynamite that was being unloaded did not go off.

They finally unloaded all of their cargo and loaded up with a bunch of brass shell casings and returned to the States in January 1945.

His next troop was on black oil T-2 tanker called the SS *Broadriver* and they made put 100.000 miles on that tanker in a year, making trips between Panama and the fleet off of Japan and one trip to the Persian Gulf to a place called RAS *Tanura* returning to the States April 1946.

He soon got a communication job with the State of California Communication Division from which he retired in 1974. The state of California had a very modest communication system but had a lot of money saved up during the war and he helped build a huge communication system for the Highway Patrol, Forestry, Fish and Game, Beaches and Parks, Narcotic and a statewide microwave system before he retired.

GEOFFREY W. FAIRFAX, was born in Stockton, CA Oct. 2, 1921. Grew up in Mill Valley, CA. Graduated Marin J. College, King's Point Maritime Academy. Duty, WWII, in Pacific, delivering munitions. Served aboard Kelso Victory. After war graduated U.C. Berkeley, CA, architecture. Later achieved FFAA for work accomplished.

Married 1947, had two sons and one daughter. Responsible architecturally for design of San Francisco Golden Gateway, married student housing at U.C. Berkeley, Stanford, Coast Guard personnel housing at Pt. Reyes lighthouse area, Safeways on west coast, numerous shopping centers, hospitals, etc.

1965 moved to Honolulu, restoration of Iolani Palace, other state of Hawaii public projects. Designed undergrounding of Honolulu utilities. Was supervising architect of Sea Ranch, CA, projects in Manila, Malaysia, Idaho, and California. In 1976 moved to Roche Harbor, San Juan Island, WA, but commuting to Pacific Rim to complete projects. Died suddenly and unexpectedly of heart attack at Roche Harbor, May 28, 1978, age 56. Grandfather of.

Son, Christopher Fairfax decided to join Merchant service and has been shipping for last few years, Ocean Ships, Inc., Houston. Chris lives in Everett, WA. Married, divorced and has no children.

HAROLD E. FALETTE, sailed on the SS *Grove City Victory* between November 1945 and March 1946. "This was the only West Coast trip he made and it was an exciting one. They had a fire in the paint locker, ran aground in the Straits of Malacca and just missed a mine leaving Shanghai" (TAL 4/92, p.5).

Harold resides in Granville, IL.

ROBERT E. FALL, was born Aug. 15, 1925 in Oakland, CA. He received his seaman papers by way of the Sailor Union of Pacific training schooner the invader in San Francisco January 1943.

His first trip to sea was ordinary seaman aboard the *Jacques Laramie* a brand new liberty out of Richman Kaiser Ship Yard II.

Other ships he sailed on where *Michael Casey* (Gilbert Islands 1943), *Sea Pike* (Marshall Island 1944), *John Phillbury* (Chile 1944), *Edwin M. Stanton* (New Guinea-Admiral Island 1944-1945), *Wide Awake* (Philippines 1945), *Sea Hunter* (Japan-Korea 1945), *Marine Leopard* (Turn 21 in Panama Aug. 15, 1946), *Thomas Lyons* (Japan 1947), P&T Trader (Rio-Buenos Aires 1947), *General M.C. Meigs* 1947-1948), (P&T Navigator), Rio Buenos Aries 1948), *Edmund Mallett* (Alaska 1948), *Joel Chandler Harris* (Coast Wise 1950).

His last ship he was hurt and it ended his sailing days. He is retired and lives in San Pedro, CA.

HAROLD FALLICK, was born Feb. 9, 1927, graduated from Peekskill High School in 1944. Joined U.S. Maritime Service in December 1944. Trained at Sheepshead Bay and Hoffman Island Radio School in New York. Shipped out as a radio operator in 1945 on the SS *Lincoln Steffens,* returning the troops from Europe; 1947 sailed on SS *Santa Barbara* and SS *William T. Howell.* He found a home on the M/V *Mormac Dale* from 1948 to 1952, with a stop in Korea when the Navy chartered her.

He left going to sea to say home with his wife and two daughters, one of which he named Melinda Dale. He worked as an electrical and electronic designer and senior project manager for Sparkman and Stephens N.A. and M. Rosenblatt & Sons, Inc., two large naval architect firms until 1970, when he joined the City of New York's Department of Ports and terminals as an assistant commissioner/director of operations. In 1992 this department was reorganized out of existence and he was transferred to the City of New York's Department of General Services.

CHARLES D. FELL, sailed as 3rd assistant engineer, on SS *Henry Knox.* Left Philadelphia on March 18, 1943. Was torpedoed June 19, 1943 by two Japanese subs in Indian Ocean. Survivors landed on the Maldive Islands 11 days later.

Certificate of discharge is displayed in AMMV museum aboard the SS *John W. Brown.*

GEORGE J. FELSHEIM, was born Feb. 20, 1923 in Arcadia, WI. Enrollment at Chicago, IL Nov. 19, 1942 - April 10, 1943. Training at Maritime Service Training Station, Sheepshead Bay, NY, Section 142.

Served with U.S. Army transport, *Yarmouth,* Boston, MA April 10, 1943 (North Atlantic), San Francisco, CA Dec. 23, 1943.

Served on M.S. *American Packer,* (oiler), January 1944-June 1944, ship #241055, San Francisco, CA (Pacific); *Cities Service Kansas* (fireman/mtr) June 1944-August 1944, New York, NY (South Atlantic), *Sea Owl,* (oiler/jr. engineer) September 1944-May 1945, ship #245730, New York, NY (Atlantic), M.U. *Sea Witch,* (Jr. engineer), June 1945-August 1945, Ship #239681, San Francisco, CA (Pacific), *Mormac Moon* (asst. electrician), October 1945-January 1946, ship #240203, New York, NY (Atlantic).

He is resides in Cincinnati, OH.

PAUL E. FELSHEIM, was born Jan. 19, 1925 in Arcadia, WI. Graduated from Sheepshead Bay, NY, Oct.

28, 1943. He sailed on the USAT *Yarmouth* November-December 1943, SS *AC Rubel,* December 1943-March 1944, SS *Cape Neddick,* April-July 1944, MS *American Manufacturer* July-August 1944, SS *Luray Victory,* September-December 1944, MS *Cape Romano,* January-February 1945, SS *Hym Salom* on February-April 1945, SS *Gauntlet* May-November 1945.

Following the war he sailed on SS *Joshua Seney* November 1945-January 1946, MS *Shooting Star,* March-July 1946, SS *Marine Tiger,* September-December 1946, SS *Jonathan Worth,* December 1946-July 1947, SS *William Edwards,* September-April 1948, SS *Pan Virginia* June-August 1948, SS *Eastport,* September-December 1948, SS *Santa Elisa,* December 1948-June 1949, SS *Exilona,* August 1949-July 1950.

He sailed on the Great Lakes steamers: DZ *Norton* September-December 1950, stmr. *Harry L. Findley,* May-November 1952, *Col. James Pickands,* June-August 1953.

Retired from the U.S. Geological Survey in 1990 after 32 years of service. Paul lives with wife Dolores in South St. Paul, MN. He has two married daughters and three grandchildren.

VINCENT T. FINAN, sailed as master during WWII, Korean and Vietnam Wars. Received war wounds and taken as POW. Ship was sunk. Has the Victory and Philippine Defense Medals, Atlantic, Pacific, Mediterranean and Middle East War Zone Bars.

He is married to Mary. They have a member of AMMV JWB Chapter. He resides in Columbia, MD.

WILLIAM E. FINNEN, graduated from USMMA February 1944. Sailed on SS *John Spencer,* SS *Malcom Stewart,* SS *Samuel DeChamplain,* SS *John C. Smith,* SS *Loma Victory,* and SS *Alden Bessie.* Holds Atlantic and Pacific War Zone Bars. Was bombed at Okinawa and was involved in invasion of Europe.

WALTER S. FINNEY, JR., member of Armed Guard. Sailed on the SS *John Constantine* in 1943 crossing the equator and initiated into the Solemn Mysteries of the Ancient Order of the Deep. Sailed on M/S *Talisee* crossing the equator on May 14, 1944 and again initiated into the Solemn Mysteries of the Ancient Order of the Deep. Completed anti-aircraft gunnery course March 14, 1945 (see Appendix).

Walter resides in Shirley, AR.

ROBERT (BOB) FIRCHAU, attended USMSTS Hoffman Island Radio School. Graduated in Section R-27.

He resides in Glen Ellyn, IL.

DUANE R. FISHER, sailed as AB and fireman during WWII and Korean War.

Married to Juanita and they reside in Pasadena, MD. He is a member of AMMV JWB Chapter.

WALTER FLETCHER, attended USMSTS at Sheepshead Bay September 1944. Served in deck and engine departments until October 1946.

He resides in Philadelphia, PA.

JOSEPH PINKNEY FORD, was born July 14, 1927 in Brownfield (Tippah County) MS. He was sworn in Birmingham, AL May 1945. USMTS, St. Fla May 1945-June 1945.

Served as messman/utilityman on board the SS *Hibueras* (No. LA) Aug. 18, 1945 to Aug. 28, 1945, *John B. Joyce* (NO LA), Sept. 15, 1945 to Nov. 30, 1945, *Daniel Heister,* (NO LA), Feb. 12, 1946 to April 16, 1946, *Henry T. Scott,* May 24, 1946 to June 2, 1946, *Wallace M. Tyler* (Galveston, TX) June 7,

1946 to Sept. 12, 1946, *Thompson Lykes* (NO LA), Nov. 5, 1946 to Dec. 20, 1946, *San Jose* (Mobole and NOLA), Feb. 1, 1947 to March 8, 1947, the most beautiful merchant ship, he had ever seen. It was a USN Cruiser hull and engine, etc., but converted to a cargo ship. Because USN didn't need it.

His memorable experiences include the ports of Rio De Janeiro, Rouen France, Triesta, February storm in N. Atlantic.

Married October 1951. They have six children and seven grandchildren. (His wife is Earlens Cannon of Oxford, MS).

Joseph is a pharmacist, Big B Drug Co., Pensacola, FL. Graduated from Ole Miss School of Pharmacy in 1951.

CALVIN L. FOSTER, was born Feb. 13, 1926 in Leavenworth, KS. Joined Merchant Marine in 1943, age 17. Took training Sheepshead Bay, NY.

Ships sailed: *The Dallas,* T-2, 1942, "FMWT", two trips to New Guinea. *Arthur L. Perry,* liberty, 1944, "FMWT" convoy to Liverpool, *David A. Curry,* liberty, 1945, "FMWT", convoy to Philippines. *M.V. Anacapa,* sea tug, 1945, (oiler), towed dry-dock to Pearl Harbor, *Joseph N. Dinand,* liberty, 1945-1946, (oiler), *Fort Clatsop,* T2, 1946, act. jr. 3rd engineer.

Continued sailing until 1953. He has held 3rd, 2nd, and 1st asst. Marine Engr. License. Sailed with Lykes Lines, various C1 cargo ships until end of sea-going career. Commissioned ensign, U.S.N.R., 1950, ready reserve.

Employed with U.S. Bureau of Prisons. Held positions of operating engineer, chief engineer, chief of mechanical services at various federal institutions. Last position was facilities manager. Retired after 26 years service.

CARLTON A. FOSTER, was born May 1, 1917, Lynn, MA. He joined the Merchant Marines February 1944 in San Francisco, CA.

Served on SS *Cape Canaveral* 1944, junior third mate, Pacific, SS *Abram S. Hewitt,* 1944-1945, 3rd mate, Pacific; SS *Jose J. Acosta* 1945-1946, 3rd mate, Pacific.

His memorable experiences include graduation day July 1944, U.S. Maritime Officers School, Alameda, CA. SS *Abram Hewitt* landed 500 troops of the Amer Cal Div. January 1945. Invasion Lingayen Gulf, Philippines.

Employed for 27 years federal employment Benicia Arsenal, CA.

Married and two children, four grandsons. He retired October 1963.

JOSEPH G. FRANCIS, SR., sailed as AB and tankerman during WWII. Has Atlantic and Middle East War Zone Bars.

Married to Goldie and they reside in Baltimore, MD. He is a member of AMMV JWB Chapter.

WILLIAM E. FRASURE, JR., was born June 26, 1927 in Wilmington, OH. Graduated from Wilmington High School. Joined U.S. Maritime Service Training Station at Sheepshead Bay, Brooklyn, NY July 3, 1945.

Ships sailed: *Lake Charles Victory,* deck dept., two trips North Atlantic to Le Havre, France, 1945. Then sailed on *African Sun* , C-1, deck dept., South Atlantic to Capetown South African and Durbin. Upon their return to New York City, they were the first ship turned back over to the American South African Lines from the War Shipping Administration 1946. Then sailed for Grace Lines *Santa Lenore,* C-1 deck dept., South Atlantic, East and West of South America went through Panama Canal Zone 12 times 1946-1947.

He married Wanda L. Powless Dec. 25, 1947 in Washington, C.H. Ohio became parents of four children and now have four grandchildren and two great grandchildren.

Worked for National Cash Register and National Life Insurance Co. 1948-1950.

Became a nursing home owner and administrator 100 bed, 1950-1972 and did computer accounting for nursing homes 1972-1982 then owner and manager of a private club Frasure's Chateau Club with a membership of over 1500, 1985-1991. Turned the club over to his son Wm. E. Frasure III and then retired at age 64, Jan. 1, 1992. He now resides with his wife in New Smyrna Beach, FL.

GORDON J. FRAZER, was born Sept. 9, 1927 in Milwaukee, WI and attended school there.

Sea Scout Volunteer U.S. Navy Recruiting Station Milwaukee age 14 in 1942. First went to sea on the Great Lakes age 15 on the SS *Milwaukee Clipper* as bell boy and the SS *Sierra* as deckhand.

Joined the United States Maritime Service June 13, 1944 age 16 years old. Sent to USMS Training Station Sheepshead Bay, Brooklyn, NY. After basic training, transferred to ships company, Boat Training Division with cruise aboard the USMSTS *American Navigator.*

Then to USMS Radio Training School, Hoffman Island, NY graduating warrant radio electrician, USMS at age 17.

Then assigned via War Shipping Administration RMO and flown U.S. Naval Transportation Service to Coco Solo, Panama Canal Zone. Stationed BOQ *Margaritta* until assigned as radio operator aboard the SS *Pendleton* a war-time T-2 turbo electric tanker.

Then six months spent island hopping in the South Pacific including Marshall, Society, Samoan, Marianna, Admiralty, Philippine, Midway Islands and Pearl Harbor.

Then sailed with United States Lines from 1946 to 1951. Thereafter 19 years with Cities Service Oil Company until retirement at age 42 in 1970 having delivered military supplies for both the Korean and Vietnam conflicts.

Also aboard the USNS *Elko Victory* during Vietnam.

A total of 27 years of wars, storms, hurricanes and typhoons in the Atlantic, Pacific and Indian Oceans and a fire and a collision at sea thrown in for good measure the remembrance of calm azure seas, beautiful sunsets and exotic ports still prevail.

After retirement, Gordon ran his own business, a tourist attraction Onyx Cave, near Hamburg, PA until 1977.

He also received his FAA pilots license and flew as commercial pilot CFI single engine, multi engine and glider for Kutztown Aviation Service, Kutztown, PA.

He now resides in Wyomissing, PA with his wife, the former Dolores S. Smith of Hamburg, PA.

He has a cottage on Lake Wallenpaupack in the Pocono Mountains where he "Captains" his 24 foot pontoon boat during the summers. He is a member of the U.S. Merchant Marine Veterans WWII, Keystone and Dennis A. Roland Chapters of the American Merchant Marine Veterans the American Legion and the Coast Guard Auxiliary.

IRA M. "FLARE" FREDRICKSEN, was born May 14, 1925, in Sparta, WI. Graduated Sheepshead Bay USMSTC, May 1943. Sailed as able seaman/quartermaster USAT *Cableship Restorer,* connecting Aleutian Islands to Alaska with underwater communications cable, 1943. Two voyages, T2 tanker *Mokino del Rey,* Aruba and Cartagena to New Guinea and southwest Pacific 1944. Three Atlantic crossings to England, tanker *Bulkfuel* 1944, and liberty ship *George A. Custer* to Antwerp, 1945. Enlisted U.S. Army 1945, Philippines as stockade sergeant. Enlisted 1947, 32nd Div., WNG, discharge first sergeant 1960.

Career in dairy sales/marketing. Retired 1990, as military sales manager, Land O Lakes, Inc. Active in Boy Scouting (Silver Beaver recipient), Writers Group (has had prose and poetry published), various Merchant Marine and Veterans organizations. He has five children and lives with wife Doris in Plymouth, WI.

RICHARD A. FREED, was born Feb. 2, 1924 in Providence, RI. Joined Merchant Marine in March 1944.

Served on SS *Oliver Wolcott,* March 1944-October 1944, SS *Ralph W. Emerson,* October 1944-July 1945. Officers Training School, New London, CT, August 1945, SS *Abbot Mills,* September 1945 to January 1946.

The *Oliver Wolcott* carried military supplies and Coast Guard personnel to England in March 1944. Outfitted in Glasgow, Scotland as a troopship. Sent to Cardiff, Wales where they loaded artillery, ammunitions and over 400 troops from the 29th Arty. Div. Late in the day of the 4th of June they assembled in a massive convoy in Barry Roads at the entrance of the Severn River on the West Coast. The original D Day landing was scheduled for June 5, but because of heavy seas, wind and rain it was rescheduled for the early morning of June 6. Because of the delay and the fact that they had already put to sea and were well into the English Channel the entire convoy had to go in circles for 24 hours. It was impossible for them to go back to Barry Roads, find Anchorage and start all over again. They also had to tow a WWI Hog Islander freighter that had been torpedoed a year earlier and could not be repaired. Its bottoms had been loaded with explosive charges and it was manned by volunteers from the Merchant Marine and Armed Guard. One June 6 early in the day they towed this derelict freighter into a line about 300 yards from the beach under fire from German shore batteries. With the aid of Dutch and Norwegian tugs it was set in place and the charges were set off, sinking the freighter in a line with other similar ships for the purpose of forming a breakwater to make landing operations less difficult. They were unable to land the troops at this time because of the heavy fire from German shore batteries and the fact that the infantry was pinned down on the beaches. They then moved offshore to about 3,000 years and came back in about 12 hours later when the first wave moved up to the top of the beach. There were many, many casualties that first few days both on land and at sea, but the toughest job was those kids that had to hit the beaches and dig the enemy out inch by inch.

He served in the European, Pacific and Mediterranean Combat Zones. Served on the *Abbot Mills* when it was mined in the Adriatic. They abandoned the *Mills* as a total loss and they repatriated on the SS *Hoke Smith.*

Founder and Chairman of Board of Johnson Fuel Service, Inc.

Married Alice Livesey, and they had eight children and 19 grandchildren.

DONALD C. (DON) FRIEDMANN, entered USMSTS at Sheepshead Bay on June 25, 1945 as AS. Graduated as steward's mate second class Sept. 7, 1945. Was in Marine hospital on Ellis Island during August and September 1945 and saw back of Statue of Liberty everyday. Sailed on the SS *F. Marion Crawford, Grenville M. Dodge,* and *Chilton Seam,* all liberties.

Donald resides in Owinngs Mills, MD and is a member of AMMV JWB Chapter; Project Liberty Shp, Radio and Historic Committees.

ROBERT FUHRER, was born Aug. 13, 1926 in New York City. December 1944 entered U.S. Merchant Marine Academy, Kings Point.

Served on *Logan's Fort, Madaket, Cape Sebastian,* cadet-midshipman, England, Pacific, Brazil, Puerto Rico; *Robin Kirk, Robin Trent,* 3rd engineer, South Africa, East Africa; *Calusa, Sovac Alladin, Sovac Pegasus,* 3rd engineer, Texas, East Coast of U.S., Saudia Arabia, Kuwait, Israel, Venezuela; *Beatrice,* 3rd engineer, Puerto Rico.

His memorable experience occurred while on the SS *Logan's Fort.* Their convoy from Charleston, SC to New York City was attacked by German subs early April 1, 1945.

He was employed at New York Naval Shipyard; Long Beach Naval Shipyard, Naval Weapons Station, Seal Beach, CA; RCA Van Nuys, CA; Rockwell International, Rocketdyne Div.

Married to Joan Alice and they have son Bruce, and daughter Karen. Both are married and they have five grandkids. Robert retired December 1990.

Now spends time traveling, playing tennis, sketching, taking various college classes and square dancing.

HARRY S. FUNK, was in Normandy invasion. Sailed as third mate and chief mate. Served on SS *Cotton Mather* and SS *Cyrus H.K. Curtis.*

Harry resides in Wilmington, DE.

DON J. GAGNE, sailed aboard the *Arthur M. Huddell* as 2nd radio officer from September 1944 to January 1945 on voyage to London.

He is member of Project Liberty Ship.

Don resides in Boielly, NJ.

EDWARD ALLEN GALLAGHER, was born in Jersey City, NJ on Jan. 28, 1920. He died July 9, 1989.

Enlisted United States Maritime Service Officers School, (United States Merchant Marine), Fort Trumbull, New London, CT, on April 15, 1943. Graduated Aug. 13, 1943 as ensign, 3rd assistance engineer. Attended United States Maritime Service Turbo Engineering School, Syracuse, NY and United States Maritime Service Turbo Electric Installation School, Chester, PA. In 1949 he received his second assistance engineer's license, 1952 his first assistance engineer's license, in 1965 his chief engineer's license. Held the rank of lieutenant Jr. in 1945; lieutenant in 1950.

Sailed Atlantic, Mediterranean-Middle East, Pacific War Zones; Korean and Vietnam War Zones. Tankers, freighters, Lash and cruise ships. Retired Jan. 1, 1985.

Merchant Marine awards to civilians: Atlantic War Zone Medal, Mediterranean-Middle East War Zone Medal, Pacific War Zone Medal, Merchant Marine Service Emblem and Honorable Button, United States Merchant Marine World War Two Victory Medal, Presidential Testimonial Letter on World War II services; Korean War Zone Medal, Vietnam War Zone Medal.

Military service: January 1940-1943, enlisted in the United States Navy and trained at Navy Training Station, Newport, Rhode Island. Served aboard the USS *Tuscaloosa,* heavy cruiser; (President Roosevelt sailed on it). Military service awards: American Defense with two Stars, American Theater, European-African Middle East with two Bars, and World War II Armed Forces (military) Victory Medal.

On March 10, 1946 he married Pauline Sapanara of Belmar, NJ. They were married for 43 years.

He was a member in the United States Navy League, a warrant officer in the sea cadets in charge of the clothing center at the Naval Training Center, Orlando, FL, American Legion Post 19, Veterans of Foreign Wars Post 2093, Elks Club 1079; and American Merchant Marine Veterans, Gulfstream Chapter. *Submitted by his wife, Mrs. Pauline Gallagher; a member in the United States Merchant Marine Veterans of World War II; East Central Florida Chapter.*

HIRAM GALLOP, JR., was born Feb. 27, 1913 in Manteo, NC. Mother, Matilda Midgett Gallop. He was the oldest of 14 children, five boys and nine girls.

Attended Maury High School, Norfolk, VA. Worked as paperboy, worked in stores and gas stations.

First went to sea in 1929 as an oiler on U.S.E.D. SS *Chinook* sea going *Hopper Dredge* until 1933.

Next sailed on *Moore McCormick Lines* from Dec. 27, 1933 until May 1, 1935 working in the engine department.

He was in the Columbian navy from May 2, 1935 until Jan. 20, 1936 working as an oiler.

For approximately six years, he was an oiler-watertender in the Engine Department for United States Coast Guard.

From May 12, 1937 until April 28, 1939, he was an AB, bos'n and carpenter for A.H. Bull SS Company.

From April 28, 1939 until May 25, 1941 he worked as boatswain, pumpman, third mate and dispatcher for Esso Oil Company on various vessels.

Received Gold Medal and Silver Cup in International Life Boat Races on Sept. 9, 1939.

Worked again for A.H. Bull S.S. Company from June 1, 1941 until Jan. 1, 1944 served as third mate, second mate, chief mate and master.

Worked with D.W. Pugh SS Company as captain aboard the SS *Joyce Kilmer* on Jan. 9, 1944. Went to Italy, three ports. Returned with 75 ship convoy with Navy commodore aboard. Commended by naval and company officials. Second trip was to North Russia with two shuttles from Liverpool, Glasgow and Russia.

May 10, 1945 the war was over.

June 1, 1945 worked several ships as master to

Europe and Asia. Last ship worked was the SS *Durango Victory,* running to Vietnam.

Retired Dec. 29, 1969 and became a businessman. Commercial and party boat fishing, marina and restaurant.

Keeps his license up to date and he will be 80 years old on Feb. 27, 1993.

Hold recommendations from all assignments and hopes to be a Dare County commissioner soon.

FRANK L. GARDNER, JR., sailed as chief engineer during WWII, Korean Conflict and Vietnam. Attended Sheepshead Bay. Completed several courses in Marine Engineering. In USMS from June of 1946, (Sheepshead Bay August to September.) Sailed on the USAT *General M.L. Hersey* in December 1946 in the North Sea which as German mines. Sailed on the liberty ship SS *Strathcape* when 22 years old as 2nd assistant engineer.

He received Atlantic, Korean and Vietnam Ribbons, Certificate of Substantially Continuous Service in the United States Merchant Marine issue August 4, 1948 for service June 19, 1946 to September 3, 1947.

Married to Janet and they reside in Smyrna, DE. He is a member of AMMV JWB Chapter.

ELMORE E. (BUD) GATES, received Certificate of Registry as a purser and pharmacist mate on Oct. 13, 1944. Seaman's certificate obtained on Sept. 10, 1942. Has nine certificates of discharge for the following ports: New York, Newport News, Norfolk, Yonkers, Baltimore, and Philadelphia.

Married to Ester and they have son Ross who is a radio amateur, N8GMY and resides in Norton Shores, MI.

Mr. Gates was released from active duty with the USMS as an ensign on Oct. 30, 1945.

He served on the following vessels: *Brette Harte,* Nov. 23, 1942 to July 13, 1943 and Oct. 31, 9144 to April 29, 1945; *Amos Kendall,* Aug. 5, 1943 to May 31, 1944; and *Thomas Symons,* May 28, 1945 to Oct. 9, 1945.

LESTER L. GATTON, was born Oct. 1, 1917 in Secretary, MD. He joined the Merchant Marine when he was 19 years old, Dec. 7, 1936 at Baltimore, MD. Served on many ships, all motor vessels and oiler to chief engineer, Inland.

Served on *City of Salisbury,* oiler, coastwide, NY-Jacksonville; SS *Edwin M. Stanton,* wiper, foreign; LT-64, motor vessel, 1st asst. engr., New York to Baltimore, U.S. Army Transportation Corps; ST-935, motor vessel, chief engineer, Southwest Pacific, New Orleans to Balboa, CZ.

Some of his memorable experiences include sinking of motor vessel *E. Madison Hall* in fog. Collided with a oil barge, March 31, 1942. Went ashore March 1946.

He went to work for Bethlehem Steel Co. for 30 years in hot strip mill, Sparrows Point Plant, retired July 1, 1976.

Married for 52 years and has two daughters and two sons. He has had two heart attacks and two strokes.

JOSEPH P. GAUZZA, was born June 24, 1927 in District of Columbia. He joined the Merchant Marine June 1943 in Sheepshead Bay, NY. Served on *Thomas Cresap* (liberty), messman, Baltimore, Oran, NA, Naples, Anzio;

Little Big Horn (T2), O.S., A.B., Bos'n, Antwerp, South America, and Pacific; *Sarazan* (Hog Islander), OS, Cuba, U.S. Philippines; *Blum* (T2), AB, Aruba, Curasol.

His memorable experiences include invasion of Anzio. Attacks from torpedo planes and "Big Burtha" gun on RR track in mountains.

Skilled in design service including contract interiors, graphic, architectural and lighting. Single with three sons and five grandchildren. Still working in above field. Involved in restoration *J.W. Brown* -Baltimore.

AMMV charter member JWB Chapter Oct. 14, 1989.

REV. FREDERICK P. GEHRING, C.M., was born in Brooklyn, NY. Educated by the Vincentian Fathers from high school through the seminary, ordained in 1930, Father Gehring was first assigned to the mission fields of China. Communist activity there prevented his arrival until 1933. After spending six years in Kiangzi Province, Father Gehring returned to the United States to become a member of the Miraculous Medal Novena Band and continued to preach Marian devotion until 1942 when he entered military service as a Navy chaplain.

Known as the "Padre of Guadalcanal" for his zeal and devotion to "his boys" during service, Father Gehring was the first Navy chaplain to receive the Legion of Merit from the President of the United States, and the Presidential Unit Citation for heroic rescue work behind enemy lines. He is the author of the famous book, "A Child of Miracles," the story of Patsy Li, a native orphan who was cared for by the Marines. Father Gehring accompanied Admiral Halsey to Hollywood for the making of the film, "The Gallant Hours," a story depicting the war torn land of Guadalcanal and a priest's devotion to his Faith, his Country, and his beloved man.

Following release from service in 1946, Father Gehring became in succession, Director of the Vincentian China Missions in the Eastern Province; Student counselor at St. John's University, Jamaica, NY; pastor and religious superior at St. Vincent's Church, Philadelphia, PA. It is from this last appointment that Father Gehring rejoins the Miraculous Medal Novena Band. Father Gehring is now in residence at St. Vincent's Seminary, Philadelphia, PA.

Father Gehring at one time was National Chaplain of the First Marine Division Association. He is at present National Chaplain of the Guadalcanal Campaign Veterans.

THOMAS R. GIBSON, was born March 6, 1924. He joined the Merchant Marine in St. Paul, MN, December 1942.

Served on SS *Irving M. Scott,* radio operator, Pacific; SS *Joseph Lane,* radio operator, Pacific; SS *Cape Saunders,* Pacific, Indian Ocean, radio operator; SS *Edwin Thacher,* radio operator, Gulf of Mexico; SS *Francis J. O'Gara,* radio operator, Pacific, Atlantic; MV *Overseas Joyce,* radio operator, East Coast to Japan.

He is professional engineer, in Pennsylvania, Maryland, Massachusetts, New York and California.

Married and has five children and five grandchildren. He retired in December 1990. Gibson is the volunteer treasurer of Project Liberty Ship (SS *John W. Brown*).

ROBERT V. GILES, was born April 15, 1919. Graduated at age 18, Omaha, NE. Worked on R.E.A. & P.W.A. jobs, 1938 and 1939, worked on government defense jobs 1940-1943. Enrolled in Maritime in Denver, CO, Oct. 29, 1943, was sent to Catalina Island for training.

Ships sailed: *Charles John Seghers* (utilityman) Liberty ship, 1944 to Milne Bay, New Guinea, Rockland Victory Ships, (So. Pacific) (cook & baker), 1944, *Fort Donelson (cook)* tanker, 1945, to Ulithi and Guam, South Pacific, *Yamhill* (purser) tanker, 1945 - two trips, Panama to Pearl Harbor - back through Panama Canal to Curacoa, West Indies, back to South Pacific, Eniwetok, Manila Bay.

At Catalina, he was put in the Steward's Department because he did not have 20-20 vision. Got tired of cooking with Bole Weevils in the flour and wormy raisins in the cinnamon rolls. Took and passed test for purser, staff officer on April 28, 1945.

He has honorable discharge from USCG Merchant Marine, belongs to China Coaster's Chapter of AMMV. Joined American Legion.

Has stayed and raised family in Los Angeles area. Worked in building trades as pipefitter. Helped build first missile bases in California. He is retired and has income property. He also belongs to U.S. Merchant Marine Veterans of World War II.

RICHARD D. GILLELEN, was born in Los Angeles, May 29, 1910. Was gust at christening of his future ship, the 10,500-ton cargo-carrier, *Charles H. Windham,* the 166th Liberty ship built in 26 days by California Shipbuilding Corporation. Ship ran aground in harbor due to list caused by imbalanced loading. While at sea, enroute from Hobart Tasmania to Bombay, India on Friday, June 18, 1943, tires in hold number  three caught fire. Steam smothering line system used to control acrid sulphur fumes and ship, which had been fighting heavy seas, altered course for nearest port; Freemantle, Australia.

At 3:03 p.m, June 19, 1943, a British plane approached the *Windham* and signalled her to hold course as a tug would meet her shortly. *Windham* arrived at Freemantle. Fire finally extinguished by local fire department. Ship eventually sailed for Melbourne, Australia where it was chartered by the U.S. Army Transport Service and passengers were re-imbursed and cargo was re-routed via other carriers.

Employed as accountant with the State of California and retired June 1972 because of stroke. Gillelen died June 28, 1990

DR. MICHAEL GILLEN, New York project coordinator of the Liberty Log is retired. (TUD, Spring 1992, p.4).

WAYNE H. GJERSETH, is the author of World War II Generation United States Merchant Marine. The authors experience before, during and after the war are documented in this book. He served as oiler on the SS *William Paca* from May 12, 1943-Nov. 22, 1943; SS *James Caldwell* from March 23, 1944-May 21, 1945 and on the SS *Madawaska Victory* from Sept. 2, 1945 to Nov. 14, 1945 as junior 3rd assistant engineer and 3rd assistant engineer. Wayne entered the USMS Dec. 2, 1942 and attended Hoffman Island and Sheepshead Bay (Gjerseth, 1991).

He has a Certificate of Substantially Continuous Service in the USMM for service from Dec. 22, 1942 to Nov. 27, 1946.

FRANCIS (FRANK) GLYNN, sailed as deck engineer and 3rd assistant engineer during WWII. Has the Atlantic War Zone Bar. Attended USMS Officers School at New London, CT.

He is married to Amelia. He is a member of AMMV JWB Chapter. They reside in Crofton, MD.

ROBERT J. GODFREY, was born Oct. 1, 1927 in Milwaukee, WI. He joined the Merchant Marine June 1945 in Sheepshead Bay. He received engine room training at Sheepshead Bay, NY.

Served on troopship *Andrew Hamilton,* oiler, New York, Marseilles and France; tankers *Capachee Canyon, Bennington, Fort Washington;* cargo, *Cable Splice, Coastal Hearld,* oiler and junior engineer.

His memorable experience includes being on a troopship (liberty) with no cargo or ballast. They were in the worst storm in the North Atlantic. Several soldiers had to be fed intravenously.

Married and has three sons and eight grandkids. He retired April 2, 1947. Retired locomotive engineer for 40 years (1947-1987). Retired and now living in Northern Michigan, winters in Florida.

DON GOODENOW, "seeking contract with anyone that sailed on the SS *William R. Davie.*" We sailed from New York in January 1943 to HamptonRoads, VA from make-up of convoy to the Mediterranean. This writer was a cadet on the liberty ship, but was removed by breeches buoy to the Coast Guard cutter *Ingham* in mid-Atlantic. The writer has made contact with several crew members of the *Ingham* that remember the incident. Anyone remembering this convoy please contact: Don Goodenow, 3218 Sunnybrook Drive, Charlotte, NC 28210." (TUD Spring 1992, p.4):

ROBERT C. GORDON, was born May 15, 1928 in New York City. They joined the Merchant Marine May 1944 at Sheepshead Bay, NY.

Served on M/S *Chester Sun,* wiper, act fireman, act oiler.

Joined ship in Panama in Pacific, Atlantic, Indian Ocean. Ship built in 1928. Sundoxford diesel, 7/8 knots-tanker.

Enlisted in U.S. Army after Merchant Marine service. Served in Europe three years in ordinary Military Police 93rd M.P. Balt.

Divorced and has three children, two sons and one daughter. His youngest son is 16 years old and an Eagle Scout.

Owner of electric service. Repairs radio, TV, stereo, VCR, camcorder. Certified technician. Scout master

JOHN T. (JACK) GOSNELL, resides in Monkton, MD and is a member of AMMV JWB Chapter.

KEN GOSSETT, was born 1927 in Dallas, TX where he lived until senior year in high school. Graduated in Pasadena, CA and trained in maritime service on Long Beach ship in 1945. Sailed as steward. 1946: *Highflyer* (South America); *Laura Drake Gill* (Hawaii); 1947: *Joshua L. Chamberlain* (Saigon, New Zealand, Australia, New Guinea, Indonesia, South Africa); *Manukai* (Hawaii); 1948: *Henry J. Raymond* (Hawaii); 1948 and 1949: *Contest* (Japan, Philippines, Hong Kong, Okinawa, Guam); 1950: *Flying Dragon* (Far East); *Lurline* (Hawaii); and *Santa Flavia* (South America).

Drafted off ship 1951 into Army at Camp Roberts, CA to 1953 (first sergeant). Entered business as salesman, manager and owner of several companies in painting industry.

Member of Inglewood Exchange Club, Inglewood Salvation Army Board, Inglewood YMCA Board, and longtime board member of Inglewood/Airport Area Chamber of Commerce. He lives with his wife of 33 years, Tita, in Thousand Oaks, CA.

ROBERT N. GOTTSHALL, wailed on *W.M. Burton, Gulf Gem, Pennsylvanian, J.L.M. Curry, Noah Webster, Charles Folger, Bulkcrude, Daniel Huger, Barbara Frietchie, Nelson W. Aldrich, William L. McLean* and *Clyde Austin Dunning.* Ports of call include Russia, England, North Africa, Italy, Dutch West Indies and France. Donated artifacts to PLS.

Robert resides in Doylestown, PA.

STUART M. GRAHAM, was born Oct. 1, 1917. Attended the universities of Iowa and Arkansas. Received training at the following USMS Schools. Hoffman Island, New York, NY, 1942; Officers School, New London, CT, 1944; Officers School, San Francisco, CA 1944.

Ships sailed include the *Cape Henlopenn* (C1), FWT-1942; *Lawton B. Evans,* liberty, oiler, 1943; *Henry C. Lomb,* liberty, oiler, 1943-1944; *Potero Hills,* T2 tanker, 3rd engineer, 1944-1945; *El Morro,* T2 tanker, 3rd eng. 1945-1946.

Cape Henlopen, Philadelphia to Alexandria, Egypt. Sailed unarmed and unescorted for seven months. South Atlantic, Pacific, South Pacific and Indian Oceans. Towed into Baltimore drydock sternfirst at conclusion of voyage. Casualties.

Lawton B. Evans, New York to Oran, Algiers. Participated in invasion of Sicily at Gila. Casualties.

Henry C. Lomb, New York City to Murmansk, Russia and return. Some enemy activity but no harm to the ship.

Potero Hills, San Pedro, CA to various islands in Pacific and South Pacific.

El Morro, Galveston, TX to various islands in South Pacific and shuttle to Persian Gulf.

Awarded "The 40th Anniversary of the Victory in the Great Patriotic War (World War II)" by Russian Ambassador Dec. 8, 1942. Several awards prior.

Retired October 1975. Terr. manager, Houston General Insurance Group, Ft. Worth, TX.

Married and has one son Stuart Jr., MD. He is enjoying retirement with wife. His hobby is golf. He has a nine hole pitching course on his premises.

JOSEPH E. GRAY, enrolled in the USMS at Washington, DC on Aug. 7, 1944. Completed the course of training for apprentice seamen in the coal passer brach at the USMSTS, St. Petersburg, FL and was enrolled in the grade of A.S. on Sept. 25, 1944. His training included six hours of elementary gunnery. His certificate of efficiency to lifeboatmen were issued Oct. 4, 1944. He sailed as wiper and oiler on SS *Samuel T. Darling,* SS *Samuel Mitchell,* SS *Thomas Say,* and SS *Gulfbreeze.*

He was a member of the National Maritime Union. Awarded the Pacific War Zone Bar.

ROBERT N. GRAY, served as sergeant U.S. Airforce. Returned from Bremerhaven, Germany to port of New York on *Lt. John J. Ray* in 1948.

Robert resides in Berlin, NJ.

HENRY C. (HARRY) GRIEB, was born Aug. 13, 1918 in Honolulu Territory of Hawaii. Lt./Cdr. USMS I.D.

Grieb attended wartime extension courses in Marine diesel engineering given by Stanford University and the Samuel Gompers Trade School. Grieb received USCG license as Marine Diesel Engineer, subsequently signing on as chief engineer on the ATS tug, "S.T. 470" which sailed from S.F. to Milne Bay, New Guinea via Pearl Harbor. Next Grieb sailed as first assistant engineer, on the C-1s M/V *Cape Pillar* from S.F. to Ulithi via Pearl Harbor, in convoy as a Navy supply ship. Grieb's last assignment was a first assistant on M/V *Cape Spencer* on intercoastal voyage from S.F. to NYC.

Grieb joined the California Highway Patrol in 1948 and served at various California stations as patrolman, field sergeant and commander. Grieb retired from the C.H.P. in 1970 after 22 years of service.

Grieb was active in the 1960s in the Civil Air Patrol. His last assignment was as major and squadron commander of an organization that did much search and rescue duty, also training cadets to become interested in the flying as a career in U.S.A.F.

Grieb is a charter life member of the USMMV WWII, *Lane Victory,* San Pedro, CA. He is also active in donating and the restoration of the historical liberty ship, *Jeremiah O'Brien* in San Francisco Bay.

JAMES WILLIAM GRIFFITH, sailed as radio officer on the USNS *Suamico,* SS *Windjammer Polly* and the SS *Carbide Texas City.* Formerly served in U.S. Navy.

MERRILL E. GROELLE, sailed as purser-pharmacist mate during WWII. Attended Sheepshead Bay, Aug. 4, 1944. Holds Atlantic and Mediterranean East War Zone Bars and Combat Bar. He is skilled in administrative, management and fund raising.

His sister, Dorothea Ballou, is his next of kin. She resides on Cambree, CA. He is member AMMV JWB Chapter. He resides in Merrill E. Groelle, Frederick, MD.

HERBERT B. GROH, resides in Catonsville, MD. He is a member of AMMV Charter Member JWB Chapter Oct. 14, 1989.

ROBBY N. GUNSTREAM, was born April 3, 1925. Outbreak of WWII attending Pasadena Nazarene College preparing for the ministry. Gave up Ministerial Deferment to join the Merchant Marine in 1943.

Graduated Marine Cooks and Stewards, Long Beach, CA. Licensed as 2nd cook and baker.

Ships sailed: *Cape Martin* - C1 - 1944. Steward's Department invasion of Guam. *Golden West* - C2 - 1944, fireman water tender to the end of the war 1945. All sailings through the South Pacific.

Returned to Pasadena Nazarene College September 1945. Married Dorothy Jean Poole May 1946. Graduated together 1949. Next 30 years pastored two churches in Los Angeles and Temple City, CA. He has two children: son, Robby D. Gunstream of Missoula, MT. Daughter, Judy Lynn Onken of Temple City, CA. Agent for New York Life Insurance Co. from 1976 to present.

WILLIAM FREDERICK HABER, graduated from Kings Point in April 1942. Sailed during WWII as cadet and 3rd assistant engineer. Awarded the following decorations for Merchant Marine service: Merchant Marine Emblem, Pacific and Atlantic War Zone Bars, Combat and Defense Bars, Victory Medal, Honorable Service Button, and Presidential Testimonial Letter. Also was awarded the China War Memorial Medal which the Government of the Republic of China especially decreed as a token of appreciation for the contributions made by Americans in the China theater during WWII.

Retired from the U.S. Naval Surface Warfare Center in November 1975 with the following medals: American Defense Service Medal, American Campaign Medal, European African Middle Eastern Campaign Medal and World War II Victory Medal.

Married to Katherine. They reside in Silver Spring, MD. He is a member of AMMV JWB Chapter.

CLIFTON L. HAGENBUCH, JR., was born Dec. 22, 1924, in Pittsburgh, PA. Graduated from Wilkinsburg High School. April 1943 went to Sheepshead Bay Maritime Training School, Brooklyn, NY obtaining Lifeboat Certificate on Aug. 13, 1943. September 1943 was sent to the U.S. Merchant Marine Cadet Corps, basic school, San Mateo, CA as a deck cadet.

Met Mildred Louise Moore, yeoman, U.S. Navy, stationed on Terminal Island, San Pedro, CA and they married on Nov. 23, 1944 in Long Beach, CA. Resigned from the Cadet Corps and obtained his able bodied seaman's papers.

The rest of the war was spent aboard tankers, mostly Union Oil from Los Angeles, CA as AB. SS *Charles Nelson,* SS *A.C. Rubel,* SS *Fort Williams,* SS *Cathwood,* SS *Klamath Falls,* SS *Paul M. Gregg,* SS *George Berkeley* and the SS *Santa Paula.*

After the war he worked for the Todd Shipyard as heavy rigger, then as an accountant for Wilmington Gasoline Company and Standard Oil of California all located in Southern California.

1955 formed the Westminster Insurance Agency as broker and agent in Westminster, CA. 1974 admitted to the State Bar of California and practiced law in San Juan Capistrano, CA until retirement Jan. 1, 1990.

They have two adult children, Stephen L. Hagenbuch and Anita Fox Dryland. They have five grandchildren.

Presently the wife spends most of her time playing golf and he has gone to the club circle with magic shows.

He resides in San Clemente, CA.

PAUL HAJOSTEK, was born Jan. 15, 1927 in Donora, PA. He joined the Merchant Marines at the age of 15, and trained at Hoffman Island. He had his 16th birthday in Africa, and later took part in the invasion of Anzio. In 1953 he went into the fuel oil delivery business. Retired in 1981. He currently works for the city of New York, operating engineers local 14B as a high pressure boiler operator, living on Staten Island, NY with wife Virginia and two daughters.

He served on liberty ships, *William Mulholland, Peter Minuit, Augustus Merriman, George A. Custer* and *Nelson W. Aldrich,* as messman, night utility and O.S. from 1943 to 1945 in Atlantic and invasion of Anzio and Russia. Served on victory ships *Stamford Victory, James Manning, Montclair Victory,* 1945 through 1946 as deck maintenance, and AB, in the Atlantic.

RAYMOND T. HALEY, was born July 17, 1928, educated in Bayonne, NJ - August 1943 assigned to *J.A. Moewinkle* (tanker). Back to school in September 1943 (Oh Well!).

Wartime ships sailed: *W.H. Libby* (wiper), tanker, June 1944-July 1944: then in Deck Department as O.S. and A.B. until December 1944. *Elisha Walker* (tanker) December, 1944-December 1945 as messman. Served primarily in Atlantic and Mediterranean-Middle East Theatres. Also served on *Esso Bolivar, Esso Parkersburg, F.H. Bedford, Jr., Esso Baytown, Esso Annapolis, Esso Allentown, Esso Concord, Peter Hurll.*

Continued going to sea until December 1950. Then worked in time study until 1959. Since 1959 has been in data processing. Currently director of payroll services for a major service bureau in New York city.

Presently living in Toms River, NJ with wife Claire.

L. BERTRAND HALSEMA, Dutch, Jax, FL, mess captain. Trumbull 4101-D. 1942: tourist business blackout holdup! Classmate St. Johns Lightship sinking. Mobile-Keys, port anchoring nights. Bauxite "rustbucket" "minutemen", Mississippi mouth sinkings. USO admittance refusals. 1943:

Marine Insurance's sending Germany sailings! Alcoa's plane, plant hold up. Hull bombing: 3K munitions, 80-P, manning guns. Watches days, shipyard tacking nights. Liverpool wedding. Stormy torpedo net rescue. Harrimans Hog Islanders. Drybowl compass. Cuban ragged Guajiros, bohios. "Apprentice" pilots: 50 years! Pancake Tues. Lemons. 1944: Belly robber chow theft D-day Manchester. Canadian Corvett Savior sinking. Antwerp V-bombing, LeHavre destruction, Marseilles shootings. 10K porpoise migration. X mas weeks: day watches, nightmating 24 hours! 1946: UUsitalo Finnish hospital coffee. Kiel freeze. Crossing: QE-1 portbound. U.K. snobbery, bus conductor: "No silk purses from sows ears (council housers)! MCC-UNAM-CSM- SDIS. Praising seafarers, radical NMvers. Honesty courage antidiscrimination. Texaco Portland explosion.

ALFRED L. HAMEL, born July 16, 1924 in Providence, RI. He joined the Merchant Marine in New York City, 1942. Hamel served aboard the SS *Joseph Story* from March 1944 to March 1945 as OS. He made 25 trips from Southampton to France; nine trips to Utah Omaha Beachhead; one trip to Cherbourg; one trip to LeHarve; 14 trips to Roven, all with soldiers and equipment.

His memorable experiences include serving on the SS *John Wayne* from April 1943 to Oct. 1943; Boston (Castle Is.), 8,500 tons 500 lb. demolition bombs to Newport, Memleuthshire, SW England - unloaded. Reloaded same cargo and unloaded at Brendesi, Italy.

Was in the U.S. Army April 1945 to Dec. 1945.

Member of the Providence Police Dept. 1944 to 1973. State of Rhode Island Stationary Engineer 1973-1986, now retired.

RICHARD P. HAMM, sailed as OS, wiper and AB during WWII on the SS *George Berkeley* from Oct. 13, 1944 to Aug. 3, 1945. Has USCG-Merchant Marine discharge and DD-214. Has the Merchant Marine Emblem, Atlantic, Pacific, Mediterranean, and Middle East War Zone Bars.

Married to Nancy and is a member of AMMV JWB Chapter. They reside in Frederick, MD.

JAMEEL HAMOUD, was born in Philadelphia, PA, July 20, 1920. He went to school there. He received his bachelor's of science degree from Temple University, and his masters degree from Antioch University.

He received his seaman's papers in 1937, but he did not go to sea until July 1942. At that time he joined the U.S. Maritime Service. He did his boot training in Curtis Bay, MD. Left the training school with a fireman and water tender endorsement. His first ship was out of 1700 Fleet Street, Baltimore, MD, from the National Maritime Union Hall.

As an unlicensed person, some of the trips he made were: on a tanker, refueling Navy escort vessels in a convoy running between Trinidad in the West Indies and Brazil, South America.

The Persian Gulf run, from the U.S. to Iran Persia, carrying ammo. On a tanker carrying aviation fuel from the U.S. to England, during WWII.

In February 1945, he went to Officers Training School in New London, CT. After he completed the course. He went back to Philadelphia, PA. It was there he joined the Marine Engineers Beneficial Association.

During his licensed years, he sailed on ships that carried ammo from the U.S. to Japan and Korea, and from Japan to Korea. This was during the Korean War.

He sailed on ships carrying ammo, from the U.S. to Vietnam when the French were fighting, and also when the U.S. was fighting there.

He made voyages in peaceful areas also. He went to countries in South America, crossing the Equator many times. He visited countries in the Far East. Countries that were at peace. To get there he had to cross the International Date Line. There were other countries at peace that he visited, such as countries in Europe, countries in the Middle East and countries in Africa.

He ended up with an officers rating in the U.S. Naval Reserve, and the U.S. Maritime Service.

He retired from life at sea in 1966. From the National Marine Engineers Beneficial Association. He is now a retiree.

ROBERT A. HAMPSHIRE, sailed as O.S., A.B., 3rd mate and 2nd mate from October 1941 to August 1945. Attended Fort Trumbull May 4, 1943 to Oct. 12, 1943. Graduated as ensign. Sailed around the world. Awarded Atlantic and Pacific War Zone Bars.

Married to Mrs. Ellen Stebbing. They reside in Baltimore, MD. He is a member of AMMV JWB Chapter.

JIM W. HANABURY, was born Sept. 12, 1918 in New Haven, CT. He joined the Merchant Marine March 1943 in San Antonio, TX. Training in St. Petersburg, FL in Maritime Service.

Served on the *Arizonian,* ordinary, So. America - Rio and Buenos Aries; *John Martin Miller,* AB, North Atlantic-Scotland and England; Frank A. Munsey, AB, France, Pacific Islands.

His memorable experiences include collision off Grandbanks - AB, North Atlantic, England. On ammunition ship - attacked by Germany surface craft in North Sea.

Employed as public school teacher, Corpus Christi, TX. He is a widower, volunteer U.S. Coast Guard Auxiliary.

JAMES MERTZ HANBERRY, was born March 6, 1923, DeQuincy, LA, died March 5, 1986. Married to Lynette Abercrombie Hanberry, they had two sons, James Mertz Hanberry II, Joseph Lee Hanberry, a daughter

Lorri Lynn Perdue, and two grandsons James Mertz Hanberry III and Jeremy Wayne Perdue.

His enlistment in the U.S. Merchant Marine Sept. 1, 1943, in Mobile, AL, continued until Aug. 31, 1948. Advancing his rating to ensign at his discharge, he began serving as an ordinary seaman on SS *Lake Sapor*. Assigned to eleven ships, final discharge was as third mate on the SS *Alcoa Pegasus*.

Awarded to him: the Merchant Marine Combat Bar, Mediterranean Middle East War Zone Bar, Atlantic War Zone Bar, and Pacific War Zone Bar.

J. Mertz Hanberry graduated from Woodrow Wilson College of law, he was a civilian employee for thirty-one years, and retired as a contracting officer for CNET on Aug. 18, 1981.

WILLIAM L. HANGER, attended Sheepshead Bay. Sailed as wiper, F/W and acting oiler during WWII. Awarded the Mediterranean-Middle East War Zone Bar.

He is married to Betty and they reside in Beltsville, MD. He is a member of AMMV JWB Chapter.

TORBEN BERNHARD HANSEN, sailed as messman, O.S., A.B., bosun, and 3rd mate during WWII. Attended USMSTS at Fort Trumbull September 1945. Skilled in deck seamanship electrical engineering. Awarded Atlantic, Pacific, Mediterranean Middle East War Zone Bars and Combat Bar. Sailed from October 1945 to February 1946. Served on SS *Flagstaff Victory*, SS *Henry D. Whiton*, SS *John B. Ashe*, SS *Francis Parkman*, SS *George Rogers Clark*, MS *Pennant* and MS *Roseville*.

He is married to Anita and they reside in Annapolis, MD. He is a member of AMMV JWB Chapter.

JOHN F. HARDESTY, sailed as unlicensed junior engineer, 3rd assistant engineer, 2nd assistant engineer, 1st assistant engineer and chief engineer during WWII and Korean War. MV *Staghound* was torpedoed in South Atlantic on March 3, 1943. Attended Sheepshead Bay. Graduated Officers Training School, Fort Trumbull, New London, CT in 1944.

Has Atlantic, Pacific and Far East War Zone Bars, Merchant Marine Combat Ribbon with one star and Presidential Testimonial Letter.

Married to Constance. He is a member of AMMV JWB Chapter.

CHARLES L. HARKNESS, was born Oct. 26, 1919, Muskegon, MI. First went to sea, 1938. Sailed Atlantic, Pacific and Mediterranean Middle East. During WWII he was on following ships. Engine room.

Oiler, SS *Oliver Hazard Perry*, 1942, oiler, SS *Thomas Johnson*, 1942-1943; FWT, SS *Stephan T. Mather*, 1943; FWT, SS *John A. Dix*, 1944; FWT, SS *Walt Whitman*, 1944-1945, two trips in 1945; FWT, SS *James J. O'Kelly*, 1945.

James J. O'Kelly was at Okinawa when A bomb were dropped on Japan and war ended.

Post war sailed all types ships. Liberty, victory and C-type freighters, C-4 troop ship lumber schooners, sea going salvage tug and all passenger ships.

Awarded the Merchant Marine Emblem and Victory Medal, Atlantic War Zone Bar, Pacific War Zone Bar, Mediterranean Middle East War Zone Bar.

Member MFOWW Association of Pacific until 1960. Worked 25 years as west coast longshoreman and retired from ILWU Local 13, Wilmington, CA. Retired between California and New Mexico.

Married Maria. Charter life member USMMV WWII.

CHARLES E. HARRIS, was born March 26, 1925 in Fulton, NY. He joined the Merchant Marine May 11, 1943 at Hoffman Island.

Served on many ships stationed in England, Scotland, Murmansk, Archangles, North Africa, Sicily, Italy, Persian Gulf, Guam and Saipan.

His memorable experiences include the submarine attacks, air raids, rammed a German submarine in English Channel. Loaded with ammunition.

Employed in construction and retired in 1980. He is married and has two daughters.

FRANK JAMES HART, was born Dec. 20, 1921 in Kingman, AZ. He joined the U.S. Maritime School in Port Hueme, CA, June 1942.

Stationed on SS *Degolia*, 1942, AB, Pacific; SS *White*, liberty ship, 1943, AHB, New Guinnie; SS *Cape Greig* C1, 1944, A.B., New Guinnie; SS *Rogue River* T2, 1944, A.B., England; SS *Clarksdale Victory*, February 1945, AB, Okinawa; SS *Pinebluff Victory*, Aug. 7, 1945, A.B., Philippines.

From 1945 to 1992 he has been on 30 or 40 ships, and is still sailing. His last ship was SS *President Adams*.

During the battle of New Guinnie, he picked up Samuri Sword and now he has donated it to the *Lane Victory* Museum

On the SS *Clarksdale Victory*, in 1945, during the invasion of Okinawa, carrying 10,000 tons of live ammunition. They were shelled by Japanese artillery They missed them for an hour, except for one shell which hit midship, about 10 feet from the ship, and it bent the plants. But another friend of his, that he went to high school with, wasn't so lucky. He was on another Victory Ship, and the Japanese hit it, it sank and he was killed.

In 1944, he was on the T2 tanker *Rogue River*, in a convoy to Europe. Dodging the torpedoes from the German submarine wolf pack.

1940-1941 CCC's. Belonged to Laborers Union and was operating engineer.

Married in 1948. Has three daughters, four grandchildren. Still in shipping. Still shipping as AB, Sailors Union of the Pacific.

FORREST F. HASBROUCK, was born May 22, 1917 in New Paltz, NY. Joined Merchant Marine, Sheepshead Bay, NY. He was a night foreman in a machine shop, making 40 mm antiaircraft shells for the Navy. He was a dayman on SS *Samuel Mitchell*, went through a hurricane off Cape Cod, this ship hauled Gyssum white rock to New York then to Virginia for coal to be taken to Sandy Point Marine, then on SS *Archbishop* Lanny liberty to France and Germany. This was a converted to bring forces home from LeHavre, France.

Later after the Merchant Marine, he became a butcher, after that spent 26 years working for IBM and now has been retired for 15 years.

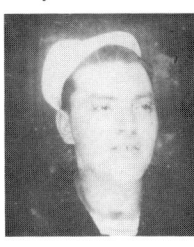

RAYMOND F. HASBROUCK, was born March 2, 1921 in New Paltz, NY. Attended "Kings Point" U.S. Merchant Marines Academy as an engine cadet and graduated December 1943.

During the war years sailed on five different "liberties", *Walt Whitman, Howard A. Kelly, Joseph L. Kemp, Janet Lord Roper* and the *Caeser Rodney*. Made many Atlantic crossings to England, Africa and Mediterranean ports. Sailing most of the time as "Second Assistant Engineer". The last trip was on the *Caesar Rodney* taking the last load of American "Lend Lease" to Russia. The load was machinery for a tire manufacturing plant, diesel generating plants and a deck load of Baldwin locomotives. They discharged in Murmansk, but had to follow an ice breaker through ice three foot thick to get to Molotvsk for their return cargo of chromium ore in the lower holes brought to the USA lumber was loaded in the between decks and on deck and discharged in Germany. Signed off April 1946. Employed by IBM Corp. for 35 years retiring in 1983.

Now living with his wife Anne in New Paltz, NY. Hobby building model Marine steam engines.

CHARLES C. HAUG, joined the Merchant Marine when he was 16 years old. He went through Sheepshead Bay in New York and came out with fireman second class and oilers papers. He also has a certificate of efficiency as a lifeboatman. In addition he also had training in elementary gunnery. He got out of Sheepshead Bay on Dec. 13, 1944 and signed on his first ship on Dec. 16, 1944. The ship was the SS *Lafcadio Hearn*. The ship was a liberty tanker. It was the dirtiest ship he was ever on. They pulled out of New York on Dec. 23, 1944. This is all he can remember about this trip. He was on the *Central Fall Victory* which was a troop transport. They had troops on deck sleeping intents nailed to the hatch covers. They hit some rough water and the waves came over the bow and collapsed the tents and the soldiers were floating around the deck in sleeping bags. All of the troops on board were sea sick. He also sailed on the SS *Ferdinand Gagnon*. All the ships he sailed on were carrying cargoes of aviation fuel or ammunition and guns. He stopped sailing after the war when the NMU went on strike. When they were out so long and he needed money he got a job with Continental Can Co. and worked for them for 39 years and retired.

He is a member of AMMV JWB Chapter and resides in White Hall, MD.

ROBERT A. HAYWOOD, was born Sept. 4, 1923. Graduated Lafayette High School, Buffalo, NY January

1942. Worked Colonial Radio and Curtiss Wright Aircraft in Buffalo in 1942, 1943, 1944. Joined the Merchant Marines 1944, age 21. Trained at Sheepshead Bay, NY.

Sailed on *Irving Babbitt*, November 1944, Atlantic; *Charles D. Poston*, April 1945, Mediterranean; *Sea Robin*, October 1945, Atlantic, *Courser*, June 1946, Pacific.

Moved to California in 1950 and worked for the Garrett Corp. Airsearch Aviation Service Co., Los Angeles for 31 years. Retiring in March 1981. He still lives in Los Angeles area with his wife Grace of 47 years. They have three children, nine grandchildren and four great grandchildren.

LEWIS C. HAZELWOOD, JR., sailed as wiper and ordinary seaman. His next of kin is his son James M. Hazelwood.

Lewis is a member of AMMV JWB Chapter and he resides in Baltimore, MD.

DAVID HEATON, was born Dec. 1, 1920 in Denver, CO. Graduated University of Denver School of Commerce May 1943. Enrolled in U.S. Maritime Service and trained at Catalina Island. Selected for officer training at Assistant Purser Hospital Corps School, Sheepshead Bay, NY. Graduated December 1943 with the rank of warrant officer.

Sailed January 1944 SS *Edwin Markham* (liberty) for Anzio, Italy beachhead. Bombed by Germany planes and bombarded by German artillery while unloading cargo. Awarded Merchant Marine Combat Bar, Atlantic and Mediterranean-Middle East War Zone Medals. Commissioned ensign USMS. SS *John A. Rawlins* (liberty) supported General MacArthur's return to the Philippines. Bombed nightly by Japanese Air Force at Leyte and Lingayen Gulf. Awarded Pacific War Zone Medal. Philippine Government awarded Philippine Liberation Medal, Presidential Unit Citation and Independance Medal. SS *Australia Victory* en route to Saipan where Japan surrendered. Awarded World War II Victory Medal. Promoted to lieutenant (j.g.) USMS.

Continued sailing after the war. SS *Australia Victory* to South Africa. Awarded Chief Purser's Certificate. SS *Gainesville Victory* to Poland, SS *Cape Hatteras* (C1) coastwise. Promoted to lieutenant USMS. Completed five voyages East Coast South America aboard Delta Line's SS *Del Mundo* (C-2). Retired from Merchant Marine and USMS Aug. 8, 1943.

E.J. HEINS, JR., was born Feb. 22, 1927 in Charleston, SC. Joined the Merchant Marine July 1944 at Charleston, SC.

Self employed, mechanical contractor.

Married to Eva and has son Eddie Heins III. He retired 1989. At present he is East Coast vice president, U.S. Merchant Marine Veterans of WWII.

WALTER G. HENDERSON, was born June 10, 1926 on a farm in Southeast Missouri. Gulf Radio School, New Orleans, LA, October 1944 to March 1945. He obtained his FCC License and Merchant Marine papers and between April 1945 and January 1947 he was on the following ships: SS *William B. Travis*, SS *LaBrea Hills*, SS *Henry L. Ellsworth*, M/V *Span Splice*. He sailed in the Atlantic, some in the Pacific, but mostly in the West Indies and South America. Then four years at Westminster College in Fulton, MO, where he graduated with a degree in physics. He liked college very much, but he was still single and he also liked going to sea. His next ships were: SS *DePauw Victory*, in June 1951 to Japan and Korea, then the North Atlantic run to Europe. From February 1953 to August 1954 he sailed on the USNS *Mission DePala*. They made trips to the Mediterranean, Coastwise and the Far East. Most of the time they were running between the Persian Gulf and Japan, Korea, Philippines, and Ceylon.

Their communications and orders were from Navy stations and he copied a schedule each six hours. In February 1955 he went to work for Western Electric/BTL/AT&T Technologies at Burlington, NC. He married a wonderful North Carolina girl in December 1955, which ended his sea life. They have three fine children and two grandchildren. He retired as a design/development engineer on special Navy projects in April 1989. He's an active radio amateur, K4GDC, and enjoy electronic repair, travel, railroading and photography.

ROBERT G. HERBERT, JR., was the solicited and unsolicited, critic and advisor of authors, artists, curators, editors and model makers. "I'll miss the crusty exchanges between Bob and Karl...two maritime giants." said the secretary of Karl Kortum, curator of the National Maritime Museum in San Francisco. A Houston newspaper columnist said, "I didn't always like what he said in his letters, but he always learned something from them." Herbert was a well known and highly respected authority on maritime history who sought perfection in himself and others. He was an avid supporter of, and he collaborated with, the likes of Marine artists John Stobart, Paul McGehee and Michael Blaser.

Born in New York City, the second son of two prominent artists, Bob Herbert grew up in Sea Cliff on the North shore of Long Island. He graduated from the New York State Nautical School (the Schoolship USS *Newport*) in 1924 and spent eight years as a watch officer in several steamship companies including the Morgan Line, American Hawaiian Steamship Co., Standard Oil of California, *Mystic SS Co.* and the Bull Line.

When he "came ashore", a year after marrying the former Elsa Karen Peulecke, also of Sea Cliff, he held an unlimited (any size - any ocean) chief mate's license.

After working as designer and production manger for Model Builders Guild of Hempstead, NY he accepted a position as model maker and section head for Norman Bel Geddes in construction the celebrated General Motors "Futurama" for the 1939 New York World's Fair. When the fair closed, Herbert became a draftsman and model maker for Gibbs and Cox where he worked on the *Fletcher* class destroyer and numerous landing craft design aspects. He was ultimately assigned to a then-secret anti-torpedo net design project for British Admiralty.

Herbert's intimate knowledge of the net design and sea-going background saw him "inducted" into the active U.S. Naval Reserve as a lieutenant, to work directly with British Admiralty on the further development, rigging and testing of anti-torpedo nets for merchant vessels. He spent the duration of the war at sea again, doing just that; rigging and testing, under battle conditions, an invention that saved thousands of Merchant Mariners' lives and hundreds of thousands of tons of allied cargo from Axis torpedoes. Herbert was promoted to lieutenant commander in 1943, a rank he also carried in the U.S. Maritime Service.

After the war, Bob Herbert went back to ship modelling as the designer and chief model maker for Marine Model Company at Halesite, Long Island. He commenced independent model building, repair and restoration in early 1950s when he and a colleague took on a French Line project which Marine Model Co. had declined. In that capacity he rebuilt, repaired, converted and constructed hundreds of display models for the French Line until they finally ceased tranatlantic passenger service.

Having repaired and restored much of the model collection at the Maritime Industry Museum at Fort Schuler (SUNY Maritime - successor to his alma mater, the New York State Nautical School), and because he was (still) so active in alumni and student activities, the museum's model gallery was dedicated to Robert G. Herbert II in 198, on the occasion of his 82nd birthday.

Among his many accomplishments, Herbert was an active "plank owner" member of South Street Seaport, for whom he drew the spar and rigging plans and supervised re-rigging of the bark PEKING. He was an outspoken and unabashed advisor to the National Maritime Historical Society and an active member and long-time supporter of Mystic Seaport. Other maritime activities included the Steamship Historical Society of America, the New York Shiplore and Model Club, the Long Island Ship Model Society, the Suffolk County Marine Museum and the Battle of the Atlantic (BATLANT) Historical Society, of which he served as chairman. He was an oft sought speaker, lecturer and reviewer of matters maritime, and he never lost his knack for accuracy and detail, in models or in the printed word.

Herbert is survived by a son, Peter, in Virginia; a daughter, Susan, in Washington State, three grandchildren and one great-granddaughter....all of whom love the sea.

KENNETH EDWARD HERMAN, was born Feb. 1, 1926, Montrose, MN. Joined the Merchant Marine Jan. 20, 1944 in Minneapolis, MN.

Served on *Stephen T. Mather*, utility, New York, NY, Philadelphia, PA; SS *George E. Hale*, wiper, Baltimore, MD to Seattle, WA; SS *Hart Crane*, FMIWT, Baltimore, MD to Mobile, AL; *Finley Peter Dunne*, messman, Baltimore, MD to New York.

He is in business for himself, carpet, mobile homes, Isle, MN. Married Marlys L. Hetland, March 20, 1946. Had two children, Eugene Barbara. Kenneth died Aug. 5, 1988. Buried Sunset Cemetery, Minneapolis, MN.

THOMAS W. HERMAN, (See Sunpaper article quote listed under Patrick L. Whalen.)

NEAL A. HESSLETON, sailed as messman and radio officer during WWII. Was strafed on *James E. Howard* in Mediterranean, rammed on *Chapel Hill Victory* in English Channel. Attended USMSTS in St. Petersburg, FL and Gallups Island Radio School in Boston.

Holds Combat Bar, Atlantic, Mediterranean and Middle East War Zone Bars. He is married to Elizabeth. They reside in Suitland, MD. He is a member of AMMV JWB Chapter.

DONALD W. HEWETT, sailed as cadet on SS *Paul Hamilton Hayne* (liberty) from Dec. 8, 1942 to Aug. 20, 1943, 3rd mate on SS *Golden State* (C-2), SS *Sirocco* (C-2) from June 17, 1944 to Aug. 17, 1944, SS *Harry Percey* (liberty) from Sept. 7, 1944 to Dec. 29, 1944, SS *John W. Brown*, (liberty) from March 28, 1945 to June 12, 1945, SS *Lone Star State* (liberty) from July 26, 1945 to June 19, 1946, and SS *Sharon Victory* from Nov. 25, 1946 to April 26, 1948. Sailed as 2nd mate on SS *Old Dominion State* (liberty) from Aug. 28, 1948 to Jan. 3, 1949. Sailed as third mate on SS *Junius Smith* from Jan. 11, 1949 to March 31, 1949.

WILLIAM RAYMOND HICKEY, resides in Palm Coast, FL and served in the Merchant Marines.

ROBERT W. HIGDON, was born June 19, 1926 in Chicago, IL. He joined the Merchant Marines October 1944 in Chicago, IL.

Served on: *Frank B. Linderman*, 3rd radio operator, Seattle, WA; *Pontotiac Victory*, 2nd radio operator, Galveston, TX.

Shipped out to *Prince Robert* for ammo and to Guam. Ship went to Marseilles, France for 101st Abn. to return to Norfolk, VA.

Radio operator, TWA, Midway Airport, Chicago, IL. Also employed for Swift Adhesives, Downers Grove, IL. Married in 1950. Retired in January 1989. Today he plays golf and tennis.

PAUL HIGGINS, "What about those of us that were in Vietnam era and rode merchant ships into the war zone and spent many months sitting on the hook discharging ammunition and other supplies for the war effort." (TAL, 4/92 p.7).

LEONARD R. HILGENBERG, resides in Camp Springs, MD and is a member of AMMV JWB Chapter.

MALCOLM L. HINCHCLIFFE, was born Feb. 10, 1920 in Lawrence, MA. Joined the Merchant Marine in Boston on Sept. 17, 1941. Trained in Florida on Squarerigger. Transferred to San Pedro, CA to take *American Sailor* to dry dock in 1942.

Sailed as AB on *HM Storey,* (a tanker), 1942; *Norluna* (cargo ship in North Atlantic) 1942; *Esso Rochester* (tanker) 1943; *Edmund Randolph* (liberty in South Pacific), 1943; Marine hospital in San Francisco, CA (injured on *Edmund Randolph*), 1943; Fort Trumbull, New London, CT (Officer Training School), 1944;

Sailed as third mate on board *William P. Duval* (liberty in North Atlantic), 1945; *Richard Rush,* (liberty in North Atlantic), 1945; *Rufus C. Dawes,* (liberty) promoted to 2nd mate, July 1945-February 1946, Philippines and Japan.

Turned ship over to Japan in Yokohama Harbor. Crew returned to SAn Pedro, CA via troop ship.

Received Veteran status in 1988 and disability pension for injury of 1943. (Pension not retroactive).

Retired in 1979, having been a real estate broker since 1950.

Presently touring USA in a motorhome with wife Dorothy of 48 years.

JOHN FRANCIS HIRD, was born Jan. 9, 1923. Continuous service discharge book issued in the port of New York recording service from Dec. 29, 1942 to Feb. 13, 1944 as deck cadet serving on the SS *Daniel Willard,* SS *Exceller,* SS *William S. Halsted,* and SS *Borinquen.* All voyages were foreign. First Aid Certificate issued at the U.S. Merchant Marine Cadet Basic School, Henderson's Point, Pass Christian, Miss. dated April 7, 1944. Issued 3rd mates license. Photographs with personal notations show John in his Midshipmen Khaki uniform on board his first ship, the SS *Daniel Willard* of Baltimore; securing lifeboats for heavy seas; Bill Bliss and Arnold Ridout loafing between watches with notation that these Mariners were killed in action; S.A. Korber (chief mate) on watch; miles of water; Captain Paige (a swell skipper); Jacob Jacobsen (2nd mate) arrested on spy charges as a Nazi; looking aft toward 'midships' over the deck cargo; looking from the bridge forward over the deck cargo; heavy seas - taken in the Great Australian Bight; Charlie Quinn (gunnery officer); SS *Santa Maria* July 1943 Dakar, Swenegal, French West Africa after striking a mine, damage 87 feet from bow to aft; "Pop and me just before I made trip to England"; John is shown in photograph of commissioning ceremonies on his first Navy ship USS *Shoshone* (AKA65); other photographs show crew members; LCM's circling the spot where the USS *Arizona* was sunk a Pearl Harbor; loading of truck and bulldozer; LST 758, photographs of natives and scenery passed by Naval Censors; John with Marine officer and three Navy nurses in dress uniforms, group photo of celebration; personnel on hospital grounds; 1946 Oldsmobile; and several photos of other individuals.

GEORGE L. HOBBS, was born April 1, 1927. Attended school in Kansas City, MO and joined Merchant Marine in 1944, training at Catalina Island, CA.

Ships sailed: *Bluejacket* C2, FWT, 1944, Pacific; *William Dean Howell,* liberty, FWT, 1945, Atlantic and Mediterranean; *Wesleyan Victory,* oiler, 1945-1946, Pacific and Atlantic; *Lane Victory,* oiler, 1948, Pacific; *Arizona Victory,* oiler, 1948, Pacific; *Tradewind,* C2, oiler-reefer oiler, 1949-1950, Pacific; *Santa Flavia,* C2, oiler, 1950-1951, Pacific; *Knox Victory Jr.,* 3rd assistant engineer, 1951-1953; Pacific, Atlantic and Mediterranean. Entered navy in 1953. Served on USS *Repose,* assistant engineer officer 1953-1954, Pacific; USS *General Breckinridge,* assistant engineering officer, 1955, Pacific.

Worked ashore as stationary engineer until retirement in 1990. Now doing volunteer work on the *Jerimiah O'Brien,* restored liberty ship. He lives in Belmont, CA with his wife Jeannette.

JOHN HODAK, was born June 30, 1918 in Kaylor, PA. Joined Merchant Marine Oct. 29, 1942 in Pittsburg, PA. Took training at Sheepshead Bay, New York City. Sailed as ordinary and able seaman on seven cargo ships.

SS *Fisher Ames,* Jan. 21, 1943-Sept. 10, 1943; *Ralph Woods Emerson,* June 7, 1944 to Aug. 4, 1944, O.S.; *Cushman K. Davis,* Aug. 25, 1944 to Feb. 18, 1945, A.B.; *Kentuckin,* Sept. 29, 1943 to Dec. 1, 1943, O.S.; *William A. Coulter,* April 1, 1945-July 3, 1945, A.B., *Matthew P. Deady,* Jan. 11, 1944, Nov. 23, 1944, A.B.; *Mary D.,* July 22, 1945 to Dec. 27, 1945, A.B.

He survived the typhoon on SS *Mary D.,* Pacific Ocean, 1945.

In 1943 he sailed around the world in submarine infested waters. Was in all war zones, two times. Received three ribbons. Survived typhoon near end of WWII in 1945 in Pacific Ocean with a broken steering. He left the Merchant Marine March 15, 1946.

He went to work as a heavy equipment operator for 22 years doing excavation on highways and airports. Retired in 1970. At present he has two acres of ground that keeps him busy.

GEORGE WILLIAM HOFERT, was born November 1920, Memphis, NY. May 14, 1940 boarded ship in Boston, MA.

Ships sailed: MV *Yankee Clipper* (wiper and motor man) Ex-Henry Ford Yacht converted to passenger ship 1940 *Cape Cod;* SS *Warrior,* (wiper and fireman) freighter 1941 Atlantic; MV *Melvin H. Baker,* (oiler), Hog Island 1941, Atlantic; SS *Yarmouth,*(oiler), passengers hip 1942 Atlantic; SS *Ipswitch,* (oiler), freighter 1942, Atlantic; SS *Alcoa Ranger,* (oiler), Hog Island, 1942, Atlantic and Arctic; SS *Joshia Bartlett,* (3rd engineer), liberty 1943, Atlantic and Mediterranean; SS *Robin-Locksley,* C-2, (Jr. engineer), Atlantic, Pacific, Indian; SS *Robin Sherwood,* (4th assistant and 2nd assistant engineer), C-2, 1944 Atlantic; SS *Hart Crane,* 1st assistant engineer), Liberty 1945, Atlantic, Indian and Mediterranean; SS *Sea Centaur,* (1st assistant engineer), C-3, 1945, Atlantic, Mediterranean, Indian, Pacific; SS *Marine Carp,* (1st asst. engineer), C-4, 1946, Atlantic, Mediterranean; SS *Sea Tarpon,* (1st assistant and chief engineer), C-3, 1946 and 1947, Atlantic, Pacific; SS *Samual Q. Brown* (2nd asst. engineer) T-2, 1947, Atlantic. SS *Robin Locksley,* (Jr. engineer, 4th assistant engineer and 1st assistant engineer), C-2, 1950-1951, Atlantic and Indian.

His memorable experiences include SS *Alcoa-Ranger* sunk July 7, 1942 near top of the world bound for Russia, SS *Joshia Bartlett* bombed in Oran, North Africa; SS *Robin Sherwood* ballast shifted, rolled to starboard 54 degrees permanent list-rolled to 70 degrees to starboard.

Worked in shipyard 10 years, New York Ship Building, Camden, NJ. Guarentee engineer, 3-MSTS ships *Barrett, Geiger, Upshure,* guarentee engineer USS *Edl-1* Norfolk. Trials for five fleet oilers, AOE's, one-DE (trial). Foreman-firerooms and engine rooms CAG-1 *Boston* and CAG-2 *Canberra.* Foreman air and hydraulics systems on the submarine USS *Bonefish.* Foreman for hydraulics on USS *Little Rock,* head of department 85-test and operation of NS *Savannah* reactor and main propulsion complex and associated equipment—just prior to criticality he was made superintendent for the whole ship. After NS *Savannah* was delivered, he was made superintendent for all testing in the shipyard. That department was later dissolved and he went on the nuclear submarines SSN 603-*Pollack,* then was transferred to SSN 604-*Haddo*; made five trial trips on SSN *Haddo.* Left the shipyard in February 1965 to go to work in Akron, OH in sales for Lucian Q. Moffitt, National and International exclusive distributors of Lucian Q Moffitt July 30, 1978 and went into business for myself as a factory representative and manufacturer of fluid lubricated bearings-rubber lined—for pumps. Sold his business as of June 30, 1990 and is semi-retired.

He is now taking in the slack.

GEORGE R. HOFFMAN, was born May 8, 1926 in Mineola, NY. Entered USMS training Sheepshead Bay, NY April 29, 1944. Assigned Flying Cloud barracks. Transferred USMSRTS, Hoffman Island. Assigned section 20-R, Northern Lights barracks. Graduated Hoffman Island March 16, 1945. Sailed as radio operator on *Madawaska Victory* April-May 1945; *Cape Comfort,* C2 June-July 1945; *Alexander Graham Bell,* liberty August-October 1945; *David C. Shanks* USATS April 1945-February 1946; *George W. Goethals* USATS March 1946-April 1947.

Married Marge Creash 1946. They have three children, Ronald, Glenn and Linda and three granddaughters Ryann, Ashley and Morgan.

Worked at LaGuardia and John F. Kennedy airports for TransWrld Airlines as ground radio operator, crew scheduler, flight attendant management until retirement January 1983. Presently residing in East Meadow, Long Island, NY.

GEORGE S. HOGAN, was born Sept. 28, 1925. He served from 1943-1955 on many ships and touched on many lands. Altogether, he served 12 years in the Navy

and USMM. He served in the USN, 6th Beach Btry. in 1943. Was discharged and obtained seaman's papers in 1944. Then shipped out on M.V. *Clevelander* coastal shipping to Canada. Later in 1944 shipped out on NMV on SS *Morris C. Fienstone*, A.B. to the Mediterranean. There their convoy was chased by an E boat along Italy's coast. Also in 1944 he was on the SS *Wildwood*, AB to Pacific waters.

The highlight of his shipping career was on SS *Edward Rutledge* Sept. 1, 1945 to Nov. 6, 1945. On an approach to Philadelphia in dense fog, he was instrumental in avoiding a collision with a hospital ship which was also with a ship bound for Yugoslavia loaded with wheat. While on look-out, he gave the bridge a hard over order to avert impact. Thank God the order was heeded, as there was no time to give details. The Captain said he would put George in for an award, which he tried to obtain but never received.

He shipped on many ships: SS *John E. Schmethzer* to Germany-came back with the troops, SS *Volunteer to Cuba*, SS *Cape John* to South America, SS *Queens Victory*-transporting horses to Poland, SS *Oglethorpe Victory*, and around the world on SS *African* (down Sept. 14, 1949 to Feb. 6, 1950). He served in Korea on SS *Central Victory* July 10, 1952 to Oct. 28, 1952. He retired his union book March 30, 1955. Sailed on many ships with boyhood friend Josphe R. Tullo.

His high school education was completed by correspondence course, then he attended Diesel-Refrigeration School and took upgrade courses at Sheepshead Bay. Until retiring in 1987, he worked in the lithograph trade. In 1990 he and his wife and two sons relocated to Virginia from New Jersey where he pursued one of his major hobbies - Civil War historical activities. Last year he had the privilege to become a member of the Virginia Defense forces where he holds the rank of staff sergeant. On his class A uniform he wears his Merchant Marine ribbons with the Merchant Marine patch worn on his right sleeve, indicating last service. Virginia Defense Forces is a cadre of National Guard.

RICHARD E. (DICK) HOLDAWAY, was born May 9, 1928 in Salt Lake City, UT. At age 16 he enlisted in the United States Maritime Service. Dick received training at Catalina Island, CA during May and June 1944.

On June 28, 1944 he was assigned to the troop ship (a former luxury liner) "SS *Monterey*" as a fireman. The SS *Monterey* sailed San Francisco July 3, 1944 on an unescorted voyage (because of her 22 knot speed) which included Honolulu, HI; Guam; Guadalcanal; Milne Bay and Oro Bay, New Guinea. While traveling from Milne Bay to Oro Bay the *Monterey* encountered a volcanic ash storm, turning day into night. The ship was under the control of an Australian pilot who managed to run the vessel onto a sandbar. After several days of effort the vessel was refloated and returned to San Francisco where it went into dry dock for repairs. Dick was unable to remain with the *Monterey* because he was hospitalized with an appendectomy. He returned to sea with the U.S. Army Transportation Service, Fort Mason, CA sailing on USAT troop ships.

His USAT ships included the *Gibson, Yarmouth, David C. Shanks, Aconagagua, Etolin, LST 802,* and *LST 553.* On these ships he progressed from fireman through water-tender, oiler, electrician, and Jr., 3rd asst., 2nd asst., and 1st asst engineer. As a crew member on these troop carrying vessels, Dick sailed the Mediterranean, Atlantic, Indian and Pacific Oceans. He sailed out of San Francisco, Los Angeles, Honolulu, New Orleans, Newport News and New York. His foreign ports of call included voyages to Italy, France, Gibraltar, Cuba, Panama, Australia, New Zealand, New Guinea, Iwo Jima, Wake Island, the Philippines, and the Solomon, Mariana, Gilbert, Marshall, Admiralty and the Caroline Islands.

Dick is a lifetime member of the U.S. Merchant Marine Veterans WWII. He is president of Kaiser International Corporation, operating the Los Angeles Dry Bulk Terminal, loading and unloading ships with coal and other products. The SS *Lane Victory*, a national historic monument, is temporarily berthed at Kaiser's Los Angeles Harbor facility. Dick's offices are in San Pedro, CA and he lives in nearby Rancho Palos Verdes.

JOSEPH E. (JOE) HOLLAND, was born on Nov. 3, 1921 in Lewistown, PA. Graduated high school, Langhorne, PA 1940. Sheepshead Bay, 1943.

Worked in Bethlehem Fairfield Fabricating Ship, Curtis Bay, MD, on the first liberty ship, SS *Patrick Henry*. Attended launching Sept. 27, 1941. Admiral Land and Mrs. Henry A. Wallace (vice-president's wife) did the honors.)

Ships he sailed on first four are liberties
Francis Drake, O.S., 1943, Iran; *William Whipple,* A.B., 1944, Iran, Australia; *John Barton Payne,* A.B., 1945, England; *Robert C. Grier,* 3rd mate; 1946, China; *Marine Fox,* quartermaster, 1945, France, all Isthmian ships.

Worked ashore 38 years C.R. Daniels Inc., Ellicott City, MD, vice-president. Retired 1988. Joined Project Liberty Ship, Baltimore, *John W. Brown.*

After 17 months working two days a week on the *Brown,* he joined MMP and in 1990 shipped out through Gleneagle Ship MGM Co., Houston. He has made three ships to Asia. Took part in Desert Storm, carrying diesel fuel for tanks and helicopters. Still active.

DELRAY HOLLEY, was born Oct. 10, 1927, Prichard, AL. Attended schools in Mobile, AL. Joined Merchant Service, Dec. 6, 1944. Received training at St. Petersburg, FL. Maritime School, Co. 51. Graduated March 26, 1945, fireman-oiler-watertender. Shipped out Maritime Shipping Pool, New Orleans, LA, MFOW Union.

Sailed three liberty ships, fireman/watertender.
Oliver Evans: From New Orleans April 10, 1945 to Panama Canal; Manila; Finchaven, New Guinea; Manila; Okinawa; Yokohama, Tokyo Bay; home to Mobile, AL Dec. 12, 1945 by way of Honolulu and Panama Canal.
John Isaacson: from Mobile Jan. 25, 1946 to Venice, Italy to New Orleans April 18, 1946.
Frank Springer: From Galveston, TX June 5, 1946 to Calcutta, India; Bahrain, Arabia; Genoa, Italy; Jacksonville, FA Dec. 9, 1946.

Truck, bus mechanic 11 years, Gulf Transport Co., Mobile. Forklift, general mechanic 33 1/2 years, International Paper Co. Retired March 1991, Mobile, AL.

Lives with wife, Elsie, in Mobile. They were married March 2, 1947.

He is president, Central Gulf Chapter, American Merchant Marine Veterans, member of U.S. Merchant Marine Veterans World War II, and member *John Brown,* Project Liberty Ship.

WILLIAM H. HOLLOWAY, resides in Arnold, MD and is a member of AMMV JWB Chapter.

LEONARD HOLOUBEK, resides in Annapolis, MD and is a member of AMMV JWB Chapter.

BRIAN H. HOPE, resides in Columbia, MD and is a member of AMMV JWB Chapter, Project Liberty Ship, chairman; Maryland Pilots Association.

MARTIN HRIVNAK, sailed as wiper on the SS *John W. Brown* to LeHavre, France with troops. Brought back German POWS and released American POWs.

He resides in Albuquerque, NM.

LEON A. HUBBARD, was born June 3, 1928 in Cambridge, MD. He joined the Merchant Marine, August 1945. Joined the U.S. Army September 1948. He was discharged from the Merchant Marine August 1948 and from the Army October 1969. His rank was OS/AB.

His memorable experiences included taking training at Sheepshead, NY. Joined the SUP and shipped out of East Coast ports as OS/AB. Sailed mostly to European ports on libertys, but made one trip on a Victory and one on a C-2, preferred libertys. Stopped sailing in August 1948 and joined the Army. Retired from Army, after 21 years in October 1969. Worked for the U.S. Government until June 1990, then retired again. Joined Project Liberty Ship, as a lifetime member, in October 1988 he has been a active volunteer ever since.

He is married and has one son and is enjoying retired life. Does a few odd jobs, but works mostly around the yard and garden. Does a little fishing, shrimping and traveling. Volunteers for the Red Cross and of course volunteer on the SS *John W. Brown* with Project Liberty Ship.

RICHARD D. HUFF, was born May 7, 1927 in Sayre, PA. Graduation from Athens High School, Athens, PA in June 1944. Joined the USMS in November 1944. Was in Sheepshead Bay, NY before attending radio school on Hoffman Island. Graduated there on July 20, 1945 with a 2nd class radio telegraphers license. Sailed on five ships.

SS *Joseph J. Kinyoun*, liberty; SS *Hutchinson I. Cone*, liberty, SS *Abraham Baldwin*, liberty; SS *James McHenry*, liberty, and MV *Gulfwing*, tanker.

He hit many ports, both here and abroad and enjoyed it thoroughly. Especially going through the Panama Canal.

He stopped sailing and went into construction in 1949. Became an equipment operator, mainly cranes and retired in 1989.

He recently lost his wife of 42 years to cancer on Dec. 30, 1992. He now resides by himself in the small town of Milan, PA, where he grew up as a child.

JARVIS T. HUGHES, was born July 6, 1924 in Baltimore, MD.

Went to work as an erector of the Bethlehem Fairfield Shipyard July 6, 1942 on his 18th birthday. Worked the midnight shift all through the war, helped to build liberty, LST and victory ship. After the war worked at the Bethlehem Key Hight Way ship repair yard for three years.

Worked at the Baltimore Gas and Electric Company for 37 years, March 10, 1949 until Aug. 8, 1986. He has been married to Jessie for 45 years and they have two daughters and two grandchildren.

Now working as a volunteer on the liberty ship *John W. Brown,* two day a week.

RICHARD PHILIP HUMM, was born Dec. 13, 1926 in Frederick, MD. He joined the Merchant Marine June 6, 1944 in Baltimore, MD.

He served on the *George Berkeley,* as wiper, OS, Baltimore, Long Beach around the world. *Issac M. Singer,* A.B. DK. Maintenance, Baltimore, Mobile "around the world"; *Crawford W. Long,* O.S., Baltimore, Rio, New York.

He is land surveyor and rental property owner. Married to Nancy and they have children, Linda, Jeannie, Suellen, and William.

Richard is retired and a life member of Project Liberty Ship.

THOMAS W. HUMM, was born Sept. 26, 1922 in Frederick, MD. Joined USMS, Sheepshead Bay, NY Sept. 28, 1943.

Served on *James Ford Rhodes,* April 1944, mess, Africa, Italy; *Janet Ford Roper,* July 1944, mess, Scotland, England, France; November 1944, Cuba.

JOHN JOSEPH HUNT, (Seán Ó Fiach) in Irish, was born in Philadelphia, PA Feb. 1, 1929. NMV Philadelphia January 1946 to 1968.

Served on *Atlantic Mariner* (Qmed); *Archers Hope, Jean Ribaut,* liberty ship, three years, 1951-1953; on the Marshal Plan - U.S. Army, Korean War mostly coastwise Texas Co. Gulf Oil. He received a honorable discharge.

Spent three years as oiler on the *Texaco California.* He finally sobered up.

Employed with the Palds Verdes School District for 15 years and retired Jan. 10, 1979. He is now single. "Doing justly. Loving Mercy and walking humbling with God!

JACKSON K. IVERSON, IEEE, EMBS, USMS, USAR, was born Oct. 14, 1929. Graduated California Maritime Academy, 1952. BS Marine Engineering, licensed 3rd engineering officer, unlimited horsepower steam, electric and diesel. Commissioned as engineering officer, U.S. Maritime Service, Korean Service.

Ships sailed, USS *Marine Serpent,* attack transport, *General Breckenridge,* troop transport, TS *Golden Bear,* USS *Grierson,* FS310 Army freight ship.

Commissioned in U.S. Army, engineering officer. Then went into design engineering, electrical, Westinghouse, Pacific Gas and Electric, Litton Systems and Hughes Aircraft Company.

Worked as design engineer or manager of the following ship systems: SSN *Nautilus,* USCG *Glacier,* SSBN *G. Washington.* Lafayette class submarines, Naval Tactical Data System (NTDS). Destroyers- DD *Spruance, Peterson,* large helicopter assault ships, Tomahawk Navy missiles and tank fire control weapons systems.

Retired from Hughes Aircraft Company in 1989 as chief engineer and program manager.

MICHAEL A. IZZO, was born June 13, 1928 in Waterbury, CT. He joined the Merchant Marine October 1944 in Sheepshead Bay, Brooklyn, NY.

Served on *Henry M. Rice,* oiler, Bari Italy, Venice, Italy.

Joined U.S. Army 1946-1966. Employed with Waterbury Fire Department for 25 years.

Married and has two daughters, one son, seven grandchildren and one great grandson. He is now retired and traveling.

EUGENE E. JACKS, was born Jan. 15, 1927 in Marin County, CA, graduated from high school in 1943 at San Francisco. After attending the University of California, Berkeley, served in Merchant Marine Jan. 10, 1945 to July 9, 1947.

Received training at U.S. Maritime Service training stations on Catalina island, CA (basic training) and Hoffman Island, NY (radio officer training).

Sailed as radio officer on Army transport ships: *David Shanks, General Morton,* and *LT-62.* Also on SS *John Lykes, Matsonia* and *Costa Rica Victory.* Sailed to Nagoya and Yokohama, Japan, Okinawa, Manila, Saipan, Guam, Honolulu, and Anchorage.

Received BS degree from University of California, Berkeley, School of Business in 1952. Retired in 1992 as senior life actuary, State of California, Department of Insurance after 32 years of service.

Lives in Marin County with his wife Joan. He has three daughters, Alison (Gegenheimer), Wendy and Marjorie and two grandsons, Andrew and Stuart Gegenheimer.

OWEN W. JACKSON, JR., sailed as O.S., A.B., 3rd mate and 2nd mate during WW II. Attended USMSTS at Hoffman Island and Fort Trumbull. Holds Atlantic, Pacific and Mediterranean War Zone Bars.

His next of kin is his daughter, Kristine E. Jackson. Owen is a member of AMMV JWB Chapter. He resides in Rockville, MD.

JACOB JACOBSEN, (See John Hird)

IGOR J. JAVROTSKY, deceased November 1988. Married to Ruth Javrotsky. He is a member of AMMV JWB Chapter and they reside in Annapolis, MD.

ROBERT GRANGER JENKINS, JR., enrolled as an AS in the USMS at the War Shipping Administration Training Organization at the Enrolling Office at 209 East Fayette Street, Baltimore, MD, on Aug. 12, 1944 at which time he was assigned to inactive duty. On Aug. 22, 1944 he was ordered to report for transfer to a USMSTS. On Oct. 13, 1944 he received his Merchant Seaman's Certificate of Identification at the port of New York. On Oct. 13, 1944 he received a rating of wiper. On Oct. 14, 1944 he received a Certification of Graduation from USMSTS at Sheepshead Bay and on Nov. 1, 1944 received release from active duty in the USMS at which time he was order to Cristobal, Canal Zone to serve on the MS *Chester Sun* which he did until Feb. 26, 1945. Copies of DD2168, WSA/USMS/USCG/USMM orders, certificates and pay slips donated to Project Liberty Ship and contained in the archives on board the *Brown.*

ROBERT L. (BOB) JENNINGS, was born June 5, 1927 in Fresno, CA. Joined the Merchant Marine June 12, 1943, (age 16), training on some old sailing vessel.

Dec. 22, 1943 SS *Tidewater,* tanker, messman, San Francisco, Brisbane, Persia, Egypt, Torrato, Italy. SS *Mericos,* tanker, *H. Whittier,* SS *Lundys Lane,* SS *M. Michael Edelstine,* troopship, SS *Algiworld,* SS *Charles S. Jones.* 1964 Vietnam, Alaska tug and barge, seatug, MV *Mowhawk.* River Tug, Cam Rahn Bay, Phan Ranh, Qui Nhon, Da Nang, Hue Vie Tau; MV *Osage* -towed ammo and PX supplies, Coastal Vietnam via Philippines.

ARTHUR JENSEN, sailed from 1941 to 1945 as wiper, cadet-midshipman, A.B., 3rd mate. Currently holds unlimited master's license issued Feb. 20, 1991.

Sailed during WWII, Korean and Vietnam Wars. Attended *John W. Brown* Metropolitan Vocational High School in New York City. Holds honorable discharge from USCG for service in USMM.

His next of kin is his daughter Teresa Rafferty. He is a member of AMMV JWB Chapter. He resides in Ellicott City, MD.

VERNER T. JENSEN, was born Nov. 18, 1920 in Denmark. He entered the Merchant Marine in 1936 in Copenhagen, Denmark.

Served on 14 different ships: SS *Harriet,* M/S *Indian Reefer,* M/T *Aristophanes* (tanker), SS *Standard* (tanker), SS *Greenville,* SS *Azra,* MS *Johnstown* (torpedoed with her June 5, 1942), SS *Washington,* SS *Santa Barbara,* SS *Flying Dragon,* SS *Augustine B. McManus* Liberty Ship, SS *MormacStar.* (He sailed on two other liberty ships.

He was awarded three Battle Stars, Combat Infantry Badge, Service Arrow Head (first Wave to hit Red Beach).

In the Army he was in the 3rd Div., 30th Inf., 3rd Bn., Co. 1. He received his American Citizenship papers in 1943.

He was married in 1950 to a beautiful woman from Oslo, Norway.

He is now an assistant manager for mobile home park.

CASEY JESUKAITIS, resides in Chicago, IL and is a member of AMMV JWB Chapter.

EDWARD L.H. JOHANNESSEN, was born Dec. 3, 1919 in San Luis Obispo, CA. Once was one of the youngest longshoremen on the San Francisco waterfront at age 16. Former member of ILA, ILWU and Masters, Mates and Pilots. Also worked for StandardOil Co. of California (Chevron) prior to WWII as a longshoreman and wharfinger assistant.

Licensed chief mate, any ocean, any tonnage. During WWII sailed as deck officer on cargo vessels and troop transports in the Atlantic, Pacific, Mediterranean War

Zones. Also served in U.S. Maritime Service as deck training officer for the U.S. Merchant Marine Cadet Corps.

After WWII resumed career with Chevron Corporation. Retired as manager, Corporate Labor Relations in 1985 after a career spanning 47 years.

Graduate of California Maritime Academy, Stanford University and University of California.

Resides with his wife of 50 years, Juliet, in Walnut, Creek, CA.

ALBERT F. JOHNSON, (See Sunpaper article quote listed below under Patrick L. Whalen.)

ANDREW C. JOHNSON, sailed as chief cook-baker, assistant electrician, wiper and messman during WWII, Korean and Vietnam Wars. Has certificate of substantially continuous service. Period of service is from Dec. 27, 1945 to Sept. 2, 1968. Sailed on following steamships. *Ethan Allen, John Vining, Anniston Victory, Del Ouro, Calvin Victory, Dick Lykes, American Leader, Gainesville Victory, Flying Independent, Linton Seam, William R. Lewis, Pan Virginia, William R. Lewis, Glamorgan Seam, Plymouth, Bulkero, Ocean Victory, George W. McCrary, Samuel F. Miller, Joseph Feuier, Arlington, Mandoil, Battle Mountain, Flying Spray, Cibao, Marine Ranger, American Courier, Marine Voyage, Marine Victory, Brase, American Reliance and Container Dispatcher.*

He is married to Dorothy. He is a member of AMMV JWB Chapter. They reside in Baltimore, MD.

BRYCE N. JOHNSON, trained as a fireman-watertender at Sheepshead Bay, July 21 through Nov. 9, 1945. He sailed the Atlantic aboard three liberty ships; SS *Nicholas D. Labadie,* Nov. 9, 1945 - April 1, 1946; SS *Thomas B. Robertson* May 11, 1946-June 24, 1946; SS *John Bartram* July 21, 1946-Oct. 3, 1946. His last voyage aboard SS *Midnight Victory* steam turbine Dec. 21, 1946 was New York to San Francisco through the Panama Canal, then on to Yokohama, Japan. They returned to San Francisco March 4, 1946 where he was discharged. Their cargos included coal, corn, bombs from Wales, military supplies, P-38s and autos.

His troops took him to Nazi submarine bunkers of LaRachelle, France, up the Seine River to Rouen, France, past the Rock of Gibraltar to the Bay of Naples and Mt. Vesuvious. A stop at Algiers gave him a good view of the Casbah.

GLEN A. JOHNSON, "he sailed on the SS *Topila,* the SS *Fort Wood,* the SS *Swan Island* and the SS *Socona.* He would enjoy hearing from anyone who sailed on these ships during 1945 and 1946" (TAL 4/92, p.5).

He resides in Beatrice, NE.

JAY L. JOHNSON, was born in Miles City, MT June 29, 1927. Enlisted in Merchant Marine Sept. 8, 1944. Basic training at Catalina, then to Radio School at Gallups Island, Boston. Upon graduation signed on the *Wellesley Victory* for her maiden voyage to Guam. Made several trips to France and Germany on the *United States Victory,*

taking German POWs back to Europe and bringing our troops home.

On March 9, 1946 he married Patricia Sellew who he had met on his first liberty from Gallups Island. Most of his working years were with the Connecticut Dept. of Corrections. Retired as a lieutenant in 1981. Since then they've been traveling the country in their motorhome. Winters in the south and summers in New England with their sons and three granddaughters. Recently they purchased a home at the Great Outdoors R.V. resort at Titusville, FL.

WARREN E. JOHNSON, was born in Richland, ND, on March 2, 1921. He left an Idaho CCC Camp to attend Maritime Service School in 1940. In 1941, Warren sailed off on the Standard Oil tanker, SS *Comet,* finishing his course work at sea. He sailed up and down the East Coast until blown out of the wtaer off the Georgia coast by a U-boat. Rescued by fishermen, the crew back on armed *Comet,* sailed out of Baltimore during the blizzard of 1942. Seven more ships carried Warren through the warring seas from Gibraltar through the South Pacific.

Liberty ship *Abel Stearns* in 1942-1943 when hit by German and Italian planes off Gibraltar; tanker *Quebec* in 1943; tanker *Pennsylvania,* 1943; liberty ship *Santiago Iglesias* in 1944; freighter *Sharon Victory* 1944-1945 carrying 7,250 tons of ammunition; tanker *Deroche* in 1945, and liberty ship *Robert Mills* in 1945-1946. He sailed for Richfield Oil one year and for U.S. Steel on the Great Lakes. Warren married Elizabeth MacPherson in 1949 and moved to Alaska. Completed electrical technician school in Chicago in 1954 and took a construction job with Hatfield Electric at Reserve Mining Company in Silver Bay, MN. Worked for Reserve from June 1955 until his retirement in 1983 as shift engineer in their power plant. He and wife reside in Silver Bay, MN.

He was awarded the Atlantic War Zone Bar, Pacific War Zone Bar, Mediterranean Middle East War Zone Bar, The Merchant Marine Combat Bar, The Merchant Marine Defense Bar, Victory Medal, Philippine Liberation Ribbon.

He has a Merchant Marine first assistant license.

FOREST JOHNSTON, sailed during WWII, Korean and Vietnam Wars as wiper, F/W, oiler and engine utility. Awarded Atlantic, Pacific, Mediterranean Middle East War Zone Bars, Merchant Marine Defense Bar, Victory Medal, Korean and Vietnam Service Bars.

He is married to Genevive. Member of AMMV JWB Chapter. He resides in Glen Burnie, MD.

CHARLES T. JONES, JR., attended the USMSST in St. Petersburg, FL and Baltimore from Sept. 6, 1943 to Dec. 22, 1943. Enrolled in the USMS with the grade of stgeward's mate second class. Released from active duty at USMSGA Baltimore on Dec. 22, 1943. Originally enrolled at Raleigh, NC. Has the Atlantic, Pacific, Mediterranean-Middle East, Vietnam War Zone Bars and Combat Bar. Sailed on the SS *Howell Lykes,* SS *Edward W. Scripps,* SS *El Salvador Victory,* S *James Hoban,* SS *Roger Griswold,* S *Samuel Griffin,* SS *Nicaragua Victory, Stephen Leacock,* and SS *Peter Minuit.* Was on matron voyage of the *Brown.*

He resides in Raleigh, NC.

HERMAN H. JONES, was born June 3, 1923, finished 10th grade, Tampa, FL. Worked for a ship chandler at Port Tampa, FL until 1943. Got his seamans papers Z-7806 in 1940 but no ship jobs open in Tampa at that time. First shipped out from New York July 1, 1943. These are the ships that he sailed on:

Axtell J. Byles, wiper, July 12, 1943; *Altair,*

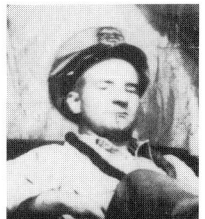 

galleyman, Aug. 28, 1943; *Standard Arrow,* galleyman, Nov. 11, 1943; *Liebre,* oiler, June 30, 1944; *R.G. Stewart,* oiler Aug. 21, 1944; *Edward L. Shea,* oiler, Oct. 30, 1944; *Pine Bluff,* oiler, Oct. 30, 1944; *York,* oiler, Dec. 16, 1944; *Emilia,* fireman, Jan.22, 1945, Hog Island; *William Wirt,* oiler, April 19, 1945; *Valdosta Victory,* jr. engineer, June 19, 1945; *Hampden Sydney Victory,* jr. engineer, Jan. 5, 1946; *Purdue Victory,* jr. engineer, March 16, 1946; *South Bend Victory,* jr. engineer, May 27, 1946; *Ethiopia Victory,* jr. engineer, July 29, 1946; *Yamhill,* pumpman-machinist, Oct. 7, 1946, T-2; *Bertram G. Goodhue,* oiler, Feb. 19, 1947; *Meredith Victory,* fireman-watertender; *Alcoa Pointer,* fireman-watertender, June 4, 1947; *Robin Hood,* oiler, Oct. 9, 1947, C-3; *Ampac California,* pumpman machinist, Feb. 14, 1948, T-2; *Evelyn,* oiler Nov. 19, 1948, liberty ship; *Mankato Victory,* oiler, April 26, 1950. FWE (finished with engines) - last trip to sea.

Worked as boiler operator and then operating engineer in four large factories in Detroit, MI. Retired from Massey Ferguson, Inc. after 20 years as operating engineer. He earned a good living in Detroit, due to his Merchant Marine Ship training and experience with boilers and steam engines. Married 1947, they raised two boys, two girls and still married and retired in Las Vegas, NV. Good place for retirees. He is a member of U.S. Merchant Marine Veterans World War II and support the *Lane Victory* restoration effort.

J. GORDON JONES, was born June 21, 1926 in Essex, Balto. County, MD. He joined the Merchant Marine February 1944, Baltimore, MD.

Served on SS *Herman Winter,* OS, Atlantic; SS *John Fiske,* O.S., Atlantic-Mediterranean; USS *Reina Mercedes,* S1/c U.S. Navy.

As a 17 year old Merchant seaman on SS *Herman Winter,* shipwrecked at Martha's Vineyard. He is now a volunteer crew member helping restore SS *John W. Brown.*

Married to Virginia and they have three sons and five grandsons. Employed with Balto County Police for 24 years. Retired as sergeant Oct. 2, 1983.

Helping restore the liberty ship *John W. Brown.*

MARY CLAIRE JONES, was born Oct. 2, 1928 in Buffalo, NY. First shipped out in June 1957 on Grace Line's passenger ship *Santa Rosa.* Remained with Grace Line until 1971 when their passenger ships were laid up. Then sailed in various capacities in the steward department on break-bulk and container vessels for export, Farrell, Moore McCormack and United State Lines.

Retired in 1987 after 30 years at sea. Now living in Hoboken, NJ.

NEIL E. JONES, sailed as oiler in 1946 on the USAT *Edmund BN. Alexander.* Attended USMMA in 1952 and sailed as 3/O on SS *Brazil.* Donated hat band he wore as an oiler with "my high pressure hat...(I needed all the help with the ladies that I could get) The band looks pretty scurvy, but I did have it dry cleaned. It should adorn some member of the black gangs steaming hat."

Neil resides in Englewood, CO.

RUDOLOPH W. JONES, sailed as radio officer during WWII. Has War Zone Bars. Attended Sheepshead Bay and Gallups Island. He is a member of AMMV JWB Chapter.

He resides in New York, NY.

ROBERT T. JORDAN, was born Aug. 3, 1922 in Chicago. Training at Catalina as fireman-watertender. Isthmian (U.S. Steel) non-union Liberty *J. Sterling Morton* three months, 1943-1944 Australia, New Caledonia, New Guinea and nearby islands, Leyte. Captain universally detested — did he realize how close he was to being fragged? No blacks (we said Negroes then) in crew, majority Southern who outdid each other in verbal fierceness re"niggers" but instantly, at Leyte, the rabid racists became close buddies with muscular Negro longshoremen unloading our ship!

Three runs from Australia to New Guinea (on Equator) with mixed cargo for Australian troops. An impressive proportion of the cargo was beer, some of which was pirated to and consumed in our cabin — the ship's pub — next to No. 4 hatch. The temperature in the cabin circa 125 degrees — metal fixtures too hot to touch.

At Aitape, a day before a major Japanese offensive on the U.S./Australian perimeter, he had foolishly wandered outside that perimeter and luckily survived.

Several in crew of the *J. Sterling Morton* (including your truly) court-martialed for "mutiny" — but he was exonerated.

ARTHUR L. JORGENSEN, was born Oct. 6, 1924. Entered the service on April 17, 1943 and graduated from the Merchant Marine Academy at Kings Point, NY, in February of 1944.

Following three months of training at Coyote Point, San Francisco, he sailed from San Pedro, CA, aboard the liberty ship *Steven H. Long,* as a second Marine engineer. Ports of call included Hobart, Tasmania, Calcutta and Buenos Aries.

He served aboard turbine-electric tankers on subsequent cruises including the SS *Markey.* Art was discharged in San Pedro in February 1946.

Following his Merchant Marine service, he completed his education at Linfield College in McMinville, OR, and began a career with Montgomery Wards that would take him throughout the Pacific Northwest. In 1962, along with his wife Margaret and five children, he settled in Fresno, CA, where he has lived since. He remains active in the restaurant business.

DALE H. KAMERER, was born in Revenna, OH on Dec. 25, 1927. He joined the Merchant Marine in Cleveland, OH in August 1944. Went to Sheepshead Bay. Sailed on the *James Ford Rhodes, John Hawthorne, Stephen A. Douglas,* and *Laura Keene* in the Atlantic and Mediterranean from 1944 until 1946. Saw the Northern Light in North Atlantic, England, France, Belgium, Italy, Spain, North Africa.

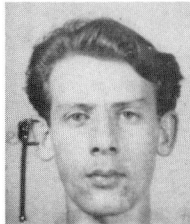

1989. He and his wife have three children, two boys and one girl. They now live in West Covina, CA. Dale works with Elks and W.C. Food Bank, doing volunteer work only.

AUSTIN C. KANE, was born in Uniontown, PA, 1918. Was graduated from Hoffman Island, NY; Ft. Trumbalcers Training School, CT, Naval Reserve. Sailed various lines on deck from Baltimore, Boston, New York, Wilmington, CA. In the early years Hitler's subs ruled the Atlantic. He treasures vivid memories of their vessel creeping along the coastline avoiding sunken ships from Cape May to Perth Amboy, NJ, so close to shore that people were visible on the beaches; exhausted Jewish families fleeing extinction dragging their few belongings aboard a British freighter in the Persian Gulf; bombs spiraling down from Nazi planes in the Mediterranean while the pom-pom guns of the convoy's escort warship forced the enemy planes too high for accurate targeting; so many faces, sights, sounds, smells that enrich and expand life.

Austin is now retired and living in Downey, CA with wife, Helen, near their two children and five grandchildren. Spend many hours in hospice volunteer work and contributes to *Lane Victory.*

JOE LIVINGSTON KARR, SR., Lt. J.G., was born Dec. 26, 1922 in Brownwood, TX. He joined the Merchant Marine in 1939, at 17 years of age. Served on SS *HM Frederickson,* 1939, ordinary seaman; *Empire* (steam tug), 1941, messman; (oil barge), 1941, ordinary seaman; SS *Simon Bolivar,* 1943, ordinary seaman; SS *New London,* 1943-1944, able seaman; *MV Cape Blanco,* 1944-1945, third mate; SS *Lakeland Victory,* 1945, third mate; *LL Abshire,* 1948, able seaman; *Henry Dawes* (tank steamer), 1948, second mate; and *CB Watson* (tank steamer), 1948, second mate. Sailed in Australia, Hawaii, India, Iran, Madagascar, Mozambique, Roi, Persian Gulf and various others locations.

In 1943 he received a bachelors degree in business administration, Southwestern University, Georgetown, TX; 1951, masters degree in education, University of Texas at El Paso; 1950-1960, doctoral studies, New Mexico State University, Las Cruces, New Mexico. Retired in 1983 after 35 years as an elementary-intermediate principal, El Paso, TX. From 1983 until the present time he has served as supervisor of student teachers at University of El Paso. Married 42 years, with five children and six grandchildren.

JOSEPH KATUSA, sailed as utility (troop) storekeeper during WWII. Attended USMSST at Sheepshead Bay. He was awarded the Atlantic, Pacific, and Mediterranean War Zone Bars, and Victory Medal. Member of AMMV (Keystone Chapter), and associate member JWB Chapter.

Married to wife, Ann. Resides at 525 Old Waynesburg Road, Carmichaels, PA.

KENNETH E. KEITH, born Sept. 4, 1925, graduated age 17, Wilmington, CA. Worked swing shift Cal. Ship Terminal Island. Age 16 helped build Liberty and Victory ships. Joined Merchant Marine 1943, age 17. Took training at Catalina Island.

Ships sailed: *Charles H. Windham* (oiler) Liberty ship, 1943, Pacific; *James E. Clements* (oiler) Liberty ship 1944, Pacific; *James Otis,* Liberty ship (deck engineer) 1944, Pacific; *Roger Sherman,* Liberty ship (deck engineer) 1944-1945, Pacific and Atlantic; *Knox,* Victory ship 1945-1946 (asst. electrician) 1945-1946.

Then worked as longshoreman in Los Angeles harbor for 25 years. Loaded Liberty and Victory ships for Korea and Vietnam.

Retired and at present is third Vice President of United Merchant Marine Veterans of WW II.

WILLIAM KELLETT, was born in Layfayette, CO, July 28, 1924. Joined the U.S. Maritime service and trained at Catalina Island February-May 1945. Sailed From San Pedro, CA, on the T-2 tanker SS *Fort George* to the South Pacific, Ulithi, Darwin, Australia, Persian Gulf, New Guinea, and the Admiralty Islands. The ship was in the Admiralties on Aug. 15, 1945, when the war ended.

Boarded the SS *Bringham Victory* in Portland, OR in November 1945. Sailed to Seattle, Vancouver, BC, Panama Canal, New York City and Philadelphia and back to Portland, OR. In March the ship sailed for Hawaii and was trapped in the tidal wave in Hilo, HI. He was a second cook and baker.

Entered the postal service in 1947 and transferred to the National Bureau of Standards in 1961 and retired with 34 years government service.

He has been working with Colorado Merchant Seaman since 1988 helping them obtain their honorable discharges.

THOMAS V. KELLY, sailed as wiper on the SS *John H. Eaton* in 1945 out of New York City and Norfolk to Brazil. Now living in Staten Island, NY.

WILLIAM P. KELLY, was born July 7, 1925 in Hibernia, NJ. He joined the Merchant Marine July 7, 1943. Took training at Hoffman Islands, NY. Served on *George Matthews* (Liberty), 1943, Atlantic; *Sahale* (Hog Islander), 1944, Atlantic; *Groverton* (Liberty), 1944, Atlantic; *Salvador* , 1944, Atlantic; *George L. Farley,* 1945, Atlantic; *Golden Eagle,* 1945, Atlantic; *Golden Eagle,* 1945, Pacific and Atlantic; *Chapel Hill Victory,* 1945, Atlantic; *Laconia Victory,* 1946, Atlantic; *Wilson Victory,* 1946, Atlantic.

His first combat experience was at Naples, Italy

when the German's bombed the port. The second scare happened when the Germans inadvertently anchored in a mine field in Agusta, Sicily. Also took part in the invasion of Anzio this trip.

His next ship was the *Sahale* which was sunk during the invasion of Normandy. He was injured and spent 30 days in an Army hospital outside of Cardiff, England. Returned to the States on the *Argentia*.

Went to work in aerospace June 1946, where he supervised all the testing on the X-15 Aircraft (first in space with human life). Retired in 1990 as production manager of a filtration company enjoying Florida.

He is married with one son who is a nuclear engineer at Diablo Canyon. His second son owns a laundromat in Florida.

HENRY M. KERON, attended Sheepshead Bay. Sailed on the *SS Arembo, SS Margaret Brent, SS Able,* and *SS Archibold Mansfield.* He is now living on Independence Drive in Burlington, NJ.

WILLIAM F. KERR, was born in Lenox, MA on Aug. 12, 1907. His father was born in Glasgow, Scotland in 1879. After passing all tests for service with the U.S. Marine Corp, he failed to get parents consent. Was to be sent to Parris Island, SC. He joined the Merchant Marine Nov. 4, 1932 at New York Barge Office as able seaman. He sailed with the Navy on USS *Bridge,* USS *Concord* as seaman first class. With the Merchant Marine on passenger, freighter, and numerous tankers. Received honorable discharge from U.S. Army, Massachusetts National Guard, U.S. Navy, U.S. Coast Guard.

Worked for Socony-Vacuum Oil Corp. Last position held with Socony was vacuum tug No. 27, as marine fireman. Have served in deck department as A.B. fireman-oiler engineers, Steward Dept. as sergeant at arms. At present time he is retired and "taking in the slack".

EDWIN R. KIESEL, was born Nov. 6, 1922 in Colorado. After graduating from Montebello High School in California, he enrolled in a Aircraft Sheet Metal course at Santa Monica Tech. Worked at North American Aviation until joining U.S. Navy Reserve in October 1942, and the Merchant Marine December 1942, having training at Catalina Island.

Ships sailed: SS *George Read* (O.S.), 1943, Tasmania, Ceylon, India, Australia, Panama; SS *Bald Hill* -tanker (A.B.), 1943, Pacific; SS *Augustine Stahl*- Liberty (A.B.), 1944, India, Australia, North Africa, Gilbraltar; SS *Solon Turman* C-1-B (deck maint.), 1944, New Guinea, Morotai, Philippines; SS *Caribbean* T-2 tanker (A.B.), 1945, South Pacific; and SS *Trinity Victory* (Bosun), 1945-46, Japan and Korea.

Ed then worked in sheet metal trade until joining the Montebello Fire Department 1950-1978 retiring as battalion chief in fire suppression. Ed lives in Paradise, CA with his wife, Marge. He has two sons and three grandchildren.

RALPH L. KILSHEIMER, graduated from USMS Radio Training Station in Section R-36 at Hoffman Island, NY. He sailed as radio officer. Skilled in computer operations. Ralph holds radio amateur license KB2DIS. He is a member of the Hoffman Island Radio Association.

JOHN J. KING, sailed as AB, third and second mate during WWII. Was injured. He has the Atlantic, Mediterranean, and Middle East War Zone Bars and Combat Bar. Attended Sheepshead Bay and Fort Trumbull.

He is married to June. A member of AMMV JWB Chapter. Now residing at Ocean City, MD.

CLAUDE F. KINNEY, JR., was born May 11, 1922 in Bremen, GA. He joined the Merchant Marine Sept. 3, 1942 in Birmingham, AL. He served on the *Horace Gray*-AB; *J.H. Drummond, R.M. Williamson*-third mate, *Fenn Victory* -third mate; *Walter F. Kraft* - third mate; *Salmon P. Chase* - third mate; *SS Mean Ticut* - O.S.; *William B. Travis*-AB; *Nathaniel Alexander;* and the *Pedro Menedez.* He made Murmansk run on *Nathaniel Alexander.* One of his most memorable experiences was getting two of his teeth pulled by a Russian woman dentist with no pain killer-Ouch!

Claude worked as a elevator mechanic for 31 years with Otis Elevation and Bagby Elevator. He retired Jan. 10, 1984. He is married to Joyce, they have four sons, Stevie, Roderick, Arnold and Lou. Now spending most of his time doing "Honey do jobs".

EDMUND B. KINTER, was born June 13, 1925, first member of Class of '45 to enlist. Trained at St. Petersburg, FL. O.S. December 1943 to March 1944 *George E. Badger;* April 1944 to May 1944 Caribbean; A.B. May 1944 to July 1944 *E. Kirby Smith;* July 1944 to August 1944 *Autossee;* August 1944 to January 1945 *Dwight L. Moody;* January 1945 to April 1945 *William Graham;* May 1945 to July 1945 *Lara;* July 1945 to October 1945 *David P. Johnson,* November 1945 to May 1946 *Isaac M. Singer.*

He managed L/W Restaurants in Pittsburgh and Butler, PA, 1946 to 1950. August 1950 to July 1952, U.S. Army served in Germany as staff sergeant, cook, Co. D, 112th Inf., 28th Div. August 1952 to November 1989 G.C. Murphy Company after working as restaurant manager various locations, retiring as home office director of food service. His current address is R D 1, Box 116, Portersville, PA 16051.

DON KIRK, sailed on Liberty Ship SS *William Pitt Fessenden.* Donated paint brush from ship. He now lives on Walker Ave. in Baltimore, MD.

DONALD THOMAS KLEVER, was born Oct. 5, 1927 in North Lawrence, OH. Joined the Merchant Marine June 20, 1944 in Cleveland, OH, O/S Acctine-Quartermast ACC AB. Served on the SS *Westward Ho,* San Francisco, CA; SS *John Bidwell,* Baltimore, MD; SS *Pocket Canyon,* AB-QM, Lone Beach, CA.

He recalls waking in early morning to general alarm, sub surfacing, which turned out to be one of theirs. Worked with the U.S. Coast Guard, railroads for 37 years. Now refinishing furniture.

JOHN J. KLOCKO, JR., was born on April 15, 1920, in Jersey City, NJ. He obtained his seaman documents in 1937, and certified eligible for appointments cadet by the U.S. Maritime Commission in 1938, after graduated from the James J. Ferris High School. Attended New York State Maritime Academy at Fort Schuyler, NY, graduating in 1941. Enlisted in the U.S. Naval Reserve in 1937, and had training cruises on USS *Texas,* USS *Quincy,* and USS *Herbert* before entering Fort Schuyler. Received third mate license in October 1941. Worked as cargo mate with Grace Line in New York thru November 1941. On Dec. 5, 1941 was hired as junior third mate for SS *Socony Vacuum,* left home Dec. 7, 1941 to join ship at Portland, ME. On Jan. 7, 1942 sailed with United Fruit Company as third mate on SS *Chiripo* and SS *Tiviess;* second mate on SS *John Walker* and SS *David G. Farragut.*

Married Miss Me A. Kuster of Jersey City, NJ. Chief officer on SS *Lorenzo De Zavala.* Obtained masters license in New York in January 1945. Joined Moor McCormac Line Feb. 24, 1945, assigned chief officer on SS *Robert Lansing.* Joined States Marine Lines on April 4, 1945 as master SS *Jose Bonidacio* to Nov. 8, 1945; relief master to April 1946. Served as assistant port captain; planning and loading supervisor for vessels on Far East run and Mediterranean-Persian Gulf run. Master SS *Evergreen State* Jan. 1, 1949 to Jan. 31, 1949. During Korean Conflict was master SS *loma Victory* and SS *Sharron Victory* from June 6, 1951 to Aug. 15, 1952.

From May 30, 1950 to June 1, 1951 and from Sept. 1, 1952 to Nov. 3, 1958, employed by Michigan Mutual Liability Company as safety engineer, providing safety surveys, programming and training supervisors of client employers in the stevedoring, manufacturing, and motor carrier industries in the greater New York area and east coast cities and ports.

Resigned on Nov. 1, 1958 to return to sea. On Nov. 7, 1958, shipped out with States Marine Lines as junior third mate on the SS *Pelican State,* continuing as second and third mate; until on a voyage leaving the Saigon River, South Vietnam, he received a cable from the U.S. Department of Labor, advising him of his selection as Maritime safety officer and assignment as Chicago district supervisor (covering an eight state area), for the Bureau of Labor Standards, Maritime Safety Program (administering the new longshoring and ship repair safety and health regulations and programs). He left the ship in Olympia on Aug. 15, 1959. He reported to Washington, D.C. on Aug. 25, 1959 for indoctrination, and on Oct. 1, 1959, reported to Chicago, IL to his assignment as Chicago district supervisor, Bureau of Labor Standards, U.S. Department of Labor. On April 28, 1963, he was reassigned to Washington, D.C. as the assistant chief longshore safety branch, Maritime Safety Division. This included reviewing all field inspection reports, citations, accident and personal injury investigation reports. Making field visits to evaluate field staff on their efforts to apply the safety regulations and in promoting safety programs and training of longshoreman engaged in loading and unloading vessels cargo. Worked with various representatives on various committees in developing various Industry Consensus Standards, as coordinated by the American National Standards Institute.

In January 1970, the Occupational Safety and Health Act became effective and the program absorbed the Maritime Safety Regulations and programs. He was assigned the Office of Chief Material Handling Safety Standards for General Industry. He was responsible for developing OSHA safety regulations for: cranes, derricks, conveyors, industrial trucks, slings, manlifts, overhead and gantry cranes; crawler, locomotive and truck cranes; helicopters; vehicle mounted elevating and rotating work platforms; servicing split rim wheels and tires for heavy duty and highway motor trucks; other material handling related matters.

He is retired from U.S. Department of Labor, OSHA, since September 1980. He and his wife continue to live in Crofton, MD; they have two daughters and one son, and enjoy seven grandchildren. He is retired from the U.S. Naval Reserves with the rank of lieutenant commander in

1968. He is a registered engineer (P.E.) in safety in the State of California. Recently he renewed his USCG license for Master, Oceans-Unlimited Issue 10-13. He is a member of U.S. Merchant Marine Veterans Assoc. and the Council of American Master Mariners Inc., and president of the Baltimore Washington Chapter.

LOUIS D. KNOLES, married to Margaret, passed away Oct. 20, 1990. His wife resides in Mount Pleasant, SC.

FRANK C. KNOLLE, was born Jan. 22, 1917 in Sonoma, CA, where he also went to high school. Joined Merchant Marines in 1944; first ship USAT *David C. Shanks*, as assistant electrician, operated in the South Pacific, moving troops from Oakland Army Base and carrying troops from Australia to the Celebes (Moratai), carried wounded from Halandia, New Guinea to San Francisco, CA. USAT *Sea Barb* 1945 as assistant electrician in South Pacific to Okinawa and Korea. MSTS *Admiral W.S. Sims* 1947, assistant electrician, Philippines, Japan, transporting troops. *Sims* ran aground July 1, 1947 in Yokohama Bay. It took nine days to refloat and 30 days to repair the hole that was torn in her bottom.

An electrical contractor in Marin County until retirement in 1969 when he bought a farm in Yolo, County, where he now lives with his wife, Gladys in Capay, CA.

STEPHEN L. KOCIS, was born on Christmas Day in 1926, graduated high school at age 17, and joined Merchant Marine. Training: basic at Sheepshead Bay, radio at Hoffman Island. Signed on *Morgan Robertson*, a Liberty, in Frisco and via Enwitok, Saipan, and Guam, anchored in Okinawa's Bruckner Bay waiting for the invasion of Japan.

Back to the States. Made several trips to Europe first on a troop carrier, the *Texarkana Victory* (chief radio operator) and then another Liberty the *Binger Herman* (only radio operator). Next, the *Pan Massachusetts*. And then nine months in the Caribbean on the MV *Emerald Knot*. Started school in 1947 and for the next three months sailed: *Gulfbird, Gulfmeadows,* and *Gulfswamp*. Married and then spent next two years in the Army (U.S. Army retired corporal) and next 35 in the Bell System. Blessed with four sons. Retired in 1988 and currently treasurer of the Hoffman Island Radio Association. Lives with wife, Jean in Flat Rock, NC.

CAPTAIN J.A. KONKEL, was born Dec. 10, 1923 in Milwaukee, WI. Joined the Merchant Marine July 1941, in Milwaukee, WI (sailing the Great Lakes). Sailed on many ships including: *Maine* (OS), *John B. Ashe* (OS),

Jason Lee, Cape Trinity, Charles Nardhoff, Sea Bass (AB), *Alcoa Planter* (AB), and various others from July 27, 1942 until May 1, 1945. He served in WWII, Korean and Vietnam Wars, with ratings from junior third mate to master.

He received the Merchant Marine Emblem, Victory Medal, Honorable Service Medal, Presidential Testimonial Letter, Philippine Defense Ribbon, Philippine Liberation Ribbon, Korean Service Bar, Vietnam Service Bar. Retired in 1968. He is married and living in Mequon, WI.

VICTOR J. KONSAVAGESEE, holder of Murmansk medal.

S.A. KORBER, See John Hird.

RUSSELL KRENCIPOCK, SR., served in Armed Guard aboard the *SS Ney McNeely* on Murmansk run in 1944. He was in great storm of 1944. Donated photos of group in Scotland on Christmas 1944, Murmansk, Aircraft Carrier in storm, and picture of SS *Billy Mitchell* taken in Algier, September 1944. The *Mitchell* was carrying all bombs. Russell now resides in McDonald, OH.

CHARLES D. KROMER, was born Nov. 1, 1923 in Scottdale, PA. Signed up for Merchant Marine in Washington, D.C. on Nov. 3, 1942. Trained at Sheepshead Bay, graduated March 1943. Ships sailed: U.S. Army Transport, *E.B. Alexander* from April 12, 1943 to June 4, 1943, ordinary seaman; U.S. Army Transport, *James Parker* from July 1, 1943 to Sept. 22, 1943, ordinary seaman; Liberty Ship, SS *William Black Yates* from Oct. 8, 1943 to Jan. 14, 1944, ordinary seaman; Liberty Ship, SS *David B. Johnson,* Jan. 29, 1944 to April 13, 1944, AB seaman; Liberty Ship, SS *Henry Middleton,* April 21, 1944 to June 12, 1944, AB seaman; Liberty Ship, *Sidney Wright,* July 7, 1944 to Nov. 7, 1944, ordinary seaman; Liberty Ship, SS *Jared Ingersoll,* Dec. 4, 1944 to Feb. 14, 1945, AB seaman. Signed up for OCS School, Fort Trumball, New London, CO. Third mates license dated July 17, 1945. Ships sailed: Alcoa freighter, SS *Charles Hull,* Aug. 17, 1945 to Oct. 8, 1945, third mate; Liberty Ship, SS *Edward W. Burton,* Nov. 7, 1945 of Feb. 6, 1946, third mate; Liberty Ship, SS *George Vickers,* Feb. 22, 1946 to Aug. 8, 1946, third then second mate; Liberty Ship, SS *Michael J. Owens,* May 9, 1947 to Oct. 28, 1947, third mate; Liberty Ship, SS *Joseph L. Meek,* April 1, 1948 to April 23, 1948, third mate. Ship then went aground in Cuba. Charles states, "War time shipping made us a superstitious lot. Some shipmates and I decided if a ship made it the first time, the odds were against it repeating, thus one trip per ship. This worked for me and I hope it worked for them". He sailed mainly the North Atlantic, Mediterranean Sea, and the Indian Ocean from Liverpool, England to Bombay, India and many ports in between.

He is now residing in Leesburg, Lake County, FL, where they are self-employed and hoping some day to retire so he and his wife, Bettie, can go back to sea, "as passengers".

MICHAEL KUCIK, sailed as AB during WWII and Korean Conflict. Married to Dorothy, now residing in Baltimore, MD. Michael is a member of AMMV JWB Chapter.

JOHN KUKTA, (See Sunpaper article quote listed under Patrick L. Whalen).

JAMES A. (JIM) LAMBERT, attended USMSTS at Sheepshead Bay. Jim was in Section 331 on July 24, 1944. Jim states, " I volunteered to serve as messman on my first trip they were needed badly..many guys did this in order to get out of six more weeks training." he went through deck training obtaining an OS endorsement. He later received an AB blue ticket. He served in the USCG for three years on DE's during the Korean War. After release from the USCG he obtained a green ticket AB endorsement and served again in the USMM during the Vietnam War. He sailed aboard the SS *William Day,* SS *Rufus W. Peckham,* SS *Walter M. Christiansen* and the SS *Dorothy*. He is a member of AMMV JWB Chapter.

WILLIAM W. LANDRETH, was born July 22, 1907. Served with USCG from 1928 to 1932. Joined Merchant Marines in 1934, Mobile, AB. Served on *John M. Schofielf* and *William Windom* (chief engineer), in the Atlantic, Pacific, and Mediterranean Oceans. Also sailed on SS *Warrior* as first assistant engineer on this vessel. Returned to the States via Australia alone (chief engineer on *William Windom,* left

Glasco with 48 ship convoy for Russia, half of this convoy did not make it; his ship made it to Murmansk.) Joined *Calvin Victory* ship as chief and converted her to haul cattle, which he did from Montreal to Belgium for food after the war. Retired in 1967. Living in Greenville, SC.

ERNEST LANGNER, was born Dec. 31, 1926 in Los Angeles, CA. Trained for Merchant Marines at Catalina in 1944. Sailed 1944 on Liberty tanker, *Alan Seeger* as fireman and oiler carrying molasses from Hawaiian Isles to San Francisco. In 1945, T-2 tankers, *Capital Reef and Rainer,* and Liberty freighter *J.W. Gibbs* as oiler in Pacific and 1946 on T-2, *Cedar Breaks* from Gulf. While on the *Alan Seeger* he recalls reworking crankpin bearing while at sea (off California coast). Also served in Korea with U.S. Army from 1950-1952.

After service he worked in electrical construction, retiring in January 1992 after 30 years. Married to Claire, they have one son and two daughters. He enjoys fly fishing, travelling.

JOHN EDWARD LAUGHTON, was born Oct. 13, 1921 in Redlands, CA. Graduated Salinas Union High School, June 1939; Salinas Junior College, May 1942; and USMM Cadet Corps at Treasure Island, San Francisco, CA, July 1942. Then at sea as cadet aboard *SS Francis Lewis,* July 1942 to April 1943; Figi Islands, New Caledonia, Australia, New Guinea, graduated USMM Academy Kings Point, NY, January 1944. At sea as third mate aboard SS *Jan P. Coen* (Liberty ship) in 1944, Eniwetok, Hawaii, Saipan, Tinian, and Guam; as second mate aboard SS *Hobbs Victory* early 1945, which was sunk by Jap Zero (kamikaze) at Okinawa on April 6, 1945; second mate aboard SS *Lafayette Victory,* May 1945 to February 1946, Okinawa, Japan, Philippines, Singapore, India, and Suez. California was home port for all of above ships and *Sudden and Christenson* was the shipping company.

Married Feb. 5, 1944 to school sweetheart Lorna Kueber and will soon celebrate their 50th wedding anniversary. They have two sons and three grandchildren. Retired from row crop farming Dec. 31, 1981 after 35 years.

CAPTAIN JOHN M. LE CATO, was born in Huntington, WV. Started sailing, coastwise, 1939, M&M Transportation Co., out of Baltimore. Third mate's license from USMS New London, 1942. First third's job SS *Norluna,* North Atlantic and Arctic, shipwrecked in Canada. Married former shipmate on graduation from

New London. Sailed Liberties, North Atlantic. Made three Murmansk runs, including "The Forgotten Convoy", eight months in North Russia. Ship: *Thomas Hartley, Crosby Noyes,* and *George Walton.*

Joined Army Transport Service as second mate, 1946, various military cargo ships and troop transports, second mate, mate and master. Mate, then master, USNS *Comet* (the mother of RORO), North Atlantic and Vietnam 1960 to 1966. Master, USNS *General Patch,* longest U.S. troop lift, Boston to Vietnam, 1966. Master, USNS *Victoria,* ballistic missile resupply ship, 1967 to 1973. Commended for two rescues on one voyage.

As of April 1992 Capt. Jack is working with a lady in Florida on an article on wartime life in Russia, some railroad history and a story of a boy's farm life in Anne Arundel County, MD. When he gets a chance he plans to summarize his WWII experience. Both Capt. Jack and his wife sailed out of Pratt Street in Baltimore for the Merchants and Miners Transportation Co. (M&M Mean and Miserable according to Capt. Jack). He was senior first mate when the company went out of business. He is now retired with his wife in Charleston, SC. Doing odd marine jobs, historical research, community service. Awarded Soviet Murmansk Jubilee Medal, 1990. Member of U.S. Merchant Marines Veterans WWII, Charleston, SC Chapter.

RICHARD LESLIE LeMASTER, was born Nov. 8, 1925 in Portsmouth, OH. Raised in educated in Denver, CO. Joined the Merchant Marine at age 17 in 1943; reported January 1944, Catalina Island. Ships served on: March 9, 1944 to May 22, 1944 SS *Mariposa,* Scullion, Los Angeles, Honolulu, Fremantle, Bombay, India; July 9, 1944 to Oct. 2, 1944 *Sarah J. Hale,* utilityman, San Francisco, Wewak, New Guinea, Lea, New Guinea, Hollandia, New Guinea, and San Francisco; Oct. 3, 1944 to Jan. 4, 1945 *John G. Todd,* utilityman, San Francisco, Port Hueneme, Pearl Harbor, Eniwetok, Guam, Saipan, Eniwetok, San Francisco; Feb. 4, 1945 to May 7, 1945 *Samuel G. Howe* (OS), San Francisco, Port Hueneme, Eniwetok, Saipan, Seattle; May 15, 1945 to June 3, 1946 *Samuel G. Howe* (OS), Honolulu, Eniwetok, Ulithi, Okinawa, Ulithi, Saipan, Guam, Iwo Jima, Matsuyama, Yokosuka, Japan, Guam, Manus, Noumea, Honolulu, San Francisco.

Memorable experiences: being at Okinawa during the typhoon in September 1945. Sailing into Matsuyama, Japan and having to sail out of there because of the fallout from the atomic bomb.

Worked at Armour & Co. and Guardian Service in Denver, CO. Moved in August 1952 to Wellington, KS. Worked at Hunter Milling Co. until September 1954. Worked as office manager at Welco Aerospace, which is now GEC Precision Corp. Remained with this company and at the present time he is corporate vice-president and general manager of the Welco Division.

Married Norma Jean Tomlins in March 1949. They have four sons and five grandchildren.

SCHLEY D. LEMMA, was born Nov. 14, 1925 in Ranger, TX. Joined U.S. Maritime Service Dec. 10, 1943 in San Antonio, YTX. Sent to St. Petersburg, FL. Spent four months permanent crew *Joseph Conrad* (square rigged sail), then to Gallup Island, Boston for radio school in April, graduating Sept. 16, 1944. Shipped from San Francisco aboard SS *H. Wier Cook* for two trips in Pacific; SS *Thomas Sully* from Houston for two trips, one to Mediterranean second to Pacific for invasion of Japan, but war ended on the way and they went to Japan; SS *North Point* tanker from Houston one trip around the world first to Venice then two trips from Baharin to Japan and to the Philippines to Houston.

He saw Hiroshima while on *Thomas Sully*. Rode out typhoon that hit Manila and a hurricane in the Atlantic three days while waste baskets rolled up the ladders. She rolled 48 degrees twice-The Lord was with them. He feels that he was one of the lucky ones, he never had to dodge a bullet or a bomb.

He graduated Howard Payne College in Brownwood, TX BS Med. 37 years public schools, four as an administrator, principal, etc. Married M. Joyce Swinney, 1948, in Beeville, TX. They have one son, three daughters, and four grandchildren. Retired in 1990. Now fishing a little, sings in church choir, and belongs to senior group in church. He has lived the last 26 years at 4233 Western, Corpus Christi, TX 78410.

MAX EMIL LEVECKE, was born Feb. 19, 1880 in Stateen, Germany. At the age of 14, he was bonded out to learn the machinist trade and upon researching the age of 18, he was conscripted into the German Navy for a period of two years.

After discharge from the Navy, he sailed for the Hamburg-American steamship line. It has been said, that one night in 1903 he put on two suits of clothes and stuffed all his personal items in his pockets and walked off of the ship. The gangway watch said, "Well, we will not be seeing you again." He migrated to St. Louis, MO and married. He became a naturalized citizen in 1910. Moved to Philadelphia and worked for the League Island Navy Yard as a machinist. During WWI, he took the examination as a first assistant marine engineer. During WWI, he sailed with the War Shipping Board on the ships SS *Bar Harbor* and SS *Kalispell* on the New York to Cuba sugar run. At the end of WWI he sailed on the first ship to Germany with a load of grain, the SS *Bannock.*

The family moved west in 1921 and finally settling in Clatskanie, OR while working at the Puget Sound Naval Shipyard as a machinist. During WWII, he sailed with the American Mail Line as a first assistant engineer on the following ships, both in the Pacific and European theatres: SS *John S. Copely,* SS *Anthony Ravalli,* and SS *Matthew Thornton.* Served as relief engineer for a number of years prior to his retirement. He is a 50 year member of the Masonic Lodge. He was cleared by the Master Mariner to his final resting place, April 20, 1973 at the age of 93. Survived by two sons, Warren of Silverton, OR and Theodore of Olympia, WA and two daughters, Louise Bigelow (deceased), and Elsie Berchard of Little Rock, AR.

HERSCHEL LEVIN, sailed as radio operator and purser during WWII. Attended Sheepshead Bay and Gallups Island Radio School. Had second class FCC Radiotelegraph license and purser papers. He is married to Rosalie and lives in Baltimore, MD. Herschel is a member of the AMMV JWB Chapter.

GEORGE W. LEWIS, JR., was born Nov. 8, 1926 in Mobile, AL. Graduated high school at age 17, and entered U.S. Maritime Service in 1945, St. Petersburg, FL; Sheepshead Bay, NY; and New Orleans, LA, with rank of ensign. Served U.S. Merchant Marine from 1945-1947, position purser-pharmacist. Ships sailed during service: *Albert A. Michelson, Xavier Victory, Harvey Cushing,* and *William Wirt.* Served in Atlantic, Mediterranean Sea and Pacific war zones. Graduated 1950, Spring Hill College, BS in chemistry, University of Alabama, chemical engineering. Served as lieutenant in U.S. Army, 31st Inf. Div. and 7th Inf. Div., Korea 1950-1952.

Civilian employment was with Scott Paper Company, National Gypsum Company and Armstrong World Industries, Inc. as plant manager from 1953-1992. He is a member of Merchant Marine Veterans of WWII, Veterans of Foreign Wars, American Legion and Navy Legion of the U.S. Lives in Mobile, AL with wife of 42 years, Gilda, they have eight children and 14 grandchildren.

FRANCESCO VITALINO LIBERATORE, was born in Brooklyn, NY. Received his Form DD 214 and Honorable Discharge Certificate DD 256 CG, on June 7, 1990. Enlisted U.S. Maritime Service (United States Merchant Marine) in 1943; trained at U.S. Maritime Service Training Center, Sheepshead Bay, Brooklyn, NY. Graduated as apprentice seaman; Fireman Second Class; training included 30 hours of Elementary Gunnery, 5". 38, 3". 50, 20mm. Sailed Atlantic, Mediterranean-Middle East, Pacific War Zones; Tankers, T2, C1, C2, MV, Hog Island, Liberty, Victory ships. A weapon of war the Liberty Ship; transportation of materials needed, ships manned by Civilians.

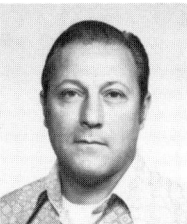

Heave Ho! My Lads, Heave Ho! (Song of the Merchant Marines, key of C (C-E).
Verse:
Give us the oil, give us the gas, give us the shells,
Give us the guns, we'll be the ones to see them thru,
Give us the tanks, give us the planes, give us the parts,
Give us the ship, give us a hip hoo-ray!
Damn the sub-ma-rine! we're the men of the merchant marine!
Chorus:
Heave Ho! my Lads, Heave Ho!
It's a long, long way to go.
It's a long, long pull with our hat-ches-full,
Brav-ing the wind, brav-ing the sea, fight-ing the treach-er-ous foe,
Heave Ho! my Lads, heave ho!
Let the sea roll high or low, we can cross an-y o-cean,
Sail an-y riv-er, give us the goods, and we'll de-li-ver,
Damn the sub-mar-ine! We're the men of the merchant ma-rine! Heave-rine!

Merchant Marines awards to Civilians: Atlantic War Zone Medal, Mediterranean Middle East War Zone Medal, Pacific War Zone Medal, Combat Bar with Stars. Merchant Marine Service Emblem and Honorable Button, Merchant Marine Victory Medal World War II. Presidential Testimonial letter on WWII services; Vietnam Service Medal, New York State Conspicuous Service Cross Medal (Military Cross), United States Bicentennial Memorial Medal. Foreign Government awards: The Royal Yugoslav Commemorative War Cross 1941-1945, Medaille Commemorative Belge, established by the Kingdom of Belgium to commemorate the War years 1940-1945; Medaille de la France Liberaee, established by Decree of the Republic of France on Dec. 12, 1947 and given the aforementioned name on June 16, 1948, Medilee Commemorative de la Reconnaissance (Gratitude) of the

Kingdom of Belgium, China Memorial War Medal. Retired in 1988 after 45 years of Sea Service. Life member of the USMMVWW II, the SS *Lane* Victory; a national historical landmark, National Park Service, Department of the Interior, a Living Memorial Monument dedicated to all those who lost their lives at sea. It is recorded in the Historical Registry in the same category as the Memorial Ship *USS Arizona*. Representative of Florida and Chapter Organizer. The names of Florida Chapters are: East Central Florida, Sanford Tamps/St. Petersburg, Space Coast, Miami, South West, Sanford, Tamps/St., Petersburg, Space Coast, Miami, South West, Satellite Beach, Cape Canaveral, Daytona Beach, Cocoa, Edgewater, New Smyrna Beach, Port Orange and Orlando. President of the East Central Florida Chapter established July 4, 1991.

The valuable and often valiant service of the American Merchant Marine has long been recognized. That service has now been recognized as having veterans status; presented on behalf of a grateful nation. Issued pursuant to Public Law 95-202 (1988) for service in the "American Merchant Marine in Oceangoing Service during Dec. 7, 1941 to Aug. 15, 1945." Bill H.R. 44, known as "The Merchant Marine Fairness and Memorial Act of 1989", will extend this cutoff date to Dec. 31, 1946; the same date as all other branches of service. General Douglas MacArthur said, "I will hold no branch in higher esteem than the Merchant Marine Service."

JOHN FRANCIS LIBERATORE, was born April 29, 1929, Crown Heights, Brooklyn, NY. He hopes to receive his Form DD 214 and Honorable Discharge Certificate DD 256 CG, after Bill H.R. 44, known as "The Merchant Marine Fairness and Memorial Act of 1989, is passed.

He had a small part of the Merchant Marines history, but one in which he will never forget. At the age of 17, he signed on as Acting AB and shipped out of Baltimore, MD on the Liberty ship SS *Abeil Foster,* for Matson Navigation Lines bound for Trieste, Italy, March to June 1946.

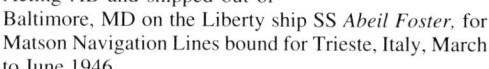

His only experience with DANGER was the mines in the Mediterranean and Adriatic Seas. The fellowship aboard ship was gracious and one he will never forget. The experience of working aboard ship, steering and observing sunrises and sunsets at sea is one he will cherish. They returned to the U.S.A. to Norfolk, VA. Then he had to go into the military USAF for his tour of duty. He did not return to the Merchant Marine service but he is proud to be a small part of a first great history book of the U.S. Merchant Marines Veterans of WWII.

Merchant Marine awards to civilians: Atlantic War Zone Medal, Mediterranean-Middle East War Zone Medal, Merchant Marine Service Emblem and Honorable Button, Merchant Marine Victory Medal WWII. Presidential Testimonial letter on WWII services; U.S. Bicentennial Memorial Medal. A member of the East Central Florida Chapter, Orlando, FL. General Douglas MacArthur said, "I hold no branch in higher esteem than the Merchant Marine."

FRANCIS LIS, was born June 15, 1927 in Goodyear, CT. From 1943 to 1944, helped build destroyer escorts at Walsh-Kaiser Shipyard, Rhode Island. Sheepshead Bay, NY, August 1944, U.S. Maritime service. Ships sailed with Merchant Marine: *George Bellows* (OS), October 1944-April 1945; *Pan Massachusetts* (AB), June 1945-August 1945; *Sedalia Victory* (deck maint.), September 1945-December 1945; *Salmon Knot* (AB), January 1946-

March 1946; and *Silver Star* (Carp.), May 1946-July 1946. Served with U.S. Marine Corp in Hawaii from 1946-1948.

Putman Technical School, Connecticut, 1948; graduated Architectural Department, 1952. Married, had two children. Worked for Architectural firms Worchester, MA and private practice 1952-1959. Moved to Claremont, CA, had two more children. Continued full-time in the field of architecture through 1974; thereafter practicing part-time. Founding member of U.S. Merchant Marine Veterans WWII. Retired and residing in Claremont, CA.

JAMES R. LITTLETON, sailed as OS, AB, F/W, wiper and deck maintenance during WWII. Has discharge from Army Transportation Corps and USCG. He is married to Josephine and they live in St. Leonard, MD. James is a member of AMMV JWB Chapter.

HERMAN C. LITZ, was born March 28, 1925 in Baltimore, MD. Graduated from Mt. St. Joseph High School, June 1943. Sworn into USMS Baltimore, MD, June 1943. Trained at Sheepshead Bay, NY, July 6, 1943, graduating October 1943. He sailed on the SS *Kenmar* (fireman); SS *Charles M. Schwab* (oiler); SS *Blue Ridge Victory* (oiler); SS *Vassar Victory* (oiler); SS *Cooper Union Victory* (oiler); SS *Honduras Victory* (junior. engineer).

Retired from Sherwin Williams Paint Company in 1986. Presently doing volunteer work aboard the SS *John W. Brown*. Resides in Glen Burnie, MD, with wife, Betty, whom he married in 1946. He is a member of AMMV JWB Chapter.

MAURICE LIZOTTE, sailed as OS, AB, 3rd mate, 2nd mate, and chief mate. Holds masters license. Sailed during Vietnam War. Attended Maritime Institute Graduate Studies. He holds various Merchant Marine and Navy decorations. He is married to Pauline and resides in Pasadena, CA. He is a member of AMMV JWB Chapter.

VICTOR LLUIS

HAROLD LOCKTOV, was born March 2, 1922 in San Francisco, CA. Joined the Merchant Marine in 1941. Served on the *Alcoa Pathfinder* (torpedoed), *John C. Plainworth, George Bancroft, Seton Hall Victory, Cape Johnson,* and various other ships during his service time.

He has been employed as a toy salesman for 40 years, still working. Now living in Piedmont, CA.

ARTHUR L. LOGAN, was born June 1, 1918 in Lake County, OH. Attended school in Leroy Township and Painesville, OH. Joined the Merchant Marine April 15, 1937 at Fairport, OH. First shipped out as ordinary seaman in April 1937. Sailed as ordinary and able bodied seaman until 1942, then attended USMS Officers Candidate School at Fort Trumball, New London, CT.

Shipped as third, second and chief mate, including two voyages to Murmansk, Russia as chief mate of the SS *John J. Abel,* official number 243096. Continued as chief mate various ships until April 1949 when he became captain of a Liberty ship. Went to Panama Canal Zone as pilot-in-training on Sept. 19, 1951. Piloted in the Canal until 1963 when was promoted to assistant port captain, Cristobal. Was transferred to Balboa in February 1965, where he was promoted to senior assistant port captain and then to port captain on Jan. 9, 1972 until retirement June 17, 1978. Since retirement Art and his wife of 50 years, Maxine, have made their home in Titusville, FL.

EDWARD LONC, was born April 3, 1920 in Toledo, OH. Joined Merchant Marine at Sheepshead Bay Sept. 29, 1942. Edward served on the *Covalt* (fireman), *Ann Skakel* (watertender), *Newton D. Baker,* and various other ships. Honorably discharged. He was awarded the Merchant Marine Emblem, Atlantic War Zone Bar, Pacific War Zone Bar, Mediterranean-Middle East War Zone Bar. He recalls the Invasion of France on the SS *Marine Raven*.

Married to wife Carolyn for 45 years, they have two sons. Worked at Dana Corporation for 36 years. Retired in 1977.

FLOYD LEE LOTKER, JR., was born in Kansas City, MO, graduated from St. John's Military Academy, Salina, KS, and was attending Kansas State University when enlisting in the USMS at Omaha, NE, July 1941. Boot training was at Hoffman Island, New York. Two weeks were spent learning seamanship aboard the USS *Vema* (three masted schooner formerly owned by Barbara Hutton) and remainder of time on the USS *Empire State,* a converted Hog-Islander, finishing January 1942 as an able bodied seaman with coxswain rating, a month after Pearl Harbor attack.

Before the formation of the USOs, the Seaman's Episcopal Institute in New York City, was "home away from home" to seaman with their physical, social, intellectual, and spiritual needs being met. Some 500,000 pieces of mail wee handled annually by it's post office. Father Larson was the Chaplain and through him, he met his wife of 49 years.

The *Toteco,* a converted tanker was his first assignment. Made two trips to Mexico along Torpedo Alley (East Coast) for crude oil, February-May 1942.

He served May 1942-January 1943, as an AB on SS

George Wythe, a new Liberty ship. Her maiden voyage to Panama with supplies, then a seven month trip to Karachi and Bombay, India with bombs, ammunition, and planes. Unescorted, as their cargo was too dangerous for a convoy.

On returning, he was accepted into the seventh class of Officer Training School at Fort Trumball, New London, CT, graduating in June 1943 as ensign in the USMS and Naval Reserve.

July 1943, as third officer aboard the SS *Cape Charles,* a new CIA vessel, they loaded bombs, ammunition. planes, and supplies, out in mid-New York Harbor, because of the explosive nature of the cargo, and headed for the Persian Gulf via Panama Canal and Australia, returning to San Pedro, CA and drydock. Experienced the "Roaring Forties".

Returned to New York City for Upgrading school and earned his second mate's license. He was reassigned as lieutenant junior grade, to teach navigation at OCS at Fort Trumball from April 1944 to March 1946, with summer assignment at Baltimore, MD, instructing cadets on-board navigation aboard USS *American Navigator,* cruising the Chesapeake Bay, as the Atlantic had too much U-boat activity. He was honorably discharged in March 1946.

He took berths on the SS *Cape Alexander* and M.V. *Cape Barrow,* both as second officer, during 1946 and 1947. When the latter was sold to a foreign country, he left for the sea for his hometown, Oberlin in Western Kansas, and took over his family's homestead, a wheat and cattle ranch.

MATTHEW J. LOUGHRAN, was born June 20, 1927, Long Island City, NY. Rejected by Navy, Marine and Coast Guard June 1944 because of defective vision. Someone told him about the U.S. Maritime Service and was accepted as a stewards mate second class on July 10, 1944. He started his training on July 17, 1944 at Sheepshead Bay, NY and graduated in Section 344 on Sept. 13, 1944. Sailed as officers messman on the SS *Fred W. Weller;* SS *Esso Camden;* SS *Esso Rochester;* SS *Esso Raleigh;* and MS *Esso Pittsburgh* which struck an unknown object suffering damage which required a portion of the crew to be taken off by the Canadian Corvette, K-133, HMCS *Quesnel;* and the SS *A.C. Bedford.* All the ships were tankers operated by Standard Oil of New Jersey.

In December 1945 he was called for the draft but was rejected. He was called again and rejected. Finally in April 1946 he was drafted into the Army and took basic training at Fort Dix, NJ. He was assigned to the Medical Corp and sent to Letterman General Hospital and served as supply clerk and promoted to corporal. On April 12, 1947 he was discharged for the convenience of the government. His time spent in the Army was calculated into his retirement from the U.S. Post Office (1950-1982) but not his time in the U.S. Maritime Service or U.S. Merchant Marine. He also belongs to the Combat Merchant Mariners WWII. He has ship logos of all the ships he sailed on as well as Armed Guard Reports. He was one of the 17 rescued by HMCS *Quesnel.* He is currently residing at Deer Park NY with wife, Johanna.

WILLIAM R. LOWE, was born Aug. 28, 1925 in Glencoe, AL. Took training at St. Petersburg 1944 and Sheepshead Bay 1945. Ships sailed: U.S. Army Hospital ships *Charles A. Stafford* and *Jarrett M. Huddleston* (messman), 1945, out of Charleston. Liberty ships: *Francis M. Smith* (utility), 1945; *Robert S. Lovett* (act. AB), 1945-1946; *Elbridge Gerry* (act. AB), 1946; *William Brewster* (act. fm/wt), 1946, out of New Orleans. Cruise liner *Del Norte* (OS), 1947, out of New Orleans.

Bill then worked for the retail variety store chains, S.H. Kress, J.J. Newberry and McCrory Stores until

retiring in 1984. Bill lives with wife, Annie Laura in Birmingham, AL.

CHARLES W. LUCAS, AKA CHARLES WILLIAM LUCAS, JR, was born Feb. 2, 1918 in Honolulu, HI, the son of Charles Williams and Mona Hind (Holmes). Student of Menlo School and College, 1935-1937. Attended Princeton, Boston University, and Harvard. Merchant Marines Service: Hawaiian water 1937-1938, SS *Humuula* and SS *Hawaii;* August 1944 U.S. Maritime Service Officers School, New London, CT, granted third mates license, seaman second class USMS at time of entry. Served aboard SS *Nathan B. Forrest* as third mate from Feb. 5, 1945 to May 22, 1945; SS *Linfield Victory* as third mate from July 3, 1945 to Jan. 17, 1946. Awarded Merchant Marine Emblem, Atlantic War Zone Bar, Pacific War Zone Bar.

Among the most memorable experiences was August 1945, en route to Leyte Gulf aboard ammunition ship *Linfield Victory,* USS *Indianapolis* reported sunk in their area; next report received was bombing of Hiroshima, several days before arriving at Leyte...hundreds of ships were making ready for the Invasion of Japan. The bombing of Hiroshima resulted in them being at Ammunition Anchorage for 128 days before being ordered to Eniwetok..finally to San Francisco by Christmas. Victory at last!

Married Jacqueline A. Cooper, Aug. 17, 1957; children, Deborah (Mrs. John M. Williams, David L.- sales manager Hawaiian Tuna Packers, Ltd., Honolulu, 1937 to 1940; assistant treasurer, Maine Boat Yards Assoc., Ellsworth, ME, 1942-44; asst. treasurer Mt. Desert Boat Yard, Inc. (ME), 1943-44; asst. comptroller, Camden Shipbldg. and Marine Ry. Co.(ME), 1944; co-owner, The Ranch House restaurant, Honolulu, 1947-49; C.W. Lucas Jr. Co., Noroton, CO distributor industrial products, 1950-52; manager marketing services, Pratt and Whitney, West Hartford, CO, 1953-1958; president, Hawaii Drug Co., Honolulu, 1958-1985; president, director Lucas and Co. Inc., Honolulu. Served as deck officer U.S. Merchant Marine, 1944-46. Now enjoying retirement in the Pacific Northwest.

WALTER W. LUIKART, was born Nov. 11, 1925 in New Castle, PA. Went to Hoffman Island Dec. 2, 1943 for deck training. Ships sailed: SS *Burkshire* (OS); SS *Exchange* (OS-troop ship), Atlantic Ocean; SS *Nicholas Herkimer* (shuttled English Channel for eight months); SS *William Moody,* March 1945 to July 1945 to India, South Africa and New York; SS *Frederick Kummer,* August 1945 to November 1945; SS *Westminister Victory,* December 1945 to February 1946 (troop ship) two trips in Atlantic; SS *Christopher Gadson,* third mate, April 1946 to May 1946; SS *William Thornton,* third mate, June 1946 to September 1946; SS *Nicholas Biddle,* November 1946 to March 1947. Went to work as printer on the New Castle News for 38 years.

PHIL NATHANIEL LYON, was born Aug. 31, 1924 in San Francisco, CA. Joined the Merchant Marine on his 18th birthday. He was one, the first of four brothers to ship in the Merchant Marines in WWII. He made three trips

with two of his brothers. Took training at Sheepshead Bay, NY, fireman, oiler, watertender. Later assistant electrician, deck engineer, and deep sea crane operator for Scrips Inst. Oceanography, San Diego. First ship sailed was a sea tramper, March 1943, the *SS Wisconsin,* under Panamanian flag as not up to quality to sail under the American flag. Foreign vessel, originally German built. Had seen duty in WWI. There were very few English speaking aboard. All engine valves and equipment was still in German language. An old scotch boiler; had eight boilers. Four expansion engine. American flag ships aboard and sailed were the *Liberty, Zona Gale,* July-December 1943. SS *Lurline* August 1944 to September 1944 to Brisbane, Philippines and home.SS *Matsonia; Edward J. O'Brien,* January-July 1944; Cape Catoche January-April 1945.

Most memorable trip was aboard the SS *Edward J. O'Brien* when they they were aboard at anchor in Bombay, India April 14, 1944 when an ammunition carrying vessel caught fire blowing up the stern, then later the forward end of the ship. Several other ships were also sunk, not one officer of the ship survived the holocaust, and most of the crew were lost as well as thousands that gathered at the docks to see the fire. The story is told in the book called *The Great Bombay Explosion,* which he read at a later date after the war. They slipped into Bombay because a ship south of them was torpedoed. Last sailed with Scripts, three trips. The last one was called the Eurydice Expedition, September 1974 to July 1975, 18 ports, almost 30,000 miles throughout the Pacific, Adman Sea and Indian Ocean. Sailed as oiler, handling the cranes, wherewith they dredged the Challenger Deep Trench off the Philippine Islands March 28, 1975. The deepest dredge ever at that time. Nearly seven miles down.

At present he is barbering. He went to Bible college and was in the ministry for some years, raising a family, etc. He is also incorporating with others at a new church, in Rich, CA.

DONALD MAXWELL MACE, sailed as an oiler during WWII on SS *George W. Woodwardd* from April 15, 1944 to Nov. 24, 1944; SS *Justin S. Morrill* from Jan. 3, 1945 to April 2, 1945; and the SS *Kemp P. Battle* from May 5, 1945 to July 17, 1945. Has Atlantic, Mediterranean, and Middle East War Zone Bars. Attended Sheepshead Bay. Donald is married to Jean and lives in Monkton, MD. He is a member of AMMV JWB Chapter.

RALPH E. MACY, was born Sept. 14, 1927 in Vermillion, SD. Joined U.S. Maritime Service in December 1944 in Los Angeles, CA. Finished basic (boot camp) at Catalina Island, CA. Graduated Sept. 14, 1945 from Hoffman Island Radio School, NY. Sailed on SS *Kodiak Victory* from San Francisco to Japan and back. In December 1945 they nearly hit floating mines off Okinawa. Then sailed on troop ship SS *Sea Marlin* with German PWs from Portland, OR, to Liverpoort, England then to France to bring back American G.I.'s to New York.

Went home to South Dakota, got married and was in trucking business for 43 years. Later sold out, went back to Florida on SS *Galveston Bay* which he is presently on until October 1993. He is married to Lenette (43 years) and has four children and five grandchildren.

GEORGE J. MACZALI, was born March 17, 1928 in Hillside, NH. In 1943, he quit school to join the Navy, then Marine Corps. Discharged from both for being underage. Joined USMS, Sheepshead Bay, NY, sent to Hoffman Island Radio School, graduated (R-007) and shipped out. First two ships assigned as second radio operator were Liberty's, both torpedoed and sunk. Thereafter, sailed on tankers until the end of WWII.

In 1947, sat for New York State Regency Board High School Completion Exams and college entrance examinations for Newark College of Engineering, graduated with a BS (electrical engineering). Returned to sea, sailing as chief radio or sole radio officer on passenger, firefighters but mainly tankers until retired from the sea.

1967, Marine service engineer with ITT MacKay Marine; coastal station operator with ITT World Communications, KLC, Galveston Radio; 1983, Marine service manager with RMCA, Houston, TX, 1984-1990, Communications officer, City of Houston, TX, Office of Emergency Management Operations Center.

Presently, on staff as Marine Radio survey inspector for Marine survey agency, Houston; treasurer of the Lone Star Chapter of the AMMV. George lives and rejoices in his marital relationship with Dorothy in Richmond, TX.

WILLIAM J. MAHER, was born March 3, 1914 in Worcester, MA. Graduated Clark University 1936. First went to sea 1936, deck seaman, freighter *M.S. Ward*, Jamaica, Panama Canal, Pitcairn Island, Australia-Sidney, Brisbane, Melbourne, Adalaide, Wyalla. East Coast, Quebec, Montreal, Canada. Took part in National Maritime Union strike. Graduate U.S. Sheepshead Bay Maritime Station, sailed on *William H. Ashley*, Liberty Ship, 1944, from New York to San Francisco, third mate. Sailed on troop ship *Thomas H. Barry*, 1945, Boston to England and France.

Awarded Atlantic and Pacific War Zone Bars, and Merchant Marine Service Emblem. After the war, active in real estate, development, banking, plastic manufacturing, pipe manufacturing, mergers and acquisitions. Lived in Worcester, MA, Cape Cod, Ft. Lauderdale, New York, and travelled to about 30 countries in Europe, African Asia, North and South America. Lives with his wife, Miriam (Mimi) in Ft. Lauderdale and Cape Cod.

WILLIAM D. MALPASS, has been a Charter Member of JWB Chapter of AMMV since Oct. 14, 1989.

EDWARD C. MARCH, was born July 3, 1920 at Philadelphia, PA. Started to sea in 1937, going from ordinary seaman to master. First ship was *Nantucket* (cargo), others prewar being *Dorothy Cahill* (cargo), *Major Wheeler* (cargo), *Evelyn* (cargo), and *Carrabulle* (tanker). Also spent season on the Great Lakes. Served during WWII in *Catahoula* (tanker-when torpedoed), *Edwin Christenson* (cargo), *John C. Freemont* (Liberty), *Fluor Spar* (cargo), *Badger State* (cargo), *Kettle Creek* (tanker), *Cyrus T. Brady* (Liberty), *Colabee* (cargo), and *Joseph G. Cannon* (Liberty trooper). Graduated Officer Candidate School, Fort Trumball, during war. Was wounded and taken as POW. Was on board SS *Catahoula*, April 5, 1942, when she was torpedoed.

Holds the Mariners Medal, Combat Bar with star, Victory Medal, Merchant Marine Defense Bar, Atlantic, Mediterranean Middle East, and Pacific War Zone Bars. After war sailed with Weyerhaeuser, Olympia, Bull and United States lines as well as a tug, some ferries, and some piloting. Instructor at United States Maritime Service Institute 1952-54. In marine safety work until 1980 and a consultant until 1989. Married to Carol. Retired and living at Millville (Ocean View), DE.

DANIEL MARIN, attended John W. Brown High School Ship from 1956-59. From 1959-63, he served in the U.S. Navy. Served in Merchant Marine for two and one-half years. Served on Mobile Oil tankers as messman and with MSTS as OS and AB. Now living in Newark, DE.

GILBERT D. MARKLE, was born June 27, 1928 in Youngwood, PA. Presently resides in Greensburg, PA. Worked as a wood pattern maker apprentice for Walworth Co., maker of valves-fittings, before joined the Maritime Service, enlisting in Pittsburgh, PA. Boot camp training was at Sheepshead Bay, NY and American Mariner training ship. Was sent to Baltimore and shipped out on the SS *Gulf Breeze*, Aug. 29, 1945 as watertender-fireman; SS *Thomas J. Jarvis*, Nov. 23, 1945, as oiler; SS *Thomas J. Jarvis* Feb. 6, 1946; SS *Stage Dood Canteen*, May 18, 1946; SS *Richard J. Hopkins*, Aug. 21, 1946; SS *Richard J. Hopkins*, Nov. 5, 1946; SS *John Chester Kendall*, Feb. 3, 1947; SS *E.A. Burnett*, April 22, 1947; and SS *E.A. Burnett*, June 20, 1947. He was discharged at Norfolk, VA, Aug. 10, 1947.

Awarded the Atlantic War Zone Bar. Returned to Walworth Co. completing his apprenticeship, then went to General Motors Fischer Body Div. as a wood pattern maker where he is presently employed for the last 40 years in various positions. Married to Margaret.

FRANK WILLIAM MARTILIK, (deceased), was born Dec. 15, 1915 in Pennsylvania. Two Continuous Discharge Books issued by U.S. Shipping commissioner in port of Philadelphia, PA showing 163 voyages between June 21, 1937 and Feb. 23, 1960 starting out as messboy then serving as OS, deck maintenance, AB, third mate, second mate, and chief mate. Served on SS *Cities Service Oklahoma*, SS *Hadnot*, C.S. *Empire*, SS *Watertown*, SS *Halo*, SS *Cities Service Koolmotor*, MS *Chester Sun*, MS *Northern Sun*, SS *Delaware Sun*, SS *Pennsylvania Sun*, MS *Brandywine*, MS *Sun*, MS *Texas Sun*, MS *Southern Sun*, MS *American Sun*, MS *Michigan Sun*, MS *Pacific Sun*, MS *Sunoco*, SS *Ohio Sun*, MS *Dynafuel*, MS *Mystic Sun*, SS *Maumic Sun*, SS *Ohio Sun*, SS *Maryland Sun*, SS *Mercury Sun*, and SS *Western Sun*.

All voyages except two or three were coastwise mostly out of Marcus Hook, PA. Ten, 15, 20, and 25 year service emblems were received by Frank from the Sun Oil Co. Was initiated into the Ancient Order of the Deep while serving on the MS *Texas Sun*. Attended Naval Damage Control Training Center Fire Fighters School at the U.S. Naval Base in Philadelphia. On Aug. 7, 1944 Frank received a commission as a lieutenant (j.g.) (D) in the United States Maritime Service. On Dec. 10, 1947 he received the USMM WWII Victory Medal, Service Button, and Presidential Testimonial Letter. Was also awarded the Atlantic, Pacific, and Mediterranean-Middle East War Zoner Bars.

Uniform and other artifacts donated to Project Liberty Ship by wife, Sophia. John A. Swineck, Project Liberty Ship member, Engine Department is wife's cousin.

ROBERT LEE MARTIN, JR. was born in Howardsville, VA on June 26, 1926; died Sept. 16, 1985 in Bristol, VA.

He enlisted in the U.S. Maritime Service, (U.S.

Merchant Marine) at Norfolk, VA on Nov. 6, 1944. Trained at U.S. Maritime Service Training Center, Sheepshead Bay, Brooklyn, NY. Graduated as steward's mate second class (St. M2c). His training also included 30 hours of elementary gunnery, 5" .38, 3" . 50, 20 mm. Released from active duty on Dec. 17, 1944 at U.S. Maritime Service Graduate Station, Boston, MA. All training conducted by War Shipping Administration Training Organization, U.S. Maritime Service. Service number 4414-33715; 2-615599.

December 17, 1944, he signed Coastwise Articles and sailed as saloon messman on the SS *Glen White* at Boston, MA. Ship's official number 216529 and the class of vessel was steam. A 10 day trip; and discharged when the vessel returned to Boston Dec. 27, 1944. His medical shot record; Form WAS-Med.2 (2)-record and immunizations and blood type read: Nov. 7, 1944 blood type-O, Nov. 7, 1944 Smallpox, Typhus Nov. 20, 1944, Typhoid Nov 20, 1944, Tetanus toxoid Nov. 28, 1944, Yellow fever Nov. 28, 1944.

He sailed on the Liberty ship, SS *Charles Carrol*, as gun crew messman. Signing foreign articles on Feb. 3, 1945 to May 4, 1945. Sailed from Norfolk, VA, coastwise to Philadelphia, and foreign; returning to New York. Vessel official number 241299, class of vessel - steam.

He sailed two war zones, Atlantic and Mediterranean-Middle East. The Liberty ship: transportation of materials needed, ships manned by civilians.

On Dec. 17, 1944 he filled out form, Certificate of Designation or Change of Beneficiary, Second Seamen's War Risk Policy by U.S.A. War Shipping Administration; "War Risk Life Insurance". "You may designate one or more of the following person, but no one else: (a) Your wife (b) your children (c) Your parents (d) your brothers and sisters (e) Your grandparents and grandchildren (f) Your nephews or nieces (g) Your aunts or uncles." "This designation will remain in force until a new certificate is made out by the insured."

Merchant Marine Awards to civilians: Atlantic War Zone Medal, Mediterranean-Middle East War Zone Medal, Merchant Marine World War II Victory Medal, Merchant Marine Service Emblem and Honorable Button, Presidential Testimonial Letter on WWII services. *Submitted by Robert Lee Martin, Jr. Longwood, CA. Via Frank and Edna Liberatore.*

LOUIS MARTON, a member of AMMV JWB Chapter, resides at 896 Timber Ridge, Hanover, MD.

NORMAN A. MATHEWS, sailing history covers period from Sept. 26, 1941 to June 19, 1957. Service from Jan. 9, 1948 to June 19, 1957 was obtained under name of Norman Mathus Arminger. Sailed as wiper, storekeeper, oiler, deck engineer, electrician, FWT, and deck utility on the following ships: *Esso Providence*, *American Trader*, *Thomas H. Wheller*, *Richard Alvey*, *Rufus W. Peckham*, *John Banvard*, *Richard Rush*, *George H. Dern*, *Andrew Furuseth*, *John S. Sargent*, *Turk's Head*, *Elezar Lord*, *Fairport*, *Steel Vendor*, *Pioneer Mail*, *Salem Maritime*, *Dorothy*, *P&T Adventurer*, *China Mail*, *B.F. Irvine*, *Sea Serpent*, *Sylvester Pattie*, *Washington Mail*, *Longview Victory*, and *Barbara*. Also served on *LST 973* and *898* for Headquarters, 52nd Transportation Medium Port, *Philcom APO 900*. Was boiler mechanic on *APO 331* for Headquarters, Ryukyus Command. Served on the USNS *AKL-32(E)*, *General C.G. Morton (A)*, and *General J. Pope* for the Military Sea Transport Service Pacific, San Francisco, CA. Awarded Murmansk Medal and other decorations. Holder of Murmansk Medal. AMMV Charter Member JWB Chapter Oct. 14, 1989.

DOUGLAS W. MATTHIA, a member of AMMV JWB Chapter, residing in Baltimore, MD.

RAYMOND B. MAURSTAD, was born April 4, 1928 in St. Paul, MN. Riggers helper and electricians helper Puget Sound Naval Shipyard 1944. Trained Catalina Island; graduated Gallups Island Maritime Radio School

Boston Harbor April 1945. First ship was the Liberty SS *David Lubin*, Okinawa Invasion. 1946 on Wake Island with PAA; 1947 with U.S. Lines moving displaced persons from Europe to U.S. and South America and with Northwest Airlines Minneapolis and Grand Forks, ND.

In 1948 he married and was with Western Union; 1949-50 with U.S. Training Mission in Korea. Alerted General Douglas MacArthur via amateur radio on the invasion from the North. Wife Marion pregnant and evacuated to Japan. First child, Murray born in Tokyo. 1951-57 T2 coastal tankers and cargo Europe, Africa, Central America and Greenland. Daughter Deborah was born Brooklyn 1951; son, Mitchell, Long Island, NY, 1953. 1956 on T2 *Robert E. Hopkins;* first ship to respond to SOS from SS *Andrea Doria* and MV *Stockholm* in collision and fourth ship at scene taking survivors. Two years on SS *African Dawn* to West, South and East Africa. 1957-60 three years Press Wireless Hicksville and Center-Reach, Long Island, NY; 1960 with CBS Ch.10 TV station KOOL Phoenix, AZ and disc jockey KBUZ Radio Mesa, AZ. 1960-89 with Remington Rand Univac/Sperry Univac; retired as director in 1989. Son, Matthew was born Minneapolis in 1963. 1989 to date; shipboard radio officer on Texaco coastal tankers. Four children and five grandchildren; resides with artist wife Marion in Coon Rapids, MN. Active Gallups Island Radio Association, Society of Wireless Pioneers and American Merchant Marine Veterans WWII. Amateur radio call signs: HL1CE, W2JNA, ELOC, ZD4CE, 9G1CE, WOBNM, presently W3HUV.

JOSEPH LOYE MAXWELL, was born Feb. 4, 1916 in Eastanollee, GA. Entered U.S. Navy 1943; 1944 Regional Enrolling Office, Atlanta, GA, Fort Trumball Class 3604D. Sailed the Atlantic on the *Raymond Vail Ingersoll* (Liberty), as third mate; *Gertrude Kellogg* (tanker), second mate, West Indies; *Frostburg Victory* (troop transport), second mate, Atlantic-Mediterranean; *Mission San Juan* (tanker), chief mate, Atlantic Coastwise.

While on his eight to 12 watch sighted a westbound hospital ship ablaze with deck floodlights and Red Cross steaming through the middle of their east bound 672 ship convoy.

Employed as manufacturer's representative in the Florida territory. Licensed GRI real estate broker, with no plans to retire. Married for over 50 years, they have one son, one daughter, four grandsons, one granddaughter and two great-granddaughters. He is a Christian serving God in his everyday life. A 40 year eteran adult volunteer in the Boy Scouts of America. Awarded the Silver Beaver and is a vigil honor member of The Order of the Arrow. Charter member of East Central Florida Chapter of the USMMV WWII. Sixteen years perfect attendance in Rotary International.

MILTON N. MCCAFFERTY was born March 22, 1921 in Ohio. Joined the Merchant Marine in Port Hueneme, CA, 1942. Sailed on the *Esso Little Rock* (OS), *Jonathon P. Dolliver* (AB), *SS Egg Harbor* (AB), *Cyrus W. Field* (AB), *Inglewood Hills* (third mate), *Alan Seeger* (third mate), *Charlotte P. Gilman* (second mate), USNT *Schulkill* (second mate), USNT *Pecos* (second mate), and USNT *Sebec* (second mate). All voyages from 1942 to 1950 were very memorable for him and some were very exciting. Milton married in 1945, they had two daughters and one son. Lived in Gardena, CA. Now retired and living in Carlsbad, CA at 4545 Triesti Drive.

RICHARD D. MCCAMY SR was born Sept. 25, 1926 in Scottsboro, AL. Joined the Merchant Marine November 1943 in Mobile, AL. He served on *Alcoa Pilot* as water tender in the Gulf; *Benjamin Bourne* as oiler in Atlantic and North Sea; *Cape Romain* as fireman, Mediterranean; and *Charles A. Warfield* as fireman, Atlantic.

Since service he has been in heating and air conditioning (1950-1991). Married wife Mary in 1949. They have one son and one daughter. Member of Sanford, Florida Chapter of MM Veterans WWII.

R.A. McCLEAN, Captain McClean sailed as deck cadet on the *SS Henry Baldwin* from Nov. 9, 1942 to May 24, 1943. He is a member of National Liberty Ship Memorial, SS *Jeremiah O'Brien*. Now residing on Puritan Circle, Tampa, FL.

JERRY McCLISH, was born July 15, 1920 at Windfall, IN. Joined U.S. Maritime Service June, 1940. Ships served on were tankers, freighters, etc. He received Radio Officers training at the Gallups Island Resident Radio School. He arrived there July 4, 1940 and was in the first group to graduate. He was at sea when Pearl Harbor was bombed. Shot at once by submarine some 80 miles south of Mobile, AL. Also shot at by U.S. Navy, *Cristobal Colon,* when they did not answer a challenge immediately. Was aground in submarine alley for nearly three weeks. Finally a Merrit-Chapman tug from New York got them off. That was in the Caribbean in early 1942.

After Maritime Service, he spent some five years with Pan American flying as radio officer on the clippers. From then on, he did many things including being chief radio engineer for the Cook County (Chicago) Sheriff's Police. Quit the whole business in 1964 and spent some 15 years beach combing in the Bahamas. Is now an artist. President of the International Society of Marine Painters. Conducting workshops local and foreign. Pictures in Boston Marine Museum and other places. Have donated a print of the *Jeremiah O'Brien* made for the Gallups Island Radio Association. They have them for sale.

He has a whole box full of ribbons and assorted First Places, Best in Show, and on down through Honorable Mentions. Some of the competitions where first place ribbons have been received are: Beach Art Association, Longboat Key Art Center, United First Federal Invitational, International Society of Marine Painters, Gold Coast Watercolor Society, American Professional League, and Salmagundi Club.

JAMES C. McCOLLOM, sailed as chief mate during WWII and survived two sinkings. Graduated from Massachusetts Maritime Academy. Hold all War Zone Bars. He is a member of AMMV JWB Chapter, residing in Silver Spring, MD.

LEE (SPARKS) McCLURE, sailed on SS *George M. Bibb*. He is a member of National Liberty Ship Memorial, SS *Jeremiah O'Brien*. He now lives in Sedalia, MO.

GLEN B. McCURDY, was born March 25, 1918. After getting hurt on a construction job in San Francisco, CA, he came back to Detroit and worked in a department store. Now service would take him so he quit his job and went to Miami. Went to U.S.A. office and 24 hours later he was aboard his first ship, and four hours later was at sea.

Took the SS *Jonathon Trumbull* with a load of wealth to Antwerp and picked up troops to take to the Pacific. Two days out of port the Jap was over. Ship was sent to Boston and he signed off. Sailed on the USS *Jonathon Trumbull,* SS *Pueblo* (messman), SS *Dixiano, WW Bruce, African Sun,* SS *Gauntlet, Sunset Hill*. Remembers being at shore at Utah Beach and unable to get back to ship until the next morning.

Married his wife Mildred May 12, 1945. They have one daughter Glenda, one son Peter and two grandchildren. He has done construction work, worked as warehouseman and many other jobs in his life time. Works as Santa at mall on Christmas. Now residing in Detroit, MI.

JACK McCUSKER, was third mate on the SS *John Witherspoon* in convoy PQ-17. Of 44 ships in the convoy only 11 got through. Jack has since written many books on this convoy including *"Memories of the Russian Run"* (VWOA News Letter, Winter 1992).

JACK McDERMOTT, sailed in the Armed Guard on the SS *Joseph Pulitzer* and the SS *William Mulhavand* during 1943-44. He visited the *Brown* on April 4, 1992. He is now living on Atlantic Ave., Margate, NJ.

LEONARD A. McGINNIS, SR., was born June 24, 1926 in Warrens, WI. He joined the Merchant Marine in March 1944, Portland, OR. Served on the SS *Extavia* (second cook), South Pacific; SS *Toloa* (cook), Aleutian Islands; *MV Cape*, SS *Corrillo,* Italy-France; SS *James Roy Wells,* Belgium; SS *Courser*, China-Philippines and Australia. His ship hit mines in Solomon Islands; bombed in New Guinea ports; and was attached to third fleet in Philippine Islands supplying food to invasion fleet for Philippines.

Worked as shipyard welder in Portland, OR or OTR truck driver for 35 years. Married with one son and two daughters. Now volunteer driver for Red Cross and food bank driver.

VERNE M. McGREW, was born Aug. 17, 1924 in Pittsburgh, PA. Joined U.S. Merchant Marine in February 1943, attended U.S. Merchant Marine Academy in New York, NY. Sailed as cadet and first assistant during WWII on: SS *Fort Dearborn,* SS *Billy Sunday,* SS *Longview Victory,* SS *Sea Snipe,* SS *Fort Lane,* SS *Fort Stephenson,* and SS *Esso Pankersburg* on the Pacific, Mediterranean, North Atlantic and Pacific Oceans. In 1943 while on SS *Billy Sunday* he made acting second engineer. When ship lost third and second assistant engineers. Ran aground on Bay of Bengal while he was watch engineer-full ahead to emergency full astern-engine intakes plugged. Safety of ship declared. Has Atlantic, Pacific, and Mediterranean War Zone Bars.

Verne married Peggy and they had six sons and one daughter. Retired insurance broker; raising Hereford cattle and floral greenhouses.

ROBERT McCLAREN, sailed as F/W from 1955-57 with Esso Shipping Company. He is now living on McIntosh Drive, Dunkirk, MD.

LEE McMICHAEL, was born Sept. 25, 1918 in Rice's Landing, PA. In May of 1942, he went to sea aboard the Army Transport Ship *State of Virginia*, which supplied troops, food and material to the islands of the West Indies. Their home port was Trinidad. The sailors at the USO would bet them they wouldn't make it back, as the German "U" boats were sinking ships by the dozen.

After that he served on the Liberty Ships, *William D Moseley, Charles Carroll,* and the *John Sedgwick;* then went to Officers Training School in New London. In November 1944, he served on a Liberty Ship as third mate, going to Leghorn, Italy (can't remember the name of the ship), then signed on again as second mate. In July 1945, he signed on the SS *Pennsylvania* to the Pacific and was in Pearl Harbor when the war ended.

He married his wife, Marjorie, in May of 1944, and they have six children and 12 grandchildren. He retired from Wheeling-Pittsburgh Steel Company in 1980. They reside at 41 Thelma Drive, West Newton, PA 15089.

WILLIAM H. McMILLION, graduated from Hoffman Island as radio officer, with Class 31-R. He is now living on Anderson Street, Lewisburg, WV.

JOSEPH MELLON, sailed as AB on *E.H. Blum,* a tanker. According to Joe this was the longest ship in the world. He is now living in Gloucester, NJ.

FRED MERLINO, was born in Sutersville, PA on June 18, 1920. Enlisted in the Merchant Marines Dec. 1, 1942 in Pittsburgh, PA. Graduated from Seaman's School at Sheepshead Bay, NY. The following are the ships Fred sailed on: MS *Bostonian*, April 27, 1943-June 19, 1943 (messman and fireman); *Grenville M. Dodge,* Aug. 6, 1943-Nov. 26, 1943 (wiper); SS *Pierre Gibault,* Dec. 30, 1943-March 16, 1944 (wiper); SS *Benjamin H. Grierson,* April 10, 1944-June 10, 1944 (oiler); *Frank J. Sprague,* July 14, 1944-March 30, 1945 (fireman and watertender); *Russell A. Algier,* May 19, 1945-March 19, 1946 (oiler).

He was awarded the Merchant Marine Emblem, Atlantic War Zone Bar, Pacific War Zone Bar, Mediterranean-Middle East War Zone Bar, and Philippine Liberation with stars. After his discharge, he remained in Sutersville, married and had three children. He went to work for the U.S. Steel Mill, retiring in June 1982. He now does volunteer work for the Sportsman Club and also St. Charles Borromeo Church which he is a member of.

CAPTAIN K.O. MEYER, Deceased, TAL 4/92, p.5.

CARL L. MICHEL, Donated items which included a blue bunk spread was standard Maritime Commission issue to all Liberty and other MARAD ship and an instruction manual for the 2500 HP Liberty Ship engine. This manual was used by Carl in his position as outside machinist foreman at Todd Shipyard, Brooklyn Div. or better known as Erie Basin. A photo of a Liberty, the SS *Joseph Hooker,* designated a troopship, with a Christmas tree between the aft end of the stack and the raised boom, was also donated. Another photo donated is of a USN Electronics Liberty Ship named, *The Coasters,* or *Harbor Island.* During WWI Carl sailed on Liberty's for three years. After the war, returned to Todd Shipyards and worked on and repaired the Liberty's right on through the late 1960s when they became scarce. He now lives in Kalispell, MT.

CHARLES E. MILLER, born Jan. 29, 1927 in Saint Mary's, PA. Joined Merchant Marine in 1943 at Pass Christian, MS, graduating from USMMA December 1947. Sailed on SS *Santa Cecilia,* Grace Line, European Theatre as cadet midshipman; SS *Potrero Hills,* L.A. Tankers, Corp. Atlantic and Pacific as cadet midshipman; Liberty Ship SS *John Lind,* American Foreign SS Co., Atlantic, Pacific, Black Sea and Mediterranean as third engineer. He recalls transporting troops and war supplies to and from Europe in a convoy in the North Sea and hauling bulk chrome ore from Navorozish, Russia as a payment for lend lease, and taking sugar from Cuba to Japan.

Employed by General Electric Co. for 37 years, project manager for both Maine, Naval and Central Station power plants both domestic and international. Retired in July 1988. Married 42 years, they have two sons, one daughter, and three grandchildren. Now in building and grounds contract maintenance, and enjoying golf.

DAVID H. MILLER, was born Sept. 6, 1920 in Ft. Myers, FL; attended Landon High School, Jacksonville, Fl. Helped build Liberty Ships in 1942, as ship fitter layout, first class in Jacksonville. Joined the Merchant Marine in Jacksonville, FL, 1944. Rated as ABS at Camp Blanding, FL, based on experience as seaman on Banana Boat, Cananova at Jacksonville. U.S. Government Dredge Welaka in Lake Okeechobee, FL. Also Arundel Dredging Corporation from Baltimore, MD in port of West Palm Beach. He sailed on the *Simon Willard* (AB) in the sub-infested waters hauling ammunition into European Theatre as helmsman and lookout, and a second ship which he can't recall. Retired August, 1945.

Worked for Railway Express from 1945 to 1975. Married Corrine Miller Jan. 1, 1938, they have six children, 18 grandchildren, and six great-great grandchildren. Today, he is working for his son, Wayne Miller, as delivery service to gun shops and gun ranges in Jacksonville.

DONALD C. MILLER, was born June 27, 1927; attended school in Columbus, OH. Joined Merchant Marine in 1944 at Cincinnati, OH. Trained at Sheepshead Bay, NY. Ships: *Robert Dale Owen* (OS), Liberty Ship, 1944, Atlantic and Mediterranean; *Pontotoc Victory* (AB), 1945, Atlantic; *Nishmaha* (AB), Hog Islander, 1945, Atlantic; *Atenas* (AB), 1945, Atlantic; *Gulf Gem* (QM), tanker, 1945; *Cacalilao* (QM), tanker, 1946; *Richard J.*

Cleveland (QM), Liberty tanker, 1946; *Petersburg* (QM), T-2, 1946, Atlantic and Gulf of Mexico.

Retired from major department store as camera buyer in 1988 after 35 years of service. Activities include woodworking, gardening, and travel. Visited the west coast in 1991 and enjoyed going aboard the *Lane Victory, Jeremiah O'Brien,* and *Queen Mary.* Member of USMMV WWII. Now resides in Groverport, OH with wife, Mary. They have three children and six grandchildren. They will celebrate their golden wedding anniversary in 1995.

ORVAL I. MILLER, was born July 6, 1923 in Saskatchewan, Canada. Attended Southern California public schools. Graduated from California Maritime Academy in 1943. Served aboard: *TS Golden Bear* (midshipman); SS *Richard J. Cleveland,* Liberty tanker, third engineer, Atlantic and Pacific Oceans, Caribbean and Bering Seas; SS *Bandelier,* T-2 tanker, third engineer, South Pacific Islands; SS *West Coast,* steam schooner, first engineer, Coastwise, Central and North America; SS *Barbara Olson,* steam schooner, first engineer, Coastwise, Northwest lumber trade; SS *Loyola Victory,* third engineer, Intercoastal; and SS *Aberdeen Victory,* second engineer, Intercoastal and Orient. In 1959, he became a real property appraiser and Deputy Riverside county assessor. Retirement came after 27 years, the last 11 years as chief appraiser.

Currently a volunteer crew member helping to restore and operate the SS *Lane Victory,* the U.S. Merchant Marine Veterans of WWII memorial ship in San Pedro, CA.

RAY MILLER, attended Sheepshead Bay Engineering School December 1944 to May 1945. Sailed during WWII, Korean War and peacetime as oiler, refrigeration engineer. Holds the Pacific War Zone Bar, WWII Victory Medal, Korean War Zone Bar and Good Conduct Medal, U.S. Army. Sailed on the SS *Joseph McKenna, George McKay* and SS *Frederick Bouchard,* Liberty's, SS*Virginian,* SS *Duke Victory,* SS *DePauw Victory,* USNS *General M.L. Hershey, TAP 148,* Troopship; UNS *General W.C. Langfilt, TAP 151,* Troopship; SS *General R.E. Caldaw, TAP 139,* Troopship; and USNS *General RF.M. Blatchford, TAP 153.* He has one daughter, Regina Rae Miller. Member of AMMV VA and JWB Chapters. Now living in Hampton, VA.

WILLIAM H.C. MILLER, a member of AMMV JWB Chapter. Now living in Baltimore, MD.

DONALD F. MILEY, sailed on the SS *Joseph Story* and the *William F. Empey.* Served 20 years as captain of Weyerhauser Liberty's, six on intercoastal trade. Visited the *Brown* on May 1, 1992. Donald now lives at Rt. 2, Box 3220, Lopez Island, WA.

JOHN W. MINER, a member of AMMV JWB Chapter, now living on Chardel Rd. in Baltimore, MD.

STANLEY M. (MAC) MISNER, was born Jan. 11, 1928 in Wichita, KS. Joined the Merchant Marine in 1944. He trained on Catalina Island and then took his first ship, the SS *Broad River,* a T-2 tanker. He worked in the engine room as a wiper and helped the fireman and watertender so

that he could get his papers upgraded. They were at sea three months and hauled airplane fuel to somewhere in the South Pacific. His second ship was the SS *Tillamook,* a T-2 tanker, and he served on board as a wiper to start and then as fireman and watertender, but did not ever get his official papers. When off duty, some of the time he would help the third engineer testing for hot bearings in motors and checking the thrust bearing at the main shaft.

They were at sea for 362 days, if he remembers correctly. If they would have been at sea four more days, they would not have had to pay any taxes, but their captain, would not hear of it and even threatened the crew not to cause any breakdowns. Once they were coming into Panama Harbor and their captain was drinking. They rammed another ship and spent three months in dry dock getting their bow and starboard side repaired. After they left Panama they went all over the South Pacific including the Persian Gulf area. They took diesel fuel to a small island of the Palau Islands and while they were leaving there, they got off course and came within a few miles of Japan's largest airbase. Thank goodness they did not see them due to it being at night or he would not be around.

They were at sea when the war ended, so the captain (a new one) broke out a case of whiskey and they all got polluted to say the least, including their gun crew. They started shooting up all their ammo and almost melted the 20 mm gun barrels. They were throwing anything that would float over the side to shoot at. What a day that was!

When they returned to the States, he returned to his home in Wichita, KS, where he was born. He got married in 1950 and one month later was drafted into the Army as a forward observer and sent to Korea for eight months on the front lines. He states, "I know, God has had his hand on me all the way, or I would never have made it through it all."

He owned his own business for several years in Seattle, selling industrial batteries and chargers. Was in battery business for 30 years. He is now retired, living in L.A. area. Travelling some, fishing a lot. He has four sons, 13 grandchildren and lives alone.

JOSEPH D. MONIAK, was born Feb. 2, 1926 in Cleveland, OH. Joined the Merchant Marine March 1, 1944. Sailed on the *William A. Henry* as messman from San Francisco to Coos Bay, OR, then to Calcuta, India; *George W. Campbell,* as messman, Africa, Italy, France; *James Fergus* (OS), Europe; *Abbot L. Mills* (OS), Europe; *Stephen A. Douglas* as acting AB seaman, Yugoslavia. The *Abbot L. Mills* was mined in the Adriatic Sea.

He is married to Alice and lives in Brecksville, OH. Now retired after working as carpenter and purchasing manager. Enjoying his grandchildren and playing golf.

MIKE MOLINARI, served in the Armed Guard on the SS *Andrew Carnegie* (VWOA News Letter, Winter 1992).

CLIFFORD B. (CLIFF) MOORE, (4514-17879), was born July 12, 1927, in Memphis, TN, and went to Memphis Technical High School. Joined Merchant Marine on June 25, 1945, in Birmingham, AL; trained at the U.S. Maritime Station, Sheepshead Bay, NY. Graduated at Norfolk, VA Station on Aug. 11, 1945, as steward's mate second class. First trip was on the SS *Fairfax* on Aug. 11, 1945, to Puerto Rico, Cuba, Jamaica, and back to New York on Aug. 28, 1945. Second trip on the SS *Chippana* from New Orleans, LA on Sept. 15, 1945, to Panama Canal, Columbia, the Equator, Ecuador, Peru, Chile, and back to Texas City, TX on Nov. 19, 1945. In January 1946, he signed aboard the SS *Exceller* in New York, but they did not sail. Last trip was aboard the SS *Sea Porpoise* sailing from New York on Feb. 25, 1946, to Le Harve, France and back to New York on March 22, 1946.

Returned to Memphis, TN, and belonged to the Tennessee Air National Guard in 1948 through 1950. Owned own repair business; industrial plant engineer; hotel district engineer until retirement in 1986. Married on Aug. 27, 1948, has three children and six grandchildren. Presently retired and living in Senatobia, MS.

EDWARD D. MOORE, attended USMSTS at Sheepshead Bay in April 1944 in Section 153 and Section 19E in engine training. Sailed on SS *Corinth,* T2 tanker, in 1944, USAH *Aleda E. Lutz,* and USAHS *St. Mihiel* from 1945-46.

WILLIAM H. MOORE, a member of AMMV JWB Chapter, now living on East Oak Road, Vineland, NH 08360

EDWIN H. MORAN, a member of AMMV JWB Chapter, now residing on Phillis Drive, Clinton, MD 20735.

WILLIAM P. MORINO, sailed as chief radio officer aboard the *Arthur M. Huddell* from September 1944 to January 1945 to London, England. He was from Columbus, OH. Second operator was Don Gagne.

LELAND P. MORRIS, JR., sailed aboard American Flag Merchant Ships during WWII. He is a member of AMMV JWB Chapter, now living on Virginia Ave., Baltimore, MD 21236.

JOHANNES MUTTIK, was born Aug. 19, 1918 in Estonia. Joined the Merchant Marine in New York, NY, March 1943. He sailed on the *William S. Coddington, Sam Houston II, Exequer* (troop transport), *Pan Maine, White Bird Canyon,* and others. He remembers the Invasion of Normandy aboard the SS *Exequer* with 1st Div. of Texas Rangers and riding out a hurricane in Okinawa that swept barges one-half mile inland in 1945.

He has been married to Teresa since 1949. Retired in 1968, working as maintenance painter for Westinghouse Electric.

CHARLES MYERS, sailed as AB during WWII. Attended Sheepshead Bay, September 1942. Has Atlantic, Pacific, Mediterranean-Middle East War Zone Ribbons and Merchant Marine Service Bar. He is married to Elaine. A member of AMMV JWB Chapter and now living in Severna Park, MD.

JACK B. NAVARRE was born Nov. 21, 1925 in Detroit, MI. He joined the Merchant Marine November 1943, in Detroit. Assigned to U.S Merchant Marine Cadet Basic School, San Matee, CA, January to April 1944. Ships served in: SS *Canada Victory* (engine cadet) April 1944-February 1945, Victory ship, South and Central Pacific; SS *Sea Flasher* (oiler), March 1945-June 1945, C-3 troopship, Okinawa; SS *Sea Partridge* (oiler), June 1945-September 1945, C-3 troopship, Philippine Islands; SS *Costa Rica Victory* (fireman/watertender) September 1945-November 1945, Victory ship, Mediterranean Sea

ports; SS *Malvern Hill* and SS *Bennington* (oiler), December 1945 to April 1946, T-2 tankers, Venezuela and West Indies, coastwise; Great Lakes ships, second and third assistant engineer, 1947-1949, Great Lakes ports.

He graduated from Howe Military School, Howe, IN, 1943 and Walsh College, Troy, MI, finance and accounting in 1951. Worked in accounting and controllership positions in manufacturing companies in Detroit to 1964. 1964 to 1990, Management consultant with AT Kearney, Inc., Chicago, IL-an international general management consulting firm; retired in 1990.

Joined U.S. Military Sealift Command, Atlantic, September 1990. Served in U.S. Naval Hospital Ship *Comfort* in Persian Gulf during Desert Storm until end of facilities. Presently still in MSG; last ship was the USNS *Henry J. Kaiser* T-AO 187 in deployments in the Mediterranean and Red Sea.

WILLIAM STANLEY NELSON, was born May 1, 1921 in Greeley, CO. Joined Merchant Marine May 1942, Denver, CO. Took training at Port Hueneme, CA, under U.S. Coast Guard. He sailed on the *Richard Stockton* (fireman and watertender), Liberty ship, 1942-1943, Pacific, Indian Ocean, Caribbean Sea, Tasman Sea, Arabian Sea, Atlantic; *Trade Wind* (ordinary seaman-able seaman), C-2 refer freighter, 1943, Pacific, Tasman Sea, Caribbean Sea, Atlantic; *M.E. Lombardi* (able seaman), Standard of California tanker, 1943, Pacific, Gulf of Alaska; *W.H. Berg* (able seaman), Standard of California tanker, 1944-1945, Pacific; *Santa Catalina* (able seaman), C-2 refer freighter, 1945, Pacific; *Franklin H. King* (able seaman), Liberty ship, 1945, Pacific.

Served in U.S Air Force on B-29s; worked for Texaco Oil Co. and for Woodard Governor Co., as machinist until his retirement.

Married to Norma, they have one son and one daughter. Today, he raises stock cattle, travelling, and enjoying Colorado.

JOHN O. NESSER, was born Sept. 29, 1923 in Sharon Township, Franklin County, OH. Graduated from high school; signed up in the U.S. Maritime Service December 1942 in Columbus, OH. Sworn in Dec. 25, 1942 in Cincinnati, OH. Sent to USMS training station in Sheepshead Bay, New York City, NY for engine room training.

Sailed out of Boston on the *Emma Willard* to Avonmouth, Wales to New York. Sailed out of New York on the *Emma Willard* to Norfolk, VA, to Algiers, to Palermo, Sicily, to Naples, Sardina, Newburg, New York. On the *John Trumbull* to Algiers, Naples, Algiers, Anzio, Bizerte, to off of Leghorn to Naples to the Invasion of Southern France to Oran, Norfolk. Went to USMS Training School at New London, CO. Graduated marine engineer ensign rating.

Sent to Los Angeles, CA, sailed on the *Niantic Victory* to Cebu, Philippines to Subic Bay to Sasabo, Japan to San Diego, CA to New York City on Jan. 31, 1946. Retired USMM number 48643. Lives in Sharon Township, Franklin County, OH, with his wife of 48 years. Retired from Riverside Methodist Hospital in 1985 as supervisor of HVAC section.

WILLIAM F. NESSER, was born Feb. 4, 1920 in Columbus, OH. His first ship in September 1937 an old Hogg Islander converted into a passenger ship, destination South America.

In July 1941, started Officers Training School at an USCG base in Alemeda, CA and received his third mate's license the day after Pearl Harbor.

In February 1942, signed on the SS *West Gotomska,* for Archangel, USSR, and 15 months later paid off in New York. Made several North Atlantic voyages including one shuttle to Ghent with crackers for the Low Countries. One week later on way home, VE day occurred.

Continued to sail until 1954, including the SS *Malden Victory,* from New Orleans to Pusan, Korea. From 1956 through July 1964, was captain and port captain, Baroid Div., National Lead Company. Directly from there became a Marine surveyor and worked full-time until 1985 when he semi-retired. Since then he does part-time work in the field. He has been married for 51 years, has three children, eight grandchildren, and one great-granddaughter.

CLARENCE W. NEWCOMER, was born Oct. 26, 1926 in Manheim, PA. Graduated high school at age 17, Manheim Central High School. Joined the Merchant Marine Oct. 24, 1944 in Philadelphia, PA. Training was at Sheepshead Bay, NY. Sailed during WWII on the following ships: SS *Marine Robin,* C-4 transport, (AO mess/crew mess), Atlantic, Dec. 15, 1944 to May 13, 1945; SS *Helen Hunt Jackson,* Liberty ship, (AO mess/storekeeper, Atlantic and Mediterranean, June 12, 1945 to Nov. 21, 1945; SS *Cornelius Harnett,* Liberty ship, (storekeeper/crew mess), Atlantic, Jan. 2, 1946 to May 1, 1946. Served two years in USAF 1950 to 1952. Holds Atlantic War Zone Bar.

Married to Mildred, they have four children, 10 grandchildren, and 12 great-grandchildren. Retired from sales, American Chicle Div., Warner Lambert, Co.

PHIL NEWMAN, is looking for any crew member who served on the SS *Juan Pablo Durate* in 1942. He may be contacted c/o The Anchor Light. He is a crew member on board the *Lane Victory.*

PETER JAMES NICHOLAROPOULOS, was born Oct. 4, 1920 at Ipswich, MA. He joined the Merchant Marine in 1943 at age 22. Ships sailed: *Robert Luckenback* (wiper); *Massachusetts* (fireman); *Tennessee* (oiler); *Bethoke* (oiler); *Indiana* (fireman); and *Morris Sigman* (fireman). He sailed to North Hampton, Cherbourg, Le Harve, Port Said, Cairo, Alexandria and various other places. He achieved the rank of chief petty officer. While

aboard the *Robert Luckenback* it was attacked by a German "U" boat enroute to Cypress. He was discharged in 1948.

He married his wife, Catherine in 1951. They have three sons, James, Charles, and Thomas.

After discharge he joined the Teamsters Union Local 42, in Lynn, MA. He was a truck driver and later became business agent for Local 42. Retired October 1984. Spending his winters in Florida. He is a life member of Project Liberty Ship in Baltimore. He is a member of American Merchant Marine Veterans in Centerville, MA, and a member of U.S. Merchant Marine Veterans of WWI, San Pedro, CA.

WAYNE LOUIS NICHOL, was born Aug. 16, 1922 in Sanilac County, MI. Entered Naval Reserve Sept. 28, 1942. Attended Marine Engineering school in Baltimore, MD. Received a fireman's certificate. Called to active duty March 20, 1943 and trained at Great Lakes and Gulf Port, MS. Served in the South Pacific aboard Liberty Ships, *James H. McClintock,* SS *Edwin Bellamy,* and MS *Pennant* (Danish).

After discharge in 1946, he returned to Michigan to go into the building trade until his semi-retirement in 1988. Spends six months in Michigan and six in Florida with his wife Madalyn whom he met while attending school in Baltimore.

CLARENCE W. NICHOLS, sailed as junior engineer, pumpman from Oct. 10, 1943 to Jan. 1, 1972, then retired. Sailed during WWII. He has one brother Vernon W. Nichols, who lives in Mount Holly Springs, PA. Clarence is a member of American Merchant Marine Veterans JWB Chapter. Now living in Falling Waters, WV.

PAUL J. NICHOLSON, was born Nov. 10, 1927 in Evanston, IL Enrolled USMS September 1944, age 16 years, trained at Sheepshead Bay, Hoffman Island Radio School; graduated April 30, 1945. First ship was *Wake Forest Victory,* as assistant radio operator.

His love of the sea led P.J. to make it his career. From Pacific combat, Okinawa 1945, to Shanghai with AV-Gas for China National forces and Germany with supplies for Berlin Airlift with NATO forces. Korean War and Vietnam Conflict. Served 32 years with Moore-McCormack Lines, 20 years on the *Mormacmail*, a total of 43 years continuous sea service, sailing on Victory's, Liberty's, C2, C3, C4, C5, Mariners, supertankers, and OBOs. First retired in 1987, reactivated for "Desert Storm", retired 1991. Always devoted to basic tenet of "safety of life at sea".

Married 44 years to Marion. Family Jay, Lee Anne and Corey, and grandchildren live in Toronto, Canada. He is a member of VWOA, USMM WWII, Midwest Chapter, HIRA, GIRA.

FRANK J. NIEDERMEIER, was born April 13, 1907 at St. Gallen, Switzerland. First USMC 1942, one year. Officers Cook 1st class. Sheepshead Bay, Brooklyn, NY. Sailed on six ships 1943-1946. Lost two ships, was chief cook on all.

Some of the ships sailed with: SS *James Oliver,* *Cape Possession, Richard Henry Dana,* SS *Russian Victory, Walace E. Farrington, Matsonia, Alcoa Pathfinder,* 1941-42 Deputy Zone Commander Air Raid Warden 86 Str. New York City. Employed: Brown Derby, Hollywood, CA. 1947 and Triftys Etc., Aircrafts Bg. N.A.A., Northrup-Hughes, Sprague Engineer Co. Gardena, CA.

CAPTAIN DAVID M. NILSSON, (deceased), died at the hands of the Japanese. His ship the SS *Sebastian Cermeno* was sunk off of Madagascar.

CONRAD NILSEN, Captain Nilsen was one of the moving forces behind Project Liberty Ship having joined in 1979 and served as co-director for several years. He died at the age of 70 on Sept. 26, 1990 after falling down a flight of stairs. He was former president of the Council of American Master Mariners. He was 16 when he first went to sea in 1936. After receiving his master's license in 1943 he commanded nine Liberties: *Rufus W. Peckham, Tristram Dalton, SM Babcock, Edward Livingston, Charles P. Steinmertz, Charles Sumner, John Wise, Henry L. Benning,* and *Morris Hilquit;* all for the A.H. Bull Lines. Captain Nilsen was in 17 convoys.

After the war he continued to sail with the Bull Lines and then sail for Sea-Land for 12 years. He commanded ships for PRMMI on the Puerto Rico run.

THOMAS J. NOAKES, was born July 31, 1928, grew up in Corpus Christi, TX. Joined Maritime Service Aug. 1, 1944 at age 16, in Denver, CO, trained on Catalina Island. Sailed on *Lost Hills,* 1944 (T4), *Fort George,* 1945 (T2), *Mission San Luis Obispo,* 1945 (T2), *Glacier Park,* 1946 (T2), *Hawaiian Banker,* 1947 (C3), *Marine Swallow,* 1947 (C4), *Sunset,* 1947 (T2), *Ampac Los Angeles,* 1948 (Lib.), *R. Ney McNeeley,* 1948 (Lib.), *M.E. Comerford,* 1948 (Lib.), *John Goode,* 1948 (Lib. tanker),*W.E. Downing,* 1949 (T2), *Hawaiian Pilot,* 1950 (C3). Messman, OS, AB, deck maintenance, and Bosun.

Enlisted in U.S. Army December 1950 in Mule Pack Artillery and Germany. Discharged December 1953. Graduated Barnes Business College, Denver. Accounting and Business Admn. Controller for electrical supplies distributor. Married and has two children and three grandchildren. He has been a Boy Scout Scoutmaster since 1966.

MELVIN CLAY NORRIS, was born Jan. 31, 1930 in Pasadena, CA. Went to school at 109th St. Elementary, David Starr Jordon in Watts, and Los Angeles Pacific College in Highland Park, CA. Applied to and received first papers for Merchant Marine Jan. 28, 1938. No ships to be had (Depression). Worked for Douglas Aircraft Long Beach, CA prior to and for the first part of the war. Shipped out as ordinary seaman then able bodied then bosun. Last shipped out on the *Santa Paula* in 1947.

He was charged with jumping ship in Australia. Stood trial with Coast Guard, Calcutta, India. Charges were dismissed in Philadelphia.

Had Mel's Industrial Catering for 35 years, retiring in 1982. Have been enjoying travelling, fishing, hunting, billiards and sail boat races. Renewed shipping papers in

1990, tried for service during Desert Storm, but was turned down because of hearing loss.

Married to Pauline, they have daughter, Leticia, one son, Brock, grandson, David, and granddaughters, Kelsay and Lacee.

RICHARD A. O'DELL, spent ten years at sea from March 2, 1936 to March 2, 1946. Sailed on two liberties, the *E. Kirby Smith* and *Samuel F.B. Morse*. Was told in August 1991 that he has asbestosis in both lungs which he feels he contacted aboard ship.

He resides in South San Francisco, CA.

HAROLD R. ODOM, was born in Bainbridge, GA, March 24, 1926. Moved to Tallahassee, FL 1928. Attended schools in Tallahassee, graduated June 1943 at 17. Joined U.S. Maritime Service in St. Petersburg December 1943.

Ships served on: *Thomas Tracy,* coal collier (o.s.) May 1944, coastwise. *David Lubin,* liberty ship (o.s.) July 1944, Italy (attended up-grade school in Baltimore); *Edward Livingston,* liberty ship (A.B.) November 1944, Philippines. *Fairfax,* troop ship (A.B.) June 1945, Italy. *George Leonard,* liberty ship (A.B.) August 1945, Italy. *Milford Victory,* (A.B.) November 1945, France. *James McHenry,* liberty ship (A.B.) January 1946, Italy. *Edward Richardson,* liberty ship (A.B.) July 1946, Holland.

Entered college in 1946 and graduated from the University of Florida in 1951, employed for several years as construction engineer and for the past 23 years have practiced architecture in Tallahassee.

ALBERT OFFREDO, was born Dec. 3, 1915 in Trenton, NJ. January 26, 1939 entered Merchant Marine service at 26 years old. October 10, 1944 officers training San Pedro, CA second mate. September 6, 1944, lieutenant-navigator. August 15, 1945 honorably discharged. August 10, 1946 married Ruth. May 15, 1954, elected president Local 230 UAW, Maywood, CA 10 years. April 1, 1957, labor relations consultant at Blue Cross South Carolina, 24 years. January 1, 1981, retired. December 21, 1990 died at 75 years.

Al developed malaria at India where the rats were big as babies. In the basement of a British hospital, the captain wanted to leave Al, but Gene Yocum and mates would not board ship without him. Gene would bring and feed Al juice and soup from the ship. After many years Al finally mentioned they carried dangerous cargo in foreign water.

On the light side Gene and Al went dancing in a cold country and got so hot they removed their pink long johns and wrapped same and checked them, well they left and forgot them. For years they wondered what the checkers thought.

Served on the *Paul Shoup, Oliver Hazard Perry, Frank Joseph Irwin, William James, Willet M. Hays, Koloa Victory, Occidental Victory* and received the Merchant Marine Emblem, Atlantic War Zone Bar, Pacific War Zone Bar, Mediterranean Middle East War Zone Bar.

KALEVI A. OLKIO, sailed as AB, bosun, and 3rd mate. Sailed during WWII. While a member of the gun crew fought against a German submarine November 1942 while on board Norwegian tanker MS *Minister Wedell,* sailing towards West Africa. The ship was torpedoed on the following trip in 1943.

Hold two medals from Norway and one Combat Bar with three stars. Has Atlantic Mediterranean Middle East and Pacific War Zone Bars.

He is married to Juta. He is a member of AMMV JWB Chapter. Resides in Baltimore, MD.

JOHN L. OLSON, was born May 14, 1910 in San Jose, CA. Joined the Merchant Marines in 1929 in San Francisco, CA. Served as fireman, oiler, watertender, third assistant, second assistant and first assistant.

The South Pacific was involved with all these ships, with one exception, the *Ethiopia Victory,* which carried ammunition from Seattle to Pearl Harbor, Hawaiian Islands.

The other merchant ships carried arms, ammunition, airplane fuel, material and equipment, and troops to enhance the winning of the war.

The places and islands that were involved were the Fiji Islands, New Caledonia, New Hebrides, New Guinea, Admiralty, Philippines, New Zealand and Australia. They were on a 24 hour alert most of the time and without any destroyer escort and were ready for anything. There were several very frightening experiences that occurred but they managed to come through safely.

They also acted as a prison ship for a short duration, carrying 200 Japanese prisoners from Noumea, New Caledonia to Auckland, New Zealand, where they were interned.

RICHARD M. OLSEN, CAPT., (THL, April 1992, p.5)

KENNETH R. ORANGERS, Served on SS *Tabitha Brown* (liberty) in armed guard as gunner from December 1943 to February 1944. Left ship at Anzio Beach Feb. 2, 1944. He resides in Pennsauken, NJ.

BILL A. OWENS, SR., was born Dec. 31, 1925 in Oklahoma City, OK. Left high school in 1943 to join Merchant Marines. Took training at Catalina Island, CA (Sec. 51-5). Sent to U.S. Merchant Marine Graduate Station in Portland, OR.

Ships sailed - all in steward department: SS *Richmond,* coastwise tanker, 1944; SS *Cape Catoche,* South Pacific, 1944; SS *Benjamin F. Coston,* liberty, Atlantic, 1944; *John McLaughlin,* liberty, Pacific, 1945; *Edwin H. Duff,* liberty, Gulf of Mexico, 1945.

After war contracted appliance delivery for wholesale distributor for 30 years (delivering the goods). Now retired.

In May 1944 they were aboard the SS *Cape Catoche* in the South Pacific, somewhere in the Russell Islands. They were anchored in the bay awaiting dock space. They had been warned about sharks and barracuda in the water, so they couldn't go swimming. Chips had built a small boat out of 1 x 12 boards, with a long pole and a five gallon milk can for an outrigger. Two crew members (he wishes he could remember their names) and he started rowing over toward the beach. The bow was up high and the two other guys were worried they wouldn't see them, so they stood up and started waving their arms. The boat turned over, spilling them in the water, and the two guys panicked. Both were trying to get on top of the five gallon milk can. "I'll bet that was a funny sight for the crew on board!" One of the crew members from the L.C.I. got in the water and helped him push the boat on over to the beach. The other guys got aboard the L.C.I. and went to the beach.

KARL E. OWENS, was born March 15, 1927. At age 15 worked on steam driven river boats at the port of St. Louis. (Federal Barge Line) as oiler and striker. December 1942-1944 went to Wisconsin. Picked up a sub for the Navy. Took it to New Orleans, while there went to the U.S. Coast Guard. Picked up seam. - (USS *Rock Submarine*). Shipped out of NM Union 44.

Steam ships that he sailed on: SS *Keith Vauter,* wiper, 1944, London England; SS *Telfair Stockton,* wiper, 1944, North Africa; SS *William A. Dobson,* oiler, 1945, LeHavre, France; *Lake Sapor,* oiler, 1945, Brazil S.A.; SS *Frank Lever,* oiler, 1945, Japan and China; SS *Benjamin Huntington,* DK engineer, 1946, Italy; SS *K.I. Luckenbach,* DK. engineer, 1946, Sweden-Norway; SS *Francis Scott Key,* DK engineer, 1947, Germany; SS *John Hanson,* oiler, 1947, Holland-Belgium; SS *James Gunn,* DK engineer, 1947, Italy; SS *Mathew Sheehan,* DK engineer, 1948, Germany; SS *W.S. Jennings,* DK engineer, 1948-1950, Germany; SS *African Endeavor,* eng. maintenance, 1950-1951, South Africa; SS *Edward N. Hurley,* oiler, 1951, Germany; SS *Tuleuette Low,* DK engineer, 1951, Germany; SS *Tucon Victory,* Jr. engineer and 2nd engineer, 1951, India.

1951-1953 worked Bethlehem Steel. Shipped Baltimore as trial delivery engineer. 1953-1955 U.S. Army-101st Airborne.

1955-1961 worked for Foster Engineering Co. as guarante engineer on all air craft carriers.

1962-1970 rebuilds foreign sports cars. 1971-1981 supervisor maintenance Otis Elevator Foundry, London, OH. Retired in 1981 in London, OH.

His memorable experiences includes WWII - up convoy at Halifax Canada before going to Europe 1944. After getting under way off the coast of Island, they were attacked by German U-boats (submarines). Blew up a tanker, an ammo ship and some freighters. The seamen that were picked up had to be taken back to Germany to a prison camp as they couldn't stop any ships to pick up anyone.

In LeHavre, France they were shot at by snipers, while unloading cargo, while anchored in harbor.

Today he is has a complete repair shop - rebuilding foreign sports cars at his home in London, OH.

JOSEPH OSTROFF, sailed as radio officer. Attended Sheepshead Bay, Gallups Island and Hoffman Island.

CAPTAIN PAIGE, See John Hird.

RICHARD E. PALACIOS, was born May 12, 1928 in Rochester, NY. Joined the Merchant Marine U.S. Maritime Service 1944, Sheepshead Bay. Served on the *Carl B. Eielson* (liberty) as fireman in Atlantic, Mediterranean, Casablanca.

His memorable experience includes his 17th birthday in Naples. Served four years in U.S. Army 1950-1951, Korea. Graduated Purdue University, 1957. Married and has one child. He is a public school teacher after 34 years.

JOSEPH F. PARKES, was born May 1, 1925 in Philadelphia, PA. Joined Merchant Marine Service in 1942 ships sailed: SS *Abner Nash,* liberty 1942-1943, messman; SS *Mills Spring,* T-2, October 1943, OS; SS *Spotslyvania,* T-2, December, 1943, OS.

Authorized the following decorations for U.S. Merchant Marine service: Merchant Marine Emblem, Atlantic War Zone Bar, Mediterranean Middle East War Zone Bar, Meritorious Service Medal, Victory Medal, Honorable Service Button and Presidential Testimonial Letter.

His memorable experience includes crossing the Pacific in hurricane like weather, landing British Marines and cargo on July 10, 1943 at Augusta Bay, Sicily.

Joined the United States Marine Corps in 1944 through 1950. Joined Federal Service in May of 1950. Retired in 1980 from U.S. Customs Service as district director of Patrol Division for the Port of San Juan, Puerto Rico. Member of U.S. Merchant Marine Veterans of WWII. He resides in Lake Mary, FL with wife Cielo.

JOHN VERNE PARKS, was born April 7, 1926 in San Raphael, CA. He joined the Merchant Marine May 29, 1943 in San Pedro, CA. Served on the *John S. Casement,* o.s.; *Ben B. Lindsey,* o.s.; *Cape Saunders,* A.B.; *Lyman Beecher,* A.B. Stationed in New Zealand, India, Ceylon, Arabia, Dutch E. Indies, Italy, Holland, Gibraltar, Hawaii, Egypt, Australia, New Guinea, Africa, Spain, Tasmania, Algeria, Tunisia, and Morocco.

His memorable experience includes receiving the Atlantic War Zone Bars, Pacific War Zone Bar, Mediterranean Middle East War Zone Bar.

Joined the Merchant Marine at age 17 and had traveled around the world three times before his 19th birthday.

Married and has one son. He retired Aug. 3, 1945 and is still traveling.

EVERETT C. PARRIS, was born July 3, 1925, in Elk Mountain, NC, graduated age 17, French Broad School, Alexander, NC. Worked as TAC welder, Newport News Shipbuilding and Drydock Co. for six months. Joined Merchant Marines July 1943 age 18. Basic training at Hoffman Island, NY, plus Cook and Baker School.

Ships sailed: *Lawton B. Evans* (3rd cook), liberty ship, 1943, Mediterranean; *Winding Gulf,* (OS), 1944, Atlantic; *Cartago* (OS), 1944, Atlantic; *Cornelius Harnett* (AB), 1944, Pacific; *Charles J. Folger* (AB), 1945, Pacific; *Eugene Field* (deck engineer), 1945, Atlantic.

Discharged from Merchant Marine 1946.

Trained as printer in Asheville, NC. Worked as printer, *Greenville News,* SC and *Charlotte Observer,* NC. Moved to Arlington, VA in 1949. Worked at *Evening Star* Newspaper for 18 years. Worked for the government printing office from 1967 to retirement in 1989. Resides with wife, Barbara in Fairfax, VA. Has two sons, Gregory and Kevin and daughter, Deborah; six grandchildren.

FRANK J. PARRIS, JR., was a student on the SS *John W. Brown,* from 1953-1956, engine room. He graduated June 25, 1956.

He resides in Bellmawr, NJ.

J.W. PEARSON, began his sea-going career several years prior to World War II as an ordinary seaman (OS) aboard a number of cargo ships and tankers, the first being the SS *Jean.* The first photograph is of Pearson at the age of 22 as an able seaman (AB) painting gray camouflage aboard the SS *Exmouth* while at sea en-route from Capetown to Colombo on Pearl Harbor day - Dec. 7, 1941. They carried as part of their cargo, a deck load of P-40 airplanes to Rangoon, Burma for the AVG. Homeward bound, among their the freight was 2,000 monkeys from Calcutta to Boston - voyage of 68 days.

He spent the entire war years as a deck officer aboard the liberty ships *Lew Wallace, John Whiteaker, Nathan B. Forrest* and the *Thomas Eakins.* On Dec. 7, 1945 he received his license as master and shortly became master of the SS *Thomas Eakins* and a number of Lykes Lines vessels, the last being the SS *Charles Lykes.*

In 1958 he left the SS *Charles Lykes* to become a pilot in the Port of Houston. After 30 years as pilot of approximately 8,000 ships, he retired to his ranch near Yoakum, TX.

Having held a aircraft pilot license for more than 40 years, he still enjoys flying at the age of 73 is in the process of rebuilding a PT-17 (Steaman). Who says you have to sit in a rocking chair when you retired?

NILS L. (WHITEY) PEARSON, was born Oct. 25, 1917, Bronx, NY. Joined U.S. Navy Nov. 9, 1937, training at Newport, Rhode Island. Assigned to USS *Savannah,* a new light cruiser. Made coxswain, assigned to #3 motor launch. During tour of service, went to the South Pacific March 1941, an to Australia and New Zealand. The ship was then assigned convoy duty in the North Atlantic, from Agenda, Newfoundland to Land's End, England, to the Azores, then to Bermuda for R&R, back north to pick up another convoy to England. Honorably discharged Nov. 10, 1941.

Employed at Brooklyn Navy Yard as rigger/diver, first diver to go down to inspect the SS *Normandy* after she caught fire and rolled over at the pier. Signed on as A.B. with Moran Towing and Transportation Company, on the *Agnes Moran,* coast-wise out of New York City. Shipped out to the Pacific on a liberty, SS *Edmund Randolph* (boatswain) February 1943, to November 19, liberty ships, SS *Ring Lardner* (boatswain) January, 1944 to October, 1944; tanker, SS *Baldhill* (A.B.) November, 1944 to December, 1944; tanker S.S. *Bear Paw* (maintenance A.B.) January, 1945 to March 1945; tanker SS *Pequot Hill (*boatswain) April 1945 to November 1945, charged with mutiny on this vessel, cleared and paid off as acting chief mate.

Settled in Hawthorne, CA, with wife, Mary, and daughter, Karen. Employed at General Petroleum Corporation, at the Mobil Oil refinery at Torrance, CA. Relocated at Big Bear City, CA, where a chinchilla ranch was established; developed a chinchilla pelt marketing organization, served as international president; elected director of a newly formed public agency, Big Bear City Community Services District, serving three four-year terms, also served one year as president; currently serving as president of The Farm Mutual Water Company, at Lake Elsinore, CA.

Active since 1989 in restoration of S.S. *Lane Victory,* a National Historic Landmark, being restored by the U.S. Merchant Marine Veterans WWII, in San Pedro, CA.

Nils and his wife, Mary, celebrated their 50th anniversary in 1991.

JAMES CLAY PECKHAM, was born Aug. 2, 1916, Lufkin, TX. Married Angie Fay Whalin, Oct. 30, 1936, two sons, James Henry, who made one Merchant Marine trip with his father, and Thomas Jan, a pilot of executive plane for an oil company in Arabia.

Sailed on tanker, S.S. *Red Canyon* (pumpman), April 1945, out of San Pedro, CA, to South Pacific, Guam, Manila. Was in Philippines when WWII ended. Sailed other vessels during Korean War; was in De Nang and Battle of TET, Vietnam. Worked up from pumpman to chief engineer before retiring in 1977, due to a heart attack at sea.

Employed as engineer during construction of the Stardust Hotel in Las Vegas, Nevada, 1953 and 1954.

Active, Adventure Club of Los Angeles and Sons of the American Revolution, and hobbies as health permits.

Since 1989, a volunteer for the restoration of the SS *Lane Victory,* a National Historic Landmark, being restored by the U.S. Merchant Marine Veterans of WWII in San Pedro, CA. Also active in Sun City Chapter of MMVWWII as organizer; wife, Angie, served as Commodore of the group.

James and Angie now reside in Quail Valley, CA. *Submitted by James C. Peckham*

ARTHUR S. PETERSON, sailed as fireman, oiler, wiper, 3rd assistant engineer during WWII. Has Merchant Marine Emblem, Atlantic, Mediterranean, Middle East War Zone Bars and Combat Bar. Attended USMSTS at St. Petersburg, FL and New London, CT.

He is married to Katherine and is a member of AMMV JWB Chapter. They reside in Baltimore, MD.

DAVID H. PETERSON, was born Nov. 11, 1927, Milwaukee, WI. Enlisted in U.S. Army, Jan. 31, 1949, Danville, IL.

Completed basic training at Camp Breckenridge, KY, May 1949, was assigned to Camp Younghans, Japan, with the Service Btry., 49th FA Bn., 7th Inf. Div.

Landed at Inchon, Korea, September 1950, making an amphibious landing on the East Coast of Korea at Iwon, pushed north to the Yalu River. He later was evacuated from Hungnam, North Korea, with his unit. Attaining rank of sergeant, ammunition supply specialist, he was awarded the Army Commendation Medal, Korean Service Medal with five Battle Stars, and returned to U.S. in November 1951. Discharged at Ft. Hamilton, NY, May 1955.

Retiring from Rockwell International, Space Division, Houston, 1989, David resides in Hitchcock, TX, with his wife Dorothy.

He is a member of a number of patriotic organizations, and of the 7th Infantry Division Association.

LOUIS ERICK PETERSON, was born April 2, 1913, at Bellingham, WA. First went to sea in Merchant Marine, 1932 (engine department).

Attended hydro-electric school at Seattle, WA in 1937 and worked on shore until return to Merchant Marine in 1940 as licensed engineer.

Assigned to various vessels carrying general cargos, including military supplies for the Adak Island landings and the Attu Island operation in 1942-1943.

Completed U.S. maritime turbo-electric training in 1944, prior to receiving chief engineer assignments.

Subsequently assigned to the SS *Mariscal Sucre*, which became involved in South Pacific convoys to the Marshal Islands, Saipan and Tinian. And finally in the Okinawa invasion in 1945.

After the end of WWII, continued working steadily with the Merchant Marine as port engineer and chief engineer, until retirement in 1975.

Married to Marie and has son Lee and daughter Marlene. He is a farmer part-time.

LYLE J. PHILBRICK, was born in Clyde, KS on April 6, 1924. Graduated from high school in Clyde on May 27, 1943. He joined Maritime Service at Sheepshead Bay on Feb. 22, 1944 at the age of 19. He took engine room training.

The first assigned ship was the *Stephen W. Kearney*, which went to ETO, did ferrying and waited for D Day at Omaha Beach head. He then returned to Kansas after the invasion. The second ship was the *John Hatherone*. After the war with Germany was over, he was discharged from service in New York on May 31, 1945.

He returned to Kansas where he retired from the insurance business in 1986.

Lyle is presently vice president of U.S. Merchant Marine Veterans World War II, Wichita, KS.

ALEX M. PHILLIAN, was born Oct. 27, 1917 in Hartford, CT. At age five, family moved to Paterson, NJ. Educated in Paterson Public Schools.

Worked for Dept. of Agriculture on tree preservation and later with New Jersey Bell Telephone Company as lineman and repairman.

Entered Sheepshead Bay Training Station in March 1944. Trained at Hoffman Island Radio School and graduated as warrant radio electrician.

First run was to Murmansk, Russia in convoy aboard SS *Caesar Rodney*. Aided in transporting Norwegian refugees to Scotland. Next assignment was aboard SS *Jean Baptiste Le Moyne* — a liberty tanker assigned to refueling escort ships in convoy. Runs included Italy, Palestine (visited Holy Land), Malta and Gibralter, where they walked to the top of the rock with British Buddies on VE Day.

Then on to Panama, Aruba, Curacao and Hawaii. Returned after VJ Day through Panama and on to Norfolk, VA.

Left the ship and the sea in November 1945. Returned home to work with telephone. Put a daughter and two sons through college.

Active in union work and social services. Retired in 1982 with 42 years of service.

Presently treasurer of County Labor Council.

Reside in West Paterson, NJ with wife Victoria.

On Dec. 8, 1992, received Medal of Gratitude from the Russian government in Washington, DC.

CAPTAIN CLAUDE D. PHILLIPS, was born June 24, 1923, Mayport, Duval, FL. Completed high school. Sea career began as galley boy on the U.S. Army Corps of Engineers seagoing dredge SS *San Pablo*, Aug. 11, 1941 through Jan. 16, 1942. Thereafter sailed continuously on gasoline tankers throughout WWII.

Service awards received were Atlantic War Zone Bar, Mediterranean Middle East War Zone Bar, Pacific War Zone Bar, Merchant Marine Defense Bar, and the Merchant Marine Combat Bar.

Held commissions in the U.S. Maritime Commission and the USNR. Came up "through the Hawse Pipe". First license issued by U.S. Dept. of Commerce, Steamboat Inspection Service, April 1944. Obtained Unlimited Masters License, Oceans, in October 1947, with endorsements as first class pilot on various rivers and harbors of the U.S. Gulf and Atlantic coasts.

Achieved first command as master, SS *Pan Florida*, January 1948. Subsequently sailed on various vessels of the Pan American Petroleum and Transport Company Fleet (American Oil Company) until promoted to port captain, August 1954. Assigned to New York office until 1970 and held various positions in fleet management. Served as docking pilot/mooring master at numerous offshore moorings, and at terminals in Long Island Sound, New York/New Jersey Harbor, and Chesapeake Bay including Baltimore.

Attended U.S. Naval Fire Fighting School, Philadelphia, and subsequently organized/conducted shipboard/shoreside tanker fire fighting training programs for the benefit of crews, terminal personnel, harbor and port authorities at ports on the east coast from Portland, ME to Wilmington, NC. Attended Fairleigh Dickinson University evening school, Madison, NJ campus working towards a BS in business. Program not completed due to increased travel requirements of job.

June 1970 transferred to Amoco Corporate Headquarters, Chicago, IL as vice president. Fleet included some 30 vessels ranging in size from tugs, barges, coastal product tankers and crude oil carriers from 80mdwt to VLCC<s of 280mdwt. Transported crude oil, refined petroleum products, chemicals, dry bulk cargo (grain and coal etc.) as required by affiliated companies, and on the open international charter market.

Retired in 1985 as president and CEO of Amoco Transport Co. Responsible for long range planning and development including new construction, purchase and sale, and chartering. Also administration, operations, maintenance and repair.

During shoreside tenure was actively involved in numerous U.S. and International Trade Associations, Professional organizations, and Maritime Safety (regulatory and advisory) groups and bodies, including: the Executive Committee, Oil Companies International Marine Forum, (OCIMF); Crystal; board of directors, International Tanker Owners Association, (TOVALOP); board of trustees, United Seamens Service; American Institute of Merchant Shipping, (AIMS); Insurance Committee, London Steamship Mutual Insurance Association; London; board of directors, Tanker Service Committee; American Petroleum Institute; Society of Naval Architects and Marine Engineers; board of managers, American Bureau of Shipping; life member and president (1963) Marine Square Club; life member (#63-L) Council of American Master Mariners; life member, Marine Society of the City of New York; and member, Federation of American Controlled Shipping, (FACS).

On Oct. 22, 1983, received the Distinguished Service Citation of the Robert L. Hague Post, American Legion, for "Outstanding Service to Country and the American Maritime Industry" at the Legions 43 Annual Guard of Honor Ball, Waldorf Astoria Hotel, New York City.

Current activities and memberships include: The Propeller Club; Charter Life Member, U.S. Merchant Marine Veterans of WWII; Heckscher Drive Community Club; various masonic bodies and Morocco Temple A.A.O.N.M.S.; life member, Beaches Area Historical Society; Member, American Bureau of Shipping; chairman of the board and president, Jacksonville Maritime Museum Society, and the Mayport Presbyterian Church. Last license was unlimited master, Oceans, Issue #8-11, issued by U.S. Coast Guard, New York, July 1, 1983, (expired July 1988).

Claude is married to Clara Elizabeth Ogilivie. Together they have five children and eight grandchildren. They are enjoying retirement on the banks of the beautiful St. Johns River, Jacksonville, FL about a mile from the Atlantic Ocean. There's fishing and all of the usual water activities, including observing the steady flow of passing ships, commercial and pleasure craft, and reminiscing about old times and good friends.

MARVIN LAVERNE PHILP, (PHIL), was born March 19, 1927. Joined Merchant Marine in 1944. Trained at Sheepshead Bay, Brooklyn, NY and Lake Ponchartrain, LA.

Ships sailed: *Tugsatoco* (wiper) 1945, Gulf of Mexico; *A.S. Hansen* (wiper) tanker, 1945, Gulf of Mexico, *Esso Aruba* (wiper) tanker 1945. Six trips to Aruba plus two trips to Panama. Sub chased them into Guantanamo, Cuba-waited for convoy to New York.

Esso *Raleigh* (fireman/wt) tanker, 1945-1946, Aruba, Panama; *Wm. Tilghman* (fireman/wt) liberty, 1946, Cardiff, Wales; Bristol, England, and Lisbon, Portugal; *Emilia* (fireman and oiler/wt) Hog Islander 1946-1946, Brazil. British Guyana-Trinidad, Hilton (oiler) 1947 Cuba.

November 1947 left Hilton to buy bar and restaurant in Ft. Johnson, NY.

Married Rosemary Partridge in 1949. Two sons went into school photography business in Syracuse, NY in 1960 until retirement in 1986. Joined the Oswego Maritime Foundation and is helping build and 85 ft. tall ship in Oswego, NY.

WARREN A. PHILP, was born Aug. 13, 1928. Joined the Merchant Marines on his 16th birthday in 1944. Trained at Sheepshead Bay, Brooklyn, NY and Lake Ponchartrain, LA.

Ships sailed: *A.S. Hansen* (wiper) tanker, 1945 Gulf of Mexico; *Esso Aruba* (wiper) tanker 1945, Aruba, Caribbean, *Esso Utica* (fireman/wt.) tanker 1945, Pacific, Manila; *Eleazar Wheelock* (fireman/wt) liberty 1945, Le Havre France and Antwerp, Belgium; *Josiah Bartlett* (oiler), liberty 1946, London, England and Genoa, Italy. Signed off the *Bartlett* on Aug. 20, 1946. Went into bar and restaurant business in 1947 in Ft. Johnson, NY.

Married Peggy Lindburg in 1950. They have one daughter.

Drafted and served in Korea from 1951 to 1953 with the 187th Abn. as a paratrooper and received the Purple Heart. Went to work at General Electric Co. in Schenectady, NY until his death of cancer on March 30, 1983 at age 54.

GLENN A. PHINNEY, nephew of Geoff Fairfax, graduate of California Maritime Academy, Vallejo, CA, 1961, engineer. Born Oct. 7, 1940 in Oakland, CA. Grew up in Vallejo, CA. First job after graduation from CMA, "Cynthia Olsen", beer cargo to Hawaii. Sea duty, various ships through MEBA, received 2nd engineer license. 1st? Left Merchant Service in 1964 to attend San Francisco State, graduate business administration and accounting. Married 1965.

Has two daughters and one son. (Sean Phinney now beginning fourth year at USNA, Annapolis.)

Glenn now is CPA, owns business, Management Consulting, Controllership Services in Belmont, CA. Remarried 1983. Lives in San Mateo, CA. Avid '49er fan, serious student of wines, wine culture and wine production. *Submitted by Barbara Fairfax Phinney, sister of Geoffrey Fairfax, aunt of Christopher Fairfax, and mother of Glenn Phinney.*

JOHN E. PINKERTON, sailed during WWII. Member of AMMV JWB Chapter.

John resides in Severn, MD.

EDWARD PLEULER, JR., graduated from Gallups Island. Sailed as radio officer on board the SS *Alcoa Banner* in 1942 on Russian Run (VWOA News Letter, Winter 1992).

KEITH MARSHALL POORE, sailed as F/W, oiler, 3rd assistant engineer, acting 2nd and first assistant engineer. Sailed during WWII. Attended Hoffman Island basic training and Ft. Trumbull, USMS Officers School.

Married to Phyllis. He is a member of AMMV JWB Chapter. Keith resides in Rockville, MD.

WARREN PORTER, attended USMSTS at St. Petersburg. Served in engineer department as oiler, 3rd assistant engineer and 2nd assistant engineer from 1945-1950.

Warren resides in Oceanview, DE.

ROBERT F. PRATT, was born Sept. 17, 1926 in Cuyahoga Falls, OH. First went to sea in May 1944 aboard the lumber schooner *Charles L. Wheeler, Jr.* (293 feet long, built in 1918) as fireman transporting war supplies out to the Aleutian Islands.

Served as 3rd assistant engineer aboard the liberty ship *Sylvester Pattie* carrying bulk wheat to China in October 1945. Also aboard were ten passengers bound for Shanghai (these were the first passengers carried to China after the war). The ship and crew were then loaned to the Chinese for nine months to haul coal from North China to Tsingtao, Shanghai and Hong Kong. Served three years (1948-1951) on the *Sea Splendor* an orion steamship Co. C-2 out of New York as second assistant engineer.

Two years in U.S. Army in Korea (1952-1954). Received a BSME degree from the UN of Washington in 1958 and spent the next 30 years working for General Electric Co. building nuclear power plants.

Retired in April 1989 to Brookings, OR where he built his own retirement home on top of a mountain overlooking the Pacific Ocean. He and his wife enjoy visiting with their seven children and five grandchildren who are located in the San Francisco Bay area. The wonderlust is still present however, and he and his wife are often found aboard freighters (as passengers) taking voyages to all parts of the world.

EARL H. PREECE, resides in Annapolis, MD and is a member of AMMV JWB Chapter.

WILLIAM N. PRESTON, JR., sailed as master during Desert Storm and Desert Sortie. Attended Suny Maritime College.

He is married to Teresa and they reside in Arlington, VA. William is a member of AMMV JWB Chapter.

THOMAS B. PUCKETT, sailed as 2nd mate during WWII. Has Atlantic, Mediterranean Middle East War Zone Bars and Combat Bars. Attended U.S. Merchant Marine Academy, 1943.

He is married to Doris and they reside in Elkridge, MD. He is also a member of AMMV JWB Chapter.

ROBERT C. PUIG, was born April 18, 1924 in Alameda, CA. He joined the Merchant Marine Oct. 26, 1942 in San Francisco.

Served on the SS *Gabriel Franchere*, liberty, ordinary seaman, New Caledonia; SS *Golden West*, CII cargo, able seaman, various South Pacific Islands; SS *Cape Junction*, CI cargo, able seaman, various South Pacific Islands; SS *Golden West*, CII cargo, able seaman, Philippine Islands.

His memorable experience includes being chased into Jacksonville, FL by a German submarine wolf pack.

He has been purchasing director for Catholic School Dept. in San Francisco for 20 years. Married 39 years and has three sons, four grandchildren, three girls and one boy. Operations manager impact Southern California. Still going strong.

ROGER H. PUTNAM, was born June 29, 1924, in Oakland, CA. Graduated from high school at Tulare Union in 1942. Accepted for training as a midshipman in the California Maritime Academy in January 1943. Graduated as a third mate in 1944. First ship as third mate was the *William R. Gibson*, U.S. Army Transport Service. Next was the C-2 troopship, SS *Young America*. After the war in 1946, Roger sailed on the liberty ship, *George C. Perkins*, to Europe, South America and Canada carrying United Nations relief cargoes.

After completing enough sea time for a continuous service discharge, Roger attended college at the University of California, Santa Barbara and received a BA degree in 1951. Graduate school was next at San Jose State and Fresno State, and then teaching in Visalia, CA. The seven years prior to retirement in 1981, were as the head counselor in junior high school. Roger is now retired and living in Tulare, CA.

JOHN M. QUAGLIANO, was born Jan. 1, 1921 on Staten Island, NY. Joined Merchant marine in January 1942 in New York.

Ships sailed: Hawaiian Shipper, SS *Ballot;* Liberty ships, SS *Tabitha Brown*, SS *John McLoughlin*, SS *John Steele,* and *R.C. Brennan.*

He was an engine room worker and belonged to the Marine firemen, oilers, wipers, and water tenders union. (M.F.O.W.W.)

John received the Merchant Marine Combat Bar (with stars) as well as the Atlantic, Pacific, Mediterranean Middle Eastern War Zone Bars and a Presidential Testimonial Letter from President Harry S. Truman. He also received a Commemorative Medal from the Russian government for his service on Allied convoys to Murmansk, Russia (SS *Ballot* 1942-1943). He served through-out WWII and received a honorable discharge for his service.

In 1954 he went to work for the city of New York onboard tug boats as oiler in 1968. He transferred to the Staten Island Ferry retiring in 1978.

John was a native Staten Islander and enjoyed his family and traveling with his wife Jennie of 44 years.

John passed away Nov. 7, 1992. He will be missed by his family, but never forgotten. *Submitted by John M. Quagliano, Jr. U.S. Merchant Marine Deck Officer*

CHARLES QUINN, (See John Hird), gunnery officer.

GERALD F. QUINLAN, was born Oct. 13, 1916 in San Francisco. Joined the Merchant Marine March 1939 in San Francisco.

Served on SS *President Coolidge*, purser, Pacific; MV *Fort Royal,* purser, Atlantic; SS *President Grant*, purser, Pacific.

His memorable experience includes torpedoed and sunk SS *Walter Camp*, January 1944.

Employed with American President Steamship Lines.

Married and retired Jan. 30, 1980.

HENRY G. QUIRK, was born in Brighton, MA, Sept. 7, 1926. At age 16 on Sept. 17, entered U.S. Maritime Service, Sheepshead Bay, Brooklyn, Manhattan Beach, NY. Finished training on SS *American Engineer*, Baltimore, MD until March 1943. Assigned to first ship SS *Michigan* and torpedoed and sunk 30 miles off Oran North Africa April 20, 1943. Repatriated on SS *Delnorte* after 16 days Oran. New York, 22 days. No discharge or pay for that period of time. Next ship same captain, a coincidence, SS *John McLaughlin,* England and Scotland. SS *Fisher Ames,* England and Scotland, SS *Peter Donahue,* Egypt and Persian Gulf. Damaged in Mediterranean storm. Wired and welded together at Aden. SS *Charles Robinson.*

Invasion of France, St. Lo Omaha Beach. SS *Edward L. Logan,* England. SS *Bienville,* C-2, England and France.

Returned seasoned troops and German prisoners. SS *Colin P. Kelley Jr.* June 4, 1945. Hit by German acoustic mine, English Channel enroute Belgium. Abandoned except for skeleton crew. Sank in tow along side dock, scrapped in England. Repatriated on *William Patterson* to New York. Ratings - O.S., A.B., quartermaster, boatswain.

1943 until November 1968 sailed steady as possible. Self-employed, owned and operated shoe repair shops until 1989. Member of Wood Carvers Association. Home and acre of lawn keeps his retirement time fulfilled.

JOSEPH B. RAAB, resides in Oxon Hills, MD and is a member of AMMV JWB Chapter, Membership Committee chairman.

ELMER (AL) R. RAANES, was born July 6, 1927 in San Francisco, CA. Joined the Sailors Union of the Pacific. In 1944 at the age of 16 went to sea as a ordinary seaman aboard the SS *James King*. Shuttled up and down the New Guinea coast carrying military supplies. Eventually joining the convoy with MacArthur for the invasion of Leyte Gulf, PI, carrying gas, oil and ammo. While in Palau Islands as a stand by ship, working on the Cross Tree of the Mizzen Mast he got sunstroke and fell to deck. Necessitating his removal to the hospital ship USS *Hope* becoming the first official patient of that ship. After nine months of recuperation went back to sea as a able bodied seaman on various ships.

Also went back to sea during the Korean War. In 1947 became the youngest license charter boat skipper in the San Francisco bay area. For the last 35 years has been an appliance and refrigeration technician in Union City, CA.

ANTHONY "TONY" RADSPIELER, sailed as radio officer during WWII. Served as 2nd radio officer on SS *San Francisco M. Quinones* from Dec. 20, 1944 to April 23, 1945 and chief radio officer on SS *Wild Wave* from June 9, 1945 to Aug. 15, 1945. Has USCG discharge and DD-214. Attended Gallups Island Radio School (R-28) and Sheepshead Bay, radar training. Employed as economist by Bureau of the Census, U.S. Department of Commerce, Washington, D.C. Has Atlantic and Pacific War Zone Bars and Philippine Liberation (with stars) and Merchant Marine Emblem.

Is a plank owner of the American Merchant Mariners' Memorial. He is married to Sandra and he is also a member of AMMV JWB Chapter. They reside in Columbia, MD.

HORACE RAINEY, JR., served on liberties during WWII. He resides in Columbia, TN.

CHESTER M. RAKOWSKI, attended Sheepshead Bay July, August and September of 1944. Sailed as utility messman and BR utility during WWII. Served on the SS *John W. Meldrum* and SS *Peter Donahue*. Awarded Atlantic, Pacific and Mediterranean-Middle East War Zone Bars.

His next of kin is his son Gary. Chester is a member of AMMV JWB Chapter. He resides in Baltimore, MD.

LOUIE S. RAMEY, graduated from War Shipping Administration (WSA) United States Maritime Service Training Station at Fort Trumbull, New London, CT on Sept. 18, 1942. This was graduation exercise of the third class of prospective licensed officers.

Awarded the Pacific, Atlantic, Mediterranean Middle East War Zone Bars, the Merchant Marine Defense and the Merchant Marine Combat Bars, and the Vietnam Service Bar.

Louie is a member of AMMV JWB Chapter and resides in Baltimore, MD.

V. NOBLE REDMON, JR., was born Dec. 21, 1926 in East St. Louis, IL. Joined Merchant Marine in San Francisco, CA. Received papers in July 1945. Sponsor: S.U.P. Sailed on SS *Jefferson City Victory* as an ordinary seaman. Ships sailed alone, no convoy as they were carrying high explosives to Saipan, Mariannas Islands for the 20th Air Force. July to September 1945.

His second trip was on the SS *Homer Lea* a liberty ship. He got a waiver from ordinary seaman to wiper, but signed on as an oiler. Later he made deck engineer. On this trip, October 1945 to September 1946 they sailed to Manila, PI, Finchshafen, New Guinea, back to Manila, Cebu, Manila again. From Manila they then sailed to Tokyo, Japan. From Tokyo to Sasebo and then to Yokohama, Japan, back to Tokyo and then set sail for Port Hueneme, CA. They then sailed to Portland, OR. He signed off the ship in Portland.

He made only these two trips to sea. In fact he wanted to go to sea again but there was not getting a ship at that time. He returned to Illinois, became a machinist, later a tool and die maker. Subsequently he got into aircraft electronics, this came about as a result of his hobby of amateur radio. In the aircraft industry he ultimately became an aircraft flight inspector doing first flight check-out on new jet fighter aircraft that had never been flown before.

In September 1957 he went into the commercial television broadcasting industry as an engineer. Twenty-three years later in the same television station he became the chief engineer. At this time, 35 years after joining the station he holds the position of director of technical maintenance and special projects.

He was 65 years old last December and could have retired, however, he opted to stay one more year. He plans to retired at the end of 1992.

He married Rose L. Grahmann of East St. Louis, IL, Nov. 24, 1954. They have had a good life together all these years, graced with a son and a daughter, V Noble III in 1957 and Ruth Ann in 1962. They have a granddaughter Bridget Katherine Redmon and a grandson V. Noble Redmon IV.

In a few short months he will be retired.

In retirement he hopes to pursue his favorite hobbies of amateur radio, computers and astronomy, in addition to spending time with his family. He hopes to make a couple of trips per year to the SS *Lane Victory*, as he and his wife are charter life members of the U.S. Merchant Marine Veterans of WWII. Hobbies of day's gone by, were boating on the Mississippi River and flying an airplane that he and his wife restored.

CHARLES N. REIBLE, was born Aug. 29, 1924 in Madison, WI. He joined Merchant Marine, Maritime Academy (Sheepshead Bay, NY) 1943.

Served on *Western Queen*, OS, Atlantic; *John Langdon*, A.B., Atlantic-Murmansk; *Oldham*, A.B.-bosn, Atlantic; *Bulkfuel*, A.B., Atlantic; *Robert Luckenbach*, A.B., Atlantic; *Maria Mitchell*, bosn, Pacific; *James J. Pettigrew*, A.B., Atlantic, SS *Carribean*, DK maintenance, Atlantic.

His memorable experience includes trip to Murmansk.

Married and has two children. He retired March 2, 1946.

GEORGE H. REID, was born May 23, 1924 in Birmingham, AL. He began sailing full-time aboard American flag vessels in December 1942, after sailing on foreign flag freighters during the Summers of 1940 and 1941.

Sailed as OS and AB from December 1942 to March 1944 aboard liberty ships *Nicholas Gilman*, *Theodoric Bland*, *William H. Wilmer* and *Nathanial Bacon*. Also sailed as AB aboard the T2 tanker *Lake George* during this time.

Received his third mates license and commission in the Maritime Service at the USMS Officer's Training Service at Ft. Trumbull, New London, CT in 1944. He served as second mate aboard the V-4 tug *Sombrero Key* and as third mate aboard the liberty ships *Arlie Clark* and *George Whitefield* until the end of World War II. By this time he had served in all of the war zones and had seen action in the North Atlantic, European and North African area.

He remained active as a Merchant Marine officer and harbor pilot, sailing in all grades until 1986. He has continued active as a Marine consultant and surveyor as president of his own company, Harrison Reid and Associates, Inc. He is the author of *Primer of Towing*, *Boatmen's Guide to Light Salvage, Shiphandling with Tugs,* and the revised edition of *Primer of Towing*.

He is presently the secretary of the Merchant Marine Veterans of World War II, Space Coast Branch. *Submitted by George H. Reid.*

LEE H. REYNOLDS, was born July 4, 1927 in Philadelphia, PA. Went to sea at age 17 and sailed to October 1950. Started as a messman on the SS *W.W. Mills,* a coastal tanker and rose to chief electrician in 1948 sailing on C-2's, knot ships and C-4's. His last ship, the SS *Siboney* (1948-1950), C-2, New York, Cuba-Haiti and Jamaica, a refrig. ship, served as chief elect. Worked as electrician for the New York City Transit System for five years, then 26 years in law enforcement, retiring as detective-sergeant NYCPD. Present occupation, New York City Marshal.

He found his years at sea to be the most rewarding, educational period of his life. In subsequent years after gaining B.S. and M.A. degrees this still holds. "Lets all fight to keep a growing U.S. Merchant Marine, so that other Americans can experience the Merchant Mariners life at sea. The U.S. Merchant Marines is a vital asset in war and peace."

RAYMOND C. (ROCKY) RHODES, was born Dec. 19, 1924 in Daytona, VA. Ready to sail ordinary seaman after completing Sheepshead Bay training. Received appointment to Kings Point. As cadet-midshipman, sailed one voyage to England, one to Scotland. On return, five days out of Glasgow, in hurricane Jan. 21, 1944, the SS *Jane Long* started cracking in two. Returned to Liverpool with a destroyer escort. In dry dock for repair one month.

After graduating from Kings Point, sailed in Pacific as second mate on the SS *Louis Sloss* until August 1946. Visited Eniwetok, Guam, Saipan, Manus Island, Espiritu Santo, Noumea, Wellington, Shanghai, Saigon, Manila and Yokohama. Heard on radio in 1951? that the SS *Louis Sloss* was cracking in Pacific typhoon, but survived.

B.S. chemical engineering, M.S. statistics, Virginia Polytechnic Technic Institute. Quality assurance manager, Hercules Inc. (20 years), quality assurance specialist, environmental protection agency (18 years), currently president, Environmental Quality Assurance Management, Daleville, VA.

FRANK RICCI, AB-Deck Maintenance. Made several trips: Liberty, *Gilbert Stuart*, May 13, 1943-sailed around the world carrying general cargo; Liberty, *Mark Hopkins*, Oct. 1943-second trip around the world, cargo was bulk cement; Liberty, *Carl Schury*, July 10, 1944-to Alaska; *Hibbing Victory*, Aug. 24, 1944-sailed to the islands; SS *West Wind*, Oct. 16, 1944-sailed to the islands; *Daisy Gray*, 1945-sailed to Oregon carrying cargo of lumber; *Alhandbra Victory,* 1945, around the world; SS *West Wind*, Sept. 11, 1945-stopped at several islands near Hawaii; SS *Salinas*, Oct. 26, 1951-sailed to Canada.

EDW. G. RICHARDS, was born Nov. 30, 1915 in Southampton, England; raised in Hamburg, Germany and Antwerp, Belgium; migrated to the United States July 1925; moved from Hoboken, NJ to San Francisco, CA December 1929; graduated in 1934.

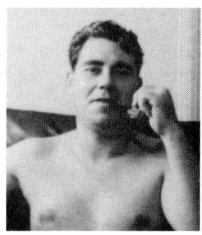 

His father was chief engineer on the SS *California* of the Panama Pacific Lines; in June of 1934 he first went to sea on the SS *California* from San Francisco to New York, then on the SS *Santa Rosa* on the Grace Line, New York to Valparaiso and return; later sailed U.S. Lines from New York to London; returned to West Coast in 1937 and sailed on oil reciprocating engine tankers.

In November 1941, he was sent as third assistant engineer for a new tanker, the SS *Charles S. Jones* of the Richfield Oil Company; sailed on the *Charles S. Jones* for most of the war until June 1934, mostly between the United States, Australia and the Persian Gulf, and on occasion, to South Africa and the Mediterranean; sailed on other tankers after June 1944, plus two trips on a liberty ship, the SS *Arthur P. Fairchild* to Europe.

Retired from the service in June 1948; at present he is retired and living in Mexico.

ARNOLD RIDOUT, see John Hird.

LOUIS RIZZO, is a member of AMMV JWB Chapter and resides in Baltimore, MD.

JOHN F. (JACK) RODGERS, III, entered the United States Maritime Service at Sheepshead Bay at age 16 attending Hoffman Island Radio School. Between 1945 and 1952 he served as radio officer aboard the *Sideling Hill, Francis Vigo, Fluor Spar, Nathaniel Alexander, Alcoa Voyager, Richard J. Hopkins, John LaFarge, George M. Bibb, Steelore, Ernest W. Gibson, Santore,* and *Henry Baldwin.*

The USMS commissioned him a lieutenant (j.g.). His awards include the Atlantic and Pacific War Zone Bars, Victory Medal, Presidential Testimonial Letter, Merchant Marine Emblem, Honorable Service Button, and National Defense Service Medal. Honorable discharges were received from the Armed Forces of the United States for his WWII Merchant Marine Service and Korean War Army Signal Corp service from 1952-1954.

Employed by the Bendix Corporation for 22 years he held positions in engineering, administration, and management. In 1977 Jack joined the faculty at Catonsville Community College and is an associate professor.

Governor Schaefer appointed him to the Maryland WWII Memorial Commission. Jack is seeking names and addresses of Maryland WWII Merchant Marine Veterans or their next of kin.

Jack and his wife, LaRue, live in Catonsville, MD. They have two daughters, Melanie and Valerie; and two grandchildren Matthew and Christine.

EARLE J. ROSSNEY, was born Dec. 14, 1927 in Dunkirk, NY. Completed training at Sheepshead Bay. Assigned to the USAT *Henry Gibbons;* made a number of trips to Marseilles and LeHavre. After the *Gibbons* was converted to carry war brides, made two trips to Belfast. Signed-on the *General Callan.* Transported troops and dependents to Leghorn, Italy and Bremerhaven, Germany.

Returned to Buffalo. Worked as a welder until drafted for the Korean "police action." Served 33 months finishing as operations sergeant for 10th Antiaircraft Group based in Seoul.

Returned to welding. Took advantage of GI Bill to earn a BA degree. Married to Peg Day in 1956 and still is. Moved to San Diego Summer of 1957. Completed BA and teaching credential requirements at San Diego State; later an MA from Long Beach State. Taught one year in Pasadena then 29 1/2 years of U.S. Government/Economics in Torrance, CA. Retired in January 1990; relocated to Temecula, CA March 1991.

He has two married daughters, two bachelor sons and no grandchildren.

JOHN DILLON ROUBIAN, was born Nov. 2, 1923 in Pasadena, CA. He entered U.S. Merchant Marine Cadet Basic School, Dec. 23, 1942 at San Mateo, CA.

Served on SS *E. J. Henry,* cadet midshipman, San Pedro, CA to New Caledonia, Australia, American Samoa; SS *George Crile,* 3rd mate, Pacific Islands (Marshall etc.); SS *Edgar W. Nye,* 2nd mate, Pacific Islands; SS *Benjamin Bonneville,* 2nd mate, Yokohama Bay, Japan.

His memorable experience includes first civilian merchant ship in Yokohama Bay after VJ Day. His mother's prayers kept him safe and he is very grateful to be alive.

Acquired chief mates license, self-employed trucking appliance technician.

Married to Rose and they have three married son and six grandchildren.

He worked for Sears Roebuck and Co. as telephone sales representative.

DARRELL F. ROUSH, Merchant Marine I.D. No. 4307-04354. Coast Guard I.D. No. Z-372101. He was born in Boulder, CO, July 17, 1925. Graduated South High School, Denver, CO, June 1943. Merchant Marine training, Catalina Island, July 1943-November 1943. Shipped out on tankers, cargo was aviation gas and oil, sometimes had airplanes on an added flight deck.

November 12, 1943 to Nov. 23, 1943, messman, SS *Mojave,* 221302, coastwise; Nov. 24, 1943 to Feb. 1, 1944, messman, SS *Mojave,* 221302, Fiji, Espirito Santos; April 14, 1944 to June 19, 1944, messman, *R.C. Stoner,* 24318, South Pacific Islands and New Zealand; July 23, 1944 to Aug. 18, 1944, galleyman, SS *Pennsylvania,* 215286, coastwise; Sept. 23, 1944 to Sept. 24, 1945, OS and AB, SS *Mobilight,* 243327, Australia, New Zealand, Tasmania, India, Ceylon (Sri Lanka), Iran, Iraq, Africa; Dec. 1, 1945 to Dec. 11, 1945, AB, SS *Syosset,* 247458, coastwise; Jan. 9, 1946 to April 4, 1946, AB, SS *Syosset,* 247458, Peru, Panama, Curacao.

Married Eddene Yeager, May 22, 1955. Owner and operator dry cleaning and laundry business in Denver, CO 1946 to 1961.

They moved to Camas, WA 1961. Owned charter fishing boats for about 15 years and work for James River Paper Company in Camas. Eddene works for Dr. Nevin, Camas dentist.

HENRY B. ROWLAND, was born Aug. 28, 1923 in Greenport, Long Island, NY. Graduated GHS 1941. Hoffman Island RDO Training School October 1944. World War II Shipboard service in Atlantic, Pacific, Mediterranean and after war, worked at coast stations SWL and KHK to earn college tuition.

Attended Rensselaer and Tri-State University. Graduated Tri-State with BS eng. in 1954. Employed as graduate E.E. the next 33 years including four years at MARAD (U.S. Maritime Administration, OSC, Washington, DC) as their engineer for Merchant Marine shipboard navigation and communications systems onboard all ongoing government subsidized commercial vessels under design and construction in this country.

Wartime experiences: The vessel he served on as radio operator was part of the last convoy to Murmansk during WWII. She was in collision on departure from that port and nearly sank before the crew was able to rig a collision mat below the waterline. They ended up having to remain in port for nine months after drydock facilities became icebound up there. While all this was happening in 1945 and early 1946, Russia cut off nearly all contacts between the West and in March 1946 the BBC announced the start of the Cold War and they realized they were caught behind the Iron Curtain. His transmitters were sealed and there was never a mail call. Their food and supplies ran out after months so their meals consisted of boiled rice every day for the next seven months.

When he left the engineering profession in 1987, he was fortunate enough to be accepted back into the shipboard fraternity, this time as an apprentice in the ROU program at their John G. Phillips (of Titanic fame) Maritime Electronics Training School at Panama City Beach, FL.

Last year he received their certificate for master radio electronics officer which as been very helpful in getting some really great shipboard jobs recently. He'll not retire.

He doesn't know why, but nothing has ever been as difficult to master as the studies at the Hoffman Island Radio School. Particularly what they had to cover for their 2nd class FCC license. He believes this says a lot for the teaching staff at Hoffman. These men remembered the Titanic and they were trained to handle the situation that he faced when he sent SOS.

JAMES M. RUCKER, was born May 18, 1926, Petersburg, VA. Trained at Sheepshead Bay and Hoffman Island Radio School. Sailed WWII in T2 tanker *Verendrye* (radio officer) to Pacific then around the world. Korean War in SS *Tainaron* and USNS Mission Loretto (radio officer) was with the merchant fleet that evacuated the X Corp from Wonsan/Hungnam area in December 1950 after the Chinese entered the war. Three voyages to Vietnam on victory ships in 1969.

Sailed continuous until 1970 then worked 16 years for Bethlehem Steel Corp., installing and maintaining

navigation and communication equipment on company ships. Retired, living in Virginia. He is company commander in Virginia State Militia.

ROBERT R. RUPPENDER, was born on June 5, 1923 in Cleveland, OH. Trained at Sheepshead Bay, NY in 1943. USAT *Fred C. Aimsworth* from Ingals Ship Building, Pascagoula, MS to South Pacific Islands and Australia. Then the liberty SS *W.A. Jones* to Cuba and London. Tug and Fire Boat in San Francisco Bay. *Gen. Geo. S. Simmons* to England and French coast invasion June 7, 1944. then the turboelectric tanker SS *Santa Maria Hills* to New Guinea. And finally the USAT *James Parker*.

Currently metallurgical engineer in aerospace in Van Nuys, CA. Married and has two children, and one grandchild. His hobby is sailing around California's Channel Islands.

JUDSON RUSS, was born June 6, 1925, WinterHaven, FL. Joined Merchant Marine 1943. Trained at Maritime Training School, St. Petersburg, FL.

Ships sailed: *Acadia*, 1943-1944, hospital ship - St. Mikiel, 1944; *Boon Island* (motor) 1944, SS *Malabar* 1944; SS *Caloria*, 1944, SS *William Asa Carter*, 1945; *John B. Gordon*, 1945, *Eugene Lykes*, 1945, *Richard J. Cleveland*, 1946; *Charles Bulfinch*, 1946.

Sailing as a wiper on board hospital ship SS *Acadia* from Charleston, SC to Oran, North Africa, stopping at Rock of Gibraltar for engine repairs. Sailing as wiper, fireman/watertender, or oiler from ports located, Gulf of Mexico and East Coast of the United States. The ships he sailed aboard introduced him to the waters of the Gulf of Mexico, Straits of Florida, North Atlantic Ocean, North Sea, Notre Dame Bay, Baltic Sea, Celtic Sea, English Channel, and the Mediterranean Sea.

He moved to Haines City, FL 1946. New and used furniture and appliance business 1946 to 1982. 1982 to present insurance agent for Capital Security Life Insurance Company living with wife Sue.

GEORGE S. (PAT) RYAN, was born Sept. 14, 1927 in Seattle, WA. Graduated Sequoia High School, Redwood City, CA and entered Merchant Marine in 1944. Trained at Catalina Island.

Ships sailed as FW/T or oiler: *St. Clair, John Lykes, Pierre Victory, Aquiprince, Santa Monica* and *A.C. Rubel* - coastwise tankers or Pacific. The *John Lykes* was a troop ship that sailed from Manila (May 1945) with women and children imprisoned at Santa Tomas during the war.

Graduated from Colorado School of Mines in 1953 and except for Army duty (1954-1956) worked in mineral exploration until 1979 when employed by U.S. Bureau of Mines and worked "Wilderness Studies" until retirement in 1990.

Presently residing in West Valley, UT with wife Elece (married 1946). Progeny: four daughters, Patrice, Laurel, Kay and Megan. Also has six grandchildren. Greatest achievement-donated 160 pints of blood.

THEODORE SADOWY, AMMV charter member JWB Chapter Oct. 14, 1989. He resides in Baltimore, MD.

CHARLES M. SALINA, was born Sept. 29, 1919 in Great Falls, MT. Graduated from high school and Gonzaga University, Spokane, WA. Electrical engineering BS. Began Merchant Marine service at Hoffman Island, NY as acting chief machinist (1943).

Ships sailed: SS *Warrior* (cargo ship) as junior engineer. (After that trip attended turbo-electric school, Schenectady, NY. Received his 3rd and 2nd engineering licenses and was acting first assistant on his last two ships). Tankers: SS *Opequon, Four Lakes, Aricharee, Somme* and *War Bonnett*.

All the tankers carried hi-test gasoline and they experienced some "close calls". Two tankers in their convoy were hit and went up in flames.

Medals received: Mediterranean Middle East War Zone Bar, Pacific War Zone Bar, Atlantic War Zone Bar, Merchant Marine Combat Bar.

Met Janet Roper Copp (1944) granddaughter of the late Jane Lord Roper, fondly known as "Mother Roper" of the Missing Seamen's Bureau which she founded, organized and headed in 1920 at the Seamen's Church Institute, 25 South Street, New York City. Married Janet Copp, December 1946.

Began his professional career with the General Electric Company, Schenectady, NY. Was director of utilities and telecommunications with Rockwell Company at the Hanford Nuclear Plant, Richland, Washington until he retired in 1984. He is still active in the engineering profession. Currently, he is chairman of the Washington State Board of Professional Engineers and Land Surveyors. He also is on the board of regents at Gonzaga University, Spokane, WA.

Celebrated their 45th wedding anniversary December 1991 with their two daughters, two sons, spouses and ten grandchildren.

ROBERT G. SAMPSON, attended USMSTS at Sheepshead Bay in 1944. Sailed during WWII as cook, baker, butcher, steward, chief, etc.

Awarded Atlantic, Pacific, Mediterranean-Middle East War Zone Bars, Combat Bar with stars, Victory Medal and citations. Has letter dated May 2, 1945, from War Shipping Administration (WSA) stating in part: "...whose seaman's certificates were lost when his ship went down, is a bona fide seaman and a survivor of a Marine disaster who was recently repatriated." Served two years in Army in Korea.

He is married and is a member of AMMV JWB Chapter. He resides in Annapolis, MD.

ROBERT B. SANFORD, resides in Annandale, VA and is a member of AMMV JWB Chapter.

V. LEE SAUNDERS, attended Chicago Institute of Technology. Skill as engineer and machinist. Sailed during WWII as chief electrician and refrigeration engineer. Ship was damaged. Awarded Atlantic and Mediterranean Middle East War Bars and Combat Bar. Has USCG discharge for USMM service and Army discharge for service on Army transport and hospital ships.

Married to Mary and they reside in Bowie, MD. He is a member of AMMV JWB Chapter.

CHARLES SCARPELLO, died Sept. 7, 1991. Graduated from the Merchant Marine Academy. Served aboard two ships that were torpedoed during WWII. He wrote an article for *The Sun* about his trip on a ship sunk in July 1942 when it was returning from Murmansk in a convoy that ran into a surfaced U-boat. His ship had suffered torpedo attacks, five days and nights of aerial attacks and frequently attacks in port before being sunk on the way home. He is survived by his wife Carmela and a daughter. Uniforms and other artifacts were donated.

He resides in Cockseyville, MD.

ED C. SCHADLER, was born Sept. 23, 1926 in Alexandria, KY. Graduated from high school Jan. 1, 1945. Joined Merchant Marine December 1944. He took his training at Sheepshead Bay in Brooklyn, NY. His section number was 33.

Ships sailed on: SS *Harry Bowen,* freighter, ordinary seaman, Atlantic; SS *Malay,* tanker, ordinary seaman, Atlantic; SS *Edward Livingston,* liberty ship, able seaman, Atlantic and Mediterranean; SS *Wendell L. Wilke,* liberty ship, able seaman, Atlantic and Mediterranean.

His memorable experience occurred while aboard the SS *Edward Livingston* at 2:00 a.m. it collided with a English freighter off the west coast of Italy.

Married and had five children. His wife and one son are now deceased. Ed retired Jan. 1, 1947.

Today he is in his 45th year as a State Farm insurance agent. He is in the Greater Cincinnati-Northern Kentucky area. The agency is one of the larger ones within the State Farm companies.

JOSEPH E. SCHALLOCK, was born Feb. 3, 1927 in New York City. He enlisted, age 17, at Sheepshead Bay, Brooklyn, NY. He graduated Dec. 23, 1944 and was then called to become a 90-day wonder.

His first ship, Dec. 23, 1944, was the Lillian Nordick. He served as 2d Class Deck Hand in the Atlantic and Europe. The last ship he served on (Jan. 13, 1948-Feb. 27, 1948) was the Santa Inez. Of the 12 ships he served on in four years, nine were liberty ships. His first ship was the first into Antwerp, Belgium after the Normandy invasion in June 1944. In 1944, his ship was part of a convoy of ten ships and three destroyers in the North Sea that were attacked by German P.T. Boats. His ship was one of the four that made it into Antwerp. They were on a shuttle run for three trips to Antwerp. Belgium and Bremon, Germany. Three days before they left port at Bremen, they were bombed by buzz bombs and V-2 bombs, setting them adrift when their pier was blown apart. He has other experiences he remembers well.

He is married to Mary Durham Schallock. He is now retired. He was a life underwriter with Mony (Mutual of New York).

CARL A. SCHARPF, was born Nov. 5, 1919. Carl graduated from the Baltimore Polytechnic Institute in 1936, and from the Johns Hopkins University in 1940. His first experiences at sea were as a wiper during summer vacations while studying mechanical engineering at Hopkins.

Shortly after Pearl Harbor, he left his job at Wright Aeronautical to sail as a fireman aboard the SS *American Seaman*. Several months later, he entered the Maritime Service Officers school at Fort Trumbull, from which he graduated as the engineering student with the highest standing and received a third assistant engineer's license, steam and diesel.

Ships sailed: *Cape San Antonio, Mormachawk, Jeremiah O'Brien, John Phillip Sousa, Hibueras, Chain and Crown, Wallowa, Fiador Knot and Marine Jumper*. In 1946 he was one of the youngest chief engineers in the Merchant Marine.

Carl ended his career as a seagoing engineer in late 1948 to accept a position as port engineer for Esso Shipping in Venezuela. Ten years later, he returned to the States and enrolled as a graduate student at the University of Arizona, majoring in heat and power. Upon obtaining a master of science degree, he worked two years at the Naval Civil Engineering Lab in charge of evaporator development.

Then followed 24 years with Bechtel Power Corporation as desalination and technology transfer manager in the States, France, Spain, and Mexico. During this period, Carl wrote two power plant textbooks in Spanish. He retired in 1986. He and his wife, Erika, whom he met while working in Paris, live in Washington State and spend winters in Arizona.

JEREMIDTH D. (JERRY) SCHENCK, attended USMSTS at Sheepshead Bay Dec. 24, 1943-April 1944. Served as O.S., A.B., and bosun. Sailed on the SS *Robert Eden*, SS *Reverdy Johnson*, SS *William Phips*, SS *John G. Brady*, SS *James Jackson* and the SS *Drew Victory*.

Jeremidth resides in Orlando, FL.

JAMES H. SCHEPANSKY, was born Sept. 25, 1926 in Detroit, MI. Enlisted in U.S. Maritime Service on April 17, 1944. Graduated from U.S. Maritime Service Training Station, Sheepshead Bay, Brooklyn, NY June 4, 1944. Member of National Maritime Union, New York City.

Ships sailed: SS *Bulklube*; Avonmouth/Bristol, England June 1944-July 1944; SS *Baldbutte*, Aruba, Curacao and Cristobal, Panama-July 1944-August 1944; SS *Mary Ashley Townsend*; Southend/Canvey Isle, England September 1944 to October 1944; SS *Abel Parker Upshure*, Augusta, Sicily-Bari, Italy-Matanzas Bay, Cuba-November 1944-February 1945; SS *James H. Price*, Antwerp, Belgium-Rouen and LeHavre, France, February 1945-August 1945.

Enlisted Army Air Force January 1946 to October 1948. Worked in auto plants and Goebel Brewery 1948-1950, Detroit, MI. Re-enlisted in USAF January 1951 and retired from the Air Force April 1968.

Enlisted in East Tawas, MI for next nine years. Worked as inventory manager for U.S. Army tank command East Detroit; equipment installer for a liquid petroleum gas company; warehouseman for Michigan National Guard and U.S. Postal Service as a clerk/carrier.

Moved to Bloomington, IN in 1977. Attended the Perkins Piano Tuner/Technician School in Cleveland/Elria, OH in 1978. Moved to Colorado Springs, CO September 1979 and then to Amarillo, TX in July 1980. Worked for Diamond Shamrock R&M Gas and Oil Company as a inserter machine operator for nine years and continued piano work until retirement in January 1990. Moved to Carson City, NE for two years. He is presently residing in Ching Valley, AZ.

WILLIAM F. SCHEPLER, was born in 1916 in Detroit, MI. He entered the California Nautical School in January 1936. He made two long cruises on the *T.V. California State* to the Carribbean and the South Pacific as an engineering cadet. He left the sea until 1942 when he entered the Maritime Service Officers' School at Alameda, CA. He graduated with his engineer's papers in 1943. He accepted duty at Avalon with the Maritime Service as a training officer. Part of that time as engineering officer on the *T.V. Barbara*.

In January 1944 he left to ship out on the tanker *Tejon* as 3rd assistant for two trips to Portland, OR. He then headed for New York to see some action. After a false start on the Liberty *Moses Auston*, he landed as 3rd assistant on the liberty troop carrier *Stephen A. Duglas* where he did see action with six months in the Mediterranean.

After a couple more maritime school to raise his license he returned to the west coast for a dream job as 2nd assistant on the old steam schooner *Astoria*, running coastwise. After six months he shipped 2nd assistant on the liberty tanker *Horace* see up to the Aleutians. Back to Richmond, CA for High Pressure Geared Turbine School. The war was over, he was a lieutenant commander USMS. He had his first assistant ticket so he swallowed the anchor and came ashore.

He tried real estate, built an adobe home in Chatsworth, CA, and took a few civil service tests for Los Angeles City that landed him in power plants and heating plants which he enjoyed.

But the travel bug was working on both he and his wife (who was also employed by the city as a recreation supervisor). So after 25 years they both took early retirement and entered the travel industry as travel agents.

They went around the world, took 18 cruises, hit all the continents but one, (and several times) and all just in time. After 18 years he suffered cardiac arrest on a trip to Maine two years ago. That slowed him down, but it hasn't stopped him yet!

LOUIS SCHIAVON, was born Nov. 16, 1919, Coalinga, CA. 1929 moved to Watsonville, CA. On Apirl 27, 1943, he went to the invader at Pier 43 in San Francisco to inquire as to what the Merchant Marine was about. Within two hours, along with Joe Partridge and Sam Earle Perkins, they found themselves ordinaries aboard the cockroach and rat infested Danish ship, SS *Day Star*. Louis, Joe and Sam became lifelong friends, and along with busun Frank Calhoun sailed several ships together. (Joe and Frank are deceased.) He was given an hour off to quit his job as a welder at general engineering.

Subsequently, sailed five liberties: *Eugene Skinner*, (o.s.) May 20, 1943; *J.H. Kinkaid*, (a.b.) Sept. 17, 1943; *George K. Fitch* (a.b.) Nov. 5, 1943; *E.A. Burnett* (a.b.-third mate), July 27, 1944; *Andrew Humphreys* (2nd mate) March 10, 1946. Interspersed, were tug, M.V. *St. Simon* (a.b.) April 1, 1944, to Vancouver then to Eniwetok with a concrete barge load of ammo. T-2 tanker *Fort Christina* (2nd mate) Sept. 27, 1945 to Feb. 28, 1946. OCS in Alameda May 16, 1945.

He lives in beautiful carefree, Arizona. Retired 1972. Has been married for 42 years and has two wonderful sons and a wonderful daughter.

SALVATORE SCHIETROMA, sailed on two liberty ships, the SS *David L. Swqaim* and the SS *Elijah Cobb*. Sailed European theater into Mediterranean and Pacific Theater of war. Served in the Armed Guard as S 1/c. Was in the invasion of North Africa, Oran, Algiers, and Tunis. Shipped out of Catania, Sicily. Was in Anzio invasion, invasion of France at Omaha and LeHavre on shuttle runs from South Hampton England to France.

ROLAND SCHIRMER, sailed as FWT, oiler, deck, engineer, and wiper during WWII and peace time. Survived two Jap suicide attacks (six planes) unscratched. Also licensed as electrician. Holds WWII Victory Medal, Philippine Liberation Ribbon, Combat Bar and Pacific War Zone Bar.

Served on the *Owen Summers* and *Narcissa Whitman* during WWII. Has honorable USCG-Merchant Marine discharge. Married to Christia.

Roland is a member of AMMV JWB Chapter and resides in New Roads, LA.

JOSEPH T. (TED) SCHMIDT, was born Aug. 22, 1925 in Newport, KY. Graduated from high school in June 1943. Joined Merchant Marines shortly after graduation at age 17. Took training at Sheepshead Bay, Brooklyn, NY.

Ships sailed SS *Bret Harte* (oiler), 1943-1944, Atlantic; SS *Edward Canby*(FWT), 1944, Atlantic; SS *John A. Dix* (oiler), 1944, Atlantic; *Daulton Mann* (oiler), 1944-1945, Atlantic and Pacific.

He spent the next 40 years as a union sheet metal worker. The last five years before retirement, he was maintenance man at a high school in Northern Kentucky. In 1979, he entered the Diaconate Formation Program at Mt. St. Mary Seminary in Cincinnati, OH. On July 3, 1983 he was ordained a permanent deacon in the Catholic Church. Since retirement, he spends most of his time in this ministry for the Archdiocese of Cincinnati. He and his wife have four children, all married with 12 (plus) grandchildren.

About two weeks after graduating from high school, he saw a movie, Action In The North Atlantic, three times in two days. This was for him. (He had already been rejected by the Marines and Navy for a physical problem). He took his physical at the USMS Recruiting Office with all his clothes on. He was 6'1" tall and weighed 124 lbs. The recruiter wrote 6'0" and 128 lbs - this was minimum. And he was off to Sheepshead Bay.

One tale of his experience as a Merchant seaman stands out from the rest - it was unique. Not many of them wound up in a POW compound . . . an American POW compound at that. He did.

In July 1943, about a month after D-Day, their ship the SS *John A. Dix*, dropped anchor off the Normandy beachhead, and waited to be unloaded. For seven days, they just sat there. Going ashore was forbidden because the "Front" wasn't that far inland. Then after the weeks' wait, the Army sent soldiers out to unload their ship. The soldiers worked in two shifts, 8 a.m. - 8 p.m. and 8 p.m. - 8 a.m. After a few days of this, his curiosity got the better of him. Here he was off the shores of France and not able to walk on the ground or meet any of the French people. So - he decided to go ashore with the night shift soldiers at 8 a.m. and come back with them at 8 p.m. He did this for four days. The first day, by himself. The second day, with a mess boy; the third day with a fireman; and the fourth day, all three of them left - and that's when they got caught. They were hitchhiking, as usual, but this time a war shipping administrator picked them up. Instead of taking them to the nearest town as the others had, he dropped them off at an enfencement - the POW compound, had them charged and fitted the POW coveralls. In the four days, three nights stay as POWs, they worked 12-14 hours a day and got little sleep at night due to the gunfire and air raids. He was given the task of digging sentry fox holes. This must have been a 'make work' project, because after digging the first one (5' deep and 3' diameter), he hid all the dirt behind some nearby bushes. Then on digging the second foxhole about 20' feet away, he was told to take its' dirt and fill up the first foxhole. This was followed by the third and fourth. Needless to say, none of the others was as neat and well-done as the first. On the fourth day, they were taken back to their ship, at their Captain's request.

Back on board ship, they were each called before the Captain. Thank God he was the man he was, a very fatherly type. First he reprimanded him for disobeying orders, not to go ashore, then telling him he could charge him with desertion. But being the man he was, he told Joseph that, as punishment, he would have to pay back the others for standing his watches while he was a POW. This equaled to eight missed watches. In order to pay them back, he was on watch with a very irregular schedule . . . 8 on, 4 off; 4 on, 4 off; 8 on, 8 off, 8 on, 4 off, 4 off, etc. It seemed that all he did for eight days was work or sleep. After it was over, he was one grateful fellow. He doesn't remember what punishment the other two fellows got, but he's quite sure it was similar. He'll never forget his time as a POW nor the Captain's kindness in meting out the punishment.

COLEMAN (COKE) SCHNEIDER, was born March 19, 1924 in Union City, NJ. Schooled in West New York, NY. As a senior in high school, helped fight the disastrous fire aboard the SS *Normandy* on Feb. 9, 1942.

Applied and accepted for USMMA Kings Point in March 1943, assigned to newly launched liberty ship SS *Jeremiah O'Brien* as cadet-midshipman, four crossings of the North Atlantic, usually loaded with munitions. Graduated 1944, sailed as 3rd mate on liberty ship *Henry S. Foote;* 2nd mate on the MV *Cape Nun* carrying a mission of mercy; grain for starving India. Returned to New York sailed as 3rd assistant on the Army Engineers MV *Goethals* to gain first class, unlimited tonnage, New York Harbor Pilot license. Came ashore to learn the manufacture of embroidery centered in Hudson County, NJ. Started first business in 1947 as manufacturer in 1951 changed to major supplier of creative designing and patterns for the industry. Began development of the first computerized tape system in 1968 for embroidery machines, now used all over the world.

Started an insignia manufacturing company in 1968 known as the All American Co., served as president again in 1982 another company known as AA World Class Corp. one of the largest insignia companies in the U.S., still serving as CEO. Provided emblems for *Jeremiah O'Brien* and *John Brown*.

Received many design awards, Man of the Year of the Schiffli Industry and Man of the Year of the Salesmens Association. Wrote and published three books on the industry in 1968, 1978 and 1991. One was translated and published in Japanese.

In his spare time he's a private pilot, instrument rated. Most likely will never retire.

CAPTAIN EDWARD SCHRETTER, graduated from Fort Trumbull. Sailed in deck department on the SS *Dunyone* which was in the secon convoy to Murmansk (VWOA News Letter, Winter 1992).

MELVERN SCHROEDER, "...strong feelings and images still command my memory... not because [the] experiences were of such extraordinary kind, [but because] the sea, as it were, became a part of me and to this day there is a compulsion to return where I belong. I developed an addiction and it won't let go ..."

He is now retired from the position of Head Cataloger for the Wichita Kansas Public School System.

CLINTON R. SCHULZ, was born Dec. 1, 1927 in International Falls, MN. He was 16 years old when attended boot camp at Sheepshead Bay, NY. Went into Marine Corps after. Served on SS *Laura Keene,* messman, France Italy. Stationed also in Corsica, Sicily, North Africa, 1944-1945.

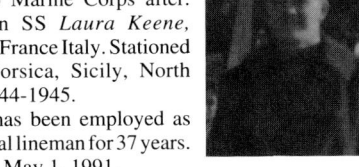

He has been employed as an electrical lineman for 37 years. He retired May 1, 1991.

ROBERT SEAGER II, served as a King's Point cadet/midshipman on the SS *George C. Childress* for about 11 months during 1943-1944. Sailed as 3rd mate on SS *Isabel*, a troop transport with a capacity for 1800 troops. From Oct. 10, 1945 to December 1945 sailed as 2nd mate on SS *Ponce de Leon*.

Remembrances: "When I sailed as 2nd mate in her (SS *Ponce de Leon*) she carried bulk cargo - grain to Bordeaux and she had "passenger accommodations" (if you could call them that!) in the 'tween-decks. Going out, we had empty 'tween decks and wheat in the lower hold. Coming home we had about 500 Air Force, ground personnel troops from the China-Burma-India Theater. Don't ask me how they got to Le Havre, but that's where we loaded them! We hit heavy gales, nearly hurricane force, coming home. With no cargo in her hold the *Ponce* bobbed like a cork. Those men began vomiting and continued to vomit for four days. I'm quoted in John Gorley Bunker, Liberty ships: *The Ugly Ducklings of World War II* (Annapolis: Naval Institute Press 1972, pp. 174-1975, on how the vessel smelled when we finally reached Hampton Roads. Awful.

Before the troops began to puke, they put out a daily "Newspaper." I saved several issues of date Dec. 12, 1945 because it had something about me in it. "Social History" it's called. It was my last trip to sea. I returned to college (Rutgers) in May 1946, then later on to graduate school in U.S. History (Ohio State, Ph.D. 1956) and a career in university teaching and administration from which I retired in 1987. I've also written several books - naval history and biography. I'm working on Henry Clay just now.

PETER SEROKA, donated artifacts that were received from Rev. Fr. Carl Warnet who was Army Chaplin aboard the hospital ship *John J. Meany*.

He now resides in Avon Lake, OH.

ARNOLD L. SERVISS, left Canton, KS in June 1945 to begin training for Merchant Marine duty. He trained on Catalina Island. In September 1945, he was ready for sea duty.

His first ship was the SS *Stephan Furdeck* and his first voyage took him from San Francisco, through the Panama Canal and up to Baltimore. While in the Carribean Sea the order came to dump the ammo overboard. In Baltimore they unloaded the Armed Guard, removed all the guns and loaded coal. The coal was taken to Trieste, Italy. They were then ordered to Bari where they were loaded with temporary air stripping material and then on to Naples to load additional army equipment and 21 officers and enlisted men to be returned to the states. They arrived in Norfolk, VA about the second week of January 1946.

The next ship was the SS *Johnston*. They sailed empty from the Brooklyn Naval Yard through the Panama Canal and on to Tocapali, Chile where they were loaded with nitrate to take to the Netherlands. Because of a labor strike it took 30 days to get their cargo unloaded and get on their way to Anthwerp, Belgium The ship was then loaded with 300 lb. bombs to be returned to the states for unloading at the San Jacinto Ordnance Depot in Texas.

He was drafted in 1948 and served with the 32nd Group, 439th Construction Engineer Bn from February 1951 to June 1952 in Korea. He was discharged in July 1952.

He is now retired (March 2, 1991) after 40 years service in military and U.D. Department of Agriculture.

WILLIAM SHAVER, sailed on board USNS *Comfort* as junior engineer during Desert Storm. Awarded U.S. Merchant Marine Expeditionary Medal. Attended U.S. Navy Engineering Schools.

His next of kin is his father, John W. Shaver. William is a member of AMMV JWB Chapter and resides in Steroselaval Province Quebec, Canada.

LESLIE E. SHELTON, was born on April 20, 1920 in Montgomery, AL where he attended school. He enlisted in the U.S. Navy in 1938 and was honorably discharged at the end of his enlistment in April of 1941. He was employed by the Department of Defense from 1941 until April 1944 when he was accepted to attend officers training at Fort Trumbull. He received his license as third assistant engineer in August of 1944 and sailed on the following vessels:

Lake Sapor, third assistant engineer, Caribbean; *Montoso,* third assistant engineer, Caribbean; *City of Alma, Jr.* third assistant engineer, Atlantic; *James F. Harrell,* third assistant engineer, Atlantic; *Charles Fort,* third assistant engineer, Atlantic and Pacific; *Stephen W. Gambrell,* third assistant engineer, Atlantic; *J. Warren Keifer,* third and second assistant engineer, Atlantic.

Returned to employment in 1947 with the Department of Defense and remained until his retirement in 1975. Leslie Shelton currently resides in Mongtomery, AL.

HAROLD AUSTIN SHERMOND, was born Feb. 20, 1921, Plainfield, NJ. Enlisted United States Maritime Service May 10, 1943.

Training: U.S. Maritime Service Training Station, Sheepshead Bay, NY (May 10, 1943-July 19, 1943); U.S. Maritime Service Upgrade School, New York, NY able seaman training (Nov. 1, 1943-Nov. 8, 1943).

Assignments: SS *Jeremiah S. Black,* ordinary seaman, Mediterranean (July 19, 1943-Oct. 20, 1943). Ports of call: Algiers, Algeria; Bizerte, Tunisia.

SS *William Eaton,* able seaman, Mediterranean, Persian Gulf and Indian Ocean. Nov. 1, 1943-June 3, 1944). Ports of call: New York, Norfolk, Suez, Egypt; Aden, Saudia Arabia; Bandar Shahpur, Iran; Bahrain, Bandar Abbas, Lourenco Marques, Mozambique; Mombasa, Kenya; Port Said, Egypt; Valetta, Malta; Bari and Taranto, Italy; Tripoli, Lybia.

SS *Mobile City,* able seaman, North Atlantic (June

26, 1944-Oct. 7, 1944) Ports of call: New York, Boston, Halifax, Oban and Methil, Scotland; London, England; Cherbourg, France; Swansea, Wales; Bangor, Ireland.

SS *Winthrop Marvin,* able seaman, North Atlantic (Nov. 9, 1944-Feb. 8, 1945) Ports of call: Boston, Halifax, Antwerp, Belgium; Portsmouth, England.

SS *Steel Engineer,* acting junior third officer, (March 20, 1945-Jan. 16, 1946) Ports of call: Savannah, Agusta, Italy; Brindisi and Bari, Italy; Port Said and Suez, Aden, Melbourne, Australia. Seattle, WA.

SS *Montgomery City,* third officer, (Feb. 25, 1946-March 27, 1946) Ports of Call: Baltimore, MD; Pastelillo and Tarafa, Cuba; Philadelphia, PA. Four of the six vessels were engaged in direct enemy action.

He received the Combat Bar, Atlantic Mediterranean, Middle East and Pacific War Zone Bars, and the Victory Medal.

Was employed for 33 years by Curtiss Wright Flight Systems. Retired in 1972. Drove charter and school bus around New Jersey and New York. Metropolitan area for 10 years. Retired to Florida 1984.

Member of USMMVWWII, International Associations of Machinists, A.F.L. C.I.O., Masonic Lodge F&AM, The Gideons International.

Married to the former Martha Ida Schulz and they have four children, John Harold, Wayne Austin, Dorothy Ida and Sarah Martha.

WILLIAM H. SHOAF, attended USMSOS at Fort Trumbull from 1944-1946. Sailed on SS *Alexander J. Dallas* and SS *Eugene Fields.* Licensed as 2nd assistant engineer. Commissioned as lieutenant, USMS.

William resides in Wilmington, DE.

MANUEL SILVIA, attended USMSTS at Sheepshead Bay, and Baltimore Navigation and Marine Engineering School. Skilled in all facets of Marine and stationary engineering operations. Sailed during WWII as coal passer (Great Lakes), utility man, fireman, oiler, 3rd assistant engineer and acting 2nd assistant engineer.

Awarded Atlantic, Pacific and Mediterranean War Zone Bars, Combat Ribbon and Mariners Medal. Retired from Potomac Electric Power Company after 39 years service as power plant operator (23 years), shift supervisor (14 1/2 years) and operation coordinator (1 1/2 years). Licensed in Maryland and D.C.

Married to Frances and they resided in Lanham Seabrock, MD. He is a member of AMMV JWB Chapter.

ROBERT EDWARD SKILLMAN, retired business executive, born Baltimore, MD Dec. 8, 1921; son of the late Thomas and Emma Catherine; wife Marian R. 1945; children Robert E. Jr. and Thomas H.; grandchildren, Matthew, Maggie, Laura, and Katie.

Educated Maryland schools. Graduate industrial electronics and communication engineering; U.S. Maritime School (purser pharmacist) at Sheepshead Bay, NY.

Ships sailed: *Old Bay Line,* passenger ship (assistant purser) 1940-1943; SS *Moses Rogers* (purser) liberty ship May 1944-December 1944, Mediterranean and Middle East; SS *Pan Maine* (purser) tanker 1945-1946 Atlantic Zone.

Received both the Atlantic and Mediterranean Middle East War Zone Bars.

Served as pier superintendent, Army Service Forces 1943-1944. Since WWII has held positions as an insurance agent, hospital purchasing director, professional pharmaceutical representative, and retired from the surgical supply business in 1983.

Since retirement have been active in the Boy Scout movement acting as council chairman, Health and Safety Committee, and also served on the Council Executive Board.

WILLIAM SKINER, (TAL, 4/92, p.2)

ANDREW F. SMITH, was born Oct. 23, 1919 in San Diego, CA. Trained Catalina Island, December 1942-1943 and first of 1944, worked for U.S. Maritime Service and Andrew Wilson, Pacific Coast director warshipping administration San Francisco.

Ships sailed: *Victor H. Kelly* (messman) tanker, 1944-1945, Pacific; *Leonardo L. Romero* (purser) liberty 1945-1946, Atlantic and English Channel, France and Wales; *Lawrence D. Tyson* (purser), liberty 1946 Atlantic and Mediterranean, Gibraltar and Italy; *William D. Moseley* (purser) liberty, 1946, Atlantic Mediterranean and Caribbean, Italy; *Lincoln Steffens,* (purser) liberty, 1946-1947, Atlantic, Irish Sea and Caribbean Island, Venezuela and British Giuana; *Alcoa Voyager* (purser) Hog Islander 1947, Atlantic, Caribbean, Trinidad and Dutch Giuana.

Worked as a letter carrier 1948-1978 until retirement in San Diego. Andy and Sylvia have two children and one grandson. They have been active in the Advent Christian Church for their lifetime.

They are proud to be charter life-member of USMMV of WWII *Lane Victory,* San Pedro.

Great moments: War's end near coast of Alaska and reunion with close buddies in Honolulu love to travel.

CHARLES C. SMITH, was born Burnet, TX Jan. 18, 1927. Graduated Burnet High School, 1943. Enlisted Texas Guard Co. C, 6th Bn. Discharged as corporal May 1944.

Enlisted U.S. Coast Guard March 1, 1945. Training at St. Pete. Assigned to T-2 tanker SS *Battle Rock* in canal zone, loaded gasoline in Venezuela. Delivered to Philippines. Others ships were SS *Spring Hill* from August 1945  to January 1947. Liberty ships *Wendell Wilkie* March 1947-May 12, 1947. Victory Ship *Czechoslovakia Victory* May 1947-September 1947; SS *Volunteer State,* September 1947-October 1947. Participated in taking rolling vehicles to Persian Gulf Sept. 7, 1990 to 18 of March 1991.

Life charter member of WWII MMVFW 8787 Austin, TX, life member Korean War Veterans Association, Washington, DC and Houston, TX.

Would like to hear from all Korean War Veterans, 1950-1953. WWII Merchant Marines 1940-1960. Charles C. Smith, 5309 Grover, Austin, TX 78756.

GORDON E. SMITH, was born Nov. 15, 1923 in Newark, NJ. He joined the Merchant Marine at Sheepshead Bay, NY May 8, 1943.

Served on ships SS *Agwiking,* wiper, nearby and foreign; *Cape Avinof,* assistant electrician, foreign; *Tivives,* elecrician, Costa Rica, Nicarauga, foreign; SS *Santa Paula,* 3rd electrician, England, France, foreign; *Coastal Harbinger,* assistant electrician, Cuba, foreign; MV *Cape Trafalgor,* assistant electrician, Mediterranean, foreign; SS *Mormaemar,* assistant electrician, South American, foreign; *Fort Bridger,* Australia, Philippines, S. Pacific, foreign; *Aguidale,* chief electrician, Cuba, foreign; *Cristobal,* 3rd electrician, Panama Canal Zone, foreign; SS *South Bend Victory,* asst. electrician, coastwise; SS *Brandon Victory,* assistant electrician, France, Foreign; *Aran J. Potheir,* deck engineer, England, foreign.

His memorable experiences include hauling war brides across the Atlantic Ocean. On a tanker, discharging fuel on the Admiralty Islands, American GIs didn't have any refreshments. They were driven down a long road where they found Australian soldiers in the middle of nowhere, selling American beer.

Employed as electrician, Pan American World Airways; owned his own business.

Lives with his wife Pat in Merritt Island, FL. They had one daughter, Sandra. Retired space center worker; treasurer space coast chapter MMVWWII.

JAMES E. SMITH, served 1942-1946. Enrolled in USMS as apprentice seaman, July 1942 in San Diego. Attended USMS Radio School at Gallups Island. Graduated March 1943. Sailed as radio officer on the following ships: *Louis Hennepin, Britain Victory* and *Haiti Victory.* Was only radio officer on the *Louis Hennepin* in 1943 on an around the world voyage. Survived German air attack at Bari, Italy in December 1943. Was also involved in action in the Pacific. Spent two years active duty and three years inactive reserve. Ended up with two years active duty in Signal Corps and was recalled in 1950 during the Korean War.

He is a member of Gallups Island Radio Association (GIRA) and U.S. Merchant Marine Veterans of World War II.

JAMES LACY SMITH, was born April 9, 1921 Pasadena, CA. Went to UCLA, 1952 and to University of Michigan.

First sailed 1941 as Maintenance Man on Standard of California (now Chevron) tanker *District of Columbia,* El Segundo, CA through the Canal to Aruba, Dutch West Indies, then to Marcos Hook, PA. US Navy aviator 1942-1943. Rejoined the Merchant Marine 1943, sailed tankers, mostly T-2, as deck hand - Ordinary, A.B., and Quartermaster.

Some ships sailed: *Mission San Luis Rey,* SS *Plattsburg, Frank G. Drum, Marcos H. Whittier,* SS *Scotts Bluff.* Longest voyage-five months 1944-45 Quartermaster SS *Scotts Bluff,* San Pedro, California to Saipan, Boston, London, Port Arthur, Texas. Left Merchant Marine in 1945. Part owner lumber yard and mill El Monte CA 1946-48. Began Civil Service career 1952 as mathematician, Aberdeen Bombing Mission, Edwards Air Force Base, CA. Retired as a mathematician with the Naval Ocean Systems Center, San Diego, CA 1975. Presently avocado grower and free-lance writer with seven grandchildren. Lives with Charlotte, wife for 49 years, in San Diego North County, CA.

JOHN D. (TEX) SMITH, was born Aug. 16, 1920 in small west Texas town of Clyde. Graduated 1938, Lubbock, TX. When war started was working on B-25s for North American aircraft, Inglewood, CA.

Joined Merchant Marine in 1942, trained in St. Petersburg, FL on the *American Seaman.* Also, was

fortunate to get to sail on the square rigged vessel, *Joseph Conrad*. She is now at berth in the museum at Mystic, CT.

Later in 1942 sailed from New Orleans to many Caribbean ports aboard the sea tow *Margaret Moran*. Once they towed a gate for one of Panama Canal locks from New Orleans.

In 1943 sailed from Portland, OR on liberty ship, SS *Donald Macleay*, to New Hebrides, Australia, and New Guinea. In April 1944 boarded the SS *Marine Eagle* (C-4) in New York harbor bound for the invasion port at Cherbourg, France.

In September 1944 went to Merchant Marine Officers School at Ft. Trumbull, New London, CT. In early 1945 boarded liberty ship SS *Edward E. Hale* as third mate bound for Manila, Lingayen Gulf, Okinawa and Tokyo. Was in Okinawa when the two A-Bombs were dropped and when the Japanese surrender was signed on the battle *Missouri*. Went to Tokyo for six months then to Portland, OR in March 1946.

Back in Lubbock, 40 years in the restaurant business and other investments, from 1946 to 1986.

Now retired and enjoying studying the Lord's word.

JOHN G. SMITH, is a member of AMMV JWB Chapter. He resides in Baltimore, MD.

LEROY J. SMITH, was born Dec. 29, 1922 in Philadelphia, PA. He joined the Merchant Marine Oct. 18, 1941 in Philadelphia, PA.

Served on the *Explorer, Theodore Sedgwick, Joshua Thomas, William Crompton, Mauvilla, Santa Rosa, William D. Moseley, City of Omaha, Lake Frugality, John W. Powell, Mormaclark, E.R. Kemp, Carol Victory, Gulfglow, Natico, Kingston, Minerva, Anstan III*.

His memorable experience includes Bombay India, December 1941. Pearl Harbor where's that?

Obtained civil engineering degree Georgia Tech. Worked as consulting engineer retiring in 19481.

Today he is getting fat and keeping his wife happy.

NATHIEL SMITH, was member of AMMV JWB Chapter. He resides in Pompano Beach, FL.

JOSEPH W. SNEDDEN, JR., was born Nov. 14, 1921, Brooklyn, NY. Schooling Brooklyn and Houston, TX. Started sea 1937.

Sailed *Ponca City* out Corpus Christi Dec. 7, 1941. *Susan Luckenbach* December 1941 to March 1943 after being sunk in Red Sea with vessel repaired in Suez. After six and a half months in Egypt. Third's license May 1943. T-2 *Chapultepec* 1944. USMS Upgrade School, New Orleans January 1945 for second's. Liberty tanker *Irwin Russell* to August 1945. Continued on liberty cargo/tankers, T-2s and victories until late 1952, when left sea as chief engineer.

Unlimited chief engineer's license July 1946 at age 24 1/2.

Commander (E) USMS.

1954 port engineer for Caribbean Steamship Co., Corpus Christi, TX. Senior P/E, superintendent maintenance and repair and superintendent Vessel Management Caribbean/Reynolds Metals-Marine Division until retirement February 1986.

Formed JWS and Associates, Marine Consultants, Surveyors and Engineers in 1984. Active in Marine business doing work for TSA, DNV, Scandinavian Underwriters, Owners and Attorneys.

DONALD W. SOBIN, (DUKE), was born Jan. 6, 1928 in Spring Valley, IL. Joined the Merchant Marines 1945 and trained at Sheepshead Bay, Brooklyn, NY. Sailed on the SS *Bienville* (stewards mate) transport, 1945, Atlantic; SS *Grove City Victory* 1945-1946 (stewards mate), Pacific.

Joined the U.S. Army and served with the 88th Blue Devil Infantry Division Occupation Forces in Italy.

Married in 1951 to Marie Perra of LaSalle, IL and worked as an industrial engineer for General Electric in Bloomington, IL for 31 years. Presently working as an associate for Diamond Star Motors, Normal, IL. Has a son, Gregory and a daughter, Nancy and one grandchild.

THOMAS SOFRANKO, chief radio officer aboard the the SS *Edward H. Crockett* which was torpedoed Sept. 29, 1944 on the Murmansk Run. He is a member of AMMV Desert Mariners Chapter.

Thomas resides in Scottsdale, AZ.

JOSEPH SOKOLICH, was born July 16, 1925. A tool & die maker apprentice at age 16 he entered U.S. Maritime training in 1943 at Sheepshead Bay, NY, graduated December 20.

Sailed February 15, -June 2, 1944 on MS *Gulfcrest*, tanker, coastwise; July 5, 1944 - Feb. 29, 1945 on SS *Caribbean* - T2 mission, tanker as oiler, fireman/watertender. Sailed the Pacific to Eniwetok Atoll, Ulithi, the Carolina Group, from Panama and Venezuela. March 28-June 4, 1945 sailed as oiler aboard liberty ship *Joseph E. Leidy*, to Antwerp, Belgium. His brother, Tom, sailed on this liberty also; the cargo-Sherman tanks, in hold, on deck everywhere! Received endorsement as junior engineer on June 5, 1945. Sailed the SS *Great Republic*, C-3 cargo, to Antwerp, Belgium, June 30-July 31, 1945; the SS *Pachadg Victory* Oct. 13, 1945 to June 5, 1946 as plumber/machinist. This ship was leased to British government for troop transport. They carried a French battalion to Saigon, Indochina, then to Sidney, Brisbane Australia; shuttled Aussie troops to Tokyo, Yokohama, Kure, Japan; crossed the equator eight times; saw the devastation at Hiroshima, Japan; returned to Liverpool, England here the ship was sold. He returned as passenger aboard a troop transport to New York.

His most memorable experience was at Eniwetok Atoll, while anchored for 30 days, he awoke one morning to see, 550 naval ships of every category, in one place at the same time. This task force was used for the invasion of the Philippines.

Retired from Merchant Marine Service, July 15, 1946. Worked as buyer/purchasing agent/purchasing manager until retiring from Crane Defense Systems, Jan. 1, 1988.

Moved to Vandalia, IL from St. Louis where he resides with his wife, Gerry on a 30 acre farm. He belongs to Vandalia CC, play golf, builds doll houses and furniture and radio controlled model airplanes.

BERMARD SOLOMON, member AMMV JWB Chapter. Resides in Germantown, MD.

JOSEPH E. SOLOMON SR. born Aug. 27, 1927 in Opelika, AL. Graduated U.S.M.T.S. St. Petersburg, FL. At the age of 16 in early 1944 he joined Merchant Marines and served as Q.M.E.D., chief steward and below, deck hand, life boatman. Ships sailed: *Joseph Conrad, Hog Islander Tampa* (coal passer), *Vernon L. Parrington, Jeremiah O'Brien, George Uhler, George Lenord, Ethiopia Victory, H.S. Astoria and Charles A. Stafford, Del Sud, Del Norte, Del Mar, Alcoa Clipper, Alcoa Corsair, Alcoa Cavalier, General Black*.

Saw combat in North Atlantic, Pacific, Murmansk to the Philippines. Holds the Mariners Medal, Gallient Ship Award, Atlantic, Pacific and Mediterranean Zones, Combat Bar, Victory Medal, Mariners Emblem and Philippine Liberation.

He returned home to begin college, but soon enlisted in the Army. Joe served in the Far East, U.S. and Germany. He was a member of the 18th Airborne Corp. In 1952 married Margie E. Wilson of Columbus, GA whom he met in Germany. Together they had six children. Upon discharge, Joe attended Auburn University. He worked for the state of California for 30 years as an electrical engineer working on the construction of the California Aquaduct. Joe and wife Margie are retired and live in Bakersfield, CA spending most of their time getting even with each other.

FRED SPEER, JR., sailed on SS *Ben Ruffin* as 3rd assistant engineer. Has "rembrances" and photos of carrying Chinese troops. This is described in "Ship and Crew Listings" published by Project Liberty Ship and in exhibit on board the SS *John W. Brown*.

HAROLD E. SPENCER, was born Corning, NY, Oct. 1, 1920. Wartime training program, U.S. Merchant Marine Academy, 1942-1943, deck cadet, *Agwimonte* (South Africa, Egypt, Sudan, Malta, East Africa, South America, Cape Horn, Panama, Cuba); 1944-1945, junior third mate, 3rd mate, 2nd mate, *Agriprince* (Gulf of Mexico, Panama, New Guinea, New Caledonia, Solomons, Guam and elsewhere in the Pacific theater); 1945-1946, 2nd mate, *Fisk Victory* (Pacific Theater, Okinawa, China, India). Post-war: degrees from University of California at Berkeley and Harvard University. Served on the faculties of Blackburn College, Carlinville, IL; Occidental College, Los Angeles, CA; University of Connecticut, Storrs, CT, from which he retired, professor emeritus, 1988. Artist, writer, and art historian.

Living with wife, Editha Hayes Spencer, artist and writer, in Ashford, CT. Four sons (David, Robert, Eric, and Mark) and nine grandchildren.

EUGENE R. SPERRY, was born Nov. 17, 1915 in Inglewood, CA.

Graduated 1934 Inglewood High School.

1934 to 1943 worked for Western Pipe and Steel and Consolidated Shipbuilders in Welmington and San Pedro.

1943 joined Merchant Marine in Welmington and received training at Catalina Island. Shipped aboard the *W.S. Miller,* oil tanker; *Cape Saint George* C2 cargo ship to New Guinea and back.

1944 joined the *Cody Victory* ship while under construction at California Shipyard in San Pedro, CA. After construction he shipped out with the *Cody Victory* from San Pedro to Melbourne, Australia, then on to Calcutta, India. From Calcutta to Port Said, Egypt by way of the Red Sea and Suez Canal.

From there they sailed across the Mediterranean Sea by the Rock of Gibraltar and out to the Atlantic and on to New Orleans; a trip around the world of 25,800 miles in 93 days unescorted carrying military supplies through all war zones!

Retired auto mechanic in Oroville, CA.

JOHN J. STANISH, was born June 20, 1926 in Brooklyn, NY. USMS April 1944. Hoffman Island Seaman Training Radio School RI. Graduated November 1944. Warrant radio electrician FCC 2nd telegraph license. Ensign (reserves) June 1945. Maiden voyage SS *John A. Quitman* November 1944 to May 1945. Murmansk. Run cruel weather, U-boat attacks, Kola Inlet, convoy loses three ships. HMS B*luebell*. Straggled several days, aircraft bombing attacks. June 1945-October 1946 five vessels Mediterranean.

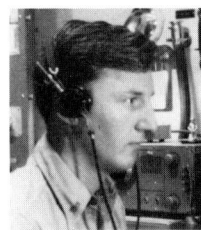 

SS *Esso Camden* October 1946 to November 1946, New York Baytown. Norfolk, Baltimore collision. Liberty cattle vessel off Annapolis fog conditions. SOS burned three hours before self extinguishing by blowing itself out.

November 1946 to August 1946 several vessels South America Mediterranean Marshall plan aid August 1949-May 1951 SS *Exilona*. First Nato Arms aid to Italy Sabotage attempt by underwater bombs by communist (Italian) non event. 1951-1986 Landlubber 1986-1993. Retired. Married Carmella and they have two sons John A. and Gary L. who live in South Carolina.

JAMES M. STANLEY, was born on April 2, 1907 in Portland, OR. He graduated in 1928 with a degree in radio engineering and a radio operator's license, and moved to California where he was in business until WWII. He renewed his radio license and joined the Merchant Marines in New Orleans in 1943.

Ships sailed included: the SS *Dan Beard* in 1943, a three-week-crossing from New York to the north of Scotland and London, which was attacked by German E boats all the way; the SS *David E. Garrett,* a liberty ship in 1944; the SS *John Ireland,* a liberty ship, which crossed the Atlantic and the Mediterranean to the Persian Gulf. Two more trips were made on the *Ireland,* the last to Murmansk, Russia; in a convoy of 38 ships, 18 were lost on the return trip of six days by constant bomber attacks. In April 1945 he sailed from Los Angeles to the South Pacific on a T-2 tanker supplying the Navy with fuel oil.

Mr. Stanley was in many small business ventures from 1946, and in 1973 retired from Santa Barbara Blueprint Co.

He joined SCORE (Service Corps of Retired Executives) a branch of the Small Business Administration as volunteer, and has held all offices in SCORE including four years as elected director of the National Board. Presently he is regional director of Veterans Affairs for California, Arizona, Nevada and Hawaii. He is the current president of the Board of the Lions Sighting and Hearing Center of Santa Barbara.

James Stanley is married and has one son, three grandsons and a granddaughter.

JOHN H. STARK, was born June 30, 1924 in New Brunswick, NJ. He joined the Merchant Marine July 1943 at Newark, NJ Served on SS *Fairfax*, T2SEA-1 Tanker, F/W Oiler; SS *Lyons Creek*, T2 Tanker, 3rd Eng.

One of his most memorable experiences is lying dead in the water north of Ireland with 150 thousand barrels of gas and a DE drops back and said 'Good Luck.'

As a Marine Engineer, he crossed the Atlantic six times and the Pacific four times. In addition, while in the service, he had the opportunity of attending USMS Officer School.

He is married and has one daughter working in the Raritan Valley Workshop. Today he is a retired professional engineer. He retired June 1985.

FRANK FRANCIS G. STEINBACH, was born July 1, 1925 in Denver, CO. He joined the Merchant Marine June 9, 1943 in Denver, CO. Completed training at Catalina Island, Oct. 21, 1943.

Served on SS *John Constantine,* liberty PO-28-43 to March 26, 1944 (wiper), Pacific; SS *William H. Allen,* liberty May 10, 1944 to Oct. 9, 1944 (fireman water tender) Pacific; SS *Nicaragua Victory,* Dec. 1, 1944 to June 15, 1945 (fireman w.t. and oiler two trips) Pacific; SS *Cape Orange* (Aug. 24, 1945 to Nov. 29, 1945) (oiler) Pacific; SS *Grange Victory* (Jan. 23, 1946 to April 26, 1946) two trips oiler coastwise and Pacific;

His memorable experiences include the Panama Canal, the Statue of Liberty, Invasion of Okinawa, the kamikazes, two trips Sidney, Australia and all the South Pacific Islands. Five years for DuPont, 35 years at Atomic Energy Plant, Rocky Flats.

Got married to Lillian with three kids and they had four; five boys and two girls. Frank retired Nov. 1, 1987, 62 years old. Today he travels, does yard work and is taking it easy.

WALTER R. STEINSIEK, resides in Laurel, MD and is a member of AMMV JWB Chapter.

NEIL M. STERUD, was born Nov. 1, 1920 in Reno, NV. Graduated from Mission High School, San Francisco December 1938. Became engine cadet, U.S. Merchant Marine Academy June 1942. Basic training at Treasure Island, CA. Went aboard liberty ship *Daniel H. Lownsdale* as engine cadet. Most of the time spent in the Mediterranean Sea, Egypt, Libya, Malta.

Graduated from USMMA, Kings Point, NY, March 1944. Went aboard *Francis W. Parker* as third engineer, April 1944. All of this trip was in the South Pacific (13 months). Returned to U.S. in 1945. He didn't sail after October 1945. Married a girl he went to junior high and high school with on Dec. 1, 1945. They raised four boys, lost the oldest one in Vietnam (he died with honors).

He went to work for Pacific Gas and Electric Co. At their Contra Costa Steam Power Plant, Antioch, CA. Retired April 1, 1982 as instrument maintenance foreman.

The *Lownsdale* was the only liberty ship that he knows of that was equipped with depth charges. Just roll off the stern no Y guns. The British installed these in Egypt just before their trip to Malta in 1942.

They lost their deck cadet Harry Quale in Tripoli, Libya due to a land mine explosion while ashore.

WINIFRED N. STILLMOCK, resides in Baltimore, MD and is a member of AMMV JWB Chapter.

GEORGE A. STINNETT, was born July 31, 1927, South Portland, ME. Joined Merchant Marine May 1944, Portland, ME. Graduated Sheepshead Bay, NY, July 1944. Signed on SS *Owen Summers* San Francisco, July 1944.

Ships served on: SS *Owen Summers,* liberty, utilityman-July 1944-March 1945, South Pacific, New Guinea, Lingayen Gulf D-Day + 2; SS *James Kearney,* liberty, messman, May 1945-July 1945, Antwerp, Belgium; SS *Townsend Harris,* liberty, O.S., July 1945, Portland, to New York; SS *Oakey Alexander,* collier, o.s., July 1945-December 1945-Portland, Norfolk, VA; SS *Pierre Victory,* victory, pantryman, January 1946-March 1946, LeHavre, France. This ship carried horse to France. SS *Diamond Island,* T2 tanker, o.s., 1946, Portland Harbor; SS *Walter Reed,* liberty, o.s., 1946; SS *George Ade,* liberty, o.s., 1946; SS *Oakey Alexander Collier,* o.s., August 1946-February 1947.

He got off this ship to be married. The morning he was to return to the ship she went on the rocks in a storm at Cape Elizabeth, ME after losing her bow off the entrance to Portland Harbor.

He married Feb. 22, 1947 to Ann Brasier. He has one daughter Gayle born June 18, 1949. He has three grandchildren and one great granddaughter.

He worked for H.P. Hood Inc. for 42 years as night clean up at the ice cream plant and as a chestman also a trailer truck driver until 1979 when they closed the ice cream plant and he transferred to the milk division as a trailer truck driver then to night clean up in the milk plant then to janitor just before his retirement Feb. 26, 1990.

Since retirement has done a little traveling and baby sitting his great granddaughter so that his granddaughter could attend college full time.

Kamikaze planes attacked the *Owen Summers* off Luzon. Heading south from Lingayen Gulf they saw a meteor streak across the sky and land in the sea and saw the steam rise from the sea. This was at night off the west coast of the Philippines.

JACK W. STIXRUD, was born Aug. 9, 1927, welder, Oregon shipyard before joining Merchant Marine, graduated Catalina June 6, 1944.

Wiper first ship *Otsego* (coal burner) fireman hurt in storm, he got fireman job and sorry, signed off that fireroom happier than when he got married.

Wiper second ship *Edward G. Acheson* (liberty ship). In convoy with full load bombs, packing blew out main engine high pressure cylinder, blind chief engineer knew repair while underway, first engineer with gloves and arms wrapped in rags forced in new packing, it worked, his hands and arms blistered from steam. Relatives deserve medal for what he did.

Fireman watertender third ship *William J. Gray* another liberty ship and last trip during WWII.

He remained fireman watertender until 1956 and strayed ashore, married twice with six children. Retired on Social Security after a few years self-employment handprinting antique art.

RAYMOND D. STORM, sailed as oiler during WWII. Has Atlantic, Pacific, Mid-East, Mediterranean Middle East War Zone Bars and Merchant Marine Emblem. Skilled as machinist and carpenter. Next of kin is wife, Virginia.

He is a member of AMMV JWB Chapter. He resides in Cockseyville, MD.

KENNETH T. STOUT, sailed as OS on the SS *John Fiske* with J. Gordon Jones, a lifelong friend.

Kenneth resides in Newport News, VA.

JACK R. STRAW, was born Nov. 27, 1923, in Jamestown, NY. Attended school in Southern California's San Fernando Valley.

First shipped out of San Pedro, February 1942. Ships sailed: *Edward J. O'Brien, David R. Francis, Oliver Wendell Holmes,* liberty ships. *Frank G. Drum, Ft. Dearborn,* tankers. C1-SS *Flyway*, SS *Nevadian*, and salvage tug SS *Viking*.

Several years after completing his Merchant Marine service in June 1946, he relocated his family to Orange County. There he worked in the vending business until 1987.

Jack considers his adventures while a merchant seaman a highlight of his life and through the years has entertained family and friends with many sea stories. Some memorable recollections involve:

Transporting 500 mules to Calcutta, India, for use on the Burma Road; Associating with a friendly fellow in Calcutta who was later identified by Army Intelligence as a Russian KGB spy; Surviving an Atlantic storm where waves knocked out radio shack windows 50 ft. above water line; and a multitude of engine room experiences.

Jack is now enjoying retirement in Pismo Beach, his collection of Maritime memorabilia, and his proximity to the Pacific.

JOHN (JACK) STRULLER, SR., was born May 3, 1926 in Brooklyn, NY. He joined the Merchant Marine July 1943, Brooklyn, NY, Sheepshead Bay, Maritime Service.

Served on T-2 tankers, liberty ships, victory ship, Army transport as fireman water tender, oiler, 2nd cook and baker and libertyman. Stationed in Atlantic, Pacific, Indian Ocean, Arabia Sea, North Sea.

He does not remember all names of ships he served on. He was a member of the SIU Union and works in the union hall in Brooklyn as a waiter for a while after the war. Later worked on passage ships SS *Puerto Rico*. Got married in 1954 quit sailing.

His memorable experience includes bombay India twice went to bombay for repairs and to unload wheat, fascinating country. Went to sea 10 years 1943 to 1954. Coming out of English channel on D day after unloading T-2 tanker at Graves End England.

He is employed with housing authority of Passaic, NY. Retired January 1991 as director of maintenance. Married and has six children and four grandchildren.

Today he is taking it easy.

JOHN D. STRUYK born July 22, 1922 in New York City and went to school on Staten Island. First went to sea in 1942 on the S.S. *Collyto*, a Dutch freighter. Doing six knots, unescorted, the *Collyto* carried military supplies from New York to Alexandria, Egypt, by way of South Africa and the Indian Ocean, a trip of seven months through German submarine infested waters. He next sailed in 1943 on the U.S. Army Transport *H. F. Alexander*, later renamed the *Gen. George S. Simonds*. John then served on the U.S. Army Transport *Lakehurst* from January 1944 to November 1945. Later, he sailed on the Great Lakes from 1953-1956, then for Military Sea Transportation Service from 1956 to 1962.

John moved to California where he worked as a mail carrier until his retirement in 1982. Since 1990, he has been an active volunteer helping in the restoration of the S.S. *Lane Victory*, a National Historic Landmark, being restored by the U.S. Merchant Marine Veterans of WW II in San Pedro, CA. John lives with wife Mary Anne in Downey, CA.

HAROLD M. STUMPH, JR., resides in Lanham, M. and is a member of AMMV JWB Chapter.

JOHN STUPI, attended Sheepshead Bay. Sailed as fireman, oiler and pumpman during WWII, Korean and Vietnam. Ship damaged. Awarded Pacific War Zone Bar, Combat Bar, Philippine Liberation.

He is a member of AMMV JWB Chapter. He resides in Randallstown, MD.

JOHN H. (JACK), SULLIVAN, was born Dec. 19, 1916 in Boston, MA. Attended Boston College, 1939. Married and has three children.

U.S. Army Military Police, honorably discharged July 10, 1943. August 1943-January 1944, U.S. Maritime Training School, Sheepshead Bay, Brooklyn, NY as ships

 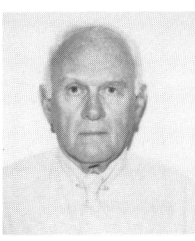

company commander, drill instructor. February 1944-July 1944, U.S. A.M.S St. Mihiel, foreign jet service. July 1944-June 1945, Army Transport Service, Boston Port of Embarkation, port agent, War Department Special disbursing agent; July 1945-June 1946, Army Transport Service, USAHS *Louis A. Milne*, USAT *President Tyler*, foreign sea service, War Department special disbursing agent and ships transportation agent. 1946 to present sales manager, C Pappas Co., Boston, MA; president and treasurer Renaissance Foods, Boston, MA; managing director, S.S. Pierce Co., Boston, MA; president and treasurer Major Restaurant Group "Charley's Eating and Drinking Saloon"; president Sullivan Enterprises, Boston, MA and Palm Beach, FL.

CHARLES A. SUSANJ, was born Dec. 17, 1927 in Bellingham, WA. In training 1945 Avalon, Catalina Island, CA.

He served on SS *Wm Sturgess*, steward's dept, Portland, OR; SS *Fair Isle*, 1946, 1,650, a.b., carried German PWs., Seattle, WA, North Atlantic by way Panama Canal.

His memorable experience includes Mid Atlantic storm six days off course one other ship in distress and can't stop because P.W.

Employed for 27 years with F.V. Eeyore Capt. Retired July 1988. Musician part-time.

ROBERT B. SWANSON, was born April 24, 1924 in Erie, PA. He joined the Merchant Marine, Hoffman Island, 194? Served on *John Paul Jones* (liberty), wiper, Liverpool, 1943; *Henry Villard* (liberty) wiper, Scotland, 1943, USSR, RA 55A; *FQ Barstow*, fireman, Colon, Aruba, Holland. Last trip to sea, troops from Japan; *Archbishop Lamy*, oiler, Naples, Moremac wave, mait oiler.

Worked in Erie, the old *Erie Dispatch, Miami Herald, Orlando Sentinel*, newspaper distributor in Gainesville, FL.

Working part time video business, Orlando, FL. He is now interested in golf and camping.

JOHN A. SWINECK, run away at age 17. Went to the Shipping Commissioners Office and applied for his seaman's papers. Received his application, filled them out and signed his daddy's name to them. Took them back, and received his seaman's papers. He had sent him to Southern Steamship Col., for his first ship. Can still hear the commissioners voice coming through the bulkheads, when he got back for pay off. Lost the *Lillian Luckenbach* March 27, 1943. A liberty ship struck them on the port

bow, took all plates from anchor to midships. Went down in 15 minutes. All hands got off safe. Returned to civilian life 1947. Went to work as stationary engineer until 1949. Married in 1947.

Still with together-called to serve USMCA, Korean Conflict. He is a life member and restoration crew SS *John W. Brown.* Now residing in South Jersey.

PETER S. SZATOSKY, (SZATKOWSKI), was born June 29, 1913 in Holyoke, MA and educated in local school systems. First went to sea in 1936 as a deckhand aboard the tanker *I.C. White,* out of Fall River, MA, sailing to Texas and Aruba. Later employed as a machinist with Pratt and Whitney. Entered wartime merchant service in 1943 and assigned to the U.S. Army transport *Monterey (I),* which unescorted delivered troops and military cargo to stations throughout the Caribbean. Peter gained his most memorable wartime experiences aboard the U.S. Army Transport *Lakehurst* from November 1943 to November 1945. He vividly recalls the North Atlantic convoys, the massive preparation for the Normandy landing and the delivery of locomotives to Cherbourg, France. Then there was the typhoon that battered Admiral Halsey's Third Fleet invasion task force in the South China Sea in June 1945. The *Lakehurst* rode out the storm at its center but sustained only minor damage.

After discharge, Peter worked as a machinist with Moore Drop Forge in Springfield, MA until his retirement in 1974. Now he and his devoted wife of 50 years Phyllis enjoy fishing, reading, and spending as much time as possible with their family including a beloved granddaughter Mary Catherine.

JOHN TAYLOR, JR., was born Jan. 23, 1920 in Greenville, MS. He died April 14, 1991. Joined Merchant Marine Sept. 8, 1942 in Mobile, AL when he was 20.

Served as 1st cook, baker, chief steward. Several ships John sailed for 29 years, SS *African Planet,* SS *Mormac Sea,* SS *Flying Trader,* SS *African Rainbow,* SS *Exchester,* SS *African Enterprise,* SS *African Neptune,* SS *Australian Gem,* SS *Australian Reef,* SS *Henry D. Whitton* and others.

Completed 11th grade, Coleman High School, Greenville, MS also at one time attended Merchant Marine School for seamen in New York.

Served during World War II, Vietnam War, Korean War. Upon retirement, made several talks in Meridian Public Schools to children about his experiences abroad with articles collection demonstrated and to many professional clubs. Loved being a Merchant seaman.

After retirement worked with MAP Program in Meridian.

Married to Mrs. Dorothy C. Taylor for 49 years. Retired in 1971.

RALPH D. TAYLOR, was born July 8, 1922. Joined Merchant Marine Dec. 8, 1942, Lansing, MI. Trained at Hoffman Island and Sheepshead Bay, NY. Sent to Great Lakes. Worked on tug SS *Liberty* and ore boat SS *Wm. A. Reiss.* Mate had Ralph and another deckhand washing hatch coamings with soogee 0200 hours while loading coal at Erie, PA. Wanted to contribute more than that to war effort so paid off and went to New York to ship out.

Shipped as AB on SS *Yankee Sword*-Hog Island, Atlantic coast. SS *Cedar Mills,* T-2 tanker, England. SS *Henry St. G Tucker,* liberty, Egypt, Yemmen, Kenya, Mozambique, South Africa, Brazil and BWI. SS *Amelia Earhart*-liberty, England. SS *Willard Hall,* liberty, Murmansk and Molotovsk, Russia (three months in Russia due to broken prop). SS *William N. Pendleton,* liberty, Philippine Islands. 3rd mate, SS *Charles J. Colden,* liberty-Chili. Ended maritime career June 1946.

Retired 1986 after career in sales and sales promotion. Resides with wife Bette in (East Tawakoni) Lone Oak, TX.

Current activities include organizing reunions for Merchant Marine Veterans.

A. JOHN TERRELL, was born Dec. 27, 1927, Pasadena, CA; BBA University of New Mexico 1952. U.S. Maritime Service, class 286, Catalina Island, 1944. He shipped out, age 16, on the SS *Iran Victory* (Aug. 30, 1944 to May 25, 1945); The first ship to load ammunition at Port Chicago after the ammo depot blew up in series of blasts (July 17, 1944) killing 320 sailors, damaging the town of Martinez, CA.

His ship sailed the Pacific to Los Negros where it joined the Fifth Fleet in a convoy heading to the Battle of Luzon. After a loss of power they were diverted to Leyte Gulf, off Tacloben, which was still under attack by the Japanese. Off Japanese held Bablethuap Island they had a fire while offloading bombs onto the *Iran Victory* from the mine damaged USS *Colorado Victory* (K227) causing his ship to take emergency action, cast off and beat a hasty retreat.

While anchored off the coast of Ulithi Island in a squall with high choppy wave action, without hesitation John jumped overboard swimming to an unmanned Navy LCVP which tore loose of it's moorings from the SS *Iran Victory.* He climbed aboard as the boat was being washed out to sea and got one of the two engines started. Working the rudder against the turning screw it took over an hour to bring the boat alongside the ship. He got a cheering welcome from the crew and a hearty thanks from the guy who "lost his boat", Navy Coxswain Smith. The crew presented John with a medal for his valor, a "tomato can lid dangling from a dirty string." He also got a chewing out from F.W. Miller, chief engineer, for not claiming the LCVP as "salvage". Weeks later he felt all the shock waves, as two Japanese kamikaze planes hit, first, a Navy signal tower on Ulithi Island, then an ammunition locker on an aircraft carrier anchored about one and a half miles away from his ammunition ship.

John served as a paratrooper with the 82nd Airborne Div. (1946-1947); serving in the 325th Glider/Parachute Infantry and Hq. and Hq. Co.; Army Reserve (1947-1951). He is a member of the U.S. Merchant Marine Veterans of World War II, a life member of the VFW and the American Legion.

John, a licensed pilot, spends time sailing and skiing with his grown children, Patricia, Marilee and Scott and his grandchildren. He is retired from U.C.L.A. where he was director of telecommunitions. He lives with his wife Betty in Newport Beach, CA.

ALBERT TERRIBILINI, was born Dec. 20, 1926. Went to school in Paterson, NJ. Joined Merchant Marines in 1944, training at Sheepshead Bay, NY.

Ships sailed: SS *Pueblo,* T-2 oil tanker, 1945 to February 1946. Sailing the Atlantic, Pacific, Middle East and Far East. *Sedalia Victory* May 1946 to January 1947 sailing the Atlantic and Pacific carrying troop to Philippines, Japan and Korea.

Came out in January 1947. Went to work for Public Service Gas Co. retiring in December 1988, after 35 years. Now working for the recycling dept. in Hawthorne, NJ.

EARL (BILL) M. TERRY, was born Dec. 10, 1920 in Chinook, MT. Graduated from Eastern Washington State College 1942. At Vancouver, WA he taught junior high school and worked swing shift at Kaiser Shipyard building merchant ships. Joined the U.S. Maritime Service at Portland, OR (1943). Received his maritime training at Catalina Island, CA. Served in his maritime training at Catalina Island, CA. Served in the South Pacific and North Pacific aboard the following vessels: SS *Columbia,* SS *Yukon,* SS *Cape Mears,* SS *Marine Falcon,* SS *Marine Shark,* SS *Barnoff,* and SS *Alaska* in the capacity of chief and second steward.

He moved to California in 1948 where for the next 37 years he was employed by the LA Board of Education as a teacher and school principal. He earned his advanced degrees at the University of Southern California.

Terry holds life memberships in the following organizations: Benevolent and protective order of Elks, Phi Delta Kappa, Associated Administrators of Los Angeles City Schools, American Legion, Navy League of the U.S. and the U.S. Merchant Marine Veterans World War II.

He retired in 1985 and resides with his wife Donnie in West Hills, CA.

ERNEST J. THOMAS, was born Aug. 4, 1915, civilian employee, War Department, Ft. Leonard Wood, MO. At age of 27 years volunteered as an apprentice seaman, Sheepshead Bay Brooklyn, NY. Then as yeoman duties aboard training ships SS *American Seaman.* Received pursers certificate. After ships were available, went to sea as AB on various vessels. SS *Theodore Sedgwick,* liberty ships, carrying tanks and planes to Port Said, Egypt.

Robert L. Vann, liberty ship, to Plymouth, England, after long delay from severe storm in North Atlantic. They could not keep up with convoy. Deck cargo was washed overboard, boat deck awash with oil as drums of oil broke, refrigerator tore loose and acted as battering ram until secured. Vessel limped into Nova Scotia. Canadian destroyer informed them they were in a mine field and were instructed to follow destroyer. When asked if there were any survivors on board, Captain signaled that they were all survivors. After repairs and replacement of rafts, they continued to England with another convoy. About a year later vessel did hit a mine and sunk off the Coast of Belgium in March 1945. Jinx ship.

SS *Examiner,* victory ship, two trips — first to Liverpool, England and second to Cardiff, Wales. SS *Henry Brown,* liberty ship to Normandy Beach Head, France via Atlanta, Orkney Island, North Sea, Straits of Dover, Isle of Wight, and English Channel. After graduating from U.S. Maritime Officers School, Fort Trumbull, New London, CT, in April 1945, certified as third mate and ensign in USMS.

Pan American Victory, victory ship, junior third mate, Eniwetok, Ulithi, Saipan, Okinawa.

SS *Charles Scribner,* liberty ship, third mate, first trip to Saipan, second trip to Vancouver, British Columbia, Colon, Panama and Rotterdam. Went into Marine Hospital, State Island, New York, for 2 1/2 months in April 1946. Problem with eyes due to contact with refugees from Japanese and German prison camps. He was at Okinawa when atom bombs were dropped on Japan. After treatment returned as civilian employee with Civil Service Accounting with U.S. Army Aviation Command until retirement in 1974.

Married to Mary and has a daughter Kathleen.

VAL A. THOMAS, was born April 23, 1923 in Fresno, CA. Joined the Merchant Marine Aug. 2, 1943 in San Francisco, CA.

Served on SS *Stephen W. Kearney,* carp, August 1943-February 1944, Tasmania, Columbo, Ceylon, Calcutta, Durban A.F., Rio De Janeiro; SS *Hiram Bingham* carp, March 1944-May 1944, South Pacific; SS *United Victory,* carp, July 1944-December 1944, invasion Pelilu; SS *Richard Oglesby,* AB February 1945-June 1945, South Pacific; *James K. Kelly,* carp, July 1945-January 1946, invasion of Leyte.

Bombed in New Guinea, October 1944. Left King George Doons in Calcutta under Jap plane attack. Japs fired torpedoes at *United Victory* at Pelilu but went under ship to land on shore.

He is ex-San Francisco Police Officer. Now in burglar alarms January 1946.

RAYMOND S. THOMPSON, was a farm boy and native of N.E. Oklahoma near Pryor. He enlisted when he was 18 and entered Sheepshead Bay, NY in October 1943. He was shipped by train to San Francisco in April of 1944. There he went on a liberty that went to New Guinea and Sydney Australia. They participated in an invasion of an island called Noemfoor. They were not hit but they fired at aircraft and a sub.

The other four ships he served on was in the Atlantic. The ports included St. Nazaire, France; Antwerp, Belgium; Bremerhaven, Germany, Wales and Cornerbrook, Newfoundland.

He left the service in August of 1946 and came to Wichita, KS where some family had settled and have been here ever since.

He worked in a warehouse, an aircraft plant, a public utility company and sales jobs. He retired in 1974.

ROGER M. THOMPSON, was born Feb. 16, 1923, at Council Grove, KS. Joined the Merchant Marines in November 1943; took basic training in St. Petersburg, FL. After basic was accepted for Radio School and sent to Gallups Island in Boston Harbor.

First sailed on SS *F.H. Hillman,* March 1944 (2nd class radio operator); July 1944 made chief radio operator and stayed on Hillman until February 1945.

Sailed on SS *Clearwater Victory* February 1945 to June 1945. All trips were in the Pacific. Was off shore when U.S. Marines took Iwo Jima; His last trip was on SS *William Coleman,* sailing from Pacific through Panama Canal to Italy and returned to New York City. Received his discharge in January 1946.

Married to Emma and have three children, five grandchildren. Retired from 22 years with Kansas Highway Patrol.

ANDREW F. THURMOND, was born Oct. 7, 1924, was in Maritime training in 1943 at Sheepshead Bay, NY. Before his high school graduation ceremony took place at Blewett High School in St. Louis, MO. In 1943 he sailed as F/man on troopship *George Washington,* up and down East Coast, through "Torpedo Junction" (windward passage) into Carribean, Panama, Trinidad, Central America, etc.

In early 1944 Andy was f/man w.t. on the troop carrying liberty ship *Richard Bassett. Bassett's* convoy was attacked by Germany torpedo planes enroute from N. Africa to Italy in this engagement of direct enemy action Andy was awarded the "Merchant Marine Combat Bar". (In this same convoy the troop carrying liberty "Paul Hamilton" was sunk with 500 men. It was two columns away from "Bassett".

In summer of 1944 Andy sailed again out of New York to North Africa and Italy on liberty ship *Richard Alvey* (cargo was military supplies tanks, trucks, etc.)

Late in 1944 Andy was oiler on T-2 tanker *Mission Buenaventura* out of Frisco. During this trip the *Buenaventura* refueled the battleship *Iowa* at an island rendezvous somewhere in the Western Pacific. After "running the equator" and through Panama to Venezuela, the *Buenaventura* returned with gas and oil to Pacific Islands in Admiralties, Carolines and Mariannas in the spring of 1945 the *Buenaventura* returned to west coast and "Andy" was accepted for engineer officer training at Fort Trumbull New London, CT.

In fall of 1945 with 3rd engineer steam and diesel license and maritime commission. Andy sailed on the passenger refrigerator ship *Antigua* with refrigerated meat for the Navy the *Antigua* sailed from Frisco with military officers to Hawaii and Pacific Islands, ending the trip in Japan shortly after the armistice. *Antigua* was then returned to the United Fruit Co. "Great White Fleet" of pre-war turbo electric twin screw "mail line" ships. It sailed from Honolulu to Costa Rica and brought refrigerated bananas through Panama to East Coast.

In early 1946 to 1947 Andy worked ashore towards a stationary steam engineers license in his home state of Missouri. In summer of 1947 Andy again sailed as third engineer on liberty ship *John Merrick.* The *Merrick* took cargo from Baltimore to France under the "Marshall Plan", then proceeded for 28 days to Argentina to load barley as cargo for India via S. Africa and Cape of Good Hope. After unloading six in Vizagapitum and Calcutta India the *Merrick* sailed empty for Australia. In Sydney the load was wheat. The trip below Australia, across the Indian Ocean, Red Sea and Suez, took the *Merrick* 47 days to N. Africa. After nine months the *Merrick* returned across the Atlantic to New York in April 1948.

Andy then acquired a St. Louis Stationary Steam Engr. License and worked for the Proctor and Gamble Mfg. Co. for 35 years.

Andy and wife Betty (his high school sweetheart and wife of 47 years) successfully raised and educated four children, then retired to Largo, FL in the summers. They have traveled 48 states in their 36 ft. motorhome.

Andy has continuously maintained his Marine Steam and Diesel Engineers License. (the current issue will be 50 years.) Also 44 years current St. Louis Stationary Steam Engineer License.

GEORGE A. TICKELL, attended Massachusetts Maritime Academy in 1943. Sailed as second mate, chief mate, and master. Next of kin is wife, Eleanor.

George is a member of AMMV JWB Chapter. He resides in Hughesville, MD.

CARMEL JOSEPH TINTLE, was born Sept. 25, 1924, Paterson, NJ. Enlisted United States Maritime Service May 1943.

Training: U.S. Maritime Service Training Station, Sheepshead Bay, NY (May 4, 1943-July 19, 1943); U.S. Maritime Service Upgrade School, New York, NY. Able Seaman training (Nov. 1, 1943-Nov. 8, 1943); U.S. Maritime Service Officers School, Fort Trumbull, New London, CT. Deck Officer Candidate Training; graduated with rank of ensign and third officer's papers (March 30, 1945-July 31, 1945).

Assignments: SS *Jeremiah S. Black,* ordinary seaman, Mediterranean (July 19, 1943-Oct. 20, 1943). Ports of call: Algiers, Algeria, Bizerte, Tunisia.

SS *William Eaton,* able seaman, Mediterranean, Persian Gulf and Indian Ocean. (Nov. 1, 1943-June 3, 1944). Ports of Call: New York, Norfolk, Suez, Egypt; Aden, Saudi Arabia; Bandar Shahpur, Iran; Bahrain, Bandar Abbas, Lourenco Marques, Mozambique; Mombasa, Kenya; Port Said, Egypt; Bari and Taranto, Italy; Tripoli, Libya.

SS *Mobile City,* able seaman, North Atlantic (June 26, 1944-Oct. 7, 1944). Ports of call: New York, Boston, Halifax, Oban and Methil, Scotland; London, England; Cherbourg, France; Swansea, Wales; Bangor, Ireland.

SS *Winthrop Marvin,* able seaman, North Atlantic (Nov. 9, 1944-Feb. 8, 1945). Ports of Call: Boston, Halifax, Antwerp, Belgium; Portsmouth, England.

SS *Henry Wynkoop,* third officer, Atlantic, Mediterranean, Middle East, Indian Ocean, Pacific (Sept. 6, 1945-May 20, 1946). Ports of Call: New York, Philadelphia, Port Said, Egypt; Bahrain Island; Ras Tanura, Saudi Arabia; Khorramshahr, Iran; Columbo, Ceylon;

Singapore, Shanghai and Tsing Tao, China. Four of the five vessels were engaged in direct enemy action.

When not taking formal training at U.S.M.S. schools and between sea assignments cited above, served as a member of temporary or as the night mate aboard ships tied up in the port of New York.

Decorations: Combat Bar, Atlantic, Mediterranean, Middle East and Pacific War Zone Bars, Victory Medal.

Graduated of Fordham University, New York. Spent six years as a journalist in New York and New Jersey and the past 40 years in public relations at both agency and corporate levels. Positions included that of staff writer and associate account executive, Carl Byoir & Associates, New York; account supervisor, Grey Public Relations, New York; Senior vice president and a director of Schenley Affiliated Brands Corp.; vice president-corporate affairs, The American Distilling Company; and currently vice president-public relations, Banfi Vintners, the U.S.' leading wine importer and a major producer in Italy; also C.E.O. of Vinum Communications, a Banfi affiliate; and publicity director of Jumby Bay, a Banfi resort property in Antigua, West Indies.

Married to the former Alice Marie Hayes; two children, Joseph and Alice Maureen; three grandchildren and one on the way.

GEORGE K. TRASK, was born Aug. 17, 1920 in East Chicago, IN. Joined USMM, June 25, 1942, Chicago, IL. Trained at Hoffman Island, NY. Graduated Oct. 16, 1942, fireman w/t. SS *Pontiac,* fireman, Great Lakes, Oct. 17, 1942 to Dec. 9, 1942; SS *Arickaree,* fireman, coastwise, tanker, March 14, 1942 to March 31, 1943; SS *Ethan Allen,* fireman, cargo ship, Oran N. Africa, returned with 200 German prisoners of war to New York; M.V. *Mercury,* oiler, July 20, 1943 to March 31, 1943, intercoastal; M.V. *Mercury,* oiler, Aug. 14, 1943 to Aug. 20, 1943, intercoastal; SS *Lee S. Overman,* oiler, Sept. 8, 1943 to Nov. 11, 1943, Preston, Cuba to Liverpool, England, load of sugar; SS *John Sharp Williams,* Jan. 1, 1944 to May 10, 1944, oiler, Murmansk, Russia, bombed and straffed all the way.

SS *Santa Maria,* junior engineer, June 23, 1944 to Aug. 4, 1944. Took, American troops to Naples, Italy.

SS *Arthur J. Tyrer,* junior engineer, Sept. 1, 1944 to Dec. 1, 1944, cargo.

USMS Ft. Trumbull OCS, Jan. 15, 1945 to May 15, 1945, grad. 3rd ass't. engineer.

SS *Chung Tung,* July 17, 1945 to Nov. 16, 1945, 3rd assistant engr., Far East, Suez Canal, Columbo Ceylon, Calcutta, India.

SS *Floyd Bennett,* erd. asst., engr., Coal to Genoa, Italy for their power station.

Youngs Sheet and Tube Co. E Chicago, IN Jan. 5, 1946 to Dec. 15, 1952, elect. maintenance.

Fresh Meadows Housing Power Plant, Jan. 6, 1952 to Oct. 16, 1958, stationary and refer. engineer.

Employed with Board of Education New York City, custodian engineer Oct. 16, 1958 to Nov. 16, 1986. Retired.

Married a girl from Brooklyn July 14, 1943. Had three daughters and four grandchildren.

Now that they have retired they have taken six cruises and traveled to England, Hawaii, Italy, Russia, Sweden, Finland, and Holland.

GLEN E. TRIMBLE, was born Oct. 7, 1924 in Agenda, KS, and graduated age 17, in 1942. Attended a NYA Radio School in Topeka, KS and worked at a munitions plant while waiting to join the Navy at age 18. Navy enlistments were full with a large backlog, so joined the Maritime Service. Boot camp in Sheepshead Bay and Radio School at Gallups Island in 1943.

Sailed three ships, *Cape Constance, Grinnell* and

Joplin Victory throughout the Pacific. First supply convoy into Leyte, PI and used as bomb warehouse for two months. Had two near misses with bombs and a kamikaze crashed at the #3 King Post. Also made the Okinawa invasion and received Mariner's Medal for shrapnel wounds. Also received Pacific Theater Ribbon, Combat Ribbon with stars, Philippine Medal of Liberation (with stars), Philippine Independence Medal, Mariners Medal (shrapnel at Leyte), and Victory Medal.

Used GI training extensively with Kansas Highway Patrol and then 20 years with Boeing on bombing, navigation and missile systems. Now retired and organizing a Kansas Chapter of USMMV WWII. Lives with wife, Bonnie, in Wichita, KS.

EDWARD van BEVERHOUDT, was born Jan. 29, 1918, in St. Thomas, Virgin Island, USA.

He joined the Merchant Marine June 4, 1944. They joined the Merchant Marine at Sheepshead Bay, NY. Served as solo radio officer on board the SS *Horace Bushnell* (KTLP A1/A2 from Feb. 2, 1945 to May 1, 1945; SS *Midnight* (KWGA) A1/A2 from May 11, 1945 to Oct. 30, 1945; SS *Maria Mitchell* (KKTA), A1/A2 from Dec. 15, 1945 to July 12, 1946; SS *Cleveland Forbes* (KWMW) A1/A2 from July 20, 1946 to Sept. 26, 1946.

His memorable experiences include his first ship, SS *Horace Bushnell;* on the Murmansk, Russia, run; was torpedoed and sunk with the loss of the engine crew. Service on the SS *Midnight* and SS *Maria Mitchell,* was in the European and North Africa theatres.

Service on the SS *Cleveland Forbes* was in the Pacific Theatres.

Graduated Ensign (R) from Hoffman Island Radio School, NY, Dec. 30, 1944. Service No. 4414-16162. Radio Certificate No. T-2-3395. Attained rank of lieutenant, JG.

After war service, employed by Department of the Army, as administrative assistant, in the Armed Forces Examining and Entrance Station (recruiting and induction center), New Haven, CT. Retired from Federal Civil Service (32 1/2 years) on Jan. 1, 1971.

Since 1971, became a certified teaching tennis professional, and Eastern Tennis umpire, up to the present.

Married to Margaret S. Robinson, Oct. 13, 1946 to the present. He is now teaching tennis part time and playing amateur senior tennis tournaments.

JOSEPH C. VILLA, AMMV Charter Member JWB Chapter Oct. 14, 1989. He resides in Baltimore, MD.

FRANK R. VITALE, was born Jan. 29, 1927, in San Francisco, CA. Graduated Sequoia High, Redwood City, CA age 17. Joined the U.S. Maritime Service (March 1945) (fireman/oiler) watertender training at Catalina Island, CA). Sailed on *T.V. Barbara*. Entered the U.S. Merchant Marine Academy, Kings Point as cadet midshipman engineer, midshipman sea duty SS *Monterey* (Matson), SS *Pres. Madison* (Apl. Graduated USMMA June 1949. Sailed 1950-1955 all engineer positions to chief engineer in Pacific and Round-the-World runs on SS *Philippine Bear,* SS *Darthmouth Victory* later renamed SS *Pres. Arthur.*

Following sea duty joined the Best Foods Div. of corn products (SF) as assistant plant engineer (1955-1961). In 1961 joined the Standford University Medical Center as chief engineer. Frank proceeded through the rank from chief to management associate, assistant administrator, associate administrator to deputy director (1961-1971).

In 1971 Frank opened the Western Region Office for Herman Smith Associates a hospital planning and management firm as its managing partner for West Coast and Pacific RIM. Frank served as managing partner from 1971 through 1988 when the firm merged with Coopers and Lybrand. Vitale continued as partner in HSA/C&L to his retirement in September 1992.

He currently serves as an executive consultant on special assignments and international engagements. Frank lives with his wife Grace in Menlo Park, CA.

A. PAUL VITOLO, attended USMSTS at Sheepshead Bay. Sailed during WWII as oiler. Hold Atlantic, Pacific and Mediterranean East War Zone Bars.

Married to Dorothy. He is a member of AMMV JWB Chapter.

Vitolo resides in Jeannette, PA.

LEO T. VOGELSANG was born in Baltimore, MD in 1927. Joined the Merchant Marine when he was 16 years old at Sheepshead Bay, New York. Graduated as an Ordinary Seaman. Served on the SS *John Singleton Mosby,* and the SS *Gulf Gem.*

Some of his memorable experiences include supplying ammunition for the "Battle of the Bulge," in Europe and refueling DEs in convoy to Italy. He also served in the USMC during WW II and Korea.

He worked 42 years for Western Maryland DSX Railroads. Now retired.

Married to Joyce Pruett with five step-children.

ORVILLE L. WAHLIN, was born Nov. 16, 1922 Estevan, Sask, Canada. Graduated high school, Maiden Rock, WI. Joined USMS and USNR Nov. 11, 1942. USMS training Hoffman Island, NY. Came out as 2nd cook and baker.

First ship USMS training ship *Vema.*

1943, SS *Garnet Huling* 1918 tanker, Galleyman, Carricou to Halifax; 1943-1944 *Alexander Wilson,* liberty, 3rd cook, Pacific, Guadalcanal, Bouganville to Chile, S.A and into Mobile, AL.

1944, *Cape Spencer,* C-1, Pacific, 2nd cook and baker.

1944-MV *Point Sur,* Pacific, chief cook and steward.

1944-1945 SS *Fallen Timbers* T-2 tanker, Pacific and Carribean, chief steward.

1944-1945 *Vernon S. Hood,* liberty, Pacific, chief steward

1945-SS *Wagon Mound,* T2, coastwise, chief steward.

1946-*Fort George,* T2 tanker, Atlantic and Pacific, chief steward.

1946-U.S. Maritime Service, Alameda, CA, chief steward, retaining, graduated lt.jg. USMS.

1947-*Signal Hills,* T2, coastwise, chief steward.

1947-*Celilo* T2, coastwise, chief steward.

1951-*William H. Aspinal,* liberty, Atlantic, chief steward.

1951-1952-*George H. Pendleton,* liberty, Atlantic, chief steward.

1952-*Southern Cities* LST-Carribean 2nd cook and baker.

1952-1953-*Alice Brown,* victory ship, Atlantic, chief cook.

1955-*Beauregard,* C-2, Atlantic, chief steward.

1955-*Southland,* Atlantic and Mediterranean, chief steward.

1955-*Bents Fort,* T-2, coastwise, chief cook.

1957-*Neva West,* C2, Atlantic and Mediterranean, chief steward.

1958-*Myriam III,* liberty, sailed around world, 2nd cook.

1959-*Bents Fort,* T2, coastwise, chief cook

1959-1960-*Fairland,* Sea Land container ship, chief steward.

MV *Timber Hitch,* missile ship, foreign chief steward.

He worked for Babcock and Wilcox Co. doing firebrick and refactory. Worked between shipping. After he quit sailing worked full time for B&W all over U.S. Retired 1984. Now does lots of fishing in his cabin cruiser, Baytown, TX. Also they ride their 1946 Indian Chief motorcycle. His wife Marjorie, RN retired in 1984 too.

NORRIS E. WAINWRIGHT, sailed during WWII. Attended Sheepshead Bay. Member AMMV JWB Chapter. He resides in Dover, DE.

BOYD WILLIAM WALKER, was born May 17, 1928, Covington, KY. Joined Merchant Marine July 1944, Cincinnati, OH. He went to school at Sheepshead Bay, Brooklyn, NY. After school on Nov. 21, 1944 he was shipped on a tug operated by the U.S. Army Transport Service the L.T. 463 and then the L.T. 493. He quit on Feb. 22, 1945. He then joined the National Maritime Union and shipped on the SS *Arthur St. Clair* March 30, 1945. They loaded a full load of bombs with the fuses on the bottom. Then went to Gent Belgium in convoy. They did not need the bombs in Europe so they sent them back to Philadelphia, PA and put the fuses on top and sent them back to the Philippines and then to Okinawa and from there to Tokyo Bay, since the war was over they came back to Houston, TX and unloaded on Feb. 6, 1946. They were the 64th merchant ship that entered Tokyo Bay after the war.

He served on the following ships from 1946 to 1988 when he retired. SS *Silas Weir Mitchell,* March 19, to Dec. 6, 1946; SS *John Leckie,* Dec. 20, to Dec. 27, 1946; SS *Newton P. Baker,* March 18, to June 17, 1947; SS *Swiftarrow,* June 28, to July 11, 1947; SS *Logans Fort,* July 15, to Aug. 9, 1947; SS *William L. Smith,* Aug. 18, to Aug. 21, 1947; SS *Matthew J. O'Brien,* Aug. 26 to Oct. 18, 1947; SS *Solon Turman,* Nov. 10, 1947 to Jan. 14, 1948; SS *Sweetwater,* Jan. 22, to Jan. 30, 1948; SS *Morgantown Victory* March 23 to June 14, 1948; MV *Knob Knot,* Aug. 1, to Oct. 20, 1948; SS *Mission Los Angeles,* Oct. 25, to Dec. 1, 1948; SS *Gulfking,* Dec. 10, 1948 to April 2, 1949; SS *Helen Hunt Jackson,* May 9 to June 19, 1949; SS *William H. Wilmer,* July 11, to Oct. 14, 1949; SS *E.W. Sinclair,* Dec. 30 to Sept. 25, 1950; SS *American Starling* Nov. 7, 1950 to Feb. 19, 1951; SS *North Heaven,* May 1, 1951 to Oct. 18, 1951; SS *American Starling,* Oct. 26, 1951 to May 7, 1952; SS *Androil,* July 2 to Aug. 4, 1952; SS *Mason Lykes,* Oct. 2, to Oct. 12, 1952; SS *Slyvia Lykes,* Oct. 15 to Oct. 29, 1952.

Inducted in the United States Army Nov. 19, 1952. Separated as sergeant Nov. 18, 1954. Received honorable discharge Nov. 1, 1960.

SS *Mission Los Angeles,* March 5, 1955 to July 18, 1955; SS *Southwind,* Dec. 10, 1955 to May 16, 1956; USNS *Tamalpais,* June 4, to Nov. 21, 1956; USNS *Kennebago,* Feb. 14, 1957 to Nov. 15, 1957; SS *Cape Cod,* Feb. 25, 1958 to April 17, 1958; USNS *Nodaway,* July 16, 1958 to March 16, 1959, motor vessel; SS *Margaret Lykes,* Sept. 18, 1959 to Nov. 14, 1960; SS *Cape Cod,* Feb. 10 to March 3, 1961; SS *Fullerton Hills,* July 12, 1961 to March 1, 1963. Scrapped Taiwan; USNS *Maumee,* Dec. 23, 1962 to April 1, 1964; USNS *Cossatot,* Oct. 8, 1964 to Oct. 19, 1964; USNS *Cossatot,* Oct. 20, 1964 to Oct. 18, 1965, 364 day trip station ship in Vietnam.

USNS *Tallulah,* April 13, 1966 to March 7, 1967; SS *Christopher Lykes,* June 5, 1967 to April 30, 1968; SS *Ruth Lykes,* July 22, 1968 to Oct. 24, 1986; 20 years on same ship.

He has made three around the world trips SS *North Heaven,* USNS *Tamalpais,* USNS *Maumee.* Have sailed as able seaman all ships except *Silas Weir Mitchell* two trips, SS *John Leckie* one trip.

Has Atlantic War Zone Bar, Pacific War Zone Bar, Vietnam Service Bar, U.S. Merchant Marine World War II Bar. He is now 64 years old.

JAMES A. WALKER, as a youngster living in Brooklyn, NY he did not do well in school because of his severe stuttering. He was failing. His dad was a chief engineer (four striper) in the Merchant Marine and he helped him get into Sheepshead Bay Maritime Academy, NY. He did well with engineering and seamanship. They had to yell their orders in a military type fashion and he discovered quickly that you cannot stutter when you yell or sing. To this day he still speaks a little louder than someone else to ensure than he doesn't stammer again.

He selected the engine room (black gang) because of the warmth, the engine fascination, and he had to yell over the typical engine room sounds. Therefore he stops stuttering. It was nice.

Not so nice was the convoy runs to Murmansk, Russia. They had to fight the cold Atlantic, the ice build up topside, and the ever present German submarine packs. Some convoys went to LeHavre, France instead but the sinkings were heavy. When you are 16 years old the thought of "your ship" being hit doesn't enter your mind. Once when they were being straffed by airplanes he heard the twang of wild bullets while he was on deck. He remember saying, "You guys are crazy to stay up here. He's going below where its safe." He had no thoughts of bombs coming through the deck or torpedoes hitting the hull in the engine room. He was just plain lucky. Nothing religious, just flat ass luck as he sees it. After a few runs in the Atlantic he went to San Francisco and sailed the Pacific until April 1946.

One run in particular he recalls was on the *Cuba Victory* ship. They sailed out of San Pedro with ammo only. No convoy at all. The ship was relatively fast (18 knots). They topped off at Honolulu and made it all the way to Calcutta without being hit. Those poor old turbines really were hard at work all the way. He has a lot of respect for the victory ships as compared to the liberty ships.

He joined the U.S. Army Air Corp in April 1946 in Fort Dix, NJ and attended mechanics school. He was put into B29s and was a flight engineer for the next 21 years. The service separated the Air Force part and he changed into the blue uniform. He flew bombers for 11 years and cargo/passenger jets for 11 more. He retired honorable in 1967.

A week after his discharge he joined McDonnell Douglas Aircraft plant in Long Beach. He taught flight engineering and pilots for another 21 years and retired in May 1992. Today he is fully retired (just like the *Lane Victory*). He and his wife of 45 years are both now on Social Security pensions but they have the Air Force retirement and Douglas retirement checks too. Life is great and they are healthy.

He donated his old Coast Guard original "Z" and "C" papers to the museum on the *Lane* plus his seamans passport, and a T2 tanker floating model. He is very proud of his MM service. He received a formal discharge from the Coast Guard in 1992 for that WW2 time and effort. He still looks at cargo ships today in Los Angeles harbor as they sail in and out and he must admit he's more than just a little envious of the crews who sail now. No torpedoes, no shells, no ice on the decks, no convoys, no military paint jobs. They even smoke on deck and all the lights are on. They have TV, video tapes, music, and fully automated machinery. The ship is air conditioned and the galleys are modern with a crew lounge. What a life (and they probably get paid more) plus the ports of call are nice. He volunteered for duty when Desert Storm came on but he was not needed on the older ships. It was just a last chance shot to sail again.

WILLIAM W. WALKER, sailed as a cook and baker during WWII, Korean and Vietnam Wars. Attended USMSTS at Sheepshead Bay, NY. Next of kin is sister, Rose Ash. She resides in Baltimore, MD. He is a member of AMMV JWB Chapter. He resides in Baltimore, MD.

EARL P. WALLACE, was born Oct. 10, 1921 in Canton, OH. Raised in Chicago from the age of nine. First sailed on the Great Lakes in 1942 in order to be close to home until the birth of his first child. He joined the Merchant Marines in 1943.

Ships sailed: *Alfred Moore,* liberty ship (OS) North Africa; *Moses Brown,* liberty ship (OS) Mediterranean; *Pan Georgia,* tanker, (OS) Coastwise Atlantic; *Rosebud,* tanker, (Deck Maintenance) North Atlantic; *Cedar Mills,* tanker (Able seaman and boatswain) South Pacific; SS *Whitehorse,* tanker, (3rd mate and acting 2nd mate) North Atlantic and North Africa. Graduated from United States Maritime Service Officers School at Fort Trumbull, CT in 1945.

Earl moved his family to California in 1950 where he became a building contractor in Manhattan Beach. Retired to Escondido in 1973 where he and his wife of 51 years now raise avocados and exotic palm trees.

WILLIAM H. WALLACE, sailed as messman, cook/baker, wiper, F/W, and butcher during WWII. Has Atlantic, Pacific and Med. War Zone Bars and USMM Certificate of Service. Attended Sheepshead Bay. Next of kin is son, William H. Wallace, Jr., of Mitchelville, MD.

Member of AMMV JWB Chapter. He resides in Churchton, MD.

RICHARD B. WALTER, resides in Hanover, PA. Member AMMV JWB Chapter.

GEORGE E. WARD, JR., was born Aug. 23, 1926. Graduated age 17, St. Louis, MO. Joined Merchant Marines

in 1945 training at Catalina Island. Was in Darwin, Australia on VJ Day on the last tip of the *Jeremiah O'Brien* which has now been restored and is currently moored at Fort Mason, San Francisco.

Sailed until 1947. Steamboated the Mississippi Summer 1948. Later served two years in the Army. Completed A.A., B.S. and M.S. degrees in Louisiana.

Worked in Germany 10 years as civilian, U.S. Army. Spent 18 years as a high school and college teacher, coach athletic director and intramural sports director before going into private business. Managed large discount houses and later owned and operated sports center, museum and a western trading post.

Lives with wife Dorothy. They have six grown children. Semi-retired at Stanton, MO. Still regularly sees Al (Bud) La Gates who was a fo'c'sle mate on the *O'Brien*.

DAVE WARFEL, was born July 19, 1925. Trained in Catalina, CA early 1943. First ship: *J.E. Gorman* to Alaska as fireman on this old Great Lakes reefer.

Then various T-2 tankers to Fiji, Guadalcanal, Tulagi, Australia, India, Ceylon, Egypt, Iran, Sicily, etc. Worked as oiler, pumpman and third assistant engineer.

Last ship: *Azalea City* (waterman line) left New Orleans heading west and went around the world to Mobile.

His memorable experience includes picking up survivors from a torpedoed ship in the Mediterranean.

He loved the sea, but felt that he would never be able to buy his own ship; so he left to go into business. After several ventures, some successful and some not so successful, he currently head up a firm that sells shipboard piping materials and donates much material to the *Lane Victory* program.

CARL WARNET, (deceased), served as Army chaplain aboard the hospital ship *John J. Meany*. Artifacts donated by Peter Seroka.

RICHARD STEACY WARREN, was born July 2, 1913, in Lancaster, PA. Graduate Franklin and Marshall College, 1935. Left Sperry Gyroscope Company on Long Island, NY in 1944 to join the Merchant Marine. Basic training at Sheepshead Bay, NY. Radio training, Section 4 R, Hoffman Island, NY.

Shipped from New Orleans, 2nd radio officer on SS *James Bowie*. She had heavy steel plates welded across the forward deck and down the sides to hold her together after her original welds gave way during a storm on a trip to England. Sailed through the canal to Eniwetok alone and then to Lingayen Gulf, PI in convoy. Returned to Seattle and their first shore leave in five months. Returned to New York and made two more trips on the SS *Abraham Lincoln*, one to Bremerhaven with a return pickup of 750 troops in LeHavre, and the other to Yugoslavia with a pick up of 600 troops in Naples. Signed off in Hampton Roads, VA Nov. 19, 1945.

Lives with wife, Anne, in Lancaster, PA. Two children, daughter and son. Retired from Hamilton Watch Company in 1976, as personnel director. Continue to serve industries as a personnel consultant but took time this year (300 hours) to build a detailed model of the SS *Abraham Lincoln*.

WILLIAM H. WEBB, attended Sheepshead Bay September 1944. Was stewards mate on several liberty ships until 1947. From 1947 to 1951 sailed on SS *America*. He resides in Mt. Laurel, NJ.

ROBERT H. WELCH, resides in Hatboro, PA and is a member of AMMV JWB Chapter.

HAROLD E. WELLINGTON, was born Sept. 29, 1924. Left Vermont and joined the Merchant Marine. Went to Sheepshead Bay, NY for training. Shipped out of the Chelsea Hotel in New York.

Ships sailed: *Edmund Fanning* (liberty ship), fireman watertender, England, July 1943; *William Eaton*, (liberty ship), fireman, watertender, Persian Gulf November 1943; *George Read*, (liberty ship) fireman watertender, Persian Gulf, June 1944. *John Ericsson* (troop ship), oiler, France, March 1945. Returning liberated POWs back to States. *John Colton* (liberty ship), oiler, France, October 1945.

Left the Merchant Marine Spring of 1946, was drafted into Army January 1949, spent a year in Fort Bliss, TX. Joined the Navy September 1950. Spent four years on the USS *Mississippi* and the USS *Iowa*. Was discharged as boilerman second class in 1954.

He is now retired living with wife at 134 Rhododendron Drive, Brevard, NC.

ARNE R. WESSLEN, was born Oct. 2, 1924. Attended San Pedro High School and graduated June 1943. Started sailing during summer vacation of 1942 and after high school graduation resumed a sea career on a full time basis. After satisfying the seatime requirement to attended the U.S. Maritime Officers School, attended the Alameda School, graduating January 1945. Until November 1946 he continued going to sea as well as upgrading his license to eventually chief mate - last renewal November 1985, were spent ashore in employment with ARCO - Atlantic Richfield Co. (Richfield Oil Corp. and Atlantic Refining Co. merged in January 1966 to form ARCO). Although working ashore, the majority of his employment was Marine related and at one stage included manager of U.S. Fleet Operations. Marine terminal and pipe line operations were other job assignments. Graduated from Los Angeles Harbor College and West Coast University.

Currently a member of the American Merchant Marine Veterans.

His memorable experiences include attendance at the U.S. Maritime Service Officers School. At sea - very routine, no hostile encounters.

He is employed at Atlantic Richfield Co. for 39 years, transportation management January 1946- November 1985. Married and has two daughters, one is a naval officer. Today he is in property management. Part-time funeral director.

JOSEPH LAWRENCE WESTBERRY, was born Feb. 20, 1906, Savannah, GA. Lived with his grandparents, at Waycross, GA, until he was 14 years old. Left Waycross, GA at an early age. When his grandmother died he went to live with his parents in St. Petersburg, Tampa, FL and Savannah, GA.

At age 18, he enlisted in the United States Marine Corps, (Aug. 6, 1924). Trained at Parris Island, SC. Duty Stations: Norfolk, VA. Honolulu, Pearl Harbor, Hawaiian Islands, Brooklyn Navy Yard, NY. Discharged May 9, 1928 at Saint Julius Creek, VA. Was in the USMC Reserve from July 23, 1928 to July 22, 1932.

Sea time: June 6, 1928, Jacksonville, FL; SS *Iroquis* of Clyde Mallory Lines. During the 1929 depression he worked in New York and married his wife Freda in 1936. Worked the Brooklyn Navy Yard until 1939.

Enlisted United States Maritime Service, (United States Merchant Marines) in 1943. Trained at United States Maritime Service Training Center, Sheepshead Bay, Brooklyn, NY. Graduated as apprentice seamen; fireman 2nd class; training included 30 hours of elementary gunnery, 5".38, 3" .50, 20mm. Shipped to USMS Graduation Station at 23rd Street, New York City, NY. On to Phila by train, (Sept. 3, 1943) signed on the SS *Vera Cruz* a T-2 tanker. Signed off in December and he joined the National Maritime Union. In 1944 he shipped on a C-2 type troop carrier ship; SS *Exchange*, American Export Lines. At 38 years of age; he stopped going to sea and worked ashore doing war material work for Bendix Aviation and Armour Can Companies. After the war, he worked in various garages.

In 1947 he went back to sea. Sailed on the SS *America*, SS *Washington*, SS *United States*, (Big U) as: fireman, oiler, plumber, plumber/machinist, and steady chief plumber machinist until they tied her up in 1970. He made the final voyage on these following ships before they laid up. SS *Marine Tiger*, SS *Uruguay*, SS *Washington*, SS *America*; and the SS *United States*. The Big U was some ship and they will never see another one like her; a Great American loss.

In 1970 sailed Far East; with U.S. Lines Company's container ship, SS *American Legion;* was refrigeration engineer until he retired in July 1981 at the age of 75.

Sailed all three war zones; Atlantic, Pacific, and Mediterranean, Middle East; ships manned by Civilians.

Awards to civilians: All three war zones medals, Merchant Marine Service Emblem and Honorable Button, Merchant Marine World War II Victory Medal. U.S. Bicentennial Memorial Medal. Member of USMMVWWII, SS *Lane Victory* and it's East Central Florida Chapter.

He and his wife Freda and they have one daughter, two grandchildren; and four great grandchildren. They live in (Co-op City), Bronx, NY.

VAGN AKTON WESTERGAARD, was born Dec. 23, 1917, Copenhagen, Denmark. Cadet on the Danish training ship *Fano* at Reykjavig, Iceland Sept. 1, 1939, when war broke out in Europe. Sailed in Danish and Swedish ships until June 1941, then joined the American Merchant Marine, NY.

Sailed: *Oklahoman*, (ab), 1941, Atlantic; *Montanan*, (ab), outside Capetown Dec. 7, 1941 on way to Suez with military cargo to the British. *Columbian* (ab) unescorted to Persian Gulf. Gun crew repelled surface attack by German submarine June 17, 1942. *George Bancroft*, (ab) liberty ship 1943 Murmansk Run, USAT *James Parker* (Jr. 3rd mate), 1943, Mediterranean. USAT *Atlantic* (trader) (2nd Mate), Southwestern Pacific. Gun crew downed Japanese bomber, at Amsterdam Isle, New Guinea Aug. 27, 1944. *Henry V. Alvarado*, (chief mate), 1945 Pacific at Samar Isle, Philippines, Aug. 15, 1945.

Korean War - *Bedford Victory* (ab) 1951, Pusan,

Inchon. Sailed ocean until 1960, then the Great Lakes until retirement 1980. First class pilot, lives in Webster Groves, MO.

LAWRENCE W. WETMORE, was born Sept. 29, 1908 in New Brunswick, Canada. Joined Merchant Marine, Boston, MA 1943.

Served on: liberty ships: *Eugene E. O'Donnell,* (purser) Atlantic; *William Phipps,* (purser), Port; *Galen L. Stone* (purser), Mediterranean-Middle East; *Calvin Austin,* purser-pharm-mate, Pacific; *Samuel Johnston* (purser-pharm-mate), Atlantic; *James G. Blaine* (purser-pharm-mate) Atlantic. Steamships *Yarmouth* and *Evangeline* (sr. purser), Carribbean cruise service.

Maritime Service Hospital Corps School, Sheepshead Bay, NY, 1945.

Memorable experience: Normandy invasion. To Utah and Omaha assault areas on *Eugene E. O'Donnell* (commanded by Capt. Harvey L. Dunning). June 4-8 1944, from Cardiff.

Vessel made seven subsequent shuttle trips to Utah and Omaha assault areas from Southampton.

Other employment: Eastern Steamship Lines, Boston, MA. RCA until retirement in 1969. Married Anna Brooking 1930. Celebrating 62nd wedding anniversary this month.

PATRICK L. WHALEN, as reported in the *The Evening Sun* of Dec. 16, 1944 Seven Naltimoreans, including Ensign Patrick L. Whalen, son of the late Patrick B. Whalen former head of the National Maritime Union (NMU) here and the Baltimore CIO were graduated this week from the Maritime Service Officer's School at Fort Trumbull, New London, CT. Two of the Baltimore graduates received certificates of merit for their work at the officer school. They are Ensign Albert F. Johnson, 7 Gwynndale Avenue, who won a certificate in Marine engines and auxiliaries and Ensign John Kukta 1942 Perlman place, who was awarded a certificate for overcoming the greatest number of articles.

Others in the class were Ensigns Carroll H. Cooper, 310 Birkwood Place; Thomas W. Herman, 2922 Grantley Road; Frank E. Douglas, 2902 Dunmurry Road, Dundalk, and Richard L. Anderson, 2726 Hugo Avenue. Ensign Anderson was graduated as a deck officer and the other six as engineers. Ensign Whalen who is 25 and first went to sea in 1937, resides at 1537 Carswell Street. His father who was the head of the seaman's committee which led a strike in Baltimore in 1936, became head of the Baltimore Branch of the Maritime Union which grew out of the strike. Later he was elected president of the Baltimore Industrial Union Council. He returned to sea in 1940 and was killed when a torpedo sunk his ship in the Indian Ocean in the spring of 1942."

EDWARD L. WHEELER, resides in Parkton, MD and is member of AMMV JWB Chapter.

RAY H. WHEELER, was born Oct. 6, 1926 in Lewiston, UT. He joined the Merchant Marine Aug. 1, 1944 in San Francisco, CA.

Served on ATS *Spindleye,* ON, Honolulu, HI; SS *Wm. McCracken,* O.S., Seattle, WA; SS *John S. Bassett,* A.B., Honolulu, HI; SS *La Brea Hills,* QM, San Pedro, CA; SS *Mission Dolorus,* QM, San Pedro, CA; SS *Pan Virginia,* purser-PH, Galvaston, TX.

His memorable experience includes four invasions, Philippine, Iwo Jima, Palue, Okinawa. Sailed seven convoys delivered 100,000 tons of shipping during war time. Served in all theatres of war in WWII.

Married in 1946 and have three children. Farmer-

rancher and self employed. Drawing disability from U.S. Govt. Vets, (DAV). He retired Nov. 19, 1977.

ROY E. WHITAKER, was born July 24, 1917 in Geneva, NY. Sworn in Dec. 15, 1943 at Buffalo, NY. Trained at Sheepshead Bay, Brooklyn, NY.

Served on *Kansan,* carpenter, New York to South Pacific, 1944; *Jose J. Acosta,* liberty ship, carpenter, New York to Pacific, 1944-1945; *Clara Barton,* liberty ship, carpenter, Boston to Antwerp, 1945; New York to Pacific, 1945.

Employed pre-war as truck driver and machinist. After the war employed as banker. He retired in 1981.

Married with three children before the war and now has seven grandchildren and eight grandchildren. He is a auto race official (raced approx. 40 years), Air Museum volunteer, travels, etc.

CLEO I. WHITE, was born Aug. 25, 1922 in Spokane, WA. Joined Merchant Marine June 9, 1942 in Spokane, WA. Ships served on: M.S. *Standard Service,* O.S., San Francisco, CA. SS *K.R. Kingsbury,* O.S., San Francisco, CA; SS *Jeremiah M. Rusk,* A.B., San Francisco, CA; MS *Island Mail,* A.B., San Francisco, CA; SS *Sea Pike,* deck maintenance, San Francisco, CA; SS *Laredo Victory,* deck maintenance, San Francisco, *Richard Yates,* deck maintenance, San Francisco; SS *Yugoslavia Victory,* deck maintenance, San Francisco, CA.

He was transported from Spokane, WA to Port Hueneme, CA on June 9, 1942 for boot training than transferred to the American Sailor at Long Beach, CA for ship training. He was than transferred to Alameda, CA and released from the Coast Guard to the Maritime Service where he shipped on ocean going merchant ships.

He was discharged from the last ship on Dec. 28, 1945. He is eligible for the Pacific War Zone Bar, Combat Bar with stars, honorable service button.

After service he became a carpenter and cattle rancher. He has a wife no children. He is retired on disability in 1982. He lives in Elk, WA.

ROBERT CRAIG WHITTEN, was born Dec. 6, 1926 in Bristol, VA to Robert Craig Whitte, Sr. and Adeline (Gerke) Whitten.

Married Sally Marie Kriz, Aug. 2, 1953 and had children Robert Craig, III, Lisa Marie Marchese and grandchildren Christopher Joseph Marchese, III, Elise Marie Marchese Paulina Marie Marchese, Andrew Robert Victor Marchese.

Attended public schools, Baltimore, County, MD 1933-1944. U.S. Merchant Marine Academy, 1944-1947; B.S. Marine Transportation; University of Buffalo, Buffalo, NY, 1947-1955; B.A., physics; Duke University, Durham, NC, 1955-1959, Ph.D, nuclear physics.

Merchant Marine Service: Engine cadet, SS *Fairwind,* January-June 1945 (three trips to UK, French ports); Jr. 3rd assistant engineer, SS *Exporter,* 1947. Both ships operated by American Export Lines.

Service in U.S. Navy 1949-1953; assistant engineer officer, USS *Elokomin* (AO55), assistant engineer officer USS *Ozbourn* (DD846), engineer officer USS *Thomas F.*

Nickel (DE-587). Qualified and served as officer of the deck (underway) in each ship. Retired from USNR in rank of commander, September 1971.

Career SRI International, 1959-1961, physicist, senior physicist. NASA-Ames Research Center, 1967-1988, research scientist. Published over 125 scientific papers in the archival literature and six books. The last one, A *Guide to Reference and Standard Atmosphere Models,* has been adopted by the American National Standards Institute and the Department of Defense as part of the National Aerospace Standards.

Association officer, National Director and Chairman, National Community Education Committee, Navy League of the United States (current); Scottish-American Military Society, Northern California Regional commander, 1988-1992; National Adjutant, 1992.

Association Membership U.S. Naval Institute, Veterans of Foreign Wars (life), Naval Reserve Association (life), Air Force Association.

Honors Associate Fellow, American Institute of Aeronautics and Astronautics Chevalier, *Sovereign and Military Order of the Temple of Jerusalem,* Grand Priory of Nova Scotia, two NASA Group Achievement Awards.

His memorable experience includes being nearly washed overboard in the North Atlantic in April 1945.

THOMAS W. WHORTON, JR., sailed as purser/ pharm. mate on the liberty ship SS *William P. Duval.*

He resides in Hockessin, DE.

GEORGE W. WICKENS, was first radio officer on SS *John W. Brown.*

HAROLD S. WILCOX, was born July 19, 1924 in Boise, ID. He joined the Merchant Marine July 1942.

Served on *William Cody,* wiper, Aug. 1942-February 1943, India, returned to New York, Pacific (New Zealand); *William Carson,* oiler, April 1943-September 1943, South America, Canal, England.

His memorable experiences include sub attack Dec. 25, 1942 off coast of Ceylon. Sub attacks in North Atlantic summer 1943 while in convoy.

Employed USMC, teacher, probation officer. Retired in 1980. Married and has three sons. He is traveling the U.S., Canada in motorhome with their dogs.

ALONZO WILLIAMS, sailed as FWT on the liberty ship SS *Davey Crockett* in 1946.

He resides in Philadelphia, PA.

BERGE C. WILLIAMS, on Pearl Harbor Dec. 7, 1941, he was already in the Merchant Marine and was the radio operator on the SS *Yorkmar,* a freighter bound from San Francisco to Panama and thence to New York. On that eventful day they were off the coast of Mexico. During his three hour watch in the morning he heard nothing concerning events at Pearl Harbor. After lunch he transmitted their weather (WX) using the general call signal of CQ (to all ships). Soon thereafter a ship nearby asked if he had heard that Pearl Harbor had been bombed.

He answered no. He took this information to the bridge and they were dumbfounded.

DONALD R. WILLIAMS, resides in Bowie, MD.

CARROLL R. WILSON, born Feb. 23, 1923 in Johnston City, IL. Joined the Merchant Marine in March 1941 in Tampa, FL.

Ships served on: SS *Glenpool*, messman; SS *John C. Calhoun*, wiper; SS *Chester*, fireman; *Samson*, AB; SS *Elijah White*, OS; *Point Arguello*, AB; SS *John Smeaton*, AB; SS *Ben Robertson*, AB; SS *Cape Corwin*, AB.

His memorable experiences include one trip when their ship was hit by something out in the Atlantic. They were to man the life boats, since it was very cold Wilson put on a rubber life saving suit so he would not freeze if he got in the water— then he discovered that it leaked when in the water. Fortunately, after the ship was checked they discovered it was not damaged and stayed with the ship.

Wilson has been a sheet metal worker, iron worker, boiler maker, etc. since leaving the Merchant Marine. He and his wife, Helen, have been married for 47 years.

DR. FRED H. WILSON, (ND, Ph.D, C.Ht., F.A.S.P.), was born Aug. 9, 1926 in Bayonne, NJ. Joined the Merchant Marine after being honorably discharged, 1944, New York, United States Navy.

He served on *Nicaragua Victory*, *Jesse Applegate* *Robert Barnes*, *Richard J. Barnes*, SS *Washington*, seaman, utilityman.

His memorable experience includes excitement of looking at all the ships in convoy as a young man. Hearing they might be under attack. Hearing that our President FDR passed away.

He is employed in private practice, three offices in psychotherapy/teacher NYS/lecturer. Doctor with sheriff's office.

Now separated. Has five children Ronald, Craig, Freda, Gary, Everette. Private practice, and clinical psychotherapist.

ANTHONY WINNICK, JR., is member of AMMV JWB Chapter. He resides in Dundalk, MD.

GEORGE C. WINTER, is member of AMMV JWB Chapter. He resides in Baltimore, MD.

RICHARD S. WISE, was born December 1926 in Wichita, KS. He joined Merchant Marine in January 1945. Trained at Catalina Island. Graduated USMS Hoffman Island Radio School.

Served on SS *Robert C. Grier*, radio officer, Pacific Ocean; SS *Brookfield*, radio officer, Atlantic, Pacific, Indian Ocean; SS *Abiqua*, radio officer, Atlantic; SS *Brookfield*, two trips round-the-world.

Most of his adult life worked as electronics engineer. Married and raised a family of four. Retired in 1992. Lives in New Brighton, MN.

ELWOOD J. WOLF, is a member of AMMV JWB Chapter. He resides in Greenbelt, MD.

FRANK PRESTON WOODING, was born May 17, 1922 in Long Island, VA. He joined the Merchant Marine July 5, 1942 in King Point, NY.

Served on S.S. *Lara*, engine cadet; USAT *General George Simmons*, JV & 3rd asst. engineer; Atlantic, Mediterranean; SS *Santia Maria*, 3rd assist. engineer, Mediterranean, SS *Santa Cecilia*, 2nd assist.

Made D Day and one Normandy invasion. General contractor. He is property management.

J.C. WOODS, born April 21, 1923 in Water Valley, MS. Joined the Merchant Marine June 1942.

Ships served on: SS *Widmea*, messman; SS *Permanen*, oiler; SS *Phillippa*, wiper and oiler; SS *Monterey*, fireman; SS *D.M Dickinson*, oiler; SS *Salina Victory*, oiler and Lu Jn. Engineer; SS *Anchorage Victory*, oiler; MV *John Erickson*, utility man; SS *President Tyler*, wiper; SS *Donald Duck Dickinson*, oiler; SS *George S. Boatwell*, oiler; *William A White*, F/M/WT.

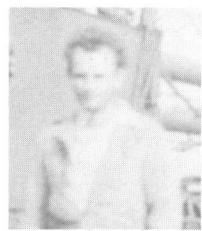 

Memorable experiences include being hit bow to bow by another ship and then beign able to get to Frisco. Another was being told their ship would not go out as scheduled but would be on stand-by a little longer. Then seeing the ship sink that had taken their ship's place when they went on stand-by. The only casualty was the man who held the same job on the sunken ship as Wood did on his ship.

LORING W. WORDELL, was born April 1, 1923, Taunton, MA. He joined the USMS Oct. 9, 1942. Received discharge from U.S. Coast Guard Aug. 15, 1945. Received discharge 1989 and recognition from U.S. Maritime Comm. He achieved the rank of chief radio officer.

His memorable experience includes seeing the destruction at Pearl Harbor. Although it was two years later it was a chilling sight. Visiting the city of Rotterdam when it was so severely damaged. Visiting the city of Manila where most of the streets were impassable because of 3' to 6' rubble from collapsed buildings. Receiving radio messages of subs sighted though they never saw them it was a constant threat.

The North Atlantic in the winter is constantly stormy and the seas are mountainous and beyond description. Experienced a typhoon on each of four voyages. It was common for the captain to write up a summary of events to be turned in at the end of a voyage. Several of these narratives complimented him for service performed beyond his normal duties.

Works in the construction trade. He worked at plumbing, carpentry and masonry. Boatbuilding, repair and maintenance. For eight years taught/owned/operated Boat Building School. He hold contractors license and a teaching certificate in the state of Massachusetts.

ROBERT R. WYATT, was born Feb. 19, 1928 in San Luis Obispo, CA. He entered Merchant Marine March 1945 in San Francisco, CA. Signed up at sup. union hall, San Francisco. Went to school, San Francisco State six weeks to learn ship board serving procedures, etc. He was 17 years old when he joined the Merchant Marine.

Served on the *Ales Hrdlicka*, messman, (F.H.), San Francisco, Port Hueneme, Leyte, Philippines; MV *Boone Island*, messman, (F.H.), San Francisco, Eniwetok, two times. SS *Cape Newenham*, ordinary seaman, San Francisco, Guam. Lost one of troops, overboard, around Wake Island. Searched until dark. Never found him.

His memorable experience includes serving in the South Pacific on the tug boat MV *Boone Island*, he was volunteered to help the Navy Armed Guard on the 3" 50 on the bow, they blew up a floating mine at 500 mi west of Guam. He was in Merchant Marine for two years. Lived 15 years in Santa Barbara, CA. Employed 34 years as construction electrician.

Married Betty Rice, June 25, 1947. They have four children, three boys, one girl and 12 grandchildren. Has resided in Arroyo Grande, CA for 22 years.

Fishing, Mexico, deer hunting. Enjoys working his three acres in the country.

SAUL B. YOCHELSON, was born Dec. 1, 1925, in Cleveland, OH. Lived in Ohio until moving to California in 1961. Educated at Ohio State University (B.E.E. 1948) and University of Illinois (M.Sc. 1950). Licenses include: ham in November 1941 (W8WSM, now WA6VEN), 2nd class radiotelephone in June 1942, 1st class radiotelephone in August 1942 and 2nd class radiotelegraph in June 1944.

Worked at Cleveland Board of Education FM radio station (WBOE) while in high school; technically was chief engineer because no else had a commercial license (all operators had departed for military!) and at WCOL in Columbus, OH in 1943 while at Ohio State. Joined Merchant Marine in July 1944 and sailed until August 1946 on the following liberty ships: *Sidney Sherman* (Mediterranean, Persian Gulf), *Bret Harte* (North Atlantic), *Daniel H. Lownsdale* (North Atlantic and Mediterranean), *Thomas H. Sumner* (North Atlantic), and *Eugene Field* (Mediterranean). Also sailed in August 1946 on the *Notre Dame Victory* to Holland.

After war and college worked as an electrical engineer at NACA in Cleveland, OH (1948-1951), Goodyear Aircraft in Akron, OH (1951-1961), Librascope in Glendale, CA (1961-1962), Lockheed Missiles and Space in Van Nuys, CA (1961-1964) and Hughes Aircraft in El Segundo and Culver City California (1964-1991).

Retired as chief scientist from Hughes in November 1961. Now active in support of the SS *Lane Victory*, ham radio, and part-time teaching at California State University, Northridge, CA.

EUGENE D. YOCUM, was born May 29, 1909. Resident of San Bernardino County from 1918 to his death in 1981. Made five trips as able bodied seaman from 1942 until end of 1943. Then, studied under Captain Thorensen in San Pedro to become third mate in March 1944. Sailed four trips in that capacity, from March 1944 to Aug. 21, 1945.

Sailed mostly victory cargo ships including: *Frank Joseph Irwin*, *Wm. James*, *Walter Wyman*, *Greenville*

Victory, Koloa Victory, and the *Occidental Victory.* Retired from shipping upon war's end.

Started his own landscape contracting business in the San Bernardino area, continuing until he passed away in February 1981, leaving a wife and one son.

ROBERT MARSHALL YOFFIE, departed St. Louis, MO, Feb. 8, 1943 and was discharged in New York, NY March 22, 1946. Served on SS *Montana, Jesse Billingsley, Walter Jennings, Charles Goodnight, Arizona, Cerro Gordo, Williamsburg).*

Sailed as messman, ordinary seaman, ablebodied seaman and quartermaster also held certificate as lifeboatman.

Survivor of SS *Montana* which was rammed and sunk of Norfolk, VA in late May 1943.

LATIMER T. YOUNG, was born Nov. 24, 1912 in New York City and grew up in Saskatchewan, Canada and Portland, OR. He attended the University of Oregon and Georgetown University. He served in the U.S. Merchant Marine for 18 years on 35 ships beginning in January 1935 and visiting at least 50 countries. His last voyage was to India in 1954 on the SS *Express.*

He sailed as a cook on the U.S. Army transport

Monterey and as chief steward on C2 cargo ships and liberty ships in the Atlantic, Pacific, Mediterranean and Middle East war zones.

Spent 32 years with the Office of Ship Construction, Maritime Administration, in Washington, DC until his retirement in 1985. He now resides in Silver Spring, MD.

ROBERT L. YOUNG, was born Nov. 25, 1921. Graduated from California Maritime Academy January 1942. Sailed as Jr. 3rd engineer on the SS *Minnisotan* to Basra. Second ship was a new liberty - *Henry Ward Beecher,* sailed as 2nd engineer. Convoy was attacked by subs off Natal Brazil hitting eight of 32 ships.

In May 1943 he sailed as 2nd engineer on the T-2 tanker, *Fort Moultrie.* Then sailed as first engineer on 3 T-

2s out of Swan Island Shipyard, Ft. Meigs, Plattsburg and White Oak. In January 1944 he received his chief engineers license and sailed as chief on the T-2 Fort Dearborn. This was two years after graduation - age 22 and at that time the youngest chief engineer in the U.S. Merchant Marine. Perhaps the youngest ever!

Spent his working years in Chicago and retired in 1980. A widower with three grown children. Lives in Fort Walton Beach, FL.

FRANK ZABROCKY, is a member of AMMV JWB Chapter. He resides in Linthicum, MD.

ANTHONY J. ZALESKI, served as gunner in U.S. Navy Armed Guard, 1943, on the SS *Haywood Brown,* SS *Wm. Richardson,* and *Alcoa Voyager.* Ports of call included Sicily, Naples, London, Glasglow, Rio de Janiero, Buneos Aries, Algiers, Oran, Port Said and Cairo.

JOSEPH ZARICKI, was born Sept. 27, 1920. Received deck training at Hoffman Island from May 30, 1942 to Oct. 18, 1942. Has certificate of substantially continuous service from May 30, 1942 to Dec. 2, 1946. Served on liberty ships SS *Pearl Harbor,* SS *Edward M. House,* SS *James R. Randall,* SS *George W. Woodward,* SS *Haverford Victory,* SS *Paulsboro,* SS *Sachem,* and the SS *Paulsboro.* Has USCG honorable discharge for Merchant Marine Service and USMM Certificate of Service.

Was awarded the Merchant Marine Emblem, Atlantic War Zone Bar, Victory Medal, Honorable Service Button, and the Presidential Testimonial Letter. Donated items for PLS archives and museums.

GEORGE ZIDIK, resides in Cockeysville, MD and is a member of JWB Chapter.

Gun Crew of Liberty Sip SS John Constantine 1943.

ACKNOWLEDGEMENTS

The sponsors and publisher of **U.S. Merchant Marine** wish to thank the hundreds of Merchant Marine veterans who contributed to this historic effort including, but not limited to:

U. S. Merchant Marine Veterans of WWII
American Merchant Marine Veterans
Gallups Island Radio Association
Hoffman Island Radio Association
Kenneth Keith
Joe Vernick
Frank and Edna Libertore
Jerry McClish
Dr. W. Rion Dixon
Jack Rodgers
Marci Hooper

The "William Tilghman" 1946. (Courtesy of M.L. Verne Philp)